African American Mosaic

A Documentary History
from the Slave Trade
to the Twenty-First Century
Volume One:
To 1877

Newly-freed slaves plant sweet potatoes while hoeing the dirt at Hopkinson's Plantation on Edisto Island in South Carolina in 1862. (*Source:* The New York Historical Society.)

African American Mosaic
A Documentary History
from the Slave Trade
to the Twenty-First Century
Volume One:
To 1877

John H. Bracey, Jr.
Manisha Sinha

University of Massachusetts, Amherst

PEARSON

Prentice
Hall

Upper Saddle River, New Jersey 07458

Library of Congress Cataloging-in-Publication Data

African American mosaic: a documetary history from the slave trade to
the twenty-first century / [compiled by] John H. Bracey, Jr., Manisha
Sinha.
     p.   cm.
Includes bibliographical references and index.
   ISBN 0–13-092287-0—ISBN 0-13-092288–9
  1. African Americans—History—Sources.   I. Bracey, John H.   II. Sinha,
Manisha.
   E184.6.A333 2004
   973'.0496073—dc22

                                         2003022536

Editorial Director: Charlyce Jones-Owen
Senior Acquisitions Editor: Charles Cavaliere
Editorial Assistant: Shannon Corliss
Marketing Manager: Heather Shelstad
Senior Marketing Assistant: Jennifer Bryant
Production Liaison: Marianne
   Peters-Riordan
Production Editor: Bruce Hobart
Permissions Coordinator: Ronald Fox
Manufacturing Buyer: Tricia Kenny

Cover Image: "Oneness" by Nelson Stevens. By
   permission of the artist, Nelson Stevens, Pro-
   fessor of Afro-American Studies, University of
   Massachusetts, Amherst
Cover Design: Bruce Kenselaar
**Composition/Full-Service Project
   Management:** Pine Tree Composition
Printer/Binder: R.R. Donnelley & Sons
   Company
Cover Printer: Phoenix Color Corp

Pearson Education LTD., London
Pearson Education Singapore, Pte. Ltd
Pearson Education, Canada, Ltd
Pearson Education–Japan
Pearson Education Australia PTY,
   Limited
Pearson Education North Asia Ltd

Pearson Educación de Mexico,
   S.A. de C.V.
Pearson Education Malaysia, Pte. Ltd
Pearson Education, Upper Saddle River,
   New Jersey

10 9 8 7 6 5 4 3 2 1
ISBN: 0-13-092287-0

Dedicated to the Spirit and Courage of the People of African Descent

and

To the memory of three pioneering scholars of the black experience
and veterans of the struggle to end racial oppression:

Herbert Aptheker
August Meier
Meyer Weinberg

Contents

FOUR
NORTH OF SLAVERY: FREE BLACK COMMUNITIES
AND ABOLITIONISM

FIVE
THE NEGRO'S CIVIL WAR

SIX
BLACK RECONSTRUCTION   **321**

INTRODUCTION   321

Acknowledgments

We would like to acknowledge the help and support of several people who helped bring this volume to fruition. First and foremost, we thank Tricia Loveland, our department secretary, who greatly assisted us at every stage in the preparation of this manuscript. We also thank Sarah Fitzgerald, our work study student, for copying some of the documents for us. It gives us great pleasure to acknowledge the support of all our colleagues and graduate students at the W. E. B. Du Bois Department of Afro-American Studies. We also thank the scores of undergraduate students at the University of Massachusetts, Amherst, whose needs inspired us to substantially revise an early edition of these volumes. We are particularly grateful to two of the original co-editors, the late Professors August Meier and Elliot Rudwick. Darlene Clark Hine, David W. Blight, and Eric Foner reviewed the table of contents and provided invaluable suggestions, for which we are indebted. We thank our editor at Prentice Hall, Charles Cavaliere, for his patience and gentle prodding to complete this manuscript. Finally, we thank our families for their forbearance while we were putting this book together.

Introduction

In the past few decades, the field of African American history has come of age. Not only is it one of the most dynamic areas in American history, containing some of the most exciting contemporary historical debates, but it is also changing the very way in which we view American history as a whole. African American history is not merely the addition of black people to a larger American historical narrative; it has its own issues and concerns. It is not merely the history of oppression and suffering but also one of overcoming tremendous odds. Finally, African American history leads us to reevaluate a "consensus" view of American history by highlighting contradictions and conflicts.

Keeping these ideas in mind, we have selected some of the most significant and representative primary documents on the black experience for this two-volume collection. These documents illustrate such enduring themes in African American history as the experience of slavery and the growth of a strong black protest tradition. They also reflect the latest research in the field, such as the distinct experience of black women and the development of African American culture and communities. Volume I, which deals with the period from the Atlantic slave trade to the end of the Civil War, covers three important watersheds in black history: the forced migration of the peoples of predominantly West and Central Africa to the New World, the black travail under slavery when African American communities and culture were formed, and emancipation when these communities were remade.

The documents are arranged topically and chronologically in six chapters. These volumes may be used in conjunction with a survey text on black history or by themselves. They are meant to stimulate students into understanding that history is not merely the rote memorization of facts, but the critical reading and interpretation of historical data. As much as possible we have used complete documents or substantial selections from longer documents. We have deliberately kept introductory commentary to a minimum, preferring to let the various "voices" speak for themselves. Documents have been reprinted without revision, except for obvious typographical errors and the capitalization of the word "Negro" throughout.

In seeking to revise the original one-volume selection of primary documents in African American history, *The Afro-Americans: Selected Documents*, edited by John H. Bracey, Jr., August Meier and the late Elliot Rudwick, we confronted the reality that we are following the footsteps of generations of black and white scholars. Despite the common misperception, there is nothing new or faddish about black history. As early as the nineteenth century, African American leaders and writers such as William Wells Brown and William C. Nell tried to chronicle the role of black people in American history in the face of unremitting racial hostility. Much of this work of necessity stressed the contributions of African Americans to the making of the American nation. The first formal work in African American history, George Washington William's *History of the Negro Race in America, 1619–1880*, was published in 1882. By the turn of the century, when the mainstream American academy and universities ignored or caricatured the black historical experience, institutes and associations for the study of black history—such as the Banneker Institute and the Negro Society for Historical Research founded by Arthur Schomburg in 1911, which lives on as the famous Schomburg Library in New York City—proliferated among African American intellectuals and historians.

The "professionalization" of the field was completed under Carter G. Woodson, the father of black history. Woodson founded the Association for the Study of Negro Life and History in 1915 (now known as the Association for the Study of African American Life and History), the *Journal of Negro History,* and the Negro History Week, which is now Black History Month. A generation of black historians, trained at historically black colleges such as Howard, Fisk, and Atlanta, devoted themselves to writing an objective history of black people following the most rigorous "scientific" standards of the day. The most original and talented of course was the great W. E. B. Du Bois, whose ideas and interpretations prefigured the contours of modern African American history. During the Second World War, when Nazism completely discredited racism in the academy and society, a new generation of black and white "revisionist" historians such as John Hope Franklin and Kenneth Stampp challenged dominant historical interpretations of slavery as a beneficent institution and Reconstruction, when former slaves acquired the right to vote briefly, as a period of corruption and black misrule.

However, it was only with the rise of the Civil Rights Movement and the explosion of social history, or the effort to write history from "the bottom up," that African American history came into its own. Increasingly, African Americans were viewed as the legitimate subjects of history or as historical actors rather than as objects or victims of history. New methodologies borrowed from the social sciences and the use of oral testimony uncovered the history of ordinary African Americans. This last phase in the maturation of black history has also been marked by its "institutionalization" in various departments and institutes in universities and colleges across the country.

Today African American history occupies a central position in American history and is instrumental in the construction of new historical synthesis in the United States. Indeed, the international dimensions of the Atlantic slave trade, the hemispheric nature of racial slavery and its aftermath, suggests—to use a phrase popularized by Hegel who sanguinely claimed that Africans had no history—"the world historical significance" of the African American experience. We offer this collection of primary documents as part of a long and ongoing effort to uncover the history of people of African descent and to reevaluate American history from the black perspective. We hope it proves useful to students of both African American and United States history.

John Bracey, Jr.
Manisha Sinha
W. E. B. Du Bois Department of Afro-American Studies
University of Massachusetts, Amherst

African American Mosaic

A Documentary History
from the Slave Trade
to the Twenty-First Century
Volume One:
To 1877

Sao Jorge da Mina (Saint George's Mine), a Portuguese fort on the Gold Coast (present-day Ghana), built in 1482. (*Source:* The Granger Collection.)

Chapter 1

Africans in the Making of the Atlantic World: The African Slave Trade and the Middle Passage

The Atlantic slave trade from mainly the west coast of Africa to the New World, or the Americas, began in the late fifteenth century, reached its peak in the eighteenth century, and lasted until the end of the nineteenth century. It was a complex undertaking that involved the destinies of four continents: Europe, Africa, and North and South America. The African slave trade was an integral part of European commercial expansion that included the plantation colonies of the New World. These plantations produced cash crops, mainly sugar, but also tobacco and rice in North America for the world market and needed substantial amounts of land and labor. After experimenting with white indentured servitude and Indian slavery, European colonists settled upon African slaves as their main source of slave labor for the plantations. This initiated the largest forced migration of human beings in world history: Ten to fifteen million have been documented by historians so far. While the African slave trade contributed to the wealth and economic growth of all the European countries that participated in it and their American colonies, it led to the drain of population from Africa and resulted in an economy that specialized in exporting slaves. Many West African

countries and Africans joined the trade in order to meet the insatiable European demand for labor.

The following selections document how the trade was conducted and the indescribable horrors of the voyage across the Atlantic known as the Middle Passage. The first three sources, by a former slave named Olaudah Equiano, the Dutch slave trader William Bosman, and Alexander Falconbridge, an English surgeon aboard a slaver, describe how Africans were captured, enslaved, and shipped across the Atlantic. The narratives of Mary Prince and Venture Smith also describe early colonial slavery in British North America. Equiano's and Smith's narratives give us insight into African life and society from which so many were torn. Many African slaves were "seasoned" in the West Indies before being shipped to the mainland British colonies in North America. Mary Prince's autobiography that describes plantation slavery in the British West Indies is also one of the very few female slave narratives from this period. Only about five to seven percent of all documented Africans who came to the New World arrived in North America. The description of the Stono Rebellion in South Carolina documents the largest rebellion of Africans in colonial America.

The Interesting Narrative of the Life of Olaudah Equiano, or Gustavus Vassa, the African

Olaudah Equiano

That part of Africa, known by the name of Guinea, to which the trade for slaves is carried on, extends along the coast above 3400 miles, from Senegal to Angola, and includes a variety of kingdoms. Of these the most considerable is the kingdom of Benin, both as to extent and wealth, the richness and cultivation of the soil, the power of its king, and the number and warlike disposition of the inhabitants. It is situated nearly under the line and extends along the coast about 170 miles, but runs back into the interior part of Africa to a distance hitherto I believe unexplored by any traveller; and seems only terminated at length by the empire of Abyssinia, near 1500 miles from its beginning. This kingdom is divided into many provinces or districts: in one of the most remote and fertile of which [called Eboe] I was born, in the year 1745, in a charming fruitful vale, named Essaka. The distance of this province from the capital of Benin and the sea coast must be very considerable; for I had never heard of white men or Europeans, nor of the sea; and our subjection to the king of Benin was little more than nominal; for every transaction of the government, as far as my slender observation extended, was conducted by the chiefs or elders of the place. The manners and government of a people who have little commerce with other countries are generally very simple; and the history of what passes in one family or village may serve as a specimen of the whole nation. My father was one of those elders or

chiefs I have spoken of, and was styled Embrenché; a term, as I remember, importing the highest distinction, and signifying in our language a mark of grandeur. This mark is conferred on the person entitled to it, by cutting the skin across at the top of the forehead, and drawing it down to the eyebrows; and, while it is in this situation, applying a warm hand, and rubbing it until it shrinks up into a thick *weal* across the lower part of the forehead. Most of the judges and senators were thus marked; my father had long borne it: I had seen it conferred on one of my brothers, and I was also *destined* to receive it by my parents. Those Embrenché, or chief men, decided disputes and punished crimes; for which purpose they always assembled together. The proceedings were generally short; and in most cases the law of retaliation prevailed. I remember a man was brought before my father, and the other judges, for kidnapping a boy; and, although he was the son of a chief or senator, he was condemned to make recompense by a man or woman slave. Adultery, however, was sometimes punished with slavery or death; a punishment which I believe is inflicted on it throughout most of the nations of Africa: so sacred among them is the honour of the marriage bed, and so jealous are they of the fidelity of their wives. Of this I recollect an instance.—A woman was convicted before the judges of adultery, and delivered over, as the custom was, to her husband to be punished. Accordingly he determined to put her to death: but it being found, just before her execution, that she had an infant at her breast; and no woman being prevailed on to perform the part of a nurse, she was spared on account of the child. The men, however, do not preserve

Source: *The Interesting Narrative of the Life of Olaudah Equiano, or Gustavus Vassa, the African,* Written by Himself. (London, 1789), pp. 32–61.

the same constancy to their wives, which they expect from them; for they indulge in a plurality, though seldom in more than two. Their mode of marriage is thus:—both parties are usually betrothed when young by their parents (though I have known the males to betroth themselves). On this occasion a feast is prepared, and the bride and bridegroom stand up in the midst of all their friends, who are assembled for the purpose, while he declares she is thenceforth to be looked upon as his wife, and that no other person is to pay any addresses to her. This is also immediately proclaimed in the vicinity, on which the bride retires from the assembly. Some time after, she is brought home to her husband, and then another feast is made, to which the relations of both parties are invited: her parents then deliver her to the bridegroom, accompanied with a number of blessings, and at the same time they tie round her waist a cotton string of the thickness of a goosequill, which none but married women are permitted to wear: she is now considered as completely his wife; and at this time the dowry is given to the new married pair, which generally consists of portions of land, slaves, and cattle, household goods, and implements of husbandry. These are offered by the friends of both parties; besides which the parents of the bridegroom present gifts to those of the bride, whose property she is looked upon before marriage; but after it she is esteemed the sole property of her husband. The ceremony being now ended, the festival begins, which is celebrated with bonfires, and loud acclamations of joy, accompanied with music and dancing.

We are almost a nation of dancers, musicians, and poets. Thus every great event, such as a triumphant return from battle, or other cause of public rejoicing, is celebrated in public dances, which are accompanied with songs and music suited to the occasion. The assembly is separated into four divisions, which dance either apart or in succession, and each with a character peculiar to itself. The first division contains the married men, who in their dances frequently exhibit feats of arms, and the representation of a battle. To these succeed the married women, who dance in the second division. The young men occupy the third; and the maidens the fourth. Each represents some interesting scene of real life, such as a great achievement, domestic employment, a pathetic story, or some rural sport; and as the subject is generally founded on some recent event, it is therefore ever new. This gives our dances a spirit and variety which I have scarcely seen elsewhere. We have many musical instruments, particularly drums of different kinds, a piece of music which resembles a guitar, and another much like a stickado. These last are chiefly used by betrothed virgins, who play on them on all grand festivals.

As our manners are simple, our luxuries are few. The dress of both sexes is nearly the same. It generally consists of a long piece of calico, or muslin, wrapped loosely round the body, somewhat in the form of a Highland plaid. This is usually dyed blue, which is our favourite colour. It is extracted from a berry, and is brighter and richer than any I have seen in Europe. Besides this, our women of distinction wear golden ornaments; which they dispose with some profusion on their arms and legs. When our women are not employed with the men in tillage, their usual occupation is spinning and weaving cotton, which they afterwards dye, and make into garments. They also manufacture earthen vessels, of which we have many kinds. Among the rest tobacco pipes, made after the same fashion, and used in the same manner, as those in Turkey.

Our manner of living is entirely plain; for as yet the natives are unacquainted with those refinements in cookery which debauch the taste: bullocks, goats, and poultry supply the greatest part of their food. These constitute likewise the principal wealth of the country, and the chief articles of its commerce. The flesh is usually stewed in a pan. To make it savory, we sometimes use also pepper, and other spices, and we have salt made of wood ashes. Our vegetables are mostly plantains, eadas, yams, beans, and Indian corn. The head of the family usually eats alone; his wives and slaves have also their separate tables. Before we taste food, we always wash our hands: indeed our cleanliness on all occasions is extreme; but on this it is an indispensable ceremony. After washing, libation is made, by pouring out a small portion of the drink on the floor, and tossing a small quantity of the food in a certain place, for the spirits of departed relations, which the natives suppose to preside over their conduct, and guard them from evil. They are totally unacquainted with strong or spiritous liquours; and their principal beverage is palm wine. This is got from a tree of that name, by tapping it at the top, and fastening a large gourd to it; and sometimes one tree will yield three or four gallons in a night. When just drawn it is of a most delicious sweetness; but in a few days it acquires a tartish and more spirituous flavour: though I never saw any one intoxicated by it. The same tree also produces nuts and oil. Our principal luxury is in perfumes; one sort of these is an odoriferous wood of delicious fragrance: the other a kind of earth; a small portion of which thrown into the fire diffuses a most powerful odour. We beat this wood into powder, and mix it with palm-oil; with which both men and women perfume themselves.

In our buildings we study convenience rather than ornament. Each master of a family has a large square piece of ground, surrounded with a moat or fence, or enclosed with a wall made of red earth tempered, which, when dry, is as hard as brick. Within this are his houses to accommodate his family and slaves; which, if numerous, frequently present the appearance of a village. In the middle stands the principal building, appropriated to the sole use of the master, and consisting of two apartments; in one of which he sits in the day with his family, the other is left apart for the reception of his friends. He has besides these a distinct apartment in which he sleeps, together with his male children. On each side are the apartments of his wives, who have also their separate day and night houses. The habitations of the slaves and their families are distributed throughout the rest of the enclosure. These houses never exceed one story in height; they are always built of wood, or stakes driven into the ground, crossed with wattles, and neatly plastered within, and without. The roof is thatched with reeds. Our dayhouses are left open at the sides; but those in which we sleep are always covered, and plastered in the inside, with a composition mixed with cow-dung, to keep off the different insects which annoy us during the night. The walls and floors also of these are generally covered with mats. Our beds consist of a platform, raised three or four feet from the ground, on which are laid skins, and different parts of a spungy tree called plaintain. Our covering is calico or muslin, the same as our dress. The usual seats are a few logs of wood; but we have benches, which are generally perfumed, to accommodate strangers; these compose the greater part of our household furniture. Houses so constructed and furnished require but little skill to erect them. Every man is a sufficient architect for the purpose. The whole neighbourhood afford their unanimous assistance in building them, and, in return, receive and expect no other recompense than a feast.

As we live in a country where nature is prodigal of her favours, our wants are few and easily supplied; of course we have few manufactures. They consist for the most part of calicoes, earthen ware, ornaments, and instruments of war and husbandry. But these make no part of our commerce, the principal articles of which, as I have observed, are provisions. In such a state money is of little use; however, we have some small pieces of coin, if I may call them such. They are made something like an anchor; but I do not remember either their value or denomination. We have also markets, at which I have been frequently with my mother. These are sometimes visited by stout, mahogany-coloured men from the south west of us: we call them

Oye-Eboe, which term signifies red men living at a distance. They generally bring us firearms, gun-powder, hats, beads, and dried fish. The last we esteemed a great rarity, as our waters were only brooks and springs. These articles they barter with us for odoriferous woods and earth, and our salt of wood-ashes. They always carry slaves through our land; but the strictest account is exacted of their manner of procuring them before they are suffered to pass. Sometimes indeed we sold slaves to them, but they were only prisoners of war, or such among us as had been convicted of kidnapping, or adultery, and some other crimes which we esteemed heinous. This practice of kidnapping induces me to think, that, notwithstanding all our strictness, their principal business among us was to trepan our people. I remember too they carried great sacks along with them, which, not long after, I had an opportunity of fatally seeing applied to that infamous purpose.

Our land is uncommonly rich and fruitful, and produces all kinds of vegetables in great abundance. We have plenty of Indian corn, and vast quantities of cotton and tobacco. Our pine apples grow without culture; they are about the size of the largest sugar-loaf, and finely flavoured. We have also spices of different kinds, particularly pepper; and a variety of delicious fruits which I have never seen in Europe; together with gums of various kinds, and honey in abundance. All our industry is exerted to improve those blessings of nature. Agriculture is our chief employment; and every one, even the children and women, are engaged in it. Thus we are all habituated to labour from our earliest years. Every one contributes something to the common stock; and as we are unacquainted with idleness, we have no beggars. The benefits of such a mode of living are obvious. The West-India planters prefer the slaves of Benin or Eboe to those of any other part of Guinea, for their hardiness, intelligence, integrity, and zeal. Those benefits are felt by us in the general healthiness of the people, and in their vigour

and activity; I might have added too in their comeliness. Deformity is indeed unknown amongst us, I mean that of shape. Numbers of the natives of Eboe now in London might be brought in support of this assertion; for, in regard to complexion, ideas of beauty are wholly relative. I remember while in Africa to have seen three negro children, who were tawny, and another quite white, who were universally regarded by myself and the natives in general, as far as related to their complexions, as deformed. Our women too were, in my eyes at least, uncommonly graceful, alert, and modest to a degree of bashfulness; nor do I remember to have ever heard of an instance of incontinence amongst them before marriage. They are also remarkably cheerful. Indeed cheerfulness and affability are two of the leading characteristics of our nation.

Our tillage is exercised in a large plain or common, some hours walk from our dwellings, and all the neighbours resort thither in a body. They use no beasts of husbandry; and their only instruments are hoes, axes, shovels, and beaks, or pointed iron to dig with. Sometimes we are visited by locusts, which come in large clouds, so as to darken the air, and destroy our harvest. This however happens rarely, but when it does, a famine is produced by it. I remember an instance or two wherein this happened. This common is oftimes the theatre of war; and therefore when our people go out to till their land, they not only go in a body, but generally take their arms with them, for fear of a surprise; and when they apprehend an invasion they guard the avenues to their dwellings, by driving sticks into the ground, which are so sharp at one end as to pierce the foot, and are generally dipt in poison. From what I can recollect of these battles, they appear to have been irruptions of one little state or district on the other, to obtain prisoners or booty. Perhaps they were incited to this by those traders who brought the European goods I mentioned amongst us. Such mode of obtaining slaves in Africa is common; and I believe more are procured this way, and by kidnapping, than any other. When a trader wants slaves, he applies to a chief for them, and tempts him with his wares. It is not extraordinary, if on this occasion he yields to the temptation with as little firmness, and accepts the price of his fellow creature's liberty with as little reluctance, as the enlightened merchant. Accordingly, he falls on his neighbours, and a desperate battle ensues. If he prevails, and takes prisoners, he gratifies his avarice by selling them; but, if his party be vanquished, and he falls into the hands of the enemy, he is put to death: for, as he has been known to foment their quarrels, it is thought dangerous to let him survive, and no ransom can save him, though all other prisoners may be redeemed. We have firearms, bows and arrows, broad two-edged swords and javelins; we have shields also, which cover a man from head to foot. All are taught the use of the weapons. Even our women are warriors, and march boldly out to fight along with the men. Our whole district is a kind of militia: on a certain signal given, such as the firing of a gun at night, they all rise in arms and rush upon their enemy. It is perhaps something remarkable, that when our people march to the field, a red flag or banner is borne before them. I was once a witness to a battle in our common. We had been all at work in it one day as usual when our people were suddenly attacked. I climbed a tree at some distance, from which I beheld the fight. There were many women as well as men on both sides; among others my mother was there and armed with a broad sword. After fighting for a considerable time with great fury, and many had been killed, our people obtained the victory, and took their enemy's Chief prisoner. He was carried off in great triumph, and, though he offered a large ransom for his life, he was put to death. A virgin of note among our enemies had been slain in the battle, and her arm was exposed in our market-place, where our trophies were always exhibited. The spoils were divided according to the merit of the warriors. Those prisoners which were not sold or redeemed we kept as slaves: but how different was their condition from that of the slaves in the West-Indies! With us they do no more work than other members of the community, even their master. Their food, cloathing, and lodging were nearly the same as theirs, except that they were not permitted to eat with those who were free born and there was scarce any other difference between them, than a superior degree of importance which the head of a family possesses in our state, and that authority which, as such, he exercises over every part of his household. Some of these slaves have even slaves under them, as their own property, and for their own use.

As to religion, the natives believe that there is one Creator of all things, and that he lives in the sun, and is girded round with a belt, that he may never eat or drink; but, according to some, he smokes a pipe, which is our own favourite luxury. They believe he governs events, especially our deaths or captivity; but, as for the doctrine of eternity, I do not remember to have ever heard of it: some however believe in the transmigration of souls in a certain degree. Those spirits, which are not transmigrated, such as our dear friends or relations, they believe always attend them, and guard them from the bad spirits of their foes. For this reason, they always, before eating, as I have observed, put some small portion of the meat, and pour some of their drink, on the ground for them; and they often make oblations of the blood of beasts or fowls at their graves. I was very fond of my mother, and almost constantly with her. When she went to make these oblations at her mother's tomb, which was a kind of small solitary thatched house, I sometimes attended her. There she made her libations, and spent most of the night in cries and lamentations. I have been often extremely terrified on these occasions. The loneliness of the place, the darkness of the night, and the ceremony of libation, naturally awful and gloomy, were heightened by my mother's lamentations; and these, concurring with the doleful cries of birds, by which these places were frequented, gave an inexpressible terror to the scene.

We compute the year from the day on which the sun crosses the line, and, on its setting that evening, there is a general shout throughout the land; at least I can speak from my own knowledge throughout our vicinity. The people at the same time make a great noise with rattles, not unlike the basket rattles used by children here, though much larger, and hold up their hands to heaven for a blessing. It is then the greatest offerings are made; and those children whom our wise men foretell will be fortunate are then presented to different people. I remember many used to come to see me, and I was carried about to others for that purpose. They have many offerings, particularly at full moons; generally two at harvest, before the fruits are taken out of the ground: and, when any young animals are killed, sometimes they offer up part of them as a sacrifice. These offerings, when made by one of the heads of a family, serve for the whole. I remember we often had them at my father's and my uncle's, and their families have been present. Some of our offerings are eaten with bitter herbs. We had a saying among us to any one of a cross temper, "That if they were to be eaten, they should be eaten with bitter herbs."

We practised circumcision like the Jews, and made offerings and feasts on that occasion in the same manner as they did. Like them also, our children were named from some event, some circumstance, or fancied foreboding at the time of their birth. I was named *Olaudah,* which, in our language, signifies vicissitude, or fortunate also; one favoured, and having a loud voice and well spoken. I remember we never polluted the name of the object of our adoration; on the contrary, it was always mentioned with the greatest reverence; and we were totally unacquainted with swearing, and all those terms of abuse and reproach which find the way so readily and copiously into the languages of more civilized people. The only

expressions of that kind I remember were "May you rot, or may you swell, or may a beast take you."

I have before remarked, that the natives of this part of Africa are extremely cleanly. This necessary habit of decency was with us a part of religion, and therefore we had many purifications and washings; indeed almost as many, and used on the same occasions, if my recollection does not fail me, as the Jews. Those that touched the dead at any time were obliged to wash and purify themselves before they could enter a dwelling-house. Every woman too, at certain times, was forbidden to come into a dwelling-house, or touch any person, or any thing we ate. I was so fond of my mother I could not keep from her, or avoid touching her at some of those periods, in consequence of which I was obliged to be kept out with her, in a little house made for that purpose, till offering was made, and then we were purified.

Though we had no places of public worship, we had priests and magicians, or wise men. I do not remember whether they had different offices, or whether they were united in the same persons but they were held in great reverence by the people. They calculated our time, and foretold events, as their name imported, for we called them Ah-affoe-way-cah, which signifies calculators, or yearly men, our year being called Ah-affoe. They wore their beards; and, when they died, they were succeeded by their sons. Most of their implements and things of value were interred along with them. Pipes and tobacco were also put into the grave with the corpse, which was always perfumed and ornamented; and animals were offered in sacrifice to them. None accompanied their funerals but those of the same profession or tribe. These buried them after sunset, and always returned from the grave by a different way from that which they went.

These magicians were also our doctors or physicians. They practised bleeding by cupping, and were very successful in healing wounds and expelling poisons. They had likewise some extraordinary method of discovering jealousy, theft, and poisoning; the success of which no doubt they derived from their unbounded influence over the credulity and superstition of the people. I do not remember what those methods were, except that as to poisoning. I recollect an instance or two, which I hope it will not be deemed impertinent here to insert, as it may serve as a kind of specimen of the rest, and is still used by the negroes in the West Indies. A young woman had been poisoned, but it was not known by whom; the doctors ordered the corpse to be taken up by some persons, and carried to the grave. As soon as the bearers had raised it on their shoulders, they seemed seized with some sudden impulse, and ran to and fro', unable to stop themselves. At last, after having passed through a number of thorns and prickly bushes unhurt, the corpse fell from them close to a house, and defaced it in the fall: and the owner being taken up, he immediately confessed the poisoning.

The natives are extremely cautious about poison. When they buy any eatable the seller kisses it all round before the buyer, to shew him it is not poisoned; and the same is done when any meat or drink is presented, particularly to a stranger. We have serpents of different kinds, some of which are esteemed ominous when they appear in our houses, and these we never molest. I remember two of those ominous snakes, each of which was as thick as the calf of a man's leg, and in colour resembling a dolphin in the water, crept at different times into my mother's night-house, where I always lay with her, and coiled themselves into folds, and each time they crowed like a cock. I was desired by some of our wise men to touch these, that I might be interested in the good omens, which I did, for they were quite harmless, and would tamely suffer themselves to be handled; and then they were put into a large open earthen pan, and set on one side of the highway. Some of our snakes, however, were poisonous: one of them crossed the road one day when I was standing on it, and passed between my feet, without offering to touch me, to the great surprise of many who saw it; and these incidents

were accounted by the wise men, and likewise by my mother and the rest of the people, as remarkable omens in my favour.

Such is the imperfect sketch my memory has furnished me with of the manners and customs of a people among whom I first drew my breath. And here I cannot forbear suggesting what has long struck me very forcibly, namely, the strong analogy which even by this sketch, imperfect as it is, appears to prevail in the manners and customs of my countrymen, and those of the Jews, before they reached the Land of Promise, and particularly the patriarchs, while they were yet in that pastoral state which is described in Genesis—an analogy, which alone would induce me to think that the one people had sprung from the other. Indeed this is the opinion of Dr. Gill, who, in his commentary on Genesis very ably deduces the pedigree of the Africans from Afer and Afra, the descendants of Abraham by Keturah his wife and concubine, (for both these titles are applied to her). It is also conformable to the sentiments of Dr. John Clarke, formerly Dean of Sarum, in his Truth of the Christian Religion: both these authors concur in ascribing to us this original. The reasonings of these gentlemen are still further confirmed by the Scripture Chronology of the Rev. Arthur Bedford; and if any further corroboration were required, this resemblance in so many respects is a strong evidence in support of the opinion. Like the Israelites in their primitive state, our government was conducted by our chiefs, our judges, our wise men, and elders; and the head of a family with us enjoyed a similar authority over his household with that which is ascribed to Abraham and the other patriarchs. The law of retaliation obtained almost universally with us as with them: and even their religion appeared to have shed upon us a ray of its glory, though broken and spent in its passage, or eclipsed by the cloud with which time, tradition, and ignorance might have enveloped it: for we had our circumcision (a rule I believe peculiar to that people): we had also our sacrifices and burnt-offerings, our washings and purifications, on the same occasions as they had.

As to the difference of colour between the Eboan Africans and the modern Jews, I shall not presume to account for it. It is a subject which has engaged the pens of men of both genius and learning, and is far above my strength. The most able and Reverend Mr. T. Clarkson, however, in his much-admired Essay on the Slavery and Commerce of the Human Species, has ascertained the cause, in a manner that at once solves every objection on that account, and, on my mind at least, has produced the fullest conviction. I shall therefore refer to that performance for the theory, contenting myself with extracting a fact as related by Dr. Mitchel. "The Spaniards, who have inhabited America, under the torrid zone, for any time, are become as dark coloured as our native Indians of Virginia, *of which I myself have been a witness.* There is also another instance of a Portuguese settlement at Mitomba, a river in Sierra Leona, where the inhabitants are bred from a mixture of the first Portuguese discoverers with the natives, and are now become, in their complexion, and in the woolly quality of their hair, *perfect negroes,* retaining however a smattering of the Portuguese language."

These instances, and a great many more which might be adduced, while they shew how the complexions of the same persons vary in different climates, it is hoped may tend also to remove the prejudice that some conceive against the natives of Africa on account of their colour. Surely the minds of the Spaniards did not change with their complexions! Are there not causes enough to which the apparent inferiority of an African may be ascribed, without limiting the goodness of God, and supposing he forbore to stamp understanding on certainly his own image, because "carved in ebony?" Might it not naturally be ascribed to their situation? When they come among Europeans, they are ignorant of their language, religion, manners, and customs. Are any pains taken to teach them these? Are they treated as men? Does not slavery itself depress the mind, and extinguish all its fire, and every noble sentiment? But, above all, what advantages do not a refined people possess over those who are rude and uncultivated? Let the polished and haughty European recollect that *his* ancestors were once, like the Africans, uncivilized, and even barbarous. Did Nature make *them* inferior to their sons? and should *they too* have been made slaves? Every rational mind answers, No. Let such reflections as these melt the pride of their superiority into sympathy for the wants and miseries of their sable brethren, and compel them to acknowledge, that understanding is not confined to feature or colour. If, when they look round the world, they feel exultation, let it be tempered with benevolence to others, and gratitude to God, "who hath made of one blood all nations of men for to dwell on all the face of the earth; and whose wisdom is not our wisdom, neither are our ways his ways."

. . . I have already acquainted the reader with the time and place of my birth. My father, besides many slaves, had a numerous family, of which seven lived to grow up, including myself and a sister, who was the only daughter. As I was the youngest of the sons, I became, of course, the greatest favourite with my mother, and was always with her; and she used to take particular pains to form my mind. I was trained up from my earliest years in the arts of agriculture and war: my daily exercise was shooting and throwing javelins; and my mother adorned me with emblems, after the manner of our greatest warriors. In this way I grew up till I was turned the age of eleven, when an end was put to my happiness in the following manner:—Generally, when the grown people in the neighbourhood were gone far in the fields to labour, the children assembled together in some of the neighbours' premises to play; and commonly some of us used to get up a tree to look out for any assailant, or kidnapper, that might come upon us; for they sometimes took those opportunities of our parents' absence, to attack and carry off as many as they could seize. One day, as I was watching at the top of a tree in our yard, I saw one of those people come into the yard of our next neighbour but one, to kidnap, there being many stout young people in it. Immediately, on this, I gave the alarm of the rogue, and he was surrounded by the stoutest of them, who entangled him with cords, so that he could not escape till some of the grown people came and secured him. But, alas! ere long it was my fate to be thus attacked, and to be carried off, when none of the grown people were nigh. One day, when all our people were gone out to their works as usual, and only I and my dear sister were left to mind the house, two men and a woman got over our walls, and in a moment seized us both; and, without giving us time to cry out, or make resistance, they stopped our mouths, tied our hands, and ran off with us into the nearest wood: and continued to carry us as far as they could, till night came on, when we reached a small house, where the robbers halted for refreshment, and spent the night. We were then unbound, but were unable to take any food; and, being quite overpowered by fatigue and grief, our only relief was some sleep, which allayed our misfortune for a short time. The next morning we left the house, and continued travelling all the day. For a long time we had kept the woods, but at last we came into a road which I believed I knew. I had now some hopes of being delivered; for we had advanced but a little way before I discovered some people at a distance, on which I began to cry out for their assistance; but my cries had no other effect than to make them tie me faster, and stop my mouth, and then they put me into a large sack. They also stopped my sister's mouth, and tied her hands; and in this manner we proceeded till we were out of the sight of these people.— When we went to rest the following night they offered us some victuals; but we refused them; and the only comfort we had was in being in one another's arms all that night, and bathing each other with our tears. But, alas! we were soon deprived of even the smallest comfort of weeping together. The next day proved a day of greater sorrow than I had yet experienced; for my sister and I were then separated, while we lay clasped in each other's arms. It was in vain that we besought

them not to part us: she was torn from me, and immediately carried away, while I was left in a state of distraction not to be described. I cried and grieved continually; and for several days I did not eat any thing but what they forced into my mouth. At length, after many days travelling, during which I had often changed masters, I got into the hands of a chieftain, in a very pleasant country. This man had two wives and some children, and they all used me extremely well, and did all they could to comfort me; particularly the first wife, who was something like my mother. Although I was a great many days journey from my father's house, yet these people spoke exactly the same language with us. This first master of mine, as I may call him, was a smith, and my principal employment was working his bellows, which were the same kind as I had seen in my vicinity. They were in some respects not unlike the stoves here in gentlemen's kitchens; and were covered over with leather; and in the middle of that leather a stick was fixed, and a person stood up, and worked it, in the same manner as is done to pump water out of a cask with a hand-pump. I believe it was gold he worked, for it was of a lovely bright yellow colour, and was worn by the women on their wrists and ancles. I was there I suppose about a month, and they at last used to trust me some little distance from the house. This liberty I used in embracing every opportunity to inquire the way to my own home: and I also sometimes, for the same purpose, went with the maidens, in the cool of the evenings, to bring pitchers of water from the springs for the use of the house. I had also remarked where the sun rose in the morning, and set in the evening, as I had travelled along; and I had observed that my father's house was towards the rising of the sun. I therefore determined to seize the first opportunity of making my escape, and to shape my course for that quarter; for I was quite oppressed and weighed down by grief after my mother and friends; and my love of liberty, ever great, was strengthened by the mortifying circumstance of not daring to eat with the free-born children, although I was mostly their companion.—While I was projecting my escape one day, an unlucky event happened, which quite disconcerted my plan, and put an end to my hopes. I used to be sometimes employed in assisting an elderly woman slave to cook and take care of the poultry; and one morning, while I was feeding some chickens, I happened to toss a small pebble at one of them, which hit it on the middle, and directly killed it. The old slave, having soon after missed the chicken, inquired after it; and on my relating the accident (for I told her the truth, because my mother would never suffer me to tell a lie) she flew into a violent passion, threatened that I should suffer for it; and, my master being out, she immediately went and told her mistress what I had done. This alarmed me very much, and I expected an instant correction, which to me was uncommonly dreadful; for I had seldom been beaten at home. I therefore resolved to fly; and accordingly I ran into a thicket that was hard by, and hid myself in the bushes. Soon afterwards my mistress and the slave returned, and, not seeing me, they searched all the house, but, not finding me, and I not making answer when they called to me, they thought I had run away, and the whole neighbourhood was raised in the pursuit of me. In that part of the country (as well as ours) the houses and villages were skirted with woods, or shrubberies, and the bushes were so thick, that a man could readily conceal himself in them, so as to elude the strictest search. The neighbours continued the whole day looking for me, and several times many of them came within a few yards of the place where I lay hid. I expected every moment, when I heard a rustling among the trees, to be found out, and punished by my master; but they never discovered me, though they were often so near that I even heard their conjectures as they were looking about for me; and I now learned from them, that any attempt to return home would be hopeless. Most of them supposed I had fled towards home; but the distance was so great, and the way so intricate, that they thought I could never reach it, and that I should be lost in the woods. When I heard this

I was seized with a violent panic, and abandoned myself to despair. Night too began to approach, and aggravated all my fears. I had before entertained hopes of getting home, and I had determined when it should be dark to make the attempt; but I was now convinced it was fruitless, and I began to consider that, if possibly I could escape all other animals, I could not those of the human kind; and that, not knowing the way, I must perish in the woods.—Thus was I like the hunted deer:

Ev'ry leaf and ev'ry whisp'ring breath
Convey'd a foe, and ev'ry foe a death.

I heard frequent rustlings among the leaves; and, being pretty sure they were snakes, I expected every instant to be stung by them.—This increased my anguish, and the horror of my situation became now quite insupportable. I at length quitted the thicket, very faint and hungry, for I had not eaten or drank any thing all the day, and crept to my master's kitchen, from whence I set out at first, and which was an open shed, and laid myself down in the ashes, with an anxious wish for death to relieve me from all my pains. I was scarcely awake in the morning when the old woman slave, who was the first up, came to light the fire, and saw me in the fire-place. She was very much surprised to see me, and could scarcely believe her own eyes. She now promised to intercede for me, and went for her master, who soon after came, and, having slightly reprimanded me, ordered me to be taken care of, and not ill-treated.

Soon after this my master's only daughter and child by his first wife sickened and died, which affected him so much that for some time he was almost frantic, and really would have killed himself had he not been watched and prevented. However, in a small time afterwards he recovered, and I was again sold. I was now carried to the left of the sun's rising, through many dreary wastes and dismal woods, amidst the hideous roarings of wild beasts.—The people I was sold to used to carry me very often, when I was tired, either on their shoulders or on their backs. I saw many convenient well-built sheds along the roads, at proper distances, to accommodate the merchants and travellers, who lay in those buildings along with their wives, who often accompany them; and they always go well armed.

From the time I left my own nation I always found somebody that understood me till I came to the sea coast. The languages of different nations did not totally differ, nor were they so copious as those of the Europeans, particularly the English. They were therefore easily learned; and, while I was journeying thus through Africa, I acquired two or three different tongues. In this manner I had been travelling for a considerable time, when one evening, to my great surprise, whom should I see brought to the house where I was but my dear sister. As soon as she saw me she gave a loud shriek, and ran into my arms.—I was quite overpowered; neither of us could speak, but, for a considerable time, clung to each other in mutual embraces, unable to do any thing but weep. Our meeting affected all who saw us; and indeed I must acknowledge, in honour of those sable destroyers of human rights, that I never met with any ill treatment, or saw any offered to their slaves, except tying them, when necessary, to keep them from running away. When these people knew we were brother and sister they indulged us to be together; and the man, to whom I supposed we belonged, lay with us, he in the middle, while she and I held one another by the hands across his breast all night; and thus for a while we forgot our misfortunes in the joy of being together: but even this small comfort was soon to have an end; for scarcely had the fatal morning appeared, when she was again torn from me for ever! I was now more miserable, if possible, than before. The small relief which her presence gave me from pain was gone, and the wretchedness of my situation was redoubled by my anxiety after her fate, and my apprehensions lest her sufferings should be greater than mine, when I could not be with

her to alleviate them. Yes, thou dear partner of all my childish sports! thou sharer of my joys and sorrows! happy should I have ever esteemed myself to encounter every misery for you, and to procure your freedom by the sacrifice of my own. Though you were early forced from my arms, your image has been always rivetted in my heart, from which neither *time nor fortune* have been able to remove it: so that while the thoughts of your sufferings have damped my prosperity, they have mingled with adversity, and increased its bitterness.—To that heaven which protects the weak from the strong, I commit the care of your innocence and virtues, if they have not already received their full reward; and if your youth and delicacy have not long since fallen victims to the violence of the African trader, the pestilential stench of a Guinea ship, the seasoning in the European colonies, or the lash and lust of a brutal and unrelenting overseer.

I did not long remain after my sister. I was again sold, and carried through a number of places, till, after travelling a considerable time, I came to a town called Tinmah, in the most beautiful country I had yet seen in Africa. It was extremely rich, and there were many rivulets which flowed through it; and supplied a large pond in the center of the town, where the people washed. Here I first saw and tasted cocoa nuts, which I thought superior to any nuts I had ever tasted before; and the trees, which were loaded, were also interspersed amongst the houses, which had commodious shades adjoining, and were in the same manner as ours, the insides being neatly plastered and whitewashed. Here I also saw and tasted for the first time sugarcane. Their money consisted of little white shells, the size of the finger nail: they are known in this country by the name of *core.* I was sold here for one hundred and seventy-two of them by a merchant who lived and brought me there. I had been about two or three days at his house, when a wealthy widow, a neighbour of his, came there one evening, and brought with her an only son, a young gentleman about my own age and size.

Here they saw me; and, having taken a fancy to me, I was bought of the merchant, and went home with them. Her house and premises were situated close to one of those rivulets I have mentioned, and were the finest I ever saw in Africa: they were very extensive, and she had a number of slaves to attend her. The next day I was washed and perfumed, and when meal-time came, I was led into the presence of my mistress, and ate and drank before her with her son. This filled me with astonishment: and I could scarce help expressing my surprise that the young gentleman should suffer me, who was bound, to eat with him who was free; and not only so, but that he would not at any time either eat or drink till I had taken first, because I was the eldest, which was agreeable to our custom. Indeed every thing here, and all their treatment of me, made me forget that I was a slave. The language of these people resembled ours so nearly, that we understood each other perfectly. They had also the very same customs as we. There were likewise slaves daily to attend us, while my young master and I, with other boys, sported with our darts and bows and arrows, as I had been used to do at home. In this resemblance to my former happy state I passed about two months, and I now began to think I was to be adopted into the family, and was beginning to be reconciled to my situation, and to forget by degrees my misfortunes, when all at once the delusion vanished; for, without the least previous knowledge, one morning early, while my dear master and companion was still asleep, I was awakened out of my reverie to fresh sorrow, and hurried away even amongst the uncircumcised.

Thus, at the very moment I dreamed of the greatest happiness, I found myself most miserable: and it seemed as if fortune wished to give me this taste of joy only to render the reverse more poignant. The change I now experienced was as painful as it was sudden and unexpected. It was a change indeed from a state of bliss to a scene which is inexpressible by me, as it discovered to me an element I had never before beheld, and till then had no idea of, and wherein such instances of hardship and cruelty continually occurred as I can never reflect on but with horror.

All the nations and people I had hitherto passed through resembled our own in their manners, customs and language: but I came at length to a country, the inhabitants of which differed from us in all those particulars. I was very much struck with this difference, especially when I came among a people who did not circumcise, and eat without washing their hands. They cooked also in iron pots, and had European cutlasses and cross bows, which were unknown to us, and fought with their fists amongst themselves. Their women were not so modest as ours, for they eat, and drank, and slept with their men. But, above all, I was amazed to see no sacrifices or offerings among them. In some of those places the people ornamented themselves with scars, and likewise filed their teeth very sharp. They wanted sometimes to ornament me in the same manner, but I would not suffer them; hoping that I might some time be among a people who did not thus disfigure themselves, as I thought they did. At last, I came to the banks of a large river, which was covered with canoes, in which the people appeared to live with their household utensils and provisions of all kinds. I was beyond measure astonished at this, as I had never before seen any water larger than a pond or a rivulet; and my surprise was mingled with no small fear when I was put into one of these canoes, and we began to paddle and move along the river. We continued going on thus till night; and when we came to land, and made fires on the banks, each family by themselves, some dragged their canoes on shore, others staid and cooked in theirs, and laid in them all night. Those on the land had mats, of which they made tents, some in the shape of little houses: In these we slept; and after the morning meal we embarked again, and proceeded as before. I was often very much astonished to see some of the women, as well as the men, jump into the water, dive to the bottom, come up again, and swim about. Thus I continued to travel, sometimes by land, sometimes by water, through different countries, and various nations, till, at the end of six or seven months after I had been kidnapped, I arrived at the sea coast. It would be tedious and uninteresting to relate all the incidents which befel me during this journey, and which I have not yet forgotten; of the various hands I passed through, and the manners and customs of all the different people among whom I lived: I shall therefore only observe, that, in all the places where I was, the soil was exceedingly rich; the pomkins, eadas, plantains, yams, &c. &c. were in great abundance, and of incredible size. There were also vast quantities of different gums, though not used for any purpose; and every where a great deal of tobacco. The cotton even grew quite wild; and there was plenty of red wood. I saw no mechanics whatever in all the way, except such as I have mentioned. The chief employment in all these countries was agriculture, and both the males and females, as with us, were brought up to it, and trained in the arts of war.

The first object which saluted my eyes when I arrived on the coast was the sea, and a slave-ship, which was then riding at anchor, and waiting for its cargo. These filled me with astonishment, which was soon converted into terror, which I am yet at a loss to describe, nor the then feelings of my mind. When I was carried on board I was immediately handled, and tossed up, to see if I were sound, by some of the crew; and I was now persuaded that I had gotten into a world of bad spirits, and that they were going to kill me. Their complexions too differing so much from ours, their long hair, and the language they spoke, which was very different from any I had ever heard, united to confirm me in this belief. Indeed, such were the horrors of my views and fears at the moment, that, if ten thousand worlds had been my own, I would have freely parted with them all to have exchanged my condition with that of the meanest slave in my own country. When I looked round the ship too, and saw a large furnace of copper boiling, and a multitude of black people of every description chained together, every one of their countenances expressing dejection and sorrow, I no longer doubted of my fate, and, quite overpowered with horror and anguish, I fell motionless on the deck and fainted. When I recovered a little, I found some black people about me, who I believed were some of those who brought me on board, and had been receiving their pay; they talked to me in order to cheer me, but all in vain. I asked them if we were not to be eaten by those white men with horrible looks, red faces, and long hair? They told me I was not; and one of the crew brought me a small portion of spirituous liquor in a wine glass; but, being afraid of him, I would not take it out of his hand. One of the blacks therefore took it from him and gave it to me, and I took a little down my palate, which, instead of reviving me, as they thought it would, threw me into the greatest consternation at the strange feeling it produced, having never tasted any such liquor before. Soon after this, the blacks who brought me on board went off, and left me abandoned to despair. I now saw myself deprived of all chance of returning to my native country, or even the least glimpse of hope of gaining the shore, which I now considered as friendly: and I even wished for my former slavery in preference to my present situation, which was filled with horrors of every kind, still heightened by my ignorance of what I was to undergo. I was not long suffered to indulge my grief; I was soon put down under the decks, and there I received such a salutation in my nostrils as I had never experienced in my life; so that with the loathsomeness of the stench, and crying together, I became so sick and low that I was not able to eat, nor had I the least desire to taste any thing. I now wished for the last friend, Death, to relieve me; but soon, to my grief, two of the white men offered me eatables; and, on my refusing to eat, one of them held me fast by the hands, and laid me across, I think, the windlass, and tied my feet, while the other flogged me severely. I had never experienced any thing of this kind before; and although, not being used to the water, I naturally feared that element the first time I saw it; yet, nevertheless, could I have got over the nettings, I would have jumped over the side, but I could not; and, besides, the crew used to watch us very closely who were not chained down to the decks, lest we should leap into the water; and I have seen some of these poor African prisoners most severely cut for attempting to do so, and hourly whipped for not eating. This indeed was often the case with myself. In a little time after, amongst the poor chained men, I found some of my own nation, which in a small degree gave ease to my mind. I inquired of these what was to be done with us? they gave me to understand we were to be carried to these white people's country to work for them. I then was a little revived, and thought, if it were no worse than working, my situation was not so desperate: but still I feared I should be put to death, the white people looked and acted, as I thought, in so savage a manner; for I had never seen among any people such instances of brutal cruelty; and this not only shewn towards us blacks, but also to some of the whites themselves. One white man in particular I saw, when we were permitted to be on deck, flogged so unmercifully with a large rope near the foremast, that he died in consequence of it; and they tossed him over the side as they would have done a brute. This made me fear these people the more; and I expected nothing less than to be treated in the same manner. I could not help expressing my fears and apprehensions to some of my countrymen: I asked them if these people had no country, but lived in this hollow place the ship? they told me they did not, but came from a distant one. "Then," said I, "how comes it in all our country we never heard of them?" They told me, because they lived so very far off. I then asked where were their women? had they any like themselves! I was told they had: "And why," said I, "do we not see them?" they answered, because they were left behind. I asked how the vessel could go? they told me they could not tell; but that there were cloths put upon the

masts by the help of the ropes I saw, and then the vessel went on; and the white men had some spell or magic they put in the water when they liked in order to stop the vessel. I was exceedingly amazed at this account, and really thought they were spirits. I therefore wished much to be from amongst them, for I expected they would sacrifice me: but my wishes were vain; for we were so quartered that it was impossible for any of us to make our escape. While we staid on the coast I was mostly on deck; and one day, to my great astonishment, I saw one of these vessels coming in with the sails up. As soon as the whites saw it, they gave a great shout, at which we were amazed; and the more so as the vessel appeared larger by approaching nearer. At last she came to an anchor in my sight, and when the anchor was let go, I and my countrymen who saw it were lost in astonishment to observe the vessel stop; and were now convinced it was done by magic. Soon after this the other ship got her boats out, and they came on board of us, and the people of both ships seemed very glad to see each other. Several of the strangers also shook hands with us black people, and made motions with their hands, signifying, I suppose, we were to go to their country; but we did not understand them. At last, when the ship we were in had got in all her cargo, they made ready with many fearful noises, and we were all put under deck, so that we could not see how they managed the vessel. But this disappointment was the least of my sorrow. The stench of the hold while we were on the coast was so intolerably loathsome, that it was dangerous to remain there for any time, and some of us had been permitted to stay on the deck for the fresh air; but now that the whole ship's cargo were confined together, it became absolutely pestilential. The closeness of the place, and the heat of the climate, added to the number in the ship, which was so crowded that each had scarcely room to turn himself, almost suffocated us. This produced copious perspirations, so that the air soon became unfit for respiration, from a variety of loathsome smells, and brought on a sickness among the slaves, of which many died, thus falling victims to the improvident avarice, as I may call it, of their purchasers. This wretched situation was again aggravated by the galling of the chains, now become insupportable; and the filth of the necessary tubs, into which the children often fell, and were almost suffocated. The shrieks of the women, and the groans of the dying, rendered the whole a scene of horror almost inconceiveable. Happily perhaps for myself I was soon reduced so low here that it was thought necessary to keep me almost always on deck; and from my extreme youth I was not put in fetters. In this situation I expected every hour to share the fate of my companions, some of whom were almost daily brought upon deck at the point of death, which I began to hope would soon put an end to my miseries. Often did I think many of the inhabitants of the deep much more happy than myself; I envied them the freedom they enjoyed, and as often wished I could change my condition for theirs. Every circumstance I met with served only to render my state more painful, and heighten my apprehensions, and my opinion of the cruelty of the whites. One day they had taken a number of fishes; and when they had killed and satisfied themselves with as many as they thought fit, to our astonishment who were on the deck, rather than give any of them to us to eat, as we expected, they tossed the remaining fish into the sea again, although we begged and prayed for some as well as we could, but in vain; and some of my countrymen, being pressed by hunger, took an opportunity, when they thought no one saw them, of trying to get a little privately; but they were discovered, and the attempt procured them some very severe floggings.

One day, when we had a smooth sea, and moderate wind, two of my wearied countrymen, who were chained together (I was near them at the time), preferring death to such a life of misery, somehow made through the nettings, and jumped into the sea: immediately another quite dejected fellow, who, on account of his illness, was suffered to be out of irons, also followed their example; and I believe many more would very soon have done the same, if they had not been prevented by the ship's crew, who were instantly alarmed. Those of us that were the most active were, in a moment, put down under the deck; and there was such a noise and confusion amongst the people of the ship as I never heard before, to stop her, and get the boat out to go after the slaves. However, two of the wretches were drowned, but they got the other, and afterwards flogged him unmercifully, for thus attempting to prefer death to slavery. In this manner we continued to undergo more hardships than I can now relate; hardships which are inseparable from this accursed trade.—Many a time we were near suffocation, from the want of fresh air, which we were often without for whole days together. This, and the stench of the necessary tubs, carried off many. During our passage I first saw flying fishes, which surprised me very much: they used frequently to fly across the ship, and many of them fell on the deck. I also now first saw the use of the quadrant. I had often with astonishment seen the mariners make observations with it, and I could not think what it meant. They at last took notice of my surprise; and one of them, willing to increase it, as well as to gratify my curiosity, made me one day look through it. The clouds appeared to me to be land, which disappeared as they passed along. This heightened my wonder: and I was now more persuaded than ever that I was in another world, and that every thing about me was magic. At last we came in sight of the island of Barbadoes, at which the whites on board gave a great shout, and made many signs of joy to us. We did not know what to think of this; but as the vessel drew nearer we plainly saw the harbour, and other ships of different kinds and sizes: and we soon anchored amongst them off Bridge Town. Many merchants and planters now came on board, though it was in the evening. They put us in separate parcels, and examined us attentively. They also made us jump, and pointed to the land, signifying we were to go there. We thought by this we should be eaten by these ugly men, as they appeared to us; and, when soon after we were all put down under the deck again, there was much dread and trembling among us, and nothing but bitter cries to be heard all the night from these apprehensions, insomuch that at last the white people got some old slaves from the land to pacify us. They told us we were not to be eaten, but to work, and were soon to go on land, where we should see many of our country people. This report eased us much; and sure enough, soon after we were landed, there came to us Africans of all languages. We were conducted immediately to the merchant's yard, where we were all pent up together like so many sheep in a fold, without regard to sex or age. As every object was new to me, every thing I saw filled me with surprise. What struck me first was, that the houses were built with bricks, in stories, and in every other respect different from those in [sic] I have seen in Africa: but I was still more astonished on seeing people on horseback. I did not know what this could mean; and indeed I thought these people were full of nothing but magical arts. While I was in this astonishment, one of my fellow prisoners spoke to a countryman of his about the horses, who said they were the same kind they had in their country. I understood them, though they were from a distant part of Africa, and I thought it odd I had not seen any horses there; but afterwards, when I came to converse with different Africans, I found they had many horses amongst them, and much larger than those I then saw. We were not many days in the merchant's custody before we were sold after their usual manner, which is this:—On a signal given, (as the beat of a drum), the buyers rush at once into the yard where the slaves are confined, and make choice of that parcel they like best. The noise and clamour with which this is attended, and the eagerness visible in the countenances of the buyers, serve not a little to increase the apprehensions of the terrified Africans, who may well be supposed to consider them as the ministers of that destruction to which they think themselves devoted. In this manner, without scruple, are relations and friends separated, most of them never to see each other again. I remember in the vessel in which I was brought over, in the men's apartment, there were several brothers, who, in the sale, were sold in different lots; and it was very moving on this occasion to see and hear their cries at parting. O, ye nominal Christians! might not an African ask you, learned you this from your God? who says unto you, Do unto all men as you would men should do unto you? Is it not enough that we are torn from our country and friends to toil for your luxury and lust of gain? Must every tender feeling be likewise sacrificed to your avarice? Are the dearest friends and relations, now rendered more dear by their separation from their kindred, still to be parted from each other, and thus prevented from cheering the gloom of slavery with the small comfort of being together and mingling their sufferings and sorrows? Why are parents to lose their children, brothers their sisters, or husbands their wives? Surely this is a new refinement in cruelty, which, while it has no advantage to atone for it, thus aggravates distress, and adds fresh horrors even to the wretchedness of slavery.

A New and Accurate Description of the Coast of Guinea Divided into the Gold, the Slave, and the Ivory Coasts

Willem Bosman

. . . The first business of one of our Factors when he comes to *Fida* [Whydah] is to satisfie the Customs of the King and the great Men, which amount to about 100 Pounds in *Guinea* value, as the Goods must yield there. After which we have free Licence to Trade, which is published throughout the whole Land by the Cryer.

But yet before we can deal with any Person, we are obliged to buy the King's whole stock of Slaves at a set price; which is commonly one third or one fourth higher than ordinary: After which we obtain free leave to deal with all his Subjects of what Rank soever. But if there happen to be no stock of Slaves, the Factor must then resolve to run the Risque of trusting the inhabitants with Goods to the value of one or two hundred Slaves; which Commodities they send into the In-land Country, in order to buy with them Slaves at all Markets, and that sometimes two hundred Miles deep in the Country: For you ought to be informed that Markets of Men are kept in the same manner as those of beasts with us.

Not a few in our Country fondly imagine that Parents here sell their Children, Men their Wives, and one Brother the other: But those who think so deceive themselves; for this never happens on any other account but that of Necessity, or some great Crime: But most of the Slaves that are offered to us are Prisoners of War, which are sold by the victors as their Booty.

When these Slaves come to *Fida,* they are put in Prison all together, and when we treat concerning buying them, they are all brought out together in a large Plain; where, by our Chirurgeons, whose Province it is, they are thoroughly examined, even to the smallest Member, and that naked too both Men and Women, without the least Distinction or Modesty. Those which are approved as good are set on one side; and the lame or faulty are set by as *Invalides,* which are here called *Mackrons.* These are such as are above five and thirty Years old, or are maimed in the Arms, Legs, Hands or Feet, have lost a Tooth, are grey-haired, or have Films over their Eyes; as well as all those which are affected with any Veneral Distemper, or with several other Diseases.

The *Invalides* and the Maimed being thrown out, as I have told you, the remainder are numbred, and it is entred who delivered them. In the mean while a burning Iron, with the Arms or Name of the Companies, lyes in the Fire; with which ours are marked on the Breast.

This is done that we may distinguish them from the Slaves of the *English, French* or others; (which are also marked with their Mark) and to prevent the *Negros* exchanging them for worse; at which they have a good Hand.

I doubt not but this Trade seems very barbarous to you, but since it is followed by meer necessity it must go on but we yet take all possible care that they are not burned too hard, especially the Women, who are more tender than the Men.

We are seldom long detained in the buying of these Slaves, because their price is established, the Women being one fourth or fifth part cheaper than the Men. The Dis-

Source: Willem Bosman, *A New and Accurate Description of the Coast of Guinea Divided into the Gold, the Slave, and the Ivory Coasts.* Translated from Dutch (London, 1705), pp. 363–365.

putes which we generally have with the Owners of these Slaves are, that we will not give them such Goods as they ask for them, especially the *Boesies* (as I have told you, the Money of this Country) of which they are very fond, though we generally make a Division on this Head in order to make one sort of Goods help off another, because those Slaves which are paid for in *Boesies* cost the Company one half more than those bought with other Goods. The Price of a Slave is commonly———

When we have agreed with the Owners of the Slaves, they are returned to their Prison; where from that time forwards they are kept at our charge, cost us two pence a day a Slave; which serves to subsist them, like our Criminals, on Bread and Water: So that to save Charges we send them on Board our Ships with the very first Opportunity; before which their Master strip them of all they have on their Backs; so that they come Aboard stark-naked as well Women as Men: In which condition they are obliged to continue, if the Master of the Ship is not so Charitable (which he commonly is) as to bestow something on them to cover their Nakedness.

You would really wonder to see how these Slaves live on Board; for though their number sometimes amounts to six or seven Hundred, yet by the careful Management of our Masters of Ships, they are so regulated that it seems incredible: And in this particular our Nation exceeds all other *Europeans;* for as the *French, Portugese* and *English* Slave-Ships, are always foul and stinking; on the contrary ours are for the most part clean and neat.

The Slaves are fed three times a Day with indifferent good Victuals, and much better than they eat in their own Country. Their Lodging-place is divided into two parts; one of which is appointed for the Men the other for the Women; each Sex being kept a-part: Here they lye as close together as is possible for them to be crouded.

We are sometimes sufficiently plagued with a parcel of Slaves, which come from a far In-land Country, who very innocently perswade one another, that we buy them only to fatten and afterwards eat them as a Delicacy.

When we are so unhappy as to be pestered with many of this sort, they resolve and agree together (and bring over the rest to their Party) to run away from the Ship, kill the *Europeans,* and set the Vessel a-shore; by which means they design to free themselves from being our Food.

I have twice met with this Misfortune; and the first time proved very unlucky to me, I not in the least suspecting it; but the Up-roar was timely quashed by the Master of the Ship and my self, by, causing the Abettor to be shot through the Head, after which all was quiet.

But the second time it fell heavier on another Ship, and that chiefly by the carelessness of the Master, who having fished up the Anchor of a departed *English* Ship, had laid it in the Hold where the Male Slaves were lodged; who, unknown to any of the Ships Crew, possessed themselves of a Hammer; with which, in a short time, they broke all their Fetters in pieces upon the Anchor: after this they came above Deck and fell upon our Men; some of whom they grievously wounded, and would certainly have mastered the Ship, if a *French* and *English* Ship had not very fortunately happened to lye by us; who perceiving by our firing a Distressed Gun, that something was in disorder on Board, immediately came to our assistance with Chalops and Men, and drove the Slaves under Deck: Notwithstanding which before all was appeased about twenty of them were killed. . . .

An Account of the Slave Trade on the Coast of Africa

Alexander Falconbridge

. . . The men Negroes, on being brought aboard the ship, are immediately fastened together, two and two, by hand-cuffs on their wrists, and by irons rivetted on their legs. They are then sent down between the decks, and placed in an apartment partitioned off for that purpose. The women likewise are placed in a separate apartment between decks, but without being ironed. And an adjoining room, on the same deck, is besides appointed for the boys. Thus are they all placed in different apartments.

But at the same time, they are frequently stowed so close, as to admit of no other posture than lying on their sides. Neither will the height between decks, unless directly under the grating, permit them the indulgence of an erect posture; especially where there are platforms, which is generally the case. These platforms are a kind of shelf, about eight or nine feet in breadth, extending from the side of the ship towards the centre. They are placed nearly midway between the decks, at the distance of two or three feet from each deck. Upon these the Negroes are stowed in the same manner as they are on the deck underneath.

In each of the apartments are placed three or four large buckets, of a conical form, being near two feet in diameter at the bottom, and only one foot at the top, and in depth about twenty-eight inches; to which, when necessary, the Negroes have recourse. It often happens, that those who are placed at a distance from the buckets, in endeavouring to get to them, tumble over their companions, in consequence of their being shackled. These acci-

dents, although unavoidable, are productive of continual quarrels, in which some of them are always bruised. In this distressed situation, unable to proceed, and prevented from getting to the tubs, they desist from the attempt; and, as the necessities of nature are not to be repelled, ease themselves as they lie. This becomes a fresh source of broils and disturbances, and tends to render the condition of the poor captive wretches still more uncomfortable. The nuisance arising from these circumstances, is not unfrequently increased by the tubs being much too small for the purpose intended, and their being usually emptied but once every day. The rule for doing this, however, varies in different ships, according to the attention paid to the health and convenience of the slaves by the captain.

About eight o'clock in the morning the Negroes are generally brought upon deck. Their irons being examined, a long chain, which is locked to a ring-bolt, fixed in the deck, is run through the rings of the shackles of the men, and then locked to another ring-bolt, fixed also in the deck. By this means fifty or sixty, and sometimes more, are fastened to one chain, in order to prevent them from rising or endeavouring to escape. If the weather proves favourable, they are permitted to remain in that situation till four or five in the afternoon, when they are disengaged from the chain, and sent down.

The diet of the Negroes, while on board, consists chiefly of horse-beans, boiled to the consistence of a pulp; of boiled yams and rice, and sometimes of a small quantity of beef or pork. The latter are frequently taken from the provisions laid in for the sailors. They sometimes make use of a sauce, composed of palm-oil, mixed with flour, water, and pepper, which the sailors call slabber-sauce. Yams are the favourite food of the Eboe, or Bight Negroes, and rice or corn, of

Source: Alexander Falconbridge, *An Account of the Slave Trade on the Coast of Africa.* (London, 1788), pp. 19–21, 22–25, 27–28, 30–31.

those from the Gold and Windward Coasts; each preferring the produce of their native soil. . . .

They are commonly fed twice a day, about eight o'clock in the morning and four in the afternoon. In most ships they are only fed with their *own food* once a day. Their food is served up to them in tubs, about the size of a small water bucket. They are placed round these tubs in companies of ten to each tub, out of which they feed themselves with wooden spoons. These they soon lose, and when they are not allowed others, they feed themselves with their hands. In favourable weather they are fed upon deck, but in bad weather their food is given them below. Numberless quarrels take place among them during their meals; more especially when they are put upon short allowance, which frequently happens, if the passage from the coast of Guinea to the West-India islands, proves of unusual length. In that case, the weak are obliged to be content with a very scanty portion. Their allowance of water is about half a pint each at every meal. It is handed round in a bucket, and given to each Negroe in a pannekin; a small utensil with a strait handle, somewhat similar to a sauce-boat. However, when the ships approach the islands with a favourable breeze, they are no longer restricted.

Upon the Negroes refusing to take sustenance, I have seen coals of fire, glowing hot, put on a shovel, and placed so near their lips, as to scorch and burn them. And this has been accompanied with threats, of forcing them to swallow the coals, if they any longer persisted in refusing to eat. These means have generally had the desired effect. I have also been credibly informed, that a certain captain in the slave trade, poured melted lead on such of the Negroes as obstinately refused their food.

Exercise being deemed necessary for the preservation of their health, they are sometimes obliged to dance, when the weather will permit their coming on deck. If they go about it reluctantly, or do not move with agility, they are flogged; a person standing by them all the time with a cat-o'-nine-tails in his hand for that purpose. Their musick, upon these occasions, consists of a drum, sometimes with only one head; and when that is worn out, they do not scruple to make use of the bottom of one of the tubs before described. The poor wretches are frequently compelled to sing also; but when they do so, their songs are generally, as may naturally be expected, melancholy lamentations to their exile from their native country.

The women are furnished with beads for the purpose of affording them some diversion. But this end is generally defeated by the squabbles which are occasioned, in consequence of their stealing them from each other.

On board some ships, the common sailors are allowed to have intercourse with such of the black women whose consent they can procure. And some of them have been known to take the inconstancy of their paramours so much to heart, as to leap overboard and drown themselves. The officers are permitted to indulge their passions among them at pleasure, and sometimes are guilty of such brutal excesses, as disgrace human nature.

The hardships and inconveniencies suffered by the Negroes during the passage, are scarcely to be enumerated or conceived. They are far more violently affected by the sea-sickness, than the Europeans. It frequently terminates in death, especially among the women. But the exclusion of the fresh air is among the most intolerable. For the purpose of admitting this needful refreshment, most of the ships in the slave-trade are provided, between the decks, with five or six air-ports on each side of the ship, of about six inches in length, and four in breadth; in addition to which, some few ships, but not one in twenty, have what they denominate *wind-sails*. But whenever the sea is rough, and the rain heavy, it becomes necessary to shut these, and every other conveyance by which the air is admitted. The fresh air being thus excluded, the Negroes rooms very soon grow intolerably hot. The confined air, rendered noxious by the effluvia exhaled from their bodies, and by being repeatedly breathed, soon produces fevers and fluxes, which generally carries off great numbers of them.

During the voyages I made, I was frequently a witness to the fatal effects of this exclusion of the fresh air. I will give one instance, as it serves to convey some idea, though a very faint one, of the sufferings of those unhappy beings whom we wantonly drag from their native country, and doom to perpetual labour and captivity. Some wet and blowing weather having occasioned the port-holes to be shut, and the grating to be covered, fluxes and fevers among the Negroes ensued. While they were in this situation, my profession requiring it, I frequently went down among them, till at length their apartments became so extremely hot, as to be only sufferable for a very short time. But the excessive heat was not the only thing that rendered their situation intolerable. The deck, that is, the floor of their rooms, was so covered with the blood and mucus which had proceeded from them in consequence of the flux, that it resembled a slaughter-house. It is not in the power of the human imagination, to picture to itself a situation more dreadful or disgusting. Numbers of the slaves having fainted, they were carried upon deck, where several of them died, and the rest were, with great difficulty, restored. It had nearly proved fatal to me also. The climate was too warm to admit the wearing of any clothing but a shirt, and that I had pulled off before I went down; notwithstanding which, by only continuing among them for about a quarter of an hour, I was so overcome with the heat, stench, and foul air, that I had nearly fainted; and it was not without assistance, that I could get upon deck. The consequence was, that I soon after fell sick of the same disorder, from which I did not recover for several months. . . .

The place allotted for the sick Negroes is under the half deck, where they lie on the bare planks. By this means, those who are emaciated, frequently have their skin, and even their flesh, entirely rubbed off, by the motion of the ship, from the prominent parts of the shoulders, elbows, and hips, so as to render the bones in those parts quite bare. And some of them, by constantly lying in the blood and mucus, that had flowed from those afflicted with the flux, and which, as before observed, is generally so violent as to prevent their being kept clean, have their flesh much sooner rubbed off, than those who have only to contend with the mere friction of the ship. The excruciating pain which the poor sufferers feel from being obliged to continue in such a dreadful situation, frequently for several weeks, in case they happen to live so long, is not to be conceived or described. Few, indeed, are ever able to withstand the fatal effects of it. The utmost skill of the surgeon is here ineffectual. If plaisters be applied, they are very soon displaced by the friction of the ship; and when bandages are used, the Negroes very soon take them off, and appropriate them to other purposes.

The surgeon, upon going between decks, in the morning, to examine the situation of the slaves, frequently finds several dead: and among the men, sometimes a dead and living Negroe fastened by their irons together. When this is the case, they are brought upon the deck, and being laid on the grating, the living Negroe is disengaged, and the dead one thrown overboard. . . .

As very few of the Negroes can so far brook the loss of their liberty, and the hardships they endure, as to bear them with any degree of patience, they are ever upon the watch to take advantage of the least negligence in their oppressors. Insurrections are frequently the consequence; which are seldom suppressed without much bloodshed. Sometimes these are successful, and the whole ship's company is cut off. They are likewise always ready to seize every opportunity for committing some act of desperation to free themselves from their miserable state; and notwithstanding the restraints under which they are laid, they often succeed.

While a ship, to which I belonged, lay in Bonny River, one evening, a short time before our departure, a lot of Negroes, consisting of about ten, was brought on board; when one of them, in a favourable moment, forced his way through the net-work on the larboard side of the vessel, jumped overboard, and was supposed to have been devoured by the sharks.

During the time we were there, fifteen Negroes belonging to a vessel from Liverpool, found means to throw themselves into the river; very few were saved; and the residue fell a sacrifice to the sharks. A similar instance took place in a French ship while we lay there.

Circumstances of this kind are very frequent. On the coast of Angola, at the River Ambris, the following incident happened:— During the time of our residing on shore, we erected a tent to shelter ourselves from the weather. After having been there several weeks, and being unable to purchase a number of slaves we wanted, through the opposition of another English slave vessel, we determined to leave the place. The night before our departure, the tent was struck; which was no sooner perceived by some of the Negroe women on board, than it was considered as a prelude to our sailing; and about eighteen of them, when they were sent between decks, threw themselves into the sea through one of the gun ports; the ship carrying guns between decks. They were all of them, however, excepting one, soon picked up; and that which was missing, was, not long after, taken about a mile from the shore. . . .

The History of Mary Prince: A West Indian Slave

Mary Prince

Oh, the trials! the trials! they make the salt water come into my eyes when I think of the days in which I was afflicted—the times that are gone; when I mourned and grieved with a young heart for those whom I loved.

It was night when I reached my new home. The house was large, and built at the bottom of a very high hill; but I could not see much of it that night. I saw too much of it afterwards. The stones and the timber were the best things in it; they were not so hard as the hearts of the owners.

Before I entered the house, two slave women, hired from another owner, who were at work in the yard, spoke to me, and asked

Source: The History of Mary Prince: A West Indian Slave. (London, 1831), pp. 192–203.

who I belonged to? I replied, "I am come to live here." "Poor child, poor child!" they both said; "you must keep a good heart, if you are to live here."

The next morning my mistress set about instructing me in my tasks. She taught me to do all sorts of household work; to wash and bake, pick cotton and wool, and wash floors, and cook. And she taught me (how can I ever forget it!) more things than these; she caused me to know the exact difference between the smart of the rope, the cart-whip, and the cow-skin, when applied to my naked body by her own cruel hand. And there was scarcely any punishment more dreadful than the blows I received on my face and head from her hard heavy fist. She was a fearful woman, and a savage mistress to her slaves.

There were two little slave boys in the house, on whom she vented her bad temper in a special manner. One of these children was a mulatto, called Cyrus, who had been bought while an infant in his mother's arms; the other, Jack, was an African from the coast of Guinea, whom a sailor had given or sold to my master. Seldom a day passed without these boys receiving the most severe treatment, and often for no fault at all. Both my master and mistress seemed to think that they had a right to ill-use them at their pleasure; and very often accompanied their commands with blows, whether the children were behaving well or ill. I have seen their flesh ragged and raw with licks.—Lick—lick—they were never secure one moment from a blow, and their lives were passed in continual fear. My mistress was not contented with using the whip, but often pinched their cheeks and arms in the most cruel manner. My pity for these poor boys was soon transferred to myself; for I was licked, and flogged, and pinched by her pitiless fingers in the neck and arms, exactly as they were. To strip me naked—to hang me up by the wrists and lay my flesh open with the cow-skin, was an ordinary punishment for even a slight offence. My mistress often robbed me too of the hours that belong to sleep. She used to sit up very late, frequently even until morning; and I had then to stand at a bench and wash during the greater part of the night, or pick wool and cotton; and often I have dropped down overcome by sleep and fatigue, till roused from a state of stupor by the whip, and forced to start up to my tasks.

Poor Hetty, my fellow slave, was very kind to me, and I used to call her my Aunt; but she led a most miserable life, and her death was hastened (at least the slaves all believed and said so), by the dreadful chastisement she received from my master during her pregnancy. It happened as follows. One of the cows had dragged the rope away from the stake to which Hetty had fastened it, and got loose. My master flew into a terrible passion, and ordered the poor creature to be stripped quite naked, not-withstanding her pregnancy, and to be tied up to a tree in the yard. He then flogged her as hard as he could lick, both with the whip and cow-skin, till she was all over streaming with blood. He rested, and then beat her again and again. Her shrieks were terrible. The consequence was that poor Hetty was brought to bed before her time, and was delivered after severe labour of a dead child. She appeared to recover after her confinement, so far that she was repeatedly flogged by both master and mistress afterwards; but her former strength never returned to her. Ere long her body and limbs swelled to a great size; and she lay on a mat in the kitchen, till the water burst out of her body and she died. All the slaves said that death was a good thing for poor Hetty; but I cried very much for her death. The manner of it filled me with horror. I could not bear to think about it; yet it was always present to my mind for many a day.

After Hetty died all her labours fell upon me, in addition to my own. I had now to milk eleven cows every morning before sunrise, sitting among the damp weeds; to take care of the cattle as well as the children; and to do the work of the house. There was no end to my toils—no end to my blows. I lay down at night and rose up in the morning in fear and sorrow; and often wished that like poor Hetty I could escape from this cruel bondage and be at rest in the grave. But the hand of God whom then I knew not, was stretched over me; and I was mercifully preserved for better things. It was then, however, my heavy lot to weep, weep, weep, and that for years; to pass from one misery to another, and from one cruel master to a worse. But I must go on with the thread of my story.

One day a heavy squall of wind and rain came on suddenly, and my mistress sent me round the corner of the house to empty a large earthen jar. The jar was already cracked with an old deep crack that divided it in the middle, and in turning it upside down to empty it, it parted in my hand. I could not help the accident, but I was dreadfully frightened, looking forward to a severe punishment. I ran crying to my mistress, "O mistress, the jar has come in two." "You have broken it, have you?" she replied; "come directly here to me." I came trembling; she stripped and flogged me long and severely with the cow-skin; as long as she had strength to use the lash, for she did not give over till she was quite tired.—When my master came home at night, she told him of my fault; and oh, frightful! how he fell a swearing. After abusing me with every ill name he could think of, (too, too bad to speak in England,) and giving me several heavy blows with his hand, he said, "I shall come home to-morrow morning at twelve, on purpose to give you a round hundred." He kept his word—Oh sad for me! I cannot easily forget it. He tied me up upon a ladder, and gave me a hundred lashes with his own hand, and master Benjy stood by to count them for him. When he had licked me for some time he sat down to take breath; then after resting, he beat me again and again, until he was quite wearied, and so hot (for the weather was very sultry), that he sank back in his chair, almost like to faint. While my mistress went to bring him drink, there was a dreadful earthquake. Part of the roof fell down, and every thing in the house went—clatter, clatter, clatter. Oh I thought the end of all things near at hand; and I was so sore with the flogging, that I scarcely cared whether I lived or died. The earth was groaning and shaking; every thing tumbling about; and my mistress and the slaves were shrieking and crying out, "The earthquake! the earthquake!" It was an awful day for us all.

During the confusion I crawled away on my hands and knees, and laid myself down under the steps of the piazza, in front of the house. I was in a dreadful state—my body all blood and bruises, and I could not help moaning piteously. The other slaves, when they saw me, shook their heads and said, "Poor child! poor child!"—I lay there till the morning, careless of what might happen, for life was very weak in me, and I wished more than ever to die. But when we are very young, death always seems a great way off, and it would not come that night to me. The next morning I was forced by my master to rise and go about my usual work, though my body and limbs were so stiff and sore, that I could not move without the greatest pain.—Nevertheless, even after all this severe punishment, I never heard the last of that jar; my mistress was always throwing it in my face.

Some little time after this, one of the cows got loose from the stake, and eat one of the sweet-potatoe slips. I was milking when my master found it out. He came to me, and without any more ado, stooped down, and taking off his heavy boot, he struck me such a severe blow in the small of my back, that I shrieked with agony, and thought I was killed; and I feel a weakness in that part to this day. The cow was frightened at his violence, and kicked down the pail and spilt the milk all about. My master knew that this accident was his own fault, but he was so enraged that he seemed glad of an excuse to go on with his ill usage. I cannot remember how many licks he gave me then, but he beat me till I was unable to stand, and till he himself was weary.

After this I ran away and went to my mother, who was living with Mr. Richard Darrel. My poor mother was both grieved and glad to see me; grieved because I had been so ill used, and glad because she had not seen me for a long, long while. She dared not receive me into the house, but she hid me up in a hole in the rocks near, and brought me food at night, after every body was asleep. My father, who lived at Crow-Lane, over the salt-water channel, at last heard of my being hid up in the cavern, and he came and took me back to my master. Oh I was loth, loth to go back; but as there was no remedy, I was obliged to submit.

When we got home, my poor father said to Cap. I——, "Sir, I am sorry that my child should be forced to run away from her owner; but the treatment she has received is enough to break her heart. The sight of her wounds has nearly broke mine.—I entreat you, for the love of God, to forgive her for running away, and that you will be a kind master to her in future." Capt. I——said I was used as well as I deserved, and that I ought to be punished for running away. I then took courage and said that I could stand the floggings no longer; that I was weary of my life, and therefore I had run away to my mother; but mothers could only weep and mourn over their children, they could not save them from cruel masters—from the whip, the rope, and the cow-skin. He told me to hold my tongue and go about my work, or he would find a way to settle me. He did not, however, flog me that day.

For five years after this I remained in his house, and almost daily received the same harsh treatment. At length he put me on board a sloop, and to my great joy sent me away to Turk's Island. I was not permitted to see my mother or father, or poor sisters and brothers, to say good bye, though going away to a strange land, and might never see them again. Oh the Buckra people who keep slaves think that black people are like cattle, without natural affection. But my heart tells me it is far otherwise.

We were nearly four weeks on the voyage, which was unusually long. Sometimes we had a light breeze, sometimes a great calm, and the ship made no way; so that our provisions and water ran very low, and we were put upon short allowance. I should almost have been starved had it not been for the kindness of a black man called Anthony, and his wife, who had brought their own victuals, and shared them with me.

When we went ashore at the Grand Quay, the captain sent me to the house of my new master, Mr. D——, to whom Captain I—— had sold me. Grand Quay is a small town upon a sandbank; the houses low and built of wood. Such was my new master's. The first person I saw, on my arrival, was Mr. D——, a stout sulky looking man, who carried me through the hall to show me to his wife and children. Next day I was put up by the vendue master to know how much I was worth, and I was valued at one hundred pounds currency.

My new master was one of the owners or holders of the salt ponds, and he received a certain sum for every slave that worked upon his premises, whether they were young or old. This sum was allowed him out of the profits arising from the salt works. I was im-

mediately sent to work in the salt water with the rest of the slaves. This work was perfectly new to me. I was given a half barrel and a shovel, and had to stand up to my knees in the water, from four o'clock in the morning till nine, when we were given some Indian corn boiled in water, which we were obliged to swallow as fast as we could for fear the rain should come on and melt the salt. We were then called again to our tasks, and worked through the heat of the day; the sun flaming upon our heads like fire, and raising salt blisters in those parts which were not completely covered. Our feet and legs, from standing in the salt water for so many hours, soon became full of dreadful boils, which eat down in some cases to the very bone, afflicting the sufferers with great torment. We came home at twelve; ate our corn soup, called *blawly,* as fast as we could, and went back to our employment till dark at night. We then shovelled up the salt in large heaps, and went down to the sea, where we washed the pickle from our limbs, and cleaned the barrows and shovels from the salt. When we returned to the house, our master gave us each our allowance of raw Indian corn, which we pounded in a mortar and boiled in water for our suppers.

We slept in a long shed, divided into narrow slips, like the stalls used for cattle. Boards fixed upon stakes driven into the ground, without mat or covering, were our only beds. On Sundays, after we had washed the salt bags, and done other work required of us, we went into the bush and cut the long soft grass, of which we made trusses for our legs and feet to rest upon, for they were so full of the salt boils that we could get no rest lying upon the bare boards.

Though we worked from morning till night, there was no satisfying Mr. D——. I hoped, when I left Capt. I——, that I should have been better off, but I found it was but going from one butcher to another. There was this difference between them: my former master used to beat me while raging and foaming with passion; Mr. D——was usually quite calm. He would stand by and give orders for a slave to be cruelly whipped, and assist in the punishment, without moving a muscle of his face; walking about and taking snuff with the greatest composure. Nothing could touch his hard heart—neither sighs, nor tears, nor prayers, nor streaming blood; he was deaf to our cries, and careless of our sufferings.—Mr. D——has often stripped me naked, hung me up by the wrists, and beat me with the cow-skin, with his own hand, till my body was raw with gashes. Yet there was nothing very remarkable in this; for it might serve as a sample of the common usage of the slaves on that horrible island.

Owing to the boils in my feet, I was unable to wheel the barrow fast through the sand, which got into the sores, and made me stumble at every step; and my master, having no pity for my sufferings from this cause, rendered them far more intolerable, by chastising me for not being able to move so fast as he wished me. Another of our employments was to row a little way off from the shore in a boat, and dive for large stones to build a wall round our master's house. This was very hard work; and the great waves breaking over us continually, made us often so giddy that we lost our footing, and were in danger of being drowned.

Ah, poor me!—my tasks were never ended. Sick or well, it was work—work—work!—After the diving season was over, we were sent to the South Creek, with large bills, to cut up mangoes to burn lime with. Whilst one party of slaves were thus employed, another were sent to the other side of the island to break up coral out of the sea.

When we were ill, let our complaint be what it might, the only medicine given to us was a great bowl of hot salt water, with salt mixed with it, which made us very sick. If we could not keep up with the rest of the gang of slaves, we were put in the stocks, and severely flogged the next morning. Yet, not the less, our master expected, after we had thus been kept from our rest, and our limbs rendered stiff and sore with ill usage, that we should still go through the ordinary tasks of the day all the same.—Sometimes we had to work all night, measuring salt to

load a vessel; or turning a machine to draw water out of the sea for the salt-making. Then we had no sleep—no rest—but were forced to work as fast as we could, and go on again all next day the same as usual. Work—work—work—Oh that Turk's Island was a horrible place! The people in England, I am sure, have never found out what is carried on there. Cruel, horrible place!

Mr. D——had a slave called old Daniel, whom he used to treat in the most cruel manner. Poor Daniel was lame in the hip, and could not keep up with the rest of the slaves; and our master would order him to be stripped and laid down on the ground, and have him beaten with a rod of rough briar till his skin was quite red and raw. He would then call for a bucket of salt, and fling upon the raw flesh till the man writhed on the ground like a worm, and screamed aloud with agony. This poor man's wounds were never healed, and I have often seen them full of maggots, which increased his torments to an intolerable degree. He was an object of pity and terror to the whole gang of slaves, and in his wretched case we saw, each of us, our own lot, if we should live to be as old.

Oh the horrors of slavery!—How the thought of it pains my heart! But the truth ought to be told of it; and what my eyes have seen I think it is my duty to relate; for few people in England know what slavery is. I have been a slave—I have felt what a slave feels, and I know what a slave knows; and I would have all the good people in England to know it too, that they may break our chains, and set us free.

Mr. D——had another slave called Ben. He being very hungry, stole a little rice one night after he came in from work, and cooked it for his supper. But his master soon discovered the theft; locked him up all night; and kept him without food till one o'clock the next day. He then hung Ben up by his hands, and beat him from time to time till the slaves came in at night. We found the poor creature hung up when we came home; with a pool of blood beneath him, and our master still licking him. But this was not the worst. My master's son was in the habit of stealing the rice and rum. Ben had seen him do this, and thought he might do the same, and when the master found out that Ben had stolen the rice and swore to punish him, he tried to excuse himself by saying that Master Dickey did the same thing every night. The lad denied it to his father, and was so angry with Ben for informing against him, that out of revenge he ran and got a bayonet, and whilst the poor wretch was suspended by his hands and writhing under his wounds, he run it quite through his foot. I was not by when he did it, but I saw the wound when I came home, and heard Ben tell the manner in which it was done.

I must say something more about this cruel son of a cruel father.—He had no heart—no fear of God; he had been brought up by a bad father in a bad path, and he delighted to follow in the same steps. There was a little old woman among the slaves called Sarah, who was nearly past work; and, Master Dickey being the overseer of the slaves just then, this poor creature, who was subject to several bodily infirmities, and was not quite right in her head, did not wheel the barrow fast enough to please him. He threw her down on the ground, and after beating her severely, he took her up in his arms and flung her among the prickly-pear bushes, which are all covered over with sharp venomous prickles. By this her naked flesh was so grievously wounded, that her body swelled and festered all over, and she died a few days later. In telling my own sorrows, I cannot pass by those of my fellow-slaves—for when I think of my own griefs, I remember theirs.

I think it was about ten years I had worked in the salt ponds at Turk's Island, when my master left off business, and retired to a house he had in Bermuda, leaving his son to succeed him in the island. He took me with him to wait upon his daughters; and I was joyful, for I was sick, sick of Turk's Island, and my heart yearned to see my native place again, my mother, and my kindred.

I had seen my poor mother during the time I was a slave in Turk's Island. One Sunday morning I was on the beach with some of the slaves and we saw a sloop come in loaded with slaves to work in the salt water. We got a boat and went aboard. When I came upon the deck I asked the black people, "Is there any one here for me?" "Yes," they said, "your mother." I thought they said this in jest—I could scarcely believe them for joy; but when I saw my poor mammy my joy was turned to sorrow, for she had gone from her senses. "Mammy," I said, "is this you?" She did not know me. "Mammy," I said, "what's the matter?" She began to talk foolishly, and said that she had been under the vessel's bottom. They had been overtaken by a violent storm at sea. My poor mother had never been on the sea before, and she was so ill, that she lost her senses, and it was long before she came quite to herself again. She had a sweet child with her—a little sister I had never seen, about four years of age, called Rebecca. I took her on shore with me, for I felt I should love her directly; and I kept her with me a week. Poor little thing! her's has been a sad life, and continues so to this day. My mother worked for some years on the island, but was taken back to Bermuda some time before my master carried me again thither.*

After I left Turk's Island, I was told by some negroes that came over from it, that the poor slaves had built up a place with boughs and leaves, where they might meet for prayers, but the white people pulled it down twice, and would not allow them even

---

*Of the subsequent lot of her relatives she can tell but little. She says, her father died while she and her mother were at Turk's Island; and that he had been long dead and buried before any of his children in Bermuda knew of it, they being slaves on other estates. Her mother died after Mary went to Antigua. Of the fate of the rest of her kindred, seven brothers and three sisters, she knows nothing further than this—that the eldest sister, who had several children to her master, was taken by him to Trinidad; and that the youngest, Rebecca, is still alive, and in slavery in Bermuda. Mary herself is now about forty-three years of age.—Ed.

a shed for prayers. A flood came down soon after and washed away many houses, filled the place with sand, and overflowed the ponds: and I do think that this was for their wickedness; for the Buckra men* there were very wicked. I saw and heard much that was very very bad at that place.

I was several years the slave of Mr. D—— after I returned to my native place. Here I worked in the grounds. My work was planting and hoeing sweet-potatoes, Indian corn, plaintains, bananas, cabbages, pumpkins, onions, &c. I did all the household work, and attended upon a horse and cow besides,—going also upon all errands. I had to curry the horse—to clean and feed him—and sometimes to ride him a little. I had more than enough to do—but still it was not so very bad as Turk's Island.

My old master often got drunk, and then he would get in a fury with his daughter, and beat her till she was not fit to be seen. I remember on one occasion I had gone to fetch water, and when I was coming up the hill I heard a great screaming; I ran as fast as I could to the house, put down the water, and went into the chamber, where I found

*Negro term for white people.

my master beating Miss D——dreadfully. I strove with all my strength to get her away from him; for she was all black and blue with bruises. He had beat her with his fist, and almost killed her. The people gave me credit for getting her away. He turned round and began to lick me. Then I said, "Sir, this is not Turk's Island." I can't repeat his answer, the words were too wicked—too bad to say. He wanted to treat me the same in Bermuda as he had done in Turk's Island.

He had an ugly fashion of stripping himself quite naked, and ordering me then to wash him in a tub of water. This was worse to me than all the licks. Sometimes when he called me to wash him I would not come, my eyes were so full of shame. He would then come to beat me. One time I had plates and knives in my hand, and I dropped both plates and knives, and some of the plates were broken. He struck me so severely for this, that at last I defended myself, for I thought it was high time to do so. I then told him I would not live longer with him, for he was a very indecent man—very spiteful, and too indecent; with no shame for his servants, no shame for his own flesh. So I went away to a neighbouring house and sat down and cried till the next morning, when I went home again, not knowing what else to do.

A Narrative of the Life and Adventures of Venture: A Native of Africa but Resident Above Sixty Years in the United States of America

Venture Smith

PREFACE

The following account of the life of Venture is a relation of simple facts, in which nothing is added in substance to what he related himself. Many other interesting and curious passages of his life might have been inserted, but on account of the bulk to which they must necessarily have swelled this narrative, they were omitted. If any should suspect the truth of what is here related, they are referred to people now living who are acquainted with most of the facts mentioned in the narrative.

The reader is here presented with an account, not of a renowned politician or warrior, but of an untutored slave, brought into this Christian country at eight years of age, wholly destitute of all education but what he received in common with domesticated animals, enjoying no advantages that could lead him to suppose himself superior to the beasts, his fellow-servants. And, if he shall derive no other advantage from perusing this narrative, he may experience those sensations of shame and indignation that will prove him to be not wholly destitute of every noble and generous feeling.

The subject of the following pages, had he received only a common education, might have been a man of high respectability and

usefulness; and had his education been suited to his genius, he might have been an ornament and an honor to human nature. It may, perhaps, not be unpleasing to see the efforts of a great mind wholly uncultivated, enfeebled and depressed by slavery, and struggling under every disadvantage. The reader may here see a Franklin and a Washington, in a state of nature, or, rather, in a state of slavery. Destitute as he is of all education, and broken by hardships and infirmities of age, he still exhibits striking traces of native ingenuity and good sense.

This narrative exhibits a pattern of honesty, prudence and industry to people of his own color; and perhaps some white people would not find themselves degraded by imitating such an example.

The following account is published in compliance with the earnest desire of the subject of it, and likewise a number of respectable persons who are acquainted with him.

CHAPTER 1

Containing an Account of His Life, from His Birth to the Time of His Leaving His Native Country

I was born at Dukandarra, in Guinea, about the year 1729. My father's name was Saungm Furro, Prince of the tribe of Dukandarra. My father had three wives. Polygamy was not uncommon in that country, especially among the rich, as every man was allowed to keep as many wives as he could maintain. By his first wife he had three chil-

---

Source: A Narrative of the Life and Adventures of Venture: A Native of Africa but Resident Above Sixty Years in the United States of America Related by Himself. (Middletown, Connecticut, 1897), pp. 11–24.

dren. The eldest of them was myself, named by my father, Broteer. The other two were named Cundazo and Soozaduka. My father had two children by his second wife, and one by his third. I descended from a very large, tall and stout race of beings, much larger than the generality of people in other parts of the globe, being commonly considerable above six feet in height, and every way well proportioned.

The first thing worthy of notice which I remember, was a contention between my father and mother, on account of my father marrying his third wife without the consent of his first and eldest, which was contrary to the custom generally observed among my countrymen. In consequence of this rupture, my mother left her husband and country, and travelled away with her three children to the eastward. I was then five years old. She took not the least sustenance along with her, to support either herself or children. I was able to travel along by her side; the other two of her offspring she carried, one on her back, the other, being a sucking child, in her arms. When we became hungry, our mother used to set us down on the ground and gather some of the fruits that grew spontaneously in that climate. These served us for food on the way. At night we all lay down together in the most secure place we could find and reposed ourselves until morning. Though there were many noxious animals there, yet so kind was our Almighty protector that none of them were ever permitted to hurt or molest us.

Thus we went on our journey until the second day after our departure from Dukandarra, when we came to the entrance of a great desert. During our travel in that, we were often affrighted with the doleful howlings and yellings of wolves, lions and other animals. After five days' travel we came to the end of this desert, and immediately entered into a beautiful and extensive interval country. Here my mother was pleased to stop and seek a refuge for me. She left me at the house of a very rich farmer. I was then, as I should judge, not less than one hundred and forty miles from my native place, separated from all my relatives and acquaintances. At this place, my mother took her farewell of me and set out for her own country. My new guardian, as I shall call the man with whom I was left, put me into the business of tending sheep immediately after I was left with him. The flock, which I kept with the assistance of a boy, consisted of about forty. We drove them every morning between two and three miles to pasture, into the wide and delightful plains. When night drew on, we drove them home and secured them in the cote. In this round I continued during my stay here. One incident which befel me when I was driving my flock from pasture, was so dreadful to me at that age, and is to this time so fresh in my memory, that I cannot help noticing it in this place. Two large dogs sallied out of a certain house and set upon me. One of them took me by the arm and the other by the thigh, and before their master could come and relieve me, they lacerated my flesh to such a degree that the scars are very visible to the present day. My master was immediately sent for. He came and carried me home, as I was unable to go myself on account of my wounds. Nothing remarkable happened afterwards until my father sent for me to return home.

Before I dismiss this country, I must first inform my reader what I remember concerning this place. A large river runs through this country in a westerly course. The land for a great way on each side is flat and level, hedged in by a considerable rise in the country at a great distance from it. It scarce ever rains there, yet the land is fertile; great dews fall in the night which refresh the soil. About the latter end of June or first of July, the river begins to rise, and gradually increases until it has inundated the country for a great distance, to the height of seven or eight feet. This brings on a slime which enriches the land surprisingly. When the river has subsided, the natives begin to sow and plant, and the vegetation is exceeding rapid. Near this rich river my guardian's land lay. He possessed, I cannot exactly tell how much, yet this I am certain of respecting it, that he owned an immense tract. He possessed likewise a great many cattle and goats. During my stay with him I was kindly used, and with as much tenderness, for what I saw, as his only son, although I was an entire stranger to him, remote from friends and relatives. The principal occupations of the inhabitants there were the cultivation of the soil and the care of their flocks. They were a people pretty similar in every respect to that of mine, except in their persons, which were not so tall and stout. They appeared to be very kind and friendly. I will now return to my departure from that place.

My father sent a man and horse after me. After settling with my guardian for keeping me, he took me away and went for home. It was then about one year since my mother brought me here. Nothing remarkable occurred to us on our journey until we arrived safe home. I found then that the difference between my parents had been made up previous to their sending for me. On my return, I was received both by my father and mother with great joy and affection, and was once more restored to my paternal dwelling in peace and happiness. I was then about six years old.

Not more than six weeks had passed after my return, before a message was brought by an inhabitant of the place where I lived the preceding year to my father, that that place had been invaded by a numerous army, from a nation not far distant, furnished with musical instruments, and all kinds of arms then in use; that they were instigated by some white nation who equipped and sent them to subdue and possess the country; that his nation had made no preparation for war, having been for a long time in profound peace; that they could not defend themselves against such a formidable train of invaders, and must, therefore, necessarily evacuate their lands to the fierce enemy, and fly to the protection of some chief; and that if he would permit them they would come under his rule and protection when they had to retreat from their own possessions. He was a kind and merciful prince, and therefore consented to these proposals.

He had scarcely returned to his nation with the message before the whole of his people were obligated to retreat from their country and come to my father's dominions. He gave them every privilege and all the protection his government could afford. But they had not been there longer than four days before news came to them that the invaders had laid waste their country, and were coming speedily to destroy them in my father's territories. This affrighted them, and therefore they immediately pushed off to the southward, into the unknown countries there, and were never more heard of.

Two days after their retreat, the report turned out to be but too true. A detachment from the enemy came to my father and informed him that the whole army was encamped not far from his dominions, and would invade the territory and deprive his people of their liberties and rights, if he did not comply with the following terms. These were, to pay them a large sum of money, three hundred fat cattle, and a great number of goats, sheep, asses, etc.

My father told the messenger he would comply rather than that his subjects should be deprived of their rights and privileges, which he was not then in circumstances to defend from so sudden an invasion. Upon turning out those articles, the enemy pledged their faith and honor that they would not attack him. On these he relied, and therefore thought it unnecessary to be on his guard against the enemy. But their pledges of faith and honor proved no better than those of other unprincipled hostile nations, for a few days after, a certain relation of the king came and informed him that the enemy who sent terms of accommodation to him, and received tribute to their satisfaction, yet meditated an attack upon his subjects by surprise, and that probably they would commence their attack in less than one day, and concluded with advising him, as he was not prepared for war, to order a speedy retreat of his family and subjects. He complied with this advice.

The same night which was fixed upon to retreat, my father and his family set off about the break of day. The king and his two younger wives went in one company, and my mother and her children in another. We left our dwellings in succession, and my father's company went on first. We directed our course for a large shrub plain, some distance off, where we intended to conceal ourselves from the approaching enemy, until we could refresh ourselves a little. But we presently found that our retreat was not secure. For having struck up a little fire for the purpose of cooking victuals, the enemy, who happened to be encamped a little distance off, had sent out a scouting party who discovered us by the smoke of the fire, just as we were extinguishing it and about to eat. As soon as we had finished eating, my father discovered the party and immediately began to discharge arrows at them. This was what I first saw, and it alarmed both me and the women, who, being unable to make any resistance immediately betook ourselves to the tall, thick reeds not far off, and left the old king to fight alone. For some time I beheld him from the reeds defending himself with great courage and firmness, till at last he was obliged to surrender himself into their hands.

They then came to us in the reeds, and the very first salute I had from them was a violent blow on the head with the fore part of a gun, and at the same time a grasp around the neck. I then had a rope put about my neck, as all the women in the thicket with me, and were immediately led to my father, who was likewise pinioned and haltered for leading. In this condition we were all led to the camp. The women and myself, being submissive, had tolerable treatment from the enemy, while my father was closely interrogated respecting his money, which they knew he must have. But as he gave them no account of it, he was instantly cut and pounded on his body with great inhumanity, that he might be induced by the torture he suffered to make the discovery. All this availed not in the least to make him give up his money, but he despised all the tortures which they inflicted, until the continued ex-

ercise and increase of torment obliged him to sink and expire. He thus died without informing his enemies where his money lay. I saw him while he was thus tortured to death. The shocking scene is to this day fresh in my memory, and I have often been overcome while thinking on it. He was a man of remarkable stature. I should judge as much as six feet and six or seven inches high, two feet across the shoulders, and every way well proportioned. He was a man of remarkable strength and resolution, affable, kind and gentle, ruling with equity and moderation.

The army of the enemy was large, I should suppose consisting of about six thousand men. Their leader was called Baukurre. After destroying the old prince, they decamped and immediately marched towards the sea, lying to the west, taking with them myself and the women prisoners. In the march, a scouting party was detached from the main army. To the leader of this party I was made waiter, having to carry his gun, etc. As we were a-scouting, we came across a herd of fat cattle consisting of about thirty in number. These we set upon and immediately wrested from their keepers, and afterwards converted them into food for the army. The enemy had remarkable success in destroying the country wherever they went. For as far as they had penetrated they laid the habitations waste and captured the people. The distance they had now brought me was about four hundred miles. All the march I had very hard tasks imposed on me, which I must perform on pain of punishment. I was obliged to carry on my head a large flat stone used for grinding our corn, weighing, as I should suppose, as much as twenty-five pounds; besides victuals, mat and cooking utensils. Though I was pretty large and stout of my age, yet these burdens were very grievous to me, being only six years and a half old.

We were then come to a place called Malagasco. When we entered the place, we could not see the least appearance of either house or inhabitants, but on stricter search found that instead of houses above ground they had dens in the sides of hillocks, contiguous to ponds and streams of water. In these we perceived they had all hid themselves, as I suppose they usually did on such occasions. In order to compel them to surrender, the enemy contrived to smoke them out with faggots. These they put to the entrance of the caves and set them on fire. While they were engaged in this business, to their great surprise some of them were desperately wounded with arrows which feel from above on them. This mystery they soon found out. They perceived that the enemy discharged these arrows through holes on the top of the dens directly into the air. Their weight brought them back, point downwards, on their enemies heads, whilst they were smoking the inhabitants out. The points of their arrows were poisoned, but their enemy had an antidote for it which they instantly applied to the wounded part. The smoke at last obliged the people to give themselves up. They came out of their caves, first spatting the palms of their hands together, and immediately after extended their arms, crossed at their wrists, ready to be bound and pinioned. I should judge that the dens above mentioned were extended about eight feet horizontally into the earth, six feet in height, and as many wide. They were arched overhead and lined with earth, which was of the clay kind and made the surface of their walls firm and smooth.

The invaders then pinioned the prisoners of all ages and sexes indiscriminately, took their flocks and all their effects, and moved on their way towards the sea. On the march, the prisoners were treated with clemency, on account of their being submissive and humble. Having come to the next tribe, the enemy laid siege and immediately took men, women, children, flocks, and all their valuable effects. They then went on to the next district, which was contiguous to the sea, called in Africa, Anamaboo. The enemies' provisions were then almost spent, as well as their strength. The inhabitants, knowing what conduct they had pursued, and what were their present in-

tentions, improved the favorable opportunity, attacked them, and took enemy, prisoners, flocks and all their effects. I was then taken a second time. All of us were then put into the castle and kept for market. On a certain time, I and other prisoners were put on board a canoe, under our master, and rowed away to a vessel belonging to Rhode Island, commanded by Captain Collingwood, and the mate, Thomas Mumford. While we were going to the vessel, our master told us to appear to the best possible advantage for sale. I was bought on board by one Robertson Mumford, a steward of said vessel, for four gallons of rum and a piece of calico, and called Venture on account of his having purchased me with his own private venture. Thus I came by my name. All the slaves that were bought for that vessel's cargo were two hundred and sixty.

CHAPTER II

Containing an Account of His Life from the Time of His Leaving Africa to That of His Becoming Free

AFTER all the business was ended on the coast of Africa, the ship sailed from thence to Barbadoes. After an ordinary passage, except great mortality by the small pox, which broke out on board, we arrived at the island of Barbadoes; but when we reached it, there were found, out of the two hundred and sixty that sailed from Africa, not more than two hundred alive. These were all sold, except myself and three more, to the planters there.

The vessel then sailed for Rhos[d?]e Island, and arrived there after a comfortable passage. Here my master sent me to live with one of his sisters until he could carry me to Fisher's Island, the place of his residence. I had then completed my eighth year. After staying with his sister some time, I was taken to my master's place to live.

When we arrived at Narraganset, my master went ashore in order to return a part of the way by land, and gave me the charge of the keys of his trunks on board of the vessel, and charged me not to deliver them up to anybody, not even to his father, without his orders. To his directions I promised faithfully to conform. When I arrived with my master's articles at his house, my master's father asked me for his son's keys, as he wanted to see what his trunks contained. I told him that my master intrusted me with the care of them until he should return, and that I had given him my word to be faithful to the trust, and could not, therefore, give him, or any other man, the keys without my master's directions. He insisted that I should deliver to him the keys on pain of punishment. But I let him know that he should not have them, let him say what he would. He then laid aside trying to get them. But notwithstanding he appeared to give up trying to obtain them from me, yet I mistrusted that he would take some time when I was off my guard, either in the daytime or at night, to get them, therefore, I slung them round my neck, and in the daytime concealed them in my bosom, and at night I always slept with them under me, that no person might take them from me without my being apprized of it. Thus I kept the keys from everybody until my master came home. When he returned he asked where VENTURE was. As I was within hearing, I came and said, "Here, sir, at your service." He asked for his keys, and I immediately took them off my neck and reached them out to him. He took them, stroked my hair, and commended me, saying in presence of his father that his young VENTURE was so faithful that he never would have been able to have taken the keys from him but by violence; that he should not fear to trust him with his whole fortune, for that he had been in his native place so habituated to keeping his word, that he would sacrifice even his life to maintain it.

The first of the time of living at my master's own place, I was pretty much employed in the house, carding wool and other household business. In this situation I continued for some years, after which my master put me to work out of doors. After many proofs of my faithfulness and honesty, my master began to put great confidence in me. My behavior had as yet been submissive and obedient. I then began to have hard tasks imposed on me. Some of these were to pound four bushels of ears of corn every night in a barrel for the poultry, or be rigorously punished. At other seasons of the year, I had to card wool until a very late hour. These tasks I had to perform when only about nine years old. Some time after, I had another difficulty and oppression which was greater than any I had ever experienced since I came into this country. This was to serve two masters. James Mumford, my master's son, when his father had gone from home in the morning and given me a stint to perform that day, would order me to do *this* and *that* business different from what my master had directed me. One day in particular, the authority which my master's son had set up had like to have produced melancholy effects. For my master having set me off my business to perform that day and then left me to perform it, his son came up to me in the course of the day, big with authority, and commanded me very arrogantly to quit my present business and go directly about what he should order me. I replied to him that my master had given me so much to perform that day, and that I must faithfully complete it in that time. He then broke out into a great rage, snatched a pitchfork and went to lay me over the head therewith, but I as soon got another and defended myself with it, or otherwise he might have murdered me in his outrage. He immediately called some people who were within hearing at work for him, and ordered them to take his hair rope and come and bind me with it. They all tried to bind me, but in vain, though there were three assistants in number. My upstart master then desisted, put his pocket handkerchief before his eyes and went home with a design to tell his mother of the struggle with young VENTURE. He told that their young VENTURE had become so stubborn that he could not control him, and asked her what he should do with him. In the meantime I recovered my temper, voluntarily caused myself to be bound by the same men who tried in vain before, and carried before my young master, that he might do what he pleased with me. He took me to a gallows made for the purpose of hanging cattle on, and suspended me on it. Afterwards he ordered one of his hands to go to the peach orchard and cut him three dozen of whips to punish me with. These were brought to him, and that was all that was done with them, as I was released and went to work after hanging on the gallows about an hour.

After I had lived with my master thirteen years, being then about twenty-two years old, I married Meg, a slave of his who was about my own age. My master owned a certain Irishman, named Heddy, who about that time formed a plan of secretly leaving his master. After he had long had this plan in meditation, he suggested it to me. At first I cast a deaf ear to it, and rebuked Heddy for harboring in his mind such a rash undertaking. But after he had persuaded and much enchanted me with the prospect of gaining my freedom by such a method, I at length agreed to accompany him. Heddy next inveigled two of his fellow-servants to accompany us. The place to which we designed to go was the Mississippi. Our next business was to lay in a sufficient store of provisions for our voyage. We privately collected out of our master's store, six great old cheeses, two firkins of butter, and one batch of new bread. When we had gathered all our own clothes and some more, we took them all about midnight and went to the water side. We stole our master's boat, embarked, and then directed our course for the Mississippi River.

We mutually confederated not to betray or desert one another on pain of death. We first steered our course for Montauk Point, the east end of Long Island. After our arrival there, we landed, and Heddy and I made an incursion into the island after fresh water, while our two comrades were left a little distance from the boat, employed in cooking. When Heddy and I had sought some time for water, he returned to our companions and I continued on looking for my object. When Heddy had performed his business with our companions who were engaged in cooking, he went directly to the boat, stole all the clothes in it, and then travelled away for East Hampton, as I was informed. I returned to my fellows not long after. They informed me that our clothes were stolen, but could not determine who was the thief, yet they suspected Heddy, as he was missing. After reproving my comrades for not taking care of our things which were in the boat, I advertised Heddy and sent two men in search of him. They pursued and overtook him at Southampton and returned him to the boat. I then thought it might afford some chance for my freedom, or at least be a palliation for my running away, to return Heddy immediately to his master, and inform him that I was induced to go away by Heddy's address. Accordingly, I set off with him and the rest of my companions for my master's, and arrived there without any difficulty. I informed my master that Heddy was the ringleader of our revolt, and that he had used us ill. He immediately put Heddy into custody, and myself and companions were well received and went to work as usual.

Not a long time passed after that before Heddy was sent by my master to New London gaol. At the close of that year I was sold to a Thomas Stanton, and had to be separated from my wife and one daughter, who was about one month old. He resided at Stonington Point. To this place I brought with me from my late master's, two johannes, three old Spanish dollars, and two thousand of coppers, besides five pounds of my wife's money. This money I got by cleaning gentlemen's shoes and drawing-boots, by catching muskrats and minks, raising potatoes and carrots, etc., and by fishing in the night, and at odd spells.

All this money, amounting to near twenty-one pounds York currency, my master's brother, Robert Stanton, hired of me, for which he gave me his note. About a year and a half after that time, my master purchased my wife and her child for seven hundred pounds old tenor. One time my master sent me two miles after a barrel of molasses, and ordered me to carry it on my shoulders. I made out to carry it all the way to my master's house. When I lived with Capt. George Mumford, only to try my strength I took upon my knees a tierce of salt containing seven bushels, and carried it two or three rods. Of this fact there are several eye witnesses now living.

Towards the close of the time I resided with this master, I had a falling out with my mistress. This happened one time when my master was gone to Long Island a-gunning. At first the quarrel began between my wife and her mistress. I was then at work in the barn, and hearing a racket in the house, induced me to run there and see what had broken out. When I entered the house, I found my mistress in a violent passion with my wife, for what she informed me was a mere trifle— such a small affair that I forbear to put my mistress to the shame of having it known. I earnestly requested my wife to beg pardon of her mistress for the sake of peace, even if she had given no just occasion for offence. But whilst I was thus saying, my mistress turned the blows which she was repeating on my wife to me. She took down her horse whip, and while she was glutting her fury with it, I reached out my great black hand, raised it up and received the blows of the whip on it which were designed for my head. Then I immediately committed the whip to the devouring fire.

When my master returned from the island, his wife told him of the affair, but for the present he seemed to take no notice of it, and mentioned not a word of it to me. Some days after his return, in the morning as I was putting on a log in the fireplace, not suspecting harm from any one, I received a most violent stroke on the crown of my head with a club two feet long and as large around as a chair post. This blow very badly wounded my head, and the scar of it remains to this day. The first blow made me have my wits about me as you may suppose, for as soon as he

went to renew it I snatched the club out of his hands and dragged him out of the door. He then sent for his brother to come and assist him, but I presently left my master, took the club he wounded me with, carried it to a neighboring justice of the peace, and complained of my master. He finally advised me to return to my master and live contented with him till he abused me again, and then complain. I consented to do accordingly. But before I set out for my master's, up he came and his brother Robert after me. The Justice improved this convenient opportunity to caution my master. He asked him for what he treated his slave thus hastily and unjustly, and told him what would be the consequence if he continued the same treatment towards me. After the justice had ended his discourse with my master, he and his brother set out with me for home, one before and the other behind me. When they had come to a by-place, they both dismounted their respective horses and fell to beating me with great violence. I became enraged at this and immediately turned them both under me, laid one of them across the other, and stamped them both with my feet what I would.

This occasioned my master's brother to advise him to put me off. A short time after this, I was taken by a constable and two men. They carried me to a blacksmith's shop and had me handcuffed. When I returned home my mistress enquired much of her waiters whether VENTURE was handcuffed. When she was informed that I was, she appeared to be very contented and was much transported with the news. In the midst of this content and joy, I presented myself before my mistress, showed her my handcuffs, and gave her thanks for my gold rings. For this my master commanded a negro of his to fetch him a large ox chain. This my master locked on my legs with two padlocks. I continued to wear the chain peaceably for two or three days, when my master asked me with contempuous hard names whether I had not better be freed from my chains and go to work. I answered him, "No." "Well, then," said he, "I will send you to the West

Indies, or banish you, for I am resolved not to keep you." I answered him, "I crossed the waters to come here and I am willing to cross them to return."

For a day or two after this not anyone said much to me, until one Hempstead Miner of Stonington asked me if I would live with him. I answered that I would. He then requested me to make myself discontented and to appear as unreconciled to my master as I could before that he bargained with him for me, and that in return he would give me a good chance to gain my freedom when I came to live with him. I did as he requested me. Not long after, Hempstead Miner purchased me of my master for fifty-six pounds lawful. He took the chain and padlocks from off me immediately after.

It may here be remembered that I related a few pages back that I hired out a sum of money to Mr. Robert Stanton, and took his note for it. In the fray between my master Stanton and myself, he broke open my chest containing his brother's note to me and destroyed it. Immediately after my present master bought me, he determined to sell me at Hartford. As soon as I became apprized of it, I bethought myself that I would secure a certain sum of money which lay by me safer than to hire it out to Stanton. Accordingly I buried it in the earth, a little distance from Thomas Stanton's, in the road over which he passed daily. A short time after, my master carried me to Hartford, and first proposed to sell me to one William Hooker of that place. Hooker asked whether I would go to the German Flats with him. I answered, "No." He said I should; if not by fair means, I should by foul. "If you will go by no other measures, I will tie you down in my sleigh." I replied to him, that if he carried me in that manner no person would purchase me, for it would be thought he had a murderer for sale. After this he tried no more, and said he would not have me as a gift.

My master next offered me to Daniel Edwards, Esq., of Hartford, for sale. But he not purchasing me, my master pawned me to him for ten pounds, and returned to Ston-

ington. After some trial of my honesty, Mr. Edwards placed considerable trust and confidence in me. He put me to serve as his cupbearer and waiter. When there was company at his house, he would send me into his cellar and other parts of his house to fetch wine and other articles occasionally for them. When I had been with him some time, he asked me why my master wished to part with such an honest negro, and why he did not keep me himself. I replied that I could not give him the reason, unless it was to convert me into cash and speculate with me as with other commodities. I hope that he can never justly say it was on account of my ill conduct that he did not keep me himself. Mr. Edwards told me that he should be very willing to keep me himself, and that he would never let me go from him to live, if it was not unreasonable and inconvenient for me to be parted from my wife and children; therefore, he would furnish me with a horse to return to Stonington, if I had a mind for it. As Miner did not appear to redeem me, I went, and called at my old master Stanton's first to see my wife, who was then owned by him. As my old master appeared much ruffled at my being there, I left my wife before I had spent any considerable time with her, and went to Col. O. Smith's. Miner had not as yet wholly settled with Stanton for me, and had before my return from Hartford given Colonel Smith a bill of sale of me. These men once met to determine which of them should hold me, and upon my expressing a desire to be owned by Colonel Smith, and upon my master's settling the remainder of the money which was due to Stanton for me, it was agreed that I should live with Colonel Smith. This was the third time of my being sold, and I was then thirty-one years old.

As I never had an opportunity of redeeming myself whilst I was owned by Miner, though he promised to give me a chance, I was then very ambitious of obtaining it. I asked my master one time if he would consent to have me purchase my freedom. He replied that he would. I was then very happy, knowing that I was at that time able to pay part of the purchase money by means of the money which I some time buried. This I took out of the earth and tendered to my master, having previously engaged a free negro man to take his security for it, as I was the property of my master, and therefore could not safely take his obligation myself. What was wanting in redeeming myself, my master agreed to wait on me for, until I could procure it for him. I still continued to work for Colonel Smith. There was continually some interest accruing on my master's note to my friend, the free negro man above named, which I received, and with some besides, which I got by fishing, I laid out in land adjoining my old master Stanton's. By cultivating this land with the greatest diligence and economy, at times when my master did not require my labor, in two years I laid up ten pounds. This my friend tendered my master for myself, and received his note for it.

Being encouraged by the success which I had met in redeeming myself, I again solicited my master for a further chance of completing it. The chance for which I solicited him was that of going out to work the ensuing winter. He agreed to this on condition that I would give him one-quarter of my earnings. On these terms I worked the following winter, and earned four pounds and sixteen shillings, one quarter of which went to my master for the privilege, and the rest was paid him on my account. I was then about thirty-five years old.

The next summer I again desired he would give me a chance of going to work. But he refused and answered that he must have my labor this summer, as he did not have it the past winter. I replied that I considered it as hard that I could not have a chance to work out when the season became advantageous, and that I must only be permitted to hire myself out in the poorest season of the year. He asked me after this what I would give him for the privilege per month. I replied that I would leave it wholly to his own generosity to determine what I should return him a month. Well then, said he, if so, two pounds a month. I answered him that if that was the least he would take I would be contented.

Accordingly I hired myself out at Fisher's Island, earning twenty pounds; thirteen pounds six shillings of which my master drew for the privilege and the remainder I paid for my freedom. This made fifty-one pounds two shillings which I paid him. In October following I went and wrought six months at Long Island. In that six month's time I cut and corded four hundred cords of wood, besides threshing out seventy-five bushels of grain, and received of my wages down only twenty pounds, which left remaining a larger sum. Whilst I was out that time, I took up on my wages only one pair of shoes. At night I lay on the hearth, with one coverlet over and another under me. I returned to my master and gave him what I received of my six months' labor. This left only thirteen pounds eighteen shillings to make up the full sum of my redemption. My master liberated me, saying that I might pay what was behind if I could ever make it convenient, otherwise it would be well. The amount of the money which I had paid my master towards redeeming my time, was seventy-one pounds two shillings. The reason of my master for asking such an unreasonable price, was, he said, to secure himself in case I should ever come to want. Being thirty-six years old, I left Colonel Smith once more for all. I had already been sold three different times, made considerable money with seemingly nothing to derive it from, had been cheated out of a large sum of money, lost much by misfortunes, and paid an enormous sum for my freedom.

CHAPTER III

Containing an Account of His Life from the Time of Purchasing His Freedom to the Present Day

My wife and children were yet in bondage to Mr. Thomas Stanton. About this time I lost a chest, containing, besides clothing, about thirty-eight pounds in paper money. It was burnt by accident. A short time after I sold all my possessions at Stonington, consisting of a pretty piece of land and one dwelling house thereon, and went to reside at Long Island. For the first four years of my residence there, I spent my time in working for various people on that and at the neighboring islands. In the space of six months I cut and corded upwards of four hundred cords of wood. Many other singular and wonderful labors I performed in cutting wood there, which would not be inferior to the one just recited, but for brevity's sake I must omit them. In the aforementioned four years, what wood I cut at Long Island amounted to several thousand cords, and the money which I earned thereby amounted to two hundred and seven pounds ten shillings. This money I laid up carefully by me. Perhaps some may inquire what maintained me all the time I was laying up my money. I would inform them that I bought nothing which I did not absolutely want. All fine clothes I despised in comparison with my interest, and never kept but just what clothes were comfortable for common days, and perhaps I would have a garment or two which I did not have on at all times, but as for superfluous finery, I never thought it to be compared with a decent homespun dress, a good supply of money and prudence. Expensive gatherings of my mates I commonly shunned, and all kinds of luxuries I was perfectly a stranger to; and during the time I was employed in cutting the aforementioned quantity of wood, I never was at the expense of six pence worth of spirits. Being after this labor forty years of age, I worked at various places, and in particular on Ram Island, where I purchased Solomon and Cuff, two sons of mine, for two hundred dollars each.

It will here be remembered how much money I earned by cutting wood in four years. Besides this, I had considerable money, amounting to all to near three hundred pounds. After this purchased a negro man, for no other reason than to oblige him, and gave for him sixty pounds. But in a short time after

he ran away from me, and I thereby lost all that I gave for him, except twenty pounds which he paid me previous to his absconding. The rest of my money I laid out in land, in addition to a farm which I owned before, and a dwelling house thereon. Forty-four years had then completed their revolution since my entrance into this existence of servitude and misfortune.

Solomon, my eldest son, being then in his seventeenth year, and all my hope and dependence for help, I hired him out to one Charles Church, of Rhode Island, for one year, on consideration of his giving him twelve pounds and an opportunity of acquiring some learning. In the course of the year, Church fitted out a vessel for a whaling voyage, and being in want of hands to man her, he induced my son to go, with the promise of giving him on his return, a pair of silver buckles, besides his wages. As soon as I heard of his going to sea, I immediately set out to go and prevent it if possible. But on my arrival at Church's, to my great grief, I could only see the vessel my son was in, almost out of sight, going to sea. My son died of the scurvy in this voyage, and Church has never yet paid me the least of his wages. In my son, besides the loss of his life, I lost equal to seventy-five pounds.

My other son being but a youth, still lived with me. About this time I chartered a sloop of about thirty tons burthen, and hired men to assist me in navigating her. I employed her mostly in the wood trade to Rhode Island, and made clear of all expenses above one hundred dollars with her in better than one year. I had then become something forehanded, and being in my forty-fourth year, I purchased my wife Meg, and thereby prevented having another child to buy, as she was then pregnant. I gave forty pounds for her.

During my residence at Long Island, I raised one year with another, ten cart loads of watermelons, and lost a great many besides by the thievishness of the sailors. What I made by the watermelons I sold there, amounted to nearly five hundred dollars. Various other methods I pursued in order to enable me to redeem my family. In the night time I fished with setnets and pots for eels and lobsters, and shortly after went a whaling voyage in the service of Col. Smith. After being out seven months, the vessel returned laden with four hundred barrels of oil. About this time I became possessed of another dwelling house, and my temporal affairs were in a pretty prosperous condition. This and my industry was what alone saved me from being expelled that part of the island in which I resided, as an act was passed by the selectmen of the place, that all negroes residing there should be expelled.

Next after my wife, I purchased a negro man for four hundred dollars. But he having an inclination to return to his old master, I therefore let him go. Shortly after, I purchased another negro man for twenty-five pounds, whom I parted with shorty after.

Being about forty-six years old, I bought my oldest child, Hannah, of Ray Mumford, for forty-four pounds, and she still resided with him. I had already redeemed from slavery, myself, my wife and three children, besides three negro men.

About the forty-seventh year of my life I disposed of all my property at Long Island, and came from thence into East Haddam, Conn. I hired myself out first to Timothy Chapman for five weeks, the earnings of which time I put up carefully by me. After this I wrought for Abel Bingham for about six weeks. I then put my money together and purchased of said Bingham ten acres of land lying at Haddam Neck, where I now reside. On this land I labored with great diligence two years, and shortly after purchased six acres more of land contiguous to my other. One year from that time I purchased seventy acres more of the same man, and paid for it mostly with the produce of my other land. Soon after I bought this last lot of land, I set up a comfortable dwelling house on my farm, and built it from the produce thereof. Shortly after I had much trouble and expense with my daughter Hannah, whose name has been before mentioned to this account. She was soon married after I redeemed her, to one Isaac, and shortly after her marriage fell sick of a mortal disease. Her husband, a dissolute and abandoned wretch, paid but little attention to her illness. I therefore thought it best to bring her to my house and nurse her there. I procured her all the aid mortals could afford, but notwithstanding this she fell a prey to her disease, after a lingering and painful endurance of it. The physician's bill for attending her illness amounted to forty pounds.

Having reached my fifty-fourth year, I hired two negro men, one named William Jacklin, and the other, Mingo. Mingo lived with me one year, and having received his wages, run in debt to me eight dollars, for which he gave me his note. Presently after he tried to run away from me without troubling himself to pay up his note. I procured a warrant, took him, and requested him to go to Justice Throop's of his own accord but he refusing, I took him on my shoulders and carried him there, distant about two miles. The justice asking me if I had my prisoner's note with me, and replying that I had not, he told me that I must return with him and get it. Accordingly, I carried Mingo back on my shoulders, but before we arrived at my dwelling, he complained of being hurt, and asked me if this was not a hard way of treating our fellow-creatures. I answered him that it would be hard thus to treat our honest fellow-creatures. He then told me that if I would let him off my shoulders, he had a pair of silver shoe-buckles, one shirt and a pocket handkerchief, which he would turn out to me. I agreed, and let him return home with me on foot; but the very following night he slipped from me, stole my horse and has never paid me even his note. The other negro man, Jacklin, being a comb-maker by trade, he requested me to set him up, and promised to reward me well with his labor. Accordingly I bought him a set of tools for making combs, and procured him stock. He worked at my house about one year, and then ran away from me with all his combs, and owed me for all his board.

Since my residence at Haddam Neck, I have owned of boats, canoes and sail vessels, not less than twenty. These I mostly employed in the fishing and trafficking business, and in these occupations I have been cheated out of considerable money by people whom I traded with taking advantage of my ignorance of numbers.

About twelve years ago, I hired a whale boat and four black men, and proceeded to Long Island after a load of round clams. Having arrived there, I first purchased of James Webb, son of Orange Webb, six hundred and sixty clams, and afterwards with the help of my men, finished loading my boat. The same evening, however, this Webb stole my boat and went in her to Connecticut river and sold her cargo for his own benefit. I thereupon pursued him, and at length recovered the boat, but for the proceed of her cargo I never could obtain any compensation.

Four years after I met with another loss, far superior to this in value, and I think by no less wicked means. Being going to New London with a grandchild, I took passage in an Indian's boat and went there with him. On our return, the Indian took on board two hogsheads of molasses, one of which belonged to Captain Elisha Hart, of Saybrook, to be delivered on his wharf. When we arrived there, and while I was gone, at the request of the Indian, to inform Captain Hart of his arrival and receive the freight for him, one hogshead of the molasses had been lost overboard by the people in attempting to land it on the wharf. Although I was absent at the time and had no concern whatever in the business, as was known to a number of respectable witnesses, I was nevertheless prosecuted by this conscientious gentleman (the Indian not being able to pay for it) and obliged to pay upwards of ten pounds lawful money, with all the costs of court. I applied to several gentlemen for counsel in this affair, and they advised me, as my adversary was rich, and threatened to carry the matter from court to court till it would cost me more than the first damages would be,—to pay the sum and submit to the injury, which I accordingly did, and he has often since insultingly taunted me with my unmerited misfortune. Such a proceeding as this committed on a de-

fenceless stranger, almost worn out in the hard service of the world, without any foundation in reason or justice, whatever it may be called in a Christian land, would in my native country have been branded as a crime equal to highway robbery. But Captain Hart was a *white gentleman,* and I a *poor African; therefore it was all right, and good enough for the black dog.*

I am now sixty-nine years old. Though once straight and tall, measuring without shoes six feet, one inch and an half, and every way well proportioned, I am now bowed down with age and hardship. My strength, which was once equal if not superior to any man whom I have ever seen, is now enfeebled so that life is a burden, and it is with fatigue that I can walk a couple of miles, stooping over my staff. Other griefs are still behind, on account of which some aged people, at least, will pity me. My eyesight has gradually failed, till I am almost blind, and whenever I go abroad one of my grandchildren must direct my way; besides for many years I have been much pained and troubled with an ulcer on one of my legs. But amidst all my griefs and pains, I have many consolations; Meg, the wife of my youth, whom I married for love and bought with my money, is still alive. My freedom is a privilege which nothing else can equal. Notwithstanding all the losses I have suffered by fire, by the injustice of knaves, by the cruelty and oppression of false-hearted friends, and the perfidy of my own countrymen whom I have assisted and redeemed from bondage, I am now possessed of more than one hundred acres of land, and three habitable dwelling houses. It gives me joy to think that I *have* and that I *deserve* so good a character, especially for *truth* and *integrity.* *(While I am now looking to the grave as my home, my joy for this world

---

*Note, the closing words in parentheses were omitted in the later editions. It is probable that both improved later, especially so in the case of Solomon, who is well spoken of by elderly men now living, as having maintained a good character.

would be full–IF my children, Cuff for whom I paid two hundred dollars when a boy, and Solomon who was born soon after I purchased his mother–If Cuff and Solomon–Oh! that they had walked in the way of their father. But a father's lips are closed in silence and in grief!–Vanity of vanities, all is vanity.)

CERTIFICATE

STONINGTON, CONN., November 3, 1798. THESE may certify, that VENTURE is a free negro man, aged about 69 years, and was, as we have ever understood, a native of Africa, and formerly a slave to Mr. James Mumford, of Fisher's Island, in the State of New York, who sold him to Mr. Thomas Stanton, 2d, of Stonington, in the State of Connecticut, and said Stanton sold said VENTURE to Col. Oliver Smith, of the aforesaid place. That said VENTURE hath sustained the character of a faithful servant, and that of a temperate, honest and industrious man, and being ever intent of obtaining his freedom, he was indulged by his master after the ordinary labor on the days of his servitude, to improve the nights in fishing and other employments to his own emolument, in which time he procured so much money as to purchase his freedom from his late master, Colonel Smith; after which he took upon himself the name of VENTURE SMITH, and has since his freedom purchased a negro woman, called Meg, to whom he was previously married, and also his children who were slaves, and said VENTURE has since removed himself and family to the town of East Haddam, in this State, where he hath purchased lands on which he hath built a house, and there taken up his abode.

NATHANIEL MINOR, ESQ.
ELIJAH PALMER, ESQ.
CAPT. AMOS PALMER
ACORS SHEFFIELD
EDWARD SMITH

The Stono Rebellion in South Carolina, 1739

(Anonymous)

In coastal Georgia and South Carolina the black population was believed to be under the influence of the Spanish settled at St. Augustine, Florida, who offered asylum to runaways from the English colonies. The slaves often found help from the Indians of the region as well. The inducements to revolt under these circumstances were quite practical, and met with a certain amount of success. The following account of the Stono insurrection of

Source: "The Stono Rebellion in South Carolina, 1739." From Allen D. Candler, ed., *The Colonial Records of the State of Georgia,* (Atlanta: Charles P. Byrd, 1913), Vol. 22, Pt. 2, pp. 232–236.

September 1739 was an anonymous enclosure in a letter dated October 9, 1739, from Gen. James Oglethorpe, founder of the colony of Georgia, to Mr. Harman Verelst, treasurer to the Trustees of Georgia. Oglethorpe requested that the account be published in the English newspapers.

Sometime since there was a Proclamation published at Augustine, in which the King of Spain (then at Peace with Great Britain) promised Protection and Freedom to all Negroes Slaves that would resort thither. Certain Negroes belonging to Captain Davis escaped to Augustine, and were received there. They were demanded by General Oglethorpe who sent Lieutenant Demere to Augustine, and the Governour assured the General of his sincere Friendship, but at the same time showed his Orders from the Court of Spain, by which he was to receive all Run away Negroes. Of this other Negroes having notice, as it is believed, from the Spanish Emissaries, four or five who were Cattel-Hunters, and knew the Woods, some of whom belonged to Captain Macpherson, ran away with His Horses, wounded his Son and killed another Man. These marched f [*sic*] for Georgia, and were pursued, but the Rangers being then newly reduced [*sic*] the Countrey people could not overtake them, though they were discovered by the Saltzburghers, as they passed by Ebenezer.[1] They reached Augustine, one only being killed and another wounded by the Indians in their flight. They were received there with great honours, one of them had a Commission given to him, and a Coat faced with Velvet. Amongst the Negroe Slaves there are a people brought from the Kingdom of Angola in Africa, many of these speak Portugueze [which Language is as near Spanish as Scotch is to English,] by reason that the Portugueze have considerable Settlement, and the Jesuits have a Mission and School in that Kingdom and many Thousands of the Negroes there profess the Roman Catholic Religion. Several Spaniards upon diverse Pretences have for some time past been strolling about Carolina, two of them, who will give no account of themselves have been taken up and committed to Jayl in Georgia. The good reception of the Negroes at Augustine was spread about, Several attempted to escape to the Spaniards, & were taken, one of them was hanged at Charles Town. In the latter end of July last Don Pedro, Colonel of the Spanish Horse, went in a Launch to Charles Town under pretence of a message to General Oglethorpe and the Lieutenant Governour.

On the 9th day of September last being Sunday which is the day the Planters allow them to work for themselves, Some Angola Negroes assembled, to the number of Twenty; and one who was called Jemmy was their Captain, they suprized a Warehouse belonging to Mr. Hutchenson at a place called Stonehow [*sic*—]; they there killed Mr. Robert Bathurst, and Mr. Gibbs, plundered the House and took a pretty many small Arms and Powder, which were there for Sale. Next they plundered and burnt Mr. Godfrey's house, and killed him, his Daughter and Son. They then turned back and marched Southward along Pons Pons, which is the Road through Georgia to Augustine, they passed Mr. Wallace's Tavern towards day break, and said they would not hurt him, for he was a good Man and kind to his Slaves, but they broke open and plundered Mr. Lemy's House, and killed him, his wife and Child. They marched on towards Mr. Rose's resolving to kill him; but he was saved by a Negroe, who having hid him went out and pacified the others. Several Negroes joyned them, they calling out Liberty, marched on with Colours displayed and two Drums beating, pursuing all the white people they met with, and killing Man Woman and Child when they could come up to them. Collonel Bull Lieutenant Governour of South Carolina, who was then riding along the Road, discovered them, was pursued, and with much difficulty escaped & raised the Countrey. They burnt Colonel Hext's house and killed his Overseer and his Wife. They then burnt Mr. Sprye's house, then Mr. Sacheverell's, and then Mr. Nash's house, all lying upon the Pons Pons Road, and killed all the white People they found in them. Mr. Bullock got off, but they burnt his House, by this time many of them were drunk with the Rum they had taken in the Houses. They increased every minute by new Negroes coming to them, so that they were above Sixty, some say a hundred, on which they halted in a field, and set to dancing, Singing and beating Drums, to draw more Negroes to them, thinking they were

---

[1]Ebenezer was the name of a religious community near Savannah, founded by German dissenters resettled in Salzburg. (*Editor's note*)

now victorious over the whole Province, having marched ten miles & burnt all before them without Opposition, but the Militia being raised, the Planters with great briskness pursued them and when they came up, dismounting; charged them on foot. The Negroes were soon routed, though they behaved boldly several being killed on the Spot, many ran back to their Plantations thinking they had not been missed, but they were there taken and [*sic*] Shot, Such as were taken in the field also, were after being examined, shot on the Spot, And this is to be said to the honour of the Carolina Planters, that notwithstanding the Provocation they had received from so many Murders, they did not torture one Negroe, but only put them to an easy death. All that proved to be forced & were not concerned in the Murders & Burnings were pardoned, And this sudden Courage in the field, & the Humanity afterwards hath had so good an Effect that there hath been no farther Attempt, and the very Spirit of Revolt seems over. About 30 escaped from the fight, of which ten marched about 30 miles Southward, and being overtaken by the Planters on horseback, fought stoutly for some time and were all killed on the Spot. The rest are yet untaken. In the whole action about 40 Negroes and 20 whites were killed. The Lieutenant Governour sent an account of this to General Oglethorpe, who met the advices on his return from the Indian Nation. He immediately ordered a Troop of Rangers to be ranged, to patrole through Georgia, placed some Men in the Garrison at Palichocolas, which was before abandoned, and near which the Negroes formerly passed, being the only place where Horses can come to swim over the River Savannah for near 100 miles, ordered out the Indians in pursuit, and a Detachment of the Garrison at Port Royal to assist the Planters on any Occasion, and published a Proclamation ordering all the Constables &c. of Georgia to pursue and seize all Negroes, with a Reward for any that should be taken. It is hoped these measures will prevent any Negroes from getting down to the Spaniards.—

SUGGESTED READINGS

Robin Blackburn, *The Making of New World Slavery: From the Baroque to the Modern, 1492–1800* (London, 1997)

Michael Carton, *Testing the Chains: Resistance to Slavery in the British West Indies* (Ithaca, N.Y., 1982)

Philip D. Curtin, *The Atlantic Slave Trade: A Census* (Madison, Wis., 1969)

Basil Davidson, *Black Mother: The Years of the African Slave Trade* (Boston, 1961)

David Eltis, *The Rise of African Slavery in the Americas* (Cambridge, England, 2000)

Daniel C. Littlefield, *Rice and Slaves: Ethnicity and the Slave Trade in Colonial South Carolina* (Baton Rouge, La., 1981)

Daniel P. Mannix and Malcolm Cowley, *Black Cargoes: A History of the Atlantic Slave Trade, 1518–1865* (New York, 1962)

Joseph C. Miller, *Way of Death: Merchant Capitalism and the Angolan Slave Trade, 1730–1830* (Madison, Wis., 1988)

C. Duncan Rice, *The Rise and Fall of Black Slavery* (London, 1975)

Walter Rodney, *How Europe Underdeveloped Africa* (Washington, 1974)

Hugh Thomas, *The Slave Trade: The Story of the Atlantic Slave Trade, 1440–1870* (New York, 1991)

John Thornton, *Africa and Africans in the Making of the Modern World, 1400–1680* (Cambridge, England, 1992)

Eric Williams, *Capitalism and Slavery* (New York, 1944)

Peter H. Wood, *Black Majority: Negroes in Colonial South Carolina from 1670 Through the Stono Rebellion* (New York, 1974)

Two black male slaves are sold in New Orleans by an auctioneer. (*Source:* The New York Historical Society.)

Chapter 2

Slavery and Race in Early America

African servitude emerged as a major institution in the colonial United States by the end of the seventeenth century. It was especially important for the production of staple crops in the southern plantation colonies, tobacco in Virginia and Maryland, rice in the Carolinas, and cotton by the end of the eighteenth century. The first document comprised of colonial laws illustrates the gradual codification of racial slavery and the degradation of Africans and Indians as separate races. The sermon by Reverend Charles Woodmason, an itinerant Baptist minister from the Carolina backcountry, gives a candid assessment of the colonists' fear and perceptions of African slaves and Native Americans.

The American Revolution led to the abolition of slavery in the northern states and the resulting growth of the free black population. Additional sources swelling the ranks of free blacks were private manumissions in the upper south states, freedom suits, self-emancipation by purchase, and natural increase in the free black community. Tens of thousands of slaves took advantage of the disruption caused by the Revolutionary War to escape slavery by running away. Many fought in both sides of the war to gain their freedom. The following documents indicate the initiative that African Americans took at this time to challenge their own enslavement. The antislavery petitions reveal the early adoption of revolutionary ideology by African Americans in order to question the existence of black slavery in the new American republic. A petition from an old slave woman, Belinda, shows that ordinary African Americans did not hesitate to use the political system to plead for their rights. Phillis Wheatley's poem is the first example of a black woman who mastered the form and style of the dominant literary genre of the day. The selections from pioneering black historian and abolitionist William C. Nell's book describe black participation in the revolutionary struggle and provide vivid portraits of some of the leading figures of this era. The clauses on slavery from the North West Ordinance and the U.S. Constitution reveal how the founding fathers tried to contain the spread of slavery while recognizing and protecting it in the constitution. Nell's book, Prince Hall's speech, Absalom Jones's petition, and Reverend Richard Allen's autobiography illuminate the growth of a sense of community among free blacks and the development of independent black institutions. Sojourner Truth's narrative documents the existence of slavery in the early north and the long struggle to abolish it.

The Statutes at Large; Being a Collection of the Laws of Virginia, From the First Session of the Legislature, in the Year 1619

"September 17th, 1630. Hugh Davis to be soundly whipped, before an assembly of Negroes and others for abusing himself to the dishonor of God and shame of Christians, by defiling his body in lying with a negro; which fault he is to acknowledge next Sabbath day."

MARCH, 1661–2—14TH

Act CII.

Run-aways. WHEREAS there are diverse loytering runaways in this country who very often absent themselves from their masters service and sometimes in a long time cannot be found, that losse of the time and the charge in the seeking them often exceeding the value of their labor: *Bee it therefore enacted* that all runaways that shall absent themselves from their said masters service, shalbe lyable to make satisfaction by service after the times by custome or indenture is expired (vizt.) double their times of service soe neglected, and if the time of their running away was in the crop or the charge of recovering them extraordinary the court shall lymitt a longer time of service proportionable to the damage the master shall make appeare he hath susteyned, and because the adjudging the time they should serve is often referred untill the time by indenture is expired, when the proofe of what is due is

very uncertaine, *it is enacted* that the master of any runaway that intends to take the benefitt of this act, shall as soone as he hath recovered him carry him to the next commissioner and there declare and prove the time of his absence, and the charge he hath bin at in his recovery, which commissioner thereupon shall grant his certificate, and the court on that certificate passe judgment for the time he shall serve for his absence; and in case any English servant shall run away in company of any negroes who are incapable of making satisfaction by addition of a time, *it is enacted* that the English soe running away in the company with them shall at the time of service to their owne masters expired, serve the masters of the said negroes for their absence soe long as they should have done by this act if they had not beene slaves, every christian in company serving his proportion; and if the negroes be lost or dye in such time of their being run away, the christian servants in company with them shall by proportion among them, either pay fower thousand five hundred pounds of tobacco and caske or fower yeares service for every negroe soe lost or dead.

DECEMBER, 1662—14TH

Act XII.

Negro womens children to serve according to the condition of the mother. (a) WHEREAS some doubts have arrisen whether children got by any Englishman upon a negro woman should be slave or free, *Be it therefore enacted and declared by this present grand assembly*, that all children borne in this country shalbe held bond or free only according to the condition of the mother,

Source: William Waller Hening, ed., *The Statutes at Large; Being a Collection of the Laws of Virginia, From the First Session of the Legislature, in the Year 1619.* (New York, 1823); Vol. I, p. 146; Vol. II, p. 116–117, 170, 260, 280–281, 481–482.

And that if any christian shall committ fornication with a negro man or woman, hee or shee soe offending shall pay double the fines imposed by the former act.

SEPTEMBER, 1667—19TH

Act III.

An act declaring that baptisme of slaves doth not exempt them from bondage. WHEREAS some doubts have risen whether children that are slaves by birth, and by the charity and piety of their owners made pertakers of the blessed sacrament of baptisme, should by vertue of their baptisme be made free; *It is enacted and declared by this grand assembly, and the authority thereof,* that the conferring of baptisme doth not alter the condition of the person as to his bondage or freedome; that diverse masters, freed from this doubt, may more carefully endeavour the propagation of christianity by permitting children, though slaves, or those of greater growth if capable to be admitted to that sacrament.

OCTOBER, 1670—22ND

Act V.

Noe Negroes nor Indians to buy christian servants. WHEREAS it hath beene questioned whither Indians or negroes manumited, or otherwise free, could be capable of purchasing christian servants. It *is enacted* that noe negroe or Indian though baptised and enjoyned their owne freedome shall be capable of any such purchase of christians, but yet not debarred from buying any of their owne nation.

JUNE, 1680—32D CHARLES II.

Act X.

An act for preventing Negroes Insurrections. WHEREAS the frequent meeting of considerable numbers of negroe slaves under pretence of feasts and burialls is judged of dangerous consequence; for prevention whereof for the future, *Bee it enacted by the kings most excellent majestie by and with the consent of the generall assembly, and it is hereby enacted by the authority aforesaid,* that from and after the publication of this law, it shall not be lawfull for any negroe or other slave to carry or arme himselfe with any club, staffe, gunn, sword or any other weapon of defence or offence, nor to goe or depart from of his masters ground without a certificate from his master, mistris or overseer, and such permission not to be granted but upon perticuler and necessary occasions; and every negroe or slave soe offending not haveing a certificate as aforesaid shalbe sent to the next constable, who is hereby enjoyned and required to give the said negroe twenty lashes on his bare back well layd on, and soe sent home to his said master, mistris or overseer. *And it is further enacted by the authority aforesaid* that if any negroe or other slave shall presume to lift up his hand in opposition against any christian, shall for every such offence, upon due proofe made thereof by the oath of the party before a magistrate, have and receive thirty lashes on his bare back well laid on. *And it is hereby further enacted by the authority aforesaid* that if any negroe or other slave shall absent himself from his masters service and lye hid and lurking in obscure places, comitting injuries to the inhabitants, and shall resist any person or persons that shalby any lawfull authority be imployed to apprehend and take the said negroe, that then in case of such resistance, it shalbe lawfull for such person or persons to kill the said negroe or slave soe lying out and resisting, and that this law be once every six months published at the respective county courts and parish churches within this colony.

Reverend Charles Woodmason's Sermon

Charles Woodmason

"We should live like Brethren in Unity."

I speak this [urging kind treatment to non-Presbyterians] on Account of the Infidels and Atheists around, who never will be perswaded to turn Religious, by any Rough treatment, or abusive Words—As also on Account of our Neighbours of the Reformed Churches in Germany. Severals of whom (as well as of my People) complain, that when they have brought their Children to this House of Worship for to be baptized Your Elders would not suffer the Minister to receive them, because the Parents were not in Church membership with You. Now Gentlemen I do not think this Treatment defensible—but rather reprehensible. . . . And I further hope, never more to hear of Your Inhospitality to Strangers, only because they are Episcopalians, and not of Your Kirk. . . .

2dly. There is an External Enemy near at Hand, which tho' not formidable either to our Religion or Liberties, still is to be guarded against. These are our *Indian* Neighbours. Common Prudence, and our Common Security, requires that We should live like Brethren in Unity, be it only to guard against any Dangers to our Lives and Properties as may arise from that Quarter.

3dly. We have an *Internal* Enemy Not less than 100 M [100,000] *Africans* below us (and more are daily importing) Over these We ought to keep a very watchful Eye, lest they surprize us in an Hour when We are not aware, and begin our Friendships towards each other in one Common Death.

Source: Reverend Charles Woodmason's Sermon, from Richard J. Hooker, ed., *The Carolina Backcountry on the Eve of the Revolution.* (Chapel Hill, NC, 1953), pp. 93–94.

To the Right Honourable William, Earl of Dartmouth, His Majesty's Principal Secretary of State for North America, & c.

Phillis Wheatley

Hail, happy day, when, smiling like the morn,
Fair *Freedom* rose *New-England* to adorn:
The northern clime beneath her genial ray,
Dartmouth, congratulates thy blissful sway:
Elate with hope her race no longer mourns,   5
Each soul expands, each grateful bosom burns,
While in thine hand with pleasure we behold
The silken reins, and *Freedom's* charms unfold.
Long lost to realms beneath the northern skies
She shines supreme, while hated faction
  dies: 10

Source: Phillis Wheatley, *Poems on Various Subjects, Religious and Moral.* (London, 1773), pp. 73–75.

Soon as appear'd the *Goddess* long desir'd,
Sick at the view, she languish'd and expir'd;
Thus from the splendors of the morning light
The owl in sadness seeks the caves of night.
No more, *America*, in mournful strain   15
Of wrongs, and grievance unredress'd complain,
No longer shall thou dread the iron chain,
Which wanton *Tyranny* with lawless hand
Had made, and with it meant t' enslave the land.
Should you, my lord, while you peruse my song,   20
Wonder from whence my love of *Freedom* sprung,
Whence flow these wishes for the common good,
By feeling hearts alone best understood,
I, young in life, by seeming cruel fate
Was snatch'd from *Afric's* fancy'd happy seat: 25

What pangs excruciating must molest,
What sorrows labour in my parent's breast?
Steel'd was that soul and by no misery mov'd
That from a father seiz'd his babe belov'd:
Such, such my case. And can I then but pray 30
Others may never feel tyrannic sway?
For favours past, great Sir, our thanks are due,
And thee we ask thy favours to renew,
Since in thy pow'r, as in thy will before,
To sooth the griefs, which thou did'st once deplore.   35
May heav'nly grace the sacred sanction give
To all thy works, and thou for ever live
Not only on the wings of fleeting *Fame,*
Though praise immortal crowns the patriot's name,
But to conduct to heav'ns refulgent fane,   40
May fiery coursers sweep th' ethereal plain,
And bear thee upwards to that blest abode,
Where, like the prophet, thou shalt find thy God.

Petitions of African Americans to Massachusetts General Court to Abolish Slavery and to the Massachusetts Legislature

PETITION OF SLAVES IN BOSTON.

Province of Massachusetts Bay.

To His Excellency, Thomas Hutchinson, Esq., Governor:—

To the Honorable, His Majesty's Council, and to the Honorable House of Representa-

---

Source: Petitions of African Americans to Massachusetts General Court to Abolish Slavery, 1773, 1777, from William Cooper Nell, *The Colored Patriots of the American Revolution* (Boston, 1855), pp. 40–41, 47–48; Petition of an African Slave to the Legislature of Massachusetts from *The American Museum, or Repository of Ancient and Modern Fugitive Pieces, Prose and Poetical* (June 1787) Vol. I, No. 6.

tives, in general court assembled at Boston, the 6th day of January, 1773:— The humble petition of many slaves living in the town of Boston, and other towns in the province, is this, namely:—

That Your Excellency and Honors, and the Honorable the Representatives, would be pleased to take their unhappy state and condition under your wise and just consideration.

We desire to bless God, who loves mankind, who sent his Son to die for their salvation, and who is no respecter of persons, that he hath lately put it into the hearts of multitudes, on both sides of the water, to bear our burthens, some of whom are men of great note and influence, who have pleaded our cause with arguments, which we hope will have their weight with this Honorable Court.

We presume not to dictate to Your Excellency and Honors, being willing to rest our cause on your humanity and justice, yet would beg leave to say a word or two on the subject.

Although some of the negroes are vicious, (who, doubtless, may be punished and restrained by the same laws which are in force against others of the King's subjects,) there are many others of a quite different character, and who, if made free, would soon be able, as well as willing, to bear a part in the public charges. Many of them, of good natural parts, are discreet, sober, honest and industrious; and may it not be said of many that they are virtuous and religious, although their condition is in itself so unfriendly to religion, and every moral virtue, except *patience?* How many of that number have there been, and now are, in this province, who had every day of their lives embittered with this most intolerable reflection, that, let their behavior be what it will, neither they nor their children, to all generations, shall ever be able to do or to possess and enjoy any thing—no, not even *life itself*—but in a manner as the *beasts* that perish!

We have no property! we have no wives! we have no children! we have no city! no country! But we have a Father in heaven, and we are determined, as far as his grace shall enable us, and as far as our degraded condition and contemptuous life will admit, to keep all his commandments; especially will we be obedient to our masters, so long as God, in his sovereign providence, shall *suffer* us to be holden in bondage.

It would be impudent, if not presumptuous, in us to suggest to Your Excellency and Honors, any law or laws proper to be made in relation to our unhappy state, which, although our greatest unhappiness, is not our *fault;* and this gives us great encouragement to pray and hope for such relief as is consistent with your wisdom, justice and goodness.

We think ourselves very happy, that we may thus address the great and general court of this province, which great and good court is to us the best judge, under God, of what is wise, just and good.

We humbly beg leave to add but this one thing more: we pray for such relief only, which by no possibility can ever be productive of the least wrong or injury to our masters, but to us will be as life from the dead.

SIR,

The efforts made by the legislative of this province in their last sessions to free themselves from slavery, gave us, who are in that deplorable state, a high degree of satisfaction. We expect great things from men who have made such a noble stand against the designs of their fellow-men to enslave them. We cannot but wish and hope Sir, that you will have the same grand object, we mean civil and religious liberty, in view in your next session. The divine spirit of freedom, seems to fire every humane breast on this continent, except such as are bribed to assist in executing the execrable plan.

We are very sensible that it would be highly detrimental to our present masters, if we were allowed to demand all that of right belongs to us for past services; this we disclaim. Even the Spaniards, who have not those sublime ideas of freedom that English men have, are conscious that they have no right to all the services of their fellowmen, we mean the Africans, whom they have purchased with their money; therefore they allow them one day in a week to work for themselves, to enable them to earn money to purchase the residue of their time, which they have a right to demand in such portions as they are able to pay for (a due appraizment of their services being first made, which always stands at the purchase money.) We do not pretend to dictate to you Sir, or to the honorable Assembly, of which you are a member: We acknowledge our obligations to you for what you have already done, but as the people of this province seem to be actuated by the principles of equity and justice, we cannot but expect your house will again take our deplorable case into serious consideration, and give us that ample relief which, as men, we have a natural right to.

But since the wise and righteous governor of the universe has permitted our fellow men to make us slaves, we bow in submission to him, and determine to behave in such a manner, as that we may have reason to expect the divine approbation of, and assistance in, our peaceable and lawful attempts to gain our freedom.

We are willing to submit to such regulations and laws as may be made relative to us, until we leave the province, which we determine to do as soon as we can from our joynt labours procure money to transport ourselves to some part of the coast of Africa, where we propose a settlement. We are very desirous that you should have instructions relative to us, from your town, therefore we pray you to communicate this letter to them, and ask this favor for us.

In behalf of our fellow slaves in this province, And by order of their Committee.

Peter Bestes,
Sambo Freeman,
Felik Holbrook,
Chester Joie.
For the Representative of the town of Thompson.

SECOND PETITION OF MASSACHUSETTS SLAVES.

The petition of a great number of negroes, who are detained in a state of slavery in the very bowels of a free and Christian country, humbly showing, —

That your petitioners apprehend that they have, in common with all other men, a natural and inalienable right to that freedom, which the great Parent of the universe hath bestowed equally on all mankind, and which they have never forfeited by any compact or agreement whatever. But they were unjustly dragged by the cruel hand of power from their dearest friends, and some of them even torn from the embraces of their tender parents,—from a populous, pleasant and plentiful country, and in violation of the laws of nature and of nations, and in defiance of all the tender feelings of humanity, brought hither to be sold like beasts of burthen, and, like them, condemned to slavery for life—

among a people possessing the mild religion of Jesus—a people not insensible of the sweets of national freedom, nor without a spirit to resent the unjust endeavors of others to reduce them to a state of bondage and subjection.

Your Honors need not to be informed that a life of slavery like that of your petitioners, deprived of every social privilege, of every thing requisite to render life even tolerable, is far worse than non-existence.

In imitation of the laudable example of the good people of these States, your petitioners have long and patiently waited the event of petition after petition, by them presented to the legislative body of this State, and cannot but with grief reflect that their success has been but too similar.

They cannot but express their astonishment that it has never been considered, that every principle from which America has acted, in the course of her unhappy difficulties with Great Britain, bears stronger than a thousand arguments in favor of your humble petitioners. They therefore humbly beseech Your Honors to give their petition its due weight and consideration, and cause an act of the legislature to be passed, whereby they may be restored to the enjoyment of that freedom, which is the natural right of all men, and their children (who were born in this land of liberty) may not be held as slaves after they arrive at the age of twenty-one years. So may the inhabitants of this State (no longer chargeable with the inconsistency of acting themselves the part which they condemn and oppose in others) be prospered in their glorious struggles for liberty, and have those blessings secured to them by Heaven, of which benevolent minds cannot wish to deprive their fellow-men.

And your petitioners, as in duty bound, shall ever pray:—

Lancaster Hill,
Peter Bess,
Brister Slenfen,
Prince Hall,
Jack Pierpont, [his × mark.]
Nero Funelo, [his × mark.]
Newport Sumner, [his × mark.]

PETITION OF BELINDA, AN AFRICAN

To the honourable the senate and house of representatives, in general court assembled: The petition of Belinda, an African, Humbly shews,

That seventy years have rolled away, since she, on the banks of the Rio de Valta, received her existence. The mountains, covered with spicy forests—vallies, loaded with the richest fruits spontaneously produced—joined to that happy temperature of air, which excludes excess, would have yielded her the most complete felicity, had not her mind received early impressions of the cruelty of men, whose faces were like the moon, and whose bows and arrows were like the thunder and the lightning of the clouds. The idea of these, the most dreadful of all enemies, filled her infant slumbers with horror, and her noon-tide moments with cruel apprehensions! But her affrighted imagination, in its most alarming extension, never represented distresses equal to what she has since really experienced: for before she had twelve years enjoyed the fragrance of her native groves, and ere she had realized that Europeans placed their happiness in the yellow dust, which she carelessly marked with her infant foot-steps—even when she, in a sacred grove, with each hand in that of a tender parent, was paying her devotion to the great Orisa, who made all things, an armed band of white men, driving many of her countrymen in chains, rushed into the hallowed shades! Could the tears, the sighs, the supplications, bursting from the tortured parental affection, have blunted the keen edge of avarice, she might have been rescued from agony, which many of her country's children have felt, but which none have ever described. In vain she lifted her supplicating voice to an insulted father, and her guiltless hands to a dishonoured deity! She was ravished from the bosom of her country, from the arms of her friends, while the advanced age of her parents rendering them unfit for servitude, cruelly separated them from her for ever.

Scenes which her imagination had never conceived of, a floating world, the sporting monsters of the deep, and the familiar meeting of billows and clouds, strove, but in vain, to divert her attention from three hundred Africans in chains, suffering the most excruciating torment; and some of them rejoicing that the pangs of death came like a balm to their wounds.

Once more her eyes were blessed with a continent: but alas! how unlike the land where she received her being! Here all things appeared unpropitious. She learned to catch the ideas, marked by the sounds of language, only to know that her doom was slavery, from which death alone was to emancipate her. What did it avail her, that the walls of her lord were hung with splendor, and that the dust trodden under foot in her native country, crouded his gates with sordid worshippers! The laws rendered her incapable of receiving property: and though she was a free moral agent, accountable for her own actions, yet never had she a moment at her own disposal! Fifty years her faithful hands have been compelled to ignoble servitude for the benefit of an Isaac Royall, until, as if nations must be agitated, and the world convulsed, for the preservation of that freedom, which the Almighty Father intended for all the human race, the present war commenced. The terrors of men, armed in the cause of freedom, compelled her master to fly, and to breathe away his life in a land, where lawless dominion sits enthroned, pouring blood and vengeance on all who dare to be free.

The face of your petitioner is now marked with the furrows of time, and her frame feebly bending under the oppression of years, while she, by the laws of the land, is denied the enjoyment of one morsel of that immense wealth, a part whereof hath been accumulated by her own industry, and the whole augmented by her servitude.

Wherefore, casting herself at the feet of your honours, as to a body of men, formed for the extirpation of vassalage, for the reward of virtue, and the just returns of honest industry—she prays that such allowance may be made her, out of the estate of colonel Royall, as will prevent her, and her more infirm daughter, from misery in the greatest extreme, and scatter comfort over the short

and downward path of their lives: and she will ever pray.

Belinda
Boston, February, 1782. (538–540).

Article 6 of the Northwest Ordinance of 1787

There shall be neither slavery nor involuntary servitude in the said territory, otherwise than in the punishment of crimes, whereof the party shall have been duly convicted: *Provided always,* That any person escaping into the same, from who labor or service is lawfully claimed in any one of the original

States, such fugitive may be lawfully reclaimed, and conveyed to the person claiming his or her labor or service as aforesaid.

Be it ordained by the authority aforesaid, That the resolutions of the 23d of April, 1784, relative to the subject of this ordinance, be, and the same are hereby, repealed, and declared null and void.

Done by the United States, in Congress assembled, the 13th day of July in the year of our Lord 1787, and their sovereignty and independence the twelfth.

Source: Article 6 of the Ordinance of 1787.

Three Clauses on Slavery from the United States Constitution, 1787

ARTICLE 1

Section 2. The House of Representatives shall be composed of Members chosen every second Year by the People of the several States, and the Electors in each State shall have the Qualifications requisite for Electors of the most numerous Branch of the State Legislature.

No Person shall be a Representative who shall not have attained to the Age of twenty-five Years, and been seven Years a Citizen of the United States, and who shall not, when elected, be an Inhabitant of that State in which he shall be chosen.

[Representatives and direct Taxes shall be apportioned among the several States which may be included within this Union, according to their respective Numbers, which shall be determined by adding to the whole Number of free Persons, including those bound to Service for a Term of Years, and excluding Indians not taxed, three fifths of all other Persons.]

Source: The United States Constitution, 1787.

Section 9. The Migration or Importation of such Persons as any of the States now existing shall think proper to admit, shall not be prohibited by the Congress prior to the Year one thousand eight hundred and eight, but a tax or duty may be imposed on such Importation, not exceeding ten dollars for each Person.

ARTICLE IV

Section 2. The Citizens of each State shall be entitled to all Privileges and Immunities of Citizens in the several States.

A Person charged in any State with Treason, Felony, or other Crime, who shall flee from Justice, and be found in another State, shall on demand of the executive Authority of the State from which he fled, be delivered up, to be removed to the State having Jurisdiction of the crime.

No Person held to Service or Labour in one State, under the Laws thereof, escaping into another, shall, in Consequence of any Law or Regulation therein, be discharged from such Service or Labour, but shall be delivered up on Claim of the Party to whom such Service or Labour may be due.

Petition of Absalom Jones and Seventy-Three Others

Absalom Jones and Others

To the President, Senate, and House of Representatives. The Petition of the People of Colour, free men, within the City and Suburbs of Philadelphia, humbly showeth,

That, thankful to God, our Creator, and to the Government under which we live, for the blessings and benefits granted to us in the enjoyment of our natural right to liberty, and the protection of our persons and property from the oppression and violence which so great a number of like colour and national descent are subject to, we feel ourselves bound, from a sense of these blessings, to continue in our respective allotments, and to lead honest and peaceable lives, rendering due submission unto the laws, and exciting and encouraging each other thereto, agreeable to the uniform advice of our friends of

Source: Petition of Absalom Jones and Seventy-Three Others. From John Parrish, *Remarks on the Slavery of Black People Addressed to the Citizens of the United States* (Philadelphia, 1806), pp. 49–51.

every denomination; yet while we feel impressed with grateful sensations for the Providential favour we ourselves enjoy, we cannot be insensible of the condition of our afflicted brethren, suffering under various circumstances, in different parts of these states; but deeply sympathizing with them, are incited by a sense of social duty, and humbly conceive ourselves authorized to address and petition you on their behalf, believing them to be objects of your representation in your public councils, in common with ourselves and every other class of citizens within the jurisdiction of the United States, according to the design of the present Constitution, formed by the General Convention, and ratified in the different states, as set forth in the preamble thereto in the following words, viz. "We, the people of the United States, in order to form a more perfect union, establish justice, insure domestic tranquillity, provide for the common defence, and to secure the blessings of liberty to ourselves and posterity, do ordain, &c." We apprehend this solemn compact is violated, by a trade carried on in a clandestine manner, to the coast of Guinea, and another equally wicked, practised openly by citizens of some of the southern states, upon the waters of Maryland and Delaware; men sufficiently callous to qualify them for the brutal purpose, are employed in kidnapping those of our brethren that are free, and purchasing others of such as claim a property in them: thus, those poor helpless victims, like droves of cattle, are seized, fettered, and hurried into places provided for this most horrid traffic, such as dark cellars and garrets, as is notorious at Northwestfork, Chestertown, Eastown, and divers other places. After a sufficient number is obtained, they are forced on board vessels, crowded under hatches, without the least commiseration, left to deplore the sad separation of the dearest ties in nature, husband from wife, and parents from children; thus packed together, they are transported to Georgia and other places, and there inhumanly exposed to sale. Can any commerce, trade, or transaction so detestably shock the feeling of man, or degrade the dignity of his nature equal to this? And how increasingly is the evil aggravated, when practised in a land high in profession of the benign doctrines of our Blessed Lord, who taught his followers to do unto others as they would they should do unto them. Your petitioners desire not to enlarge, though volumes might be filled with the sufferings of this grossly abused part of the human species, seven hundred thousand of whom, it is said, are now in unconditional bondage in these states: but conscious of the rectitude of our motives in a concern so nearly affecting us, and so effectually interesting to the welfare of this country, we cannot but address you as guardians of our rights, and patrons of equal and national liberties, hoping you will view the subject in an impartial, unprejudiced light. We do not ask for an immediate emancipation of all, knowing that the degraded state of many, and their want of education, would greatly disqualify for such a change; yet, humbly desire you may exert every means in your power to undo the heavy burdens, and prepare the way for the oppressed to go free, that every yoke may be broken. The law not long since enacted by Congress, called the Fugitive Bill, is in its execution found to be attended with circumstances peculiarly hard and distressing; for many of our afflicted brethren, in order to avoid the barbarities wantonly exercised upon them, or through fear of being carried off by those men-stealers, being forced to seek refuge by flight, they are then, by armed men, under colour of this law, cruelly treated, or brought back in chains to those that have no claim upon them. In the Constitution and the Fugitive Bill, no mention is made of black people, or slaves: therefore, if the Bill of Rights, or the Declaration of Congress are of any validity, we beseech, that as we are men, we may be admitted to partake of the liberties and unalienable rights therein held forth; firmly believing that the extending of justice and equity to all classes would be a means of drawing down the blessing of Heaven upon this land, for the peace and prosperity of which, and the real happiness of every member of the community, we fervently pray. Philadelphia, 30th of December, 1799.

Absalom Jones and others. 73 subscribers.

The Life, Experience and Gospel Labors of the Right Reverend Richard Allen

Richard Allen

I had it often impressed upon my mind that I should one day enjoy my freedom; for slavery is a bitter pill, notwithstanding we had a good master. But when we would think that our day's work was never done, we often thought that after our master's death we were liable to be sold to the highest bidder, as he was much in debt; and thus my troubles were increased, and I was often brought to weep between the porch and the altar. But I have had reason to bless my dear Lord that a door was opened unexpectedly for me to buy my time, and enjoy my liberty. When I left my master's house I knew not what to do, not being used to hard work, what business I should follow to pay my master and get my living. I went to cutting of cord wood. The first day my hands were so blistered and sore, that it was with difficulty I could open or shut them. I kneeled down upon my knees and prayed that the Lord would open some way for me to get my living. In a few days my hands recovered, and became accustomed to cutting of wood and other hardships; so I soon became able to cut my cord and a half and two cords a day. After I was done cutting, I was employed in a brick-yard by one Robert Register, at fifty dollars a month, continental money. After I was done with the brick-yard I went to days' work, but did not forget to serve my dear Lord. I used oftimes to pray sitting, standing, or lying; and while my hands were employed to earn my bread, my heart was devoted to my dear Redeemer. Sometimes I

Richard Allen, *The Life, Experience and Gospel Labors of the Right Reverend Richard Allen.* (Philadelphia, 1833), pp. 7–21.

would awake from my sleep preaching and praying. I was after this employed in driving of wagon in time of the continental war, in drawing salt from Rehobar, Sussex county, in Delaware. I had my regular stops and preaching places on the road. I enjoyed many happy seasons in meditation and prayer while in this employment.

After peace was proclaimed I then travelled extensively, striving to preach the Gospel. My lot was cast in Wilmington. Shortly after I was taken sick with the fall fever and then the pleurisy. September the 3d, 1783, I left my native place. After leaving Wilmington, I went into New-Jersey, and there travelled and strove to preach the Gospel until the spring of 1784. I then became acquainted with Benjamin Abbot, that great and good apostle. He was one of the greatest men that ever I was acquainted with. He seldom preached but what there were souls added to his labour. He was a man of as great faith as any that ever I saw. The Lord was with him, and blessed his labours abundantly. He was as a friend and father to me. I was sorry when I had to leave West Jersey, knowing I had to leave a father. I was employed in cutting of wood for Captain Cruenkleton, although I preached the Gospel at nights and on Sundays. My dear Lord was with me, and blessed my labours—glory to God—and gave me souls for my hire. I then visited East Jersey, and laboured for my dear Lord, and became acquainted with Joseph Budd, and made my home with him, near the new mills—a family, I trust, who loved and served the Lord. I laboured some time there; but being much afflicted in body with the inflammatory rheumatism, was not so successful as in some other places. I went from there to

Jonathan Bunn's, near Bennington, East Jersey. There I laboured in that neighbourhood for some time. I found him and his family kind and affectionate, and he and his dear wife were a father and mother of Israel. In the year 1784 I left East Jersey, and laboured in Pennsylvania. I walked until my feet became so sore and blistered the first day, that I scarcely could bear them to the ground. I found the people very humane and kind in Pennsylvania. I having but little money, I stopped at Cæsar Water's, at Radnor township, twelve miles from Philadelphia. I found him and his wife very kind and affectionate to me. In the evening they asked me if I would come and take tea with them; but after sitting awhile, my feet became so sore and painful that I could scarcely be able to put them to the floor. I told them that I would accept of their kind invitation, but my feet pained me so that I could not come to the table. They brought the table to me. Never was I more kindly received by strangers that I had never before seen, than by them. She bathed my feet with warm water and bran; the next morning my feet were better and free from pain. They asked me if I would preach for them. I preached for them the next evening. We had a glorious meeting. They invited me to stay till Sabbath day, and preach for them. I agreed to do so, and preached on Sabbath day to a large congregation of different persuasions, and my dear Lord was with me, and I believe there were many souls cut to the heart, and were added to the ministry. They insisted on me to stay longer with them. I stayed and laboured in Radnor several weeks. Many souls were awakened, and cried aloud to the Lord to have mercy upon them. I was frequently called upon by many inquiring what they should do to be saved. I appointed them to prayer and supplication at the throne of grace, and to make use of all manner of prayer, and pointed them to the invitation of our Lord and Saviour Jesus Christ, who has said, "Come unto me, all ye that are weary and heavy laden, and I will give you rest." Glory be to God! and now I know he

was a God at hand and left not afar off. I preached my farewell sermon, and left these dear people. It was a time of visitation from above.

. . . many were the slain of the Lord. Seldom did I ever experience such a time of mourning and lamentation among a people. There were but few coloured people in the neighbourhood—the most of my congregation was white. Some said, this man must be a man of God; I never heard such preaching before. We spent a greater part of the night in singing and prayer with the mourners. I expected I should have had to walk, as I had done before; but Mr. Davis had a creature that he made a present to me; but I intended to pay him for his horse if ever I got able. My dear Lord was kind and gracious to me. Some years after I got into business, and thought myself able to pay for the horse. The horse was too light and small for me to travel on far. I traded it away with George Huftman for a blind horse, but larger. I found my friend Huftman very kind and affectionate to me, and his family also. I preached several times at Huftman's meeting house to a large and numerous congregation.

I proceeded on to Lancaster, Pennsylvania. I found the people in general dead to religion, and scarcely a form of godliness. I went on to Little York and put up at George Tess, a saddler, and I believed him to be a man that loved and served the Lord. I had comfortable meetings with the Germans. I left Little York and proceeded on to the State of Maryland, and stopped at Mr. Benjamin Grover's; and I believed him to be a man that loved and served the Lord. I had many happy seasons with my dear friends. His wife was a very pious woman; but their dear children were strangers to vital religion. I preached in the neighbourhood for some time, and travelled Hartford circuit with Mr. Porters, who travelled that circuit. I found him very useful to me. I also travelled with Jonathan Forest and Leari Coal.

December, 1784, General Conference sat in Baltimore, the first General Conference ever held in America. The English preachers just arrived from Europe, Rev. Dr. Coke, Richard Watcoat, and Thomas Vasses. This was the beginning of the Episcopal Church amongst the Methodists. Many of the ministers were set apart in holy orders at this Conference, and were said to be entitled to the gown; and I have thought religion has been declining in the church ever since. There was a pamphlet published by some person which stated that when the Methodists were no people, then they were a people; and now they have become a people, they were no people, which had often serious weight upon my mind.

In 1785 the Rev. Richard Watcoat was appointed on Baltimore circuit. He was, I believe, a man of God. I found great strength in travelling with him—a father in Israel. In his advice he was fatherly and friendly. He was of a mild and serene disposition. My lot was cast in Baltimore, in a small meeting-house called Methodist Alley. I stopped at Richard Mould's, and was sent to my lodgings, and lodged at Mr. McCannon's. I had some happy meetings in Baltimore. I was introduced to Richard Russell, who was very kind and affectionate to me, and attended several meetings. Rev. Bishop Asberry sent for me to meet him at Henry Gaff's. I did so. He told me he wished me to travel with him. He told me that in the slave countries, Carolina and other places, I must not intermix with the slaves, and I would frequently have to sleep in his carriage, and he would allow me my victuals and clothes. I told him I would not travel with him on these conditions. He asked me my reason. I told him if I was taken sick, who was to support me? and that I thought people ought to lay up something while they were able, to support themselves in time of sickness or old age. He said that was as much as he got, his victuals and clothes. I told him he would be taken care of, let his afflictions be as they were, or let him be taken sick where he would, he would be taken care of; but I doubted whether it would be the case with myself. He smiled, and told me he would give me from then

until he returned from the eastward to make up my mind, which would be about three months. But I made up my mind that I would not accept of his proposals. Shortly after I left Hartford Circuit, and came to Pennsylvania, on Lancaster Circuit. I travelled several months on Lancaster Circuit with the Rev. Peter Morratte and Irie Ellis. They were very kind and affectionate to me in building me up; for I had many trials to pass through, and I received nothing from the Methodist connexion. My usual method was, when I would get bare of clothes, to stop travelling and go to work, so that no man could say I was chargeable to the connexion. My hands administered to my necessities. The autumn of 1785 I returned again to Radnor. I stopped at George Giger's, a man of God, and went to work. His family were all kind and affectionate to me. I killed seven beefs, and supplied the neighbours with meat; got myself pretty well clad through my own industry—thank God—and preached occasionally. The elder in charge in Philadelphia frequently sent for me to come to the city. February, 1786, I came to Philadelphia. Preaching was given out for me at five o'clock in the morning at St. George's Church. I strove to preach as well as I could, but it was a great cross to me; but the Lord was with me. We had a good time, and several souls were awakened, and were earnestly seeking redemption in the blood of Christ. I thought I would stop in Philadelphia a week or two. I preached at different places in the city. My labour was much blessed. I soon saw a large field open in seeking and instructing my African brethren, who had been a long forgotten people and few of them attended public worship. I preached in the commons, in Southwark, Northern Liberties, and wherever I could find an opening. I frequently preached twice a day, at five o'clock in the morning and in the evening, and it was not uncommon for me to preach from four to five times a day. I established prayer meetings; I raised a society in 1786 of forty-two members. I saw the necessity of erecting a place of worship for the coloured people. I proposed it to the most respectable people of colour in this city; but here I met with opposition. I had but three coloured brethren that united with me in erecting a place of worship—the Rev. Absalom Jones, William White, and Dorus Ginnings. These united with me as soon as it became public and known by the elder who was stationed in the city. The Rev. C—B— opposed the plan, and would not submit to any argument we could raise; but he was shortly removed from the charge. The Rev. Mr. W—took the charge, and the Rev. L— G—. Mr. W—was much opposed to an African church, and used very degrading and insulting language to us, to try and prevent us from going on. We all belonging to St. George's church—Rev. Absalom Jones, William White, and Dorus, Ginnings. We felt ourselves much cramped; but my dear Lord was with us, and we believed, if it was his will, the work would go on, and that we would be able to succeed in building the house of the Lord. We established prayer meetings and meetings of exhortation, and the Lord blessed our endeavours, and many souls were awakened; but the elder soon forbid us holding any such meetings; but we viewed the forlorn state of our coloured brethren, and that they were destitute of a place of worship. They were considered as a nuisance.

A number of us usually attended St. George's Church in Fourth street; and when the coloured people began to get numerous in attending the church, they moved us from the seats we usually sat on, and placed us around the wall, and on Sabbath morning we went to church and the sexton stood at the door, and told us to go in the gallery. He told us to go, and we would see where to sit. We expected to take the seats over the ones we formerly occupied below, not knowing any better. We took those seats. Meeting had begun, and they were nearly done singing, and just as we got to the seats, the elder said, "let us pray." We had not been long upon our knees before I heard considerable scuffling and low talking. I raised my head up and saw one of the trustees, H— M—, having hold of the Rev. Absalom Jones, pulling him up off of his knees, and saying, "You must get up—you must not kneel here." Mr. Jones replied, "wait until prayer is over." Mr. H— M— said "no, you must get up now, or I will call for aid and I force you away." Mr. Jones said, "wait until prayer is over, and I will get up and trouble you no more." With that he beckoned to one of the other trustees, Mr. L— S— to come to his assistance. He came, and went to William White to pull him up. By this time prayer was over, and we all went out of the church in a body, and they were no more plagued with us in the church. This raised a great excitement and inquiry among the citizens, in so much that I believe they were ashamed of their conduct. But my dear Lord was with us, and we were filled with fresh vigour to get a house erected to worship God in. Seeing our forlorn and distressed situation, many of the hearts of our citizens were moved to urge us forward; notwithstanding we had subscribed largely towards finishing St. George's Church, in building the gallery and laying new floors, and just as the house was made comfortable, we were turned out from enjoying the comforts of worshiping therein. We then hired a store room, and held worship by ourselves. Here we were pursued with threats of being disowned, and read publicly out of meeting if we did continue worship in the place we had hired; but we believed the Lord would be our friend. We got subscription papers out to raise money to build the house of the Lord. By this time we had waited on Dr. Rush and Mr. Robert Ralston, and told them of our distressing situation. We considered it a blessing that the Lord had put it into our hearts to wait upon those gentlemen. They pitied our situation, and subscribed largely towards the church, and were very friendly towards us, and advised us how to go on. We appointed Mr. Ralston our treasurer. Dr. Rush did much for us in public by his influence. I hope the name of Dr. Benjamin Rush and Mr. Robert Ralston will never be forgotten among us.

They were the two first gentlemen who espoused the cause of the oppressed, and aided us in building the house of the Lord for the poor Africans to worship in. Here was the beginning and rise of the first African church in America. But the elder of the Methodist church still pursued us. Mr. J— M— called upon us and told us if we did not erase our names from the subscription paper, and give up the paper, we would be publicly turned out of meeting. We asked him if we had violated any rules of discipline by so doing. He replied, "I have the charge given to me by the Conference, and unless you submit I will read you publicly out of meeting." We told him we were willing to abide by the discipline of the Methodist church; "and if you will show us where we have violated any law of discipline of the Methodist church, we will submit; and if there is no rule violated in the discipline, we will proceed on." He replied, "we will read you all out." We told him if he turned us out contrary to rule of discipline, we should seek further redress. We told him we were dragged off of our knees in St. George's church, and treated worse than heathens; and we were determined to seek out for ourselves, the Lord being our helper. He told us we were not Methodists, and left us. Finding we would go on in raising money to build the church, he called upon us again, and wished to see us all together. We met him. He told us that he wished us well, and that he was a friend to us, and used many arguments to convince us that we were wrong in building a church. We told him we had no place of worship; and we did not mean to go to St. George's church any more, as we were so scandalously treated in the presence of all the congregation present; "and if you deny us your name, you cannot seal up the scriptures from us, and deny us a name in heaven. We believe heaven is free for all who worship in spirit and truth." And he said, "so you are determined to go on." We told him—"yes, God being our helper." He then replied, "we will disown you all from the Methodist connex-

ion." We believed if we put our trust in the Lord, he would stand by us. This was a trial that I never had to pass through before. I was confident that the great head of the church would support us. My dear Lord was with us. We went out with our subscription paper, and met with great success. We had no reason to complain of the liberality of the citizens. The first day the Rev. Absalom Jones and myself went out we collected three hundred and sixty dollars. This was the greatest day's collection that we met with. We appointed a committee to look out for a lot—the Rev. Absalom Jones, William Gray, William Wilcher, and myself. We pitched upon a lot at the corner of Lombard and Sixth streets. They authorized me to go and agree for it. I did accordingly. The lot belonged to Mr. Mark Wilcox. We entered into articles of agreement for the lot. Afterwards the committee found a lot in Fifth street, in a more commodious part of the city, which we bought; and the first lot they threw upon my hands, and wished me to give it up. I told them they had authorized me to agree for the lot, and they were all well satisfied with the agreement I had made, and I thought it was hard that they should throw it upon my hands. I told them I would sooner keep it myself than to forfeit the agreement I had made. And so I did.

We bore much persecution from many of the Methodist connexion; but we have reason to be thankful to Almighty God, who was our deliverer. The day was appointed to go and dig the cellar. I arose early in the morning and addressed the throne of grace, praying that the Lord would bless our endeavours. Having by this time two or three teams of my own—as I was the first proposer of the African church, I put the first spade in the ground to dig a cellar for the same. This was the first African church or meeting house that was erected in the United States of America. We intended it for the African preaching house or church; but finding that the elder stationed in this city was such an opposer to our proceedings of erecting a place of worship; though the principal part of the directors of this church belonged to the Methodist connexion, the elder stationed here would neither preach for us, nor have any thing to do with us. We then held an election, to know what religious denomination we should unite with. At the election it was determined—there were two in favour of the Methodist, the Rev. Absalom Jones and myself, and a large majority in favour of the Church of England. The majority carried. Notwithstanding we had been so violently persecuted by the elder, we were in favour of being attached to the Methodist connexion; for I was confident that there was no religious sect or denomination would suit the capacity of the coloured people as well as the Methodist; for the plain and simple gospel suits best for any people, for the unlearned can understand, and the learned are sure to understand; and the reason that the Methodist is so successful in the awakening and conversion of the coloured people, the plain doctrine and having a good discipline. But in many cases the preachers would act to please their own fancy, without discipline, till some of them became such tyrants, and more especially to the coloured people. They would turn them out of society, giving them no trial, for the smallest offence, perhaps only hearsay. They would frequently, in meeting the class, impeach some of the members of whom they had heard an ill report, and turn them out, saying, "I have heard thus and thus of you, and you are no more a member of society"—without witnesses on either side. This has been frequently done, notwithstanding in the first rise and progress in Delaware State, and elsewhere, the coloured people were their greatest support; for there were but few of us free; but the slaves would toil in their little patches many a night until midnight to raise their little truck and sell to get something to support them more than what their masters gave them, but we used often to divide our little support among the white preachers of the Gospel. This was once a quarter. It was in the time of the old revolutionary war between Great Britain and the

United States. The Methodists were the first people that brought glad tidings to the coloured people. I feel thankful that ever I heard a Methodist preach. We are beholden to the Methodists, under God, for the light of the Gospel we enjoy; for all other denominations preached so high-flown that we were not able to comprehend their doctrine. Sure am I that reading sermons will never prove so beneficial to the coloured people as spiritual or extempore preaching. I am well convinced that the Methodist has proved beneficial to thousands and ten times thousands. It is to be awfully feared that the simplicity of the Gospel that was among them fifty years ago, and that they conform more to the world and the fashions thereof, they would fare very little better than the people of the world. The discipline is altered considerably from what it was. We would ask for the good old way, and desire to walk therein.

In 1793 a committee was appointed from the African Church to solicit me to be their minister, for there was no colored preacher in Philadelphia but myself. I told them I could not accept of their offer, as I was a Methodist. I was indebted to the Methodists, under God, for what little religion I had; being convinced that they were the people of God, I informed them that I could not be any thing else but a Methodist, as I was born and awakened under them, and I could go no further with them, for I was a Methodist, and would leave you in peace and love. I would do nothing to retard them in building a church as it was an extensive building, neither would I go out with a subscription paper until they were done going out with their subscription. I bought an old frame that had been formerly occupied as a blacksmith shop from Mr. Sims, and hauled it on the lot in Sixth near Lobard street, that had formerly been taken for the church of England. I employed carpenters to repair the old frame, and fit it for a place of worship. In July, 1794, Bishop Asbury being in town I solicited him to open the church for us which he accepted. The Rev. John Dickins sung and prayed, and Bishop Asbury preached. The house was called bethel agreeable to the prayer that was made. Mr. Dickins prayed that it might be a bethel to the gathering in of thousands of souls. My dear Lord was with us, so that there was many hearty Amen's echoed through the house. This house of worship has been favored with the awakening of many souls, and I trust they are in the kingdom both white and colored. Our warfare and troubles now began afresh. Mr. C. proposed that we should make over the church to the conference. This we objected to, he asserted that we could not be Methodists unless we did, we told him he might deny us their name, but they could not deny us a seat in Heaven. Finding that he could not prevail with us so to do, he observed that we had better be incorporated, then we could get any legacies that were left for us, if not, we could not. We agreed to be incorporated, he offered to draw the incorporation himself, that it would save us the trouble of paying for to get it drawn. We cheerfully submitted to his proposed plan. He drew the incorporation, but incorporated our church under the Conference, our property was then all consigned to the Conference for the present Bishops, Elders, and Ministers, &c., that belonged to the white Conference, and our property was gone. Being ignorant of incorporations we cheerfully agreed thereto, we labored about ten years under this incorporation, until J— S— was appointed to take the charge in Philadelphia, he soon waked us up by demanding the keys and books of the church, and forbid us holding any meetings except orders from him, these propositions we told him we could not agree to. He observed he was elder appointed to the charge, and unless we submitted to him, he would read us all out of meeting, we told him the house was ours we had bought it, and paid for it. He said he would let us know it was not ours, it belonged to the Conference, we took council on it; council informed us we had been taken in, according to the incorporation, it belonged to the white connexion. We

asked him if it could'nt be altered, he told us it two thirds of the society agreed to have it altered, it could be altered. He gave me a transcript to lay before them, I called the society together and laid it before them. My dear Lord was with us. It was unanimously agree to by both male and female, we had another incorporation drawn that took the church from Conference, and got it passed before the elder knew any thing about it. This raised a considerable rumpus, for the elder contended that it would not be good unless he had signed it. The elder with the Trustees of St. George's called us together, and said we must pay six hundred dollars a year for their services, or they could not serve us. We told them we were not able so to do. The Trustees of St. George's insisted that we should, or should not be supplied by their preachers, at last they made a move that they would take four hundred, we told them that our house was considerable in debt, and we poor people, and we could not agree to pay four hundred, but we agreed to give them two hundred. It was moved by one of the Trustees of St. George's that the money should be paid into their treasury, we refused paying it into their treasury, but we would pay it to the preacher that served, they made a move that the preacher should not receive the money from us. The bethel Trustees made a move that their funds should be shut and they would pay none, this caused a considerable contention, at length they withdrew their motion, the elder supplied us with preaching five times in a year for two hundred dollars. Finding that they supplied us so seldom, the Trustees of Bethel church passed a resolution that they would pay but one hundred dollars a year, as the elder only preached five times in a year for us, they called for the money, we paid him twenty-five dollars a quarter, but he being dissatisfied, returned the money back again, and would not have it unless we paid him fifty dollars. The Trustees concluded it was enough for five sermons, and said they would pay no more, the elder of St. George's was determined to preach for us no more, unless we gave him two hundred dollars, and we were left alone for upwards of one year.

Mr. S— R— being appointed to the charge of Philadelphia, declared unless we would repeal the Supplement neither he nor any white preacher travelling or local, should preach any more for us; so we were left to ourselves, at length the preachers and stewards belonging to the Academy, proposed serving us on the same terms that we had offered to the St. George's preachers, and they preached for us better than a twelve month; and then demanded $150 per year; this not being complied with, they declined preaching for us, and we were once more left to ourselves, as an edict was passed by the elder that if any local preacher should serve us, he should be expelled from the connexion. John Emory, then elder of the Academy, published a circular letter in which we were disowned by the Methodists. A house was also hired and fitted up for worship not far from Bethel, and an invitation given to all who desired to be Methodists to resort thither. But being disappointed in this plan, Robert R. Roberts, the resident elder, came to Bethel, insisted on preaching to us, and taking the spiritual charge of the congregation, for we were Methodists. He was told he should come on some terms with the Trustees: his answer was that, "He did not come to consult with Richard Allen or other trustees, but to inform the congregation that on next Sunday afternoon, he would come and take the spiritual charge." We told him he could not preach for us under existing circumstances. "However, at the appointed time he came, but having taken previous advice we had our preacher in the pulpit when he came, and the house was so fixed that he could not get but more than half way to the pulpit. Finding himself disappointed he appealed to those who came with him as witnesses that "That man (meaning the preacher) had taken his appointment." Several respectable white citizens who knew the colored people had been ill used were present, and told us not to fear for they would

see us righted, and not suffer Roberts to preach in a forcible manner, after which Roberts went away.

The next elder stationed in Philadelphia was Robert Birch, who following the example of his predecessor, came and published a meeting for himself. But the method just mentioned was adopted, and he had to go away disappointed. In consequence of this he applied to the Supreme Court for a writ of Mandamus, to know why the pulpit was denied him. Being elder, this brought on a law suit, which ended in our favor. Thus by the Providence of God we were delivered from a long, distressing and expensive suit which could not be resumed, being determined by the Supreme Court. For this mercy we desire to be unfeignedly thankful.

About this time our colored friends in Baltimore were treated in a similar manner by the white preachers and Trustees, and many of them drove away; who were disposed to seek a place of worship, rather than go to law.

Many of the colored people in other places were in a situation nearly like those of Philadelphia and Baltimore, which induced us in April 1816 to call a general meeting, by way of Conference. Delegates from Baltimore and other places which met those of Philadelphia, and taking into consideration their grievances, and in order to secure the privileges, promote union and harmony among themselves, it was resolved, "That the people of Philadelphia, Baltimore, &c. &c., should become one body, under the name of the African Methodist Episcopal Church." We deemed it expedient to have a form of discipline, whereby we may guide our people in the fear of God, in the unity of the Spirit, and in the bonds of peace, and preserve us from that spiritual despotism which we have so recently experienced—remembering that we are not to lord it over God's heritage, as greedy dogs that can never have enough. But with long suffering, and bowels of compassion to bear each other's burthens, and so fulfil the Law of Christ, praying that our mutual striving together for the promulgation of the Gospel may be crowned with abundant success.

The God of Bethel heard her cries,
He let his power be seen;
He stop'd the proud oppressors frown,
And proved himself a King.

Thou sav'd them in the trying hour,
Ministers and councils joined
And all stood ready to retain
That helpless church of thine.

Bethel surrounded by her foes,
But not yet in despair,
Christ heard her supplicating cries;
The God of Bethel heard.

A Charge Delivered to the African Lodge, June 24, 1797, at Menotomy

Prince Hall

Beloved Brethren of the African Lodge, 'Tis now five years since I deliver'd a Charge to you on some parts and points of Masonry. As one branch or superstructure on the foundation; when I endeavoured to shew you the duty of a Mason to a Mason, and charity or love to all mankind, as the mark and image of the great God, and the Father of the human race.

I shall now attempt to shew you, that it is our duty to sympathise with our fellow men under their troubles: the families of our brethren who are gone: we hope to the Grand Lodge above, here to return no more. But the cheerfulness that you have ever had to relieve them, and ease their burdens, under their sorrows, will never be forgotten by them; and in this manner you will never be weary in doing good.

But my brethren, although we are to begin here, we must not end here; for only look around you and you will see and hear of numbers of our fellow men crying out

with holy Job, Have pity on me, O my friends, for the hand of the Lord hath touched me. And this is not to be confined to parties or colours; not to towns or states; not to a kingdom, but to the kingdoms of the whole earth, over whom Christ the king is head and grand master.

Among these numerous sons and daughters of distress, I shall begin with our friends and brethren; and first, let us see them dragg'd from their native country, by the iron hand of tyranny and oppression, from their dear friends and connections, with weeping eyes and aching hearts, to a strange land and strange people, whose tender mercies are cruel; and there to bear the iron yoke of slavery & cruelty till death as a friend shall relieve them. And must not the unhappy condition of these our fellow men draw forth our hearty prayer and wishes for their deliverance from these merchants and traders, whose characters you have in the xviii chap. of the Revelations, 11, 12, & 13 verses, and who knows but these same sort of traders may in a short time, in the like manner, bewail the loss of the African traffick, to their shame and confusion: and if I mistake not, it now begins to dawn in some

Source: Prince Hall, *A Charge Delivered to the African Lodge, June 24, 1797, at Menotomy* (1797).

of the West-India islands; which puts me in mind of a nation (that I have somewhere read of) called Ethiopeans, that cannot change their skin: But God can and will change their conditions, and their hearts too; and let Boston and the world know, that He hath no respect of persons; and that that bulwark of envy, pride, scorn and contempt; which is so visible to be seen in some and felt, shall fall, to rise no more.

When we hear of the bloody wars which are now in the world, and thousands of our fellow men slain; fathers and mothers bewailing the loss of their sons; wives for the loss of their husbands; towns and cities burnt and destroy'd; what must be the heartfelt sorrow and distress of these poor and unhappy people! Though we cannot help them, the distance being so great, yet we may sympathize with them in their troubles, and mingle a tear of sorrow with them, and do as we are exhorted to—weep with those that weep.

Thus my brethren we see what a chequered world we live in. Sometimes happy in having our wives and children like olive-branches about our tables; receiving the bounties of our great Benefactor. The next year, or month, or week, we may be deprived of some of them, and we go mourning about the streets: so in societies; we are this day to celebrate this Feast of St. John's, and the next week we might be called upon to attend a funeral of some one here, as we have experienced since our last in this Lodge. So in the common affairs of life we sometimes enjoy health and prosperity; at another time sickness and adversity, crosses and disappointments.

So in states and kingdoms; sometimes in tranquility; then wars and tumults; rich today, and poor to-morrow; which shews that there is not an independent mortal on earth; but dependent one upon the other, from the king to the beggar.

The great law-giver, Moses, who instructed by his father-in-law, Jethro, an Ethiopean, how to regulate his courts of justice, and what sort of men to choose for the different offices; hear now my words, said he, I will give you counsel, and God shall be with you; be thou for the people to God-ward, that thou mayest bring the causes unto God, and thou shall teach them ordinances and laws, and shall shew the way wherein they must walk; and the work that they must do: moreover thou shall provide out of all the people, able men, such as fear God, men of truth, hating covetousness, and place such over them, to be rulers of thousands, of hundreds and of tens.

So Moses hearkened to the voice of his father-in-law, and did all that he said.—Exodus xviii. 22–24.

This is the first and grandest lecture that Moses ever received from the mouth of man; for Jethro understood geometry as well as laws, *that* a Mason may plainly see: so a little captive servant maid by whose advice Nomen, the great general of Syria's army was healed of his leprosy; and by a servant his proud spirit was brought down: 2 Kings, v, 3–14. The feelings of this little captive, for this great man, her captor, was so great, that she forgot her state of captivity, and felt for the distress of her enemy. Would to God (said she to her mistress) my lord were with the prophets in Samaria, he should be healed of his leprosy: So after he went to the prophet, his proud host was so haughty that he not only disdain'd the prophet's direction, but derided the good old prophet; and had it not been for his servant, he would have gone to his grave, with a double leprosy, the outward and the inward, in the heart, which is the worst of leprosies; a black heart is worse than a white leprosy.

How unlike was this great general's behaviour to that of as grand a character, and as well beloved by his prince as he was; I mean Obadiah, to a like prophet. See for this 1st Kings, xviii. from 7 to the 16th.

And as Obadiah was in the way, behold Elijah met him, and he knew him, and fell on his face, and said, Art not thou, my Lord, Elijah, and he told him, Yea, go and tell thy

Lord, behold Elijah is here: and so on to the 16th verse. Thus we see, that great and good men have, and always will have, a respect for ministers and servants of God. Another instance of this is in Acts viii. 27 to 31, of the European Eunuch, a man of great authority, to Philip, the apostle: here is mutual love and friendship between them. This minister of Jesus Christ did not think himself too good to receive the hand, and ride in a chariot with a black man in the face of day; neither did this great monarch (for so he was) think it beneath him to take a poor servant of the Lord by the hand, and invite him into his carriage, though but with a staff, one coat and no money in his pocket. So our Grand Master, Solomon, was not asham'd to take the Queen of Sheba by the hand, and lead her into his court, at the hour of high twelve, and there converse with her on points of masonry (for if ever there was a female mason in the world she was one) and other curious matters; and gratified her, by shewing her all his riches and curious pieces of architecture in the temple, and in his house: After some time staying with her, he loaded her with much rich presents: he gave her the right hand of affection and parted in love.

I hope that no one will dare openly (tho' in fact the behaviour of some implies as much) to say, as our Lord said on another occasion. Behold a greater than Solomon is here. But yet let them consider that our Grand Master Solomon did not divide the living child, whatever he might do with the dead one, neither did he pretend to make a law, to forbid the parties from having free intercourse with one another without the fear of censure, or be turned out of the synagogue.

Now my brethren, as we see and experience, that all things here are frail and changeable and nothing here to be depended upon: Let us seek those things which are above, which are sure and stedfast, and unchangeable, and at the same time let us pray to Almighty God, while we remain in the tabernacle, that he would give us the grace of patience and strength to bear up under all our troubles, which at this day God knows we have our share. Patience I say, for were we not possess'd of a great measure of it you could not bear up under the daily insults you meet with in the streets of Boston; much more on public days of recreation, how are you shamefully abus'd, and that at such a degree, that you may truly be said to carry your lives in your hands; and the arrows of death are flying about your heads; helpless old women have their clothes torn off their backs, even to the exposing of their nakedness; and by whom are these disgraceful and abusive actions committed, not by the men born and bred in Boston, for they are better bred; but by a mob or horde of shameless, low-lived, envious, spiteful persons, some of them not long since, servants in gentlemen's kitchings, scouring knives, tending horses, and driving chaise. 'Twas said by a gentleman who saw that filthy behaviour in the common, that in all the places he had been in, he never saw so cruel behaviour in all his life, and that a slave in the West-Indies, on Sunday or holidays enjoys himself and friends without any molestation. Not only this man, but many in town who hath seen their behaviour to you, and that without any provocations, twenty or thirty cowards fall upon one man, have wonder'd at the patience of the Blacks: 'tis not for want of courage in you, for they know that they dare not face you man for man, but in a mob, which we despise, and had rather suffer wrong than to do wrong, to the disturbance of the community and the disgrace of our reputation: for every good citizen doth honor to the laws of the State where he resides.

My brethren, let us not be cast down under these and many other abuses we at present labour under: for the darkest is before the break of day: My brethren, let us remember what a dark day it was with our African brethren six years ago, in the French West-Indies. Nothing but the snap of the whip was heard from morning to evening;

hanging, broken on the wheel, burning, and all manner of tortures inflicted on those unhappy people, for nothing else but to gratify their masters pride, wantonness and cruelty: but blessed be God, the scene is changed; they now confess that God hath no respect of persons, and therefore receive them as their friends, and treat them as brothers. Thus doth Ethiopia begin to stretch forth her hand, from a sink of slavery to freedom and equality.

Although you are deprived of the means of education; yet you are not deprived of the means of meditation; by which I mean thinking, hearing and weighing matters, men and things in your own mind, and making that judgment of them as you think reasonable to satisfy your minds and give an answer to those who may ask you a question. This nature hath furnished you with, without letter learning; and some have made great progress therein, some of those I have heard repeat psalms and hymns, and a great part of a sermon, only by hearing it read or preached and why not in other things in nature: how many of this class of our brethren that follow the seas; can foretell a storm some days before it comes; whether it will be a heavy or light, a long or short one; foretell a hurricane whether it will be destructive or moderate; without any other means than observation and consideration.

So in the observation of the heavenly bodies, this same class without a tellescope or other apparatus have through a smoak'd glass observed the eclipse of the sun: One being ask'd what he saw through his smoak'd glass? said, Saw, saw, de clipsey, or de clipseys;—and what do you think of it?—stop, dere be two;—right, and what do they look like?—Look like, why if I tell you, they look like two ships sailing one bigger than tother; so they sail by one another, and make no noise. As simple as the answers are they have a meaning, and shew, that God can out of the mouth of babes and Africans shew forth his glory; let us then love and adore him as the God who defends us and sup-

ports us and will support us under our pressures, let them be ever so heavy and pressing. Let us by the blessing of God, in whatsoever state we are, or may be in, to be content; for clouds and darkness are about him; but justice and truth is his habitation; who hath said, Vengeance is mine and I will repay it, therefore let us kiss the rod and be still, and see the works of the Lord.

Another thing I would warn you against, is the slavish fear of man, which bringest a snare, saith Solomon. This passion of fear, like pride and envy, hath slain its thousands.—What but this makes so many perjure themselves; for fear of offending them at home they are a little depending on, for some trifles: A man that is under a panic of fear, is afraid to be alone; you cannot hear of a robbery or house broke open or set on fire, but he hath an accomplice with him, who must share the spoil with him; whereas if he was truly bold, and void of fear, he would keep the whole plunder to himself: so when either of them is detected and not the other, he may be call'd to oath to keep it secret, but through fear, (and that passion is so strong) he will not confess, till the fatal cord is put on his neck; then death will deliver him from the fear of man, and he will confess the truth when it will not be of any good to himself or the community: nor is this passion of fear only to be found in this class of men, but among the great.

What was the reason that our African kings and princes have plung'd themselves and their peaceable kingdoms into bloody wars, to the destroying of towns and kingdoms, but the fear of the report of a great gun or the glittering of arms and swords, which struck these kings near the seaports with such a panic of fear, as not only to destroy the peace and happiness of their inland brethren, but plung'd millions of their fellow countrymen into slavery and cruel bondage.

So in other countries; see Felix trembling on his throne. How many Emperors and kings have left their kingdoms and best friends, at the sight of a handful of men in arms: how many have we seen that have left their estates and their friends and ran over to the stronger side as they thought: all through the fear of men; who is but a worm, and hath no more power to hurt his fellow worm, without the permission of God, than a real worm.

Thus we see my brethren, what a miserable condition it is to be under the slavish fear of men; it is of such a destructive nature to mankind, that the scriptures every where from Genesis to the Revelations warns us against it; and even our blessed Saviour himself forbids us from this slavish fear of man, in his sermon on the mount; and the only way to avoid it is to be in the fear of God: let a man consider the greatness of his power, as the maker and upholder of all things here below, and that in Him we live, and move, and have our being, the giver of the mercies we enjoy here from day to day, and that our lives are in his hands, and that he made the heavens, the sun, moon and stars to move in their various orders; let us thus view the greatness of God, and then turn our eyes on mortal man, a worm, a shade, a wafer, and see whether he is an object of fear or not, on the contrary, you will think him in his best estate, to be but vanity, feeble and a dependent mortal, and stands in need of your help, and cannot do without your assistance, in some way or other; and yet some of these poor mortals will try to make you believe they are Gods, but worship them not. My brethren let us pay all due respect to all whom God hath put in places of honor over us: do justly and be faithful to them that hire you, and treat them with that respect they may deserve; but worship no man. Worship God, this much is your duty as christians and as masons.

We see then how becoming and necessary it is to have a fellow feeling for our distress'd brethren of the human race, in their troubles, both spiritual and temporal—How refreshing it is to a sick man, to see his sympathising friends around his bed, ready to administer all the relief in their power; al-though they can't relieve his bodily pain yet they may ease his mind by good instructions and cheer his heart by their company.

How doth it cheer up the heart of a man when his house is on fire, to see a number of friends coming to his relief; he is so transported that he almost forgets his loss and his danger, and fills him with love and gratitude: and their joys and sorrows are mutual.

So a man wreck'd at sea, how must it revive his drooping heart to see a ship bearing down for his relief.

How doth it rejoice the heart of a stranger in a strange land to see the people cheerful and pleasant and are ready to help him.

How did it, think you, cheer the heart of those our poor unhappy African brethren, to see a ship commissioned from God, and from a nation that without flattery saith, that all men are free and are brethren; I say to see them in an instant deliver such a number from their cruel bolts and galling chains, and to be fed like men, and treated like brethren. Where is the man that has the least spark of humanity, that will not rejoice with them; and bless a righteous God who knows how and when to relieve the oppressed, as we see he did in the deliverance of the captives among the Algerines; how sudden were they delivered by the sympathising members of the Congress of the United States, who now enjoy the free air of peace and liberty, to their great joy and surprize, to them and their friends. Here we see the hand of God in various ways, bringing about his own glory for the good of mankind, by the mutual help of their fellow men; which ought to teach us in all our straits, be they what they may, to put our trust in Him, firmly believing, that he is able and will deliver us and defend us against all our enemies; and that no weapon form'd against us shall prosper; only let us be steady and uniform in our walks, speech and behaviour; always doing to all men as we wish and desire they would do to us in the like cases and circumstances.

Live and act as Masons, that you may die as Masons; let those despisers see, altho' many of us cannot read, yet by our searches and researches into men and things, we have supplied that defect, and if they will let us we shall call ourselves a charter'd lodge, of just and lawful Masons; be always ready to give an answer to those that ask you a question; give the right hand of affection and fellowship to whom it justly belongs let their colour and complexion be what it will: let their nation be what it may, for they are your brethren, and it is your indispensible duty so to do; let them as Masons deny this, and we & the world know what to think of them be they ever so grand: for we know this was Solomon's creed, Solomon's creed did I say, it is the decree of the Almighty, and all Ma-

sons have learnt it: plain market language and plain and true facts need no apologies.

I shall now conclude with an old poem which I found among some papers:—

Let blind admirers handsome faces praise,
And graceful features to great honor raise,
The glories of the red and white express,
I know no beauty but in holiness;
If God of beauty be the uncreate
Perfect idea, in this lower state,
The greatest beauties of an human mould
Who most resemble Him we justly hold;
Whom we resemble not in flesh and blood,
But being pure and holy, just and good:
May such a beauty fall but to my share,
For curious shape or face I'll never care.

Biographical Sketches of Crispus Attucks and Benjamin Banneker

William C. Nell

CRISPUS ATTUCKS

On the 5th of March, 1851, the following petition was presented to the Massachusetts Legislature asking an appropriation of $1,500, for the erection of a monument to the memory of CRISPUS ATTUCKS, the first martyr in the Boston Massacre of March 5th, 1770:—

To the Honorable the Senate and House of Representatives of the State of Massachusetts, in General Court assembled:

The undersigned, citizens of Boston, respectfully ask that an appropriation of fifteen

Source: Biographical Sketches of Crispus Attucks and Benjamin Banneker. From William C. Nell, *Colored Patriots of the Revolution* (Boston, 1855), pp. 13–18, 203–211.

hundred dollars may be made by your Honorable Body, for a monument to be erected to the memory of CRISPUS ATTUCKS, the first martyr of the American Revolution.

> WILLIAM C. NELL,
> CHARLES LENOX REMOND,
> HENRY WEEDEN,
> LEWIS HAYDEN,
> FREDERICK G. BARBADOES,
> JOSHUA B. SMITH,
> LEMUEL BURR.

BOSTON, Feb. 22d, 1851.

This petition was referred to the Committee on Military Affairs, who granted a hearing to the petitioners, in whose behalf appeared Wendell Phillips, Esq., and William C. Nell, but finally submitted an adverse report, on the ground that a boy, Christopher Snyder, was previously killed. Admitting this fact, (which was the result of a very different scene from that in which Attucks fell,) it does not offset the claims of Attucks, and those who made the 5th of March famous in our annals—the day which history selects as the dawn of the American Revolution.

Botta's History, and Hewes's Reminiscences (the tea party survivor), establish the fact that the colored man, ATTUCKS, was *of* and *with* the people, and was never regarded otherwise.

Botta, in speaking of the scenes of the 5th of March, says:—"The people were greatly exasperated. The multitude ran towards King street, crying, *'Let us drive out these ribalds; they have no business here!'* The rioters rushed furiously towards the Custom House; they approached the sentinel, crying, *'Kill him, kill him!'* They assaulted him with snowballs, pieces of ice, and whatever they could lay their hands upon. The guard were then called, and, in marching to the Custom House, they encountered," continues Botta, "a band of the populace, led by a mulatto named ATTUCKS, who brandished their clubs, and pelted them with snowballs. The maledictions, the imprecations, the execrations of the multitude, were horrible. In the midst of a torrent of invective from every quarter, the military were challenged to fire. The populace advanced to the points of their bayonets. The soldiers appeared like statues; the cries, the howlings, the menaces, the violent din of bells still sounding the alarm, increased the confusion and the horrors of these moments; at length, the mulatto and twelve of his companions, pressing forward, environed the soldiers, and striking their muskets with their clubs, cried to the multitude: *'Be not afraid; they dare not fire: why do you hesitate, why do you not kill them, why not crush them at once?'* The mulatto lifted his arm against Capt. Preston, and having turned one of the muskets, he seized the bayonet with his left hand, as if he intended to execute his threat. At this moment, confused cries were heard: *'The wretches dare not fire!'* Firing succeeds. ATTUCKS is slain. The other discharges follow. Three were killed,

five severely wounded, and several others slightly."

ATTUCKS had formed the patriots in Dock Square, from whence they marched up King street, passing through the street up to the main guard, in order to make the attack.

ATTUCKS was killed by Montgomery, one of Capt. Preston's soldiers. He had been foremost in resisting, and was first slain. As proof of a front engagement, he received two balls, one in each breast.

John Adams, counsel for the soldiers, admitted that Attucks appeared to have undertaken to be the hero of the night, and to lead the people. He and Caldwell, not being residents of Boston, were both buried from Faneuil Hall. The citizens generally participated in the solemnities.

The Boston *Transcript* of March 7, 1851, published an anonymous communication, disparaging the whole affair; denouncing CRISPUS ATTUCKS as a very firebrand of disorder and sedition, the most conspicuous, inflammatory, and uproarious of the misguided populace, and who, if he had not fallen a martyr, would richly have deserved hanging as an incendiary.* If the leader, ATTUCKS, deserved the epithets above applied, is it not a legitimate inference, that the citizens who followed on are included, and hence should swing in his company on the gallows? If the leader and his patriot band were *misguided,* the distinguished orators who, in after days, commemorated the 5th of March, must, indeed, have been misguided, and with them, the masses who were inspired by their eloquence; for John Hancock, in 1774, invokes the injured shades of *Maverick, Gray, Caldwell,* ATTUCKS, *Carr;* and Judge Dawes, in 1775, thus alludes to the band of "misguided incendiaries":—"The provocation of that night must be numbered among the master-springs which gave the first motion to a vast machinery,—a noble and comprehensive system of national independence."

---

*The *Transcript* of March 5th, 1855, honorably alludes to CRISPUS ATTUCKS.

Ramsay's History of the American Revolution, Vol. I., p. 22, says—"The anniversary of the 5th of March was observed with great solemnity; eloquent orators were successively employed to preserve the remembrance of it fresh in the mind. On these occasions, the blessings of liberty, *the horrors of slavery*, and the danger of a standing army, were presented to the public view. These annual orations administered fuel to the fire of liberty, and kept it burning with an irresistible flame."

The 5th of March continued to be celebrated for the above reasons, until the Anniversary of the Declaration of American Independence was substituted in its place; and its orators were expected to honor the feelings and principles of the former as having given birth to the latter.

On the 5th of March, 1776, Washington repaired to the intrenchments. "Remember," said he, "it is the 5th of March, and avenge the death of your brethren!"

In judging, then, of the merits of those who launched the American Revolution, we should not take counsel from the *Tories* of *that* or the *present* day, but rather heed the approving eulogy of Lovell, Hancock, and Warren.

Welcome, then, be every taunt that such correspondents may fling at ATTUCKS and his company, as the best evidence of their merits and their strong claim upon our gratitude! Envy and the foe do not labor to traduce any but prominent champions of a cause.

The rejection of the petition was to be expected, if we accept the axiom that a colored man never gets justice done him in the United States, except by mistake. The petitioners only asked for justice, and that the name of CRISPUS ATTUCKS might be honored as a grateful country honors other gallant Americans.

And yet, let it be recorded, the same session of the Legislature which had refused the ATTUCKS monument, granted one to ISAAC DAVIS, of Concord. Both were promoters of the American Revolution, but one was white, the other was *black;* and this is the only solution to the problem *why* justice was not fairly meted out.

BENJAMIN BANNEKER

BENJAMIN BANNEKER was born in Baltimore county, near the village of Ellicott's Mills, in the year 1732. His father was a native African, and his mother the child of natives of Africa; so that, to no admixture of the blood of the white man was he indebted for his peculiar and extraordinary abilities. His father was a slave when he married; but his wife, who was a free woman, and possessed of great energy and industry, very soon afterwards purchased his freedom. Banneker's mother was named Morton before her marriage, and belonged to a family remarkable for its intelligence. When upwards of seventy, she was still very active; and it is remembered of her, that at this advanced age, she made nothing of catching her chickens, when wanted, by running them down. A nephew of hers, Greenbury Morton, was a person of note, notwithstanding his complexion. Prior to 1809, free people of color, possessed of a certain property qualification, voted in Maryland. In that year, a law was passed, restricting the right of voting to free white males. Morton was ignorant of the law till he offered to vote at the polls in Baltimore county; and it is said, that, when his vote was refused, he addressed the crowd in a strain of pure and impassioned eloquence, which kept the audience, that the election had assembled, in breathless attention while he spoke.

When Benjamin was old enough, he was employed to assist his parents in their labor. This was at an early age, when his destiny seemed nothing better than that of a child of poor and ignorant free negroes, occupying a few acres of land, in a remote and thinly peopled neighborhood; a destiny which, certainly, at this day, is not of very brilliant promise, and which, at the time in question, must have been gloomy enough. In the intervals of toil, and when he was approaching, or had attained, manhood, he was sent to an obscure and distant country school, which he attended until he had acquired a knowledge of reading and writing, and had advanced in arithmetic as far as Double Position. In all matters, beyond these rudiments of learning, he was his own instructor. On leaving school, he was obliged to labor for years, almost uninterruptedly, for his support. But his memory being retentive, he lost nothing of the little education he had acquired. On the contrary, although utterly destitute of books, he amplified and improved his stock of arithmetical knowledge by the operation of his mind alone. He was an acute observer of every thing that he saw, or which took place around him in the natural world, and he sought with avidity information from all sources of what was going forward in society; so that he became gradually possessed of a fund of general knowledge which it was difficult to find among those, even, who were far more favored by opportunity and circumstances than he was. At first, his information was a subject of remark and wonder among his illiterate neighbors only; but, by degrees, the reputation of it spread through a wider circle; and Benjamin Banneker, still a young man, came to be thought of as one, who could not only perform all the operations of mental arithmetic with extraordinary facility, but exercise a sound and discriminating judgment upon men and things. It was at this time, when he was about thirty years of age, that he contrived and made a clock, which proved an excellent time-piece. He had seen a watch, but not a clock—such an article not yet having found its way into the quiet and secluded valley in which he lived. The watch was, therefore, his model. It took him a good while to accomplish this feat; his great difficulty, as he often used to say, being to make the hour, minute, and second hands, correspond in their motions. But the clock was finished at last, and raised still higher the credit of Banneker in his neighborhood as an ingenious man, as well as a good arithmetician.

As already stated, the basis of Banneker's arithmetical knowledge was obtained from the school book in which he had advanced as far as Double Position; but, in 1787, Mr. George Ellicott lent him Mayer's Tables, Ferguson's Astronomy, and Leadbeater's Lunar Tables. Along with these books were some astronomical instruments. Mr. Ellicott was accidentally prevented from giving Banneker any information as to the use of either books or instruments at the time he lent them; but, before he again met him, (and the interval was a brief one,) Banneker was independent of any instruction, and was already absorbed in the contemplation of the new world which was thus opened to his view. From this time, the study of astronomy became the great object of his life, and, for a season, he almost disappeared from the sight of his neighbors.

Very soon after the possession of the books already mentioned had drawn Banneker's attention to astronomy, he determined to compile an almanac, that being the most familiar use that occurred to him of the information he had acquired. Of the labor of the work, few of those can form an estimate, who would at this day commence such a task with all the assistance afforded by accurate tables and well-digested rules. Banneker had no such aid; and it is narrated as a well-known fact, that he commenced and had advanced far in the preparation of the logarithms necessary for his purpose, when he was furnished with a set of tables by Mr. George Ellicott. About this time, he began the record of his calculations, which is still in existence, and is left with the society for examination.

The first almanac which Banneker prepared, fit for publication, was for the year 1792. By this time, his acquirements had become generally known, and among others who took an interest in him was James McHenry, Esq. Mr. McHenry wrote a letter to Goddard & Angell, then the almanac publishers in Baltimore, which was probably the means of procuring the publication of the first almanac.

In their editorial notice, Messrs. Goddard & Angell say "They feel gratified in the opportunity of presenting to the public, through their press, what must be considered as an extraordinary effort of genius; a complete and accurate Ephemeris for the year 1792, calculated by a sable descendant of Africa," &c. And they further say, "That they flatter themselves that a philanthropic public, in this enlightened era, will be induced to give their patronage and support to this work, not only on account of its intrinsic merits, (it having met the approbation of several of the most distinguished astronomers of America, particularly the celebrated Mr. Rittenhouse,) but from similar motives to those which induced the editors to give this calculation the preference,—the ardent desire of drawing modest merit from obscurity, and controverting the long-established illiberal prejudice against the blacks."

The motives alluded to by Goddard & Angell, in the extracts just quoted, of doing justice to the intellect of the colored race, were a prominent object with Banneker himself; and the only occasions when he overstepped a modesty which was his peculiar characteristic, were, when he could, by so doing, "controvert the long-established illiberal prejudice against the blacks." We find him, therefore, sending a copy of his first almanac to Mr. Jefferson, the Secretary of State under General Washington, with an excellent letter, to which Mr. Jefferson made the following reply :—

Philadelphia, Aug. 31, 1791.
Sir, —I thank you sincerely for your letter of the 19th instant, and for the almanac it contained. Nobody wishes more than I do to see such proofs as you exhibit, that Nature has given to our black brethren talents equal to those of the other colors of men, and that the appearance of a want of them is owing only to the degraded condition of their existence, both in Africa and America. I can add, with truth, that no one wishes more ardently to see a good system commenced for raising the condition, both of their body and mind, to what it ought to be, as fast as the imbecility of their present existence, and other circumstances which cannot be neglected, will admit. I have taken the liberty of sending your almanac to Monsieur de Condorcet,

Secretary of the Academy of Sciences, at Paris, and members of the Philanthropic Society, because I considered it a document to which your whole color had a right, for their justification against the doubts which have been entertained of them.

I am, with great esteem, sir,
Your most obedient servant,
THO. JEFFERSON.
Mr. Benjamin Banneker, near Ellicott's
Lower Mills, Baltimore county.

When he published his first almanac, Banneker was fifty-nine years old, and had high respect paid to him by all the scientific men of the country, as one whose color did not prevent his belonging to the same class, as far as intellect went, with themselves. After the adoption of the Constitution in 1789, commissioners were appointed to run the lines of the District of Columbia, the ten miles square now occupied by the seat of government, and then called the "Federal Territory." The commissioners invited Banneker to be present at the runnings, and treated him with much consideration.

Banneker continued to calculate and publish his almanacs until 1802, and the folio already referred to and now before the society, contains the calculations clearly copied, and the figures used by him in his work. The hand-writing, it will be seen, is very good, and remarkably distinct, having a practised look, although evidently that of an old man, who makes his letters and figures slowly and carefully. His letter to Mr. Jefferson gives a very good idea of his style of composition, and his ability as a writer. The title of the almanac is here transcribed at length, as a matter of curious interest at this latter day. If it claims little of the art and elegance and wit of the almanacs of Punch or of Hood, it is, nevertheless, considering its history, a far more surprising production.

"Benjamin Banneker's Pennsylvania, Delaware, Virginia, and Maryland Almanac and Ephemeris, for the year of our Lord 1792, being Bissextile or leap year, and the sixteenth year of American Independence, which commenced

July 4, 1776: containing the motions of the Sun and Moon, the true places and aspects of the Planets, the rising and setting of the Sun, and the rising, setting, and southing, place and age of the Moon, &c. The Lunations, Conjunctions, Eclipses, Judgment of the Weather, Festivals, and remarkable days."

In 1804, Banneker died, in the seventy-second year of his age, and his remains are deposited, without a stone to mark the spot, near the dwelling which he occupied during his life-time.

During the whole of his long life, he lived respectably and much esteemed by all who became acquainted with him, but more especially by those who could fully appreciate his genius and the extent of his acquirements. Although his mode of life was regular and extremely retired, living alone, having never married,—cooking his own victuals and washing his own clothes, and scarcely ever being absent from home,—yet there was nothing misanthropic in his character; for a gentleman who knew him thus speaks of him:—"I recollect him well. He was a brave looking, pleasant man, with something very noble in his appearance. His mind was evidently much engrossed in his calculations; but he was glad always to receive the visits which we often paid to him." Another of Mr. Ellicott's correspondents writes as follows:—"When I was a boy, I became very much interested in him, (Banneker,) as his manners were those of a perfect gentleman; kind, generous, hospitable, humane, dignified and pleasing, abounding in information on all the various subjects and incidents of the day; very modest and unassuming, and delighting in society at his own house. I have seen him frequently. His head was covered with a thick suit of white hair, which gave him a very venerable and dignified appearance. His dress was uniformly of superfine drab broadcloth, made in the old style of a plain coat, with a straight collar and long waistcoat and a broad-brimmed hat. His color was not jet black, but decidedly negro. In size and personal appearance, the statue of Franklin, at the Library in Philadelphia, as seen from the street, is a perfect likeness of him."

Narrative of Sojourner Truth

Sojourner Truth

HER BIRTH AND PARENTAGE

The subject of this biography, Sojourner Truth, as she now calls herself, but whose name originally was Isabella, was the daughter of James and Betsey, slaves of one Col. Ardinburgh, Hurley, Ulster County, N.Y. Sojourner does not know in what year she was born, but knows she was liberated under the act of 1817, which freed all slaves who were forty years old and upward. Ten thousand slaves were then set at liberty. Those under forty years of age were retained in servitude ten years longer, when all were emancipated.

Col. Ardinburgh belonged to that class of people called Low Dutch.

Of her first master, she can give no account, as she must have been a mere infant when he died; and she with her parents and some ten or twelve other fellow human chat-

Source: Sojourner Truth, *Narrative of Sojourner Truth.* (Battle Creek, Michigan, 1878), pp. 13–54.

tels, became the legal property of his son, Charles Ardinburgh. She distinctly remembers hearing her father and mother say that their lot was a fortunate one, as Master Charles was the best of the family,—being, comparatively speaking, a kind master to his slaves.

James and Betsey having, by their faithfulness, docility, and respectful behaviour, won his particular regard, received from him particular favors—among which was a lot of land, lying back on the slope of a mountain, where, by improving the pleasant evenings and Sundays, they managed to raise a little tobacco, corn, or flax; which they exchanged for extras, in the articles of food or clothing for themselves and children. She has no remembrance that Saturday afternoon was ever added to their own time, as it is by *some* masters in the Southern States.

ACCOMMODATIONS

Among Isabella's earliest recollections was the removal of her master, Charles Ardinburgh, into his new house, which he had built for a hotel, soon after the decease of his father. A cellar, under this hotel, was assigned to his slaves as their sleeping apartment,—all the slaves he possessed, of both sexes, sleeping (as is quite common in a state of slavery) in the same room. She carries in her mind, to this day, a vivid picture of this dismal chamber; its only lights consisting of a few panes of glass, through which she thinks the sun never shone, but with thrice reflected rays; and the space between the loose boards of the floor, and the uneven earth below, was often filled with mud and water, the uncomfortable splashings of which were as annoying as its noxious vapors must have been chilling and fatal to health. She shudders, even now, as she goes back in memory, and revisits this cellar, and sees its inmates, of both sexes and all ages, sleeping on those damp boards, like the horse, with a little straw and a blanket; and she wonders not at the rheumatisms, and

fever-sores, and palsies, that distorted the limbs and racked the bodies of those fellow-slaves in after-life. Still, she does not attribute this cruelty—for cruelty it certainly is, to be so unmindful of the health and comfort of any being, leaving entirely out of sight his more important part, his everlasting interests,—so much to any innate or constitutional cruelty of the master, as to that gigantic inconsistency, that inherited habit among slaveholders, of expecting a willing and intelligent obedience from the slave, because he is a MAN—at the same time every thing belonging to the soul-harrowing system does its best to crush the last vestige of a man within him; and when it *is* crushed, and often before, he is denied the comforts of life, on the plea that he knows neither the want nor the use of them, and because he is considered to be little more or little *less* than a beast.

HER BROTHERS AND SISTERS

Isabella's father was very tall and straight, when young, which gave him the name of "Bomefree"—low Dutch for tree—at least, this is SOJOURNER'S pronunciation of it—and by this name he usually went. The most familiar appellation of her mother was "Mau-mau Bett." She was the mother of some ten or twelve children; though Sojourner is far from knowing the exact number of her brothers and sisters; she being the youngest, save one, and all older than herself having been sold before her remembrance. She was privileged to behold six of them while she remained a slave.

Of the two that immediately preceded her in age, a boy of five years, and a girl of three, who were sold when she was an infant, she heard much; and she wishes that all who would fain believe that slave parents have not natural affection for their offspring could have listened as *she* did, while Bomefree and Mau-mau Bett,—their dark cellar lighted by a blazing pine-knot,—would sit for hours, recalling and recounting every endearing, as well as harrowing circumstance that taxed memory could supply, from the histories of those dear departed ones, of whom they had been robbed, and for whom their hearts still bled. Among the rest, they would relate how the little boy, on the last morning he was with them, arose with the birds, kindled a fire, calling for his Mau-mau to "come, for all was now ready for her"—little dreaming of the dreadful separation which was so near at hand, but of which his parents had an uncertain, but all the more cruel foreboding. There was snow on the ground, at the time of which we are speaking; and a large old-fashioned sleigh was seen to drive up to the door of the late Col. Ardinburgh. This event was noticed with childish pleasure by the unsuspicious boy; but when he was taken and put into the sleigh, and saw his little sister actually shut and locked into the sleigh box, his eyes were at once opened to their intentions; and, like a frightened deer he sprang from the sleigh, and running into the house, concealed himself under a bed. But this availed him little. He was re-conveyed to the sleigh, and separated for ever from those whom God had constituted his natural guardians and protectors, and who should have found him, in return, a stay and a staff to them in their declining years. But I make no comments on facts like these, knowing that the heart of every slave parent will make its own comments, involuntarily and correctly, as soon as each heart shall make the case its own. Those who are not parents will draw their conclusions from the promptings of humanity and philanthropy:—these, enlightened by reason and revelation, are also unerring.

HER RELIGIOUS INSTRUCTION

Isabella and Peter, her youngest brother, remained, with their parents, the legal property of Charles Ardinburgh till his decease, which took place when Isabella was near nine years old.

After this event, she was often surprised to find her mother in tears; and when, in her simplicity, she inquired "Mau-mau, what makes you cry?" she would answer, "Oh, my child, I am thinking of your brothers and sisters that have been sold away from me." And she would proceed to detail many circumstances respecting them. But Isabella long since concluded that it was the impending fate of her only remaining children, which her mother but too well understood, even then, that called up those memories from the past, and made them crucify her heart afresh.

In the evening, when her mother's work was done, she would sit down under the sparkling vault of heaven, and calling her children to her, would talk to them of the only Being that could effectually aid or protect them. Her teachings were delivered in Low Dutch, her only language, and, translated into English, ran nearly as follows:—

"My children, there is a God, who hears and sees you." "A *God*, mau-mau! Where does he live?" asked the children. "He lives in the sky," she replied; "and when you are beaten, or cruelly treated, or fall into any trouble, you must ask help of him, and he will always hear and help you." She taught them to kneel and say the Lord's prayer. She entreated them to refrain from lying and stealing, and to strive to obey their masters.

At times, a groan would escape her, and she would break out in the language of the Psalmist—"Oh Lord, how long?" "Oh Lord, how long?" And in reply to Isabella's question—"What ails you, mau-mau?" her only answer was, "Oh, a good deal ails me"—"Enough ails me." Then again, she would point them to the stars, and say, in her peculiar language, "Those are the same stars, and that is the same moon, that look down upon your brothers and sisters, and which they see as they look up to them, though they are ever so far away from us, and each other."

Thus, in her humble way, did she endeavor to show them their Heavenly Father, as the only being who could protect them in their perilous condition; at the same time, she would strengthen and brighten the chain of family affection, which she trusted extended itself sufficiently to connect the widely scattered members of her precious flock. These instructions of the mother were treasured up and held sacred by Isabella, as our future narrative will show.

THE AUCTION

At length, the never-to-be-forgotten day of the terrible auction arrived, when the "slaves, horses, and other cattle" of Charles Ardinburgh, deceased, were to be put under the hammer, and again change masters. Not only Isabella and Peter, but their mother, was now destined to the auction block, and would have been struck off with the rest to the highest bidder, but for the following circumstance: A question arose among the heirs, "Who shall be burdened with Bome-free, when we have sent away his faithful Mau-mau Bett?" He was becoming weak and infirm; his limbs were painfully rheumatic and distorted—more from exposure and hardship than from old age, though he was several years older than Mau-mau Bett: he was no longer considered of value, but must soon be a burden and care to some one. After some contention on the point at issue, none being willing to be burdened with him, it was finally agreed, as most expedient for the heirs, that the price of Mau-mau Bett should be sacrificed, and she receive her freedom, on condition that she take care of and support her faithful James,—faithful, not only to her as a husband, but proverbially faithful as a slave to those who would not willingly sacrifice a dollar for *his* comfort, now that he had commenced his descent into the dark vale of decrepitude and suffering. This important decision was received as joyful news indeed to our ancient couple, who were the objects of it, and who were trying to prepare their hearts for a severe struggle, and one altogether new to them, as they had never before been separated; for, though ignorant, helpless, crushed

in spirit, and weighed down with hardship and cruel bereavement, they were still human, and their human hearts beat within them with as true an affection as ever caused a human heart to beat. And their anticipated separation now, in the decline of life, after the last child had been torn from them, must have been truly appalling. Another privilege was granted them—that of remaining occupants of the same dark, humid cellar I have before described: otherwise, they were to support themselves as they best could. And as her mother was still able to do considerable work, and her father a little, they got on for some time very comfortably. The strangers who rented the house were humane people, and very kind to them; they were not rich, and owned no slaves. How long this state of things continued, we are unable to say, as Isabella had not then sufficiently cultivated her organ of time to calculate years, or even weeks or hours. But she thinks her mother must have lived several years after the death of Master Charles. She remembers going to visit her parents some three or four times before the death of her mother, and a good deal of time seemed to her to intervene between each visit.

At length her mother's health began to decline—a fever-sore made its ravages on one of her limbs, and the palsy began to shake her frame; still, she and James tottered about, picking up a little here and there, which, added to the mites contributed by their kind neighbors, sufficed to sustain life, and drive famine from the door.

DEATH OF MAU-MAU BETT

One morning, in early autumn, (from the reason above mentioned, we cannot tell what year,) Mau-mau Bett told James she would make him a loaf of rye-bread, and get Mrs. Simmons, their kind neighbor, to bake it for them, as she would bake that forenoon. James told her he had engaged to rake after the cart for his neighbors that morning; but before he commenced, he would pole off some apples from a tree near, which they were allowed to gather; and if she could get some of them baked with the bread, it would give it a nice relish for their dinner. He beat off the apples, and soon after, saw Mau-mau Bett come out and gather them up.

At the blowing of the horn for dinner, he groped his way into his cellar, anticipating his humble, but warm and nourishing meal; when, lo! instead of being cheered by the sight and odor of fresh-baked bread and the savory apples, his cellar seemed more cheerless than usual, and at first neither sight nor sound met eye or ear. But, on groping his way through the room, his staff, which he used as a pioneer to go before, and warm him of danger, seemed to be impeded in its progress, and a low, gurgling, choking sound proceeded from the object before him, giving him the first intimation of the truth as it was, that Mau-mau Bett, his bosom companion, the only remaining member of his large family, had fallen in a fit of the palsy, and lay helpless and senseless on the earth! Who among us, located in pleasant homes, surrounded with every comfort, and so many kind and sympathizing friends, can picture to ourselves the dark and desolate state of poor old James—penniless, weak, lame, and nearly blind, as he was at the moment he found his companion was removed from him, and he was left alone in the world, with no one to aid, comfort, or console him? for she never revived again, and lived only a few hours after being discovered senseless by her poor bereaved James.

LAST DAYS OF BOMEFREE

Isabella and Peter were permitted to see the remains of their mother laid in their last narrow dwelling, and to make their bereaved father a little visit, ere they returned to their servitude. And most piteous were the lamentations of the poor old man, when, at last, *they* also were obliged to bid him "Farewell!" Juan Fernandes, on his desolate island, was not so pitiable an object as this poor lame man. Blind and crippled, he was too superannuated to think for a moment of taking care of himself, and he greatly feared no persons would interest themselves in his behalf. "Oh," he would exclaim, "I had thought God would take me first,—Mau-mau was so much smarter than I, and could get about and take care of herself;—and I am *so old*, and *so helpless*. What *is* to become of me? I can't do any thing more—my children are all gone, and here I am left helpless and alone." "And then, as I was taking leave of him," said his daughter, in relating it, "he raised his voice, and cried aloud like a child—*Oh, how he* DID *cry!* I HEAR it *now*—and remember it as well as if it were but yesterday—*poor old man!!!* He thought *God* had done it all—and my heart bled within me at the sight of his misery. He begged me to get permission to come and see him sometimes, which I readily and heartily promised him." But when all had left him, the Ardinburghs, having some feeling left for their faithful and favorite slave, "took turns about" in keeping him—permitting him to stay a few weeks at one house, and then a while at another, and so around. If, when he made a removal, the place where he was going was not too far off, he took up his line of march, staff in hand, and asked for no assistance. If it was twelve or twenty miles, they gave him a ride. While he was living in this way, Isabella was twice permitted to visit him. Another time she walked twelve miles, and carried her infant in her arms to see him, but when she reached the place where she hoped to find him, he had just left for a place some twenty miles distant, and she never saw him more. The last time she *did* see him, she found him seated on a rock, by the-road side, alone, and far from any house. He was then migrating from the house of one Ardinburgh to that of another, several miles distant. His hair was white like wool—he was almost blind—and his gait was more a creep than a walk—but the weather was warm and pleasant, and he did not dislike the journey. When Isabella addressed him, he recognized her voice, and was exceeding glad to see her. He was assisted to mount the wagon, was carried back to the famous cellar of which we have spoken, and there they held their last earthly conversation. He again, as usual, bewailed his loneliness,—spoke in tones of anguish of his many children, saying, "They are all taken away from me! I have now not one to give me a cup of cold water—why should I live and not die?" Isabella, whose heart yearned over her father, and who would have made any sacrifice to have been able to be with, and take care of him, tried to comfort, by telling him that "she had heard the white folks say, that all the slaves in the State would be freed in ten years, and that then she would come and take care of him." "I would take just as good care of you as Mau-mau would, if she was here"—continued Isabel. "Oh, my child," replied he, "I cannot *live* that long." "Oh *do*, daddy, do live, and I will take such *good* care of you," was her rejoinder. She now says, "Why, I thought then, in my ignorance, that he *could* live, if he *would*. I just as much thought so, as I ever thought *any* thing in my life—and I *insisted* on his living: but he shook his head, and insisted he could not."

But before Bomefree's good constitution would yield either to age, exposure, or a strong desire to die, the Ardinburghs again tired of him, and offered freedom to two old slaves—Cæsar, brother of Mau-mau Bett, and his wife Betsey—on condition that they should take care of James. (I was about to say, "their brother-in-law"—but as slaves are neither *husbands* nor *wives* in law, the idea of their being brothers-in-law is truly ludicrous.) And although they were too old and infirm to take care of themselves, (Cæsar having afflicted for a long time with fever-sores, and his wife with the jaundice,) they eagerly accepted the boon of freedom, which had been the life-long desire of their souls—though at a time when emancipation was to them little more than destitution, and was a freedom more to be desired by the master

than the slave. Sojourner declares of the slaves in their ignorance, that "their thoughts are no longer than her finger."

DEATH OF BOMEFREE

A rude cabin, in a lone wood, far from any neighbors, was granted to our freed friends, as the only assistance they were now to expect. Bomefree, from this time, found his poor needs hardly supplied, as his new providers were scarce able to administer to their *own* wants. However, the time drew near when things were to be decidedly worse rather than better; for they had not been together long, before Betty died, and shortly after, Cæsar followed her to "that bourne from whence no traveller returns"—leaving poor James again desolate, and more helpless than ever before; as, this time, there was no kind family in the house, and the Ardinburghs no longer invited him to their homes. Yet, lone, blind and helpless as he was, James for a time lived on. One day, an aged colored woman, named Soan, called at his shanty, and James besought her, in the most moving manner, even with tears, to tarry awhile and wash and mend him up, so that he might once more be decent and comfortable; for he was suffering dreadfully with the filth and vermin that had collected upon him.

Soan was herself an emancipated slave, old and weak, with no one to care for her; and she lacked the courage to undertake a job of such seeming magnitude, fearing she might herself get sick, and perish there without assistance; and with great reluctance, and a heart swelling with pity, as she afterwards declared, she felt obliged to leave him in his wretchedness and filth. And shortly after her visit, this faithful slave, this deserted wreck of humanity, was found on his miserable pallet, frozen and stiff in death. The kind angel had come at last, and relieved him of the many miseries that his fellow-man had heaped upon him. Yes, he had died, chilled and starved, with none to speak a kindly word, or do a kindly deed for him, in that last dread hour of need!

The news of his death reached the ears of John Ardinburgh, a grandson of the old Colonel; and he declared that "Bomefree, who had ever been a kind and faithful slave, should now have a *good* funeral." And now, gentle reader, what think you constituted a good funeral? Answer—some black paint for the coffin, and—a jug of ardent spirits! What a compensation for a life of toil, of patient submission to repeated robberies of the most aggravated kind, and, also, far more than murderous neglect!! Mankind often vainly attempt to atone for unkindness or cruelty to the living, by honoring the same after death; but John Ardinburgh undoubtedly meant *his* pot of paint and jug of whisky should act as an opiate on his slaves, rather than on his own seared conscience.

COMMENCEMENT OF ISABELLA'S TRIALS IN LIFE

Having seen the sad end of her parents, so far as it relates to *this* earthly life, we will return with Isabella to that memorable auction which threatened to separate her father and mother. A slave auction is a terrible affair to its victims, and its incidents and consequences are graven on their hearts as with a pen of burning steel.

At this memorable time, Isabella was struck off, for the sum of one hundred dollars, to one John Nealy, of Ulster County, New York; and she has an impression that in this sale she was connected with a lot of sheep. She was now nine years of age, and her trials in life may be dated this period. She says, with emphasis, "*Now the war begun.*" She could only talk Dutch—and the Nealys could only talk English. Mr. Nealy could *understand* Dutch, but Isabel and her mistress could neither of them understand the language of the other—and this, of itself, was a formidable obstacle in the way of a *good* understanding

between them, and for some time was a fruitful source of dissatisfaction to the mistress, and of punishment and suffering to Isabella. She says, "If they sent me for a fryingpan, not knowing what they meant, perhaps I carried them the pot-hooks and trammels. Then, oh! how angry mistress would be with me!" Then she suffered "*terribly—terribly,*" with the cold. During the winter her feet were badly frozen, for want of proper covering. They gave her a plenty to eat, and also a plenty of whippings. One Sunday morning, in particular, she was told to go to the barn; on going there, she found her master with a bundle of rods, prepared in the embers, and bound together with cords. When he had tied her hands together before her, he gave her the most cruel whipping she was ever tortured with. He whipped her till the flesh was deeply lacerated, and the blood streamed from her wounds—and the scars remain to the present day, to testify to the fact. "And now," she says, "when I hear 'em tell of whipping women on the bare flesh, it makes *my* flesh crawl, and my very hair rise on my head! Oh! my God!" she continues, "what a way is this of treating human beings?" In these hours of her extremity, she did not forget the instructions of her mother, to go to God in all her trials, and every affliction; and she not only remembered, but obeyed: going to him, "and telling him all—and asking Him if He thought it was right," and begging him to protect and shield her from her persecutors.

She always asked with an unwavering faith that she should receive just what she plead for,—"And now," she says, "though it seems *curious*, I do not remember ever asking for any thing but what I got it. And I always received it as an answer to my prayers. When I got beaten, I never knew it long enough beforehand to pray; and I always thought if I only had *had* time to pray to God for help, I should have escaped the beating." She had no idea God had any knowledge of her thoughts, save what she told him; or heard her prayers, unless they were spoken audibly. And consequently, she could not pray unless she had time and opportunity to go by herself, where she could talk to God without being overheard.

TRIALS CONTINUED

When she had been at Mr. Nealy's several months, she began to beg God most earnestly to send her father to her, and as soon as she commenced to pray, she began as confidently to look for his coming, and, ere it was long, to her great joy, he came. She had no opportunity to speak to him of the troubles that weighed so heavily on her spirit, while he remained; but when he left, she followed him to the gate, and unburdened her heart to him, inquiring if he could not do something to get her a new and better place. In this way the slaves often assist each other, by ascertaining who are kind to their slaves, comparatively; and then using their influence to get such a one to hire or buy their friends; and masters, often from policy, as well as from latent humanity, allow those they are about to sell or let, to choose their own places, if the persons they happen to select for masters are considered safe *pay.* He promised to do all he could, and they parted. But, every day, as long as the snow lasted, (for there was snow on the ground at the time) she returned to the spot where they separated, and walking in the tracks of her father had made in the snow, repeated her prayer that "God would help her father get her a new and better place."

A long time had not elapsed, when a fisherman by the name of Scriver appeared at Mr. Nealy's, and inquired of Isabel "If she would like to go and live with him." She eagerly answered "Yes," nothing doubting but he was sent in answer to her prayer; and she soon started off with him, walking while he rode; for he had bought her at the suggestion of her father, paying one hundred and five dollars for her. He also lived in Ulster County, but some five or six miles from Mr. Nealy's.

Scriver, besides being a fisherman, kept a tavern for the accommodation of people of his own class—for his was a rude, uneducated family, exceedingly profane in their language, but, on the whole, an honest, kind and well-disposed people.

They owned a large farm, but left it wholly unimproved; attending mainly to their vocations of fishing and inn-keeping. Isabella declares she can ill describe the life she led with them. It was a wild, out-of-door kind of life. She expected to carry fish, to hoe corn, to bring roots and herbs from the wood for beers, go to the Strand for a gallon of molasses or liquor as the case might require, and "browse around," as she expresses it. It was a life that suited her well for the time—being as devoid of hardship or terror as it was of improvement; a need which had not yet become a want. Instead of improving at this place, morally, she retrograded, as their example taught her to curse; and it was here that she took her first oath. After living with them about a year and a half, she was sold to one John J. Dumont, for the sum of seventy pounds. This was in 1810. Mr. Dumont lived in the same county as her former masters, in the town of New Paltz, and she remained with him till a short time previous to her emancipation by the State, in 1828.

HER STANDING WITH HER NEW MASTER AND MISTRESS

Had Mrs. Dumont possessed that vein of kindness and consideration for the slaves, so perceptible in her husband's character, Isabella would have been as comfortable here, as one had *best* be, if one *must* be a slave. Mr. Dumont had been nursed in the very lap of slavery, and being naturally a man of kind feelings, treated his slaves with all the consideration he did his *other* animals, and *more*, perhaps. But Mrs. Dumont, who had been born and educated in a non-slaveholding family, and, like many others, used only to work-people, who, under the most stimulating of human motives, were willing to put forth their every energy, could not have patience with the creeping gait, the dull understanding, or see any cause for the listless manners and careless, slovenly habits of the poor down-trodden outcast—entirely forgetting that every high and efficient motive had been removed far from him; and that, had not his very intellect been crushed out of him, the slave would find little ground for aught but hopeless despondency. From this source arose a long series of trials in the life of our heroine, which we must pass over in silence; some from motives of delicacy, and others, because the relation of them might inflict undeserved pain on some now living, whom Isabel remembers only with esteem and love; therefore, the reader will not be surprised if our narrative appear somewhat tame at this point, and may rest assured that it is not for want of facts, as the most thrilling incidents of this portion of her life are from various motives suppressed.

One comparatively trifling incident she wishes related, as it made a deep impression on her mind at the time—showing, as *she* thinks, how God shields the innocent, and causes them to triumph over their enemies, and also how she stood between master and mistress. In her family, Mrs. Dumont employed two white girls, one of whom, named Kate, evinced a disposition to "lord it over" Isabel, and, in her emphatic language, "to *grind her down.*" Her master often shielded her from the attacks and accusations of others, praising her for her readiness and ability to work, and these praises seemed to foster a spirit of hostility to her, in the minds of Mrs. Dumont and her white servant, the latter of whom took every opportunity to cry up her faults, lessen her in the esteem of her master and increase against her the displeasure of her mistress, which was already more than sufficient for Isabel's comfort. Her master insisted that she could do as much work as half a dozen common people, and do it well, too; whilst her mistress insisted that the first was true, only because it ever came from her hand but half performed. A good deal of feeling arose from this difference of opinion, which was getting to rather an uncomfortable height,

when, all at once, the potatoes that Isabel cooked for breakfast assumed a dingy, dirty look. Her mistress blamed her severely, asking her master to observe "a fine specimen of Bell's work!"—adding, "it is the way *all* her work is done." Her master scolded also this time, and commanded her to be more careful in future. Kate joined with zest in the censures, and was very hard upon her. Isabella thought that she had done all she well could to have them nice; and became quite distressed at these appearances, and wondered what she should do to avoid them. In this dilemma, Gertrude Dumont, (Mr. D.'s eldest child, a good, kind-hearted girl of ten years, who pitied Isabel sincerely), when she heard them all blame her so unsparingly, came forward, offering her sympathy and assistance; and when about to retire to bed, on the night of Isabella's humiliation, she advanced to Isabel, and told her, if she would wake her early next morning, she would get up and attend to her potatoes for her, while she (Isabella) went to milking, and they would see if they could not have them *nice,* and not have "Poppee," her word for father, and "Matty," her word for mother, and all of 'em, scolding so terribly.

Isabella gladly availed herself of this kindness, which touched her to the heart, amid so much of an opposite spirit. When Isabella had put the potatoes over to boil Getty told her she would herself tend the fire, while Isabel milked. She had not long been seated by the fire, in performance of her promise, when Kate entered, and requested Gertrude to go out of the room and do something for her, which she refused, still keeping her place in the corner. While there, Kate came sweeping about the fire, caught up a chip, lifted some ashes with it, and dashed them into the kettle. Now the mystery was solved, the plot discovered! Kate was working a little too fast at making her mistress's words good, at showing that Mrs. Dumont and herself were on the right side of the dispute, and consequently at gaining power over Isabella. Yes, she was quite too fast, inasmuch as she had overlooked the little figure of justice, which sat in the corner, with scales nicely balanced, waiting to give all their dues.

But the time had come when she was to be overlooked no longer. It was Getty's turn to speak now. "Oh, Poppee! oh, Poppee!" said she, "Kate has been putting ashes in among the potatoes! I saw her do it! Look at those that fell on the outside of the kettle! You can now see what made the potatoes so dingy every morning, though Bell washed them clean!" And she repeated her story to every new comer, till the fraud was made as public as the censure of Isabella had been. Her mistress looked blank, and remained dumb—her master muttered something which sounded very like an oath—and poor Kate was so chop-fallen, she looked like a convicted criminal, who would gladly have hid herself (now that the baseness was out), to conceal her mortified pride and deep chagrin.

It was a fine triumph for Isabella and her master, and she became more ambitious than ever to please him; and he stimulated her ambition by his commendation, and by boasting of her to his friends, telling them that "*that* wench" (pointing to Isabel) "is better to me than a *man*—for she will do a good family's washing in the night, and be ready in the morning to go into the field, where she will do as much at raking and binding as my best hands." Her ambition and desire to please were so great, that she often worked several nights in succession, sleeping only short snatches, as she sat in her chair; and some nights she would not allow herself to take any sleep, save what she could get resting herself against the wall, fearing that if she sat down, she would sleep too long. These extra exertions to please, and the praises consequent upon them, brought upon her head the envy of her fellow-slaves, and they taunted her with being the "*white folks' nigger*." On the other hand, she received a larger share of the confidence of her master, and many small favors that were by them unattainable. I asked her if her master, Dumont, ever whipped her? She answered,

"Oh yes, he sometimes whipped me soundly, though never cruelly. And the most severe whipping he ever give me was because *I* was cruel to a cat." At this time she looked upon her master as a *God*; and believed that he knew of and could see her at all times, even as God himself. And she used sometimes to confess her delinquencies, from the conviction that he already knew them, and that she should fare better if she confessed voluntarily: and if any one talked to her of the injustice of her being a slave, she answered them with contempt and immediately told her master. She then firmly believed that slavery was right and honorable. Yet she *now* sees very clearly the false position they were all in, both masters and slaves; and she looks back, with utter astonishment, at the absurdity of the claims so arrogantly set up by the masters, over beings designed by God to be as free as kings; and at the perfect stupidity of the slave, in admitting for one moment the validity of these claims.

In obedience to her mother's instructions, she had educated herself to such a sense of honesty, that, when she had become a mother, she would sometimes whip her child when it cried to her for bread, rather than give it a piece secretly, lest it should learn to take what was not its own! And the writer of this knows, from personal observation, that the slaveholders of the South feel it to be a *religious duty* to teach their slaves to be honest, and never to take what is not their own! Oh consistency, art thou not a jewel? Yet Isabella glories in the fact that she was faithful and true to her master; she says, "It made me true to God"—meaning, that it helped to form in her a character that loved truth, and hated a lie, and had saved her from the bitter pains and fears that are sure to follow in the wake of insincerity and hypocrisy.

As she advanced in years, an attachment sprung up between herself and a slave named Robert. But his master, an Englishman by the name of Catlin, anxious that no one's property but his own should be enhanced by the increase of his slaves, forbade Robert's visits to Isabella, and commanded him to take a wife among his fellow-servants. Notwithstanding this interdiction, Robert, following the bent of his inclinations, continued his visits to Isabel, though very stealthily, and, as he believed, without exciting the suspicion of his master; but one Saturday afternoon, hearing that Bell was ill, he took the liberty to go and see her. The first intimation *she* had of his visit was the appearance of her master, inquiring "if she had seen Bob." On her answering in the negative, he said to her, "If you see him, tell him to take care of himself, for the Catlins are after him." Almost at that instant, Bob made his appearance; and the first people he met were his old and his young masters. They were terribly enraged at finding him there, and the eldest began cursing, and calling upon his son to *"Knock down* the d——d black rascal," at the same time, they both fell upon him like tigers, beating him with the heavy ends of their canes, bruising and mangling his head and face in the most awful manner, and causing the blood, which streamed from his wounds, to cover him like a slaughtered beast, constituting him a most shocking spectacle. Mr. Dumont interposed at this point, telling the ruffians they could no longer thus spill human blood on *his* premises—he would have "no niggers killed there." The Catlins then took a rope they had taken with them for the purpose, and tied Bob's hands behind him in such a manner, that Mr. Dumont insisted on loosening the cord, declaring that no brute should be tied in *that* manner, where *he* was. And as they led him away, like the greatest of criminals, the more humane Dumont followed them to their homes, as Robert's protector; and when he returned, he kindly went to Bell, as he called her, telling her he did not think they would strike him any more, as their wrath had greatly cooled before he left them. Isabella had witnessed this scene from her window, and was greatly shocked at the murderous treatment of poor Robert, whom she truly loved, and whose only crime, in the eye of his persecutors, was his affection for her. This beating, and we know not what after

treatment, completely subdued the spirit of its victim, for Robert ventured no more to visit Isabella, but like an obedient and faithful chattel, took himself a wife from the house of his master. Robert did not live many years after his last visit to Isabel, but took his departure to that country, where "they neither marry nor are given in marriage," and where the oppressor cannot molest.

ISABELLA'S MARRIAGE

Subsequently, Isabella was married to a fellow-slave, named Thomas, who had previously had two wives, one of whom, if not both, had been torn from him and sold far away. And it is more than probable, that he was not only allowed but encouraged to take another at each successive sale. I say it is probable, because the writer of this knows from personal observation, that such is the custom among slaveholders at the present day; and that in a twenty months' residence among them, we never knew any one to open the lip against the practice; and when we severely censured it, the slaveholder had nothing to say; and the slave pleaded that, under existing circumstances, he could do no better.

Such an abominable state of things is silently tolerated, to say the least, by slaveholders—deny it who may. And what is that religion that sanctions, even by its silence, all that is embraced in the *"Peculiar Institution?"* If there *can* be any thing more diametrically opposed to the religion of Jesus, than the working of this soul-killing system—which is as truly sanctioned by the religion of America as are her ministers and churches—we wish to be shown where it can be found.

We have said, Isabella was married to Thomas—she was, after the fashion of slavery, one of the slaves performing the ceremony for them; as no true minister of Christ *can* perform, as in the presence of God, what he knows to be a mere *farce, a mock* marriage, unrecognized by any civil law, and liable to be annulled any moment, when the interest or caprice of the master should dictate.

With what feelings must slaveholders expect us to listen to their horror of amalgamation in prospect, while they are well aware that we know how calmly and quietly they contemplate the present state of licentiousness their own wicked laws have created, not only as it regards the slave, but as it regards the more privileged portion of the population of the South?

Slaveholders appear to me take the same notice of the vices of the slave, as one does of the vicious disposition of his horse. They are often an inconvenience; further than that, they care not to trouble themselves about the matter.

ISABELLA AS A MOTHER

In process of time, Isabella found herself the mother of five children, and she rejoiced in being permitted to be the instrument of increasing the property of her oppressors! Think, dear reader, without a blush, if you can, for one moment, of a *mother* thus willingly, and with *pride,* laying her own children, the "flesh of her flesh," on the altar of slavery—a sacrifice to the bloody Moloch! But we must remember that beings capable of such sacrifices are not mothers; they are only "things," "chattels," "property."

But since that time, the subject of this narrative has made some advances from a state of chattelism towards that of a woman and a mother; and she now looks back upon her thoughts and feelings there, in her state of ignorance and degradation, as one does on the dark imagery of a fitful dream. One moment it seems but a frightful illusion; again it appears a terrible reality. I would to God it *were* but a dreamy myth, and not, as it now stands, a horrid reality to some three millions of chattelized human beings.

I have already alluded to her care not to teach her children to steal, by her example; and she says, with groanings that cannot be written, "The Lord only knows how many times I let my children go hungry, rather than take secretly the bread I liked not to ask

for." All parents who annul their preceptive teachings by their daily practices would do well to profit by her example.

Another proof of her master's kindness of heart is found in the following fact. If her master came into the house and found her infant crying (as she could not always attend to its wants and the commands of her mistress at the same time), he would turn to his wife with a look of reproof, and ask her why she did not see the child taken care of; saying, most earnestly, "I will not hear this crying; I can't bear it, and I will not hear any child cry so. Here, Bell, take care of this child, if no more work is done for a week." And he would linger to see if his orders were obeyed, and not countermanded.

When Isabella went to the field to work, she used to put her infant in a basket, tying a rope to each handle, and suspending the basket to a branch of a tree, set another small child to swing it. It was thus secure from reptiles, and was easily administered to, and even lulled to sleep, by a child too young for other labors. I was quite struck with the ingenuity of such a baby-tender, as I have sometimes been with the swinging hammock the native mother prepares for her sick infant—apparently so much easier than aught we have in our more civilized homes; easier for the child, because it gets the motion without the least jar; and easier for the nurse, because the hammock is strung so high as to supersede the necessity of stooping.

SLAVEHOLDER'S PROMISES

After emancipation had been decreed by the State, some years before the time fixed for its consummation, Isabella's master told her if she would do well, and be faithful, he would give her "free papers," one year before she was legally free by statute. In the year 1826, she had a badly diseased hand, which greatly diminished her usefulness; but on the arrival of July 4, 1827, the time specified for her receiving her "free papers," she claimed the fulfillment of her master's promise; but he refused granting it, on account (as he alleged) of the loss he had sustained by her hand. She plead that she had worked all the time, and done many things she was not wholly able to do, although she knew she had been less useful than formerly; but her master remained inflexible. Her very faithfulness probably operated against her now, and he found it less easy than he thought to give up the profits of his faithful Bell, who had so long done him efficient service.

But Isabella inwardly determined that she would remain quietly with him only until she had spun his wool—about one hundred pounds—and then she would leave him, taking the rest of the time to herself. "Ah!" she says, with emphasis that cannot be written, "the slaveholders are TERRIBLE for promising to give you this or that, or such and such a privilege, if you will do thus and so; and when the time of fulfillment comes, and one claims the promise, they, forsooth, recollect nothing of the kind; and you are, like as not, taunted with being a LIAR; or, at best, the slave is accused of not having performed *his* part or condition of the contract." "Oh!" said she, "I have felt as if I could not live through the *operation* sometimes. Just think of us! *so* eager for our pleasures, and just foolish enough to keep feeding and feeding ourselves up with the idea that we should get what had been thus fairly promised; and when we think it is almost in our hands, find ourselves flatly denied! Just think! how *could* we beat it? Why, there was Charles Brodhead promised his slave Ned, that when harvesting was over, he might go and see his wife, who lived some twenty or thirty miles off. So Ned worked early and late, and as soon as the harvest was all in, he claimed the promised boon. His master said, he had merely told him he "would *see* if he could go, when the harvest was over; but now he saw that he *could not go.*" But Ned, who still claimed a positive promise, on which he had fully depended, went on cleaning his shoes. His master asked him if he intended going, and on his replying "yes," took up a sled-stick that lay near him,

and gave him such a blow on the head as broke his skull, killing him dead on the spot. The poor colored people all felt struck down by the blow. Ah! and well they might. Yet it was but one of a long series of bloody, and other most effectual blows, struck against their liberty and their lives.* But to return from our digression.

The subject of this narrative was to have been free July 4, 1827, but she continued with her master till the wool was spun, and the heaviest of the "fall's work" closed up, when she concluded to take her freedom into her own hands, and seek her fortune in some other place.

HER ESCAPE

The question in her mind, and one not easily solved, now was, "How can I get away?" So, as was her usual custom, she "told God she was afraid to go in the night, and in the day every body would see her." At length, the thought came to her that she could leave just before the day dawned, and get out of the neighborhood where she was known before the people were much astir. "Yes," said she, fervently, "that's a good thought! Thank you, God, for *that* thought!" So, receiving it as coming direct from God, she acted upon it, and one fine morning, a little before daybreak, she might have been seen stepping stealthily away from the rear of Master Dumont's house, her infant on one arm and her wardrobe on the other; the bulk and weight of which, probably, she never found so convenient as on the present occasion, a cotton handkerchief containing both her clothes and her provisions.

As she gained the summit of a high hill, a considerable distance from her master's, the sun offended her by coming forth in all his pristine splendor. She thought it never was

*Yet no official notice was taken of his more than brutal murder.

so light before; indeed, she thought it much too light. She stopped to look about her, and ascertain if her pursuers were yet in sight. No one appeared, and, for the first time, the question came up for settlement, "Where, and to whom, shall I go?" In all her thoughts of getting away, she had not once asked herself whither she should direct her steps. She sat down, fed her infant, and again turned her thoughts to God, her only help, she prayed him to direct her to some safe asylum. And soon it occurred to her, that there was a man living somewhere in the direction she had been pursuing, by the name of Levi Rowe, whom she had known, and who, she thought, would be likely to befriend her. She accordingly pursued her way to his house, where she found him ready to entertain and assist her, though he was then on his death-bed. He bade her partake of the hospitalities of his house, said he knew of two good places where she might get in, and requested his wife to show her where they were to be found. As soon as she came in sight of the first house, she recollected having seen it and its inhabitants before, and instantly exclaimed, "That's the place for me; I shall stop there." She went there, and found the good people of the house, Mr. and Mrs. Van Wagener, absent, but was kindly received and hospitably entertained by their excellent mother, till the return of her children. When they arrived, she made her case known to them. They listened to her story, assuring her they never turned the needy away, and willingly gave her employment.

She had not been there long before her old master, Dumont, appeared, as she had anticipated; for when she took French leave of him, she resolved not to go too far from him, and not put him to as much trouble in looking her up—for the latter he was sure to do—as Tom and Jack had done when they ran away from him, a short time before. This was very considerate in her, to say the least, and a proof that like begets like." He had often considered *her* feelings, though not always, and she was equally considerate.

When her master saw her, he said, "Well, Bell, so you've run away from me." "No, I did not *run* away; I walked away by daylight, and all because you had promised me a year of my time." His reply was, "You must go back with me." Her decisive answer was, "No, I *won't* go back with you." He said, "Well, I shall take the *child.*" This also was as stoutly negatived.

Mr. Isaac S. Van Wagener then interposed, saying, he had never been in the practice of buying and selling slaves; he did not believe in slavery; but, rather than have Isabella taken back by force, he would buy her services for the balance of the year—for which her master charged twenty dollars, and five in addition for the child. The sum was paid, and her master Dumont departed; but not till he had heard Mr. Van Wagener tell her not to call him master,—adding, "there is but *one* master; and he who is *your* master is *my* master." Isabella inquired what she *should* call him? He answered, "Call me Isaac Van Wagener, and my wife is Maria Van Wagener." Isabella could not understand this, and thought it a *mighty change*, as it most truly was from a master whose word was law, to simple Isaac S. Van Wagener, who was master to *no* one. With these noble people, who, though they could not be the masters of slaves, were undoubtedly a portion of God's nobility, she resided one year, and from them she derived the name of Van Wagener; he being her last master in the eye of the law, and a slave's surname is ever the same as his master; that is, if he is allowed to have any other name than Tom, Jack, or Guffin. Slaves have sometimes been severely punished for adding their master's name to their own. But when they have no particular title to it, it is no particular offence.

ILLEGAL SALE OF HER SON

A little previous to Isabel's leaving her old master, he had sold her child, a boy of five years, to a Dr. Gedney, who took him with him as far as New York city, on his way to

England; but finding the boy too small for his service, he sent him back to his brother, Solomon Gedney. This man disposed of him to his sister's husband, a wealthy planter, by the name of Fowler, who took him to his own home in Alabama.

This illegal and fraudulent transaction had been perpetrated some months before Isabella knew of it, as she was now living at Mr. Van Wagener's. The law expressly prohibited the sale of any slave out of the State—and all minors were to be free at twenty-one years of age; and Mr. Dumont had sold Peter with the express understanding, that he was soon to return to the State of New York, and be emancipated at the specified time.

When Isabel heard that her son had been sold South, she immediately started on foot and alone, to find the man who had thus dared, in the face of all law, human and divine, to sell her child out of the State; and if possible, to bring him to account for the deed.

Arriving at New Paltz, she went directly to her former mistress, Dumont, complaining bitterly of the removal of her son. Her mistress heard her through, and then replied—"*Ugh!* a *fine* fuss to make about a little *nigger!* Why, haven't you as many of 'em left as you can see to and take care of? A pity 'tis, the niggers are not all in Guinea!! Making such a halloo-balloo about the neighborhood; and all for a paltry nigger!!!" Isabella heard her through, and after a moment's hesitation, answered, in tones of deep determination—"*I'll have my child again*" "Have *your child* again!" repeated her mistress—her tone big with contempt, and scorning the absurd idea of her getting him. "How can you get him? And what have you to support him with, if you could? Have you any money?" "No," answered Bell, "I have no money, but God has enough, or what's better! And I'll have my child again." These words were pronounced in the most slow, solemn and determined measure and manner. And in speaking of it, she says, "Oh, my

God! I know'd I'd have him agin. I was sure God would help me to get him. Why, I felt so *tall within*—I felt as if the *power of a nation* was with me!"

The impressions made by Isabella on her auditors, when moved by lofty or deep feeling, can never be transmitted to paper (to use the words of another) till by some Daguerrian art, we are enabled to transfer the look, the gesture, the tones of voice, in connection with the quaint, yet fit expressions used, and the spirit-stirring animation that, at such a time, pervades all she says.

After leaving her mistress, she called on Mrs. Gedney, mother of him who had sold her boy; who, after listening to her lamentations, her grief being mingled with indignation at the sale of her son, and her declaration that she would have him again—said, "Dear me! What a disturbance to make about your child! What, is *your* child better than *my* child? My child is gone out there, and yours is gone to live with her, to have enough of everything, and to be treated like a gentleman!" And here she laughed at Isabel's absurd fears, as she would represent them to be. "Yes," said Isabel, "*your* child has gone there, but she is *married* and my boy has gone as a *slave*, and he is too little to go so far from his mother. Oh, I must have my child." And here the continued laugh of Mrs. G. seemed to Isabel, in this time of anguish and distress, almost demoniacal. And well it was for Mrs. Gedney, that, at that time, she could not even dream of the awful fate awaiting her own beloved daughter, at the hands of him whom she had chosen as worthy the wealth of her love and confidence, and in whose society her young heart had calculated on a happiness, purer and more elevated than was ever conferred by a kingly crown. But, alas! she was doomed to disappointment, as we shall relate by and by. At this point, Isabella earnestly begged of God that he would show to those about her that He was her helper; and she adds, in narrating, "And He *did*; or, if He did not show them, he did me."

IT IS OFTEN DARKEST
JUST BEFORE DAWN

This homely proverb was illustrated in the case of our sufferer; for, at the period at which we have arrived in our narrative, to her the darkness seemed palpable, and the waters of affliction covered her soul; yet light was about to break in upon her.

Soon after the scenes related in our last chapter, which had harrowed up her very soul to agony, she met a man (we would like to tell you *who*, dear reader, but it would be doing him no kindness, even at the present day, to do so), who evidently sympathized with her, and counselled her to go to the Quakers, telling her they were already feeling very indignant at the fraudulent sale of her son, and assuring her that they would readily assist her, and direct her what to do. He pointed out to her two houses, where lived some of those people, who formerly, more than any other sect, perhaps, lived out the principles of the gospel of Christ. She wended her way to their dwellings, was listened to, unknown as she personally was to them, with patience, and soon gained their sympathies and active co-operation.

They gave her lodgings for the night; and it is very amusing to hear her tell of the "nice, high, clean, white, *beautiful* bed" assigned her to sleep in, which contrasted so strangely with her former pallets, that she sat down and contemplated it, perfectly absorbed in wonder that *such* a bed should have been appropriated to one like herself. For some time she thought that she would lie down beneath it, on her usual bedstead, the floor. "I did, indeed," says she, laughing heartily at her former self. However, she finally concluded to make use of the bed, for fear that not to do so might injure the feelings of her good hostess. In the morning, the Quaker saw that she was taken and set down near Kingston, with directions to go to the Court House, and enter complaint to the Grand Jury.

By a little inquiry, she found which was the building she sought, went into the door, and taking the first man she saw of imposing appearance for the *grand* jury, she commenced her complaint. But he very civilly informed her there was no Grand Jury there; she must go up stairs. When she had with some difficulty ascended the flight through the crowd that filled them, she again turned to the *"grandest"* looking man she could select, telling him she had come to enter a complaint to the Grand Jury. For his own amusement, he inquired what her complaint was; but, when he saw it was a serious matter, he said to her, "This is no place to enter a complaint—go in there," pointing in a particular direction.

She then went in, where she found the Grand Jurors indeed sitting, and again commenced to relate her injuries. After holding some conversation among themselves, one of them rose, and bidding her follow him, led the way to a side office, where he heard her story, and asked her "if she could *swear* that the child she spoke of was her son?" "Yes," she answered, "I *swear* it's my son." "Stop, stop!" said the lawyer, "you must swear by this book"—giving her a book, which she thinks must have been the Bible. She took it, and putting it to her lips, began again to swear it was her child. The clerks, unable to preserve their gravity any longer, burst into an uproarious laugh; and one of them inquired of lawyer Chip of what use it could be to make *her* swear. "It will answer the law," replied the officer. He then made her comprehend just what he wished her to do, and she took a lawful oath, as far as the outward ceremony could make it one. All can judge how far she understood its spirit and meaning.

He now gave her a writ, directing her to take it to the constable of New Paltz, and have him serve it on Solomon Gedney. She obeyed, walking, or rather *trotting*, in her haste, some eight or nine miles.

But while the constable, through mistake, served the writ on a brother of the real culprit, Solomon Gedney slipped into a boat, and was nearly across the North River, on whose banks they were standing, before the dull Dutch constable was aware of his mistake. Solomon Gedney, meanwhile, consulted a lawyer, who advised him to go to Alabama and bring back the boy, otherwise it might cost him fourteen years' imprisonment, and a thousand dollars in cash. By this time, it is hoped he began to feel that selling slaves unlawfully was not so good a business as he had wished to find it. He secreted himself till due preparations could be made, and soon set sail for Alabama. Steamboats and railroads had not then annihilated distance to the extent they now have, and although he left in the fall of the year, spring came ere he returned, bringing the boy with him—but holding on to him as his property. It had ever been Isabella's prayer, not only that her son might be returned, but that he should be delivered from bondage, and into her own hands, lest he should be punished out of mere spite to her, who was so greatly annoying and irritating to her oppressors; and if her suit was gained, her very triumph would add vastly to their irritation.

She again sought advice of Esquire Chip, whose counsel was, that the aforesaid constable serve the before-mentioned writ upon the right person. This being done, soon brought Solomon Gedney up to Kingston, where he gave bonds for his appearance at court, in the sum of $600.

Esquire Chip next informed his client, that her case must now lie over till the next session of the court, some months in the future. "The law must take its course," said he.

"What! wait another court! wait *months?*" said the persevering mother. "Why, long before that time, he can go clear off, and take my child with him—no one knows where. I *cannot* wait; I *must* have him *now*, whilst he is to be had." "Well," said the lawyer, very coolly, "if he puts the boy out of the way, he must pay $600—one half of which will be yours;" supposing, perhaps, that $300 would pay for a "heap of children," in the eye of a slave who never, in all her life, called a dollar her own. But in this instance, he was mistaken in his reckoning. She assured him, that she had not been seeking money, neither would money satisfy her; it was her son, and her son alone she wanted, and her son she must have. Neither could she wait court, not she. The lawyer used his every argument to convince her, that she ought to be very thankful for what they had done for her; that it was a great deal, and it was but reasonable that she should now wait patiently the time of the court.

Yet she never felt, for a moment, like being influenced by these suggestions. She felt confident she was to receive a full and literal answer to her prayer, the burden of which had been—"O Lord, give my son into my hands, and that speedily! Let not the spoilers have him any longer." Notwithstanding, she very distinctly saw that those who had thus far helped her on so kindly were *wearied* of her, and she feared God was wearied also. She had a short time previous learned that Jesus was a Saviour, and an intercessor; and she thought that if Jesus could but be induced to plead for her in the present trial, God would listen to *him*, though he were wearied of *her* importunities. To him, of course, she applied. As she was walking about, scarcely knowing whither she went, asking within herself, "Who will show me any good, and lend a helping hand in this matter," she was accosted by a perfect stranger, and one whose name she has never learned, in the following terms: "Halloo, there; how do you get along with your boy? do they give him up to you?" She told him all, adding that now every body was tired, and she had none to help her. He said, "Look here! I'll tell you what you'd better do. Do you see that stone house yonder?" pointing in a particular direction. "Well, lawyer Demain lives there, and do you go to him, and lay your case before him; I think he'll help you. *Stick to him.* Don't give him peace till he does. I feel sure if you press him, he'll do it for you." She needed no further urging, but trotted off at her peculiar gait in the direction of his house, as fast as possible,—and she was not encumbered with stockings, shoes, or any other heavy article of dress. When she had told him her story, in her impassioned manner, he look at her a few moments, as if to ascertain if he were contemplating a new variety of the genus homo, and then told her, if she would give him five dollars, he would get her son for her, in twenty-four hours. "Why," she replied, "*I* have no *money*, and never had a dollar in my life!" Said he, "If you will go to those Quakers in Poppletown, who carried you to court, they will help you to five dollars in cash, I have no doubt; and you shall have your son in twenty-four hours, from the time you bring me that sum." She performed the journey to Poppletown, a distance of some ten miles, very expeditiously; collected considerable more than the sum specified by the barrister; then, shutting the money tightly in her hand, she trotted back, and paid the lawyer a larger fee than he had demanded. When inquired of by people what she had done with the overplus, she answered, "Oh, I got it for lawyer Demain, and I gave it to him." They assured her she was a *fool* to do so; that she should have kept all over five dollars, and purchased herself shoes with it. "Oh, I do not want money or clothes now, I only want my son; and if five dollars will get him, more will *surely* get him." And if the lawyer had returned it to her, she avers she would not have accepted it. She was perfectly willing he should have every coin she could raise, if he would but restore her lost son to her. Moreover, the five dollars he required were for the remuneration of him who should go after her son and his master, and not for his own services.

The lawyer now renewed his promise, that she should have her son in twenty-four hours. But Isabella, having no idea of this space of time, went several times in a day, to ascertain if her son had come. Once, when the servant opened the door and saw her, she said, in a tone expressive of much surprise, "Why, this woman's come again?" She then wondered if she went too often. When the lawyer appeared, he told her the twenty-four hours would not expire till the next morning; if she would call then, she would

see her son. The next morning saw Isabel at the lawyer's door, while he was yet in his bed. He now assured her it was morning till noon; and that before noon her son would be there, for he had sent the famous "Matty Styles" after him, who would not fail to have the boy and his master on hand in due season, either dead or alive; of that he was sure. Telling her she need not come again; he would himself inform her of their arrival.

After dinner, he appeared at Mr. Rutzer's (a place the lawyer had procured for her, while she awaited the arrival of her boy), assuring her, her son had come; but that he stoutly denied having any mother, or any relatives in that place; and said, "she must go over and identify him." She went to the office, but at sight of her the boy cried aloud, and regarded her as some terrible being, who was about to take him away from a kind and loving friend. He knelt, even, and begged them, with tears, not to take him away from his dear master, who had brought him from the dreadful South, and been so kind to him.

When he was questioned relative to the bad scar on his forehead, he said, "Fowler's horse hove him." And of the one on his cheek, "That was done by running against the carriage." In answering these questions he looked imploringly at his master, as much as to say, "If they are falsehoods, you bade me say them; may they be satisfactory to you, at least."

The justice, noting his appearance, bade him forget his master and attend only to him. But the boy persisted in denying his mother, and clinging to his master, saying his mother did not live in such a place as that. However, they allowed the mother to identify her son; and Esquire Demain pleaded that he claimed the boy for her, on the ground that he had been sold out of the State, contrary to the laws in such cases made and provided—spoke of the penalties annexed to said crime, and of the sum of money the delinquent was to pay, in case any one chose to prosecute him for the offence he had committed. Isabella, who was sitting in a corner, scarcely daring to breathe, thought within herself, "If I can but get the boy, the $200 may remain for whoever else chooses to prosecute—*I* have done enough to make myself enemies already"—and she trembled at the thought of the formidable enemies she had probably arrayed against herself—helpless and despised as she was. When the pleading was at an end, Isabella understood the Judge to declare, as the sentence of the Court, that the "boy be delivered into the hands of the mother—having no other master, no other controller, no other conductor, but his mother." This sentence was obeyed; he was delivered into her hands, the boy meanwhile begging, most piteously, *not* to be taken from his dear master, saying she was not his mother, and that his mother did not live in such a place as that. And it was some time before lawyer Demain, the clerks, and Isabella, could collectively succeed in calming the child's fears, and in convincing him that Isabella was not some terrible monster, as he had for the last months, probably, been trained to believe; and who, in taking him away from his master, was taking him from all good, and consigning him to all evil.

When at last kind words and *bon bons* had quieted his fears, and he could listen to their explanations, he said to Isabella—"Well, you *do* look like my mother *used* to;" and she was soon able to make him comprehend some of the obligations he was under, and the relation he stood in, both to herself and his master. She commenced as soon as practicable to examine the boy, and found, to her utter astonishment, that from the crown of his head to the sole of his foot, the callosities and indurations on his entire body were most frightful to behold. His back she described as being like her fingers, as she laid them side by side.

"Heavens! what is all *this?*" said Isabel. He answered, "It is where Fowler whipped, kicked, and beat me." She exclaimed, "Oh, Lord Jesus, look! see my poor child! Oh Lord, 'render unto them double' for all this! Oh my God! Pete, how *did* you bear it?"

"Oh, this is nothing, mammy—if you should see Phillis, I guess you'd *scare!* She had a little baby, and Fowler cut her till the milk as well as blood ran down *her* body. You would *scare* to see Phillis, mammy."

When Isabella inquired, "What did Miss Eliza say, Pete, when you were treated so badly?" he replied, "Oh, mammy, she said she wished I was with Bell. Sometimes I crawled under the stoop, mammy, the blood running all about me, and my back would stick to the boards; and sometimes Miss Eliza would come and grease my sores, when all were abed and asleep."

SUGGESTED READINGS

Ira Berlin, *Many Thousands Gone: The First Two Centuries of Slavery in North America* (Cambridge, Mass., 1998)

Kathleen M. Brown, *Good Wives, Nasty Wenches and Anxious Patriarchs: Gender Race and Power in Colonial Virginia* (Chapel Hill, N.C., 1996)

Sylvia R. Frey, *Water from the Rock: Black Resistance in a Revolutionary Age* (Princeton, 1991)

Carol V. R. George, *Segregated Sabbaths: Richard Allen and the Emergence of Independent Black Churches, 1760–1840* (New York, 1973)

Michael A. Gomez, *Exchanging our Country Marks: The Transformation of African Identities in the Colonial and Antebellum South* (Chapel Hill, N.C., 1998)

Winthrop D. Jordan, *White Over Black: American Attitudes Towards the Negro, 1550–1812* (New York, 1968)

Sydney Kaplan and Emma Nogrady Kaplan, *The Black Presence in the Era of the American Revolution* (Amherst, Mass., 1989)

Duncan J. MacLeod, *Slavery, Race, and the American Revolution* (London, 1974)

Edmund Morgan, *American Slavery, American Freedom: The Ordeal of Colonial Virginia* (New York, 1975)

Philip D. Morgan, *Slave Counterpoint: Black Culture in the Eighteenth Century Chesapeake and Lowcountry* (Chapel Hill, N.C., 1998)

Nell Irvin Painter, *Sojourner Truth: A Life, A Symbol* (New York, 1996)

Shane White, *Somewhat More Independent: The End of Slavery in New York City, 1770–1810* (Athens, Ga., 1995)

Arthur Zilversmit, *The First Emancipation: The Abolition of Slavery in the North* (Chicago, 1967)

Slave laborers work at the first cotton gin. (Courtesy of the Library of Congress.)

Chapter 3

The Peculiar Institution: Slavery in the Old South

Despite the democratic promise of the American Revolution, the institution of slavery became even more firmly fixed in the southern part of the country. The first document on Gabriel's conspiracy reveals how slaves tried to extend the revolutionary tradition to challenge slavery. The invention of the cotton gin and the spread of cotton production in the deep south and across the Mississippi ended the expectation that slavery would gradually disappear from the country. Selections from Frederick Law Olmsted's book and the instructions to an overseer in a cotton plantation reveal the daily existence of slaves in the Old South. Around ninety percent of the African American population remained enslaved until the Civil War. African Americans survived the rigors of slavery by creating their own families and communities. A distinct black culture and black version of Christianity grew in the slave quarters. A common theme throughout the history of slavery was the efforts of slaves to resist their enslavement or to lessen the burdens of slavery. Slaves' actions could range from day-to-day resistance to slavery, to running away, and to individual and collective acts of physical resistance such as slave rebellions.

The slave narratives of Frederick Douglass, Harriet Jacobs, and Solomon Northrup describe slavery in the south from the viewpoint of slaves themselves. As such, they are not only firsthand accounts of slavery in the Old South but also effective indictments of the slave system. The spirituals provide us with a brief glimpse into the cultural life and religious worldview of antebellum slaves. The selections from Olmsted, William Still's book on the underground railroad, the confessions of Nat Turner, and William C. Nell's descriptions of Madison Washington and the Dismal Swamp runaways reveal some major forms and instances of slave resistance in the south. While some slaves resisted slavery openly, many developed strong communities and families that gave them an alternative sense of self-worth and identity, which helped them to confront the horrors of slavery.

Gabriel's Conspiracy, 1800

At a court of Oyer and Terminer, called and held for the county of Henrico at the Courthouse, on Thursday the Eleventh day of September, 1800, for the trial of Michael alias Mike, a negro man slave the property of Judith Owen of the said county, charged with conspiracy and insurrection.

Present: Daniel L. Hylton, Miles Selden, Bowler Cocke, Hezekial Henley, Benjamin Goode, Pleasant Younghusband and George Williamson, Gent. Justices.

The said negro man Michael alias Mike, was set to the Bar in custody, and being arraigned of the premises said he was in nowise guilty of the crime with which he stands accused, whereupon sundry witnesses being charged, sworn and examined, and the prisoner heard in his defence by James Rind, Gent., counsel assigned him by the court, on consideration whereof, it is the opinion of the court that the said Michael alias Mike, is guilty of the crime with which he stands charged, and for the same that he be hanged by the neck until he be dead, and that execution of this sentence be done and performed on him the said Michael alias Mike, on tomorrow, being the twelfth instant, at the usual place of execution. The court valued the said slave at one hundred pounds.

The minutes of the foregoing trial and proceedings were signed by the above named justices.

A Copy—Teste:
Adam Craig, C.H.C.

Henrico County Court, on September 11th, sentences John, a negro man slave, the property of Mary Jones, of Hanover, to death on charge of conspiracy and insurrection, and orders that he be hung at the usual place of execution on the 12th inst.

Henrico County Court, on Sept. 11th, sentences Solomon, a negro man slave, the property of Thomas H. Prosser, of Henrico, to death on charge of conspiracy and insurrection, and orders that he be hung on the 12th instant at the usual place of execution.

Henrico County Court, on September 11th, sentences Nat, a negro man slave, the property of Anne Parsons, of Henrico, to death on charge of conspiracy and insurrection, and orders that he be hung on the 12th instant at the usual place of execution.

Henrico County Court, on September 11th, sentences Isaac, a negro man slave, the property of Wm. Burton, of Henrico, to death on charge of conspiracy and insurrection, and orders that he be hung on the 12th instant at the usual place of execution.

Henrico County Court, on September 11th, sentences Will, a negro man slave, the property of John Mosby, Senior, of Henrico, to death on charge of conspiracy and insurrection, and orders that he be hung on the 12th instant at the usual place of execution.

EVIDENCE AGAINST THE NEGROES TRIED SEPTEMBER 11TH

Solomon's Case. —Ben, the property of Thos. H. Prosser, deposed: That the prisoner at the bar made a number of swords for the purpose of carrying into execution the plan of an insurrection which was planned by Gabriel, a negro man, the property of said Prosser, and that the said Solomon was to be Treasurer. In the first place, Mr. Prosser and

Source: Gabriel's Conspiracy, 1800." From H. W. Flournoy ed., *Calendar of Virginia State Papers and Other Manuscripts from January 1, 1799, to December 31, 1807* (Richmond, 1890), 9: 140–144, 150–152.

Mr. Johnson were to be killed and their arms seized upon; then they were to resort to and kill all the White Neighbours. This plan to be executed on the Saturday night on which there was such a great fall of rain. The place of meeting was near Prosser's Blacksmith's shop in the woods. After Murdering the Inhabitants of the Neighbourhood, the assembly were to repair to Richmond and Seize upon the Arms and Ammunition—to-wit, the Magazine. Gabriel was to command at commencement of the business. The swords made by the prisoner were to be distributed by s'd Gabriel; swords have been making ever since last Harvest. 1,000 men was to be raised from Richmond, 600 from Ground Squirrel Bridge, and 400 from Goochland. Meetings were frequently held at William Young's under pretext of attending preachment, and at other times—viz., at Fish feast and at Barbacues, to concert the plan of Insurrection. The Rain which fell on Saturday night, the 30th August, prevented the carrying the said plan into Execution. Swords made by the prisoner were to be used by Horsemen, two hundred of whom were appointed, but it was expected there would be 400. Gabriel and Solomon, the prisoner, kept lists of the names of the conspirators; that he heard Lewis Barrel spoken of as one of Town's Negroes concerned. That he in conversation with Jack Bowler, otherwise called Jack Ditcher, it appeared that two white Frenchmen was the first instigators of the Insurrection, but whose names he did not hear.

Pharoah, the property of Philip Sheppard, deposed: That the prisoner at the bar on Saturday, the 30th August, enquired of this deponent whether the light horse of Richmond were out, he being then from Richmond, who informed him that he had seen some at Col. Goodall's tavern. The prisoner remarked that the business of the insurrection had so far advanced that they were compelled, even if discovered, to go forward with it; that he had four swords then to finish, which he must complete by the time of his company meeting that evening, which would consist of 1,000 men, to wit: negroes.

Will's Case. —Ben, the property of T. H. Prosser, deposed: That the prisoner brought two scythe blades to Gabriel for the purpose of having them made into swords, and that four swords were made out of them by Solomon at request of Gabriel; that the said Will acknowledged in the presence of the deponent, in conversation with Gabriel, that he was concerned in the conspiracy and insurrection, and that he wanted the appointment of captain of the foot, but this being refused him, he was to act as a horseman; that the whites were to be murdered and killed indiscriminately, except [?] none of whom were to be touched.

Toby, the property of John Holman, deposed: That the prisoner proposed to join and fight the whites; that he had joined, and had to carry two scythe blades to Soloman to be made into swords; he was determined to kill his master; that he had his master's sorrel horse set apart for him to act upon as a horseman; that there was to be a grand meeting of the negroes near Prosser's, from whence they were to proceed and take the town; that 5,000 blacks were to meet the prisoner at the bar, and that all the blacks who did not join would be put to death; that he intended to kill his master on Saturday night, the 30th August last; that the prisoner had an appointment as captain, but was turned out, being under size.

John's Case. —Daniel, property of John Williamson, deposed: That the deponent being at plough at home, the prisoner, who at that time worked at the penitentiary and was passing by, invited him to come to a great barbecue which was to be made by the negroes at Half Sink; and upon being informed that the purport of the barbecue was to concert measures for raising an insurrection and murdering and killing the whites and taking the country, of which he had no doubt, as Gabriel, and Solomon, and himself, being a captain, being at the head of the business; that the said John said he had a number of men at the Penitentiary, and was going up to Caroline, where he expected to raise several hundred; that they were to seize upon the arms at the penitentiary, and that all negroes who did not join in the insurrection would and should be put to death. That the whites were to be put to death indiscriminately.

Charles, property of Wm. Winston, deposed: That about three weeks ago the prisoner gave this deponent an invite to a barbecue to be at Mr. Moore's school-house, which was made on a particular occasion, but was not made known to him, the deponent, which invitation this deponent refused to accept.

Isaac's Case. —Ben, the property of T. H. Prosser, deposed, that the prisoner informed him the deponent, that he had joined Prosser's Gabriel, in order to take Richmond and that he the prisoner, was one of the foot soldiers; that he was if possible to supply himself with a sword which if he could not do, Gabriel was to furnish him, and he the prisoner, was determined either to kill or be killed.

Dan'l, the property of Wm. Burton, deposed, that the prisoner informed the deponent, on Friday the 29th August last, that he the prisoner, had been informed by Nanny, wife to Gabriel, that 1000 men were to meet said Gabriel near Prosser's Tavern the ensuing night, and that he also was to be one of them, for the purpose of murdering the White Citizens; that the Governor had in some measure, got an alarm of this business, and had caused the arms which had been kept in the Capitol to be removed to the Penitentiary—that they should not mind the guards which were placed over the arms as they were determined to rush through them and take both them and the magazine—that he communicated this information to the overseer that an army of negroes were raising aginst the whites, with an injunction to the said overseer to keep the communication secret, the blacks were determined to kill every black who should not aid in, and join them in the insurrection. The prisoner was much intoxicated at the time of the conversation and information above.

Michael's Case. —Ben, the property of T. H. Prosser, deposed: That about a fortnight before time appointed for the insurrection, the prisoner being on his way to Richmond, employed Gabriel to make him a sword, which was to be used by him in fighting the whites under the command of Gabriel, as a foot soldier; that he called on the Saturday evening appointed for carrying the plot into execution, the prisoner applied at the house of Gabriel and obtained his sword, and promised to meet the Sunday night at the Tobacco house of Mr. Prosser, that being too rainy an evening for carrying their. . . .

Pharoah, the property of Philip Sheppard, deposed: That in the week preceding the Saturday appointed for an insurrection, the prisoner informed him that Gabriel was to furnish him a sword, which he would call and get on Saturday evening ensuing; that he had joined the party.

Ned, the property of Judith Owen, deposed: That the prisoner informed him he had been requested by Gabriel to join him in an insurrection, which he had rejected, promising said Gabriel should he see the business progress well he would afterward join him.

William Gentry deposed: That he and Mr. Glenn being in pursuit of Gabriel and just on the return from said Gabriel's habitation, fell in with the prisoner, who they were about to take up when he fled into the woods; that being pursued by Mr. Glenn, was taken some time before the deponent arrived, and that Mr. Glenn informed him that a scythe blade made into the form of a sword was produced by the prisoner, with which he made battle against said Glenn, who had overcome the prisoner and had then the said sword in his possession.

Nat's Case. —Ben, the property of T. H. Prosser, deposed: That the prisoner had joined Gabriel to fight the White people, and for that purpose purchased a sword from one William, belonging to Ben Mosby; that upon falling in with Gabriel and this deponent, he informed Gabriel that he had his sword, and left it at the warehouse; that he had a stick in his hand, and, flourishing it in his hand, observed that thus he would wield his sword. This was about three weeks previous to the time appointed for the commencement of the insurrection. That the said Gabriel and the prisoner agreed that the prisoner should bear the rank of a captain, the said prisoner remarking that all the Warehouse boys had joined, and he would go on to get as many as he could until the appointed time.

Washington, belonging to Benj. Mosby, deposed: That he sold a sword to the prisoner, who informed him he wanted to stand Guard with it at the Warehouse, where he then lived and had the care of.

[Sept. 12, Henrico]—Henrico County Court sentences Frank, a negro man slave, the property of Thos. H. Prosser, to death on charge of conspiracy and insurrection, and orders him to be hung on the 15th instant at the usual place of execution.

Henrico County Court sentences Martin, a negro man slave, the property of Thos. H. Prosser, to death on charge of conspiracy and insurrection, and orders him to be hung on the 15th instant at the usual place of execution.

Henrico County Court sentences Billy, a negro man slave, the property of Roger Gregory, of Henrico, to death on charge of conspiracy and insurrection, and orders that he be hung on the 15th instant at the usual place of execution.

Henrico County Court sentences Charles, a negro man slave, the property of Roger Gregory, of Henrico, to death on charge of conspiracy and insurrection, and orders him to be hung on the 15th instant at the usual place of execution.

CONFESSION OF SOLOMON

Communications made to the subscribers by Solomon, the property of Thomas H. Prosser, of Henrico, now under sentence of death for plotting an insurrection.

My brother Gabriel was the person who influenced me to join him and others in order that (as he said) we might conquer the white people and possess ourselves of their property. I enquired how we were to effect it. He said by falling upon them (the whites) in the dead of night, at which time they would be unguarded and unsuspicious. I then enquired who was at the head of the plan. He said Jack, alias Jack Bowler. I asked him if Jack Bowler knew anything about carrying on war. He replied he did not. I then enquired who he was going to employ. He said a man from Caroline who was at the siege of Yorktown, and who was to meet him (Gabriel) at the Brook and to proceed on to Richmond, take, and then fortify it. This man from Caroline was to be commander and manager the first day, and then, after exercising the soldiers, the command was to be resigned to Gabriel. If Richmond was taken without the loss of many men they were to continue there some time, but if they sustained any considerable loss they were to bend their course for Hanover Town or York, they were not decided to which, and continue at that place as long as they found they were able to defend it, but in the event of a defeat or loss at those places they were to endeavor to form a junction with some negroes which, they had understood from Mr. Gregory's overseer, were in rebellion in some quarter of the country. This information which they had gotten from the overseer, made Gabriel anxious, upon which he applied to me to make scythe-swords, which I did to the number of twelve. Every Sunday he came to Richmond to provide ammunition and to find where the military stores were deposited. Gabriel informed me, in case of success, that they intended to subdue the whole of the country where slavery was permitted, but no further.

The first places Gabriel intended to attack in Richmond were, the Capitol, the Magazine, the Penitentiary, the Governor's house and his person. The inhabitants were to be massacred, save those who begged for quarter and agreed to serve as soldiers with them. The reason why the insurrection was to be made at this particular time was, the discharge of the number of soldiers, one or two months ago, which induced Gabriel to believe the plan would be more easily executed.

Given under our hands this 15th day of September, 1800.

GERVAS STORRS,
JOSEPH SELDEN.

CONFESSIONS OF BEN ALIAS BEN WOOLFOLK

[Sept. 17]—The first time I ever heard of this conspiricy was from Mrs. Ann Smith's George; the second person that gave me information was Samuel alias Samuel Bird, the property of Mrs. Jane Clarke. They asked me last spring to come over to their houses on a Friday night. It was late before I could get there; the company had met and dispersed. I inquired where they were gone, and was informed to see their wives. I went after them and found George; he carried me and William (the property of William Young) to Sam Bird's, and after we got there he (Sam) enquired of George if he had any pen and ink; he said no—he had left it at home. He brought out his list of men, and he had Elisha Price's Jim, James Price's Moses, Sally Price's Bob, Denny Wood's Emanuel. After this George invited me to come and see him the next night, but I did not go. The following Monday night William went over and returned with a ticket for me; likewise one for Gilbert. The Thursday night following, both George and Sam Bird came to see me. Bowler's Jack was with us. We conversed untill late in the night upon the subject of the meditated war. George said he would try to be ready by the 24th of August, and the following Sunday he went to Hungry meeting-house to enlist men. When I saw him again he informed me he had enlisted 37 men there. The Sunday after he went to Manchester, where he said he had recruited 50-odd men. I never saw him again untill the ser-

mon at my house, which was about three weeks before the rising was to take place. On the day of the sermon, George called on Sam Bird to inform how many men he had; he said he had not his list with him, but he supposed about 500.

George wished the business to be deferred some time longer. Mr. Prosser's Gabriel wished to bring on the business as soon as possible. Gilbert said the summer was almost over, and he wished them to enter upon the business before the weather got too cold. Gabriel proposed that the subject should be referred to his brother Martin to decide upon. Martin said there was this expression in the Bible, delays breed danger; at this time, he said, the country was at peace, the soldiers were discharged, and the arms all put away; there was no patroling in the country, and that before he would any longer bear what he had borne, he would turn out and fight with his stick. Gilbert said he was ready with his pistol, but it was in need of repair; he gave it to Gabriel, who was put it in order for him. I then spoke to the company and informed them I wished to have something to say. I told them that I had heard in the days of old, when the Israelites were in service to King Pharoah, they were taken from him by the power of God, and were carried away by Moses. God had blessed him with an angel to go with him, but that I could see nothing of that kind in these days. Martin said in reply: I read in my Bible where God says if we will worship Him we should have peace in all our land; five of you shall conquer an hundred, and a hundred a thousand of our enemies. After this they went on consultation upon the time they should execute the plan. Martin spoke and appointed for them to meet in three weeks, which was to be of a Saturday night. Gabriel said he had 500 bullets made. Smith's George said he was done the corn and would then go on to make as many cross-bows as he could. Bowler's Jack said he had got 50 spiers or bayonets fixed at the end of sticks. The plan was to be a follows: We were all to meet at the briery spot on the

Brook; 100 men were to stand at the Brook bridge; Gabriel was to take 100 more and go to Gregory's tavern and take the arms which were there; 50 more were to be sent to Rocketts to set that on fire, in order to alarm the upper part of the town and induce the people to go down there; while they were employed in extinguishing the fire Gabriel and the other officers and soldiers were to take the Capitol and all the arms they could find and be ready to slaughter the people on their return from Rocketts. Sam Bird was to have a pass as a free man and was to go to the nation of Indians called Catawbas to persuade them to join the negroes to fight the white people. As far as I understood all the whites were to be massacred, except the Quakers, the Methodists, and the Frenchmen, and they were to be spared on account as they conceived of their being friendly to liberty, and also they had understood that the French were at war with this country for the money that was due them, and that an army was landed at South Key, which they hoped would assist them. They intended also to spare all the poor white women who had no slaves.

The above communications are put down precisely as delivered to us by Ben, alias Ben Woolfolk. Given under our hands this 17th day of September, 1800.

GERVAS STORRS,
JOSEPH SELDEN.

A Journey in the Seaboard Slave States with Remarks on Their Economy

Frederick Law Olmstead

A TOBACCO PLANTATION

Half an hour after this I arrived at the negro-quarters—a little hamlet of ten or twelve small and dilapidated cabins. Just beyond them was a plain farm-gate, at which several negroes were standing; one of them, a well-made man, with an intelligent countenance and prompt manner, directed me how to find my way to his owner's house. It was still nearly a mile distant; and yet, until I ar-

Source: Frederick Law Olmsted, *A Journey in the Seaboard Slave States with Remarks on Their Economy.* (New York, 1856), pp. 88–91, 186–194, 418–422, 424–436.

rived in its immediate vicinity, I saw no cultivated field, and but one clearing. In the edge of this clearing, a number of negroes, male and female, lay stretched out upon the ground near a small smoking charcoal pit. Their master afterwards informed me that they were burning charcoal for the plantation blacksmith, using the time allowed them for holidays—from Christmas to New Year's—to earn a little money for themselves in this way. He paid them by the bushel for it. When I said that I supposed he allowed them to take what wood they chose for this purpose, he replied that he had five hundred acres covered with wood, which he would be very glad to have any one burn, or clear off in any way. Cannot some Yankee contrive a method of concentrating some of the valuable properties of this old-field pine, so that they may be profitably brought into use in more cultivated regions? Charcoal is now brought to New York from Virginia; but when made from pine it is not very valuable, and will only bear transportation from the banks of the navigable rivers, whence it can be shipped, at one movement, to New York. Turpentine does not flow in sufficient quantity from this variety of the pine to be profitably collected, and for lumber it is of very small value.

Mr. W.'s house was an old family mansion, which he had himself remodeled in the Grecian style, and furnished with a large wooden portico. An oak forest had originally occupied the ground where it stood; but this having been cleared and the soil worn out in cultivation by the previous proprietors, pine woods now surrounded it in every direction, a square of a few acres only being kept clear immediately about it. A number of the old oaks still stood in the rear of the house, and, until Mr. W. commenced his improvements, there had been some in its front. These, however, he had cut away, as interfering with the symmetry of his grounds, and in place of them had planted ailanthus trees in parallel rows.

On three sides of the outer part of the cleared square there was a row of large and comfortable-looking negro-quarters, stables, tobacco-houses, and other offices, built of logs.

Mr. W. was one of the few large planters, of his vicinity, who still made the culture of tobacco their principal business. He said there was a general prejudice against tobacco, in all the tide-water region of the State, because it was through the culture of tobacco that the once fertile soils had been impoverished; but he did not believe that, at the present value of negroes, their labor could be applied to the culture of grain, with any profit, except under peculiarly favorable circumstances. Possibly, the use of guano might make wheat a paying crop, but he still doubted. He had not used it, himself. Tobacco required fresh land, and was rapidly

exhausting, but it returned more money, for the labor used upon it, than anything else; enough more, in his opinion, to pay for the wearing out of the land. If he was well-paid for it, he did not know why he should not wear out his land.

His tobacco-fields were nearly all in a distant and lower part of his plantation; land which had been neglected before his time, in a great measure, because it had been sometimes flooded, and was, much of the year, too wet for cultivation. He was draining and clearing it, and it now brought good crops.

He had had an Irish gang draining for him, by contract. He thought a negro could do twice as much work, in a day, as an Irishman. He had not stood over them and seen them at work, but judged entirely from the amount they accomplished: he thought a good gang of negroes would have got on twice as fast. He was sure they must have "trifled" a great deal, or they would have accomplished more than they had. He complained much, also, of their sprees and quarrels. I asked why he should employ Irishmen, in preference to doing the work with his own hands. "It's dangerous work (unhealthy?), and a negro's life is too valuable to be risked at it. If a negro dies, it's a considerable loss, you know."

He afterwards said that his negroes never worked so hard as to tire themselves—always were lively, and ready to go off on a frolic at night. He did not think they ever did half a fair day's work. They could not be made to work hard: they never would lay out their strength freely, and it was impossible to make them do it.

This is just what I have thought when I have seen slaves at work—they seem to go through the motions of labor without putting strength into them. They keep their powers in reserve for their own use at night, perhaps.

Mr. W. also said that he cultivated only the coarser and lower-priced sorts of tobacco, because the finer sorts required more pains-taking and discretion than it was possible to make a large gang of negroes use.

"You can make a nigger work," he said, *"but you cannot make him think."*

LOSS OF PROFIT TO THE EMPLOYER, FROM THE ILLNESS OR DISABILITY, REAL OR COUNTERFEITED, OF THE LABORER TO WORK

This, to the employer of free laborers, need be nothing. To the slave-master it is of varying consequence: sometimes small, often excessively embarrassing, and always a subject of anxiety and suspicion. I have never made the inquiry on any plantation where as many as twenty negroes were employed together, that I have not ascertained that one or more of the field-hands was not at work on account of some illness, strain, bruise or wound, of which he or she was complaining; and in such cases I have hardly ever heard the proprietor or overseer fail to express his suspicion that the invalid was really as well able to work as any one else on the plantation. It is said to be nearly as difficult to form a satisfactory diagnosis of negroes' disorders, as it is of infants', because their imagination of symptoms is so vivid, and because not the smallest reliance is to be placed on their accounts of what they have felt or done. If a man is really ill, he fears lest he should be thought to be simulating, and therefore exaggerates all his pains, and locates them in whatever he supposes to be the most vital parts of his system.

Frequently the invalid slaves will neglect or refuse to use the remedies prescribed for their recovery. They will conceal pills, for instance, under their tongue, and declare they have swallowed them, when, from their producing no effect, it will be afterwards evident that they have not. This general custom I heard ascribed to habit, acquired when they were not very disagreeably ill, and were loth to be made quite well enough to have to go to work again.

Amusing incidents, illustrating this difficulty, I have heard narrated, showing that the slave rather enjoys getting a severe wound that lays him up:—he has his hand crushed by the fall of a piece of timber, and after the pain is alleviated, is heard to exclaim, "Bress der Lord—der haan b'long to masser—don't reckon dis chile got no more corn to hoe dis yaar, no how."*

Mr. H., of North Carolina, observed to me, in relation to this difficulty, that a man who had had much experience with negroes could generally tell, with a good deal of certainty, by their tongue, and their pulse, and their general aspect, whether they were really ill or not.

"Last year," said he, "I hired out one of my negroes to a rail-road contractor. I suppose he found that he had to work harder than he would on the plantation, and became discontented, and one night he left the camp without asking leave. The next day he stopped at a public-house, and told the people he had fallen sick working on the rail-road, and was going home to his master. They suspected he had run away, and, as he had no pass, they arrested him and sent him to the jail. In the night the sheriff sent me word that there was a boy, who said he belonged to me, in the jail, and he was very sick indeed, and I had better come and take care of him. I immediately suspected how it was, and, as I was particularly engaged, I

---

*It is, perhaps, well I should say that this soliloquy was repeated to me by a Virginia planter, as if it had occurred within his own hearing. A similar illustration of the pleasure with which a slave finds himself exempted from labor, having been mentioned in the "Key to Uncle Tom's Cabin," the Reverend E. J. Stearns, of St. John's College, Maryland, in a rejoinder to that work, thinks it unnecessary to deny the truth of it, but, with the usual happy keenness of clerical controversialists, settles the matter without being personally disrespectful to Mrs. Stowe's authority, by quoting the *final* authority:—"'No man ever hated his own flesh, but nourisheth it, and cherisheth it;' *and again,* 'So ought men to love their wives as their own bodies.'"

did not go near him till towards night, the next day. When I came to look at him, and heard his story, I felt quite sure in my own mind that he was not sick; but, as he pretended to be suffering very much, I told the sheriff to give him plenty of salts and senna, and to be careful that he did not get much of anything to eat. The next day I got a letter from the contractor, telling me that my nigger had run away, without any cause. So I rode over to the jail again, and told them to continue the same treatment until the boy got a good deal worse or a good deal better. Well, the rascal kept it up for a week, all the time groaning so you'd think he couldn't live many hours longer; but, after he had been in seven days, he all of a sudden said he'd got well, and he wanted something to eat. As soon as I heard of it, I sent them word to give him a good paddling,* and handcuff him, and send him back to the rail-road. I had to pay them for taking up a runaway, besides the sheriff's fees, and a week's board of the boy to the county."

But the same gentleman admitted that he had sometimes been mistaken, and had made men go to work when they afterwards proved to be really ill; therefore, when one of his people told him he was not able to work, he usually thought, "very likely he'll be all the better for a day's rest, whether he's really ill or not," and would let him off without being very particular in his examination. Lately he had been getting a new overseer, and when he was engaging him, he told him that this was his way. The overseer replied, "It's my way, too, now; it didn't use to be, but I had a lesson. There was a nigger one day at Mr.—'s who was sulky, and complaining; he said he couldn't work. I looked at his tongue, and it was right clean, and I thought it was nothing but damned sulkiness so I paddled him, and made him go to

*Not something to eat, but punishment with an instrument like a ferule.

work; but, two days after, he was under ground. He was a good eight hundred dollar nigger, and it was a lesson to me about taming possums, that I ain't agoing to forget in a hurry."

The liability of women, especially, to disorders and irregularities which cannot be detected by exterior symptoms, but which may be easily aggravated into serious complaints, renders many of them nearly valueless for work, because of the ease with which they can impose upon their owners. "The women on a plantation," said one extensive Virginian slave-owner to me, "will hardly earn their salt, after they come to the breeding age: they don't come to the field, and you go to the quarters and ask the old nurse what's the matter, and she says, 'Oh, she's not well, master; she's not fit to work, sir;' and what can you do? You have to take her word for it that something or other is the matter with her, and you dare not set her to work; and so she lay up till she feels like taking the air again, and plays the lady at your expense."

I was on one plantation where a woman had been excused from any sort of labor for more than two years, on the supposition that she was dying of phthisis. At last the overseer discovered that she was employed as a milliner and dress-maker by all the other colored ladies of the vicinity; and upon taking her to the house, it was found that she had acquired a remarkable skill in these vocations. She was hired out the next year to a fashionable dress-maker in town, at handsome wages; and as, after that, she did not again "raise blood," it was supposed that when she had done so before it had been by artificial means. Such tricks every army and navy surgeon is familiar with.

The interruption and disarrangement of operations of labor, occasioned by slaves "running away," frequently causes great inconvenience and loss to those who employ them. It is said to often occur when no immediate motive can be guessed at for it—when the slave has been well-treated, well-fed, and not over-worked; and when he will be sure to suffer hardship from it, and be subject to severe punishment on his return, or if he is caught.

This is often mentioned to illustrate the ingratitude and especial depravity of the African race. I should suspect it to be, if it cannot be otherwise accounted for, the natural instinct of freedom in a man, working out capriciously, as the wild instincts of domesticated beasts and birds sometimes do.

But the learned Dr. Cartwright, of the University of Louisiana, believes that slaves are subject to a peculiar form of mental disease, termed by him *Drapetomania*, which, like a malady that cats are liable to, manifests itself by an irrestrainable propensity to *run away;* and in a work on the diseases of negroes, highly esteemed at the South for its patriotism and erudition, he advises planters of the proper preventive, and curative measures to be taken for it.

He asserts that, "with the advantage of proper medical advice, strictly followed, this troublesome practice of running away, that many negroes have, can be almost entirely prevented." Its symptoms and the usual empirical practice on the plantations are described: "Before negroes run away, unless they are frightened or panic-struck, they become sulky and dissatisfied. The cause of this sulkiness and dissatisfaction should be inquired into and removed, or they are apt to run away or fall into the negro consumption." When sulky or dissatisfied without cause, the experience of those having most practice with *drapetomania,* the Doctor thinks, has been in favor of "whipping them *out of it.*" It is vulgarly called, "whipping the devil *out of them,*" he afterwards informs us.

Another droll sort of "indisposition," thought to be peculiar to the slaves, and which must greatly affect their value, as compared with free laborers, is described by Dr. Cartwright, as follows:

"DYSÆSTHESIA ÆTHIOPICA, or Hebetude of Mind and Obtuse Sensibility of Body. * * * From the careless movements of the individuals affected with this complaint, they are apt to do much mischief, which appears as if intentional, but is mostly owing to the stupidity of mind and insensibility of the nerves induced by the disease. Thus they break, waste, and destroy everything they handle—abuse horses and cattle—tear, burn, or rend their own clothing, and, paying no attention to the rights of property, steal others to replace what they have destroyed. They wander about at night, and keep in a half nodding state by day. They slight their work—cut up corn, cane, cotton, and tobacco, when hoeing it, as if for pure mischief. They raise disturbances with their overseers, and among their fellow-servants, without cause or motive, and seem to be insensible to pain when subjected to punishment. * * *

"When left to himself, the negro indulges in his natural disposition to idleness and sloth, and does not take exercise enough to expand his lungs and vitalize his blood, but dozes out a miserable existence in the midst of filth and uncleanliness, being too indolent, and having too little energy of mind, to provide for himself proper food and comfortable clothing and lodging. The consequence is, that the blood becomes so highly carbonized and deprived of oxygen that it not only becomes unfit to stimulate the brain to energy, but unfit to stimulate the nerves of sensation distributed to the body. * * *

"This is the disease called *Dysæsthesia* (a Greek term expressing the dull or obtuse sensation that always attends the complaint). When roused from sloth by the stimulus of hunger, he takes anything he can lay his hands on, and tramples on the rights as well as on the property of others, with perfect indifference. When driven to labor by the compulsive power of the white man, he performs the task assigned to him in a headlong, careless manner, treading down with his feet or cutting with his hoe the plants he is put to cultivate—breaking the tools he works with, and spoiling everything he touches that can be injured by careless handling. Hence the overseers call it 'rascality,' supposing that the mischief is intentionally done. * * *

"The term, 'rascality,' given to this disease by overseers, is founded on an erroneous hypothesis, and leads to an incorrect empirical treatment, which seldom or never cures it."

There are many complaints described in Dr. Cartwright's treatise, to which the negroes, in Slavery, seem to be peculiarly subject.

"More fatal than any other is congestion of the lungs, *peripneumonia notha,* often called cold plague, etc. * * *

"The *Frambæsia,* Piam, or Yaws, is a *contagious* disease, communicable by contact among those who greatly neglect cleanliness. It is supposed to be communicable, in a modified form, to the white race, among whom it resembles pseudo syphilis, or some disease of the nose, throat, or larynx. * * *

"Negro-consumption, a disease almost unknown to medical men of the Northern States and of Europe, is also sometimes fearfully prevalent among the slaves. 'It is of importance,' says the Doctor, 'to know the pathognomic signs in its early stages, not only in regard to its treatment, but to detect impositions, as negroes, afflicted with this complaint are often for sale; the acceleration of the pulse, on exercise, incapacitates them for labor, as they quickly give out, and have to leave their work. This induces their owners to sell them, although they may not know the cause of their inability to labor. Many of the negroes brought South, for sale, are in the incipient stages of this disease; they are found to be inefficient laborers, and are sold in consequence thereof. The effect of superstition—a firm belief that he is poisoned or conjured—upon the patient's mind, already in a morbid state (dyæsthesia), and his health affected from hard usage overtasking or exposure, want of wholesome food, good clothing, warm, comfortable lodging, with the distressing idea (sometimes) that he is an object of hatred or dislike, both to his master or fellow-servants, and has no one to befriend him, tends directly to generate that erythism of mind which is the essential cause of negro-consumption.' * * * 'Remedies should be assisted by removing the *original cause* of the dissatisfaction or trouble of mind, and by using every means to make the patient comfortable, satisfied and happy.'"

Longing for home generates a distinct malady, known to physicians as *Nostalgia,* and there is an analogy between the treatment commonly employed to cure it and that recommended in this last advice of Dr. Cartwright, which is very suggestive. . . .

A RICE PLANTATION

Mr. X. has two plantations on the river, besides a large tract of poor pine forest land, extending some miles back upon the upland, and reaching above the malarious region. In the upper part of this pine land is a house, occupied by his overseer during the malarious season, when it is dangerous for any but negroes to remain during the night in the vicinity of the swamps or rice-fields. Even those few who have been born in the region, and have grown up subject to the malaria, are generally weakly and short-lived. The negroes do not enjoy as good health on rice plantations as elsewhere; and the greater difficulty with which their lives are preserved, through infancy especially, shows that the subtle poison of the miasma is not innocuous to them; but Mr. X. boasts a steady increase of his negro stock of five percent. per annum, which is better than is averaged on the plantations of the interior.

As to the degree of danger to others, "I would as soon stand fifty feet from the best Kentucky rifleman and be shot at by the hour, as to spend a night on my plantation in summer," a Charleston gentleman said to me. And the following two instances of the deadly work it sometimes does were mentioned to me by another: A party of six ladies and gentlemen went out of town to spend a day at the mansion of a rice-planter, on an island. By an accident to their boat, their return before night was prevented, and they went back and shut themselves within the house, had fires made, around which they sat all night, and took every other precaution to guard against the miasma. Nevertheless, four of them died from its effects, within a week; and the other two suffered severely. Two brothers owned a plantation on which they had spent the winter; one of them, as summer approached, was careful to go to another residence every night; the other delayed to do so until it was too late. One morning he was found to be ill; a physician could not be procured until late in the afternoon, by which time his recovery was hopeless. The sick man besought his brother not to hazard his own life by remaining with him; and he was obliged, before the sun set, to take the last farewell, and leave him with the servants, in whose care, in the course of the night, he died.

The plantation which contains Mr. X.'s winter residence, has but a small extent of rice land, the greater part of it being reclaimed upland swamp soil, suitable for the culture of Sea Island cotton, which, at the present market, might be grown upon it with profit. But, as his force of slaves has ordinarily been more profitably engaged in the rice-fields, all this has been for many years "turned out," and is now overgrown with pines. The other plantation contains over five hundred acres of rice-land, fitted for irrigation; the remainder is unusually fertile, reclaimed upland swamp, and some hundred acres of it are cultivated for maize and Sea Island cotton.

There is a "negro settlement" on each; but both plantations, although a mile or two apart, are worked together as one, under one overseer—the hands being drafted from one to another as their labor is required. Somewhat over seven hundred acres are at the present time under the plow in the two plantations: the whole number of negroes is two hundred, and they are reckoned to be equal to about one hundred prime hands—an unusual strength for that number of all classes. The overseer lives, in winter, near the settlement of the larger plantation, Mr. X. near that of the smaller.

It is an old family estate, inherited by Mr. X.'s wife, who, with her children, were born and brought up upon it in close intimacy with the negroes, a large proportion of whom were also included in her inheritance, or have been since born upon the estate. Mr. X. himself is a New England farmer's son, and has been a successful merchant and manufacturer. He is also a religious man, without the dementifying bigotry or self-important humility, so frequently implied by that appellation to a New Englander, but generous, composed and cheerful in disposition, as well as conscientious.

The patriarchal institution should be seen here under its most favorable aspects; not only from the ties of long family association, common traditions, common memories, and, if ever, common interests, between the slaves and their rulers, but, also, from the practical talent for organization and administration, gained among the rugged fields, the complicated looms, and the exact and comprehensive counting-houses of New England, which directs the labor.

The house-servants are more intelligent, understand and perform their duties better, and are more appropriately dressed, than any I have seen before. The labor required of them is light, and they are treated with much more consideration for their health and comfort than is usually given to that of free domestics. They live in brick cabins, adjoining the house and stables, and one of these, into which I have looked, is neatly and comfortably furnished. Several of the house-servants, as is usual, are mulattoes, and good-looking. The mulattoes are generally preferred for in-door occupations. Slaves brought up to house-work dread to be employed at field-labor; and those accustomed to the comparatively unconstrained life of the negro-settlement, detest the close control and careful movements required of the house-servants. It is a punishment for a lazy field-hand, to employ him in menial duties at the house, as it is to set a sneaking sailor to do the work of a cabin-servant; and it is equally a punishment to a neglectful house-servant, to banish him to the field-gangs. All the household economy is, of course, carried on in a style appropriate to a wealthy gentleman's residence—not more so, nor less so, that I observe, than in an establishment of similar grade at the North.

It is a custom with Mr. X., when on the estate, to look each day at all the work going on, inspect the buildings, boats, embankments and sluice-ways, and examine the sick. Yesterday I accompanied him in one of these daily rounds.

After a ride of several miles through the woods, in the rear of the plantations, we came to his largest negro-settlement. There was a street, or common, two hundred feet wide, on which the cabins of the negroes fronted. Each cabin was a framed building, the walls boarded and whitewashed on the outside, lathed and plastered within, the roof shingled; forty-two feet long, twenty-one feet wide, divided into two family tenements, each twenty-one by twenty-one; each tenement divided into three rooms—one, the common household apartment, twenty-one by ten; each of the others (bed-rooms), ten by ten. There was a brick fire-place in the middle of the long side of each living room, the chimneys rising in one, in the middle of the roof. Besides these rooms, each tenement had a cock-loft, entered by steps from the household room. Each tenement is occupied, on an average, by five persons. There were in them closets, with locks and keys, and a varying quantity of rude furniture. Each cabin stood two hundred feet from the next, and the street in front of them being two hundred feet wide, they were just that distance apart each way. The people were nearly all absent at work, and had locked their outer doors, taking the keys with them. Each cabin has a front and back door, and each room a window, closed by a wooden shutter, swinging outward, on hinges. Between each tenement and the next house, is a small piece of ground, inclosed with palings, in which are coops of fowl with chickens, hovels for nests, and for sows with pig. There were a great many fowls in the street. The negroes' swine are allowed to run in the woods, each owner having his own distinguished by a peculiar mark. In the rear of the yards were gardens—a half-acre to each family. Internally the cabins appeared dirty and disordered, which was rather a pleasant indication that their home-life was not much interfered with, though I found certain police regulations were enforced. . . .

Mr. X. went to Tom's Sue's cabin, looked at the boy, and, concluding that he was well, though he lay abed, and pretended to cry with pain, ordered him to go out to work. Then, meeting the overseer, who was just riding away, on some business off the plantation, he remained some time in conversation with him, while I occupied myself in making a sketch of the nursery and the street of the settlement in my note-book. On the verandah and the steps of the nursery, there were twenty-seven children, most of them infants, that had been left there by their mothers, while they were working their tasks in the fields. They probably make a visit to them once or twice during the day, to nurse them, and receive them to take to their cabins, or where they like, when they have finished their tasks—generally in the middle of the afternoon. The older children were fed with porridge, by the general nurse. A number of girls, eight or ten years old, were occupied in holding and tending the youngest infants. Those a little older—the crawlers—were in the pen, and those big enough to toddle were playing on the steps, or before the house. Some of these, with two or three bigger ones, were singing and dancing about a fire that they had made on the ground. They were not at all disturbed or interrupted in their amusement by the presence of their owner and myself. At twelve years of age, the children are first put to regular field-work; until then no labor is required of them, except, perhaps, occasionally, they are charged with some light kind of duty, such as frightening birds from corn. When first sent to the field, one-quarter of an able-bodied hand's day's work is ordinarily allotted to them, as their task.

But very few of the babies were in arms; such as were not, generally lay on the floor, rolling about, or sat still, sucking their thumbs. The nurse was a kind-looking old negro woman, with, no doubt, philoprogenitiveness well developed; but she paid very little attention to them, only sometimes chiding the older ones for laughing or singing too loud. I watched for half an hour, and in all that time not a baby of them began to cry; nor have I ever heard one, at two or three other plantation-nurseries which I have visited. I remember, in Amsterdam, to have seen two or three similar collections of children, voluntarily deposited by their mothers, who went out from home to work. These seemed to be looked out for by two or three poor women, who probably received a small fee for their trouble, from the parent thus relieved. Not being able to converse in Dutch, I could get no particular information about it; but I especially noticed, in each case, that there was no crying or fretting. On the contrary, they appeared to be peculiarly well-disposed and jolly, as if they were already on the straight road to the right place, and were fully satisfied with the vehicles they had got to drive through the world. They had, in short, thus early learned that it did not do any good to cry—for the nurse couldn't, if she would, feed, or cuddle, or play with one every time she was wanted to. I make a note of it, as indicating how young the little twig is bent, how early the formation of habits commences, and that, even in babyhood, the "product of happiness is to be found, not so much in increasing your numerator, as in lessening your denominator."

From the settlement, we drove to the "mill"—not a flouring mill, though I believe there is a run of stones in it—but a monster barn, with more extensive and better machinery for threshing and storing rice, driven by a steam-engine, than I have ever seen used for grain on any farm in Europe or America before. Adjoining the mill-house were shops and sheds, in which blacksmiths, carpenters, and other mechanics—all slaves, belonging to Mr. X.—were at work. He called my attention to the excellence of their workmanship, and said that they exercised as much ingenuity and skill as the ordinary mechanics that he was used to employ in New England. He pointed out to me some carpenter's work, a part of which

had been executed by a New England mechanic, and a part by one of his own hands, which indicated that the latter was much the better workman.

I was gratified by this, for I had been so often told, in Virginia, by gentlemen, anxious to convince me that the negro was incapable of being educated or improved to a condition in which it would be safe to trust him with himself—that no negro-mechanic could ever be taught, or induced to work carefully or nicely—that I had begun to believe it might be so.

We were attended through the mill-house by a respectable-looking, orderly, and gentlemanly-mannered mulatto, who was called, by his master, "the watchman." His duties, however, as they were described to me, were those of a steward, or intendant. He carried, by a strap at his waist, a very large number of keys, and had charge of all the stores of provisions, tools, and materials of the plantations, as well as of all their produce, before it was shipped to market. He weighed and measured out all the rations of the slaves and the cattle; super-intended the mechanics, and himself made and repaired, as was necessary, all the machinery, including the steam-engine.

In all these departments, his authority was superior to that of the overseer. The overseer received his private allowance of family provisions from him, as did also the head-servant at the mansion, who was his brother. His responsibility was much greater than that of the overseer; and Mr. X. said, he would trust him with much more than he would any overseer he had ever known.

Anxious to learn how this trustworthiness and intelligence, so unusual in a slave, had been developed or ascertained, I inquired of his history, which was, briefly, as follows.

Being the son of a favorite house-servant, he had been, as a child, associated with the white family, and received by chance something of the early education of the white children. When old enough, he had been employed, for some years, as a waiter; but, at his own request, was eventually allowed to learn the blacksmith's trade, in the plantation-shop. Showing ingenuity and talent, he was afterwards employed to make and repair the plantation cotton-gins. Finally, his owner took him to a steam-engine builder, and paid $500 to have him instructed as a machinist. After he had become a skillful workman, he obtained employment, as an engineer; and for some years continued in this occupation, and was allowed to spend his wages for himself. Finding, however, that he was acquiring dissipated habits, and wasting all his earnings, Mr. X. eventually brought him, much against his inclinations, back to the plantations. Being allowed peculiar privileges, and given duties wholly flattering to his self-respect, he soon became contented; and, of course, was able to be extremely valuable to his owner.

I have seen another slave-engineer. The gentleman who employed him told me that he was a man of talent, and of great worth of character. He had desired to make him free, but his owner, who was a member of the Board of Brokers, and of Dr.——'s Church, in New York, believed that Providence designed the negro race for slavery, and refused to sell him for that purpose. He thought it better that he (his owner) should continue to receive two hundred dollars a year for his services, while he continued able to work, and then he should feel responsible that he did not starve, or come upon the public for a support, in his old age. The man himself, having light and agreeable duties, well provided for, furnished with plenty of spending money in gratuities by his employer, patronized and flattered by the white people, honored and looked up to by those of his own color, was rather indifferent in the matter; or even, perhaps, preferred to remain a slave, to being transported for life, to Africa.

The watchman was a fine-looking fellow: as we were returning from church, on Sunday, he had passed us, well-dressed and well-mounted, and as he raised his hat, to salute us, there was nothing in his manner or appearance, except his color, to distinguish him from a gentleman of good-breeding and fortune.

When we were leaving the house, to go to church, on Sunday, after all the white family had entered their carriages, or mounted their horses, the head house-servant also mounted a horse—as he did so, slipping a coin into the hands of the boy who had been holding him. Afterwards, we passed a family of negroes, in a light wagon—the oldest among them driving the horse. On my inquiring if the slaves were allowed to take horses to drive to church, I was informed that, in each of these three cases, the horses belonged to the negroes who were driving or riding them. The old man was infirm, and Mr. X. had given him a horse, to enable him to move about. He was probably employed to look after the cattle at pasture, or at something in which it was necessary, for his usefulness, that he should have a horse: I say this, because I afterwards found, in similar cases on other plantations, that it was so.

But the watchman and the house-servant had bought their horses with money. The watchman was believed to own three horses; and, to account for his wealth, Mr. X.'s son told me that his father considered him a very valuable servant, and frequently encouraged him in his good behavior, with handsome gratuities. He receives, probably, considerably higher wages, in fact (in the form of presents), than the white overseer. He knew his father gave him two hundred dollars at once, a short time ago. The watchman has a private house, and, no doubt, lives in considerable luxury.

Will it be said, "therefore, Slavery is neither necessarily degrading nor inhumane?" On the other hand, so far as it is not, there is no apology for it. It may be that this fine fellow, if he had been born a freeman, would be no better employed than he is here; but, in that case, where is the advantage? Certainly not in the economy of the arrangement. And if he was self-dependent, and if, especially, he had to provide for the present and future of those he loved, and was able to do so, would he not necessarily live a happier, stronger, better, and more respectable man?

But, to arrive at this conclusion, we have had to suppose such a state of society for the free laborer as to make it a matter of certainty that by the development of industry, talent, and providence, he is able to provide for himself and for those whose happiness is linked with his own.

As a general rule, this is the case in all free-labor countries. Nowhere, I suspect, are the exceptions to it so frequent as are the exceptions to humane and generous treatment of slaves by their masters. Nevertheless, it is the first duty of those who think Slavery wrong to remove to the utmost all such excuse for it as is to be found in the occasional hardships and frequent debasement and ignorance of the laboring class in free communities.

After passing through tool-rooms, corn-rooms, mule-stables, store-rooms, and a large garden, in which vegetables to be distributed among the negroes, as well as for the family, are grown, we walked to the rice-land. It is divided by embankments into fields of about twenty acres each, but varying somewhat in size, according to the course of the river. The arrangements are such that each field may be flooded independently of the rest, and they are subdivided by open ditches into rectangular plats of a quarter acre each. We first proceeded to where twenty or thirty women and girls were engaged in raking together, in heaps and winrows, the stubble and rubbish left on the field after the last crop, and burning it. The main object of this operation is to kill all the seeds of weeds, or of rice, on the ground. Ordinarily it is done by tasks—a certain number of the small divisions of the field being given to each hand to burn in a day; but owing to a more than usual amount of rain having fallen lately, and some other causes, making the work harder in some places than others, the women were now working by the day, under the direction of a "driver," a negro man, who walked about among them, taking care that they left noth-

ing unburned. Mr. X. inspected the ground they had gone over, to see whether the driver had done his duty. It had been sufficiently well burned, but, not more than quarter as much ground had been gone over, he said, as was usually burned in task-work,—and he thought they had been very lazy, and reprimanded them for it. The driver made some little apology, but the women offered no reply, keeping steadily, and it seemed sullenly, on at their work.

In the next field, twenty men, or boys, for none of them looked as if they were full-grown, were plowing, each with a single mule, and a light, New-York-made plow. The soil was very friable, the plowing easy, and the mules proceeded at a smart pace; the furrows were straight, regular, and well turned. Their task was nominally an acre and a quarter a day; somewhat less actually, as the measure includes the space occupied by the ditches, which are two to three feet wide, running around each quarter of an acre. The plowing gang was superintended by a driver who was provided with a watch; and while we were looking at them he called out that it was twelve o'clock. The mules were immediately taken from the plows, and the plow-boys mounting them, leapt the ditches, and cantered off to the stables, to feed them. One or two were ordered to take their plows to the blacksmith, for repairs.

FOOD

The plowmen got their dinner at this time: those not using horses do not usually dine till they have finished their tasks; but this, I believe, is optional with them. They commence work at sunrise, and at about eight o'clock have breakfast brought to them in the field, each hand having left a bucket with the cook for that purpose. All who are working in connection leave their work together, and gather in a social company about a fire, where they generally spend about half an hour, at breakfast time. The provisions furnished them consist mainly of meal, rice and vegetables, with salt and molasses, and occasionally bacon, fish, and coffee. The allowance is a peck of meal, or an equivalent quantity of rice per week, to each working hand, old or young, besides small stores. Mr. X. says that he has lately given a less amount of meat than is now usual on plantations, having observed that the general health of the negroes is not as good as formerly, when no meat at all was customarily given them. The general impression among planters is, that the negroes work much better for being supplied with three or four pounds of bacon a week.

Leaving the rice-land, we went next to some of the upland fields, where we found several other gangs of negroes at work; one entirely of men engaged in ditching; another of women, and another of boys and girls, "listing" an old corn-field with hoes. All of them were working by tasks, and were overlooked by negro drivers. They all labored with greater rapidity and cheerfulness than any slaves I have before seen; and the women struck their hoes as if they were strong, and well able to engage in muscular labor. The expression of their faces was generally repulsive, and their *tout ensemble* anything but agreeable to the eye. The dress of most of them was uncouth and cumbrous, dirty and ragged; reefed up, as I have once before described, at the hips, so as to show their heavy legs, wrapped round with a piece of old blanket, in lieu of leggings or stockings. Most of them worked with bare arms, but wore strong shoes on their feet, and handkerchiefs on their heads; some of them were smoking, and each gang had a fire burning on the ground, near where they were at work, to light their pipes and warm their breakfast by. Mr. X. said this was always their custom, even in summer. To each gang a boy or girl was also attached, whose business it was to bring water for them to drink, and to go for anything required by the driver. The drivers would frequently call back a hand to go over again some piece of his or her task that had not been worked to his satisfaction, and were constantly calling

to one or another, with a harsh and peremptory voice, to strike harder or hoe deeper, and otherwise taking care that the work was well done. Mr. X. asked if Little Sam ("Tom's Sue's Sam") worked yet with the "three-quarter" hands, and learning that he did, ordered him to be put with the full hands, observing that though rather short, he was strong and stout, and, being twenty years old, well able to do a man's work.

The field-hands are all divided into four classes, according to their physical capacities. The children beginning as "quarter-hands," advancing to "half-hands," and then to "three-quarter hands;" and, finally, when mature, and able-bodied, healthy and strong, to "full hands." As they decline in strength, from age, sickness, or other cause, they retrograde in the scale, and proportionately less labor is required of them. Many, of naturally weak frame, never are put among the full hands. Finally, the aged are left out at the annual classification, and no more regular field-work is required of them, although they are generally provided with some light, sedentary occupation. I saw one old woman picking "tailings" of rice out of a heap of chaff, an occupation at which she was literally not earning her salt. Mr. X. told me she was a native African, having been brought when a girl from the Guinea coast. She spoke almost unintelligibly; but after some other conversation, in which I had not been able to understand a word she said, he jokingly proposed to send her back to Africa. She expressed her preference to remain where she was, very emphatically. "Why?" She did not answer readily, but being pressed, threw up her palsied hands, and said furiously, "I lubs 'ou mas'r, oh, I lubs 'ou. I don't want go 'way from 'ou."

The field hands, are nearly always worked in gangs, the strength of a gang varying according to the work that engages it; usually it numbers twenty or more, and is directed by a driver. As on most large plantations, whether of rice or cotton, in Eastern Georgia and South Carolina, nearly all ordinary and regular work is performed *by tasks:* that is to say, each hand has his labor for the day marked out before him, and can take his own time to do it in. For instance, in making drains in light, clean meadow land, each man or woman of the full hands is required to dig one thousand cubic feet; in swamp-land that is being prepared for rice culture, where there are not many stumps, the task for a ditcher is five hundred feet; while in a very strong cypress swamp, only two hundred feet is required; in hoeing rice, a certain number of rows, equal to one-half or two-thirds of an acre, according to the condition of the land; in sowing rice (strewing in drills), two acres; in reaping rice (if it stands well), three-quarters of an acre; or, sometimes a gang will be required to reap, tie in sheaves, and carry to the stack-yard the produce of a certain area, commonly equal to one fourth the number of acres that there are hands working together. Hoeing cotton, corn, or potatoes; one half to one acre. Threshing; five to six hundred sheaves. In plowing rice-land (light, clean, mellow soil) with a yoke of oxen, one acre a day, including the ground lost in and near the drains—the oxen being changed at noon. A cooper, also, for instance, is required to make barrels at the rate of eighteen a week. Drawing staves; 500 a day. Hoop poles; 120. Squaring timber; 100 ft. Laying worm-fence; 50 panels per hand. Post and rail do., posts set 2½ to 3 ft. deep, 9 ft. apart, nine or ten panels per hand. In getting fuel from the woods, (pine, to be cut and split,) one cord is the task for a day. In "mauling rails," the taskman selecting the trees (pine) that he judges will split easiest, one hundred a day, ends not sharpened.

These are the tasks for first class able-bodied men, they are lessened by one quarter for three quarter hands, and proportionately for the lighter classes. In allotting the tasks, the drivers are expected to put the weaker hands, where (if there is any choice in the appearance of the ground, as where certain rows in hoeing corn would be less weedy than others,) they will be favored.

These tasks certainly would not be considered excessively hard, by a Northern laborer; and, in point of fact, the more industrious and active hands finish them often by two o'clock. I saw one or two leaving the field soon after one o'clock, several about two; and between three and four, I met a dozen women and several men coming home to their cabins, having finished their day's work.

Under this "Organization of Labor," most of the slaves work rapidly and well. In nearly all ordinary work, custom has settled the extent of the task, and it is difficult to increase it. The driver who marks it out, has to remain on the ground until it is finished, and has no interest in over-measuring it; and if it should be systematically increased very much, there is danger of a general stampede to the "swamp"—a danger the slave can always hold before his master's cupidity. In fact, it is looked upon in this region as a proscriptive right of the negroes to have this incitement to diligence offered them; and the man who denied it, or who attempted to lessen it, would, it is said, suffer in his reputation, as well as experience much annoyance from the obstinate "rascality" of his negroes. Notwithstanding this, I have heard a man assert, boastingly, that he made his negroes habitually perform double the customary tasks. Thus we get a glimpse again of the black side. If he is allowed the power to do this, what may not a man do?

Instructions to an Overseer in a Cotton Plantation

Alexander Telfair

Instructions by Alexander Telfair, of Savannah, Ga., to the overseer of his plantation near Augusta, dated June 11, 1832. MS. in the possession of the Georgia Historical Society, trustee for the Telfair Academy of Arts and Sciences, Savannah.

Rules and directions for my Thorn Island Plantation by which my overseers are to govern themselves in the management of it.—ALEXANDER TELFAIR.

(The directions in this book are to be strictly attended to.)

1. The allowance for every grown Negro however old and good for nothing, and every young one that works in the field, is a peck of corn each week, and a pint of salt, and a piece of meat, not exceeding fourteen pounds, per month.
2. No Negro to have more than Fifty lashes inflicted for any offence, no matter how great the crime.
3. The sucking children, and all other small ones who do not work in the field, draw a half allowance of corn and salt.
4. You will give tickets to any of the negroes who apply for them, to go any where about the neighborhood, but do not allow them to go off it without, nor suffer any strange negroes to come on it without a pass.
5. The negres to be tasked when the work allows it. I require a reasonable days work, well done—the task to be regulated by the state of the ground and the strength of the negro.
6. The cotton to be weighed every night and the weights set down in the Cotton Book. The product of each field to be set down sepa-

rately—as also the produce of the different corn fields.
7. You will keep a regular journal of the business of the plantation, setting down the names of the sick; the beginning, progress, and finishing of work; the state of the weather; Births, Deaths, and every thing of importance that takes place on the Plantation.
8. You are responsible for the conduct of all persons who visit you. All others found on the premises who have no business, you will take means to run off.
9. Feed every thing plentifully, but waste nothing.
10. The shade trees in the present clearings are not to be touched; and in taking in new ground, leave a thriving young oak or Hickory Tree to every Five Acres.
11. When picking out cotton, do not allow the hands to pull the Boles off the Stalk.
12. All visiting between this place and the one in Georgia is forbidden, except with Tickets from the respective overseers, and that but very seldom. There are none who have husbands or wives over there, and no connexions of the kind are to be allowed to be formed.
13. No night-meeting and preaching to be allowed on the place, except on Saturday night & Sunday morn.
14. Elsey is allowed to act as midwife, to black and white in the neighborhood, who send for her. One of her daughters to stay with the children and take charge of her business until she returns. She draws a peck of corn a week to feed my poultry with.
15. All the Land which is not planted, you will break up in the month of September. Plough it deep so as to turn in all the grass and weeds which it may be covered with.
16. If there is any fighting on the Plantation, whip all engaged in it—for no matter what the cause may have been, all are in the wrong.
17. Elsey is the Doctoress of the Plantation. In case of extraordinary illness, when she thinks she can do no more for the sick, you will employ a Physician.

Source: Instructions to an Overseer in a Cotton Plantation. From Ulrich B. Phillips, *Plantation and Frontier 1649–1863*, Vol. I (New York, 1910), pp. 126–129.

18. My Cotton is packed in Four & a half yard Bags, weighing each 300 pounds, and the rise of it.
19. Neither the Cotton nor Corn stalks to be burnt, but threshed and chopped down in every field on the plantation, and suffered to lie until ploughed in in the course of working the land.
20. Billy to do the Blacksmith work.
20. [sic] The trash and stuff about the settlement to be gathered in heaps, in broken, wet days to rot; in a word make manure of every thing you can.
21. A Turnip Patch to be planted every year for the use of the Plantation.
22. The Negroes measures for Shoes to be sent down with the name written on each, by my Raft hands, or any other certain conveyance, to me, early in October. All draw shoes, except the children, and those that nurse them.
23. Write me the last day of every month to Savannah, unless otherwise directed. When writing have the Journal before you, and set down in the Letter every thing that has been done, or occurred on the Plantation during the month.
24. Pease to be planted in all the Corn, and plenty sowed for seed.
25. When Picking Cotton in the Hammock and Hickory Ridge, weigh the Tasks in the field, and hawl the Cotton home in the Wagon.
26. The first picking of Cotton to be depended on for seed. Seed sufficient to plant two Crops to be saved, and what is left, not to be thrown out of the Gin House, until you clean it out before beginning to pick out the new Crop.
27. A Beef to be killed for the negroes in July, August and September. The hides to be tanned at home if you understand it, or put out to be tanned on shares.
28. A Lot to be planted in Rye in September, and seed saved every year. The Cow pens to be moved every month to tread the ground for this purpose.
29. When a Beef is killed, the Fifth quarter except the hide to be given to Elsey for the children.
30. Give the negroes nails when building or repairing their houses when you think they need them.
31. My Negroes are not allowed to plant Cotton for themselves. Every thing else they may plant, and you will give them tickets to sell what they make.
32. I have no Driver. You are to task the negroes yourself, and each negro is responsible to you for his own work, and nobodys else.
33. The Cotton Bags to be marked A. T. and numbered.
34. I leave my Plantation Shot Gun with you.
35. The Corn and Cotton stalks to be cut, and threshed down on the land which lies out to rest, the same as if it was to be planted.

The Life and Times of Frederick Douglass

Frederick Douglas

... Very soon after I went to Baltimore to live, Master Hugh succeeded in getting me hired to Mr. William Gardiner, an extensive shipbuilder on Fell's Point. I was placed there to learn to calk, a trade of which I already had some knowledge, gained while in Mr.

Hugh Auld's shipyard. Gardiner's, however, proved a very unfavorable place for the accomplishment of the desired object. Mr. Gardiner was that season engaged in building two large man-of-war vessels, professedly for the Mexican government. These vessels were to be launched in the month of July of that year, and in failure thereof Mr. Gardiner would forfeit a very considerable sum of money. So, when I entered the shipyard, all was hurry and driving. There were in the yard about one hundred men; of these, sev-

Source: Frederick Douglass, *The Life and Times of Frederick Douglass.* (Hartford, 1882), pp. 202–219, 223–227.

enty or eighty were regular carpenters—privileged men. There was no time for a raw hand to learn anything. Every man had to do that which he knew how to do, and in entering the yard Mr. Gardiner had directed me to do whatever the carpenters told me to do. This was placing me at the beck and call of about seventy-five men. I was to regard all these as my masters. Their word was to be my law. My situation was a trying one. I was called a dozen ways in the space of a single minute. I needed a dozen pairs of hands. Three or four voices would strike my ear at the same moment. It was "Fred, come help to cant this timber here,"—"Fred, come carry this timber yonder,"—"Fred, bring that roller here,"—"Fred, go get a fresh can of water,"—"Fred, come help saw off the end of this timber,"—"Fred, go quick and get the crow-bar,"—"Fred, hold on the end of this fall,"—"Fred, go to the blacksmith's shop and get a new punch,"—"Halloo, Fred! run and bring me a cold chisel,"—"I say, Fred, bear a hand, and get up a fire under the steam box as quick as lightning,"—"Hullo, nigger! come turn this grindstone,"—"Come, come, move, move! and bowse this timber forward,"—"I say, darkey, blast your eyes! why don't you heat up some pitch?"—"Halloo! halloo! halloo! (three voices at the same time)"—"Come here; go there; hold on where you are. D—n you, if you move I'll knock your brains out!" Such, my dear reader, is a glance at the school which was mine during the first eight months of my stay at Gardiner's shipyard.

At the end of eight months Master Hugh refused longer to allow me to remain with Gardiner. The circumstance which led to this refusal was the committing of an outrage upon me, by the white apprentices of the shipyard. The fight was a desperate one, and I came out of it shockingly mangled. I was cut and bruised in sundry places, and my left eye was nearly knocked out of its socket. The facts which led to this brutal outrage upon me illustrate a phase of slavery which was destined to become an important element in the overthrow of the slave system, and I may

therefore state them with some minuteness. That phase was this—the conflict of slavery with the interests of white mechanics and laborers. In the country this conflict was not so apparent, but in cities, such as Baltimore, Richmond, New Orleans, Mobile, etc., it was seen pretty clearly. The slaveholders, with a craftiness peculiar to themselves, by encouraging the enmity of the poor laboring white man against the blacks, succeeded in making the said white man almost as much a slave as the black slave himself. The difference between the white slave and the black slave was this: the latter belonged to one slaveholder, while the former belonged to the slaveholders collectively. The white slave had taken from him by indirection what the black slave had taken from him directly and without ceremony. Both were plundered, and by the same plunderers. The slave was robbed by his master of all his earnings, above what was required for his bare physical necessities, and the white laboring man was robbed by the slave system of the just results of his labor, because he was flung into competition with a class of laborers who worked without wages. The slaveholders blinded them to this competition by keeping alive their prejudice against the slaves as *men*—not against them as *slaves*. They appealed to their pride, often denouncing emancipation as tending to place the white working man on an equality with Negroes, and by this means they succeeded in drawing off the minds of the poor whites from the real fact, that by the rich slave-master they were already regarded as but a single remove from equality with the slave. The impression was cunningly made that slavery was the only power that could prevent the laboring white man from falling to the level of the slave's poverty and degradation. To make this enmity deep and broad between the slave and the poor white man, the latter was allowed to abuse and whip the former without hindrance. But, as I have said, this state of affairs prevailed mostly in the country. In the City of Baltimore there were not unfrequent murmurs that educating slaves to be mechanics might, in the end, give slave-masters power to dispense altogether with the services of the poor white man. But with characteristic dread of offending the slaveholders, these poor white mechanics in Mr. Gardiner's shipyard, instead of applying the natural, honest remedy for the apprehended evil, and objecting at once to work there by the side of the slaves, made a cowardly attack upon the free colored mechanics, saying they were eating the bread which should be eaten by American freemen, and swearing that they, the mechanics, would not work with them. The feeling was really against having their labor brought into competition with that of the colored freeman, and aimed to prevent him from serving himself, in the evening of life, with the trade with which he had served his master, during the more vigorous portion of his days. Had they succeeded in driving the black freemen out of the shipyard, they would have determined also upon the removal of the black slaves. The feeling was, about this time, very bitter toward all colored people in Baltimore (1836), and they—free and slave—suffered all manner of insult and wrong.

Until a very little while before I went there, white and black carpenters worked side by side in the shipyards of Mr. Gardiner, Mr. Duncan, Mr. Walter Price, and Mr. Robb. Nobody seemed to see any impropriety in it. Some of the blacks were first-rate workmen and were given jobs requiring the highest skill. All at once, however, the white carpenters swore that they would no longer work on the same stage with Negroes. Taking advantage of the heavy contract resting upon Mr. Gardiner to have the vessels for Mexico ready to launch in July, and of the difficulty of getting other hands at that season of the year, they swore that they would not strike another blow for him unless he would discharge his free colored workmen. Now, although this movement did not extend to me *in form*, it did reach me in *fact*. The spirit which is awakened was one of malice and bitterness toward colored people

generally, and I suffered with the rest, and suffered severely. My fellow-apprentices very soon began to feel it to be degrading to work with me. They began to put on high looks and to talk contemptuously and maliciously of "the niggers," saying that they would take the "country," and that they "ought to be killed." Encouraged by workmen who, knowing me to be a slave, made no issue with Mr. Gardiner about my being there, these young men did their utmost to make it impossible for me to stay. They seldom called me to do anything without coupling the call with a curse, and Edward North, the biggest in everything, rascality included, ventured to strike me, whereupon I picked him up and threw him into the dock. Whenever any of them struck me I struck back again, regardless of consequences. I could manage any of them singly, and so long as I could keep them from combining I got on very well.

In the conflict which ended my stay at Mr. Gardiner's I was beset by four of them at once—Ned North, Ned Hayes, Bill Stewart, and Tom Humphreys. Two of them were as large as myself, and they came near killing me, in broad daylight. One came in front, armed with a brick; there was one at each side and one behind, and they closed up all around me. I was struck on all sides, and while I was attending to those in front I received a blow on my head from behind, dealt with a heavy handspike. I was completely stunned by the blow, and fell heavily on the ground among the timbers. Taking advantage of my fall they rushed upon me and began to pound me with their fists. With a view of gaining strength, I let them lay on for awhile after I came to myself. They had done me little damage, so far, but finally getting tired of that sport I gave a sudden surge, and despite their weight I rose to my hands and knees. Just as I did this one of their number planted a blow with his boot in my left eye, which for a time, seemed to have burst my eyeball. When they saw my eye completely closed, my face covered with blood, and I staggering under the stunning blows they had given me, they left me. As soon as I gathered strength I picked up the handspike and madly enough attempted to pursue them, but here the carpenters interfered and compelled me to give up my pursuit. It was impossible to stand against so many.

Dear reader, you can hardly believe the statement, but it is true and therefore I write it down—that no fewer than fifty white men stood by and saw this brutal and shameful outrage committed, and not a man of them all interposed a single word of mercy. There were four against one, and that one's face was beaten and battered most horribly, and no one said, "That is enough," but some cried out, "Kill him! kill him! kill the d—n nigger! knock his brains out! he struck a white person!" I mention this inhuman outcry to show the character of the men and the spirit of the times at Gardiner's shipyard, and, indeed, in Baltimore generally, in 1836. As I look back to this period, I am almost amazed that I was not murdered outright, so murderous was the spirit which prevailed there. On two other occasions while there I came near losing my life. On one of these, I was driving bolts in the hold through the keelson, with Hayes. In its course the bolt bent. Hayes cursed me and said that it was my blow which bent the bolt. I denied this and charged it upon him. In a fit of rage he seized an adze and darted toward me. I met him with a maul and parried his blow, or I should have lost my life.

After the united attack of North, Stewart, Hayes, and Humphreys, finding that the carpenters were as bitter toward me as the apprentices, and that the latter were probably set on by the former, I found my only chance for life was in flight. I succeeded in getting away without an additional blow. To strike a white man was death by lynch law, in Gardiner's shipyard, nor was there much of any other law toward the colored people at that time in any other part of Maryland.

After making my escape from the shipyard I went straight home and related my story to Master Hugh, and to his credit I say it, that his conduct, though he was not a religious man, was every way more humane than that of his brother Thomas, when I went to him in a somewhat similar plight, from the hands of his "Brother Edward Covey." Master Hugh listened attentively to my narration of the circumstances leading to the ruffianly assault, and gave many evidences of his strong indignation at what was done. He was a rough but manly-hearted fellow, and at this time his best nature showed itself.

The heart of my once kind mistress Sophia was again melted in pity towards me. My puffed-out eye and my scarred and blood-covered face moved the dear lady to tears. She kindly drew a chair by me, and with friendly and consoling words, she took water and washed the blood from my face. No mother's hand could have been more tender than hers. She bound up my head and covered my wounded eye with a lean piece of fresh beef. It was almost compensation for all I suffered, that it occasioned the manifestation once more of the originally characteristic kindness of my mistress. Her affectionate heart was not yet dead, though much hardened by time and circumstances.

As for Master Hugh, he was furious, and gave expression to his feelings in the forms of speech usual in that locality. He poured curses on the whole of the shipyard company, and swore that he would have satisfaction. His indignation was really strong and healthy, but unfortunately it resulted from the thought that his rights of property, in my person, had not been respected, more than from any sense of the outrage perpetrated upon me *as a man*. I had reason to think this from the fact that he could, himself, beat and mangle when it suited him to do so.

Bent on having satisfaction, as he said, just as soon as I got a little the better of my bruises, Master Hugh took me to Esquire Watson's office on Bond street, Fell's Point, with a view to procuring the arrest of those who had assaulted me. He gave to the magistrate an account of the outrage as I had related it to him, and seemed to expect that a warrant would at once be issued for the arrest of the lawless ruffians. Mr. Watson heard all that he had to say, then coolly inquired, "Mr. Auld, who saw this assault of which you speak?" "It was done, sir, in the presence of a shipyard full of hands." "Sir," said Mr. Watson, "I am sorry, but I cannot move in this matter, except upon the oath of white witnesses." "But here's the boy; look at his head and face," said the excited Master Hugh; "*they* show what has been done." But Watson insisted that he was not authorized to do anything, unless white witnesses of the transaction would come forward and testify to what had taken place. He could issue no warrant, on my word, against white persons, and if I had been killed in the presence of a *thousand blacks*, their testimony combined would have been insufficient to condemn a single murderer. Master Hugh was compelled to say, for once, that this state of things was too bad, and he left the office of the magistrate disgusted.

Of course it was impossible to get any white man to testify against my assailants. The carpenters saw what was done, but the actors were but the agents of their malice, and did only what the carpenters sanctioned. They had cried with one accord, "Kill the nigger! kill the nigger!" Even those who may have pitied me, if any such were among them, lacked the moral courage to volunteer their evidence. The slightest show of sympathy or justice toward a person of color was denounced as abolitionism, and the name of abolitionist subjected its hearer to frightful liabilities. "D——n abolitionists," and "kill the niggers," were the watchwords of the foul-mouthed ruffians of those days. Nothing was done, and probably would not have been, had I been killed in the affray. The laws and the morals of the Christian city of Baltimore afforded no protection to the sable denizens of that city.

Master Hugh, on finding that he could get no redress for the cruel wrong, withdrew me from the employment of Mr. Gardiner and took me into his own family, Mrs. Auld kindly taking care of me and dressing my wounds until they were healed and I was ready to go to work again.

While I was on the Eastern Shore, Master Hugh had met with reverses which overthrew his business and had given up shipbuilding in his own yard, on the City Block, and was now acting as foreman of Mr. Walter Price. The best that he could do for me was to take me into Mr. Price's yard, and afford me the facilities there for completing the trade which I began to learn at Gardiner's. Here I rapidly became expert in the use of calkers' tools, and in the course of a single year, I was able to command the highest wages paid to journeymen calkers in Baltimore.

The reader will observe that I was not of some pecuniary value to my master. During the busy season I was bringing six and seven dollars per week. I have sometimes brought him as much as nine dollars a week, for wages were a dollar and a half per day.

After learning to calk, I sought my own employment, made my own contracts, and collected my own earnings—giving Master Hugh no trouble in any part of the transactions to which I was a party.

Here, then, were better days for the Eastern Shore slave. I was free from the vexatious assaults of the apprentices at Gardiner's, free from the perils of plantation life, and once more in favorable condition to increase my little stock of education, which had been at a dead stand since my removal from Baltimore. I had on the Eastern Shore been only a teacher, when in company with other slaves, but now there were colored persons here who could instruct me. Many of the young calkers could read, write, and cipher. Some of them had high notions about mental improvement, and the free ones on Fell's Point organized what they called the "East Baltimore Mental Improvement Society." To this society, notwithstanding it was intended that only free persons should attach themselves, I was admitted, and was several times assigned a prominent part in its debates. I owe much to the society of these young men.

The reader already knows enough of the ill effects of good treatment on a slave to anticipate what was now the case in my improved condition. It was not long before I began to show signs of disquiet with slavery, and to look around for means to get out of it by the shortest route. I was living among freemen, and was in all respects equal to them by nature and attainments. Why should I be a slave? There was no reason why I should be the thrall of any man. Besides, I was now getting, as I have said, a dollar and fifty cents per day. I contracted for it, worked for it, collected it; it was paid to me, and it was rightfully my own; and yet upon every returning Saturday night, this money—my own hard earnings, every cent of it—was demanded of me and taken from me by Master Hugh. He did not earn it—he had no hand in earning it—why, then should he have it? I owed him nothing. He had given me no schooling, and I had received from him only my food and raiment, and for these, my services were supposed to pay from the first. The right to take my earnings was the right of the robber. He had the power to compel me to give him the fruits of my labor, and this *power* was his only right in the case. I became more and more dissatisfied with this state of things, and in so becoming I only gave proof of the same human nature which every reader of this chapter in my life—slaveholder, or non-slaveholder—is conscious of possessing.

To make a contented slave, you must make a thoughtless one. It is necessary to darken his moral and mental vision, and, as far as possible, to annihilate his power of reason. He must be able to detect no inconsistencies in slavery. The man who takes his earnings must be able to convince him that he has a perfect right to do so. It must not depend upon mere force—the slave must know no higher law than his master's will. The whole relationship must not only demonstrate to his mind its necessity, but its absolute rightfulness. If there be one crevice through which a single drop can fall, it will certainly rust off the slave's chain. . . .

My condition during the year of my escape (1838) was comparatively a free and easy one, so far, at least, as the wants of the physical man were concerned, but the reader will bear in mind that my troubles from the beginning had been less physical than mental, and he will thus be prepared to find that slave life was adding nothing to its charms for me as I grew older, and became more and more acquainted with it. The practice of openly robbing me, from week to week, of all my earnings, kept the nature and character of slavery constantly before me. I could be robbed by indirection, but this was too open and barefaced to be endured. I could see no reason why I should, at the end of each week, pour the reward of my honest toil into the purse of my master. My obligation to do this vexed me, and the manner in which Master Hugh received my wages vexed me yet more. Carefully counting the money, and rolling it out dollar by dollar, he would look me in the face, as if he would search my heart as well as my pocket, and reproachfully ask me, "Is that all?"—implying that I had perhaps kept back part of my wages, or, if not so, the demand was made possibly to make me feel that after all, I was an "unprofitable servant." Draining me of the last cent of my hard earnings, he would, however, occasionally, when I brought home an extra large sum, dole out to me a sixpence or shilling, with a view, perhaps, of kindling my gratitude. But it had the opposite effect. It was an admission of my right to the whole sum. The fact that he gave me any part of my wages, was proof that he suspected I had a right to the whole of them, and I always felt uncomfortable after having received anything in this way, lest his giving me a few cents might possibly ease his conscience, and make him feel himself to be a pretty honorable robber after all.

Held to a strict account, and kept under a close watch—the old suspicion of my running away not having been entirely removed—to accomplish my escape seemed a very difficult thing. The railroad from Baltimore to Philadelphia was under regulations so stringent that even *free* colored travelers were almost excluded. They must have free papers; they must be measured and carefully examined before they could enter the cars, and could go only in the daytime, even when so examined. The steamboats were under regulations equally stringent. And still more, and worse than all, all the great turnpikes leading northward were beset with kidnappers—a class of men who watched the newspapers for advertisements for runaway slaves, thus making their living by the accursed reward of slave-hunting.

My discontent grew upon me, and I was on a constant lookout for means to get away. With money I could easily have managed the matter, and from this consideration I hit upon the plan of soliciting the privilege of hiring my time. It was quite common in Baltimore to allow slaves this privilege, and was the practice also in New Orleans. A slave who was considered trustworthy could, by regularly paying his master a definite sum at the end of each week, dispose of his time as he liked. It so happened that I was not in very good odor, and was far from being a trustworthy slave. Nevertheless, I watched my opportunity when Master Thomas came to Baltimore (for I was still his property, Hugh only acting as his agent), in the spring of 1838, to purchase his spring supply of goods, and applied to him directly for the much coveted privilege of hiring my time. This request Master Thomas unhesitatingly refused to grant and charged me, with some sternes, with inventing this strategem to make my escape. He told me I could go nowhere but he would catch me, and, in the event of my running away, I might be assured that he should spare no pains in his efforts to recapture me. He recounted, with a good deal of eloquence, the many kind offices he had done me, and exhorted me to be contented and obedient. "Lay out no plans for the future," said he. "If you behave yourself properly, I will take care of you." Kind and considerate as this offer was, it failed to soothe me into repose. In spite of all Master Thomas had said and in spite of my own efforts to the contrary, the injustice and wicked-ness of slavery were always uppermost in my thoughts and strengthening my purpose to make my escape at the earliest moment possible.

About two months after applying to Master Thomas for the privilege of hiring my time, I applied to Master Hugh for the same liberty, supposing him to be unacquainted with the fact that I had made a similar application to Master Thomas and had been refused. My boldness in making this request fairly astounded him at first. He gazed at me in amazement. But I had many good reasons for pressing the matter, and, after listening to them awhile, he did not absolutely refuse but told me that he would think of it. There was hope for me in this. Once master of my own time, I felt sure that I could make, over and above my obligation to him, a dollar or two every week. Some slaves had, in this way, made enough to purchase their freedom. It was a sharp spur to their industry, and some of the most enterprising colored men in Baltimore hired themselves in that way.

After mature reflection, as I suppose it was, Master Hugh granted me the privilege in question, on the following terms: I was to be allowed all my time; to make all bargains for work, and to collect my own wages; and in return for this liberty, I was required or obliged to pay him three dollars at the end of each week, and to board and clothe myself, and buy my own calking tools. A failure in any of these particulars would put an end to the privilege. This was a hard bargain. The wear and tear of clothing, the losing and breaking of tools, and the expense of board, made it necessary for me to earn at least six dollars per week to keep even with the world. All who are acquainted with calking know how uncertain and irregular that employment is. It can be done to advantage only in dry weather, for it is useless to put wet oakum into a ship's seam. Rain or shine, however, work or no work, at the end of each week the money must be forthcoming.

Master Hugh seemed, for a time, much pleased with this arrangement, and well he might be, for it was decidedly in his favor. It relieved him of all anxiety concerning me. His money was sure. He had armed my love of liberty with a lash and a driver far more efficient than any I had before known, for, while by this arrangement, he derived all the benefits of slave-holding without its evils, I endured all the evils of being a slave, and yet suffered all the care and anxiety of a responsible freeman. "Nevertheless," thought I, "it is a valuable privilege—another step in my career toward freedom." It was something even to be permitted to stagger under the disadvantages of liberty, and I was determined to hold on to the newly gained footing by all proper industry. I was ready to work by night as by day, and being in the possession of excellent health, I was not only able to meet my current expenses, but also to lay by a small sum at the end of each week. All went on thus from the month of May till August; then, for reasons which will become apparent as I proceed, my much valued liberty was wrested from me.

During the week previous to this calamitous event, I had made arrangements with a few young friends to accompany them on Saturday night to a camp meeting, to be held about twelve miles from Baltimore. On the evening of our intended start for the campground, something occurred in the shipyard where I was at work which detained me unusually late, and compelled me either to disappoint my friends, or to neglect carrying my weekly dues to Master Hugh. Knowing that I had the money and could hand it to him on another day, I decided to go to camp-meeting and, on my return, to pay him the three dollars for the past week. Once on the campground, I was induced to remain one day longer than I had intended when I left home. But as soon as I returned I went directly to his home on Fell Street to hand him his (my) money. Unhappily the fatal mistake had been made. I found him exceedingly angry. He exhibited all the signs of apprehension and wrath which a slaveholder might be surmised to exhibit on the supposed escape of a favorite slave. "You rascal! I have a great mind to give you a sound whipping. How dare you go out

of the city without first asking and obtaining my permission?" "Sir," I said, "I hired my time and paid you the price you asked for it. I did not know that it was any part of the bargain that I should ask you when or where I should go." "You did not know, you rascal! You are bound to show yourself here every Saturday night." After reflecting a few moments, he became somewhat cooled down, but, evidently greatly troubled, said: "Now, you scoundrel, you have done for yourself; you shall hire your time no longer. The next thing I shall hear of will be your running away. Bring home your tools at once. I'll teach you how to go off in this way."

Thus ended my partial freedom. I could hire my time no longer. I obeyed my master's orders at once. The little taste of liberty which I had had—although as it will be seen, that taste was far from being unalloyed—by no means enhanced my contentment with slavery. Punished by Master Hugh, it was now my turn to punish him. "Since," thought I, "you will make a slave of me, I will await your order in all things." So, instead of going to look for work on Monday morning, as I had formerly done, I remained at home during the entire week, without the performance of a single stroke of work. Saturday night came, and he called upon me as usual for my wages. I, of course, told him I had done no work, and had no wages. Here we were at the point of coming to blows. His wrath had been accumulating during the whole week, for he evidently saw that I was making no effort to get work, but was most aggravatingly awaiting his orders in all things. As I look back to this behavior of mine, I scarcely know what possessed me, thus to trifle with one who had such unlimited power to bless or blast me. Master Hugh raved, and swore he would "get hold of me," but wisely for him, and happily for me, his wrath employed only those harmless, impalpable missiles which roll from a limber tongue. In my desperation I had fully made up my mind to measure strength with him in case he should attempt to execute his threat. I am glad there was no occasion for this, for resistance to him could not have ended so happily for me as it did in the case of Covey. Master Hugh was not a man to be safely resisted by a slave, and I freely own that in my conduct toward him, in this instance, there was more folly than wisdom. He closed his reproofs by telling me that hereafter I need give myself no uneasiness about getting work—he would himself see to getting work for me, and enough of it at that. This threat, I confess, had some terror in it, and on thinking the matter over during the Sunday, I resolved not only to save him the trouble of getting me work, but that on the third day of September I would attempt to make my escape. His refusal to allow me to hire my time therefore hastened the period of my flight. I had three weeks in which to prepare for my journey.

Once resolved, I felt a certain degree of repose, and on Monday morning, instead of waiting for Master Hugh to seek employment for me, I was up by break of day, and off to the shipyard of Mr. Butler, on the City Block, near the drawbridge. I was a favorite with Mr. Butler, and, young as I was, I had served as his foreman, on the float stage, at calking. Of course I easily obtained work, and at the end of the week, which, by the way, was exceedingly fine, I brought Master Hugh nine dollars. The effect of this mark of returning good sense on my part was excellent. He was very much pleased; he took the money, commended me, and told me that I might have done the same thing the week before. It is a blessed thing that the tyrant may not always know the thoughts and purposes of his victim. Master Hugh little knew my plans. The going to camp meeting without asking his permission, the insolent answers to his reproaches, and the sulky deportment of the week after being deprived of the privilege of hiring my time, had awakened the suspicion that I might be cherishing disloyal purposes. My object, therefore, in working steadily was to remove suspicion, and in this I succeeded admirably. He probably thought that I was never better satisfied with my condition than at the very time I was planning my escape. The second week

passed, and I again carried him my full week's wages—*nine dollars*—and so well pleased was he that he gave me *twenty-five cents!* and bade me "make good use of it." I told him I would do so, for one of the uses to which I intended to put it was to pay my fare on the "underground railroad."

Things without went on as usual, but I was passing through the same internal excitement and anxiety which I had experienced two years and a half before. The failure in that instance was not calculated to increase my confidence in the success of this, my second attempt, and I knew that a second failure could not leave me where my first did. I must either get to the far north or be sent to the far south. Besides the exercise of mind from this state of facts, I had the painful sensation of being about to separate from a circle of honest and warm-hearted friends. The thought of such a separation, where the hope of ever meeting again was excluded, and where there could be no correspondence, was very painful. It is my opinion that thousands more would have escaped from slavery but for the strong affection which bound them to their families, relatives, and friends. The daughter was hindered by the love she bore her mother and the father by the love he bore his wife and children, and so on to the end of the chapter. I had no relations in Baltimore, and I saw no probability of ever living in the neighborhood of sisters and brothers, but the thought of leaving my friends was the strongest obstacle to my running away. The last two days of the week, Friday and Saturday, were spent mostly in collecting my things together for my journey. Having worked four days that week for my master, I handed him six dollars on Saturday night. I seldom spent my Sundays at home, and for fear that something might be discovered in my conduct, I kept up my custom and absented myself all day. On Monday, the third day of September, 1838, in accordance with my resolution, I bade farewell to the city of Baltimore, and to that slavery which had been my abhorrence from childhood. . . .

It was the custom in the State of Maryland to require of the free colored people to have what were called free papers. This instrument they were required to renew very often, and by charging a fee for this writing, considerable sums from time to time were collected by the State. In these papers the name, age, color, height, and form of the free man were described, together with any scars or other marks upon his person which could assist in his identification. This device of slaveholding ingenuity, like other devices of wickedness, in some measure defeated itself—since more than one man could be found to answer the same general description. Hence many slaves could escape by personating the owner of one set of papers, and this was often done as follows: A slave nearly or sufficiently answering the description set forth in the papers, would borrow or hire them till he could by their means escape to a free state, and then, by mail or otherwise, return them to the owner. The operation was a hazardous one for the lender as well as for the borrower. A failure on the part of the fugitive to send back the papers would imperil his benefactor, and the discovery of the papers in possession of the wrong man would imperil both the fugitive and his friend. It was therefore an act of supreme trust on the part of a freeman of color thus to put in jeopardy his own liberty that another might be free. It was, however, not unfrequently bravely done, and was seldom discovered. I was not so fortunate as to sufficiently resemble any of my free acquaintances as to answer the description of their papers. But I had one friend—a sailor—who owned a sailor's protection, which answered somewhat the purpose of free papers—describing his person and certifying to the fact that he was a free American sailor. The instrument had at its head the American eagle, which at once gave it the appearance of an authorized document. This protection did not, when in my hands, describe its bearer very accurately. Indeed, it called for a man much darker than myself, and close examination of it would have caused my arrest at the start.

In order to avoid this fatal scrutiny in the part of the railroad official, I had arranged with Isaac Rolls, a hackman, to bring my baggage to the train just on the moment of starting, and jumped upon the car myself when the train was already in motion. Had I gone into the station and offered to purchase a ticket, I should have been instantly and carefully examined, and undoubtedly arrested. In choosing this plan upon which to act, I considered the jostle of the train, and the natural haste of the conductor in a train crowded with passengers, and relied upon my skill and address in playing the sailor as described in my protection, to do the rest. One element in my favor was the kind feeling which prevailed in Baltimore and other seaports at the time, towards "those who go down to the sea in ships." "Free trade and sailors' rights" expressed the sentiment of the country just then. In my clothing I was rigged out in sailor style. I had on a red shirt and a tarpaulin hat and black cravat, tied in sailor fashion, carelessly and loosely about my neck. My knowledge of ships and sailors' talk came much to my assistance, for I knew a ship from stem to stern, and from keelson to crosstrees, and could talk sailor like an "old salt."

On sped the train, and I was well on the way to Havre de Grace before the conductor came into the Negro car to collect tickets and examine the papers of his black passengers. This was a critical moment in the drama. My whole future depended upon the decision of this conductor. Agitated I was while this ceremony was proceeding, but still, externally at least, I was apparently calm and self-possessed. He went on with his duty—examining several colored passengers before reaching me. He was somewhat harsh in tone and peremptory in manner until he reached me, when, strangely enough, and to my surprise and relief, his whole manner changed. Seeing that I did not readily produce my free papers, as the other colored persons in the car had done, he said to me in a friendly contrast with that observed towards the others, "I suppose you have your free papers?" To which I answered.

"No, sir; I never carry my free papers to sea with me." "But you have something to show that you are a free man, have you not?" "Yes, sir," I answered; "I have a paper with the American eagle on it, that will carry me round the world." With this I drew from my deep sailor's pocket my seaman's protection, as before described. The merest glance at the paper satisfied him, and he took my fare and went on about his business. This moment of time was one of the most anxious I ever experienced. Had the conductor looked closely at the paper, he could not have failed to discover that it called for a very different looking person from myself, and in that case it would have been his duty to arrest me on the instant and send me back to Baltimore from the first station. When he left me with the assurance that I was all right, though much relieved, I realized that I was still in great danger—I was still in Maryland, and subject to arrest at any moment. I saw on the train several persons who would have known me in any other clothes, and I feared they might recognize me, even in my sailor rig, and report me to the conductor, who would then subject me to a closer examination, which I knew well would be fatal to me.

Though I was not a murderer fleeing from justice, I felt, perhaps, quite as miserable as such a criminal. The train was moving at a very high rate of speed for that time of railroad travel, but to my anxious mind, it was moving far too slowly. Minutes were hours, and hours were days during this part of my flight. After Maryland I was to pass through Delaware—another slave state, where slavecatchers generally awaited their prey, for it was not in the interior of the state, but on its borders, that these human hounds were most vigilant and active. The border lines between slavery and freedom were the dangerous ones for the fugitives. The heart of no fox or deer, with hungry hounds on his trail, in full chase, could have beaten more anxiously or noisily than did mine from the time I left Baltimore till I reached Philadelphia. The passage of the Susquehanna River at Havre de Grace was at that time made by ferryboat, on board of which I met a young colored man by the name of Nichols, who came very near betraying me. He was a hand on the boat, but instead of minding his own business, he insisted upon knowing me, and asking me dangerous questions as to where I was going, and when I was coming back, etc. I got away from my old and inconvenient acquaintance as soon as I could decently do so, and went to another part of the boat. Once across the river I encountered a new danger. Only a few days before I had been at work on a revenue cutter, in Mr. Price's shipyard, under the care of Captain McGowan. On the meeting at this point of the two trains, the one going south stopped on the track just opposite to the one going north, and it so happened that this Captain McGowan sat at a window where he could see me very distinctly, and would certainly have recognized me had he looked at me but for a second. Fortunately, in the hurry of the moment, he did not see me, and the trains soon passed each other on their respective ways. But this was not the only hair-breadth escape. A German blacksmith, whom I knew well, was on the train with me, and looked at me very intently as if he thought he had seen me somewhere before in his travels. I really believe he knew me, but had no heart to betray me. At any rate he saw me escaping and held his peace.

The last point of imminent danger, and the one I dreaded most, was Wilmington. Here we left the train and took the steamboat for Philadelphia. In making the change I again apprehended arrest, but no one disturbed me, and I was soon on the broad and beautiful Delaware, speeding away to the Quaker City. On reaching Philadelphia in the afternoon I inquired of a colored man how I could get on to New York? He directed me to the Willow Street depot, and thither I went, taking the train that night. I reached New York Tuesday morning, having completed the journey in less than twenty-four hours. Such is briefly the manner of my escape from slavery—and the end of my experience as a slave. . . .

Twelve Years a Slave: Narrative of Solomon Northrup

Solomon Northrup

After we were all on board, the brig Orleans proceeded down James River. Passing into Chesapeake Bay, we arrived next day opposite the city of Norfolk. While lying at anchor, a lighter approached us from the town, bringing four more slaves. Frederick, a boy of eighteen, had been born a slave, as also had Henry, who was some years older. They had both been house servants in the city. Maria was a rather genteel looking colored girl, with a faultless form, but ignorant and extremely vain. The idea of going to New-Orleans was pleasing to her. She entertained an extravagantly high opinion of her own attractions. Assuming a haughty mien, she declared to her companions, that immediately on our arrival in New-Orleans, she had no doubt, some wealthy single gentleman of good taste would purchase her at once!

But the most prominent of the four, was a man named Arthur. As the lighter approached, he struggled stoutly with his keepers. It was with main force that he was dragged aboard the brig. He protested, in a loud voice, against the treatment he was receiving, and demanded to be released. His face was swollen, and covered with wounds and bruises, and, indeed, one side of it was a complete raw sore. He was forced, with all haste, down the hatchway into the hold. I caught an outline of his story as he was borne struggling along, of which he afterwards gave me a more full relation, and it was as follows: He had long resided in the city of Norfolk, and was a free man. He had a family living there, and was a mason by

trade. Having been unusually detained, he was returning late one night to his house in the suburbs of the city, when he was attacked by a gang of persons in an unfrequented street. He fought until his strength failed him. Overpowered at last, he was gagged and bound with ropes, and beaten, until he became insensible. For several days they secreted him in the slave pen at Norfolk—a very common establishment, it appears, in the cities of the South. The night before, he had been taken out and put on board the lighter, which, pushing out from shore, had awaited our arrival. For some time he continued his protestations, and was altogether irreconcilable. At length, however, he became silent. He sank into a gloomy and thoughtful mood, and appeared to be counseling with himself. There was in the man's determined face, something that suggested the thought of desperation.

After leaving Norfolk the hand-cuffs were taken off, and during the day we were allowed to remain on deck. The captain selected Robert as his waiter, and I was appointed to superintend the cooking department and the distribution of food and water. I had three assistants, Jim, Cuffee and Jenny. Jenny's business was to prepare the coffee, which consisted of corn meal scorched in a kettle, boiled and sweetened with molasses. Jim and Cuffee baked the hoe-cake and boiled the bacon.

Standing by a table, formed of a wide board resting on the heads of the barrels, I cut and handed to each a slice of meat and a "dodger" of the bread, and from Jenny's kettle also dipped out for each a cup of the coffee. The use of plates was dispensed with, and their sable fingers took the place of knives and forks. Jim and Cuffee were very demure and attentive to business, somewhat

Source: Solomon Northrup, *Twelve Years a Slave: Narrative of Solomon Northrup.* (Auburn and Buffalo, 1854), pp. 65–78, 161–175, 208–222.

inflated with their situations as second cooks, and without doubt feeling that there was a great responsibility resting on them. I was called steward—a name given me by the captain.

The slaves were fed twice a day, at ten and five o'clock—always receiving the same kind and quantity of fare, and in the same manner as above described. At night we were driven into the hold, and securely fastened down.

Scarcely were we out of sight of land before we were overtaken by a violent storm. The brig rolled and plunged, until we feared she would go down. Some were sea-sick, others on their knees praying, while some were fast holding to each other, paralyzed with fear. The sea-sickness rendered the place of our confinement loathsome and disgusting. It would have been a happy thing for most of us—it would have saved the agony of many hundred lashes, and miserable deaths at last—had the compassionate sea snatched us that day from the clutches of remorseless men. The thought of Randall and little Emmy sinking down among the monsters of the deep is a more pleasant contemplation than to think of them as they are now, perhaps, dragging out lives of unrequited toil.

When in sight of the Bahama Banks, at a place called Old Point Compass, or the Hole in the Wall, we were becalmed three days. There was scarcely a breath of air. The waters of the gulf presented a singularly white appearance, like lime water.

In the order of events, I come now to the relation of an occurrence, which I never call to mind but with sensations of regret. I thank God, who has since permitted me to escape from the thralldom of slavery, that through his merciful interposition I was prevented from imbruing my hands in the blood of his creatures. Let not those who have never been placed in like circumstances, judge me harshly. Until they have been chained and beaten—until they find themselves in the situation I was, borne away from home and family towards a land of bondage—let them refrain from saying what they would not do for liberty. How far I should have been justified in the sight of God and man, it is unnecessary now to speculate upon. It is enough to say that I am able to congratulate myself upon the harmless termination of an affair which threatened, for a time, to be attended with serious results.

Towards evening, on the first day of the calm, Arthur and myself were in the bow of the vessel, seated on the windlass. We were conversing together of the probable destiny that awaited us, and mourning together over our misfortunes. Arthur said, and I agreed with him, that death was far less terrible than the living prospect that was before us. For a long time we talked of our children, our past lives, and of the probabilities of escape. Obtaining possession of the brig was suggested by one of us. We discussed the possibility of our being able, in such an event, to make our way to the harbor of New-York. I knew little of the compass; but the idea of risking the experiment was eagerly entertained. The chances, for and against us, in an encounter with the crew, was canvassed. Who could be relied upon, and who could not, the proper time and manner of the attack, were all talked over and over again. From the moment the plot suggested itself I began to hope. I revolved it constantly in my mind. As difficulty after difficulty arose, some ready conceit was at hand, demonstrating how it could be overcome. While others slept, Arthur and I were maturing our plans. At length, with much caution, Robert was gradually made acquainted with our intentions. He approved of them at once, and entered into the conspiracy with a zealous spirit. There was not another slave we dared to trust. Brought up in fear and ignorance as they are, it can scarcely be conceived how servilely they will cringe before a white man's look. It was not safe to deposit so bold a secret with any of them, and finally we three resolved to take upon ourselves alone the fearful responsibility of the attempt.

At night, as has been said, we were driven into the hold, and the hatch barred down. How to reach the deck was the first difficulty that presented itself. On the bow of the brig, however, I had observed the small boat lying bottom upwards. It occurred to me that by secreting ourselves underneath it, we would not be missed from the crowd, as they were hurried down into the hold at night. I was selected to make the experiment, in order to satisfy ourselves of its feasibility. The next evening, accordingly, after supper, watching my opportunity, I hastily concealed myself beneath it. Lying close upon the deck, I could see what was going on around me, while wholly unperceived myself. In the morning, as they came up, I slipped from my hiding place without being observed. The result was entirely satisfactory.

The captain and mate slept in the cabin of the former. From Robert, who had frequent occasion, in his capacity of waiter, to make observations in that quarter, we ascertained the exact position of their respective berths. He further informed us that there were always two pistols and a cutlass lying on the table. The crew's cook slept in the cook galley on deck, a sort of vehicle on wheels, that could be moved about as convenience required, while the sailors, numbering only six, either slept in the forecastle, or in hammocks swung among the rigging.

Finally our arrangements were all completed. Arthur and I were to steal silently to the captain's cabin, seize the pistols and cutlass, and as quickly as possible despatch him and the mate. Robert, with a club, was to stand by the door leading from the deck into the cabin, and, in case of necessity, beat back the sailors, until we could hurry to his assistance. We were to proceed then as circumstances might require. Should the attack be so sudden and successful as to prevent resistance, the hatch was to remain barred down; otherwise the slaves were to be called up, and in the crowd, and hurry, and confusion of the time, we resolved to regain our liberty

or lose our lives. I was then to assume the unaccustomed place of pilot, and, steering northward, we trusted that some lucky wind might bear us to the soil of freedom.

The mate's name was Biddee, the captain's I cannot now recall, though I rarely ever forget a name once heard. The captain was a small, genteel man, erect and prompt, with a proud bearing, and looked the personification of courage. If he is still living, and these pages should chance to meet his eye, he will learn a fact connected with the voyage of the brig, from Richmond to New Orleans, in 1841, not entered on his log-book.

We were all prepared, and impatiently waiting an opportunity of putting our designs into execution, when they were frustrated by a sad and unforeseen event. Robert was taken ill. It was soon announced that he had the small-pox. He continued to grow worse, and four days previous to our arrival in New-Orleans he died. One of the sailors sewed him in his blanket, with a large stone from the ballast at his feet, and then laying him on a hatchway, and elevating it with tackles above the railing, the inanimate body of poor Robert was consigned to the white waters of the gulf.

We were all panic-stricken by the appearance of the small-pox. The captain ordered lime to be scattered through the hold, and other prudent precautions to be taken. The death of Robert, however, and the presence of the malady, oppressed me sadly, and I gazed out over the great waste of waters with a spirit that was indeed disconsolate.

An evening or two after Robert's burial, I was leaning on the hatchway near the forecastle, full of desponding thoughts, when a sailor in a kind voice asked me, why I was so down-hearted. The tone and manner of the man assured me, and I answered, because I was a freeman, and had been kidnapped. He remarked it was enough to make any one down-hearted, and continued to interrogate me until he learned the particulars of my whole history. He was evidently much interested in my behalf, and, in the blunt speech of a sailor, swore he would aid me all he could, if it "split his timbers." I requested him to furnish me pen, ink and paper, in order that I might write to some of my friends. He promised to obtain them—but how I could use them undiscovered was a difficulty. If I could only get into the forecastle while his watch was off, and the other sailors asleep, the thing could be accomplished. The small boat instantly occurred to me. He thought we were not far from Balize, at the mouth of the Mississippi, and it was necessary that the letter be written soon, or the opportunity would be lost. Accordingly, by arrangement, I managed the next night to secret myself again under the long-boat. His watch was off at twelve. I saw him pass into the forecastle, and in about an hour followed him. He was nodding over a table, half asleep, on which a sickly light was flickering, and on which also was a pen and sheet of paper. As I entered he aroused, beckoned me to a seat beside him, and pointed to the paper. I directed the letter to Henry B. Northup, of Sandy Hill—stating that I had been kidnapped, was then on board the brig Orleans, bound for New-Orleans; that it was then impossible for me to conjecture my ultimate destination, and requesting he would take measures to rescue me. The letter was sealed and directed, and Manning, having read it, promised to deposit it in the New-Orleans post-office. I hastened back to my place under the long-boat, and in the morning, as the slaves came up and were walking around, crept out unnoticed and mingled with them.

My good friend, whose name was John Manning, was an Englishman by birth, and a noble-hearted generous sailor as ever walked a deck. He had lived in Boston—was a tall, well-built man, about twenty-four years old, with a face somewhat pockmarked, but full of benevolent expressions.

Nothing to vary the monotony of our daily life occurred, until we reached New-Orleans. On coming to the levee, and before the vessel was made fast, I saw Manning leap on shore and hurry away into the city. As he started off he looked back over his shoulder significantly, giving me to understand the object of his errand. Presently he returned, and passing close by me, hunched me with his elbow, with a peculiar wink, as much as to say, "it is all right."

The letter, as I have since learned, reached Sandy Hill. Mr. Northup visited Albany and laid it before Governor Seward, but inasmuch as it gave no definite information as to my probable locality, it was not, at that time, deemed advisable to institute measures for my liberation. It was concluded to delay, trusting that a knowledge of where I was might eventually be obtained.

A happy and touching scene was witnessed immediately upon our reaching the levee. Just as Manning left the brig, on the way to the post-office, two men came up and called aloud for Arthur. The latter, as he recognized them, was almost crazy with delight. He could hardly be restrained from leaping over the brig's side; and when they met soon after, he grasped them by the hand, and clung to them a long, long time. They were men from Norfolk, who had come on to New-Orleans to rescue him. His kidnappers, they informed him, had been arrested, and were then confined in the Norfolk prison. They conversed a few moments with the captain, and then departed with the rejoicing Arthur.

But in all the crowd that thronged the wharf, there was no one who knew or cared for me. Not one. No familiar voice greeted my ears, nor was there a single face that I had ever seen. Soon Arthur would rejoin his family, and have the satisfaction of seeing his wrongs avenged: my family, alas, should I ever see them more? There was a feeling of utter desolation in my heart, filling it with a despairing and regretful sense, that I had not gone down with Robert to the bottom of the sea.

Very soon traders and consignees came on board. One, a tall, thin-faced man, with light complexion and a little bent, made his appearance, with a paper in his hand. Burch's gang, consisting of myself, Eliza and her children, Harry, Lethe, and some others, who had joined us at Richmond, were consigned to him. This gentleman was Mr. Theophilus Freeman. Reading from his paper, he called, "Platt." No one answered. The name was called again and again, but still there was no reply. Then Lethe was called, then Eliza, then Harry, until the list was finished, each one stepping forward as his or her name was called.

"Captain, where's Platt?" demanded Theophilus Freeman.

The captain was unable to inform him, no one being on board answering to that name.

"Who shipped *that* nigger?" he again inquired of the captain, pointing to me.

"Burch," replied the captain.

"Your name is Platt—you answer my description. Why don't you come forward?" he demanded of me, in an angry tone.

I informed him that was not my name; that I had never been called by it, but that I had no objection to it as I knew of.

"Well, I will learn you your name," said he; "and so you won't forget it either by—," he added.

Mr. Theophilus Freeman, by the way, was not a whit behind his partner, Burch, in the matter of blasphemy. On the vessel I had gone by the name of "Steward," and this was the first time I had ever been designated as Platt—the name forwarded by Burch to his consignee. From the vessel I observed the chain-gang at work on the levee. We passed near them as we were driven to Freeman's slave pen. This pen is very similar to Goodin's in Richmond, except the yard was enclosed by plank, standing upright, with ends sharpened, instead of brick walls.

Including us, there were now at least fifty in this pen. Depositing our blankets in one of the small buildings in the yard, and having been called up and fed, we were allowed to saunter about the enclosure until night, when we wrapped our blankets round us and laid down under the shed, or in the loft, or in the open yard, just as each one preferred.

It was but a short time I closed my eyes that night. Thought was busy in my brain.

Could it be possible that I was thousands of miles from home—that I had been driven through the streets like a dumb beast—that I had been chained and beaten without any mercy—that I was even herded with a drove of slaves, a slave myself? Were the events of the last few weeks realities indeed?—or was I passing only through the dismal phases of a long, protracted dream? It was no illusion. My cup of sorrow was full to over-flowing. Then I lifted up my hands to God, and in the still watches of the night, surrounded by the sleeping forms of my companions, begged for mercy on the poor, forsaken captive. To the Almighty Father of us all—the freeman and the slave—I poured forth the supplications of a broken spirit, imploring strength from on high to bear up against the burden of my troubles, until the morning light aroused the slumberers, ushering in another day of bondage.

Edwin Epps, of whom much will be said during the remainder of this history, is a large, portly, heavy-bodied man with light hair, high cheek bones, and a Roman nose of extraordinary dimensions. He has blue eyes, a fair complexion, and is, as I should say, full six feet high. He has the sharp, inquisitive expression of a jockey. His manners are repulsive and coarse, and his language gives speedy and unequivocal evidence that he has never enjoyed the advantages of an education. He has the faculty of saying most provoking things, in that respect even excelling old Peter Tanner. At the time I came into his possession, Edwin Epps was fond of the bottle, his "sprees" sometimes extending over the space of two whole weeks. Latterly, however, he had reformed his habits, and when I left, was as strict a specimen of temperance as could be found on Bayou Boeuf. When "in his cups," Master Epps was a roystering, blustering, noisy fellow, whose chief delight was in dancing with his "niggers," or lashing them about the yard with his long whip, just for the pleasure of hearing them scream and scream, as the great welts were planted on their backs. When sober, he was silent, reserved and cunning, not beating us indiscriminately, as in his drunken moments, but sending the end of his rawhide to some tender spot of a lagging slave, with a sly dexterity peculiar to himself.

He had been a driver and overseer in his younger years, but at this time was in possession of a plantation on Bayou Huff Power, two and a half miles from Holmesville, eighteen from Marksville, and twelve from Cheneyville.[1] It belonged to Joseph B. Roberts,[2] his wife's uncle, and was leased by Epps. His principal business was raising cotton, and in as much as some may read this book who have never seen a cotton field, a description of the manner of its culture may not be out of place.

The ground is prepared by throwing up beds or ridges, with the plough—back-furrowing, it is called. Oxen and mules, the latter almost exclusively, are used in ploughing. The women as frequently as the men perform this labor, feeding, currying, and taking care of their teams, and in all respects doing the field and stable work, precisely as do the ploughboys of the North.

The beds, or ridges, are six feet wide, that is, from water furrow to water furrow. A plough drawn by one mule is then run along the top of the ridge or center of the bed, making the drill, into which a girl usually drops the seed, which she carries in a bag hung round her neck. Behind her comes a mule and harrow, covering up the seed, so that two mules, three slaves, a plough and

harrow, are employed in planting a row of cotton. This is done in the months of March and April. Corn is planted in February. When there are no cold rains, the cotton usually makes its appearance in a week. In the course of eight or ten days afterwards the first hoeing is commenced. This is performed in part, also, by the aid of the plough and mule. The plough passes as near as possible to the cotton on both sides, throwing the furrow from it. Slaves follow with their hoes, cutting up the grass and cotton, leaving hills two feet and a half apart. This is called scraping cotton. In two weeks more commences the second hoeing. This time the furrow is thrown towards the cotton. Only one stalk, the largest, is now left standing in each hill. In another fortnight it is hoed the third time, throwing the furrow towards the cotton in the same manner as before, and killing all the grass between the rows. About the first of July, when it is a foot high or thereabouts, it is hoed the fourth and last time. Now the whole space between the rows is ploughed, leaving a deep water furrow in the center. During all these hoeings the overseer or driver follows the slaves on horseback with a whip, such as has been described. The fastest hoer takes the lead row. He is usually about a rod in advance of his companions. If one of them passes him, he is whipped. If one falls behind or is a moment idle, he is whipped. In fact, the lash is flying from morning until night, the whole day long. The hoeing season thus continues from April until July, a field having no sooner been finished once, than it is commenced again.

In the latter part of August begins the cotton picking season. At this time each slave is presented with a sack. A strap is fastened to it, which goes over the neck, holding the mouth of the sack breast high, while the bottom reaches nearly to the ground. Each one is also presented with a large basket that will hold about two barrels. This is to put the cotton in when the sack is filled. The baskets are carried to the field and placed at the beginning of the rows.

---

[1] Bayou Huff Power, Huffpower, or Huffpauir—various spellings are used—is a tiny waterway threading its way through the southern end of Avoyelles Parish. The stream divides the present town of Bunkie, founded in 1882.

[2] Joseph Benjamin Robert was a brother of Mrs. Epps's mother, Rosella Robert, nee Robert. Mary Elvina Epps's parents were first cousins. Not the least of Northup's accomplishments was his unfailing accuracy in citing the tangled relationships of the Boeuf relatives.

When a new hand, one unaccustomed to the business, is sent for the first time into the field, he is whipped up smartly, and made for that day to pick as fast as he can possibly. At night it is weighed, so that his capability in cotton picking is known. He must bring in the same weight each night following. If is [sic] falls short, it is considered evidence that he has been laggard, and a greater or less number of lashes is the penalty.

An ordinary day's work is considered two hundred pounds. A slave who is accustomed to picking, is punished, if he or she brings in a less quantity than that. There is a great difference among them as regards this kind of labor. Some of them seem to have a natural knack, or quickness, which enables them to pick with great celerity, and with both hands, while others, with whatever practice or industry, are utterly unable to come up to the ordinary standard. Such hands are taken from the cotton field and employed in other business. Patsey, of whom I shall have more to say, was known as the most remarkable cotton picker on Bayou Boeuf. She picked with both hands and with such surprising rapidity, that five hundred pounds a day was not unusual for her.

Each one is tasked, therefore, according to his picking abilities, none, however, to come short of two hundred weight. I, being unskillful always in that business, would have satisfied my master by bringing in the latter quantity, while on the other hand, Patsey would surely have been beaten if she failed to produce twice as much.

The cotton grows from five to seven feet high, each stalk having a great many branches, shooting out in all directions, and lapping each other above the water furrow.

There are few sights more pleasant to the eye, than a wide cotton field when it is in the bloom. It presents an appearance of purity, like an immaculate expanse of light, new-fallen snow.

Sometimes the slave picks down one side of a row, and back upon the other, but more usually, there is one on either side, gathering all that has blossomed, leaving the un-opened bolls for a succeeding picking. When the sack is filled, it is emptied into the basket and trodden down. It is necessary to be extremely careful the first time going through the field, in order not to break the branches off the stalks. The cotton will not bloom upon a broken branch. Epps never failed to inflict the severest chastisement on the unlucky servant who, either carelessly or unavoidably, was guilty in the least degree in this respect.

The hands are required to be in the cotton fields as soon as it is light in the morning, and, with the exception of ten or fifteen minutes, which is given them at noon to swallow their allowance of cold bacon, they are not permitted to be a moment idle until it is too dark to see, and when the moon is full, they often times labor till the middle of the night. They do not dare to stop even at dinner time, nor return to the quarters, however late it be, until the order to halt is given by the driver.

The day's work over in the field, the baskets are "toted," or in other words, carried to the gin-house, where the cotton is weighed. No matter how fatigued and weary he may be—no matter how much he longs for sleep and rest—a slave never approaches the gin-house with his basket of cotton but with fear. If it falls short in weight—if he has not performed the full task appointed him, he knows that he must suffer. And if he has exceeded it by ten or twenty pounds, in all probability his master will measure the next day's task accordingly. So, whether he has too little or too much, his approach to the gin-house is always with fear and trembling. Most frequently they have too little, and therefore it is they are not anxious to leave the field. After weighing, follow the whippings; and then the baskets are carried to the cotton house, and their contents stored away like hay, all hands being sent in to tramp it down. If the cotton is not dry, instead of taking it to the gin-house at once, it is laid upon platforms, two feet high, and some three times as wide, covered with boards or plank, with narrow walks running between them.

This done, the labor of the day is not yet ended, by any means. Each one must then attend to his respective chores. One feeds the mules, another the swine—another cuts the wood, and so forth; besides, the packing is all done by candle light. Finally, at a late hour, they reach the quarters, sleepy and overcome with the long day's toil. Then a fire must be kindled in the cabin, the corn ground in the small hand-mill, and supper, and dinner for the next day in the field, prepared. All that is allowed them is corn and bacon, which is given out at the corncrib and smoke-house every Sunday morning. Each one receives, as his weekly allowance, three and a half pounds of bacon, and corn enough to make a peck of meal. That is all— no tea, coffee, sugar, and with the exception of a very scanty sprinkling now and then, no salt. I can say, from a ten years' residence with Master Epps, that no slave of his is ever likely to suffer from the gout, superinduced by excessive high living. Master Epps' hogs were fed on *shelled* corn—it was thrown out to his "niggers" in the ear. The former, he thought, would fatten faster by shelling, and soaking it in the water—the latter, perhaps, if treated in the same manner, might grow too fat to labor. Master Epps was a shrewd calculator, and knew how to manage his own animals, drunk or sober.

The corn mill stands in the yard beneath a shelter. It is like a common coffee mill, the hopper holding about six quarts. There was one privilege which Master Epps granted freely to every slave he had. They might grind their corn nightly, in such small quantities as their daily wants required, or they might grind the whole week's allowance at one time, on Sundays, just as they preferred. A very generous man was Master Epps!

I kept my corn in a small wooden box, the meal in a gourd; and, by the way, the gourd is one of the most convenient and necessary utensils on a plantation. Besides supplying the place of all kinds of crockery in a slave cabin, it is used for carrying water to the fields. Another, also, contains the dinner. It dispenses with the necessity of pails, dippers, basins, and such tin and wooden superfluities altogether.

When the corn is ground, and fire is made, the bacon is taken down from the nail on which it hangs, a slice cut off and thrown upon the coals to broil. The majority of slaves have no knife, much less a fork. They cut their bacon with the axe at the woodpile. The corn meal is mixed with a little water, placed in the fire, and baked. When it is "done brown," the ashes are scraped off, and being placed upon a chip, which answers for a table, the tenant of the slave hut is ready to sit down upon the ground to supper. By this time it is usually midnight. The same fear of punishment with which they approach the gin-house, possesses them again on lying down to get a snatch of rest. It is the fear of oversleeping in the morning. Such an offence would certainly be attended with not less than twenty lashes. With a prayer that he may be on his feet and wide awake at the first sound of the horn, he sinks to his slumbers nightly.

The softest couches in the world are not to be found in the log mansion of the slave. The one whereon I reclined year after year, was a plank twelve inches wide and ten feet long. My pillow was a stick of wood. The bedding was a course blanket, and not a rag or shred beside. Moss might be used, were it not that it directly breeds a swarm of fleas.

The cabin is constructed of logs, without floor or window. The latter is altogether unnecessary, the crevices between the logs admitting sufficient light. In stormy weather the rain drives through them, rendering it comfortless and extremely disagreeable. The rude door hangs on great wooden hinges. In one end is constructed an awkward fire-place.

An hour before day light the horn is blown. Then the slaves arouse, prepare their breakfast, fill a gourd with water, in another deposit their dinner of cold bacon and corn cake, and hurry to the field again. It is an offence invariably followed by a flogging, to be found at the quarters after daybreak. Then the fears and labors of another day begin; and until its close there is no such thing as rest. He fears he will be caught lagging through the day; he fears to approach the gin-house with his basket-load of cotton at night; he fears, when he lies down, that he will oversleep himself in the morning. Such is a true, faithful, unexaggerated picture and description of the slave's daily life, during the time of cotton-picking, on the shores of Bayou Boeuf.

In the month of January, generally, the fourth and last picking is completed. Then commences the harvesting of corn. This is considered a secondary crop, and receives far less attention than the cotton. It is planted, as already mentioned, in February. Corn is grown in that region for the purpose of fattening hogs and feeding slaves; very little, if any, being set to market. It is the white variety, the ear of great size, and the stalk growing to the height of eight, and often times ten feet. In August the leaves are stripped off, dried in the sun, bound in small bundles, and stored away as provender for the mules and oxen. After this the slaves go through the field, turning down the ear, for the purpose of keeping the rains from penetrating to the grain. It is left in this condition until after cotton-picking is over, whether earlier or later. Then the ears are separated from the stalks, and deposited in the corncrib with the husks on; otherwise, stripped of the husks, the weevil would destroy it. The stalks are left standing in the field.

The Carolina, or sweet potato, is also grown in that region to some extent. They are not fed, however, to hogs or cattle, and are considered but of small importance. They are preserved by placing them upon the surface of the ground, with a slight covering of earth or cornstalks. There is not a cellar on Bayou Boeuf. The ground is so low it would fill with water. Potatoes are worth from two to three "bits," or shillings a barrel; corn, except when there is an unusual scarcity, can be purchased at the same rate.

As soon as the cotton and corn crops are secured, the stalks are pulled up, thrown into piles and burned. The ploughs are started at the same time, throwing up the beds again, preparatory to another planting. The soil, in the parishes of Rapides and Avopelles, and throughout the whole country, so far as my observation extended, is of exceeding richness and fertility. It is a kind of marl, of a brown or reddish color. It does not require those invigorating composts necessary to more barren lands, and on the same field the same crop is grown for many succeessive years.

Ploughing, planting, picking cotton, gathering the corn, and pulling and burning stalks, occupies the whole of the four seasons of the year. Drawing and cutting wood, pressing cotton, fattening and killing hogs, are but incidental labors.

In the month of September or October, the hogs are run out of the swamps by dogs, and confined in pens. On a cold morning, generally about New Year's day, they are slaughtered. Each carcass is cut into six parts, and piled one above the other in salt, upon large tables in the smoke-house. In this condition it remains a fortnight, when it is hung up, and a fire built, and continued more than half the time during the remainder of the year. This thorough smoking is necessary to prevent the bacon from becoming infested with worms. In so warm a climate it is difficult to preserve it, and very many times myself and my companions have received our weekly allowance of three pounds and a half, when it was full of these disgusting vermin.

Although the swamps are overrun with cattle, they are never made the source of profit, to any considerable extent. The planter cuts his mark upon the ear, or brands his initials upon the side, and turns them into the swamps, to roam unrestricted within their almost limitless confines. They are the Spanish breed, small and spike-horned. I have known of droves being taken from Bayou Boeuf, but it is of very rare occurrence. The value of the best cows is about five dollars each. Two quarts at one milking, would be considered an unusual large quantity. They furnish little tallow, and that of a soft, inferior quality. Notwithstanding the great number of cows that throng the swamps, the planters are indebted to the North for their cheese and butter, which is purchased in the New-Orleans market. Salted beef is not an article of food either in the great house, or in the cabin.

Master Epps was accustomed to attend shooting matches for the purpose of obtaining what fresh beef he required. These sports occurred weekly at the neighboring village of Holmesville.[3] Fat beeves are driven thither and shot at, a stipulated price being demanded for the privilege. The lucky marksman divides the flesh among his fellows, and in this manner the attending planters are supplied.

The great number of tame and untamed cattle which swarm the woods and swamps of Bayou Boeuf, most probably suggested that appellation to the French, inasmuch as the term, translated, signifies the creek or river of the wild ox.

Garden products, such as cabbages, turnips and the like, are cultivated for the use of the master and his family. They have greens and vegetables at all times and seasons of the year. "The grass withereth and the flower fadeth" before the desolating winds of autumn in the chill northern latitudes, but perpetual verdure overspreads the hot lowlands, and flowers bloom in the heart of winter, in the region of Bayou Boeuf.

There are no meadows appropriated to the cultivation of the grasses. The leaves of the corn supply a sufficiency of food for the laboring cattle, while the rest provide for themselves all the year in the evergrowing pasture.

There are many other peculiarities of climate, habit, custom, and of the manner of living and laboring at the South, but the foregoing, it is supposed, will give the reader an insight and general idea of life on a cotton plantation in Louisiana. The mode of cultivating cane, and the process of sugar manufacturing, will be mentioned in another place.

In consequence of my inability in cotton-picking, Epps was in the habit of hiring me out on sugar plantations during the season of cane-cutting and sugar-making. He received for my services a dollar a day, with the money supplying my place on his cotton plantation. Cutting cane was an employment that suited me, and for three successive years I held the lead row at Hawkins', leading a gang of from fifty to an hundred hands.[4]

In a previous chapter the mode of cultivating cotton is described. This may be the proper place to speak of the manner of cultivating cane.

The ground is prepared in beds, the same as it is prepared for the reception of the cotton seed, except it is ploughed deeper. Drills are made in the same manner. Planting commences in January, and continues until April. It is necessary to plant a sugar field only once in three years. Three crops are taken before the seed or plant is exhausted.

Three gangs are employed in the operation. One draws the cane from the rick, or stack, cutting the top and flags from the stalk, leaving only that part which is sound and healthy. Each joint of the cane has an eye, like the eye of a potato, which sends forth a sprout when buried in the soil. Another gang lays the cane in the drill, placing two stalks side by side in such manner that

[3]A frontier landing and shipping point on Bayou Boeuf in the western part of Avoyelles Parish. The little settlement apparently included several stores, a saloon, and a postoffice (some "Holmesville" postmarks survive). It is noted on early maps. No trace of the settlement exists today on the weed-grown banks of the Boeuf.

[4]Cutting cane on the lead row was a signal honor for which there was considerable competition. The pace setter could have no prouder badge of manhood than this—to strip the stalks of flags, cut the stalk and stack it across the rows faster than anybody else.

joints will occur once in four or six inches. The third gang follows with hoes, drawing earth upon the stalks, and covering them to the depth of three inches.

In four weeks, at the farthest, the sprouts appear above the ground, and from this time forward grow with great rapidity. A sugar field is hoed three times, the same as cotton, save that a greater quantity of earth is drawn to the roots. By the first of August hoeing is usually over. About the middle of September, whatever is required for seed is cut and stacked in ricks, as they are termed. In October it is ready for the mill or sugar-house, and then the general cutting begins. The blade of a cane-knife is fifteen inches long, three inches wide in the middle and tapering towards the point and handle. The blade is thin; and in order to be at all serviceable must be kept very sharp. Every third hand takes the lead of two others, one of whom is on each side of him. The lead hand, in the first place, with a blow of his knife shears the flags from the stalk. He next cuts off the top down as far as it is green. He must be careful to sever all the green from the ripe part, inasmuch as the juice of the former sours the molasses, and renders it unsalable. Then he severs the stalk at the root, and lays it directly behind him. His right and left hand companions lay their stalks, when cut in the same manner, upon his. To every three hands there is a cart, which follows, and the stalks are thrown into it by the younger slaves, when it is drawn to the sugar-house and ground.

If the planter apprehends a frost, the cane is winrowed. Winrowing is the cutting the stalks at an early period and throwing them lengthwise in the water furrow in such a manner that the tops will cover the butts of the stalks. They will remain in this condition three weeks or a month without souring, and secure from frost. When the proper time arrives, they are taken up, trimmed and carted to the sugar-house.

In the month of January the slaves enter the field again to prepare for another crop. The ground is now strewn with the tops, and flags cut from the past year's cane. On a dry day fire is set to this combustible refuse, which sweeps over the field, leaving it bare and clean, and ready for the hoes. The earth is loosened about the roots of the old stubble, and in process of time another crop springs up from the last year's seed. It is the same the year following; but the third year the seed has exhausted its strength, and the field must be ploughed and planted again. The second year the cane is sweeter and yields more than the first, and the third year more than the second.

During the three seasons I labored on Hawkins' plantation, I was employed a considerable portion of the time in the sugar-house. He is celebrated as the producer of the finest variety of white sugar. The following is a general description of his sugar-house and the process of manufacture:

The mill is an immense brick building, standing on the shore of the bayou. Running out from the building is an open shed, at least an hundred feet in length and forty or fifty feet in width. The boiler in which the stream is generated is situated outside the main building; the machinery and engine rest on a brick pier, fifteen feet above the floor, within the body of the building. The machinery turns two great iron rollers, between two and three feet in diameter and six or eight feet in length. They are elevated above the brick pier, and roll in towards each other. An endless carrier, made of chain and wood, like leathern belts used in small mills, extends from the iron rollers out of the main building and through the entire length of the open shed. The carts in which the cane is brought from the field as fast as it is cut, are unloaded at the sides of the shed. All along the endless carrier are ranged slave children, whose business it is to place the cane upon it, when it is conveyed through the shed into the main building, where it falls between the rollers, is crushed, and drops upon another carrier that conveys it out of the main building in an opposite direction, depositing it in the top of a chimney upon a fire beneath, which consumes it. It is necessary to burn it in this manner, because otherwise it would soon fill the building, and more especially because it would soon sour and engenger disease. The juice of the cane falls into a conductor underneath the iron rollers, and is carried into a reservoir. Pipes convey it from thence into five filterers, holding several hogsheads each. These filterers are filled with bone-black, a substance resembling pulverized charcoal. It is made of bones calcinated in close vessels, and is used for the purpose of decolorizing, by filtration, the cane juice before boiling. Through these five filters it passes in succession, and then runs into a large reservoir underneath the ground floor, from whence it is carried up, by means of a steam pump, into a clarifier made of sheet iron, where it is heated by steam until it boils. From the first clarifier it is carried in pipes to a second and a third, and thence into close iron pans, through which tubes pass, filled with steam. While in a boiling state it flows through three pans in succession, and is then carried in other pipes down to the coolers on the ground floor. Coolers are wooden boxes with sieve bottoms made of the finest wire. As soon as the syrup passes into the coolers, and is met by the air, it grains, and the molasses at once escapes through the sieves into a cistern below. It is then white or loaf sugar of the finest kind—clear, clean, and as white as snow. When cool, it is taken out, packed in hogsheads, and is ready for market. The molasses is then carried from the cistern into the upper story again, and by another process converted into brown sugar.

There are larger mills, and those constructed differently from the one thus imperfectly described, but none, perhaps, more celebrated than this anywhere on Bayou Boeuf. Lambert, of New Orleans, is a partner of Hawkins.[5] He is a man of vast wealth, holding, as I have been told, an interest in over forty different sugar plantations in Louisiana.

The only respite from constant labor the slave has through the whole year, is during the Christmas holidays. Epps allowed us three—others allow four, five and six days, according to the measure of their generosity. It is the only time to which they look forward with any interest or pleasure. They are glad when night comes, not only because it brings them a few hours repose, but because it brings them one day nearer Christmas. It is hailed with equal delight by the old and the young; even Uncle Abram ceases to glorify Andrew Jackson, and Patsey forgets her many sorrows, amid the general hilarity of the holidays. It is the time of feasting, and frolicking, and fiddling—the carnival season with the children of bondage. They are the only days when they are allowed a little restricted liberty, and heartily indeed do they enjoy it.

It is the custom for one planter to give a "Christmas supper," inviting the slaves from neighboring plantations to join his own on the occasion; for instance, one year it is given by Epps, the next by Marshall, the next by Hawkins, and so on. Usually from three to five hundred are assembled, coming together on foot, in carts, on horseback, on mules, riding double and triple, sometimes a boy and girls, at others a girl and two boys,

---

[5]P. A. Champomier, in his *Statement of Sugar Made in Louisiana in 1849–1850* (New Orleans, 1850), does not list a Hawkins mill. The "Lambert" Northup refers to was very likely William Lambeth. In Avoyelles Parish alone in 1849 Lambeth is listed with sugar production at Leinster Plantation (Lambeth and Wells) on Bayou Huffpower, at Meredith Plantation (Lambeth and H. P. Robert) on Bayou Clair, and at Lucky Hit Plantation (Lambeth and Cullum) on Bayou Clair. A few miles north of W. P. Ford's Boeuf plantation in Rapides Parish was a large mill owned by Lambeth with a planter named Maddox. Northup may have confused Lambeth with a local planter named David Lambert. See *U.S. Census* of Avoyelles Parish, 1850.

and at others again a boy, a girl and an old woman. Uncle Abram astride a mule, with Aunt Phebe and Patsey behind him, trotting towards a Christmas supper, would be no uncommon sight on Bayou Boeuf.

Then, too, "of all days i' the year," they array themselves in their best attire. The cotton coat has been washed clean, the stump of a tallow candle has been applied to the shoes, and if so fortunate as to possess a rimless or a crownless hat, it is placed jauntily on the head. They are welcomed with equal cordiality, however, if they come bare-headed and bare-footed to the feast. As a general thing, the women wear handkerchiefs tied about their heads, but if chance has thrown in their way a fiery red ribbon, or a cast-off bonnet of their mistress' grandmother, it is sure to be worn on such occasions. Red—the deep blood red—is decidedly the favorite color among the enslaved damsels of my acquaintance. If a red ribbon does not encircle the neck, you will be certain to find all the hair of their woolly heads tied up with red strings of one sort or another.

The table is spread in the open air, and loaded with varieties of meat and piles of vegetables. Bacon and corn meal at such times are dispensed with. Sometimes the cooking is performed in the kitchen on the plantation, at others in the shade of wide branching trees. In the latter case, a ditch is dug in the ground, and wood laid in and burned until it is filled with glowing coals, over which chickens, ducks, turkeys, pigs, and not unfrequently the entire body of a wild ox are roasted. They are furnished also with flour, of which biscuits are made, and often with peach and other preserves, with tarts, and every manner and description of pies, except the mince, that being an article of pastry as yet unknown among them. Only the slave who has lived all the years on his scanty allowance of meal and bacon, can appreciate such suppers. White people in great numbers assemble to witness the gastronomical enjoyments.

They seat themselves at the rustic table— the males on one side, the females on the other. The two between whom there may have been an exchange of tenderness, invariably manage to sit opposite; for the omnipresent Cupid disdains not to hurl his arrows into the simple hearts of slaves. Unalloyed and exulting happiness lights up the dark faces of them all. The ivory teeth, contrasting with their black complexions, exhibits two long, white streaks the whole extent of the table. All round the bountiful board a multitude of eyes roll in ecstacy. Giggling and laughter and the clattering of cutlery and crockery succeed. Cuffee's elbow hunches his neighbor's side, impelled by an involuntary impulse of delight; Nelly shakes her finger at Sambo and laughs, she knows not why, and so the fun and merriment flow on.

When the viands have disappeared, and the hungry maws of the children of toil are satisfied, then, next in the order of amusement, is the Christmas dance. My business on these gala days always was to play on the violin. The African race is a music-loving one, proverbially; and many there were among my fellow-bondsmen whose organs of tune were strikingly developed, and who could thumb the banjo with dexterity; but at the expense of appearing egotistical, I must, nevertheless, declare, that I was considered the Ole Bull of Bayou Boeuf. My master often received letters, sometimes from a distance of ten miles, requesting him to send me to play at a ball or festival of the whites. He received his compensation, and usually I also returned with many picayunes jingling in my pockets—the extra contributions of those to whose delight I had administered. In this manner I became more acquainted than I otherwise would, up and down the bayou. The young men and maidens of Holmesville always knew there was to be a jollification somewhere, whenever Platt Epps was seen passing through the town with his fiddle in his hand. "Where are you going now, Platt?" and "What is coming off tonight, Platt?" would be interrogatories issuing from every door and window, and many a time when there was no special hurry, yielding to pressing importunities, Platt would draw his bow, and sitting astride his mule, perhaps, discourse musically to a crowd of delighted children, gathered around him in the street.

Alas! had it not been for my beloved violin, I scarcely can conceive how I could have endured the long years of bondage. It introduced me to great houses—relieved me of many days' labor in the field—supplied me with conveniences for my cabin—with pipes and tobacco, and extra pair of shoes, and oftentimes led me away from the presence of a hard master, to witness scenes of jollity and mirth. It was my companion—the friend of my bosom—triumphing loudly when I was joyful, and uttering its soft, melodious consolations when I was sad. Often, at midnight, when sleep had fled affrighted from the cabin, and my soul was disturbed and troubled with the contemplation of my fate, it would sing me a song of peace. On holy Sabbath days, when an hour or two of leisure was allowed, it would accompany me to some quiet place on the bayou bank, and, lifting up its voice, discourse kindly and pleasantly indeed. It heralded my name round the country—made me friends, who, otherwise would not have noticed me—gave me an honored seat at the yearly feasts, and secured the loudest and heartiest welcome of them all at the Christmas dance. The Christmas dance! Oh, ye pleasure-seeking sons and daughters of idleness, who move with measured step, listless and snail-like, through the slow winding cotillon, if ye wish to look upon the celerity, if not the "poetry of motion"—upon genuine happiness, rampant and unrestrained—go down to Louisiana and see the slaves dancing in the starlight of a Christmas night.

On that particular Christmas I have now in my mind, a description whereof will serve as a description of the day generally, Miss Lively and Mr. Sam the first belonging to Stewart, the latter to Roberts, started the ball. It was well known that Sam cherished an ardent passion for Lively, as also did one of Marshall's and another of Carey's boys; for Lively was *lively* indeed, and a heart-breaking coquette withal. It was a victory for Sam Roberts, when, rising from the repast, she gave him her hand for the first "figure" in preference to either of his rivals. They were somewhat crest-fallen, and shaking their heads angrily, rather intimated they would like to pitch into Mr. Sam and hurt him badly. But not an emotion of wrath ruffled the placid bosom of Samuel as his legs flew like drum-sticks down the outside and up the middle, by the side of his bewitching partner. The whole company cheered them vociferously, and, excited with the applause, they continued "tearing down" after all the others had become exhausted and halted a moment to recover breath. But Sam's super-human exertions overcame him finally, leaving Lively alone, yet whirling like a top. Thereupon one of Sam's rivals, Pete Marshall, dashed in, and, with might and main, leaped and shuffled and threw himself into every conceivable shape, as if determined to show Miss Lively and all the world that Sam Roberts was of no account.

Pete's affection, however, was greater than his discretion. Such violent exercise took the breath out of him directly, and he dropped like an empty bag. Then was the time for Harry Carey to try his hand; but Lively also soon out-winded him, amidst hurrahs and shouts, fully sustaining her well-earned reputation of being the "fastest gal" on the bayou.

One "set" off another takes its place, he or she remaining on the floor longest receiving the most uproarious commendation, and so the dancing continues until broad daylight. It does not cease with the sound of the fiddle, but in that case they set up a music peculiar to themselves. This is called "patting," accompanied with one of those unmeaning songs, composed rather for its adaptation to a certain tune or measure, than for the purpose of expressing any distinct idea. The patting is performed by striking the hands on the knees, then striking the hands together, then striking the right shoulder with one hand, the left with the other—all the while keeping time with the feet, and singing, perhaps, this song:

"Harper's creek and roarin' ribber,
Thar, my dear, we'll live forebber;
　　Den we'll go to de Ingin Nation,
　　All I want in dis creation,
　　Is pretty little wife and big plantation.
Chorus. Up dat oak and down dat ribber,
　　Two overseers and one little nigger"

Or, if these words are not adapted to the tune called for, it may be that "Old Hog Eye" *is*—a rather solemn and startling specimen of versification, not, however, to be appreciated unless heard at the South. It runneth as follows:

"Who's been here since I've been gone?
Pretty little gal wid a josey on.
　　Hog eye!
　　Old Hog Eye.
　　And Hosey too!
Never see de like since I was born,
Here comes a little gal wid a josey on
　　Hog Eye!
　　Old Hog Eye!
　　And Hosey too!"

Or, maybe the following, perhaps, equally nonsensical, but full of melody, nevertheless, as it flows from the Negro's mouth:

"Ebo Dick and Jurdan's Jo,
Them two niggers stole my yo'.
Chorus. Hop Jim along,
　　Walk Jim along,
　　Talk Jim along," &c.
Old black Dan, as black as tar,
He dam glad he was not dar.
　　Hop Jim along," &c.

During the remaining holidays succeeding Christmas, they are provided with passes, and permitted to go where they please within a limited distance, or they may remain and labor on the plantation, in which case they are paid for it. It is very rarely, however, that the latter alternative is accepted. They may be seen at these times hurrying in all directions, as happy looking mortals as can be found on the face of the earth. They are different beings from what they are in the field; the temporary relaxation, the brief deliverance from fear, and from the lash, producing an entire metamorphosis in their appearance and demeanor. In visiting, riding, renewing old friendships, or, perchance, reviving some old attachment or pursuing whatever pleasure may suggest itself, the time is occupied. Such is "southern life as it is," *three days in the year,* as I found it—the other three hundred and sixty-two being days of weariness, and fear, and suffering, and unremitting labor.

Marriage is frequently contracted during the holidays, if such an institution may be said to exist among them. The only ceremony required before entering into that "holy estate," is to obtain the consent of the respective owners. It is usually encouraged by the masters of female slaves. Either party can have as many husbands or wives as the owner will permit, and either is at liberty to discard the other at pleasure. The law in relation to divorce, or to bigamy, and so forth, is not applicable to property of course. If the wife does not belong on the same plantation with the husband, the latter is permitted to visit her on Saturday nights, if the distance is not too far. Uncle Abram's wife lived seven miles from Epps', on Bayou Huff Power. He had permission to visit her once a fortnight, but he was growing old, as has been said, and truth to say, had latterly well nigh forgotten her. Uncle Abram had no time to spare from his meditations on General Jackson—connubial dalliance being well enough for the young and thoughtless, but unbecoming a grave and solemn philosopher like himself.

Incidents in the Life of a Slave Girl

Harriet Jacobs

I

Childhood

I was born a slave; but I never knew it till six years of happy childhood had passed away. My father was a carpenter, and considered so intelligent and skilful in his trade, that, when buildings out of the common line were to be erected, he was sent for from long distances, to be head workman. On condition of paying his mistress two hundred dollars a year, and supporting himself, he was allowed to work at his trade, and manage his own affairs. His strongest wish was to purchase his children; but, though he several times offered his hard earnings for that purpose, he never succeeded. In complexion my parents were a light shade of brownish yellow, and were termed mulattoes. They lived together in a comfortable home; and, though we were all slaves, I was so fondly shielded that I never dreamed I was a piece of merchandise, trusted to them for safe keeping, and liable to be demanded of them at any moment. I had one brother, William, who was two years younger than myself—a bright, affectionate child. I had also a great treasure in my maternal grandmother, who was a remarkable woman in many respects. She was the daughter of a planter in South Carolina, who, at his death, left her mother and his three children free, with money to go to St. Augustine, where they had relatives. It was during the Revolutionary War; and they were captured on their passage, carried back, and sold to different purchasers. Such

Source: Harriet Jacobs, *Incidents in the Life of a Slave Girl.* (Boston, 1861), pp. 11–20, 23–27, 44–57, 83–89, 97–104, 118–121, 147–151, 183–186, 193–196, 224–229, 237–241.

was the story my grandmother used to tell me; but I do not remember all the particulars. She was a little girl when she was captured and sold to the keeper of a large hotel. I have often heard her tell how hard she fared during childhood. But as she grew older she evinced so much intelligence, and was so faithful, that her master and mistress could not help seeing it was for their interest to take care of such a valuable piece of property. She became an indispensable personage in the household, officiating in all capacities, from cook and wet nurse to seamstress. She was much praised for her cooking; and her nice crackers became so famous in the neighborhood that many people were desirous of obtaining them. In consequence of numerous requests of this kind, she asked permission of her mistress to bake crackers at night, after all the household work was done; and she obtained leave to do it, provided she would clothe herself and her children from the profits. Upon these terms, after working hard all day for her mistress, she began her midnight bakings, assisted by her two oldest children. The business proved profitable; and each year she laid by a little, which was saved for a fund to purchase her children. Her master died, and the property was divided among his heirs. The widow had her dower in the hotel, which she continued to keep open. My grandmother remained in her service as a slave; but her children were divided among her master's children. As she had five, Benjamin, the youngest one, was sold, in order that each heir might have an equal portion of dollars and cents. There was so little difference in our ages that he seemed more like my brother than my uncle. He was a bright, handsome lad, nearly white; for he inherited the complexion my grandmother had derived from Anglo-Saxon ancestors. Though only ten years old, seven hundred and twenty dollars were paid for him. His sale was a terrible blow to my grandmother; but she was naturally hopeful, and she went to work with renewed energy, trusting in time to be able to purchase some of her children. She had laid up three hundred dollars, which her mistress one day begged as a loan, promising to pay her soon. The reader probably knows that no promise or writing given to a slave is legally binding; for, according to Southern laws, a slave, *being* property, can *hold* no property. When my grandmother lent her hard earnings to her mistress, she trusted solely to her honor. The honor of a slaveholder to a slave!

To this good grandmother I was indebted for many comforts. My brother Willie and I often received portions of the crackers, cakes, and preserves, she made to sell; and after we ceased to be children we were indebted to her for many more important services.

Such were the unusually fortunate circumstances of my early childhood. When I was six years old, my mother died; and then, for the first time, I learned, by the talk around me, that I was a slave. My mother's mistress was the daughter of my grandmother's mistress. She was the foster sister of my mother; they were both nourished at my grandmother's breast. In fact, my mother had been weaned at three months old, that the babe of the mistress might obtain sufficient food. They played together as children; and, when they became women, my mother was a most faithful servant to her whiter foster sister. On her deathbed her mistress promised that her children should never suffer for any thing; and during her lifetime she kept her word. They all spoke kindly of my dead mother, who had been a slave merely in name, but in nature was noble and womanly. I grieved for her, and my young mind was troubled with the thought who would now take care of me and my little brother. I was told that my home was now to be with her mistress; and I found it a happy one. No toilsome or disagreeable duties were imposed upon me. My mistress was so kind to me that I was always glad to do her bidding, and proud to labor for her as much as my young years would permit. I would sit by her side for hours, sewing diligently, with a heart as free from care as that of any free-born white child. When she thought I was tired, she would send me out to run and jump; and away I bounded, to gather berries or flowers to decorate her room. Those were happy days—too happy to last. The slave child had no thought for the morrow; but there came that blight, which too surely waits on every human being born to be a chattel.

When I was nearly twelve years old, my kind mistress sickened and died. As I saw the cheek grow paler, and the eye more glassy, how earnestly I prayed in my heart that she might live! I loved her; for she had been almost like a mother to me. My prayers were not answered. She died, and they buried her in the little churchyard, where, day after day, my tears fell upon her grave.

I was sent to spend a week with my grandmother. I was now old enough to begin to think of the future; and again and again I asked myself what they would do with me. I felt sure I should never find another mistress so kind as the one who was gone. She had promised my dying mother that her children should never suffer for any thing; and when I remembered that, and recalled her many proofs of attachment to me, I could not help having some hopes that she had left me free. My friends were almost certain it would be so. They thought she would be sure to do it, on account of my mother's love and faithful service. But, alas! we all know that the memory of a faithful slave does not avail much to save her children from the auction block.

After a brief period of suspense, the will of my mistress was read, and we learned that she had bequeathed me to her sister's daughter, a child of five years old. So vanished our hopes. My mistress had taught me the precepts of God's Word: "Thou shalt love thy neighbor as thyself." "Whatsoever ye would that men should do unto you, do ye even so unto them." But I was her slave, and I suppose she did not recognize me as her neighbor. I would give much to blot out from my memory that one great wrong. As a child, I loved my mistress; and, looking back on the happy days I spent with her, I try to think with less bitterness of this act of injustice. While I was with her, she taught me to read and spell; and for this privilege, which so rarely falls to the lot of a slave, I bless her memory.

She possessed but few slaves; and at her death those were all distributed among her relatives. Five of them were my grandmother's children, and had shared the same milk that nourished her mother's children. Notwithstanding my grandmother's long and faithful service to her owners, not one of her children escaped the auction block. These God-breathing machines are no more, in the sight of their masters, than the cotton they plant, or the horses they tend.

II

The New Master and Mistress

Dr. Flint, a physician in the neighborhood, had married the sister of my mistress, and I was now the property of their little daughter. It was not without murmuring that I prepared for my new home; and what added to my unhappiness, was the fact that my brother William was purchased by the same family. My father, by his nature, as well as by the habit of transacting business as a skilful mechanic, had more of the feelings of a freeman than is common among slaves. My brother was a spirited boy; and being brought up under such influences, he early detested the name of master and mistress. One day, when his father and his mistress had happened to call him at the same time, he hesitated between the two; being perplexed to know which had the strongest claim upon his obedience. He finally concluded to go to his mistress. When my father reproved him for it, he said, "You both called me, and I didn't know which I ought to go to first."

"You are *my* child," replied our father, "and when I call you, you should come immediately, if you have to pass through fire and water."

Poor Willie! He was now to learn his first lesson of obedience to a master. Grandmother tried to cheer us with hopeful words, and they found an echo in the credulous hearts of youth.

When we entered our new home we encountered cold looks, cold words, and cold treatment. We were glad when the night came. On my narrow bed I moaned and wept, I felt so desolate and alone.

I had been there nearly a year, when a dear little friend of mine was buried. I heard her mother sob, as the clods fell on the coffin of her only child, and I turned away from the grave, feeling thankful that I still had something left to love. I met my grandmother, who said, "Come with me, Linda;" and from her tone I knew that something sad had happened. She led me apart from the people, and then said, "My child, your father is dead." Dead! How could I believe it? He had died so suddenly I had not even heard that he was sick. I went home with my grandmother. My heart rebelled against God, who had taken from me mother, father, mistress, and friend. The good grandmother tried to comfort me. "Who knows the ways of God?" said she. "Perhaps they have been kindly taken from the evil days to come." Years afterwards I often thought of this. She promised to be a mother to her grandchildren, so far as she might be permitted to do so; and strengthened by her love, I returned to my master's. I thought I should be allowed to go to my father's house the next morning; but I was ordered to go for flowers, that my mistress's house might be decorated for an evening party. I spent the day gathering flowers and weaving them into festoons, while the dead body of my father was lying within a mile of me. What cared my owners for that? he was merely a piece of property. Moreover, they thought he had spoiled his children, by teaching them to feel that they were human beings. This was blasphemous doctrine for a slave to teach; presumptuous in him, and dangerous to the masters.

The next day I followed his remains to a humble grave beside that of my dear mother. There were those who knew my father's worth, and respected his memory.

My home now seemed more dreary than ever. The laugh of the little slave-children sounded harsh and cruel. It was selfish to feel so about the joy of others. My brother moved about with a very grave face. I tried to comfort him, by saying, "Take courage, Willie; brighter days will come by and by."

"You don't know any thing about it, Linda," he replied. "We shall have to stay here all our days; we shall never be free."

I argued that we were growing older and stronger, and that perhaps we might, before long, be allowed to hire our own time, and then we could earn money to buy our freedom. William declared this was much easier to say than to do; moreover, he did not intend to *buy* his freedom. We held daily controversies upon this subject.

Little attention was paid to the slaves' meals in Dr. Flint's house. If they could catch a bit of food while it was going, well and good. I gave myself no trouble on that score, for on my various errands I passed my grandmother's house, where there was always something to spare for me. I was frequently threatened with punishment if I stopped there; and my grandmother, to avoid detaining me, often stood at the gate with something for my breakfast or dinner. I was indebted to *her* for all my comforts, spiritual or temporal. It was *her* labor that supplied my scanty wardrobe. I have a vivid recollection of the linsey-woolsey dress given me every winter by Mrs. Flint. How I hated it! It was one of the badges of slavery. . . .

When I had been in the family a few weeks, one of the plantation slaves was brought to town, by order of his master. It was near night when he arrived, and Dr. Flint ordered him to be taken to the work house, and tied up to the joist, so that his feet would just escape the ground. In that situation he was to wait till the doctor had taken his tea. I shall never forget that night. Never before, in my life, had I heard hundreds of blows fall, in succession, on a human being. His piteous groans, and his "O, pray don't, massa," rang in my ear for months afterwards. There were many conjectures as to the cause of this terrible punishment. Some said master accused him of stealing corn; others said the slave had quarrelled with his wife, in presence of the overseer, and had accused his master of being the father of her child. They were both black, and the child was very fair.

I went into the work house next morning, and saw the cowhide still wet with blood, and the boards all covered with gore. The poor man lived, and continued to quarrel with his wife. A few months afterwards Dr. Flint handed them both over to a slave-trader. The guilty man put their value into his pocket, and had the satisfaction of knowing that they were out of sight and hearing. When the mother was delivered into the trader's hands, she said, "You *promised* to treat me well." To which he replied, "You have let your tongue run too far; damn you!" She had forgotten that it was a crime for a slave to tell who was the father of her child.

From others than the master persecution also comes in such cases. I once saw a young slave girl dying soon after the birth of a child nearly white. In her agony she cried out, "O Lord, come and take me!" Her mistress stood by, and mocked at her like an incarnate fiend. "You suffer, do you?" she exclaimed. "I am glad of it. You deserve it all, and more too."

The girl's mother said, "The baby is dead, thank God; and I hope my poor child will soon be in heaven, too."

"Heaven!" retorted the mistress. "There is no such place for the like of her and her bastard."

The poor mother turned away, sobbing. Her dying daughter called her, feebly, and as she bent over her, I heard her say, "Don't grieve so, mother; God knows all about it; and He will have mercy upon me."

Her sufferings, afterwards, became so intense, that her mistress felt unable to stay; but when she left the room, the scornful smile was still on her lips. Seven children called her mother. The poor black woman had but the one child, whose eyes she saw closing in death, while she thanked God for taking her away from the greater bitterness of life.

III

The Slaves' New Year's Day

Dr. Flint owned a fine residence in town, several farms, and about fifty slaves, besides hiring a number by the year.

Hiring-day at the south takes place on the 1st of January. On the 2d, the slaves are expected to go to their new masters. On a farm, they work until the corn and cotton are laid. They then have two holidays. Some masters give them a good dinner under the trees. This over, they work until Christmas eve. If no heavy charges are meantime brought against them, they are given four or five holidays, whichever the master or overseer may think proper. Then comes New Year's eve; and they gather together their little alls, or more properly speaking, their little nothings, and wait anxiously for the dawning of day. At the appointed hour the grounds are thronged with men, women, and children, waiting, like criminals, to hear their doom pronounced. The slave is sure to know who is the most humane, or cruel master, within forty miles of him.

It is easy to find out, on that day, who clothes and feeds his slaves well; for he is surrounded by a crowd, begging, "Please, massa, hire me this year. I will work *very* hard, massa."

If a slave is unwilling to go with his new master, he is whipped, or locked up in jail, until he consents to go, and promises not to run away during the year. Should he chance to change his mind, thinking it justifiable to violate an extorted promise, woe unto him if he is caught! The whip is used till the blood flows at his feet; and his stiffened limbs are put in chains, to be dragged in the field for days and days!

If he lives until the next year, perhaps the same man will hire him again, without even giving him an opportunity of going to the hiring-ground. After those for hire are disposed of, those for sale are called up.

O, you happy free women, contrast *your* New Year's day with that of the poor bond-woman! With you it is a pleasant season, and the light of the day is blessed. Friendly wishes meet you every where, and gifts are showered upon you. Even hearts that have been estranged from you soften at this season, and lips that have been silent echo back, "I wish you a happy New Year." Children bring their little offerings, and raise their rosy lips for a caress. They are your own, and no hand but that of death can take them from you.

But to the slave mother New Year's day comes laden with peculiar sorrows. She sits on her cold cabin floor, watching the children who may all be torn from her the next morning; and often does she wish that she and they might die before the day dawns. She may be an ignorant creature, degraded by the system that has brutalized her from childhood; but she has a mother's instincts, and is capable of feeling a mother's agonies.

On one of these sale days, I saw a mother lead seven children to the auction-block. She knew that *some* of them would be taken from her; but they took *all*. The children were sold to a slave-trader, and their mother was bought by a man in her own town. Before night her children were all far away. She begged the trader to tell her where he intended to take them; this he refused to do. How *could* he, when he knew he would sell them, one by one, wherever he could command the highest price? I met that mother in the street, and her wild, haggard face lives to-day in my mind. She wrung her hands in anguish, and exclaimed, "Gone! All gone! Why *don't* God kill me?" I had no words wherewith to comfort her. Instances of this kind are of daily, yea, of hourly occurrence.

Slaveholders have a method, peculiar to their institution, of getting rid of *old* slaves, whose lives have been worn out in their service. I knew an old woman, who for seventy years faithfully served her master. She had become almost helpless, from hard labor and disease. Her owners moved to Alabama, and the old black woman was left to be sold to any body who would give twenty dollars for her.

V

The Trials of Girlhood

During the first years of my service in Dr. Flint's family, I was accustomed to share some indulgences with the children of my mistress. Though this seemed to me no more than right, I was grateful for it, and tried to merit the kindness by the faithful discharge of my duties. But I now entered on my fifteenth year—a sad epoch in the life of a slave girl. My master began to whisper foul words in my ear. Young as I was, I could not remain ignorant of their import. I tried to treat them with indifference or contempt. The master's age, my extreme youth, and the fear that his conduct would be reported to my grandmother, made him bear this treatment for many months. He was a crafty man, and restored to many means to accomplish his purposes. Sometimes he had stormy, terrific ways, that made his victims tremble; sometimes he assumed a gentleness that he thought must surely subdue. Of the two, I preferred his stormy moods, although they left me trembling. He tried his utmost to corrupt the pure principles my grandmother had instilled. He peopled my young mind with unclean images, such as only a vile monster could think of. I turned from him with disgust and hatred. But he was my master. I was compelled to live under the same roof with him—where I saw a man forty years my senior daily violating the most sacred commandments of nature. He told me I was his property; that I must be subject to his will in all things. My soul revolted against the mean tyranny. But where could I turn for protection? No matter whether the slave girl be as black as ebony or as fair as her mistress. In either case, there is no shadow of law to protect her from insult, from violence, or even from death; all these are inflicted by fiends who bear the shape of men. The mistress, who ought to protect the helpless victim, has no other feelings towards her but those of jealousy and rage. The degradation, the wrongs, the vices, that grow out of slavery, are more than I can describe. They are greater than you would willingly believe. Surely, if you credited one half the truths that are told you concerning the helpless millions suffering in this cruel bondage, you at the north would not help to tighten the yoke. You surely would refuse to do for the master, on your own soil, the mean and cruel work which trained bloodhounds and the lowest class of whites do for him at the south.

Every where the years bring to all enough of sin and sorrow; but in slavery the very dawn of life is darkened by these shadows. Even the little child, who is accustomed to wait on her mistress and her children, will learn, before she is twelve years old, why it is that her mistress hates such and such a one among the slaves. Perhaps the child's own mother is among those hated ones. She listens to violent outbreaks of jealous passion, and cannot help understanding what is the cause. She will become prematurely knowing in evil things. Soon she will learn to tremble when she hears her master's footfall. She will be compelled to realize that she is no longer a child. If God has bestowed beauty upon her, it will prove her greatest curse. That which commands admiration in the white woman only hastens the degradation of the female slave. I know that some are too much brutalized by slavery to feel the humiliation of their position; but many slaves feel it most acutely, and shrink from the memory of it. I cannot tell how much I suffered in the presence of these wrongs, nor how I am still pained by the retrospect. My master met me at every turn, reminding me that I belonged to him, and swearing by heaven and earth that he would compel me to submit to him. If I went out for a breath of fresh air, after a day of unwearied toil, his footsteps dogged me. If I knelt by my mother's grave, his dark shadow fell on me even there. The light heart which nature had given me became heavy with sad forebodings. The other slaves in my master's house noticed the change. Many of them pitied me; but none dared to ask the cause. They had no need to inquire. They knew too well the guilty practices under that roof; and they were aware that to speak of them was an offence that never went unpunished.

I longed for some one to confide in. I would have given the world to have laid my head on my grandmother's faithful bosom, and told her all my troubles. But Dr. Flint swore he would kill me, if I was not as silent as the grave. Then, although my grandmother was all in all to me, I feared her as well as loved her. I had been accustomed to look up to her with a respect bordering upon awe. I was very young, and felt shamefaced about telling her such impure things, especially as I knew her to be very strict on such subjects. Moreover, she was a woman of a high spirit. She was usually very quiet in her demeanor; but if her indignation was once roused, it was not very easily quelled. I had been told that she once chased a white gentleman with a loaded pistol, because he insulted one of her daughters. I dreaded the consequences of a violent outbreak; and both pride and fear kept me silent. But though I did not confide in my grandmother, and even evaded her vigilant watchfulness and inquiry, her presence in the neighborhood was some protection to me. Though she had been a slave, Dr. Flint was afraid of her. He dreaded her scorching rebukes. Moreover, she was known and patronized by many people; and he did not wish to

have his villainy made public. It was lucky for me that I did not live on a distant plantation, but in a town not so large that the inhabitants were ignorant of each other's affairs. Bad as are the laws and customs in a slaveholding community, the doctor, as a professional man, deemed it prudent to keep up some outward show of decency.

O, what days and nights of fear and sorrow that man caused me! Reader, it is not to awaken sympathy for myself that I am telling you truthfully what I suffered in slavery. I do it to kindle a flame of compassion in your hearts for my sisters who are still in bondage, suffering as I once suffered.

I once saw two beautiful children playing together. One was a fair white child; the other was her slave, and also her sister. When I saw them embracing each other, and heard their joyous laughter, I turned sadly away from the lovely sight. I foresaw the inevitable blight that would fall on the little slave's heart. I knew how soon her laughter would be changed to sighs. The fair child grew up to be a still fairer woman. From childhood to womanhood her pathway was blooming with flowers, and overarched by a sunny sky. Scarcely one day of her life had been clouded when the sun rose on her happy bridal morning.

How had those years dealt with her slave sister, the little playmate of her childhood? She, also, was very beautiful; but the flowers and sunshine of love were not for her. She drank the cup of sin, and shame, and misery, whereof her persecuted race are compelled to drink.

In view of these things, why are ye silent, ye free men and women of the north? Why do your tongues falter in maintenance of the right? Would that I had more ability! But my heart is so full, and my pen is so weak! There are noble men and women who plead for us, striving to help those who cannot help themselves. God bless them! God give them strength and courage to go on! God bless those, every where, who are laboring to advance the cause of humanity!

VI

The Jealous Mistress

I would ten thousand times rather that my children should be the half-starved paupers of Ireland than to be the most pampered among the slaves of America. I would rather drudge out my life on a cotton plantation, till the grave opened to give me rest, than to live with an unprincipled master and a jealous mistress. The felon's home in a penitentiary is preferable. He may repent, and turn from the error of his ways, and so find peace; but it is not so with a favorite slave. She is not allowed to have any pride of character. It is deemed a crime in her to wish to be virtuous.

Mrs. Flint possessed the key to her husband's character before I was born. She might have used this knowledge to counsel and to screen the young and the innocent among her slaves; but for them she had no sympathy. They were the objects of her constant suspicion and malevolence. She watched her husband with unceasing vigilance; but he was well practised in means to evade it. What he could not find opportunity to say in words he manifested in signs. He invented more than were ever thought of in a deaf and dumb asylum. I let them pass, as if I did not understand what he meant; and many were the curses and threats bestowed on me for my stupidity. One day he caught me teaching myself to write. He frowned, as if he was not well pleased; but I suppose he came to the conclusion that such an accomplishment might help to advance his favorite scheme. Before long, notes were often slipped into my hand. I would return them, saying, "I can't read them, sir." "Can't you?" he replied; "then I must read them to you." He always finished the reading by asking, "Do you understand?" Sometimes he would complain of the heat of the tea room, and order his supper to be placed on a small table in the piazza. He would seat himself there with a well-satisfied smile, and tell me to stand by and brush away the flies. He would eat very slowly, pausing between the mouthfuls. These intervals were employed in describing the happiness I was so foolishly throwing away, and in threatening me with the penalty that finally awaited my stubborn disobedience. He boasted much of the forbearance he had exercised towards me, and reminded me that there was a limit to his patience. When I succeeded in avoiding opportunities for him to talk to me at home, I was ordered to come to his office, to do some errand. When there, I was obliged to stand and listen to such language as he saw fit to address to me. Sometimes I so openly expressed my contempt for him that he would become violently enraged, and I wondered why he did not strike me. Circumstanced as he was, he probably thought it was better policy to be forbearing. But the state of things grew worse and worse daily. In desperation I told him that I must and would apply to my grandmother for protection. He threatened me with death, and worse than death, if I made any complaint to her. Strange to say, I did not despair. I was naturally of a buoyant disposition, and always I had a hope of somehow getting out of his clutches. Like many a poor, simple slave before me, I trusted that some threads of joy would yet be woven into my dark destiny.

I had entered my sixteenth year, and every day it became more apparent that my presence was intolerable to Mrs. Flint. Angry words frequently passed between her and her husband. He had never punished me himself, and he would not allow any body else to punish me. In that respect, she was never satisfied; but, in her angry moods, no terms were too vile for her to bestow upon me. Yet I, whom she detested so bitterly, had far more pity for her than he had, whose duty it was to make her life happy. I never wronged her, or wished to wrong her; and one word of kindness from her would have brought me to her feet.

After repeated quarrels between the doctor and his wife, he announced his intention to take his youngest daughter, then four years old, to sleep in his apartment. It was necessary that a servant should sleep in the same room, to be on hand if the child stirred. I was selected for that office, and informed for what purpose that arrangement had been made. By managing to keep within sight of people, as much as possible, during the day time, I had hitherto succeeded in eluding my master, though a razor was often held to my throat to force me to change this line of policy. At night I slept by the side of my great aunt, where I felt safe. He was too prudent to come into her room. She was an old woman, and had been in the family many years. Moreover, as a married man, and a professional man, he deemed it necessary to save appearances in some degree. But he resolved to remove the obstacle in the way of his scheme; and he thought he had planned it so that he should evade suspicion. He was well aware how much I prized my refuge by the side of my old aunt, and he determined to dispossess me of it. The first night the doctor had the little child in his room alone. The next morning, I was ordered to take my station as nurse the following night. A kind Providence interposed in my favor. During the day Mrs. Flint heard of this new arrangement, and a storm followed. I rejoiced to hear it rage.

After a while my mistress sent for me to come to her room. Her first question was, "Did you know you were to sleep in the doctor's room?"

"Yes, ma'am."

"Who told you?"

"My master."

"Will you answer truly all the questions I ask?"

"Yes, ma'am."

"Tell me, then, as you hope to be forgiven, are you innocent of what I have accused you?"

"I am."

She handed me a Bible, and said, "Lay your hand on your heart, kiss this holy book, and swear before God that you tell me the truth."

I took the oath she required, and I did it with a clear conscience.

"You have taken God's holy word to testify your innocence," said she. "If you have

deceived me, beware! Now take this stool, sit down, look me directly in the face, and tell me all that has passed between your master and you."

I did as she ordered. As I went on with my account her color changed frequently, she wept, and sometimes groaned. She spoke in tones so sad, that I was touched by her grief. The tears came to my eyes; but I was soon convinced that her emotions arose from anger and wounded pride. She felt that her marriage vows were desecrated, her dignity insulted; but she had no compassion for the poor victim of her husband's perfidy. She pitied herself as a martyr; but she was incapable of feeling for the condition of shame and misery in which her unfortunate, helpless slave was placed.

Yet perhaps she had some touch of feeling for me; for when the conference was ended, she spoke kindly, and promised to protect me. I should have been much comforted by this assurance if I could have had confidence in it; but my experiences in slavery had filled me with distrust. She was not a very refined woman, and had not much control over her passions. I was an object of her jealousy, and, consequently, of her hatred; and I knew I could not expect kindness or confidence from her under the circumstances in which I was placed. I could not blame her. Slaveholders' wives feel as other women would under similar circumstances. The fire of her temper kindled from small sparks, and now the flame became so intense that the doctor was obliged to give up his intended arrangement.

I knew I had ignited the torch, and I expected to suffer for it afterwards; but I felt too thankful to my mistress for the timely aid she rendered me to care much about that. She now took me to sleep in a room adjoining her own. There I was an object of her especial care, though not of her especial comfort, for she spent many a sleepless night to watch over me. Sometimes I woke up, and found her bending over me. At other times she whispered in my ear, as though it was her husband who was speaking to me, and listened to hear what I would answer. If she startled me, on such occasions, she would glide stealthily away; and the next morning she would tell me I had been talking in my sleep, and ask who I was talking to. At last, I began to be fearful for my life. It had been often threatened; and you can imagine, better than I can describe, what an unpleasant sensation it must produce to wake up in the dead of night and find a jealous woman bending over you. Terrible as this experience was, I had fears that it would give place to one more terrible.

My mistress grew weary of her vigils; they did not prove satisfactory. She changed her tactics. She now tried the trick of accusing my master of crime, in my presence, and gave my name as the author of the accusation. To my utter astonishment, he replied, "I don't believe it: but if she did acknowledge it, you tortured her into exposing me." Tortured into exposing him! Truly, Satan had no difficulty in distinguishing the color of his soul! I understood his object in making this false representation. It was to show me that I gained nothing by seeking the protection of my mistress; that the power was still all in his own hands. I pitied Mrs. Flint. She was a second wife, many years the junior of her husband; and the hoary-headed miscreant was enough to try the patience of a wiser and better woman. She was completely foiled, and knew not how to proceed. She would gladly have had me flogged for my supposed false oath; but, as I have already stated, the doctor never allowed any one to whip me. The old sinner was politic. The application of the lash might have led to remarks that would have exposed him in the eyes of his children and grandchildren. How often did I rejoice that I lived in a town where all the inhabitants knew each other! If I had been on a remote plantation, or lost among the multitude of a crowded city, I should not be a living woman at this day.

The secrets of slavery are concealed like those of the Inquisition. My master was, to my knowledge, the father of eleven slaves.

But did the mothers dare to tell who was the father of their children? Did the other slaves dare to allude to it, except in whispers among themselves? No, indeed! They knew too well the terrible consequences.

My grandmother could not avoid seeing things which excited her suspicions. She was uneasy about me, and tried various ways to buy me; but the neverchanging answer was always repeated: "Linda does not belong to *me*. She is my daughter's property, and I have no legal right to sell her." The conscientious man! He was too scrupulous to *sell* me; but he had no scruples whatever about committing a much greater wrong against the helpless young girl placed under his guardianship, as his daughter's property. Sometimes my persecutor would ask me whether I would like to be sold. I told him I would rather be sold to any body than to lead such a life as I did. On such occasions he would assume the air of a very injured individual, and reproach me for my ingratitude. "Did I not take you into the house, and make you the companion of my own children?" he would say. "Have I ever treated you like a negro? I have never allowed you to be punished, not even to please your mistress. And this is the recompense I get, you ungrateful girl!" I answered that he had reasons of his own for screening me from punishment, and that the course he pursued made my mistress hate me and persecute me. If I wept, he would say, "Poor child! Don't cry! don't cry! I will make peace for you with your mistress. Only let me arrange matters in my own way. Poor, foolish girl! you don't know what is for your own good. I would cherish you. I would make a lady of you. Now go, and think of all I have promised you."

I did think of it.

Reader, I draw no imaginary pictures of southern homes. I am telling you the plain truth. Yet when victims make their escape from this wild beast of Slavery, northerners consent to act the part of bloodhounds, and hunt the poor fugitive back into his den, "full of dead men's bones, and all uncleanness." Nay, more, they are not only willing, but proud, to give their daughters in marriage to slaveholders. The poor girls have romantic notions of a sunny clime, and of the flowering vines that all the year round shade a happy home. To what disappointments are they destined! The young wife soon learns that the husband in whose hands she has placed her happiness pays no regard to his marriage vows. Children of every shade of complexion play with her own fair babies, and too well she knows that they are born unto him of his own household. Jealousy and hatred enter the flowery home, and it is ravaged of its loveliness.

Southern women often marry a man knowing that he is the father of many little slaves. They do not trouble themselves about it. They regard such children as property, as marketable as the pigs on the plantation; and it is seldom that they do not make them aware of this by passing them into the slavetrader's hands as soon as possible, and thus getting them out of their sight. I am glad to say there are some honorable exceptions.

I have myself known two southern wives who exhorted their husbands to free those slaves towards whom they stood in a "parental relation;" and their request was granted. These husbands blushed before the superior nobleness of their wives' natures. Though they had only counselled them to do that which it was their duty to do, it commanded their respect, and rendered their conduct more exemplary. Concealment was at an end, and confidence took the place of distrust.

Though this bad institution deadens the moral sense, even in white women, to a fearful extent, it is not altogether extinct. I have heard southern ladies say of Mr. Such a one, "He not only thinks it no disgrace to be the father of those little niggers, but he is not ashamed to call himself their master. I declare, such things ought not to be tolerated in any decent society!"

X

A Perilous Passage in the Slave Girl's Life

. . . And now, reader, I come to a period in my unhappy life, which I would gladly forget if I could. The remembrance fills me with sorrow and shame. It pains me to tell you of it; but I have promised to tell you the truth, and I will do it honestly, let it cost me what it may. I will not try to screen myself behind the plea of compulsion from a master; for it was not so. Neither can I plead ignorance or thoughtlessness. For years, my master had done his utmost to pollute my mind with foul images, and to destroy the pure principles inculcated by my grandmother, and the good mistress of my childhood. The influences of slavery had had the same effect on me that they had on other young girls; they had made me prematurely knowing, concerning the evil ways of the world. I knew what I did, and I did it with deliberate calculation.

But, O, ye happy women, whose purity has been sheltered from childhood, who have been free to choose the objects of your affection, whose homes are protected by law, do not judge the poor desolate slave girl too severely! If slavery had been abolished, I, also, could have married the man of my choice; I could have had a home shielded by the laws; and I should have been spared the painful task of confessing what I am now about to relate; but all my prospects had been blighted by slavery. I wanted to keep myself pure; and, under the most adverse circumstances, I tried hard to preserve my self-respect; but I was struggling alone in the powerful grasp of the demon Slavery; and the monster proved too strong for me. I felt as if I was forsaken by God and man; as if all my efforts must be frustrated; and I became reckless in my despair.

I have told you that Dr. Flint's persecutions and his wife's jealousy had given rise to some gossip in the neighborhood. Among others, it chanced that a white unmarried gentleman had obtained some knowledge of the circumstances in which I was placed. He knew my grandmother, and often spoke to me in the street. He became interested for me, and asked questions about my master, which I answered in part. He expressed a great deal of sympathy, and a wish to aid me. He constantly sought opportunities to see me, and wrote to me frequently. I was a poor slave girl, only fifteen years old.

So much attention from a superior person was, of course, flattering; for human nature is the same in all. I also felt grateful for his sympathy, and encouraged by his kind words. It seemed to me a great thing to have such a friend. By degrees, a more tender feeling crept into my heart. He was an educated and eloquent gentleman; too eloquent, alas, for the poor slave girl who trusted in him. Of course I saw whither all this was tending. I knew the impassable gulf between us; but to be an object of interest to a man who is not married, and who is not her master, is agreeable to the pride and feelings of a slave, if her miserable situation has left her any pride or sentiment. It seems less degrading to give one's self, than to submit to compulsion. There is something akin to freedom in having a lover who has no control over you, except that which he gains by kindness and attachment. A master may treat you as rudely as he pleases, and you dare not speak; moreover, the wrong does not seem so great with an unmarried man, as with one who has a wife to be made unhappy. There may be sophistry in all this; but the condition of a slave confuses all principles of morality, and, in fact, renders the practice of them impossible.

When I found that my master had actually begun to build the lonely cottage, other feelings mixed with those I have described. Revenge, and calculations of interest, were added to flattered vanity and sincere gratitude for kindness. I knew nothing would enrage Dr. Flint so much as to know that I favored another; and it was something to triumph over my tyrant even in that small

way. I thought he would revenge himself by selling me, and I was sure my friend, Mr. Sands, would buy me. He was a man of more generosity and feeling than my master, and I thought my freedom could be easily obtained from him. The crisis of my fate now came so near that I was desperate. I shuddered to think of being the mother of children that should be owned by my old tyrant. I knew that as soon as a new fancy took him, his victims were sold far off to get rid of them; especially if they had children. I had seen several women sold, with his babies at the breast. He never allowed his offspring by slaves to remain long in sight of himself and his wife. Of a man who was not my master I could ask to have my children well supported; and in this case, I felt confident I should obtain the boon. I also felt quite sure that they would be made free. With all these thoughts revolving in my mind, and seeing no other way of escaping the doom I so much dreaded, I made a headlong, plunge. Pity me, and pardon me, O virtuous reader! You never knew what it is to be a slave; to be entirely unprotected by law or custom; to have the laws reduce you to the condition of a chattel, entirely subject to the will of another. You never exhausted your ingenuity in avoiding the snares, and eluding the power of a hated tyrant; you never shuddered at the sound of his footsteps, and trembled within hearing of his voice. I know I did wrong. No one can feel it more sensibly than I do. The painful and humiliating memory will haunt me to my dying day. Still, in looking back, calmly, on the events of my life, I feel that the slave woman ought not to be judged by the same standard as others.

The months passed on. I had many unhappy hours. I secretly mourned over the sorrow I was bringing on my grandmother, who had so tried to shield me from harm. I knew that I was the greatest comfort of her old age, and that it was a source of pride to her that I had not degraded myself, like most of the slaves. I wanted to confess to her that I was no longer worthy of her love; but I could not utter the dreaded words.

As for Dr. Flint, I had a feeling of satisfaction and triumph in the thought of telling *him*. From time to time he told me of his intended arrangements, and I was silent. At last, he came and told me the cottage was completed, and ordered me to go to it. I told him I would never enter it. He said, "I have heard enough of such talk as that. You shall go, if you are carried by force; and you shall remain there."

I replied, "I will never go there. In a few months I shall be a mother."

He stood and looked at me in dumb amazement, and left the house without a word. I thought I should be happy in my triumph over him. But now that the truth was out, and my relatives would hear of it, I felt wretched. Humble as were their circumstances, they had pride in my good character. Now, how could I look them in the face? My self-respect was gone! I had resolved that I would be virtuous, though I was a slave. I had said, "Let the storm beat! I will brave it till I die." And now, how humiliated I felt!

I went to my grandmother. My lips moved to make confession, but the words stuck in my throat. I sat down in the shade of a tree at her door and began to sew. I think she saw something unusual was the matter with me. The mother of slaves is very watchful. She knows there is no security for her children. After they have entered their teens she lives in daily expectation of trouble. This leads to many questions. If the girl is of a sensitive nature, timidity keeps her from answering truthfully, and this well-meant course has a tendency to drive her from maternal counsels. Presently, in came my mistress, like a mad woman, and accused me concerning her husband. My grandmother, whose suspicions had been previously awakened, believed what she said. She exclaimed, "O Linda! has it come to this? I had rather see you dead than to see you as you now are. You are a disgrace to your dead mother." She tore from my fingers my mother's wedding ring and her silver thimble. "Go away!" she exclaimed, "and

never come to my house, again." Her reproaches fell so hot and heavy, that they left me no chance to answer. Bitter tears, such as the eyes never shed but once, were my only answer. I rose from my seat, but fell back again, sobbing. She did not speak to me; but the tears were running down her furrowed cheeks, and they scorched me like fire. She had always been so kind to me! *So* kind! How I longed to throw myself at her feet, and tell her all the truth! But she had ordered me to go, and never to come there again. After a few minutes, I mustered strength, and started to obey her. With what feelings did I now close that little gate, which I used to open with such an eager hand in my childhood! It closed upon me with a sound I never heard before.

Where could I go? I was afraid to return to my master's. I walked on recklessly, not caring where I went, or what would become of me. When I had gone four or five miles, fatigue compelled me to stop. I sat down on the stump of an old tree. The stars were shining through the boughs above me. How they mocked me, with their bright, calm light! The hours passed by, and as I sat there alone a chilliness and deadly sickness came over me. I sank on the ground. My mind was full of horrid thoughts. I prayed to die; but the prayer was not answered. At last, with great effort I roused myself, and walked some distance further, to the house of a woman who had been a friend of my mother. When I told her why I was there, she spoke soothingly to me; but I could not be comforted. I thought I could bear my shame if I could only be reconciled to my grandmother. I longed to open my heart to her. I thought if she could know the real state of the case, and all I had been bearing for years, she would perhaps judge me less harshly. My friend advised me to send for her. I did so; but days of agonizing suspense passed before she came. Had she utterly forsaken me? No. She came at last. I knelt before her, and told her the things that had poisoned my life; how long I had been persecuted; that I saw no way of escape; and in an hour of extremity I had become desperate. She listened in silence. I told her I would bear any thing and do any thing, if in time I had hopes of obtaining her forgiveness. I begged of her to pity me, for my dead mother's sake. And she did pity me. She did not say, "I forgive you;" but she looked at me lovingly, with her eyes full of tears. She laid her old hand gently on my head, and murmured, "Poor child! Poor child!"

XII

Fear of Insurrection

Not far from this time Nat Turner's insurrection broke out; and the news threw our town into great commotion. Strange that they should be alarmed, when their slaves were so "contented and happy"! But so it was.

It was always the custom to have a muster every year. On that occasion every white man shouldered his musket. The citizens and the so-called country gentlemen wore military uniforms. The poor whites took their places in the ranks in every-day dress, some without shoes, some without hats. This grand occasion had already passed; and when the slaves were told there was to be another muster, they were surprised and rejoiced. Poor creatures! They thought it was going to be a holiday. I was informed of the true state of affairs, and imparted it to the few I could trust. Most gladly would I have proclaimed it to every slave; but I dared not. All could not be relied on. Mighty is the power of the torturing lash.

By sunrise, people were pouring in from every quarter within twenty miles of the town. I knew the houses were to be searched; and I expected it would be done by country bullies and the poor whites. I knew nothing annoyed them so much as to see colored people living in comfort and respectability; so I made arrangements for them with especial care. I arranged every thing in my grandmother's house as neatly as possible. I put white quilts on the beds, and decorated some of the rooms with flowers. When all was

arranged, I sat down at the window to watch. Far as my eye could reach, it rested on a motley crowd of soldiers. Drums and fifes were discoursing martial music. The men were divided into companies of sixteen, each headed by a captain. Orders were given, and the wild scouts rushed in every direction, wherever a colored face was to be found.

It was a grand opportunity for the low whites, who had no negroes of their own to scourge. They exulted in such a chance to exercise a little brief authority, and show their subserviency to the slaveholders; not reflecting that the power which trampled on the colored people also kept themselves in poverty, ignorance, and moral degradation. Those who never witnessed such scenes can hardly believe what I know was inflicted at this time on innocent men, women, and children, against whom there was not the slightest ground for suspicion. Colored people and slaves who lived in remote parts of the town suffered in an especial manner. In some cases the searchers scattered powder and shot among their clothes, and then sent other parties to find them, and bring them forward as proof that they were plotting insurrection. Every where men, women, and children were whipped till the blood stood in puddles at their feet. Some received five hundred lashes; others were tied hands and feet, and tortured with a bucking paddle, which blisters the skin terribly. The dwellings of the colored people, unless they happened to be protected by some influential white person, who was nigh at hand, were robbed of clothing and every thing else the marauders thought worth carrying away. All day long these unfeeling wretches went round, like a troop of demons, terrifying and tormenting the helpless. At night, they formed themselves into patrol bands, and went wherever they chose among the colored people, acting out their brutal will. Many women hid themselves in woods and swamps, to keep out of their way. If any of the husbands or fathers told of these outrages, they were tied up to the public whipping post, and cruelly scourged for telling lies about white men. The consternation was universal. No two people that had the slightest tinge of color in their faces dared to be seen talking together.

I entertained no positive fears about our household, because we were in the midst of white families who would protect us. We were ready to receive the soldiers whenever they came. It was not long before we heard the tramp of feet and the sound of voices. The door was rudely pushed open; and in they tumbled, like a pack of hungry wolves. They snatched at every thing within their reach. Every box, trunk, closet, and corner underwent a thorough examination. A box in one of the drawers containing some silver change was eagerly pounced upon. When I stepped forward to take it from them, one of the soldiers turned and said angrily, "What d'ye foller us fur? D'ye s'pose white folks is come to steal?"

I replied, "You have come to search; but you have searched that box, and I will take it, if you please."

At that moment I saw a white gentleman who was friendly to us; and I called to him, and asked him to have the goodness to come in and stay till the search was over. He readily complied. His entrance into the house brought in the captain of the company, whose business it was to guard the outside of the house, and see that none of the inmates left it. This officer was Mr. Litch, the wealthy slaveholder whom I mentioned, in the account of neighboring planters, as being notorious for his cruelty. He felt above soiling his hands with the search. He merely gave orders; and, if a bit of writing was discovered, it was carried to him by his ignorant followers, who were unable to read.

My grandmother had a large trunk of bedding and table cloths. When that was opened, there was a great shout of surprise; and one exclaimed, "Where'd the damned niggers git all dis sheet an' table clarf?"

My grandmother, emboldened by the presence of our white protector, said, "You may be sure we didn't pilfer 'em from *your* houses."

"Look here, mammy," said a grim-looking fellow without any coat, "you seem to feel mighty gran' 'cause you got all them 'ere fixens. White folks oughter have 'em all."

His remarks were interrupted by a chorus of voices shouting, "We's got 'em! We's got 'em! Dis 'ere yaller gal's got letters!"

There was a general rush for the supposed letter, which, upon examination, proved to be some verses written to me by a friend. In packing away my things, I had overlooked them. When their captain informed them of their contents, they seemed much disappointed. He inquired of me who wrote them. I told him it was one of my friends. "Can you read them?" he asked. When I told him I could, he swore, and raved, and tore the paper into bits. "Bring me all your letters!" said he, in a commanding tone. I told him I had none. "Don't be afraid," he continued, in an insinuating way. "Bring them all to me. Nobody shall do you any harm." Seeing I did not move to obey him, his pleasant tone changed to oaths and threats. "Who writes to you? half free niggers?" inquired he. I replied, "O, no; most of my letters are from white people. Some request me to burn them after they are read, and some I destroy without reading."

An exclamation of surprise from some of the company put a stop to our conversation. Some silver spoons which ornamented an old-fashioned buffet had just been discovered. My grandmother was in the habit of preserving fruit for many ladies in the town, and of preparing suppers for parties; consequently she had many jars of preserves. The closet that contained these was next invaded, and the contents tasted. One of them, who was helping himself freely, tapped his neighbor on the shoulder, and said, "Wal done! Don't wonder de niggers want to kill all de white folks, when dey live on 'sarves" [meaning preserves]. I stretched out my hand to take the jar, saying, "You were not sent here to search for sweetmeats."

"And what *were* we sent for?" said the captain, bristling up to me. I evaded the question.

The search of the house was completed, and nothing found to condemn us. They next proceeded to the garden, and knocked about every bush and vine, with no better success. The captain called his men together, and, after a short consultation, the order to march was given. As they passed out of the gate, the captain turned back, and pronounced a malediction on the house. He said it ought to be burned to the ground, and each of its inmates receive thirty-nine lashes. We came out of this affair very fortunately; not losing any thing except some wearing apparel.

Towards evening the turbulence increased. The soldiers, stimulated by drink, committed still greater cruelties. Shrieks and shouts continually rent the air. Not daring to go to the door, I peeped under the window curtain. I saw a mob dragging along a number of colored people, each white man, with his musket upraised, threatening instant death if they did not stop their shrieks. Among the prisoners was a respectable old colored minister. They had found a few parcels of shot in his house, which his wife had for years used to balance her scales. For this they were going to shoot him on Court House Green. What a spectacle was that for a civilized country! A rabble, staggering under intoxication, assuming to be the administrators of justice!

The better class of the community exerted their influence to save the innocent, persecuted people; and in several instances they succeeded, by keeping them shut up in jail till the excitement abated. At last the white citizens found that their own property was not safe from the lawless rabble they had summoned to protect them. They rallied the drunken swarm, drove them back into the country, and set a guard over the town.

The next day, the town patrols were commissioned to search colored people that lived out of the city; and the most shocking outrages were committed with perfect impunity. Every day for a fortnight, if I looked out, I saw horsemen with some poor panting negro tied to their saddles, and compelled by the lash to keep up with their speed, till they arrived at the jail yard. Those who had

been whipped too unmercifully to walk were washed with brine, tossed into a cart, and carried to jail. One black man, who had not fortitude to endure scourging, promised to give information about the conspiracy. But it turned out that he knew nothing at all. He had not even heard the name of Nat Turner. The poor fellow had, however, made up a story, which augmented his own sufferings and those of the colored people.

The day patrol continued for some weeks, and at sundown a night guard was substituted. Nothing at all was proved against the colored people, bond or free. The wrath of the slaveholders was somewhat appeased by the capture of Nat Turner. The imprisoned were released. The slaves were sent to their masters, and the free were permitted to return to their ravaged homes. Visiting was strictly forbidden on the plantations. The slaves begged the privilege of again meeting at their little church in the woods, with their burying ground around it. It was built by the colored people, and they had no higher happiness than to meet there and sing hymns together, and pour out their hearts in spontaneous prayer. Their request was denied, and the church was demolished. They were permitted to attend the white churches, a certain portion of the galleries being appropriated to their use. There, when every body else had partaken of the communion, and the benediction had been pronounced, the minister said, "Come down, now, my colored friends." They obeyed the summons, and partook of the bread and wine, in commemoration of the meek and lowly Jesus, who said, "God is your Father, and all ye are brethren."...

When Dr. Flint learned that I was again to be a mother, he was exasperated beyond measure. He rushed from the house, and returned with a pair of shears. I had a fine head of hair; and he often railed about my pride of arranging it nicely. He cut every hair close to my head, storming and swearing all the time. I replied to some of his abuse, and he struck me. Some months before, he had pitched me down stairs in a fit of passion; and the injury I received was so serious that I was unable to turn myself in bed for many days. He then said, "Linda, I swear by God I will never raise my hand against you again;" but I knew that he would forget his promise.

After he discovered my situation, he was like a restless spirit from the pit. He came every day; and I was subjected to such insults as no pen can describe. I would not describe them if I could; they were too low, too revolting. I tried to keep them from my grandmother's knowledge as much as I could. I knew she had enough to sadden her life, without having my troubles to bear. When she saw the doctor treat me with violence, and heard him utter oaths terrible enough to palsy a man's tongue, she could not always hold her peace. It was natural and motherlike that she should try to defend me; but it only made matters worse.

When they told me my new-born babe was a girl, my heart was heavier than it had ever been before. Slavery is terrible for men; but it is far more terrible for women. Superadded to the burden common to all, *they* have wrongs, and sufferings, and mortifications peculiarly their own.

Dr. Flint had sworn that he would make me suffer, to my last day, for this new crime against *him*, as he called it; and as long as he had me in his power he kept his word. On the fourth day after the birth of my babe, he entered my room suddenly, and commanded me to rise and bring my baby to him. The nurse who took care of me had gone out of the room to prepare some nourishment, and I was alone. There was no alternative. I rose, took up my babe, and crossed the room to where he sat. "Now stand there," said he, "till I tell you to go back!" My child bore a strong resemblance to her father, and to the deceased Mrs. Sands, her grandmother. He noticed this; and while I stood before him, trembling with weakness, he heaped upon me and my little one every vile epithet he could think of. Even the grandmother in her grave did not escape his curses. In the midst of his vituperations I fainted at his feet. This recalled him to his senses. He took the baby from my arms, laid it on the bed, dashed cold water in my face, took me up, and shook me violently, to restore my consciousness before any one entered the room. Just then my grandmother came in, and he hurried out of the house. I suffered in consequence of this treatment; but I begged my friends to let me die, rather than send for the doctor. There was nothing I dreaded so much as his presence. My life was spared; and I was glad for the sake of my little ones. Had it not been for these ties to life, I should have been glad to be released by death, though I had lived only nineteen years.

Always it gave me a pang that my children had no lawful claim to a name. Their father offered his; but, if I had wished to accept the offer, I dared not while my master lived. Moreover, I knew it would not be accepted at their baptism. A Christian name they were at least entitled to; and we resolved to call my boy for our dear good Benjamin, who had gone far away from us. . . .

. . . I went forth into the darkness and rain. I ran on till I came to the house of the friend who was to conceal me.

Early the next morning Mr. Flint was at my grandmother's inquiring for me. She told him she had not seen me, and supposed I was at the plantation. He watched her face narrowly, and said, "Don't you know any thing about her running off?" She assured him that she did not. He went on to say, "Last night she ran off without the least provocation. We had treated her very kindly. My wife liked her. She will soon be found and brought back. Are her children with you?" When told that they were, he said, "I am very glad to hear that. If they are here, she cannot be far off. If I find out that any of my niggers have had any thing to do with this damned business, I'll give 'em five hundred lashes." As he started to go to his father's, he turned round and added, persuasively, "Let her be brought back, and she shall have her children to live with her."

The tidings made the old doctor rave and storm at a furious rate. It was a busy day for them. My grandmother's house was searched from top to bottom. As my trunk was empty, they concluded I had taken my clothes with me. Before ten o'clock every vessel northward bound was thoroughly examined, and the law against harboring fugitives was read to all on board. At night a watch was set over the town. Knowing how distressed my grandmother would be, I wanted to send her a message; but it could not be done. Every one who went in or out of her house was closely watched. The doctor said he would take my children, unless she became responsible for them; which of course she willingly did. The next day was spent in searching. Before night, the following advertisement was posted at every corner, and in every public place for miles round:—

"$300 Reward! Ran away from the subscriber, an intelligent, bright, mulatto girl, named Linda, 21 years of age. Five feet four inches high. Dark eyes, and black hair inclined to curl; but it can be made straight. Has a decayed spot on a front tooth. She can read and write, and in all probability will try to get to the Free States. All persons are forbidden, under penalty of the law, to harbor or employ said slave. $150 will be given to whoever takes her in the state, and $300 if taken out of the state and delivered to me, or lodged in jail.

DR. FLINT.". . .

XVIII

Months of Peril

The search for me was kept up with more perseverance than I had anticipated. I began to think that escape was impossible. I was in great anxiety lest I should implicate the friend who harbored me. I knew the consequences would be frightful; and much as I dreaded being caught, even that seemed better than causing an innocent person to suffer for kindness to me. A week had passed in terrible suspense, when my pursuers came into such close vicinity that I concluded they

had tracked me to my hiding-place. I flew out of the house, and concealed myself in a thicket of bushes. There I remained in an agony of fear for two hours. Suddenly, a reptile of some kind seized my leg. In my fright, I struck a blow which loosened its hold, but I could not tell whether I had killed it; it was so dark, I could not see what it was; I only knew it was something cold and slimy. The pain I felt soon indicated that the bite was poisonous. I was compelled to leave my place of concealment, and I groped my way back into the house. The pain had become intense, and my friend was startled by my look of anguish. I asked her to prepare a poultice of warm ashes and vinegar, and I applied it to my leg, which was already much swollen. The application gave me some relief, but the swelling did not abate. The dread of being disabled was greater than the physical pain I endured. My friend asked an old woman, who doctored among the slaves, what was good for the bite of a snake or a lizard. She told her to steep a dozen coppers in vinegar, over night, and apply the cankered vinegar to the inflamed part.*

I had succeeded in cautiously conveying some messages to my relatives. They were harshly threatened, and despairing of my having a chance to escape, they advised me to return to my master, ask his forgiveness, and let him make an example of me. But such counsel had no influence with me. When I started upon this hazardous undertaking, I had resolved that, come what would, there should be no turning back. "Give me liberty, or give me death," was my motto. When my friend contrived to make known to my relatives the painful situation I

---

*The poison of a snake is a powerful acid, and is counteracted by powerful alkalies, such as potash, ammonia, &c. The Indians are accustomed to apply wet ashes, or plunge the limb into strong lye. White men, employed to lay out railroads in snaky places, often carry ammonia with them as an antidote.—Editor.

had been in for twenty-four hours, they said no more about my going back to my master. Something must be done, and that speedily; but where to turn for help, they knew not. God in his mercy raised up "a friend in need.". . .

XXIII

Still in Prison

When spring returned, and I took in the little patch of green the aperture commanded, I asked myself how many more summers and winters I must be condemned to spend thus. I longed to draw in a plentiful draught of fresh air, to stretch my cramped limbs, to have room to stand erect, to feel the earth under my feet again. My relatives were constantly on the lookout for a chance of escape; but none offered that seemed practicable, and even tolerably safe. The hot summer came again, and made the turpentine drop from the thin roof over my head.

During the long nights I was restless for want of air, and I had no room to toss and turn. There was but one compensation; the atmosphere was so stifled that even mosquitos would not condescend to buzz in it. With all my detestation of Dr. Flint, I could hardly wish him a worse punishment, either in this world or that which is to come, than to suffer what I suffered in one single summer. Yet the laws allowed *him* to be out in the free air, while I, guiltless of crime, was pent up here, as the only means of avoiding the cruelties the laws allowed him to inflict upon me! I don't know what kept life within me. Again and again, I thought I should die before long; but I saw the leaves of another autumn whirl through the air, and felt the touch of another winter. In summer the most terrible thunder storms were acceptable, for the rain came through the roof, and I rolled up my bed that it might cool the hot boards under it. Later in the season, storms sometimes wet my clothes through and through, and that was not comfortable when the air grew

chilly. Moderate storms I could keep out by filling the chinks with oakum.

But uncomfortable as my situation was, I had glimpses of things out of doors, which made me thankful for my wretched hiding-place. One day I saw a slave pass our gate, muttering, "It's his own, and he can kill it if he will." My grandmother told me that woman's history. Her mistress had that day seen her baby for the first time, and in the lineaments of its fair face she saw a likeness to her husband. She turned the bondwoman and her child out of doors, and forbade her ever to return. The slave went to her master, and told him what had happened. He promised to talk with her mistress, and make it all right. The next day she and her baby were sold to a Georgia trader.

Another time I saw a woman rush wildly by, pursued by two men. She was a slave, the wet nurse of her mistress's children. For some trifling offence her mistress ordered her to be stripped and whipped. To escape the degradation and the torture, she rushed to the river, jumped in, and ended her wrongs in death.

Senator Brown, of Mississippi, could not be ignorant of many such facts as these, for they are of frequent occurrence in every Southern State. Yet he stood up in the Congress of the United States, and declared that slavery was "a great moral, social, and political blessing; a blessing to the master, and a blessing to the slave!"

I suffered much more during the second winter than I did during the first. My limbs were benumbed by inaction, and the cold filled them with cramp. I had a very painful sensation of coldness in my head; even my face and tongue stiffened, and I lost the power of speech. Of course it was impossible, under the circumstances, to summon any physician. My brother William came and did all he could for me. Uncle Phillip also watched tenderly over me; and poor grandmother crept up and down to inquire whether there were any signs of returning life. I was restored to consciousness by the dashing of cold water in my face, and found myself leaning against my brother's arm, while he bent over me with streaming eyes. He afterwards told me he thought I was dying, for I had been in an unconscious state sixteen hours. I next became delirious, and was in great danger of betraying myself and my friends. To prevent this, they stupefied me with drugs. I remained in bed six weeks, weary in body and sick at heart. How to get medical advice was the question. William finally went to a Thompsonian doctor, and described himself as having all my pains and aches. He returned with herbs, roots, and ointment. He was especially charged to rub on the ointment by a fire; but how could a fire be made in my little den? Charcoal in a furnace was tried, but there was no outlet for the gas, and it nearly cost me my life. Afterwards coals, already kindled, were brought up in an iron pan, and placed on bricks. I was so weak, and it was so long since I had enjoyed the warmth of a fire, that those few coals actually made me weep. I think the medicines did me some good; but my recovery was very slow. Dark thoughts passed through my mind as I lay there day after day. I tried to be thankful for my little cell, dismal as it was, and even to love it, as part of the price I had paid for the redemption of my children. Sometimes I thought God was a compassionate Father, who would forgive my sins for the sake of my sufferings. At other times, it seemed to me there was no justice or mercy in the divine government. I asked why the curse of slavery was permitted to exist, and why I had been so persecuted and wronged from youth upward. These things took the shape of mystery, which is to this day not so clear to my soul as I trust it will be hereafter.

XXV

Competition in Cunning

Dr. Flint had not given me up. Every now and then he would say to my grandmother that I would yet come back, and voluntarily surrender myself; and that when I did, I could be purchased by my relatives, or any one who wished to buy me. I knew his cunning nature too well not to perceive that this was a trap laid for me; and so all my friends understood it. I resolved to match my cunning against his cunning. In order to make him believe that I was in New York, I resolved to write him a letter dated from that place. I sent for my friend Peter, and asked him if he knew any trustworthy seafaring person, who would carry such a letter to New York, and put it in the post office there. He said he knew one that he would trust with his own life to the ends of the world. I reminded him that it was a hazardous thing for him to undertake. He said he knew it, but he was willing to do any thing to help me. I expressed a wish for a New York paper, to ascertain the names of some of the streets. He run his hand into his pocket, and said, "Here is half a one, that was round a cap I bought of a pedler yesterday." I told him the letter would be ready the next evening. He bade me good by, adding, "Keep up your spirits, Linda; brighter days will come by and by."

My uncle Phillip kept watch over the gate until our brief interview was over. Early the next morning, I seated myself near the little aperture to examine the newspaper. It was a piece of the New York Herald; and, for once, the paper that systematically abuses the colored people, was made to render them a service. Having obtained what information I wanted concerning streets and numbers, I wrote two letters, one to my grandmother, the other to Dr. Flint. I reminded him how he, a gray-headed man, had treated a helpless child, who had been placed in his power, and what years of misery he had brought upon her. To my grandmother, I expressed a wish to have my children sent to me at the north, where I could teach them to respect themselves, and set them a virtuous example; which a slave mother was not allowed to do at the south. I asked her to direct her answer to a certain street in Boston, as I did not live in New York, though I went there sometimes. I dated these letters ahead, to allow for the time it would take to carry them, and sent a memorandum of the date to the messenger. When my friend came for the letters, I said, "God bless and reward you, Peter, for this disinterested kindness. Pray be careful. If you are detected, both you and I will have to suffer dreadfully. I have not a relative who would dare to do it for me." He replied, "You may trust to me, Linda. I don't forget that your father was my best friend, and I will be a friend to his children so long as God lets me live."

It was necessary to tell my grandmother what I had done, in order that she might be ready for the letter, and prepared to hear what Dr. Flint might say about my being at the north. She was sadly troubled. She felt sure mischief would come of it. I also told my plan to aunt Nancy, in order that she might report to us what was said at Dr. Flint's house. I whispered it to her through a crack, and she whispered back, "I hope it will succeed. I shan't mind being a slave all *my* life, if I can only see you and the children free."

I had directed that my letters should be put into the New York post office on the 20th of the month. On the evening of the 24th my aunt came to say that Dr. Flint and his wife had been talking in a low voice about a letter he had received, and that when he went to his office he promised to bring it when he came to tea. So I concluded I should hear my letter read the next morning. I told my grandmother Dr. Flint would be sure to come, and asked her to have him sit near a certain door, and leave it open, that I might hear what he said. The next morning I took my station within sound of that door, and remained motionless as a statue. It was not long before I heard the gate slam, and the well-known footsteps enter the house. He seated himself in the chair that was placed for him, and said, "Well, Martha, I've brought you a letter from Linda. She has sent me a letter, also. I know exactly where to find her; but I don't choose to go to Boston for her. I had rather she would come back of her own accord, in a respectable manner. Her uncle Phillip is the best person to go for her. With *him*, she would feel per-

fectly free to act. I am willing to pay his expenses going and returning. She shall be sold to her friends. Her children are free; at least I suppose they are; and when you obtain her freedom, you'll make a happy family. I suppose, Martha, you have no objection to my reading to you the letter Linda has written to you."

He broke the seal, and I heard him read it. The old villain! He had suppressed the letter I wrote to grandmother, and prepared a substitute of his own, the purport of which was as follows:—

"Dear Grandmother: I have long wanted to write to you; but the disgraceful manner in which I left you and my children made me ashamed to do it. If you knew how much I have suffered since I ran away, you would pity and forgive me. I have purchased freedom at a dear rate. If any arrangement could be made for me to return to the south without being a slave, I would gladly come. If not, I beg of you to send my children to the north. I cannot live any longer without them. Let me know in time, and I will meet them in New York or Philadelphia, whichever place best suits my uncle's convenience. Write as soon as possible to your unhappy daughter.

Linda."

"It is very much as I expected it would be," said the old hypocrite, rising to go. "You see the foolish girl has repented of her rashness, and wants to return. We must help her to do it, Martha. Talk with Phillip about it. If he will go for her, she will trust to him, and come back. I should like an answer tomorrow. Good morning, Martha."

XXIX

Preparations for Escape

I hardly expect that the reader will credit me, when I affirm that I lived in that little dismal hole, almost deprived of light and air, and with no space to move my limbs, for nearly seven years. But it is a fact; and to me a sad one, even now; for my body still suffers from the effects of that long imprisonment, to say nothing of my soul. Members of my family, now living in New York and Boston, can testify to the truth of what I say.

Countless were the nights that I sat late at the little loophole scarcely large enough to give me a glimpse of one twinkling star. There, I heard the patrols and slave-hunters conferring together about the capture of runaways, well knowing how rejoiced they would be to catch me.

Season after season, year after year, I peeped at my children's faces, and heard their sweet voices, with a heart yearning all the while to say, "Your mother is here." Sometimes it appeared to me as if ages had rolled away since I entered upon that gloomy, monotonous existence. At times, I was stupefied and listless; at other times I became very impatient to know when these dark years would end, and I should again be allowed to feel the sunshine, and breathe the pure air.

After Ellen left us, this feeling increased. Mr. Sands had agreed that Benny might go to the north whenever his uncle Phillip could go with him; and I was anxious to be there also, to watch over my children, and protect them so far as I was able. Moreover, I was likely to be drowned out of my den, if I remained much longer; for the slight roof was getting badly out of repair, and uncle Phillip was afraid to remove the shingles, lest some one should get a glimpse of me. When storms occurred in the night, they spread mats and bits of carpet, which in the morning appeared to have been laid out to dry; but to cover the roof in the daytime might have attracted attention. Consequently, my clothes and bedding were often drenched; a process by which the pains and aches in my cramped and stiffened limbs were greatly increased. I revolved various plans of escape in my mind, which I sometimes imparted to my grandmother, when she came to whisper with me at the trapdoor. The kind-hearted old woman had an intense sympathy for runaways. She had

known too much of the cruelties inflicted on those who were captured. Her memory always flew back at once to the sufferings of her bright and handsome son, Benjamin, the youngest and dearest of her flock. So, whenever I alluded to the subject, she would groan out, "O, don't think of it, child. You'll break my heart." I had no good old aunt Nancy now to encourage me; but my brother William and my children were continually beckoning me to the north.

And now I must go back a few months in my story. I have stated that the first of January was the time for selling slaves, or leasing them out to new masters. If time were counted by heart-throbs, the poor slaves might reckon years of suffering during that festival so joyous to the free. On the New Year's day preceding my aunt's death, one of my friends, named Fanny, was to be sold at auction, to pay her master's debts. My thoughts were with her during all the day, and at night I anxiously inquired what had been her fate. I was told that she had been sold to one master, and her four little girls to another master, far distant; that she had escaped from her purchaser, and was not to be found. Her mother . . . lived in a small tenement belonging to my grandmother, and built on the same lot with her own house. Her dwelling was searched and watched, and that brought the patrols so near me that I was obliged to keep very close in my den. The hunters were somehow eluded; and not long afterwards Benny accidentally caught sight of Fanny in her mother's hut. He told his grandmother, who charged him never to speak of it, explaining to him the frightful consequences; and he never betrayed the trust. Aggie little dreamed that my grandmother knew where her daughter was concealed, and that the stooping form of her old neighbor was bending under a similar burden of anxiety and fear; but these dangerous secrets deepened the sympathy between the two old persecuted mothers.

My friend Fanny and I remained many weeks hidden within call of each other; but she was unconscious of the fact. I longed to have her share my den, which seemed a more secure retreat than her own; but I had brought so much trouble on my grandmother, that it seemed wrong to ask her to incur greater risks. My restlessness increased. I had lived too long in bodily pain and anguish of spirit. Always I was in dread that by some accident, or some contrivance, slavery would succeed in snatching my children from me. This thought drove me nearly frantic, and I determined to steer for the North Star at all hazards. At this crisis, Providence opened an unexpected way for me to escape. My friend Peter came one evening, and asked to speak with me. "Your day has come, Linda," said he. "I have found a chance for you to go to the Free States. You have a fortnight to decide." The news seemed too good to be true; but Peter explained his arrangements, and told me all that was necessary was for me to say I would go. I was going to answer him with a joyful yes, when the thought of Benny came to my mind. I told him the temptation was exceedingly strong, but I was terribly afraid of Dr. Flint's alleged power over my child, and that I could not go and leave him behind. Peter remonstrated earnestly. He said such a good chance might never occur again; that Benny was free, and could be sent to me; and that for the sake of my children's welfare I ought not to hesitate a moment. I told him I would consult with uncle Phillip. My uncle rejoiced in the plan, and bade me go by all means. He promised, if his life was spared, that he would either bring or send my son to me as soon as I reached a place of safety. I resolved to go, but thought nothing had better be said to my grandmother till very near the time of departure. But my uncle thought she would feel it more keenly if I left her so suddenly. "I will reason with her," said he, "and convince her how necessary it is, not only for your sake, but for hers also. You cannot be blind to the fact that she is sinking under her burdens." I was not blind to it. I knew that my concealment was an ever-present source of anxiety, and that the older she grew the more nervously fear-

ful she was of discovery. My uncle talked with her, and finally succeeded in persuading her that it was absolutely necessary for me to seize the chance so unexpectedly offered.

The anticipation of being a free woman proved almost too much for my weak frame. The excitement stimulated me, and at the same time bewildered me. I made busy preparations for my journey, and for my son to follow me. I resolved to have an interview with him before I went, that I might give him cautions and advice, and tell him how anxiously I should be waiting for him at the north. Grandmother stole up to me as often as possible to whisper words of counsel. She insisted upon my writing to Dr. Flint, as soon as I arrived in the Free States, and asking him to sell me to her. She said she would sacrifice her house, and all she had in the world, for the sake of having me safe with my children in any part of the world. If she could only live to know *that* she could die in peace. I promised the dear old faithful friend that I would write to her as soon as I arrived, and put the letter in a safe way to reach her; but in my own mind I resolved that not another cent of her hard earnings should be spent to pay rapacious slaveholders for what they called their property. And even if I had not been unwilling to buy what I had already a right to possess, common humanity would have prevented me from accepting the generous offer, at the expense of turning my aged relative out of house and home, when she was trembling on the brink of the grave.

I was to escape in a vessel; but I forbear to mention any further particulars. I was in readiness, but the vessel was unexpectedly detained several days. Meantime, news came to town of a most horrible murder committed on a fugitive slave, named James. Charity, the mother of this unfortunate young man, had been an old acquaintance of ours. I have told the shocking particulars of his death, in my description of some of the neighboring slaveholders. My grandmother, always nervously sensitive about runaways, was terribly frightened. She felt sure that a similar fate awaited me, if I did not desist from my enterprise. She sobbed, and groaned, and entreated me not to go. Her excessive fear was somewhat contagious, and my heart was not proof against her extreme agony. I was grievously disappointed, but I promised to relinquish my project.

XXX

Northward Bound

I never could tell how we reached the wharf. My brain was all of a whirl, and my limbs tottered under me. At an appointed place we met my uncle Phillip, who had started before us on a different route, that he might reach the wharf first, and give us timely warning if there was any danger. A row-boat was in readiness. As I was about to step in, I felt something pull me gently, and turning round I saw Benny, looking pale and anxious. He whispered in my ear, "I've been peeping into the doctor's window, and he's at home. Good by, mother. Don't cry; I'll come." He hastened away. I clasped the hand of my good uncle, to whom I owed so much, and of Peter, the brave, generous friend who had volunteered to run such terrible risks to secure my safety. To this day I remember how his bright face beamed with joy, when he told me he had discovered a safe method for me to escape. Yet that intelligent, enterprising, noble-hearted man was a chattel! liable, by the laws of a country that calls itself civilized, to be sold with horses and pigs! We parted in silence. Our hearts were all too full for words!

Swiftly the boat glided over the water. After a while, one of the sailors said, "Don't be down-hearted, madam. We will take you safely to your husband, in ——." At first I could not imagine what he meant; but I had presence of mind to think that it probably referred to something the captain had told him; so I thanked him, and said I hoped we should have pleasant weather.

When I entered the vessel the captain came forward to meet me. He was an elderly man, with a pleasant countenance. He showed me to a little box of a cabin, where sat my friend Fanny. She started as if she had seen a spectre. She gazed on me in utter astonishment, and exclaimed, "Linda, can this be *you?* or is it your ghost?" When we were locked in each other's arms, my overwrought feelings could no longer be restrained. My sobs reached the ears of the captain, who came and very kindly reminded us, that for his safety, as well as our own, it would be prudent for us not to attract any attention. He said that when there was a sail in sight he wished us to keep below; but at other times, he had no objection to our being on deck. He assured us that he would keep a good lookout, and if we acted prudently, he thought we should be in no danger. He had represented us as women going to meet our husbands in ——. We thanked him, and promised to observe carefully all the directions he gave us.

Fanny and I now talked by ourselves, low and quietly, in our little cabin. She told me of the sufferings she had gone through in making her escape, and of her terrors while she was concealed in her mother's house. Above all, she dwelt on the agony of separation from all her children on that dreadful auction day. She could scarcely credit me, when I told her of the place where I had passed nearly seven years. "We have the same sorrows," said I. "No," replied she, "you are going to see your children soon, and there is no hope that I shall ever even hear from mine."

The vessel was soon under way, but we made slow progress. The wind was against us. I should not have cared for this, if we had been out of sight of the town; but until there were miles of water between us and our enemies, we were filled with constant apprehensions that the constables would come on board. Neither could I feel quite at ease with the captain and his men. I was an entire stranger to that class of people, and I had heard that sailors were rough, and sometimes cruel. We were so completely in their power, that if they were bad men, our situation would be dreadful. Now that the captain was paid for our passage, might he not be tempted to make more money by giving us up to those who claimed us as property? I was naturally of a confiding disposition, but slavery had made me suspicious of everybody. Fanny did not share my distrust of the captain or his men. She said she was afraid at first, but she had been on board three days while the vessel lay in the dock, and nobody had betrayed her, or treated her otherwise than kindly.

The captain soon came to advise us to go on deck for fresh air. His friendly and respectful manner, combined with Fanny's testimony, reassured me, and we went with him. He placed us in a comfortable seat, and occasionally entered into conversation. He told us he was a Southerner by birth, and had spent the greater part of his life in the Slave States, and that he had recently lost a brother who traded in slaves. "But," said he, "it is a pitiable and degrading business, and I always felt ashamed to acknowledge my brother in connection with it." As we passed Snaky Swamp, he pointed to it, and said, "There is a slave territory that defies all the laws." I thought of the terrible days I had spent there, and though it was not called Dismal Swamp, it made me feel very dismal as I looked at it.

I shall never forget that night. The balmy air of spring was so refreshing! And how shall I describe my sensations when we were fairly sailing on Chesapeake Bay? O, the beautiful sunshine! the exhilarating breeze! and I could enjoy them without fear or restraint. I had never realized what grand things air and sunlight are till I had been deprived of them.

Ten days after we left land we were approaching Philadelphia. The captain said we should arrive there in the night, but he thought we had better wait till morning, and go on shore in broad daylight, as the best way to avoid suspicion.

I replied, "You know best. But will you stay on board and protect us?"

He saw that I was suspicious, and he said he was sorry, now that he had brought us to the end of our voyage, to find I had so little confidence in him. Ah, if he had ever been a slave he would have known how difficult it was to trust a white man. He assured us that we might sleep through the night without fear; that he would take care we were not left unprotected. Be it said to the honor of this captain, Southerner as he was, that if Fanny and I had been white ladies, and our passage lawfully engaged, he could not have treated us more respectfully. My intelligent friend, Peter, had rightly estimated the character of the man to whose honor he had intrusted us.

The next morning I was on deck as soon as the day dawned. I called Fanny to see the sun rise, for the first time in our lives, on free soil; for such I *then* believed it to be. We watched the reddening sky, and saw the great orb come up slowly out of the water, as it seemed. Soon the waves began to sparkle, and everything caught the beautiful glow. Before us lay the city of strangers. We looked at each other, and the eyes of both were moistened with tears. We had escaped from slavery, and we supposed ourselves to be safe from the hunters. But we were alone in the world, and we had left dear ties behind us; ties cruelly sundered by the demon Slavery.

Five African American Spirituals

Were You There When They Crucified My Lord?

Were you there, when they crucified my Lord?
Were you there, when they crucified my Lord?
Oh, sometimes, it causes me to tremble, tremble,
    tremble.
Were you there, when they crucified my Lord?

Were you there, when they nailed him to the tree?   5
Were you there, when they nailed him to the tree?
Oh, sometimes, it causes me to tremble, tremble,
    tremble.
Were you there, when they nailed him to the tree?

Were you there, when they pierced him in the side?
Were you there, when they pierced him in the
    side?   10
Oh, sometimes, it causes me to tremble, tremble,
    tremble.
Were you there, when they pierced him in the side?

Were you there, when the sun refused to shine?
Were you there, when the sun refused to shine?
Oh, sometimes, it causes me to tremble, tremble,
    tremble.   15
Were you there, when the sun refused to shine?

Were you there, when they laid him in the tomb?
Were you there, when they laid him in the tomb?
Oh, sometimes, it causes me to tremble, tremble,
    tremble.
Were you there, when they laid him in the tomb?   20

Go Down, Moses

Go down, Moses,
Way down in Egyptland
Tell old Pharaoh
To let my people go.

When Israel was in Egyptland   5
Let my people go
Oppressed so hard they could not stand
Let my people go.

Go down, Moses,
Way down in Egyptland   10
Tell old Pharaoh
"Let my people go."

Source: J. Rosamund Johnson & James Weldon Johnson, eds. *The Book of American Negro Spirituals & The Second Book of Negro Spirituals* (New York, 1925, 1926).

"Thus saith the Lord," bold Moses said,
"Let my people go;
If not I'll smite your first-born dead   15
Let my people go.

"No more shall they in bondage toil,
    Let my people go;
Let them come out with Egypt's spoil,
    Let my people go."   20

The Lord told Moses what to do
    Let my people go;
To lead the children of Israel through,
    Let my people go.

Go down, Moses,   25
    Way down in Egyptland,
Tell old Pharaoh,
    "Let my people go!"

Swing Low, Sweet Chariot

Swing low, sweet chariot,
Coming for to carry me home,
Swing low, sweet chariot,
Coming for to carry me home.

I looked over Jordan and what did I see   5
Coming for to carry me home,
A band of angels, coming after me,
Coming for to carry me home.

If you get there before I do,
Coming for to carry me home,   10
Tell all my friends I'm coming too,
Coming for to carry me home.

Swing low, sweet chariot,
Coming for to carry me home,
Swing low, sweet chariot,   15
Coming for to carry me home.

Steal Away to Jesus

Steal away, steal away, steal away to Jesus,
Steal away, steal away home,
I ain't got long to stay here.

My Lord, He calls me,
He calls me by the thunder,   5
The trumpet sounds within-a my soul,
I ain't got long to stay here.

Steal away, steal away, steal away to Jesus,
Steal away, steal away home,
I ain't got long to stay here.   10

Green trees a-bending,
Po' sinner stands a-trembling,
The trumpet sounds within-a my soul,
I ain't got long to stay here.

Steal away, steal away, steal away to Jesus,   15
Steal away, steal away home,
I ain't got long to stay here.

Oh, Freedom!

Oh, freedom,
Oh, freedom,
Oh, freedom over me!
An' befo' I'd be a slave,
I'll be buried in my grave,   5
An' go home to my Lord an' be free.

No mo' moanin',
No mo' moanin',
No mo' moanin' over me!
An' befo' I'd be a slave,   10
I'll be buried in my grave,
An' go home to my Lord an' be free.

No mo' weepin',
No mo' weepin',

No mo' weepin' over me!   15
An' befo' I'd be a slave,
I'll be buried in my grave,
An' go home to my Lord an' be free.

There'll be singin',
There'll be singin',   20
There'll be singin' over me!
An' befo' I'd be a slave,

I'll be buried in my grave,
An' go home to my Lord an' be free.

There'll be shoutin',   25
There'll be shoutin',
There'll be shoutin' over me!
An' befo' I'd be a slave,
I'll be buried in my grave,
An' go home to my Lord an' be free.   30

There'll be prayin',
There'll be prayin',
There'll be prayin' over me!
An' befo' I'd be a slave,
I'll be buried in my grave,   35
An' go home to my Lord an' be free.

Slave Resistance and Discipline

Frederick Law Olmsted

RUNAWAYS IN THE SWAMP

While driving in a chaise from Portsmouth to Deep-river, I picked up on the road a jaded looking negro, who proved to be a very intelligent and good-natured fellow. His account of the lumber business, and of the life of the lumbermen in the swamps, in answer to my questions, was clear and precise, and was afterwards verified by information obtained from his master.

He told me that his name was Joseph, that he belonged to a church in one of the inland counties, and that he was hired out by the trustees of the church to his present master. He expressed entire contentment with his lot, but showed great unwillingness to be sold to go on to a plantation. He liked to "mind himself," as he did in the swamps. Whether he would still more prefer to be entirely his own master, I did not ask.

The Dismal Swamps are noted places of refuge for runaway negroes. They were

Source: "Slave Resistance and Discipline." From Frederick Law Olmsted, *A Journey in the Seaboard Slave States With Remarks on their Economy* (New York, 1856), pp. 159–163, 194–202.

formerly peopled in this way much more than at present; a systematic hunting of them with dogs and guns having been made by individuals who took it up as a business about ten years ago. Children were born, bred, lived and died here. Joseph Church told me he had seen skeletons, and had helped to bury bodies recently dead. There were people in the swamps still, he thought, that were the children of runaways, and who had been runaways themselves all their lives. What a life it must be; born outlaws; educated self-stealers; trained from infancy to be constantly in dread of the approach of a white man as a thing more fearful than wild-cats or serpents, or even starvation.

There can be but few, however, if any, of these "natives" left. They cannot obtain the means of supporting life without coming often either to the outskirts to steal from the plantations, or to the neighborhood of the camps of the lumbermen. They depend much upon the charity or the wages given them by the latter. The poorer white men, owning small tracts of the swamps, will sometimes employ them, and the negroes frequently. In the hands of either they are liable to be betrayed to the negro-hunters. Joseph said that they had huts in "back places," hidden by bushes, and difficult of access; he had, apparently, been himself quite intimate with them. When the shingle negroes employed them, he told me, they made them get up logs for them, and would give them enough to eat, and some clothes, and perhaps two dollars a month in money. But some, when they owed them money, would betray them, instead of paying them.

DISMAL NIGGER HUNTING

I asked if they were ever shot. "Oh, yes," he said, "when the hunters saw a runaway, if he tried to get from them, they would call out to him, that if he did not stop they would shoot, and if he did not, they would shoot, and sometimes kill him.

"But some on 'em would rather be shot than be took, sir," he added, simply.

A farmer living near the swamp confirmed this account, and said he knew of three or four being shot in one day.

No particular breed of dogs is needed for hunting negroes: blood-hounds, fox-hounds, bull-dogs, and curs were used,* and one white man told me how they were trained for it, as if it were a common or notorious practice. They are shut up when puppies, and never allowed to see a negro except while training to catch him. A negro is made to run from them, and they are encouraged to follow him until he gets into a tree, when meat is given them. Afterwards they learn to follow any particular negro by scent, and then a shoe or a piece of clothing is taken off a negro, and they learn to find by scent who it belongs to, and to *tree* him, etc. I don't think they are employed in the ordinary driving in the swamp, but only to overtake some particular slave, as soon as possible after it is discovered that he has fled from a plantation. Joseph said that it was easy for the drivers to tell a fugitive from a regularly employed slave in the swamps.

"How do they know them?"

"Oh, dey looks *strange.*"

"How do you mean?"

"*Skeared* like, you know, sir, and kind 'o strange, cause dey hasn't much to eat, and ain't decent [not decently clothed], like we is."

When the hunters take a negro who has not a pass, or "free papers," and they don't know whose slave he is, they confine him in jail, and advertise him. If no one claims him within a year he is sold to the highest bidder, at a public sale, and this sale gives title in law against any subsequent claimant.

The form of the advertisements used in such cases is shown by the following, which are cut from North Carolina newspapers, published in counties adjoining the Dismals.

---

*I have since seen a pack of negro-dogs, chained in couples, and probably going to the field. They were all of a breed, and in appearance between a Scotch stag-hound and a fox-hound.

Such advertisements are quite as common in the papers of many parts of the Slave States as those of horses or cattle "Taken up" in those of the North:

WAS TAKEN UP and committed to the Jail of Halifax County, on the 26th day of May, a dark colored boy, who says his name is JORDAN ARTIS. Said boy says he was born free, and was bound out to William Beale, near Murfrees-boro', Hertford County, N. C., and is now 21 years of age. The owner is requested to come forward, prove property, pay charges, and take the said boy away, within the time pre-scribed by law; otherwise he will be dealt with as the law directs.

O. P. SHELL, Jailer.
Halifax County, N. C., June 8, 1855.

TAKEN UP,

AND COMMITTED to the Jail of New Hanover County, on the 5th of March, 1855, a Negro Man, who says his name is EDWARD LLOYD. Said negro is about 35 or 40 years old, light complected, 5 feet 9½ inches high, slim built, upper fore teeth out; says he is a Mason by trade, that he is free, and belongs in Alexandria, Va., that he served his time at the Mason business under Mr. Wm. Stuart, of Alexandria. He was taken up and committed as a runaway. His owner is notified to come forward, prove property, pay charges, and take him away, or he will be dealt with as the law directs.

E. D. HALL, Sheriff.

In the same paper with the last are four advertisements of Runaways: two of them, as specimens, I transcribe.

$200 REWARD.

RAN AWAY from the employ of Messrs. Holmes & Brown, on Sunday night, 20th inst., a negro man named YATNEY or MEDICINE, belonging to the undersigned. Said boy is stout built, about 5 feet 4 inches high, 22 years old, and dark complected, and has the appear-ance, when walking slow, of one leg being a little shorter than the other. He was brought from Chapel Hill, and is probably lurking ei-ther in the neighborhood of that place, or Beatty's Bridge, in Bladen County.

The above reward will be paid for evidence sufficient to convict any white person of har-boring him, or a reward of $25 for his appre-hension and confinement in any Jail in the State, so that I can get him, or for his delivery to me in Wilmington.

J. T. SCHONWALD.

RUNAWAY

FROM THE SUBSCRIBER, on the 27th of May, his negro boy ISOME. Said boy is about 21 years of age; rather light complexion; very coarse hair; weight about 150; hight about 5 feet 6 or 7 inches; rather pleasing countenance; quick and easy spoken; rather a downcast look. It is thought that he is trying to make his way to Franklin county, N. C., where he was hired in Jan. last, of Thomas J. Blackwell. A lib-eral Reward will be given for his confinement in any Jail in North or South Carolina, or to any one who will give information where he can be found.

W. H. PRIVETT,
Canwayboro', S. C.

Handbills, written or printed, offering re-wards for the return of Runaway slaves, are to be constantly seen at nearly every court-house, tavern, and post-office in the South-ern States. The frequency with which these losses must occur, however, on large planta-tions, is most strongly evidenced by the fol-lowing paragraph from the domestic-news columns of the *Fayetteville Observer*. A man who would pay these prices must anticipate frequent occasion to use his purchase.

"Mr. J. L. Bryan, of Moore county, sold at public auction, on the 20th instant, a pack of ten hounds, trained for hunting runaways, for the sum of $1,540. The highest price paid for any one dog was $301; lowest price, $75; aver-age for the ten, $154. The terms of sale were six months' credit, with approved security, and interest from date."

The newspapers of the Southwestern States frequently contain advertisements similar to the following, which is taken from the *West Tennessee Democrat:*

BLOOD-HOUNDS.—I have TWO of the FINEST DOGS for CATCHING NEGROES in the Southwest. They can take the trail TWELVE HOURS after the NEGRO HAS PASSED, and catch him with ease. I live just four miles southwest of Boliver, on the road leading from Boliver to Whitesville. I am ready at all times to catch runaway negroes.—March 2, 1853.

DAVID TURNER.

DISCIPLINE

Under the slave system of labor, discipline must always be maintained by physical power. A lady of New York, spending a winter in a Southern city, had a hired slave-servant, who, one day, refused outright to perform some ordinary light domestic duty required of her. On the lady's gently remonstrating with her, she immediately replied: "You can't make me do it, and I won't do it: I aint afeard of you whippin' me." The servant was right; the lady could not whip her, and was too tender-hearted to call in a man, or to send her to the guard-house to be whipped, as is the custom with Southern ladies, when their patience is exhausted, under such circumstances. She endeavored, by kindness and by appeals to the girl's good sense, to obtain a moral control over her; but, after suffering continual annoyance and inconvenience, and after an intense trial of her feelings, for some time, she was at length obliged to go to her owner, and beg him to come and take her away from the house, on any terms. It was no better than having a lunatic or a mischievous and pilfering monomaniac quartered upon her.*

---

*The *Richmond American* has a letter from Raleigh, N. C., dated Sept. 18 which says: "On yesterday morning, a beautiful young lady, Miss Virginia Frost, daughter of Austin Frost, an engineer on the Petersburg and Weldon Rail-road, and residing in this city, was shot by a negro girl, and killed instantly. Cause—reproving her for insolent language."

But often when courage and physical power, with the strength of the militia force and the army of the United States, if required, at the back of the master, are not wanting, there are a great variety of circumstances that make a resort to punishment inconvenient, if not impossible.

Really well-trained, accomplished, and docile house-servants are seldom to be purchased or hired at the South, though they are found in old wealthy families rather oftener than first-rate English or French servants are at the North. It is, doubtless, a convenience to have even moderately good servants who cannot, at any time of their improved value or your necessity, demand to have their pay increased, or who cannot be drawn away from you by prospect of smaller demands and kinder treatment at your neighbor's; but I believe few of those who are incessantly murmuring against this healthy operation of God's good law of supply and demand would be willing to purchase exemption from it, at the price with which the masters and mistresses of the South do. They would pay, to get a certain amount of work done, three or four times as much, to the owner of the best sort of hired slaves, as they do to the commonest, stupidest Irish domestic drudges at the North, though the nominal wages by the week or year, in Virginia, are but little more than in New York.

The number of servants usually found in a Southern family, of any pretension, always amazes a Northern lady. In one that I visited, there were exactly three negroes to each white, and this in a town, the negroes being employed solely in the house.

A Southern lady, of an old and wealthy family, who had been for some time visiting a friend of mine in New York, said to her, as she was preparing to return home: "I can not tell you how much, after being in your house so long, I dread to go home, and to have to take care of our servants again. We have a much smaller family of whites than you, but we have twelve servants, and your two accomplish a great deal more, and do their work a great deal better than our twelve. You think your girls are very stupid, and that they give you much trouble: but it is as nothing. There is hardly one of our servants that can be trusted to do the simplest work without being stood over. If I order a room to be cleaned, or a fire to be made in a distant chamber, I never can be sure I am obeyed unless I go there and see for myself. If I send a girl out to get anything I want for preparing the dinner, she is as likely as not to forget what is wanted, and not to come back till after the time at which dinner should be ready. A hand-organ in the street will draw all my girls out of the house; and while it remains near us I have no more command over them than over so many monkeys. The parade of a military company has sometimes entirely prevented me from having any dinner cooked; and when the servants, standing in the square looking at the soldiers, see my husband coming after them, they only laugh, and run away to the other side, like playful children.* And, when I reprimand them, they only say they don't mean to do anything wrong, or they wont do it again, all the time laughing as though it was all a joke. They don't mind it at all. They are just as playful and careless as any willful child; and they never will do any work if you don't compel them."

The slave employer, if he finds he has been so unfortunate as to hire a sulky servant, that cannot be made to work to his advantage, has no remedy but to solicit from his owner a deduction from the price he has agreed to pay for his labor, on the same ground that one would from a livery-stable keeper, if he had engaged a horse to go a journey, but found that he was not strong or skillful enough to keep him upon the road. But, if the slave is the property of his employer, and becomes "rascally," the usual remedy is that which the vet-

*In the city of Columbia, S.C., the police are required to prevent the negroes from running in this way after the military. Any negro neglecting to leave the vicinity of a parade, when ordered by a policeman or any military officer, is required, by the ordinance, to be whipped at the guard-house.

erinary surgeon recommended when he was called upon for advice how to cure a balky horse: "*Sell* him, my lord." "Rascals" are "sent South" from Virginia, for the cure or alleviation of their complaint, in much greater numbers than consumptives are from the more Northern States.

"How do you manage, then, when a man misbehaves, or is sick?" I have been often asked by Southerners, in discussing this question.

If he is sick, I simply charge against him every half day of the time he is off work, and deduct it from his wages. If he is careless, or refuses to do what in reason I demand of him, I discharge him, paying him wages to the time he leaves. With new men in whom I have not confidence, I make a written agreement, before witnesses, on engaging them, that will permit me to do this. As for "rascality," I never had but one case of anything approaching to what you call so. A man insolently contradicted me in the field: I told him to leave his job and go to the house, took hold and finished it myself, then went to the house, made out a written statement of account, counted out the balance in money due him, gave him the statement and the money, and told him he must go. He knew that he had failed of his duty, and that the law would sustain me, and we parted in a friendly manner, he expressing regret that his temper had driven him from a situation which had been agreeable and satisfactory to him. The probability is, that this single experience educated him so far that his next employer would have no occasion to complain of his "rascality;" and I very much doubt if any amount of corporeal punishment would have improved his temper in the least.

That slaves have to be "humored" a great deal, and that they very frequently can not be made to do their master's will, I have seen much evidence. Not that they often directly refuse to obey an order, but, when they are directed to do anything for which they have a disinclination, they undertake it in such a way that the desired result is sure not to be accomplished. In small particulars for which a laborer's discretion must be trusted to in every-day work, but more especially when emergencies require some extraordinary duties to be performed, they are much less reliable than the ordinary run of laborers employed on our farms in New York. They can not be driven by fear of punishment to do that which the laborers in free communities do cheerfully from their sense of duty, self-respect, or regard for their reputation and standing with their employer. A gentleman who had some free men in his employment in Virginia, that he had procured in New York, told me that he had been astonished, when a dam that he had been building began to give way in a freshet, to see how much more readily than negroes they would obey his orders, and do their best without orders, running into the water waist deep, in mid-winter, without any hesitation or grumbling.

The manager of a large candle-factory in London, in which the laborers are treated with an unusual degree of confidence and generosity, writes thus in a report to his directors:

"The present year promises to be a very good one as regards profit, in consequence of the enormous increase in the demand for candles. No mere driving of the men and boys, by ourselves and those in authority under us, would have produced the sudden and very great increase of manufacture, necessary for keeping pace with this demand. It has been effected only by the hearty good-will with which the factory has worked, the men and boys making the great extra exertion, which they saw to be necessary to prevent our getting hopelessly in arrears with the orders, as heartily as if the question had been, how to avert some difficulty threatening themselves personally. One of the foremen remarked with truth, a few days back: 'To look on them, one would think each was engaged in a little business of his own, so as to have only himself affected by the results of his work.' "

A farmer in Lincolnshire, England, told me that once, during an extraordinary harvest season, he had had a number of laborers at work without leaving the field or taking any repose for sixty hours—he himself working

with them, and eating and drinking only with them during all the time. Such services men may give voluntarily, from their own regard to the value of property to be saved by it, or for the purpose of establishing their credit as worth good wages; but to require it of slaves would be intensely cruel, if not actually impossible. A man can work excessively on his own impulse as much easier than he can be driven to by another, as a horse travels easier in going towards his accustomed stable than in going from it. I mean—and every man who has ever served as a sailor or a soldier will know that it is no imaginary effect—that the actual fatigue, the waste of bodily energy, the expenditure of the physical capacity, is greater in one case than the other.

Sailors and soldiers both, are led by certain inducements to place themselves within certain limits, and for a certain time, both defined by contract, in a condition resembling, in many particulars, that of slaves; and, although they are bound by their voluntary contract and by legal and moral considerations to obey orders, the fact that force is also used to secure their obedience to their officers, scarcely ever fails to produce in them the identical vices which are complained of in slaves. They obey the letter, but defeat the intention of orders that do not please them, they are improvident, wasteful, reckless: they sham illness, and as Dr. Cartwright gives specific medical appellations to discontent, laziness, and rascality, so among sailors and soldiers, when men suddenly find themselves ill and unable to do their duty in times of peculiar danger, or when unusual labor is required, they are humorously said to be suffering under an attack of the powder-fever, the cape-fever, the ice-fever, the coast-fever, or the reefing-fever. The counteracting influences to these vices, which it is the first effort of every good officer to foster, are, first, regard to duty; second, patriotism; third, *esprit du corps*, or professional pride; fourth, self-respect, or personal pride; fifth, self-interest, hope of promotion, or of bounty, or of privileges in mitigation of their hard service, as reward for excellence. Things are never quickly done at sea, unless they are done with a will, or "cheerly," as the sailor's word is—that is, cheerfully. An army is never effective in the field when depressed in its *morale*.

None of these promptings to excellence can be operative, except in a very low degree, to counteract the indolent and vicious tendencies of the Slavery, much more pure than the slavery of the army or the ship, by which the exertions of the Virginia laborer are obtained for his employer.

It is very common, among the Virginians, to think that the relation of free-laborers to their employers is, by the effect of circumstances, rendered very little less slavish than that of their own slaves to them. It is true that in many respects the position of agricultural laborers, in some parts of England and other countries (where the land is owned and rented only in excessively large quantities, and the principle of competition has, therefore, very little influence to counteract the power of the capitalists to prevent a man's getting his living by labor, except on their conditions), approaches, in the degree of their moral subjection, to that of slaves.

But this is true only in a very few districts, nowhere in the United States, unless it be in the Slave States, where sometimes similar causes produce somewhat similar effects upon the poor whites. And, everywhere, the services rendered by the free-laborers are rendered not from fear of punishment, are claimed not by right of force, but are rendered in obedience to, and claimed by express right of, a contract voluntarily made: consequently, compared with that of the slave, their labor is actively, cheerfully, and discreetly given. Circumstances may have made it necessary for the laborer to accept the terms offered by the employer; but those circumstances no more constitute slavery than do the circumstances, which induce merchants and manufacturers in towns to pay what they deem extravagant prices for flour, render them the slaves of the farmers, who say to them, "Pay these prices, or go without."

It is a very low mind that cannot appreciate the difference between services rendered from such motives and under such obliga-

tions, honorable, manly, and just obligations, voluntarily entered into, and the services of a slave, rendered from fear that he shall be whipped if he does not render them.

The employer of a free-laborer no more dare whip him than the laborer dare whip the employer. Their rights are equal, in all respects, before the law, and the claim of the laborer to his stipulated wages, his tacitly stipulated diet and lodging, is just as good, and renders him just as truly the owner of his employer, as the claim of the employer upon the free-laborer for his stipulated measure, by days or months, of muscular labor, and his tacitly stipulated exercise of skill and discretion, render him the owner of his employé. The man who would work cheerfully and to the best of his discretion, for the employer, in one case is a fool; the man who would not work cheerfully and to the best of his discretion, for his employer, in the other is dishonest and imprudent.

The following is from the organ of the New York city Know Nothings, of Feb. 21, 1855: "If to rise with the lark and labor the live-long day, saddled with care, loaded down with anxiety, until we sink under the burden, is freedom, then we are not slaves. If to do half this work, without any of its cares, or troubles, with the full quota of pleasure, is the want of it, then who would be free?"

Such a view of life is not only disgraceful to a man, but the prevalence of such ideas, however patriotic may be the foundation on which they have been cultivated, is most pernicious to the character of our own laboring-class, and to all industry into which competition can enter. There are some badly-educated American women who choose to die as seam-stresses, rather than to live as cooks or chamber-maids, because they are taught by such writers that the position of a servant, or of those who sell their labor and skill by measure of time and not by measure of amount, is worse than that of slaves. Even prostitution is felt to be less a disgrace than this false parallel to Slavery, and so, unconsciously deluded by this false analogy, they answer this writer's question, actually preferring death to this imaginary degradation.

The Underground Railroad

William Still

Although the name of Henry Box Brown has been echoed over the land for a number of years, and the simple facts connected with his marvelous escape from slavery in a box published widely through the medium of anti-slavery papers, nevertheless it is not unreasonable to suppose that very little is generally known in relation to this case.

Briefly, the facts are these, which doubtless have never before been fully published—

Brown was a man of invention as well as a hero. In point of interest, however, his case is no more remarkable than many others. Indeed, neither before nor after escaping did he suffer one-half what many others have experienced.

He was decidedly an unhappy piece of property in the city of Richmond, Va. In the condition of a slave he felt that it would be impossible for him to remain. Full well did he know, however, that it was no holiday task to escape the vigilance of Virginia slave-hunters, or the wrath of an enraged master for committing the unpardonable sin of attempting to escape to a land of liberty. So Brown counted well the cost before venturing upon this hazardous undertaking. Ordinary modes of travel he concluded might prove disastrous to his hopes; he, therefore, hit upon a new invention altogether, which was to have himself boxed up and forwarded to Philadelphia direct by express. The size of the box and how it was to be made to fit him most comfortably, was of his own ordering. Two feet eight inches deep, two feet wide, and three feet long were the exact dimensions of the box, lined with baize. His resources with regard to food and water consisted of the following:

One bladder of water and a few small biscuits. His mechanical implement to meet the death-struggle for fresh air, all told, was one large gimlet. Satisfied that it would be far better to peril his life for freedom in this way than to remain under the galling yoke of Slavery, he entered his box, which was safely nailed up and hooped with five hickory hoops, and was then addressed by his next friend, James A. Smith, a shoe dealer, to Wm. H. Johnson, Arch street, Philadelphia, marked, "This side up with care." In this condition he was sent to Adams' Express office in a dray, and thence by overland express to Philadelphia. It was twenty-six hours from the time he left Richmond until his arrival in the City of Brotherly Love. The notice, "This side up, &c.," did not avail with the different expressmen, who hesitated not to handle the box in the usual rough manner common to this class of men. For a while they actually had the box upside down, and had him on his head for miles. A few days before he was expected, certain intimation was conveyed to a member of the Vigilance Committee that a box might be expected by the three o'clock morning train from the South, which might contain a man. One of the most serious walks he ever took—and they had not been a few—to meet and accompany passengers, he took at half past two o'clock that morning to the depot. Not once, but for more than a score of times, he fancied the slave would be dead. He anxiously looked while the freight was being unloaded from the cars, to see if he could recognize a box that might contain a man; one alone had that appearance, and he confessed it really seemed as if there was the scent of death about it. But on inquiry, he soon learned that it was not the one he was looking after, and he was free to say he experienced a marked sense of relief. That same afternoon, however, he received from Richmond a telegram, which read thus.

William Still, *The Underground Railroad*. (Philadelphia: Porter and Coates, 1872), pp. 81–84.

"Your case of goods is shipped and will arrive to-morrow morning."

At this exciting juncture of affairs, Mr. McKim, who had been engineering this important undertaking, deemed it expedient to change the programme slightly in one particular at least to insure greater safety. Instead of having a member of the Committee go again to the depot for the box, which might excite suspicion, it was decided that it would be safest to have the express bring it direct to the Anti-Slavery Office.

But all apprehension of danger did not now disappear, for there was no room to suppose that Adams' Express office had any sympathy with the Abolitionist or the fugitive, consequently for Mr. McKim to appear personally at the express office to give directions with reference to the coming of a box from Richmond which would be directed to Arch street, and yet not intended for that street, but for the Anti-Slavery office at 107 North Fifth street, it needed of course no great discernment to foresee that a step of this kind was wholly impracticable and that a more indirect and covert method would have to be adopted. In this dreadful crisis Mr. McKim, with his usual good judgment and remarkably quick, strategical mind, especially in matters pertaining to the U. G. R. R., hit upon the following plan, namely, to go to his friend, E. M. Davis,* who was then extensively engaged in mercantile business, and relate the circumstances. Having daily intercourse with said Adams' Express office, and being well acquainted with the firm and some of the drivers, Mr. Davis could, as Mr. McKim thought, talk about "boxes, freight, etc.," from any part of the country without risk. Mr. Davis heard Mr. McKim's plan and instantly approved of it, and was heartily at his service.

"Dan, an Irishman, one of Adams' Express drivers, is just the fellow to go to the depot

*E. M. Davis was a member of the Executive Committee of the Pennsylvania Anti-Slavery Society and a long-tried Abolitionist, son-in-law of James and Lucretia Mott.

after the box," said Davis. "He drinks a little too much whiskey sometimes, but he will do anything I ask him to do, promptly and obligingly. I'll trust Dan, for I believe he is the very man." The difficulty which Mr. McKim had been so anxious to overcome was thus pretty well settled. It was agreed that Dan should go after the box next morning before daylight and bring it to the Anti-Slavery office direct, and to make it all the more agreeable for Dan to get up out of his warm bed and go on this errand before day, it was decided that he should have a five dollar gold piece for himself. Thus these preliminaries having been satisfactorily arranged, it only remained for Mr. Davis to see Dan and give him instructions accordingly, etc.

Next morning, according to arrangement, the box was at the Anti-Slavery office in due time. The witnesses present to behold the resurrection were J. M. McKim, Professor C. D. Cleveland, Lewis Thompson, and the writer.

Mr. McKim was deeply interested; but having been long identified with the Anti-Slavery cause as one of its oldest and ablest advocates in the darkest days of slavery and mobs, and always found by the side of the fugitive to counsel and succor, he was on this occasion perfectly composed.

Professor Cleveland, however, was greatly moved. His zeal and earnestness in the cause of freedom, especially in rendering aid to passengers, knew no limit. Ordinarily he could not too often visit these travelers, shake them too warmly by the hand, or impart to them too freely on his substance to aid them on their journey. But now his emotion was overpowering.

Mr. Thompson, of the firm of Merrihew & Thompson—about the only printers in the city who for many years dared to print such incendiary documents as anti-slavery papers and pamphlets—one of the truest friends of the slave, was composed and prepared to witness the scene.

All was quiet. The door had been safely locked. The proceedings commenced. Mr. McKim rapped quietly on the lid of the box and called out, "All right!" Instantly came the answer from within, "All right, sir!"

The witnesses will never forget that moment. Saw and hatchet quickly had the five hickory hoops cut and the lid off, and the marvellous resurrection of Brown ensued. Rising up in his box, he reached out his hand, saying, "How do you do, gentlemen?" The little assemblage hardly knew what to think or do at the moment. He was about as wet as if he had come up out of the Delaware. Very soon he remarked that, before leaving Richmond he had selected for his arrival-hymn (if he lived) the Psalm beginning with these words: *"I waited patiently for the Lord, and He heard my prayer."* And most touchingly did he sing the psalm, much to his own relief, as well as to the delight of his small audience.

He was then christened Henry Box Brown, and soon afterwards was sent to the hospitable residence of James Mott and E. M. Davis, on Ninth street, where, it is needless to say, he met a most cordial reception from Mrs. Lucretia Mott and her household. Clothing and creature comforts were furnished in abundance, and delight and joy filled all hearts in that strong-hold of philanthropy.

As he had been so long doubled up in the box he needed to promenade considerably in the fresh air, so James Mott put one of his broad-brim hats on his head and tendered him the hospitalities of his yard as well as his house, and while Brown promenaded the yard flushed with victory, great was the joy of his friends.

After his visit at Mr. Mott's, he spent two days with the writer, and then took his departure for Boston, evidently feeling quite conscious of the wonderful feat he had performed, and at the same time it may be safely said that those who witnessed this strange resurrection were not only elated at his success, but were made to sympathize more deeply than ever before with the slave. Also the noble-hearted Smith who boxed him up was made to rejoice over Brown's victory, and was thereby encouraged to render similar service to two other young bondmen, who appealed to him for deliverance. But, unfortunately, in this attempt the undertaking proved a failure. Two boxes containing the young men alluded to above, after having been duly expressed and some distance on the road, were, through the agency of the telegraph, betrayed, and the heroic young fugitives were captured in their boxes and dragged back to hopeless bondage. Consequently, through this deplorable failure, Samuel A. Smith was arrested, imprisoned, and was called upon to suffer severely. . . .

The Confessions of Nat Turner

Nat Turner

Source: The Confessions of Nat Turner, The Leader of the Late Insurrection in Southampton, Va., As fully and voluntarily made to Thomas R. Gray, In the prison where he was confined. (Baltimore: Lucas & Deaver, 1831).

Agreeable to his own appointment, on the evening he was committed to prison, with permission of the jailer, I visited Nat on Tuesday the 1st November, when, without being questioned at all, he commenced his narrative in the following words:—

Sir,—You have asked me to give a history of the motives which induced me to undertake the late insurrection, as you call it—To do so I must go back to the days of my infancy, and even before I was born. I was thirty-one years of age the 2nd of October last, and born the property of Benj. Turner, of this county. In my childhood a circumstance occurred which made an indelible impression on my mind, and laid the ground work of that enthusiasm, which has terminated so fatally to many, both white and black, and for which I am about to atone at the gallows. It is here necessary to relate this circumstance—trifling as it may seem, it was the commencement of that belief which has grown with time, and even now, sir, in this dungeon, helpless and forsaken as I am, I cannot divest myself of. Being at play with other children, when three or four years old, I was telling them something, which my mother overhearing, said it had happened before I was born—I stuck to my story, however, and related somethings which went, in her opinion, to confirm it—others being called on were greatly astonished, knowing that these things had happened, and caused them to say in my hearing, I surely would be a prophet, as the Lord had shown me things that had happened before my birth. And my father and mother strengthened me in this my first impression, saying in my presence, I was intended for some great purpose, which they had always thought from certain marks on my head and breast—[a parcel of excrescences which I believe are not at all uncommon, particularly among Negroes, as I have seen several with the same. In this case he has either cut them off or they have nearly disappeared]—My grandmother, who was very religious, and to whom I was much attached—my master, who belonged to the church, and other religious persons who visited the house, and whom I often saw at prayers, noticing the singularity of my manners, I suppose, and my uncommon intelligence for a child, remarked I had too much sense to be raised, and if I was, I would never be of any service to any one as a slave—To a mind like mine, restless, inquisitive and observant of every thing that was passing, it is easy to suppose that religion was the subject to which it would be directed, and although this subject principally occupied my thoughts—there was nothing that I saw or heard of to which my attention was not di-

rected—The manner in which I learned to read and write, not only had great influence on my own mine, [sic] as I acquired it with the most perfect ease, so much so, that I have no recollection whatever of learning the alphabet—but to the astonishment of the family, one day, when a book was shewn to me to keep me from crying, I began spelling the names of different objects—this was a source of wonder to all in the neighborhood, particularly the blacks—and this learning was constantly improved at all opportunities—when I got large enough to go to work, while employed, I was reflecting on many things that would present themselves to my imagination, and whenever an opportunity occurred of looking at a book, when the school children were getting their lessons, I would find many things that the fertility of my own imagination had depicted to me before; all my time, not devoted to my master's service, was spent either in prayer, or in making experiments in casting different things in moulds made of earth, in attempting to make paper, gun-powder, and many other experiments, that although I could not perfect, yet convinced me of its practicability if I had the means.* I was not addicted to stealing in my youth, nor have ever been—Yet such was the confidence of the Negroes in the neighborhood, even at this early period of my life, in my superior judgment, that they would often carry me with them when they were going on any roguery, to plan for them. Growing up among them, with this confidence in my superior judgment, and when this, in their opinions, was perfected by Divine inspiration, from the circumstances already alluded to in my infancy, and which belief was ever afterwards zealously inculcated by the austerity of my life and manners, which became the subject of remark by white and black.—Having soon discovered to be great, I must appear so, and therefore studiously avoided mixing in soci-

*When questioned as to the manner of manufacturing those different articles, he was found well informed on the subject.

ety, and wrapped myself in mystery, devoting my time to fasting and prayer—By this time, having arrived to man's estate, and hearing the scriptures commented on at meetings, I was struck with that particular passage which says: "Seek ye the kingdom of Heaven and all things shall be added unto you." I reflected much on this passage, and prayed daily for light on this subject—As I was praying one day at my plough, the spirit spoke to me, saying "Seek ye the kingdom of Heaven and all things shall be added unto you." *Question*— what do you mean by the Spirit. *Ans.* The Spirit that spoke to the prophets in former days—and I was greatly astonished, and for two years prayed continually, whenever my duty would permit—and then again I had the same revelation, which fully confirmed me in the impression that I was ordained for some great purpose in the hands of the Almighty. Several years rolled round, in which many events occurred to strengthen me in this my belief. At this time I reverted in my mind to the remarks made of me in my childhood, and the things that had been shewn me—and as it had been said of me in my childhood by those by whom I had been taught to pray, both white and black, and in whom I had the greatest confidence, that I had too much sense to be raised, and if I was, I would never be of any use to any one as a slave. Now finding I had arrived to man's estate, and was a slave, and these revelations being made known to me, I began to direct my attention to this great object, to fulfill the purpose for which, by this time, I felt assured I was intended. Knowing the influence I had obtained over the minds of my fellow servants, (not by the means of conjuring and such like tricks—for to them I always spoke of such things with contempt) but by the communion of the Spirit whose revelations I often communicated to them, and they believed and said my wisdom came from God. I now began to prepare them for my purpose, by telling them something was about to happen that would terminate in fulfilling the great promise that had been made to me—About this time I was placed under an overseer, from whom I ranaway—and

after remaining in the woods thirty days, I returned, to the astonishment of the Negroes on the plantation, who thought I had made my escape to some other part of the country, as my father had done before. But the reason of my return was, that the Spirit appeared to me and said I had my wishes directed to the things of this world, and not to the kingdom of Heaven, and that I should return to the service of my earthly master—"For he who knoweth his Master's will, and doeth it not, shall be beaten with many stripes, and thus have I chastened you." And the Negroes found fault, and murmured against me, saying that if they had my sense they would not serve any master in the world. And about this time I had a vision—and I saw white spirits and black spirits engaged in battle, and the sun was darkened—the thunder rolled in the Heavens, and blood flowed in streams—and I heard a voice saying, "Such is your luck, such you are called to see, and let it come rough or smooth, you must surely bare it. I now withdrew myself as much as my situation would permit, from the intercourse of my fellow servants, for the avowed purpose of serving the Spirit more fully—and it appeared to me, and reminded me of the things it had already shown me, and that it would then reveal to me the knowledge of the elements, the revolution of the planets, the operation of tides, and changes of the seasons. After this revelation in the year of 1825, and the knowledge of the elements being made known to me, I sought more than ever to obtain true holiness before the great day of judgment should appear, and then I began to receive the true knowledge of faith. And from the first steps of righteousness until the last, was I made perfect; and the Holy Ghost was with me, and said, "Behold me as I stand in the Heavens"— and I looked and saw the forms of men in different attitudes—and there were lights in the sky to which the children of darkness gave other names than what they really were—for they were the lights of the Savior's hands, stretched forth from east to west, even as they were extended on the cross on Calvary for the redemption of sinners. And I wondered greatly at these miracles, and prayed to be informed of a certainty of the meaning thereof—and shortly afterwards, while laboring in the field, I discovered drops of blood on the corn as though it were dew from heaven—and I communicated it to many, both white and black, in the neighborhood—and I then found on the leaves in the woods hieroglyphic characters, and numbers, with the forms of men in different attitudes, portrayed in blood, and representing the figures I had seen before in the heavens. And now the Holy Ghost had revealed itself to me, and made plain the miracles it had shown me—For as the blood of Christ had been shed on this earth, and had ascended to heaven for the salvation of sinners, and was now returning to earth again in the form of dew—and as the leaves on the trees bore the impression of the figures I had seen in the heavens, it was plain to me that the Savior was about to lay down the yoke he had borne for the sins of men, and the great day of judgment was at hand. About this time I told these things to a white man, (Etheldred T. Brantley) on whom it had a wonderful effect—and he ceased from his wickedness, and was attacked immediately with a cutaneous eruption, and blood oozed from the pores of his skin, and after praying and fasting nine days, he was healed, and the Spirit appeared to me again, and said, as the Savior had been baptised so should we be also—and when the white people would not let us be baptised by the church, we went down into the water together, in the sight of many who reviled us, and were baptised by the Spirit—After this I rejoiced greatly, and gave thanks to God. And on the 12th of May, 1828, I heard a loud noise in the heavens, and the Spirit instantly appeared to me and said the Serpent was loosened, and Christ had laid down the yoke he had borne for the sins of men, and that I should take it on and fight against the Serpent, for the time was fast approaching when the first should be last and the last should be first. *Ques.* Do you not find yourself mistaken now? *Ans.* Was not Christ crucified? And by signs in the heavens that it would make known to me when I should

commence the great work—and until the first sign appeared, I should conceal it from the knowledge of men—And on the appearance of the sign, (the eclipse of the sun last February) I should arise and prepare myself, and slay my enemies with their own weapons. And immediately on the sign appearing in the heavens, the seal was removed from my lips, and I communicated the great work laid out for me to do, to four in whom I had the greatest confidence, (Henry, Hark, Nelson, and Sam)—It was intended by us to have begun the work of death on the 4th July last—Many were the plans formed and rejected by us, and it affected my mind to such a degree, that I fell sick, and the time passed without our coming to any determination how to commence—Still forming new schemes and rejecting them, when the sign appeared again, which determined me not to wait longer.

Since the commencement of 1830, I had been living with Mr. Joseph Travis, who was to me a kind master, and placed the greatest confidence in me; in fact, I had no cause to complain of his treatment to me. On Saturday evening, the 20th of August, it was agreed between Henry, Hark and myself, to prepare a dinner the next day for the men we expected, and then to concert a plan, as we had not yet determined on any. Hark, on the following morning, brought a pig, and Henry brandy, and being joined by Sam, Nelson, Will and Jack, they prepared in the woods a dinner, where, about three o'clock, I joined them.

Q. Why were you so backward in joining them.
A. The same reason that had caused me not to mix with them for years before.

I saluted them on coming up, and asked Will how came he there, he answered, his life was worth no more than others, and his liberty as dear to him. I asked him if he thought to obtain it? He said he would, or lose his life. This was enough to put him in full confidence. Jack, I knew, was only a tool in the hands of Hark, it was quickly agreed we should commence at home (Mr. J. Travis') on that night, and until we had armed and equipped ourselves, and gathered sufficient force, neither age nor sex was to be spared, (which was invariably adhered to). We remained at the feast, until about two hours in the night, when we went to the house and found Austin; they all went to the cider press and drank, except myself. On returning to the house, Hark went to the door with an axe, for the purpose of breaking it open, as we knew we were strong enough to murder the family, if they were awaked by the noise; but reflecting that it might create an alarm in the neighborhood, we determined to enter the house secretly, and murder them whilst sleeping. Hark got a ladder and set it against the chimney, on which I ascended, and hoisting a window, entered and came down stairs, unbarred the door, and removed the guns from their places. It was then observed that I must spill the first blood. On which, armed with a hatchet, and accompanied by Will, I entered my master's chamber, it being dark. I could not give a death blow, the hatchet glanced from his head, he sprang from the bed and called his wife, it was his last word, Will laid him dead, with a blow of his axe, and Mrs. Travis shared the same fate, as she lay in bed. The murder of this family, five in number, was the work of a moment, not one of them awoke; there was a little infant sleeping in a cradle, that was forgotten, until we had left the house and gone some distance, when Henry and Will returned and killed it; we got here, four guns that would shoot, and several old muskets, with a pound or two of powder. We remained some time at the barn, where we paraded; I formed them in a line as soldiers, and after carrying them through all the manoeuvres I was master of marched them off to Mr. Salathul Francis', about six hundred yards distant. Sam and Will went to the door and knocked. Mr. Francis asked who was there, Sam replied it was him, and he had a letter for him, on which he got up and came to the door; they immediately seized him, and dragging him out a little from the door, he was dispatched by repeated blows on the

head; there was no other white person in the family. We started from there for Mrs. Reese's, maintaining the most perfect silence on our march, where finding the door unlocked, we entered, and murdered Mrs. Reese in her bed, while sleeping; her son awoke, but it was only to sleep the sleep of death, he had only time to say who is that, and he was no more. From Mrs. Reese's we went to Mrs. Turner's, a mile distant, which we reached about sunrise, on Monday morning. Henry, Austin, and Sam, went to the still, where, finding Mr. Peebles, Austin shot him, and the rest of us went to the house; as we approached, the family discovered us, and shut the door. Vain hope! Will, with one stroke of his axe, opened it, and we entered and found Mrs. Turner and Mrs. Newsome in the middle of a room, almost frightened to death. Will immediately killed Mrs. Turner, with one blow of his axe. I took Mrs. Newsome by the hand, and with the sword I had when I was apprehended, I struck her several blows over the head, but not being able to kill her, as the sword was dull. Will turning around and discovering it, despatched her also. A general destruction of property and search for money and ammunition, always succeded the murders. By this time my company amounted to fifteen, and nine men mounted, who started for Mrs. Whitehead's, (the other six were to go through a by way to Mr. Bryant's, and rejoin us at Mrs. Whitehead's,) as we approached the house we discovered Mr. Richard Whitehead standing in the cotton patch, near the lane fence; we called him over into the lane, and Will, the executioner, was near at hand, with his fatal axe, to send him to an untimely grave. As we pushed on to the house, I discovered some one run round the garden, and thinking it was some of the white family, I pursued them, but finding it was a servant girl belonging to the house, I returned to commence the work of death, but they whom I left, had not been idle; all the family were already murdered, but Mrs. Whitehead and her daughter Margaret. As I came round to the door I saw Will pulling Mrs. Whitehead out of the house, and at the step he nearly severed her head from her body, with his broad axe. Miss Margaret, when I discovered her, had concealed herself in the corner, formed by the projection of cellar cap from the house; on my approach she fled, but was soon overtaken, and after repeated blows with a sword, I killed her by a blow on the head, with a fence rail. By this time, the six who had gone by Mr. Bryant's, rejoined us, and informed me they had done the work of death assigned them. We again divided, part going to Mr. Richard Porter's, and from thence to Nathaniel Francis', the others to Mr. Howell Harris', and Mr. T. Doyle's. On my reaching Mr. Porter's, he had escaped with his family. I understood there, that the alarm had already spread, and I immediately returned to bring up those sent to Mr. Doyle's, and Mr. Howell Harris'; the party I left going on to Mr. Francis', having told them I would join them in that neighborhood. I met these sent to Mr. Doyle's and Mr. Harris' returning, having met Mr. Doyle on the road and killed him; and learning from some who joined them that Mr. Harris was from home, I immediately pursued the course taken by the party gone on before, but knowing they would complete the work of death and pillage at Mr. Francis' before I could get there, I went to Mr. Peter Edwards', expecting to find them there, but they had been here also. I then went to Mr. John T. Barrow's, they had been here and murdered him. I pursued on their track to Capt. Newit Harris', where I found the greater part mounted, and ready to start; the men now amounting to about forty, shouted and hurraed as I rode up, some were in the yard, loading their guns, others drinking. They said Captain Harris and his family had escaped, the property in the house they destroyed, robbing him of money and other valuables. I ordered them mount and march instantly, this was about nine or ten o'clock, Monday morning. I proceeded to Mr. Levi Waller's, two or three miles distant. I took my station in the rear, and as it was my object to carry terror and devastation wherever we went, I placed fifteen or twenty of the best armed and most relied on, in front, who generally approached the houses as fast as their horses could run; this was for two purposes, to prevent escape and strike terror to the inhabitants—on this account I never got to the houses, after leaving Mrs. Whitehead's, until the murders were committed, except in one case. I sometimes got in sight in time to see the work of death completed, viewed the mangled bodies as they lay, in silent satisfaction, and immediately started in quest of other victims—Having murdered Mrs. Waller and ten children, we started for Mr. William Williams'—having killed him and two little boys that were there; while engaged in this, Mrs. Williams fled and got some distance from the house, but she was pursued, overtaken, and compelled to get up behind one of the company, who brought her back, and after showing her the mangled body of her lifeless husband, she was told to get down and lay by his side, where she was shot dead. I then started for Mr. Jacob Williams, where the family were murdered—Here he found a young man named Drury, who had come on business with Mr. Williams—he was pursued, overtaken and shot. Mrs. Vaughan was the next place we visited—and after murdering the family here, I determined on starting for Jerusalem—Our number amounted now to fifty or sixty, all mounted and armed with guns, axes, swords and clubs—On reaching Mr. James W. Parker's gate, immediately on the road leading to Jerusalem, and about three miles distant, it was proposed to me to call there, but I objected, as I knew he was gone to Jerusalem, and my object was to reach there as soon as possible; but some of the men having relations at Mr. Parker's it was agreed that they might call and get his people. I remained at the gate on the road, with seven or eight; the others going across the field to the house, about half a mile off. After waiting some time for them, I became impatient, and started to the house for them, and on our return we were met by a party of white men, who had pursued our blood-stained track, and who had fired on those at the gate, and dispersed them, which I knew nothing of, not having been at the time rejoined by any of them—Immediately on discovering the whites, I ordered my men to halt and form, as they appeared to be alarmed—The white men, eighteen in number, approached us in about one hundred yards, when one of them fired, (this was against the positive orders of Captain Alexander P. Peete, who commanded, and who had directed the men to reserve their fire until within thirty paces)—And I discovered about half of them retreating, I then ordered my men to fire and rush on them; the few remaining stood their ground until we approached within fifty yards, when they fired and retreated. We pursued and overtook some of them who we thought we left dead; (they were not killed) after pursuing them about two hundred yards, and rising a little hill, I discovered they were met by another party, and had halted, and were reloading their guns, (this was a small party from Jerusalem who knew the Negroes were in the field, and had just tied their horses to await their return to the road, knowing that Mr. Parker and family were in Jerusalem, but knew nothing of the party that had gone in with Captain Peete; on hearing the firing they immediately rushed to the spot and arrived just in time to arrest the progress of these barbarous villians, and save the lives of their friends and fellow citizens). Thinking that those who retreated first, and the party who fired on us at fifty or sixty yards distant, had all fallen back to meet others with ammunition. As I saw them reloading their guns, and more coming up than I saw at first, and several of my bravest men being wounded, the others became panick struck and squandered over the field; the white men pursued and fired on us several times. Hark had his horse shot under him, and I caught another for him as it was running by me; five or six of my men were wounded, but none left on the field; finding myself defeated here I instantly determined to go through a private way, and cross the Nottoway river at the Cypress Bridge, three miles below Jerusalem, and attack that place in the rear, as I expected they would look for me on the other road, and I had a great desire to get there to procure arms and ammunition. After going a short distance in this private way, accompanied by about twenty men, I overtook two or three who told me the others were dispersed in every direction. After trying in vain to collect a sufficient force to proceed to Jerusalem, I determined to return, as I was sure they would make back to their old neighborhood, where they would rejoin me, make new recruits, and come down again. On my way back, I called at Mrs. Thomas's, Mrs. Spencer's, and several other places, the white families having fled, we found no more victims to gratify our thirst for blood, we stopped at Majr. Ridley's quarter for the night, and being joined by four of his men, with the recruits made since my defeat, we mustered now about forty strong. After placing out sentinels, I laid down to sleep, but was quickly roused by a great racket; starting up, I found some mounted, and others in great confusion; one of the sentinels having given the alarm that we were about to be attacked, I ordered some to ride round and reconnoitre, and on their return the others being more alarmed, not knowing who they were, fled in different ways, so that I was reduced to about twenty again; with this I determined to attempt to recruit, and proceed on to rally in the neighborhood, I had left. Dr. Blunt's was the nearest house, which we reached just before day; on riding up the yard, Hark fired a gun. We expected Dr. Blunt and his family were at Maj. Ridley's, as I knew there was a company of men there; the gun was fired to ascertain if any of the family were at home; we were immediately fired upon and retreated, leaving several of my men. I do not know what became of them, as I never saw them afterwards. Pursuing our course back and coming in sight of Captain Harris', where we had been the day before, we discovered a party of white men at the house, on which all deserted me but two (Jacob and Nat), we concealed ourselves in the woods until near night, when I sent them in search of Henry, Sam, Nelson, and Hark, and directed them to rally all they could, at the place we had had our dinner the Sunday before, where they would find me, and I accordingly returned there as soon as it was dark and remained until Wednesday evening, when discovering white men riding around the place as though they were looking for some one, and none of my men joining me, I concluded Jacob and Nat had been taken, and compelled to betray me. On this I gave up all hope for the present; and on Thursday night after having supplied myself with provisions from Mr. Travis's, I scratched a hole under a pile of fence rails in a field, where I concealed myself for six weeks, never leaving my hiding place but for a few minutes in the dead of night to get water which was very near; thinking by this time I could venture out, I began to go about in the night and eaves drop the houses in the nieghborhood; pursuing this course for about a fortnight and gathering little or no intelligence, afraid of speaking to any human being, and returning every morning to my cave before the dawn of day. I know not how long I might—have led this life, if accident had not betrayed me, a dog in the neighborhood passing by my hiding place one night while I was out, was attracted by some meat I had in my cave, and crawled in and stole it, and was coming out just as I returned. A few nights after, two Negroes having started to go hunting with the same dog, and passed that way, the dog came again to the place, and having just gone out to walk about, discovered me and barked, on which thinking myself discovered, I spoke to them to beg concealment. On making myself known they fled from me. Knowing then they would betray me, I immediately left my hiding place, and was pursued almost incessantly until I was taken a fortnight afterwards by Mr. Benjamin Phipps, in a little hole I had dug out with my sword, for the purpose of concealment, under the top of a fallen tree. On Mr. Phipps' discovering the place of my concealment, he cocked his gun and aimed at me. I requested him not to shoot and I would give up, upon which he demanded my sword. I delivered it to him, and he brought me to prison. During the time I was pursued, I had many hair breadth escapes, which your time will not permit you to relate. I am here loaded with chains, and willing to suffer the fate that awaits me.

I here proceeded to make some inquiries of him, after assuring him of the certain death that awaited him, and that concealment would only bring destruction on the innocent as well as guilty, of his own color, if he knew of any extensive or concerted plan. His answer was, I do not. When I questioned him as to the insurrection in North Carolina happening about the same time, he denied any knowledge of it; and when I looked him in the face as though I would search his inmost thoughts, he replied, "I see sir, you doubt my word; but can you not think the same ideas, and strange appearances about this time in the heaven's might prompt others, as well as myself, to this undertaking." I now had much conversation with and asked him many questions, having forborne to do so previously, except in the cases noted in parenthesis; but during his statement, I had, unnoticed by him, taken notes as to some particular circumstances, and having the advantage of his statement before me in writing, on the evening of the third day that I had been with him, I began a cross examination, and found his statement corroborated by every circumstance coming within my own knowledge or the confessions of others who had been either killed or executed, and whom he had not seen nor had any knowledge since 22d of August last, he expressed himself fully satisfied as to the impracticability of his attempt. It has been said he was ignorant and cowardly, and that his object was to murder and rob for the purpose of obtaining money to make his escape. It is notorious, that he was never known to have a dollar in his life; to swear an oath, or drink a drop of spirits. As to his ignorance, he certainly never had the advantages of education, but he can read and write (it was taught him by his parents) and for natural intelligence and quickness of apprehension, is surpassed by few men I have ever seen. As to his being a coward, his reason as given for not resisting Mr. Phipps, shews the decision of his character. When he saw Mr. Phipps present his gun, he said he knew it was impossible for him to escape as the woods were full of men; he therefore thought it was better to surrender, and trust to fortune for his escape. He is a complete fanatic, or plays his part most admirably. On other subjects he possesses an uncommon share of intelligence, with a mind capable of attaining any thing; but warped and perverted by the influence of early impressions. He is below the ordinary stature, though strong and active, having the true Negro face, every feature of which is strongly marked. I shall not attempt to describe the effect of his narrative, as told and commented on by himself, in the condemned hole of the prison. The calm, deliberate composure with which he spoke of his late deeds and intentions, the expression of his fiend-like face when excited by enthusiasm, still bearing the stains of the blood of helpless innocence about him; clothed with rags and covered with chains; yet daring to raise his manacled hands to heaven, with a spirit soaring above the attributes of man; I looked on him and my blood curdled in my veins.

I will not shock the feelings of humanity, nor wound afresh the bosoms of the disconsolate sufferers in this unparalleled and inhuman massacre, by detailing the deeds of their fiend-like barbarity. There were two or three who were in the power of these wretches, had they known it, and who escaped in the most providential manner. There were two whom they thought they left dead on the field at Mr. Parker's, but who were only stunned by the blows of their guns, as they did not take time to re-load when they charged on them. The escape of a little girl who went to school at Mr. Waller's, and where the children were collecting for that purpose, excited general sympathy. As their teacher had not arrived, they were at play in the yard, and seeing the Negroes approach, she ran up on a dirt chimney, (such as are common to log houses,) and remained there unnoticed during the massacre of the eleven that were killed at this place. She remained on her hiding place till just before the arrival of a party, who were in pursuit of the murderers, when she came down and fled to a swamp, where, a mere child as she was, with the horrors of the late scene before her, she lay concealed until the next day, when seeing a party go up to the house, she came up, and on being asked how she escaped, replied with the utmost simplicity, "The Lord helped her." She was taken up behind a gentleman of the party, and returned to the arms of her weeping mother. Miss Whitehead concealed herself between the bed and the mat that supported it, while they murdered her sister in the same room, without discovering her. She was afterwards carried off, and concealed for protection by a slave of the family, who gave evidence against several of them on their trial. Mrs. Nathaniel Francis, while concealed in a closet heard their blows, and the shrieks of the victims of these ruthless savages; they then entered the closet, where she was concealed, and went out without discovering her. While in this hiding place, she heard two of her women in a quarrel about the division of her clothes. Mr. John T. Baron, discovering them approaching his house, told his wife to make her escape, and scorning to fly, fell fighting on his own threshold. After firing his rifle, he discharged his gun at them, and then broke it over the villain who first approached him, but he was overpowered, and slain. His bravery, however, saved from the hands of these monsters, his lovely and amiable wife, who will long lament a husband so deserving of her love. As directed by him, she attempted to escape through the garden, when she was caught and held by one of her servant girls, but another coming to her rescue, she fled to the woods, and concealed herself. Few indeed, were those who escaped their work of death. But fortunate for society, the hand of retributive justice has overtaken them; and not one that was known to be concerned has escaped.

The Commonwealth, vs. Nat Turner
Charged with making insurrection, and plotting to take away the lives of divers free white persons, &c. on the 22d of August, 1831.

The court composed of—, having met for the trial of Nat Turner, the prisoner was brought in and arraigned, and upon his arraignment pleaded *Not guilty;* saying to his counsel, that he did not feel so.

On the part of the Commonwealth, Levi Waller was introduced, who being sworn, deposed as follows: (*agreeably to Nat's own Confession.*) Col. Trezvant* was then introduced, who being sworn, narrated Nat's Confession to him, as follows: (*his Confession as given to Mr. Gray.*) The prisoner introduced no evidence, and the case was submitted without argument to the court, who having found him guilty, Jeremiah Cobb, Esq. Chairman, pronounced the sentence of the court, in the following words: Nat Turner! Stand up. Have you any thing to say why sentence of death should not be pronounced against you?

Ans. I have not. I have made a full confession to Mr. Gray, and I have nothing more to say.

Attend then to the sentence of the court. You have been arraigned and tried before this court, and convicted of one of the highest crimes in our criminal code. You have been convicted of plotting in cold blood, the indiscriminate destruction of men, of helpless women, and of infant children. The evidence before us leaves not a shadow of doubt, but that your hands were often imbrued in the blood of the innocent; and your own confession tells us that they were stained with the blood of a master; in your own language, "too indulgent." Could I stop here, your crime would be sufficiently aggravated. But the original contriver of a plan, deep and deadly, one that never can be effected, you managed so far to put it into execution, as to deprive us of many of our most valuable citizens; and this was done when they were asleep, and defenseless; under circumstances shocking to humanity. And while upon this part of the subject, I cannot but call your attention to the poor misguided wretches who have gone before you. They are not few in number—they were your bosom associates; and the blood of all cries aloud, and calls upon you, as the author of their misfortune. Yes! You forced them unprepared, from Time to Eternity. Borne down by this load of guilt, your only justification is, that you were led away by fanaticism. If this be true, from my soul I pity you; and while you have my sympathies, I am, nevertheless called upon to pass the sentence of the court. The time between this and your execution, will necessarily be very short; and your only hope must be in another world. The judgment of the court is, that you be taken hence to the jail from whence you came, thence to the place of execution, and on Friday next, between the hours of 10 A.M. and 2 P.M. be hung by the neck until you are dead! dead! and may the Lord have mercy upon your soul.

A list of persons murdered in the Insurrection, on the 21st and 22nd of August, 1831. Joseph Travers and wife and three children, Mrs. Elizabeth Turner, Hartwell Prebles, Sarah Newsome, Mrs. P. Reese and son William, Trajan Doyle, Henry Bryant and wife and child, and wife's mother, Mrs. Catharine Whitehead, son Richard and four daughters and grandchild, Salathiel Francis, Nathaniel Francis' overseer and two children, John T. Barrow, George Naughan, Mrs. Levi Waller and ten children, William Williams, wife and two boys, Mrs. Caswell Worrell and child, Mrs. Rebecca Vaughan, Ann Eliza Vaughan, and son Arthur, Mrs. John K. Williams and child, Mrs. Jacob Williams and three children, and Edwin Drury—amounting to fifty-five.

*The committing Magistrate.

Outlyers and Rebels

William C. Nell,

MADISON WASHINGTON

An American slaver, named the *Creole*, well manned and provided in every respect, and equipped for carrying slaves, sailed from Virginia to New Orleans, on the 30th October, 1841, with a cargo of one hundred and thirty-five slaves. When eight days out, a portion of the slaves, under the direction of one of their number, named Madison Washington, succeeded, after a slight struggle, in gaining command of the vessel. The sagacity, bravery and humanity of this man do honor to his name; and, but for his complexion, would excite universal admiration. Of the twelve white men employed on board the well-manned slaver, only one fell a victim to their atrocious business. This man, after discharging his musket at the negroes, rushed forward with a handspike, which, in the darkness of the evening, they mistook for another musket; he was stabbed with a *bowie knife wrested from the captain*. Two of the sailors were wounded, and their wounds were dressed by the negroes. The captain was also injured, and he was put into the forehold, and his wounds dressed; and his wife, child and niece were unmolested. It does not appear that the blacks committed a single act of robbery, or treated their captives with the slightest unnecessary harshness; and they declared, at the time, that all they had done was for their freedom. The vessel was carried into Nassau, and the British authorities at that place refused to consign the liberated slaves again to bondage, or even to surrender the "mutineers and murderers" to perish on Southern gibbets.

Source: "Outlyers and Rebels." From William C. Nell, *Colored Patriots of the Revolution* (Boston, 1855), pp. 226–229.

THE VIRGINIA MAROONS.*

The great Dismal Swamp, which lies near the Eastern shore of Virginia, and, commencing near Norfolk, stretches quite into North Carolina, contains a large colony of negroes, who originally obtained their freedom by the grace of God and their own determined energy, instead of the consent of their owners, or by the help of the Colonization Society. How long this colony has existed, what is its amount of population, what portion of the colonists are now fugitives, and what the descendants of fugitives, are questions not easily determined; nor can we readily avail ourselves of the better knowledge undoubtedly existing in the vicinity of this colony, by reason of the decided objections of those best enabled to gratify our curiosity—to some extent, at least—to furnishing any information whatever, lest it might be used by Abolitionists for their purposes,—as one of them frankly said when questioned about the matter. Nevertheless, some facts, or, at least, an approximation towards the truth of them, are known respecting this singular community of blacks, who have won their freedom, and established themselves securely in the midst of the largest slaveholding State of the South; for, from this extensive Swamp, they are very seldom, if now at all, reclaimed. The chivalry of Virginia, so far as I know, have never yet ventured on a slave-hunt in the Dismal Swamp, nor is it, probably, in the power of that State to capture or expel these fugitives from it. This may appear extravagant; but when it is known how long a much less numerous band of Indians held the everglades of Florida against the forces of the United

*From an article in the "Liberty Bell" for 1853, by Edmund Jackson.

States, and how much blood and treasure it cost to expel them finally, we may find a sufficient excuse for the forbearance of the "Ancient Dominion" towards this community of fugitives domiciliated in their midst.

From the character of the population, it is reasonable to infer that the United States Marshal has never charged himself with the duty of taking the census of the Swamp; and we can only estimate the amount of population, by such circumstances as may serve to indicate it. Of these, perhaps the trade existing between the city of Norfolk and the Swamp may furnish the best element of computation. This trade between the Swamp merchants and the fugitives is wholly contraband, and would subject the white participants to fearful penalties, if they could only be enforced; for, throughout the slave States, it is an offence, by law, of the gravest character, to have any dealings whatever with runaway negroes. But, "You no catch 'em, you no hab 'em," is emphatically true in the Dismal Swamp, where trader and runaway are alike beyond the reach of Virginia law. An intelligent merchant, of near thirty years' business in Norfolk, has estimated the value of slave property lost in the Swamp, at one and a half million dollars. This city of refuge, in the midst of society, has endured from generation to generation, and is likely to continue until slavery is abolished throughout the land. A curious anomoly this community certainly presents; and its history and destiny are alike suggestive of curiosity and interest.

SUGGESTED READINGS

John W. Blassingame, *The Slave Community: Plantation Life in the Antebellum South* (New York, 1972)

Douglas R. Egerton, *Gabriel's Rebellion: The Virginia Slave Conspiracies of 1800 and 1802* (Chapel Hill, N.C., 1993)

Elizabeth Fox-Genovese, *Within the Plantation Household: Black and White Women in the Old South* (Chapel Hill, N.C., 1988)

Eugene D. Genovese, *Roll, Jordan, Roll: The World the Slaves Made* (New York, 1974)

Herbert G. Gutman, *The Black Family in Slavery and Freedom, 1750–1925* (New York, 1976)

Walter Johnson, *Soul By Soul: Life Inside the Antebellum Slave Market* (Cambridge, Mass., 1999)

Jacqueline Jones, *Labor of Love, Labor of Sorrow: Black Women, Work, and the Family from Slavery to the Present* (New York, 1985)

Charles W. Joyner, *Down By the Riverside: A South Carolina Slave Community* (Urbana, Ill., 1984)

Lawrence Levine, *Black Culture and Black Consciousness: Afro-American Folk Thought From Slavery to Freedom* (New York, 1977)

Leslie Howard Owens, *This Species of Property: Slave Life and Culture in the Old South* (New York, 1976)

Albert J. Raboteau, *Slave Religion: The "Invisible Institution" in the Antebellum South* (New York, 1978)

Brenda E. Stevenson, *Life in Black and White: Family and Community in the Slave South* (New York, 1996)

Sterling Stuckey, *Slave Culture: Nationalist Theory and the Foundations of Black America* (New York, 1987)

Thomas L. Webber, *Deep Like the Rivers: Education in the Slave Quarter Community, 1831–1865* (New York, 1978)

Deborah Gray White, *Ar'n't I a Woman?: Female Slaves in the Plantation South* (New York, 1985)

An 1845 portrait of Frederick Douglass. (*Source:* The Boston Athenaeum.)

Chapter

4

North of Slavery: Free Black Communities and Abolitionism

North of slavery, a small free black community occupied an anomalous position between slavery and freedom. Despite the fact that most northern free blacks faced discrimination in every walk of life by law and custom, they developed a strong and vocal tradition of activism that contributed to the strength of the abolition movement. In addition, they sought to address the problem of racial inequality they faced in their everyday lives. Even though a majority of northern blacks were denied citizenship rights and confined to mostly menial positions in the northern economy, unlike free blacks in the south, they were able to develop strong community institutions that allowed them to protest both slavery and racial discrimination.

The selections from Joseph Wilson's book on free blacks in Philadelphia describe one antebellum free black community and its institutions. William C. Nell's book provides a portrait of two early black abolitionists, James Forten and John Vashon, and offers an introduction into the range of antebellum

free black protest activities. David Walker's "Appeal" is one of the earliest and most radical statements that hints at the possibility of the violent destruction of slavery. Maria Stewart, the first American woman to speak publicly, reveals in her speech the active role assumed by black women from the start. Henry Highland Garnet, a former slave and abolitionist, calls for slave resistance in overthrowing slavery. The appeal by Robert Purvis and the speech by Frederick Douglass, the most well-known black abolitionist leader, articulate most eloquently the black abolitionist perspective. The last two documents, which contain the address of the emigration convention led by black abolitionist Martin Delaney and the speech of John S. Rock, illustrate the growing frustration of many antebellum black activists during the decade before the Civil War when proslavery forces seemed to be triumphant. The free black community's political activism was out of proportion to their small numbers.

Selections from Joseph Wilson, Sketches of the Higher Classes of Colored Society in Philadelphia

The prejudiced world has for a long time been in error, in judging of what may be termed the *home condition,* or social intercourse, of the higher classes of colored society, by the specimens who in the every day walks of life are presented to their view as the "hewers of wood and the drawers of water." This rash mode of judgment—the forming an opinion of the beauty of the landscape merely by the heavy shading in the foreground of the picture, has long been the source of many groundless and unjust aspersions against their general character, and one which common justice requires should be removed. It is equally erroneous to adjudge all to be saints, because of the few good; as to suppose all are in a state of servitude and degradation, because it is not denied that the majority are in close approximation to that condition. With the latter, however, I profess not to concern myself here; but may say with great propriety, in passing, that many of those even who are usually regarded in this light, are far more "sinned against, than sinning;" and if their homes could be visited, they would be seen to present an air of neatness and the evidences of comfort which would be quite astonishing, when compared with their limited advantages for securing them.

Among the higher classes there is no want of a knowledge of the good things of this life, or of the ability so to arrange the means at their disposal, as to make them productive of the most substantial good, present and prospective. Unlike fashionable people

Selections from Joseph Wilson, *Sketches of the Higher Classes of Colored Society in Philadelphia.* By a Southerner. (Philadelphia: Merrihew & Thompson, 1841), pp. 53–65, 93–111, 114–15.

of other communities, they mostly live within their incomes, from whatever resources derived; and hence, if they do not appear to make very rapid advances in the road to wealth, they manage well to maintain even appearances, and support such comforts, conveniencies and luxuries, as they appear to have for a long period been uniformly accustomed to. In this way they avoid many of the embarrassments that are common to those whose sole claim to "fashion" consists in the success they may meet with in making a commanding "show" on particular occasions. They keep up, apparently, an even tenor at all times,—seeming very wisely to consider that it is quite as proper for themselves to enjoy the fruits of their possessions or exertions, as that strangers should come in and have all heaped upon them. Not that I would represent them as being less hospitable than other people in this latitude: it does not appear that they are. Probably if trial were made—means compared—the scale in this respect at least would turn in their favor.

It will not, it is believed, be expected of the writer, in speaking of the ability of the higher classes of colored society to maintain social intercourse on terms of respectability and dignity, to give an elaborate statement or inventory of the furniture of their dwellings—its quality and cost;—the size of their market-baskets (an article, by the way, not to be lost sight of in making up the sum of a happy home!) and the usual character of their contents;—it will not be necessary to say that their parlors are carpeted and furnished with sofas, sideboards, card-tables, mirrors, &c. &c., with, in many instances, the addition of the piano forte. These, with other relative matters, governed by no particular standard, the reader is left to form such an opinion of, as he may deem most correct! I will say, however, that usually, according to pecuniary ability, they fail not to gratify themselves in this wise, to the extent and after the manner that gains observance among other people.

Visiting *sans ceremonie* does not obtain to a very great extent with the higher classes of colored society. Even among those who are otherwise intimate acquaintances, the order of unceremonious visits is but limited. They are mostly by familiar or formal invitation, or in return for others previously received. This latter observance is most rigidly adhered to by many. Such as are its more determined votaries, will not attend upon a friend, even by particular invitation, unless their last call has been acknowledged by like return. The intimacy in such instances, however, as may be readily imagined, is not very great; and it seems rational to suppose there is very little care to continue that which may exist.

The period of paying and receiving visits, is mostly confined to the evening; among the gentlemen almost entirely so. Many circumstances combine to render this arrangement most convenient and agreeable to all parties; and as the same observance is respected in nearly all conditions of society in our money-seeking country, the chief cause of its adoption will be found too obvious to require particular reference.

Casual visiting with the young men is very common. Their attendance upon the ladies is mostly confined to visiting them at their dwellings. Very little out-door amusement is resorted to, as walking or riding excursions; but the reason of the non-observance of these, and one which is quite sufficient to prohibit them, is readily traceable to its proper source. With the young ladies at home they pass their evenings agreeably if so disposed. It is rarely that the visitor in the different families where there are two or three ladies, will not find one or more of them competent to perform on the piano-forte, guitar, or some other appropriate musical instrument; and these, with singing and conversation on whatever suitable topics

that may offer, constitute the amusements of their evenings at home. The love of music is universal; it is cultivated to some extent,—vocal or instrumental,—by all; so that it is almost impossible to enter a parlor where the ear of the visitor is not, in some sort or other, greeted therewith. It is consequently made a prominent part of the amusements on all occasions of social meeting together of friends. The character of the conversation is usually varied, interesting and instructive. All the current topics of the time, appropriate and of sufficient interest, are elaborately discussed in a mild, dignified and becoming manner, in which the ladies mostly take part and contribute their full quota. The degree of promptness and ability often displayed on such occasions, is far surpassing the common opinion on this subject. The best informed persons could not but be pleasingly entertained, provided they could command sufficient courage to enable them to lay aside, for the time, the mask of prejudice, (if blinded by it,) so as to be competent to take a just and an impartial view.

If prejudiced persons were to be governed more by positive knowledge—actual demonstration—than they are by rash, hasty, groundless conclusions, very different views than at present generally obtain, would soon be formed, respecting the degree of refinement and cultivation to be found among the higher classes of colored society. The ease and grace of manner with which they are capable of bearing themselves in company—their strict observance of all the nicer etiquettes, proprieties and observances that are characteristic of the well-bred—render their society agreeable and interesting to the most fastidious in such matters; and speak loudly against the injustice that is done them, in refusing to accord to them any knowledge, possession or practice of those qualities or accomplishments.

On occasions of appointed entertainments, which are usually in the form of evening parties, the greatest order and neatness of management is observed. There is always a first and second table, both appropriately and well stored, and in a manner generally unexceptionable. The guests at the parties consist only of such individuals or families as are accustomed to entertain their host or hostess, for the time, in a similar manner in their turn. Those who are all things in reception and nothing in return,—strangers, agreeable, entertaining and *eligible* bachelors, and sojourners in the city at *board,* always of course excepted,—are considered detrimental to the harmony of social intercourse; and, consequently, are very apt to be neglected in the list of invitations, that may be issued! In this way they manage to collect a very agreeable company, all perhaps on terms of perfect agreement and intimacy. The amusements of the evening are much the same as before noticed,—music, conversation, &c.,—with the addition of exchanging "mottoes" taken from the "secrets' papers," which are to be found in plenteousness at all the regular evening parties.

The hours of retirement from the evening entertainments, are usually from ten to eleven o'clock—rarely beyond eleven. Many of the visitors leave as early as ten; and after the first movement, it is not long before the entertainers are in full and quiet possession of their parlors, recounting, as it is imagined, the incidents of the evening, and determining among themselves how every thing "passed off."

The observance of abstinence at the parties of the higher classes of colored society—total abstinence from all that has a tendency to intoxicate—is worthy of remark. So far as my observation has extended, the only drinks that are presented—if indeed there are any others seen than the pure, unadulterated ale of our first parents—may consist of lemonade, or some pleasant and wholesome syrup commingled with water. No wines of any description—not even the lightest and mildest—are ever brought forward. Whether this arises from a pure love of temperance or a disposition to avoid unnecessary expenditure, either of which is commendable, I shall not pause to inquire. But certain it is that the visitors at such times and places, who neglect to carry "merry hearts and laughing eyes" with them, will find nothing in the way of distilments to excite them after they get there. It is not intended to insinuate that there are no worshippers at the shrine of Bacchus among this class. It is to be feared there are. It will be observed, however, that I have spoken solely in relation to private entertainments, or social parties, where both sexes are present.

Enough has been said, it is conceived, on the subject of the social condition of the higher classes of colored society, to convey to the mind of the stranger reader, a sufficient outline of the actual position they occupy. They are, indeed, far in advance of the peculiar circumstances by which they are surrounded. The exceedingly illiberal, unjust and oppressive prejudices of the great mass of the white community, overshadowing every moment of their existence, is enough to crush—effectually crush and keep down—any people. It meets them at almost every step without their domiciles, and not unfrequently follows even *there.* No private enterprise of any moment,—no public movement of consequence for the general good,—can they undertake, but forth steps the relentless monster to blight it in the germ. But in the face of all this, they not only bear the burthen successfully, but possess the elasticity of mind that enables them to stand erect under their disabilities, and present a state of society of which, to say the least, none have just cause to be ashamed. . . .

The number and character of the institutions for the promotion of literature in any community, may be justly regarded as an unfailing indication of the tastes and morals of its components. . . .

Among no people, in proportion to their means and advantages, is the pursuit of knowledge more honored than among the colored inhabitants of Philadelphia. The exalted standard in the world of letters, which characterizes the favored class, is by them seconded to the utmost extent in their power. Many of them seem, in this respect, to have fully entered into the spirit of taste and refinement of those by whom they are surrounded; and their success is seen to be such, as of which they have no reason to be ashamed. The actual standard of literary acquirements, it is true, even among the best informed class, is nothing extraordinary of itself considered; they have engaged in the pursuit of knowledge more for its own sake—the adornment which it gives them—than from any relative or collateral advantages which could be expected; they have not been stimulated and encouraged to seek education as a *trade,* which would well repay their assiduity and the pecuniary cost of the pursuit: and, therefore, in the absence of all those cheering motives which impel others, to expect a higher state of advancement than they at present exhibit, would be illiberal if not unjust.

The educated man of color, in the United States, is by no means, so far as he may be affected by exterior circumstances, the *happiest* man. He finds himself in possession of abilities and acquirements which fit him for most of the useful and honorable stations in life, where such qualities are requisite; but does he find—can he even with reason anticipate—their ever being in like manner appreciated and rewarded? If there was nothing in education to recommend *itself,* well might reason be construed against the utility of the man of color's entering its paths; aye, well might *he* conclude within himself, that with the people of color "ignorance *is* bliss!" and for them it is, therefore, "folly to be wise!" "He that is robbed, let him not know it, and he is not robbed at all."

But education possesses its own intrinsic worth, which it imparts to those who enter its pursuits. Of this, colored Philadelphians seem to be fully aware; and as one important avenue towards further advancement and perfection, they have established numerous literary associations, the most prominent of which it is here proposed briefly to notice.

Among the earliest established of these institutions, stands first "The Philadelphia Library Company of Colored Persons." This Company was instituted January 1st, 1833. The number of persons present at its forma-

tion, and who signed the Constitution, were nine; whose names are here given:—Messrs. Frederick A. Hinton, James Needham, (now *Treasurer,* and who kindly furnished these particulars,) James Cornish, Robert C. Gordon, junr., John Dupee, William Whipper, J. C. Bowers, Charles Trulier, Robert Douglass, junr., and James C. Mathews;—who may be considered the founders of the first successful literary institution of this description, established by the colored classes in Philadelphia.

The object of the Company, as its title implies, was the collection of a library of useful works of every description for the benefit of its members, who might there successfully apply, without comparatively any cost, for that mental good which they could not readily obtain elsewhere. This enterprise met with great encouragement, both in the way of donations of books, pamphlets, maps, &c., and otherwise; so that in a short time a large and valuable collection was made. A systematic order of reading was then adopted by the members, to the very great advantage of those who persevered therein. In connexion with this, a system of debates was introduced, for the purpose of stimulating the members to historical and other researches, and for practising them in the arts of elocution and public speaking.

Soon after the establishment of the Library Company—their numbers having greatly augmented—application was made to the Legislature for an act of incorporation. In this they also met with speedy success—corporate existence having been granted them in the early part of 1836. From this period the Company rapidly increased in numbers and usefulness, until at the present time the roll book presents the names of about hundred (including a number of honorary) members; all of whom have partaken of its benefits.

The debating department has of late greatly improved in regard to the intelligence and ability of those who usually participate therein. Discussions of interesting subjects, take place on Tuesday of each week.

The Library at present contains nearly six hundred volumes of valuable historical, scientific and miscellaneous works, among which are several Encyclopœdias, and is a source of great mental profit to the members of the Company. Among those who took an interest in, and contributed towards the collection of the Library, was the late Right Reverend Bishop White, of the Protestant Episcopal church.

The fee of admission to membership of the institution, is such as to place it within the reach of every one disposed to connect themselves therewith. It is *one dollar;* and the monthly assessment thereafter, *twenty-five cents.*

The Company, at the present time, holds its meetings in the basement of St. Thomas' Episcopal Church, South Fifth street, where persons, so disposed, are at liberty to visit and judge for themselves of its probable character.

The progress of this institution has been marked by evidences of the most gratifying character—gratifying to all who delight to witness the progress of knowledge and refinement among their fellow-men. Many a young man of color in this community, who previous to the establishment of "The Philadelphia Library Company of Colored Persons" never dreamed of rising before a public auditory to make an address, or engage in a debate, is now enabled to do so with little or no embarrassment, and in a manner highly creditable.

The next, in the order of its formation comes "The Rush Library Company and Debating Society of Pennsylvania." This Society was formed on the 16th of December, 1836; and, as will be seen, is several years younger than its predecessor. Present at its formation there were seven persons as follows:—Messrs. John L. Hart, (now the *President*—and to whom I am indebted for these particulars,) William D. Banton, Littleton Hubert, Harrison R. Sylva, James Bird, and Charles Brister. In about two months after this beginning, the list of its members had increased to twenty-two; at which period an act of incorporation was granted by the Legislature, bearing date March 1, 1837.

The object aimed at, by the founders of the "Rush Library Company and Debating Society," was the same as that of the one first noticed. They have succeeded in collecting a handsome library, at the present time numbering two hundred volumes, and gradually increasing. Its contents are, of course, of a miscellaneous character; but all of the books are useful, and among them many valuable works. From this source the members have derived great advantages.

The debating department is also maintained with spirit—many of the members evidencing much ability in the discussion of the various questions that are brought before them. This is likewise, to the members a source of great improvement in elocution and public speaking.

The roll book of the Rush Library Company, at the time this is written, (June, 1841,) numbers thirty members, with occasional additions. Its place of meeting is at "Salters' Hall," Elizabeth street.

Those best acquainted with the affairs of this institution, are of opinion that it is "one of the most really useful, of its kind, among the colored classes, in the city;"—that others may equal it in regard to the benefits derivable therefrom, but none surpass. This opinion is, in all probability, nothing more than is justly due. If the energy and enterprise of its President may be taken as a sample of the spirit that characterizes the body of its members, there is no doubt but that "The Rush Library Company and Debating Society of Pennsylvania," will eminently keep pace, in the onward march of improvement, with the best of its contemporaries.

I shall now proceed to notice an institution which was originally composed of young men in their minority, and who were thereby excluded from membership of those previously established. It was this exclusion, if I am correctly informed, which chiefly gave rise to the now flourishing "Demosthenian Institute." This association was formed January 10, 1839, at the house of Mr. John P. Burr; at which time and place, the following named young men were elected its officers:—John E.

Burr, President; David Gordon, Vice President; Benjamin Stanley, Secretary; William Jennings, Treasurer; G. W. Gibbons, Librarian; Lewis B. Meade, E. Parkinson, Zedekiah J. Purnell, A. F. Hutchinson, and B. Hughes, the Board of Managers.

In the course of inquiries respecting the condition and progress of the "Demosthenian Institute," I have been furnished by the President, Mr. Z. J. Purnell, and the Secretary, Mr. T. S. Crouch, with a brief written history, containing particulars, and from it make the annexed extract:—

> Here [at the house of Mr. Burr] the meetings were held for nearly a year, during which time several addresses were delivered and numerous questions discussed;—but in the presence of the members only, owing to a general wish that the Institute should be made a preparatory school, until the members had gained sufficient confidence and experience, to fit them for an appearance before a public auditory. As the institute emerged from its obscurity, the number of its members rapidly augmented, till it became necessary to secure a more commodious place of meeting. Accordingly, Salter's Hall was engaged; and the first meeting of the Institute there, took place December 18th, 1839.

From the period here mentioned, to the present, the "Demosthenian Institute" has continued its meetings at "Salters' Hall;" where, though but of recent origin, it has, in the words of its President, "made a great deal of noise;" though not, it is believed, without much good reason. The addresses and course of lectures during the past season (1840–41,) show great energy and enterprise on the part of its members, and also forcibly exhibit the abiding interest which actuates them for its continued prosperity and usefulness. It should also be borne in mind, that these lectures, are the work, chiefly, of the members of the Institute; and it is very doubtful whether many of them ever ventured before the public, for such purposes, previous to becoming connected therewith.

The debating department has likewise been a source of great improvement to the young men of the "Demosthenian Institute." In this respect they have not remained in the rear of their predecessors. They are still improving, and will, ere long, be undoubtedly enabled to cope with the oldest of those in existence before them.

The members of the Institute number, at the present time, forty-two, with a gradual increase. Its Library contains over one hundred volumes, comprising many valuable historical and scientific works.*

Having now endeavored in a few words, to point out the condition and chief sources of improvement afforded by the literary associations among the gentlemen, I shall proceed briefly to glance at those in existence among the ladies. The first of these that comes under notice is "The Minerva Literary Association." This association was formed in "October, 1834." There were present at the formation thirty ladies, all of whom constituted themselves members. With this good beginning, the daughters of the goddess whose name they bear, went into immediate active opera-

---

*Shortly after this notice of the "Demosthenian Institute" was written, I was shown the first number of a very neat little paper, entitled the "Demosthenian Shield," which has been established by the enterprise of the young men who composed the Institute, and intended to be published weekly, from the time of its first appearance, (June 29, 1841.) Its subscription list numbered "over one thousand subscribers" before the first number was issued—and success, therefore, seems certain. Its typographical appearance is very neat; and, judging from No. 1, it promises dignity—which is very important—and ability in the editorial department. The whole is calculated to reflect great credit upon the *"Demosthenian Institute,"* and is a far better evidence of its onward march, in general improvement, than the brief notice we had taken of it, previous to the appearance of the "Shield." It is pleasing, therefore, to see what was said hereby so promptly corroborated.

tion; and were soon permanently organized into a school for the encouragement and promotion of polite literature. The order of their exercises were readings and recitations of original and selected pieces, together with other appropriate matters. Many of the essays and other original productions, both in prose and poetry, have been deemed highly meritorious, and at different periods have appeared in the "poets' corner" or other department of some of the friendly publications.

"The Minerva Literary Association" is composed of a large number of members at the present time. It still holds its meetings once each week as heretofore, to the improvement and edification of all who are connected with it.

There is also among the ladies "The Edgeworth Literary Association," whose object and exercises are so identically the same as those of the "Minerva," that a repetition thereof seems unnecessary. It is sufficient to say that the ladies consider them both worthy of being cherished, which is a sufficient guaranty that they are not wanting in importance and usefulness.*

The last of the literary institutions which I shall here notice, is the nondescript "Gilbert Lyceum." This institution is composed, as will be seen by the names of its founders, of individuals of both sexes, and is the first, and only one established by the colored classes of Philadelphia, for both literary and scientific pursuits. The name "Gilbert" is prefixed in honor to the gentleman of that name, who recommended its formation. It is of but recent origin,—instituted (as I am informed by Mr. R. Douglass, junr.) January 31, 1841. The persons who composed the meeting, that gave it

a "local habitation and a name," were eleven in number—as follows:—Messrs. Robert Douglass, senr., Joseph Cassey, Jacob C. White, John C. Bowers, Robert Purvis; and Mrs. Amy M. Cassey, Miss Sarah M. Douglass, Mrs. Hetty Burr, Mrs. Grace Douglass, Mrs. Harriet Purvis, and Miss Amelia Bogle.

In consequence of the late period of its formation, the "Lyceum" has not been able to do much towards effecting the objects of its formation. It has, however, already had a course of scientific and other lectures delivered before it, which generally have been well attended. It is understood, also, that the "Lyceum" proposes the collection of a cabinet of minerals, curiosities, &c., as soon as its permanent organization will admit of so doing.

The number of members at the present time are about forty—exhibiting a great increase in a short period. If governed by a proper spirit, the "Gilbert Lyceum" may no doubt be made a source of improvement to its members, not to be surpassed by any literary institution previously in existence. . . .

These short notices of the principal literary institutions, though not so full and comprehensive as was originally contemplated, will be sufficient to show that the colored classes are not at all behind the age, in their efforts to raise the standard of education and polite literature, to a much greater height among themselves than they have yet been enabled to do. Heretofore they have had to encounter innumerable discouragements, in almost every ennobling undertaking; but these there is every reason to believe, will be withdrawn, in proportion as the former shall demonstrate by their acts, the gross injustice of their infliction. This, it is contended, they have long ago done—in fact they *never deserted* the tyrannical prejudices they are constantly exposed to—but the great community have closed their eyes to this view of the case, and seem resolved that nothing short of a "miraculous working of their own salvation" shall ever secure to them those equitable and just considerations which are enjoyed by all others of a different descent. . . .

---

*It may be due to the ladies, and therefore proper to state, that I should have very cheerfully taken a more extended notice of the "Minerva," and the "Edgeworth," had I not failed in attempts to procure such authentic information, in regard to them, as was requisite to a correct detailed understanding of their condition, &c. &c.

James Forten and John Vashon

William C. Nell

JAMES FORTEN.*

JAMES FORTEN was born on the second day of September, 1766, and died on the Ides of March, 1842. He was the son of Thomas Forten, who died when James was but seven years old. His mother survived long after he had reached the years of maturity. In early life, he was marked for great sprightliness and energy of character, a generous disposition, and indomitable courage, always frank, kind, courteous, and disinterested. In the year 1775, he left school, being then about nine years of age, having received a very limited education (and he never went to school afterwards) from that early, devoted, and worldwide known philanthropist, ANTHONY BENEZET. He was then employed at a grocery store and at home, when his mother, yielding to the earnest and unceasing solicitations of her son, whose young heart fired with the enthusiasm and feeling of the patriots and revolutionists of that day, with the firmness and devotion of a Roman matron, but with a heart *then* truly deemed American, gave the boy of her promise, the child of her heart and her hopes, to his country; upon the altar of its liberties she laid the apple of her eye, the jewel of her soul.

In 1780, then in his fourteenth year, he embarked on board the *"Royal* Louis," Stephen Decatur, Senr., Commander, in the capacity of "powder-boy." Scarce wafted from his native

Source: James Forten and John Vashon. William C. Nell, *Colored Patriots of the Revolution* (Boston, 1855), pp. 166–188.

*Abridged from a eulogy on his life and character, delivered at Bethel Church, Philadelphia, March 30, 1842, by ROBERT PURVIS.

shore, and perilled upon the dark blue sea, than he found himself amid the roar of cannon, the smoke of blood, the dying and the dead. Their ship was soon brought into action with an English vessel, the Lawrence, which, after a severe fight, in which great loss was sustained on both sides, and leaving every man wounded on board the "Louis" but himself, they succeeded in capturing, and brought her into port amid the loud huzzas and acclamations of the crowds that assembled upon the occasion. Forten, sharing largely in the feeling which so brilliant a victory had inspired, with fresh courage, and an unquenchable devotion to the interests of his native land, soon reëmbarked in the same vessel. In this cruise, however, they were unfortunate; for, falling in with three of the enemy's vessels,—the Amphyon, Nymph, and Pomona,—they were forced to strike their colors, and become prisoners of war. It was at this juncture that his mind was harassed with the most painful forebodings, from a knowledge of the fact that rarely, if ever, were prisoners of his complexion exchanged; they were sent to the West Indies, and there doomed to a life of slavery. But his destiny, by a kind Providence, was otherwise. He was placed on board the Amphyon, Captain Beasly, who, struck with his open and honest countenance, made him the companion of his son. During one of those dull and monotonous periods which frequently occur on ship-board, young Beasly and Forten were engaged in a game at marbles, when, with signal dexterity and skill, the marbles were upon every trial successively displaced by the unerring hand of Forten. This excited the surprise and admiration of his young companion, who, hastening to his father, called his attention to it. Upon being questioned as to the truth of the matter, and assuring the Captain that nothing was easier for him to accomplish, the marbles were again placed in the ring, and in rapid succession he redeemed his word.

A fresh and deeper interest was from that moment taken in his behalf. Captain Beasly proffered him a passage to England, tempted him with the allurements of wealth, under the patronage of his son, who was heir to a large estate there, the advantages of a good education, and freedom, equality and happiness, for ever. "No, no!" was the invariable reply; "I am here a prisoner for the liberties of my country; *I never, never, shall prove a traitor to her interests!*" What sentiment more exalted! What patriotism more lofty, devoted, and self-sacrificing! Indeed, with him, the feeling was, "America, with all thy faults, I love thee still"; for, with a full knowledge of the wrongs and outrages which she was then inflicting upon his brethren by the "ties of consanguinity and of wrong," we see this persecuted and valiant son of hers, in the very darkest hour of his existence, when hope seemed to have departed from him, when the horrors of a hopeless West India slavery, with its whips for his shrinking flesh, and its chains for his free-born soul, could only be dissipated by severing that tie, which, by the strongest cords of love, bound him to his native land, we see him standing up in the spirit of martyrdom, with a constancy of affection, and an invincibility of purpose, for the honor of his country, that place him above the noblest of the Cæsars, and entitle him to a monument towering above that which a Bonaparte erected at the *Place Vendome*. Beasly, having failed in inducing him to go to England, soon had him consigned to that floating and pestilential hell, the frigate "Old Jersey,"—giving him, however, as a token of his regard and friendship, a letter to the Commander of the prison-ship, highly commendatory of him, and also requesting that Forten should not be forgotten on the list of exchanges. Thus (as he frequently remarked in after life) did a game of marbles save him from a life of West India servitude. In the mean while, his mother, at home, was in a state of mind bordering upon distraction, having learned that her son had been shot from the foretop of the Royal Louis; but her mind was relieved, after he had been absent nearly eight months, by his appearing in person.

To return. While on board the "Old Jersey," amid the privations and horrors incident to that receiving ship of disease and death, no less than three thousand five hundred persons died; and, according to a statement of Edwards, eleven thousand in all perished, while she remained the receptacle of the American prisoners. And here we have an instance to record of the most thrilling and stupendous exhibition of his generous and benevolent heart. Amid all that would make escape from his confinement desirable, when disease the most loathsome, death the most horrible, was around him, he was willing to and did endure all. He stifled the longings of his heart for the enjoyments of home, and for the embraces of his widowed and adored mother; yes, at a time when, if ever, self would lay in contribution every feeling of the heart, and every avenue of a generous out-going spirit be smothered, when the instincts and impulses of nature would unerringly covet in the closest scrutiny and watchfulness its own interests, James Forten, in the ardor of his own high-toned beneficence, performed an act, which, in my humble opinion, is unexcelled, perhaps without a parallel, in the annals of our country's history. It was this: An officer of the American navy was about to be exchanged for a British prisoner, when the thoughtful mind of Forten conceived the idea of an easy escape for himself in the officer's chest; but, when about to avail himself of this opportunity, a fellow-prisoner, a youth, his junior in years, his companion and associate in suffering, was thought of. He immediately urged upon him to avail himself of the chances of an escape so easy. The offer was accepted, and Forten had the satisfaction of assisting in taking down the "chest of old clothes," as it was then called, from the side of the prison ship. The individual thus fortunately rescued was Captain

Daniel Brewton,—the present incumbent in the Stewardship at the Lazaretto. I will read the certificate of Mr. Brewton in regard to this matter:—

"I do hereby certify, that James Forten was one who participated in the Revolution, in the year of our Lord one thousand seven hundred and seventy-six, and was a prisoner on board of the prison-ship 'Old Jersey,' in the year of our Lord one thousand seven hundred and eighty, with me.
      (Signed,)   Daniel Brewton."
      Philadelphia, March 15th, 1837. Acknowledged before Alderman

                              J. W. Palmer.

It was my great privilege to see, but a short time ago, this venerable and grateful friend of James Forten; to hear from his own lips a strict confirmation of the facts stated, as well as to witness the solemn scene which ensued, in his taking for the last time the hand of his dying benefactor. The old man's tears fell like rain; his stifled utterance marked the deep emotions of his almost bursting heart. Sad and dejected, with feelings that made him more ready to die than to live, he silently retired, stayed with the hope that they would soon meet in a better and a happier world.

After remaining seven months a prisoner on board this ship, young Forten obtained his release, and, without shoes upon his feet, (until he reached Trenton, where he was generously supplied,) arrived home in a wretchedly bad condition, having, among other evidences of great hard-ships endured, his hair nearly entirely worn from his head. He remained but a short time at home, when, in company with his brother-in-law, he sailed, in the ship Commerce, for London. He arrived there at a period of the greatest excitement. The great struggle between liberty and slavery had already been settled by the decision in the noted case of Somersett, when it was decreed, that the moment a slave trod the soil of Britain, "no matter in what language his doom may have been pronounced,—no matter what complexion incompatible with freedom an Indian or an African sun may have burnt upon him,—no matter in what disastrous battle his liberty may have been cloven down,—no matter with what solemnities he may have been devoted upon the altar of slavery, the first moment he touches the sacred soil of Britain, the altar and the god sink together in the dust; his body swells beyond the measure of his chains that burst from around him, and he stands redeemed, regenerated and disenthralled, by the irresistible Genius of Universal Emancipation."

But the accursed slave trade was still glutting in the blood and sinews of Afric's helpless children, and that mighty man, that prince of philanthropists, Granville Sharpe, was directing his benevolent efforts to its overthrow. At this time, the Christian feeling had awakened up an indignant nation to a determination for its destruction; and no small interest was taken in the discussions, both in and out of Parliament, by our deceased friend. It was among the many pleasing reminiscences of his life to refer to those scenes, so strikingly analogous to the trials and persecutions of the friends of freedom here, and the hypocritical sophisms of their opponents. After remaining in London about a year, he returned home, and was apprenticed, with his own consent, to Mr. Robert Bridges, sail-maker. He was not long at his trade, when his great skill, energy, diligence, and good conduct, commended him to his master, who, neither discriminating nor appreciating a man by the mere color of the skin in which he may be born, served his own interest in doing an act commensurate to the merits of young Forten, in promoting him foreman in his business. This was in his twentieth year. He continued in this capacity until 1798, when, upon the retirement of Mr. Bridges, he assumed the entire control and responsibility of the establishment. Having formed for himself a reputation for capability and industry, he found it no difficult task to secure the friendship of those, who, perceiving qualities in him which ever adorn and beautify the human character, gave him their countenance and patronage; for although it was by the force of his own unassisted genius and energy of character that he rose above those depressing influences which have ever operated against those

> "Whose hue makes a brother hate
> A brother mortal here,"—

yet he was indebted to some few stanch friends, of whose encouragement and kindness he was ever wont to speak in terms of gratitude. He continued, with great consistency of conduct, in prosecuting his business, offering up, on the altar of filial and fraternal regard, the first fruits of his labor, in purchasing a house for his mother and widowed sister, which sheltered the one until the period of her death, and now affords protection and support to the other in her declining years. With undiminished vigor of mind and body, enjoying the very best of health, he continued to give personal attention to his business until confined to his house from that disease, which, in a few months, proved fatal to him. It was during the long period of his active business life that he acquired that reputation, which ever remained unclouded, shedding abroad in its own clear sky the brightest and noblest qualities of the human heart; so courteous, polished and gentlemanly in his manners,—so intelligent, social, and interesting,—so honest, just and true in his dealings,—so kind and benevolent in his actions,—so noble and lofty in his bearing,— that none knew him but to admire, to speak of him but in praise. He lived but to cherish those noble properties of his soul, and those exalted principles of action, which ever prompted him to deeds of benevolence, patriotism and honor. Perhaps one of the strongest traits in his character was that of benevolence. With him, it was no occasional or fitful impulse, but a living principle of action. Wherever suffering humanity presented itself, a glow of generous and brotherly sympathy was excited in his heart; and not bestowing

nor graduating his gifts by the mere color of the skin, his open hand was ever ready to administer to the wants of all. Nor was this feeling confined to the giving of his worldly substance. No danger could appal him, no hindrance prevent, even at the greatest personal risk, in relieving from danger and death his fellow-man. No less than seven persons were at different times rescued from drowning by his promptness, energy and benevolence. From the Humane Society he obtained this certificate:—

> "The Managers of the Humane Society of Philadelphia, entertaining a grateful sense of the benevolent and successful exertions of James Forten in rescuing, at the imminent hazard of his life, four persons from drowning in the river Delaware at different times, to wit: one on the—day, 11th mo., 1805; a second on the—day of 1st mo., 1807; a third on the—day of 4th mo., 1810; and on the—day of 4th mo., 1821, present this Honorary Certificate as a testimony of their approbation of his meritorious conduct.
> By order of the Managers,
> JOSEPH CRUKESHANK, *President.*
> PHILADELPHIA, Fifth mo., 9th, 1821."

Of his patriotism, who doubts? He gave the best evidence of his love for his country by consecrating his life, in "the times that tried men's souls," to her liberties; and when urged by an honorable gentleman to petition his government for a pension, he promptly declined, saying, "I was a volunteer, sir." In the last war, when an invasion was threatened by the British upon our city, he was found, with twenty of his journeymen, and with hundreds of his persecuted and oppressed brethren, throwing up the redoubts on the west bank of the Schuylkill. Indeed, his interest was so strong in any matter connected with his country, that we would sometimes express our surprise at this. He would reply, "that he had drawn the spirit of her free institutions from his mother's breast, and that he had fought for her independence." With all this, however, his sensitive mind was but too truly pained at her ingratitude, in the wrongs she continued to inflict upon her unoffending and unfortunate children; believing, as he often expressed it, that she would bring down the vengeance of Heaven upon her, and quoting the fearful lines of Jefferson, "I tremble for my country when I remember that God is just, and that his justice will not sleep for ever." Perhaps no instance gave greater poignancy to his feelings than the late atrocious act of the miscalled Reform Convention. For this State, his attachments were peculiar and strong. Here he was born,—his ancestors were residents for upwards of one hundred and seventy years. He had paid a large amount of taxes, and contributed to almost every institution which adorned and beautified this large city. Here had lived a Franklin, Rush, Rawle, Wistar, Vaux, Parrish, and Shipley, the very brightest ornaments of Christian love and philanthropy. Yet no recollection of their principles, no regard for the true policy of this State, or for justice, humanity, or God, could stay the ruthless arms of those marauders upon human liberty from striking down the rights of forty thousand of her tax-paying citizens.

In the year 1800, Mr. Forten addressed a letter to Hon. George Thatcher, in reference to the law of Congress of '93, authorising the seizure of fugitive slaves. The letter was intended as an acknowledgment for Mr. Thacher's advocacy of the petition of Mr. Forten and others, remonstrating against the iniquitous law.

In the year 1817, this good man's principles were put to the test. Having, at this time, an extended influence, and being prominent in the eyes of the community as a man of singular probity and worth, extorting, even from the jaundiced heart of prejudice, involuntary respect, he was marked by the enemies of freedom, and every device, which the scheme of colonization could invent, was attempted to blind and mislead him. It was about this time, that this society of innate wickedness,

mantled in the cloak of benevolence, came stalking over the land, so specious and whining in its tone, so soft and insinuating in its low breathings, that many were deceived. But the discriminating mind of James Forten penetrated the veil that covered its deformed and damning features. The clique of clerical wolves, who had besieged him in tones of flattery, assuring him that he would become the Lord Mansfield of their "Heaven-born republic" on the western coast of Africa, was told, in the simplicity of truth, but with sarcasm the more cutting because unaffected, "That he would rather remain as James Forten, sail-maker, in Philadelphia, than enjoy the highest offices in the gift of their society." The matter, however, did not rest here with him. He foresaw what would be the evil tendencies and effects of this infamous institution, and the necessity of frustrating the designs of the leagued spirits of this dark crusade against the rapidly improving condition of his people, and of incorporating, at once and for ever, the idea in the public mind, that we were fixtures in this our native country,—"that here we were born, here we would live, and here die." With this view, and having the cooperation of some of the most intelligent of his brethren, among whom were our sterling and inflexible friend to human rights, Robert Douglass, Senr., the good-hearted Absalom Jones, and last, though not least, the founder of your church, that extraordinary man, the Rt. Rev. Bishop Allen, a meeting was called in this church, in the month of January, 1817. The house, upon the occasion, was literally crammed. Mr. Forten presided as chairman, and a beautiful preamble and resolutions, which had been previously prepared, went down, in an unanimous vote, as the death-knell to colonization. Of these resolutions, two were from the pen of Mr. Forten.

[After detailing Mr. F.'s efforts against colonization, Mr. Purvis continues:]

His hand was promptly extended to that pure Christian and exalted philanthropist, William Lloyd Garrison. He saw in him all those qualities necessary as a leader in the great enterprise; and, in his own language, considered him as a chosen instrument, in the Divine hand, to accomplish the great work of the abolition of American slavery. Indeed, such was his confidence (and justly so) in the principles of the American Anti-Slavery Society, and of the men and women who advocated them, that nothing was ever more painful to his feelings, nothing sooner excited his indignation, than the attempt to cast reproach upon them. The course pursued by Mr. Garrison he ever thought conformable to the true anti-slavery principles; and those principles, founded upon the immutability of eternal truth, had thrown around him, and all others who acted with him, the influences of its divinity. Hence, no difficulties nor dangers have intimidated them,—they have gone on, conquering and to conquer. In no restricted sense, but in its proper signification and application, he was a friend to human rights. The doctrine of "Woman's Rights," as it is called, found in him a zealous friend. He believed that those doctrines would be acknowledged universally, because, as he would say, we live in an enlightened age,—an age which tolerates a free expression of opinion, and leaves the mind to the guidance of its own inwardly revealing light, to the enjoyment of its own individuality; and, setting aside the dogmas and creeds of established usage and custom, unshackles the immortal mind, leaving it free and independent, as it was designed by its bountiful Creator. Yet, while *truth,* bright, eternal *truth,* is rising in all the gorgeousness of her transcendental supremacy, there are those who, not more egregiously than pertinaciously, cling to their blindness, their infatuation, meanness, and despotism. But woman is not a mere dependant upon man. The relation is perfectly reciprocal. God has given to both man and woman the same intellectual capacities, and made them subjects alike to the same moral government. He was a man of religion, but no bigot; the last survivor of the founders of St. Thomas's Episcopal Church, and its most liberal patron and friend; and, though connected with this in-

stitution for more than fifty years—in close communion with its ordinances for many years back,—he ever valued the spirit of Christianity, exemplified in the character of men, as being of infinitely more importance than a mere unity in doctrinal views and creeds. As a business man, none were more honest and fair—no overreaching, misrepresentations, or deceiving; and, as a remarkable fact in his history, as well as a lesson to others, he never had, as I have often heard him declare, been guilty of that genteel kind of swindling, which all sorts of *professedly* good people practice, under the gloss of the name of note-shaving.

Temperate in habits, and, more especially, an enemy to all intoxicating drinks, having never taken a glass of ardent spirit in his life, nor permitted its introduction into the premises among those he employed, he was a ready advocate of the blessed cause of temperance, and of all other great moral enterprises which are now so rife in our land. He was a member and the presiding officer of the American Moral Reform Society, from its origin to the time of his death. In a word, whatever was right, useful and patriotic, secured in him a friend, advocate and patron. In the social relations, he was the most affectionate of husbands, and the most indulgent of parents; as a friend, unwavering and steadfast in his attachments.

He was a *model,* not, as some flippant scribbler asserts, for what are called "colored men," but for all men. His example will ever be worthy of emulation, his virtues never forgotten in the community in which he lived.

Three or four thousand persons, it was believed, attended the funeral of Mr. Forten, one half of whom were white.

Among other reminiscences connected with the Revolution, Mr. Forten often alluded to the part taken by colored men in the war. He saw the regiments from Rhode Island, Connecticut and Massachusetts, when they marched through Philadelphia, to meet Cornwallis, who was then overrunning the South, and said that one or two companies of colored men were attached to each. The vessels of war of that period were all, to a greater or less extent, manned by colored men. On board the Royal Louis, in which Mr. Forten enlisted, there were twenty colored seamen; the Alliance, of thirty-six guns, Commodore Barry, the Trumbull, of thirty-two guns, Captain Nicholson, and the ships South Carolina, Confederacy, and Randolph, were all manned, in part, by colored men.

JOHN B. VASHON.*

JOHN BATHAN VASHON was born in Norfolk, Va., in 1792. His mother was a mulatto; his father, Capt. George Vashon, a white man of French ancestry, who was appointed Indian Agent under General Jackson, and retained his office under President Van Buren. Being a colored child, though the offspring of a white man of standing, there was probably no other care taken of his education than is usual with one of his class in the United States, under such circumstances. But John continued to grow a boy of observation, and, as was inseparable from his nature, to be "interested in whatever was interesting to man."

In 1812, during the struggle in which Europe was engaged to avert the danger threatened by the usurpation of Napoleon, and the disturbance of the amicable relations which, for a time, had seemed to exist between the United States and Great Britain, young Vashon, being now twenty years of age, and full of that curiosity which the ardor and romance of youth so naturally inspires, without even the poor consolation, as the only hope for an escape with life or liberty, that he was an *acknowledged American citizen,* embarked as a common seaman and soldier on board of the old war ship "Revenge," destined to cruise through the West Indies and on the coast of South America. In an engage-

ment on the coast of Brazil, Mr. Vashon, with others, was made prisoner of war by the English. Among his fellow-prisoners was young Henry Bears, now Major Henry Bears, a prominent and affluent old citizen of Pittsburg, Pa., to whom any reference may be made concerning this statement. The prisoners were all released on exchange. On Mr. Vashon's return to Virginia, he settled in Fredericksburg, from whence he removed to Dumfries, and subsequently to Leesburg. While a resident of the latter place, he volunteered in the land service, at a time when the colored people of that neighborhood were called upon to aid in the defence of their country, and prevent the British fleet from ascending the Potomac.

In 1822, he left Leesburg, with his family, (an amiable wife and two children,) and resided in Carlisle, Penn., for seven years. Here he was much respected as a useful member of the community; he was the proprietor of a public saloon, a place of general resort and accommodation for the students of Dickinson College, and the first gentlemen of the town; an extensive livery stable was also a part of the establishment.

He was not content with having served his country, but was desirous of becoming especially useful to his brethren. In 1823, but one year subsequent to his settlement in the town, he assisted in the formation of a mutual improvement association, and was immediately chosen Treasurer, in coöperation with his friend and very useful fellow-citizen, John Peck, as President. This institution was known as the "Lay Benevolent Society."

In 1829, he removed, with his family, (which now had an addition of a son,) to Pittsburg, Pa. Here, also, Mr. Vashon made himself much respected in the community, and quite useful among his brethren. The first public baths in Pittsburg, and probably the first public baths for ladies established west of the mountains, were the result of his exertions. He was among the first to promote the assembling of colored men in National Conventions; and was a prominent advocate of the equality of the white and

---

*For this account of Mr. VASHON, I am indebted to Dr. M. R. Delany, of Pittsburg.

colored races, always claiming to be an *American,*—a name which he appeared to love but little less than that of *liberty,* which it seemed to imply.

Immediately after the National Convention of Colored Men had been held in Philadelphia, Garrison's "Thoughts on Colonization" made its appearance, for which Mr. Vashon was appointed by the author an agent. Through his influence, and that of the book itself, the late Robert Bruce, D.D., then President of the University of Western Pennsylvania, and several other prominent citizens of Pittsburg, formerly earnest advocates of the Colonization Society, were happily converted to anti-slavery views. Mr. Vashon was also a faithful agent for the *Liberator* in the same district.

In 1833, the first Anti-Slavery Society west of the mountains was organized by him in the front parlor of his homestead. He also promoted the formation of an Educational Institution, and was its first President. Through his efforts, the handsome sum of twelve hundred dollars was contributed in its support, he himself giving, at one time, fifty dollars from his own purse. In 1834, he was elected President of a Temperance Society, and also of a Moral Reform Society, as a testimony to his devoted and assiduous labors in behalf of those movements.

In 1835, being in Boston when the infuriated mob attacked Mr. Garrison, dragging him like a felon through the streets, Mr. Vashon was an eye-witness to the terrible scene, which was heart-rending beyond his ability ever afterwards to express, as, of all living men, JOHN B. VASHON loved WILLIAM LLOYD GARRISON most; and this feeling of affection toward him continued, for aught that is known, till the day of his death. When the mob passed along Washington street, shouting and yelling like madmen, the apprehensions of Mr. Vashon became fearfully aroused. Presently there approached a group which appeared even more infuriated than the rest, and he beheld, in the midst of this furious throng, Garrison himself, with a rope round his neck, led on like a beast to the slaughter. He had been on the field of battle,

had faced the cannon's mouth, seen its lightnings flash and heard its thunders roar, but such a sight as this was more than the old citizen-soldier could bear, without giving vent to a flood of tears.

The next day, the old soldier, who had helped to preserve his country's liberty on the plighted faith of security to his own, but who had lived to witness freedom of speech and of the press stricken down by mob violence, and life itself in jeopardy, because that liberty was asked for him and his, with spirits crushed and faltering hopes, called to administer a word of consolation to the bold and courageous young advocate of immediate and universal emancipation. Mr. Garrison subsequently thus referred to this circumstance in his paper:—"On the day of the riot in Boston, he dined at my house, and the next morning called to see me in prison, bringing with him a new hat for me, in the place of one that was cut by the knives of the 'men of property and standing from all parts of the city.' " In this, he proved a "ministering angel" to the philanthropist in time of trouble.

Mr. Vashon was zealous in promoting the education of his children. One daughter was sent to the excellent Female Academy of Miss Sarah M. Douglass, in Philadelphia, and his son to the Oberlin Collegiate Institute, where he graduated with the first honors of his class, and delivered the valedictory. He subsequently studied in the law office of the late Hon. Walter Forward, ex-Secretary of the U. S. Treasury, and more recently Presiding Judge in the Western District of Pennsylvania.

A circumstance well worthy of record took place during the exemplary efforts of this good old American patriot in preparing his children to fill useful positions in society. During the collegiate course of his son, (his daughter having previously finished her education,) a change in his circumstances induced a friend to propose recalling his son George from college.

"I will never do it!" was the positive reply.

"How can you do otherwise? you must live," said his adviser.

"I will stint my market basket," rejoined the old gentleman.

"Yes, but you can't do without eating," continued his friend.

"No, but I can eat less, and economise by selecting cheaper articles of food," replied the devoted father.

"That will do well enough to talk about, friend Vashon, but when it comes to the test, that's another thing."

"Friend J.," replied the old gentleman, with feeling, "as God is my judge, I will live on potatoes and herring, and see the last piece of furniture sold out of my house, before my son shall be left without an education. When he comes from that school, he will have finished his education."

Finding that it was in vain to attempt to advise so contrary to his feelings and designs, his friend left him. His son did return, indeed, a scholar of the highest order, and is now Professor of Belles Lettres in Central College, McGrawville, N. Y. When he applied for admission to the bar, it was granted, after a successful examination in open Court in New York city.

Mr. Vashon was one of the Vice Presidents of the National Convention of Colored Men, held at Rochester, July, 1853, and was subsequently chosen a member of the Pennsylvania State Council. On the 8th of January, 1854, a National Convention of the old soldiers of 1812 was held in the city of Philadelphia. This gathering of veterans aroused the military fire in the old man's breast, and, never having received a pension, nor government lands, for his services, he determined on taking his seat, as a soldier delegate, among the defenders of his country. He was amply supplied with letters and certificates from distinguished gentlemen in his adopted city. In the best of spirits and hopes, he set out on his mission to the State Council and the Military Convention. He had proceeded as far as the depot, when, (he was of corpulent person,) resting on his trunk for relief from his fatigue, Death, that untiring, but ever certain messenger, unexpectedly summoned him home to his fathers.

Thus departed the good old citizen-soldier, clothed in the vesture of peace and war. In the language of one of his friends, in an editorial column, "he fell with his harness on, and died in the last act of service to his brethren, and in obedience to the summons of his country, in the person of one of her delegated warriors."

Appeal to the Colored Citizens of the World

David Walker

APPEAL. &C.

Preamble.

My dearly beloved Brethren and Fellow Citizens: Having travelled over a consider-

Source: David Walker, *Appeal to the Colored Citizens of the World.* (Boston, 1829), pp. 11–17, 48–53, 66–76, 78–79, 84–87.

able portion of these United States, and having, in the course of my travels taken the most accurate observations of things as they exist—the result of my observations has warranted the full and unshakened conviction, that we, (colored people of these United States) are the most degraded, wretched, and abject set of beings that ever lived since the world began, and I pray God, that none like us ever may live again until time shall be no more. They tell us of the Israelites in Egypt, the Helots in Sparta, and of the Roman Slaves, which last, were made up from almost every nation under heaven, whose sufferings under those ancient and heathen nations were, in comparison with ours, under this enlightened and christian nation, no more than a cypher—or in other words, those heathen nations of antiquity, had but little more among them than the name and form of slavery, while wretchedness and endless miseries were reserved, apparently in a phial, to be poured out upon our fathers, ourselves and our children by *christian* Americans!

These positions, I shall endeavour, by the help of the Lord, to demonstrate in the course of this *appeal,* to the satisfaction of the most incredulous mind—and may God Almighty who is the father of our Lord Jesus Christ, open your hearts to understand and believe the truth.

The *causes,* my brethren, which produce our wretchedness and miseries, are so very numerous and aggravating, that I believe the pen only of a Josephus or a Plutarch, can well enumerate and explain them. Upon subjects, then, of such incomprehensible magnitude, so impenetrable, and so notorious, I shall be obliged to omit a large class of, and content myself with giving you an exposition of a few of those, which do indeed rage to such an alarming pitch, that they cannot but be a perpetual source of terror and dismay to every reflecting mind.

I am fully aware, in making this appeal to my much afflicted by suffering brethren, that I shall not only be assailed by those whose greatest earthly desires are, to keep us in abject ignorance and wretchedness, and who are of the firm conviction that heaven has designed us and our children to be slaves and *beasts of burden* to them and their children.—I say, I do not only expect to be held up to the public as an ignorant, impudent and restless disturber of the public peace, by such avaricious creatures, as well as a mover of insubordination—and perhaps put in prison or to death, for giving a superficial exposition of our miseries, and exposing tyrants. But I am

persuaded, that many of my brethren, particularly those who are ignorantly in league with slave-holders or tyrants, who acquire their daily bread by the blood and sweat of their more ignorant brethren—and not a few of those too, who are too ignorant to see an inch beyond their noses, will rise up and call me cursed—Yea, the jealous ones among us will perhaps use more abject subtlety by affirming that this work is not worth perusing; that we are well situated and there is no use in trying to better our condition, for we cannot. I will ask one question here.—Can our condition be any worse?—Can it be more mean and abject? If there are any changes, will they not be for the better, though they may appear for the worse at first? Can they get us any lower? Where can they get us? They are afraid to treat us worse, for they know well, the day they do it they are gone. But against all accusations which may or can be preferred against me, I appeal to heaven for my motive in writing—who knows that my object is, if possible, to awaken in the breasts of my afflicted, degraded and slumbering brethren, a spirit of enquiry and investigation respecting our miseries and wretchedness in this *Republican Land of Liberty !!!!!*

The sources from which our miseries are derived and on which I shall comment, I shall not combine in one, but shall put them under distinct heads and expose them in their turn; in doing which, keeping truth on my side, and not departing from the strictest rules of morality, I shall endeavor to penetrate, search out, and lay them open for your inspection. If you cannot or will not profit by them, I shall have done *my* duty to you, my country and my God.

And as the inhuman system of *slavery,* is the *source* from which most of our miseries proceed, I shall begin with that *curse to nations;* which has spread terror and devastation through so many nations of antiquity, and which is raging to such a pitch at the present day in Spain and in Portugal. It had one tug in England, in France, and in the United States of America; yet the inhabitants thereof, do not learn wisdom, and erase it entirely from their dwellings and from all with whom they have to do. The fact is, the labor of slaves comes so cheap to the avaricious usurpers, and is (as they think) of such great utility to the country where it exists, that those who are actuated by sordid avarice only, overlook the evils, which will as sure as the Lord lives, follow after the good. In fact, they are so happy to keep in ignorance and degradation, and to receive the homage and the labor of the slaves, they forget that God rules in the armies of heaven and among the inhabitants of the earth, having his ears continually open to the cries, tears and groans of his oppressed people; and being a just and holy Being will at one day appear fully in behalf of the oppressed, and arrest the progress of the avaricious oppressors; for although the destruction of the oppressors God may not effect by the oppressed, yet the Lord our God will bring other destructions upon them—for not unfrequently will he cause them to rise up one against another, to be split and divided, and to oppress each other, and sometimes to open hostilities with sword in hand. Some may ask, what is the matter with this enlightened and happy people?—Some say it is the cause of political usurpers, tyrants, oppressors, &c. But has not the Lord an oppressed and suffering people among them? Does the Lord condescend to hear their cries and see their tears in consequence of oppression? Will he let the oppressors rest comfortably and happy always? Will he not cause the very children of the oppressors to rise up against them, and oftimes put them to death? "God works in many ways his "wonders to perform."

I will not here speak of the destructions which the Lord brought upon Egypt, in consequence of the oppression and consequent groans of the oppressed—of the hundreds and thousands of Egyptians whom God hurled into the Red Sea for afflicting his people in their land—of the Lor'ds suffering people in Sparta or Lacedemon, the land of the truly famous Lycurgus—nor have I time to comment upon the cause which produced the

fierceness with which Sylla usurped the title, and absolutely acted as dictator of the Roman people—the conspiracy of Cataline—the conspiracy against, and murder of Cæsar in the Senate house—the spirit with which Marc Antony made himself master of the commonwealth—his associating Octavius and Lipidus with himself in power—their dividing the provinces of Rome among themselves—their attack and defeat on the plains of Phillipi the last defenders of their liberty, (Brutus and Cassius)—the tyranny of Tiberius, and from him to the final overthrow of Constantinople by the Turkish Sultan, Mahomed II., A. D. 1453. I say, I shall not take up time to speak of the *causes* which produced so much wretchedness and massacre among those heathen nations, for I am aware that you know too well, that God is just, as well as merciful!—I shall call your attention a few moments to that *christian* nation, the Spaniards, while I shall leave almost unnoticed that avaricious and cruel people, the Portuguese, among whom all true hearted christians and lovers of Jesus Christ, must evidently see the judgments of God displayed. To show the judgments of God upon the Spaniards I shall occupy but little time, leaving a plenty of room for the candid and unprejudiced to reflect.

All persons who are acquainted with history, and particularly the Bible, who are not blinded by the God of this world, and are not actuated solely by avarice—who are able to lay aside prejudice long enough to view candidly and impartially, things as they were, are, and probably will be, who are willing to admit that God made man to serve him *alone,* and that man should have no other Lord or Lords but himself—that God Almighty is the *sole proprietor* or *master* of the WHOLE human family, and will not on any consideration admit of a colleague, being unwilling to divide his glory with another.—And who can dispense with prejudice long enough to admit that we are men, notwithstanding our *improminent noses* and *woolly heads,* and believe that we feel for our fathers, mothers, wives and children as well as they do for theirs.—I say, all who are permitted to see and believe these things, can easily recognize the judgments of God among the Spaniards. Though others may lay the cause of the fierceness with which they cut each other's throats, to some other circumstances, yet they who believe that God is a God of justice, will believe that SLAVERY *is the principal cause.*

While the Spaniards are running about upon the field of battle cutting each other's throats, has not the Lord an afflicted and suffering people in the midst of them whose cries and groans in consequence of oppression are continually pouring into the ears of the God of justice? Would they not cease to cut each others throats if they could? But how can they? The very support which they draw from government to aid them in perpetrating such enormities, does it not arise in a great degree from the wretched victims of oppression among them? And yet they are calling for *Peace!—Peace!!* Will any peace be given unto them? Their destruction may indeed be procrastinated awhile, but can it continue long while they are oppressing the Lord's people? Has He not the hearts of all men in His hand? Will he suffer one part of his creatures to go on oppressing another like brutes always, with impunity? And yet those avaricious wretches are calling for *Peace!!!!* I declare it does appear to me, as though some nations think God is asleep, or that he made the Africans for nothing else but to dig their mines and work their farms, or they cannot believe history, sacred or profane. I ask every man who has a heart and is blessed with the privilege of believing—Is not God a God of justice to all his creatures? Do you say he is? Then if he gives peace and tranquility to tyrants, and permits them to keep our fathers, our mothers, ourselves and our children in eternal ignorance and wretchedness to support them and their families, would he be to us a God of *justice?* I ask O ye *christians!!!* who hold us and our children, in the most abject ignorance and degradation, that ever a people were afflicted with since the world began—I say, if God gives you peace and tranquility, and

suffers you thus to go on afflicting us and our children, who have never given you the least provocation,—Would he be to us *a God of justice?* If you will allow that we are *men,* who feel for each other, does not the blood of our fathers and of us their children, cry aloud to the Lord of Sabaoth against you, for the cruelties and murders with which you have, and do continue to afflict us. But it is time for me to close my remarks on the suburbs, just to enter more fully into the interior of this system of cruelty and oppression.

Article I.

Our Wretchedness in Consequence of Slavery. My beloved brethren: The Indians of North and of South America—the Greeks—the Irish subjected under the king of Great Britain—the Jews that ancient people of the Lord—the inhabitants of the islands of the sea—in fine, all the inhabitants of the earth, (except however, the sons of Africa) are called *men,* and of course are, and ought to be free. But we, (coloured people) and our children are *brutes!!* and of course are and ought to be Slaves to the American people and their children forever! to dig their mines and work their farms; and thus go on enriching them, from one generation to another with our blood and our tears!!

I promised in a preceding page to demonstrate to the satisfaction of the most incredulous, that we, (colored people of these United States of America) are the *most wretched, degraded* and abject set of beings that ever *lived* since the world began, and that the white Americans having reduced us to the wretched state of *slavery,* treat us in that condition *more cruel* (they being an enlightened and christian people) than any heathen nation did any people whom it had reduced to our condition. These affirmations are so well confirmed in the minds of all unprejudiced men who have taken the trouble to read histories, that they need no elucidation from me. . . .

The Pagans, Jews and Mahometans try to make proselytes to their religions, and whatever human beings adopt their religions, they extend to them their protection. But Christian Americans not only hinder their fellow creatures, the Africans, but thousands of them will *absolutely beat a coloured person nearly to death, if they catch him on his knees, supplicating the throne of grace.* This barbarous cruelty was by all the heathen nations of antiquity, and is by the Pagans, Jews and Mahometans of the present day, left entirely to Christian Americans to inflict on the Africans and their descendants that their cup which is nearly full may be completed. I have known tyrants or usurpers of human liberty in different parts of this country take their fellow creatures, the colored people, and beat them until they would scarcely leave life in them; what for? Why they say, "The black devils had the audacity to be found *making prayers and supplications to the God who made them!!!*" Yes, I have known small collections of coloured people to have convened together, for no other purpose than to worship God Almighty, in spirit and in truth, to the best of their knowledge; when tyrants, calling themselves *patrols,* would also convene and wait almost in breathless silence for the poor coloured people to commence singing and praying to the Lord our God, and as soon as they had commenced the wretches would burst in upon them and drag them out and commence beating them as they would rattle-snakes—many of whom, they would beat so unmercifully, that they would hardly be able to crawl for weeks and sometimes for months.—Yet the American ministers send out missionaries to convert the heathen, while they keep us and our children sunk at their feet in the most abject ignorance and wretchedness that ever a people was afflicted with since the world began. Will the Lord suffer this people to proceed much longer? Will he not stop them in their career? Does he regard the heathens abroad, more than the heathens among the Americans? Surely the Americans must believe that God is partial, notwithstanding his Apostle Peter, declared before Cornelius and others that he has no respect to persons, but in every nation he that feareth God and worketh righteousness is ac-

cepted with him.—"The word," said he, "which God sent unto the children of Israel, preaching peace, by Jesus Christ, (he is the Lord of all.")* Have not the Americans the Bible in their hands? Do they believe it? Surely they do not. See how they treat us in open violation of the Bible!! They no doubt will be greatly offended with me, but if God does not awaken them, it will be, because they are superior to other men, as they have represented themselves to be. Our divine Lord and Master said "all things whatsoever ye would that men should "do unto you, do ye even so unto them." But an American minister, with the Bible in his hand, holds us and our children in the most abject slavery and wretchedness. Now I ask them, would they like for us to hold them and their children in abject slavery and wretchedness? No says one, that never can be done—you are too abject and ignorant to do it—you are not men—you were made to be slaves to us, to dig up gold and silver for us and our children. Know this, my dear sirs, that although you treat us and our children now, as you do your domestic beasts—yet the final result of all future events are known but to God Almighty alone, who rules in the armies of heaven and among the inhabitants of the earth, and who dethrones one earthly king and sits up another, as it seemeth good in his holy sight. We may attribute these vicissitudes to what we please, but the God of armies and of justice rules in heaven and in earth, and the whole American people shall see and know it yet, to their satisfaction. I have known pretended preachers of the gospel of my Master, who not only held us as their natural inheritance, but treated us with as much rigor as any Infidel or Deist in the world—just as though they were intent only on taking our blood and groans to glorify the Lord Jesus Christ. The wicked and ungodly, seeing their preachers treat us with so much cruelty, they say: our preachers, who must be right, if any body are, treat them like

*See the Acts of the Apostles, chap. x. v.—25—26.

brutes, and why cannot we?—They think it is no harm to keep them in slavery and put the whip to them, and why cannot we do the same!—They being preachers of the gospel of Jesus Christ, if it were any harm, they would surely preach against their oppression and do their utmost to erase it from the country; not only in one or two cities, but one continual cry would be raised in all parts of this confederacy, and would cease only with the complete overthrow of the system of slavery, in every part of the country. But how far the American preachers are from preaching against slavery and oppression, which have carried their country to the brink of a precipice; to save them from plunging down the side of which, will hardly be effected, will appear in the sequel of this paragraph, which I shall narrate just as it transpired. I remember a Camp Meeting in South Carolina, for which I embarked in a Steam Boat at Charleston, and having been five or six hours on the water, we at last arrived at the place of hearing, where was a very great concourse of people, who were no doubt, collected together to hear the word of God, (that some had collected barely as spectators to the scene, I will not here pretend to doubt, however, that is left to themselves and their God.) Myself and boat companions, having been there a little while, we were all called up to hear; I among the rest, went up and took my seat—being seated, I fixed myself in a complete position to hear the word of my Saviour and to receive such as I thought was authenticated by the Holy Scriptures; but to my no ordinary astonishment, our Reverend gentleman got up and told us (colored people) that slaves must be obedient to their masters—must do their duty to their masters or be whipped—the whip was made for the backs of fools, &c. Here I pause for a moment, to give the world time to consider what was my surprise, to hear such preaching from a minister of my Master, whose very gospel is that of peace and not of blood and whips, as this pretended preacher tried to make us believe. What the American preachers can think of us, I aver this day before my God, I have never been able to define. They have newspapers and monthly periodicals, which they receive in continual succession, but on the pages of which, you will scarcely ever find a paragraph respecting slavery, which is ten thousand times more injurious to this country than all the other evils put together; aud which will be the final overthrow of its government, unless something is very speedily done; for their cup is nearly full.— Perhaps they will laugh at, or make light of this; but I tell you Americans! that unless you speedily alter your course, *you* and your *Country are gone!!!!!!* For God Almighty will tear up the very face of the earth!!!! Will not that very remarkable passage of Scripture be fulfilled on Christian Americans? Hear it Americans!! "He that is unjust, let him be unjust still:—and he which is filthy, let him be filthy still: and he that is righteous, let him be righteous still; and he that is holy, let him be holy still."* I hope that the Americans may hear, but I am afraid that they have done us so much injury, and are so firm in the belief that our Creator made us to be an inheritance to them forever, that their hearts will be hardened, so that their destruction may be sure.— This language, perhaps is too harsh for the American's delicate ears. But Oh Americans! Americans!! I warn you in the name of the Lord, (whether you will hear, or forbear,) to repent and reform, or you are ruined!!!!!! Do you think that our blood is hidden from the Lord, because you can hide it from the rest of the world by sending out missionaries, and by your charitable deeds to the Greeks, Irish, &c.? Will he not publish your secret crimes on the house top? Even here in Boston, pride and prejudice have got to such a pitch, that in the very houses erected to the Lord, they have built little places for the reception of colored people, where they must sit during meeting, or keep away from the house of God; and the preachers say nothing about it—much less, go into the hedges and highways seeking the lost sheep of the house of Israel, and try to bring them in, to their Lord and Master. There

*See Revelation, chap. xxii. v. 11.

are hardly a more wretched, ignorant, miserable, and abject set of beings in all the world, than the blacks in the Southern and Western sections of this country, under tyrants and devils. The preachers of America cannot see them, but they can send out missionaries to convert the heathens, notwithstanding. Americans! unless you speedily alter your course of proceeding, if God Almighty does not stop you, I say it in his name, that you may go on and do us you please for ever, both in time and eternity—never fear any evil at all ! ! ! ! ! ! ! !

[☞**Addition.**—The preachers and people of the the United States form societies against Free Masonry and Intemperance, and write against Sabbath breaking, Sabbath mails, Infidelity, &c. &c. But the fountain head, compared with which all those other evils are comparatively nothing, and from the bloody and murderous head of which, they receive no trifling support, is hardly noticed by the Americans. This is a fair illustration of the state of society in this country—it shows what a bearing *avarice* has upon a people, when they are nearly given up by the Lord to a hard heart and a reprobate mind, in consequence of afflicting their fellow creatures. God suffers some to go on until they are ruined for ever!! Will it be the case with our brethren the whites of the United States of America? We hope not—we would not wish to see them destroyed, notwithstanding they have and do now treat us more cruel than any people have treated another, on this earth since it came from the hands of its creator (with the exception of the French and the Dutch, they treat us nearly as bad as the Americans of the United States.) The will of God must however, in spite of us, *be done.*

The English are the best friends the colored people have upon earth. Tho' they have oppressed us a little, and have colonies now in the West Indies, which oppress us *sorely,*—Yet notwithstanding they (the English) have done one hundred times more for the melioration of our condition, than all the other nations of the earth put together. The

blacks cannot but respect the English as a nation, notwithstanding they have treated us a little cruel.

There is no intelligent *black man* who knows any thing, but esteems a real English man, let him see him in what part of the world he will—for they are the greatest benefactors we have upon earth. We have here and there, in other nations, good friends. But as a nation, the English are our friends☞]. . . .

Here is a demonstrative proof, of a plan got up by a gang of slave-holders to select the free people of colour from among the slaves, that our more miserable brethren may be the better secured in ignorance and wretchedness, to work their farms and dig their mines, and thus go on enriching the christians with their blood and groans. What our brethren could have been thinking about, who have left their native land and home and gone away to Africa I am unable to say. This country is as much ours as it is the whites, whether they will admit it now or not, they will see and believe it by and by. They tell us about prejudice—what have we to do with it? Their prejudices will be obliged to fall like lightning to the ground, in succeeding generations; not, however with the will and consent of all the whites, for some will be obliged to hold on to the old adage, viz.: the blacks are not men, but were made to be an inheritance to us and our children forever !!!!!! I hope the residue of the coloured people will stand still and see the salvation of God, and the miracle which he will work for our delivery from wretchedness under the christians !!!!!!

[☞**Addition.**—If any of us see fit to go away, go to those who have been for many years, and are now our greatest earthly friends and benefactors—the English. If not so, go to our brethren, the Haytians, who, according to their word, is bound to protect and comfort us. The Americans say that we are ungrateful—but I ask them for heaven's sake, what we should be grateful to them for—for murdering our fathers and mothers?—Or do they wish us to return thanks to them for chaining and handcuffing us, branding us, cramming fire down our throats, or for keeping us in slavery, and beating us nearly or quite to death to make us work in ignorance and miseries, to support them and their families. They certainly think that we are a gang of fools. Those among them, who have volunteered their services for our redemption, though we are unable to compensate them for their labors, we nevertheless thank them from the bottom of our hearts, and have our eyes steadfastly fixed upon them, and their labors of love for God and man. But do slaveholders think that we thank them for keeping us in miseries, and taking our lives by the inches? ▨]

Before I proceed further with this scheme, I shall give an extract from the letter of that truly Reverend Divine, (Bishop Allen,) of Philadelphia, respecting this trick. At the instance of the Editor of the Freedom's Journal, he says, *"Dear Sir, I have been for several years trying to reconcile my mind to the Colonizing of Africans in Liberia, but there have always been, and there still remain great and insurmountable objections against the scheme. We are an unlettered people, brought up in ignorance, not one in a hundred can read or write, not one in a thousand has a liberal education; is there any fitness for such to be sent into a far country, among heathens, to convert or civilize them, when they themselves are neither civilized or christianized? See the great bulk of the poor, ignorant Africans in this country, exposed to every temptation before them: all for the want of their morals being refined by education and proper attendance paid unto them by their owners, or those who had the charge of them. It is said by the Southern slave-holders, that the more ignorant they can bring up the Africans, the better slaves they make, 'go and come.' Is there any fitness for such people to be colonized in a far country, to be their own rulers? Can we not

discern the project of sending the free people of colour away from their country? Is it not for the interest of the slave-holders to select the free people of colour out of the different states, and send them to Liberia? Will it not make their slaves uneasy to see free men of colour enjoying liberty? It is against the law, in some of the southern states, that a person of colour should receive an education, under a severe penalty. Colonizationists speak of America being first colonized, but is there any comparison between the two? America was colonized by as *wise, judicious* and *educated* men as the world afforded. William Penn did not want for *learning, wisdom, or intelligence.* If all the people in Europe and America were as ignorant, and in the same situation as our brethren, what would become of the world? where would be the principle or piety that would govern the people? We were *stolen* from our mother country, and brought *here.* We have *tilled* the ground and made fortunes for thousands, and still they are not weary of our services. *But they who stay to till the ground must be slaves.* Is there not land enough in America, or 'corn enough in Egypt?' Why should they send us into a far country to die? See the thousands of foreigners emigrating to America every year: and if there be ground sufficient for them to cultivate, and bread for them to eat; why would they wish to send the *first tillers* of the land away? Africans have made fortunes for thousands, who are yet unwilling to part with their services; but the free must be sent away, and those who remain must be *slaves.* I have no doubt that there are many good men who do not see as I do, and who are for sending us to Liberia; but they have not duly considered the subject—they are not men of colour. This land which we have watered with our *tears* and *our blood,* is now our *mother country,* and we are well satisfied to stay where wisdom abounds and the gospel is free.

"RICHARD ALLEN,
"Bishop of the African Methodist Episcopal
"Church in the United States."

*See Freedom's Journal for Nov. 2d, 1827—vol. 1, No. 34.

I have given you, my brethren, an extract verbatim from the letter of that godly man as you may find it on the aforementioned page of Freedom's Journal. I know that thousands and perhaps millions of my brethren in these States, have never heard of such a man as Bishop Allen—a man whom God many years ago raised up among his ignorant and degraded brethren, to preach Jesus Christ and him crucified to them—who notwithstanding, had to wrestle against principalities and the powers of darkness to diffuse that gospel with which he was endowed, among his brethren—but who having overcome the combined powers of devils and wicked men has under God planted a church among us which will be as durable as the foundation of the earth on which it stands. Richard Allen! O my God!! the bare recollection of the labours of this man, and his ministers among his deplorably wretched brethren (rendered so by the whites,) to bring them to a knowledge of the God of heaven, fills my soul with all those very high emotions which would take the pen of an Addison to portray. It is impossible, my brethren, for me to say much in this work respecting that man of God. When the Lord shall raise up coloured historians in succeeding generations, to present the crimes of this nation to the then gazing world, the Holy Ghost will make them do justice to the name of Bishop Allen, of Philadelphia. Suffice it for me to say, that the name of this very man (Richard Allen,) though now in obscurity and degradation, will notwithstanding stand on the pages of history among the greatest divines who have lived since the apostolic age, and among the African's, Bishop Allen's will be entirely pre-eminent. My brethren, search after the character and exploits of this godly man among his ignorant and miserable brethren, to bring them to a knowledge of the truth as it is in our Master. Consider upon the tyrants and false christians against whom he had to contend order to get access to his brethren. See him and his ministers in the states of New York, New Jersey, Penn. Delaware and Maryland, carrying the gladsome tidings of free and full salvation to the colored people. Tyrants and false christians however, would not allow him to penetrate far into the South for fear that he would awaken some of his ignorant brethren, whom they held in wretchedness and miseries—for fear, I say it, that he would awaken and bring them to a knowledge of their Maker. O my Master! my Master! I cannot but think upon Christian Americans!! What kind of people can they be? Will not those who were burnt up in Sodom and Gomorrah rise up in judgment against Christian Americans with the Bible in their hands, and condemn them? Will not the Scribes and Pharisees of Jerusalem, who had nothing but the laws of Moses and the Prophets to go by, rise up in judgment against Christian Americans, and condemn them* who in addition to these have a revelation from Jesus Christ the son of the living God? In fine, will not the Antediluvians, together with the whole heathen world of antiquity, rise up in judgment against Christian Americans and condemn them? The Christians of Europe and America go to Africa, bring us away, and throw us into the seas, and in other ways murder us, as they would wild beasts. The Antediluvians and heathens never dreamed of such barbarities. Now the Christians believe because they have a name to live, while they are dead, that God will overlook such things. But if he does not deceive them, it will be because he has overlooked it sure enough. But to return to this godly man, Bishop Allen. I do hereby openly affirm it to the world, that he has done more in a spiritual sense for his ignorant and wretched brethren than any other man of colour has, since the world began. And as for the greater part of the whites, it has hitherto been their greatest object and glory to keep us ignorant of our Maker, so as to make us believe that we were made to be slaves to them and their children to dig up gold and silver

*I mean those whose labors for the good, or rather destruction of Jerusalem, and the Jews. Ceased before our Lord entered the Temple, and over turned the tables of the Money Changers.

for them. It is notorious that not a few professing christians among the whites who profess to love our Lord and Saviour Jesus Christ, have assailed this man and laid all the obstacles in his way they possibly could, consistent with their profession—and what for? Why, their course of proceeding and his, clashed exactly together—they trying their best to keep us ignorant that we might be the better and more obedient slaves—while he on the other hand, doing his very best to enlighten us and teach us a knowledge of the Lord. And I am sorry that I have it to say, that many of our brethren have joined in with our oppressors, whose dearest objects are only to keep us ignorant and miserable, against this man to stay his hand. However, they have kept us in so much ignorance that many of us know no better than to fight against ourselves, and by that means strengthen the hands of our natural enemies, to rivet their infernal chains of slavery upon us and our children. I have several times called the white Americans our *natural enemies*—I shall here define my meaning of the phrase. Shem, Ham, and Japheth, together with their father Noah and wives, I believe were not natural enemies to each other. When the ark rested after the flood upon Mount Arrarat in Asia, they (eight) were all the people which could be found alive in all the earth—in fact if scriptures be true (which I believe are) there were no other living men in all the earth, notwithstanding some ignorant creatures hesitate not to tell us, that we, (the blacks) are the seed of Cain, the murderer of his brother Abel. But where those ignorant and avaricious wretches could have got their information, I am unable to declare. Did they receive it from the Bible? I have searched the Bible as well as they, if I am not as well learned as they are, and have never seen a verse which testifies whether we are the seed of Cain or of Abel.—Yet those men tell us that we are of the seed of Cain and that God put a dark stain upon us, that we might be known as their slaves!!! Now I ask those avaricious and ignorant wretches, who act more like the seed of Cain, by murdering, the whites or the blacks? How many vessel loads of human beings have the blacks thrown into the seas? How many thousand souls have the blacks murdered in cold blood to make them work in wretchedness and ignorance, to support them and their families?*—However, let us be the seed of Cain, Harry, Dick or Tom!!! God will show the whites what we are yet. I say, from the beginning, I do not think that we were natural enemies to each other. But the whites having made us so wretched, by subjecting us to slavery, and having murdered so many millions of us in order to make us work for them, and out of devilishness—and they taking our wives, whom we love as we do ourselves—our mothers who bore the pains of death to give us birth—our fathers & dear little children, and ourselves, and strip and beat us one before the other—chain, handcuff and drag us about like rattle-snakes—shoot us down like wild bears, before each other's faces, to make us submissive to and work to support them and their families. They (the whites) know well if we are *men*—and there is a secret monitor in their hearts which tells them we are—they know, I say, if we *are* men, and see them treating us in the manner they do, that there can be nothing in our hearts but death alone for them; notwithstanding we may appear cheerful, when we see them murdering our dear mothers and wives, because we cannot help ourselves. Man, in all ages and all nations of the earth, is the same. Man is a peculiar creature—he is the image of his God, though he may be subjected to the most wretched condition upon earth, yet that spirit and feeling which constitute the creature man, can never be entirely erased from his breast, because the God who made him after his own image, planted it in his heart; he cannot get rid of it. The whites knowing this, they

---

*How many millions souls of the human family have the blacks, beat nearly to death, to keep them from learning to read the Word of God and from writing. And telling lies about them, by holding them up to the world as a tribe of TALKING APES, void of *intellect!!!* incapable of LEARNING, &c.

do not know what to do; they are afraid that we, being men, and not brutes, will retaliate, and woe will be to them; therefore, that dreadful fear, together with an avaricious spirit, and the natural love in them to be called masters, (which term we will yet honour them with to their sorrow) bring them to the resolve that they will keep us in ignorance and wretchedness, as long as they possibly can* and make the best of their time while it lasts. Consequently they, themselves, (and not us) render themselves our natural enemies, by treating us so cruel. They keep us miserable now, and call us their property, but some of them will have enough of us by and by—their stomachs shall run over with us; they want us for their slaves, and shall have us to their fill. (We are all in the world together!!) I said above, because we cannot help ourselves, (viz. we cannot help the whites murdering our mothers and our wives) but this statement is incorrect—for we can help ourselves; for, if we lay aside abject servility, and be determined to act like men, and not brutes—the murderers among the whites would be afraid to show their cruel heads. But O, my God!—in sorrow I must say it, that my

---

*And still hold us up with indignity as being incapable of acquiring knowledge !!! See the inconsistency of the assertions of those wretches—they beat us inhumanly, sometimes almost to death, for attempting to inform ourselves, by reading the *Word* of our Maker, and at the same time tell us, that we are beings *void of intellect!!!!!* How admirably their practices agree with their professions in this case. Let me cry shame upon you Americans, for such outrages upon human nature!!! If it were possible for the whites always to keep us ignorant and miserable, and make us work to enrich them and their children, and insult our feelings by representing us as *talking Apes,* what would they do? But glory honour and praise to Heaven's King, that the sons and daughters of Africa, will, in spite of all the opposition of their enemies, stand forth in all the dignity and glory that is granted by the Lord to his creature man.

colour, all over the world, have a mean, servile spirit. They yield in a moment to the whites, let them be right or wrong—the reason the whites are able to keep their feet on our throats. Oh! my coloured brethren, all over the world, when shall we arise from this death-like apathy?—And be men!! You will notice, if ever we become men (I mean *respectable* men, such as other people are,) we must exert ourselves to the full. For remember, that it is the greatest desire and object of the greater part of the whites, to keep us ignorant, and make us work to support them and their families.—Here now, in the Southern and Western Sections of this country, there are at least three coloured persons for one white, why is it, that those few weak, good-for-nothing whites, are able to keep so many able men, one of whom, can put to flight a dozen whites, in wretchedness and misery? It shows at once, what the blacks are, we are ignorant, abject, servile, and mean—and the whites know it—they know that we are too servile to assert our rights as men—or they would not fool with us as they do. Would they fool with any other people as they do with us? No, they know too well that they would get themselves ruined. Why do they not bring the inhabitants of Asia to be body servants to them? They know they would get their bodies rent and torn from head to foot. Why do they not get the Aboriginies of this country to be slaves to them and their children, to work their farms and dig their mines? They know well that the Aboriginies of this country, (or Indians) would tear them from the earth. The Indians would not rest day or night, they would be up all times of night, cutting their cruel throats. But my colour, (some, not all,) are willing to stand still and be murdered by the cruel whites. In some of the West-India Islands, and over a large part of South America, there are six or eight coloured persons for one white. Why do they not take possession of those places? Who hinders them? it is not the avaricious whites—for they are too busily engaged in laying up money—derived from the blood and tears of the blacks. The fact is they are too servile, they love to have Masters too well!!!!!! Some of our brethren, too, who seeking more after self aggrandizement, than the glory of God, and the welfare of their brethren, join in with our oppressors, to ridicule and say all manner of evils falsely against our Bishop. They think, that they are doing great things, when they get in company with the whites, to ridicule and make sport of those who are labouring for their good. Poor ignorant creatures, they do not know that the sole aim and object of the whites, are only to make fools and slaves of them and put the whip to them, and make them work to support them and their families. But I do say, that no man can well be a despiser of Bishop Allen, for his public labors among us, unless he is a despiser of God and Righteousness. Thus, we see, my brethren, the two very opposite positions of those great men, who have written respecting this "Colonizing Plan," (Mr. Clay and his slave holding party,) men who are resolved to keep us in eternal wretchedness, are also bent upon sending us to Liberia. While the Reverend Bishop Allen, and his party, men who have the fear of God, and the welfare of their brethren at heart. The Bishop in particular, whose labors for the salvation of his brethren, are well known to a large part of those, who dwell in the United States, are completely opposed to the plan—and advise us to stay where we are. Now we have to determine whose advice we will take respecting this all important matter, whether we will adhere to Mr. Clay and his slave-holding party, who have always been our oppressors and murderers, and who are for colonizing us, more through apprehension than humanity, or to this godly man who has done so much for our benefit, together with the advice of all the good and wise among us and the whites. Will any of us leave our homes and go to Africa? I hope not. Let them commence their attack upon us as they did on our brethren in Ohio, driving and beating us from our country, and my soul for theirs, they will have enough of it. Let no man of us budge one step, and let slave-holders come to beat us from our country. America is more our country, than it is the whites—we have enriched it with our *blood and tears.* The greatest riches in all America have arisen from our blood and tears:—and will they drive us from our property and homes, which we have earned with our *blood?* They must look sharp or this very thing will bring swift destruction upon them. The Americans have got so fat upon our blood and groans, that they have almost forgotten the God of armies. But let them go on.

But to return to the colonizing trick. It will be well for me to notice here at once, that I do not mean indiscriminately to condemn all the members and advocates of this scheme, for I believe that there are some friends to the sons of Africa, who are laboring for our salvation, not in words only but in truth and in deed, who have been drawn into this plan. Some, more by persuasion than any thing else; while others, with humane feelings and lively zeal for our good, seeing how much we suffer from the afflictions poured upon us by unmerciful tyrants, are willing to enroll their names in any thing which they think has for its ultimate end our redemption from wretchedness and miseries; such men, with a heart truly overflowing with gratitude for their past services and zeal in our cause, I humbly beg to examine this plot minutely, and see if the end which they have in view will be completely consummated by such a course of procedure. Our friends who have been imperceptibly drawn into this plot I view with tenderness, and would not for the world injure their feelings, and I have only to hope for the future, that they will withdraw themselves from it; for I declare to them, that the plot is not for the glory of God, but on the contrary the perpetuation of slavery in this country, which will ruin them and the country forever, unless something is immediately done.

Do the colonizationists think to send us off without first being reconciled to us? Do they think to bundle us up like brutes and send us off, as they did our brethren of the State of Ohio? Have they not to be reconciled to us, or reconcile us to them, for the cruelties with which they have afflicted our fathers and us? Methinks colonizationists think they have a set of brutes to deal with, sure enough. Do they think to drive us from our country and homes, after having enriched it with our blood and tears, and keep back millions of our dear brethren, sunk in the most barbarous wretchedness, to dig up gold and silver for them and their children? Surely, the Americans must think that we are brutes, as some of them have represented us to be. They think that we do not feel for our brethren, whom they are murdering by the inches, but they are dreadfully deceived. I acknowledge that there are some deceitful and hypocritical wretches among us, who will tell us one thing while they mean another, and thus they go on aiding our enemies to oppress themselves and us. But I declare this day before my Lord and Master, that I believe there are some true-hearted sons of Africa, in this land of oppression, but pretended *liberty!!!!!*—who do in reality feel for their suffering brethren, who are held in bondage by tyrants. Some of the advocates of this cunningly devised plot of Satan represent us to be the greatest set of cut throats in the world, as though God, wants us to take his work out of his hand before he is ready. Does not vengeance belong to the Lord? Is he not able to repay the Americans for their cruelties, with which they have afflicted Africa's sons and daughters, without our interference, unless we are ordered? Is it surprising to think that the Americans, having the bible in their hands, do not believe it. Are not the hearts of all men in the hands of the God of battles? And does he not suffer some, in consequence of cruelties, to go on until they are irrecoverably lost? Now, what can be more aggravating, than for the Americans, after having treated us so bad, to hold us up to the world as such great throat cutters? It appears to me as though they are resolved to assail us with every species of affliction that their ingenuity can invent. . . .

In conclusion, I ask the candid and unprejudiced of the whole world, to search the pages of historians diligently, and see if the Antediluvians—the Sodomites—the Egyptians—the Babylonians—the Ninevites—the Carthagenians—the Persians—the Macedonians—the Greeks—the Romans—the Mahometans—the Jews—or devils, ever treated a set of human beings, as the white Christians of America do us, the blacks, or Africans.—I also ask the attention of the world of mankind to the declaration of these very American people, of the United States.

A Declaration made July 4, 1776. It says,* "When in the course of human events, it becomes necessary for one people to dissolve the political bands which have connected them with another, and to assume among the Powers of the earth, the separate and equal station to which the laws of nature and of nature's God entitle them, a decent respect for the opinions of mankind requires that they should declare the causes which impel them to the separation. We hold these truths to be self evident, that all men are created equal, that they are endowed by their Creator with certain unalienable rights; that among these are life, liberty, and the pursuit of happiness; that to secure these rights, governments are instituted among men, deriving their just powers from the consent of the governed; that whenever any form of government becomes destructive of these ends it is the right of the people to alter or to abolish it, and to institute a new government laying its foundation on such principles, and organizing its powers in such form as to them shall seem most likely to effect their safety and happiness. Prudence, indeed, will dictate that governments long established should not be changed for light and transient causes; and accordingly all experience hath shewn, that mankind are more disposed to suffer, while evils are sufferable, than to right themselves by abolishing the forms to which they are accustomed. But when a long train of abuses and usurpations, pursuing invariably the same object,

*See the Declaration of Independence of the United States.

evinces a design to reduce them under absolute despotism, it is their right, it is their duty to throw off such government, and to provide new guards for their future security." See your declaration, Americans!! Do you understand your own language? Hear your language, proclaimed to the world, July 4, 1776—"We hold these truths to be self evident—that *ALL* MEN ARE CREATED EQUAL! *that they are endowed by their Creator with certain unalienable rights; that among these are life, liberty, and the pursuit of happiness!!"* Compare your own language above, extracted from your Declaration of Independence, with your cruelties and murders inflicted by your cruel and unmerciful fathers on ourselves on our fathers and on us, men who have never given your fathers or you the least provocation!!!

Hear your language further!☞"But when a long train of abuses and usurpations, pursuing invariably the same object, evinces a design to reduce them under absolute despotism, it is their *right*, it is their *duty*, to throw off such government, and to provide new guards for their future security."

Now, Americans! I ask you candidly, was your sufferings under Great Britain one hundredth part as cruel and tyrannical as you have rendered ours under you? Some of you, no doubt, believe that we will never throw off your murderous government, and "provide new guards for our future security." If Satan has made you believe it, will

he not deceive you?* Do the whites say, I being a black man, ought to be humble, which I readily admit? I ask them, ought they not to be as humble as I? or do they think they can measure arms with Jehovah? Will not the Lord yet humble them? or will not these very coloured people, whom they now treat worse than brutes, yet under God, humble them low down enough? Some of the whites are ignorant enough to tell us, that we ought to be submissive to them, that they may keep their feet on our throats. And if we do not submit to be beaten to death by them, we are bad creatures and of course must be damned, &c. If any man wishes to hear this doctrine openly preached to us by the American preachers, let him go into the Southern and Western sections of this country—I do not speak from hearsay—what I have written, is what I have seen and heard myself. No man may think that my book is made up of conjecture—I have travelled and observed nearly the whole of those things myself, and what little I did not get by my own observation, I received from those among the whites and blacks, in whom the greatest confidence may be placed.

*The Lord has not taught the Americans that we will not some day or other throw off their chains and hand-cuffs, from our hands and feet, and their devilish lashes (which some of them shall have enough of yet) from off our backs.

Productions of Mrs. Maria W. Stewart

Maria Stewart

A LECTURE GIVEN
AT FRANKLIN HALL

Boston, September 21, 1832

Why sit we here and die? If we say we will go to a foreign land, the famine and the pestilence are there, and there we shall die. If we sit here, we shall die. Come, let us plead our cause before the whites: if they save us alive, we shall love—and if they kill us, we shall but die.

Methinks I heard a spiritual interrogation—"Who shall go forward, and take of the reproach that is cast upon the people of color? Shall it be a woman?" And my heart made this reply—"If it is thy will, be it even so, Lord Jesus?"

I have heard much respecting the horrors of slavery; but may Heaven forbid that the generality of my color throughout these United States should experience any more of its horrors than to be a servant of servants, or hewers of wood and drawers of water! Tell us no more of southern slavery; for with few exceptions, although I may be very erroneous in any opinion, yet I consider our condition but little better than that. Yet, after all, methinks there are no chains so galling as the chains of ignorance—no fetters so binding as those that bind the soul, and exclude it from the vast field of useful and scientific knowledge. O, had I received the advantages of early education, my ideas would, ere now, have expanded far and wide; but, alas! I possess nothing but moral capability—no teachings but the teachings of the Holy Spirit.

I have asked several individuals of my sex, who transact business for themselves, if, providing our girls were to give them the most satisfactory references, they would not be willing to grant them an equal opportunity with others? Their reply has been—for their own part, they had no objection; but as it was not the custom, were they to take them into their employ, they would be in danger of losing the public patronage.

And such is the powerful force of prejudice.—Let our girls possess what amiable qualities of soul they may—let their characters be fair and spotless as innocence itself—let their natural taste and ingenuity be what they may—it is impossible for scarce an individual of them to rise above the condition of servants. Ah! why is this cruel and unfeeling distinction? Is it merely because God has made our complexion to vary? If it be, O shame to soft, relenting humanity! "Tell it not in Gath! publish it not in the streets of Askelon!" Yet, after all, methinks were the American free people of color to turn their attention or more assiduously to moral worth and intellectual improvement, this would be the result:—prejudice would gradually diminish, and the whites would be compelled to day,—Unloose those fetters!

Though black their skins as shades of night,
Their hearts are pure—their souls are white.

Few white persons of either sex, who are calculated for anything else, are willing to spend their lives and bury their talents in performing mean, servile labor. And such is the horrible idea that I entertain respecting a life of servitude, that if I conceived of their being no possibility of my rising above the condition of a servant, I would gladly hail death as a welcome messenger. O, horrible

Source: Maria Stewart, *Productions of Mrs. Maria W. Stewart.* (Boston, 1835), pp. 63–72, 51–56.

idea, indeed! to possess noble souls aspiring after high and honorable acquirements, yet confined by the chains of ignorance and poverty to lives of continual drudgery and toil. Neither do I know of any who have enriched themselves by spending their lives as house-domestics, washing windows, shaking carpets, brushing boots, or tending upon gentlemen's tables. I can but die for expressing my sentiments; and I am as willing to die by the sword as the pestilence—for I am a true born American—your blood flows in my veins, and your spirit fires my breast.

I observed a piece in the Liberator a few months since, stating that the colonizationists had published a work respecting us, asserting that we were lazy and idle. I confute them on that point. Take us generally as a people, we are neither lazy nor idle; and considering how little we have to excite or stimulate us, I am almost astonished that there are so many industrious and ambitious ones to be found—although I acknowledge, with extreme sorrow, that there are some who never were and never will be serviceable to society. And have you not a similar class among yourselves?

Again—It was asserted that we were "a ragged set, crying for liberty." I reply to it, the whites have so long and so loudly proclaimed the theme of equal rights and privileges, that our souls have caught the flame also, ragged as we are. As far as our merit deserves, we feel a common desire to rise above the condition of servants and drudges. I have learnt, by bitter experience, that continual hard labor deadens the energies of the soul, and benumbs the faculties of the mind: the ideas become confined, the mind barren, and, like the scorching sands of Arabia, produces nothing—or like the uncultivated soil, brings forth thorns and thistles.

Again, continual hard labor irritates our tempers and sours our dispositions; the whole system becomes worn out with toil and fatigue; nature herself becomes almost exhausted, and we care but little whether we live or die. It is true that the free people of color throughout these United States are nei-

ther bought nor sold, nor under the lash of the cruel driver; many obtain a comfortable support; but few, if any, have an opportunity of becoming rich and independent; and the employments we most pursue are as unprofitable to us as the spider's web or the floating bubbles that vanish into air. As servants, we are respected; but let us presume to aspire any higher, our employer regards us no longer. And were it not that the King eternal has declared that Ethiopia shall stretch forth her hands unto God, I should indeed despair.

I do not consider it derogatory, my friends, for persons to live out to service. There are many whose inclination leads them to aspire no higher—and I would highly commend the performance of almost anything for an honest livelihood; but where constitutional strength is wanting, labor of this kind, in its mildest form, is painful. And doubtless many are the prayers that have ascended to Heaven from Afric's daughters for strength to perform their work. Oh, many are the tears that have been shed for the want of that strength! Most of our color have dragged out a miserable existence of servitude from the cradle to the grave. And what literary acquirements can be made, or useful knowledge derived, from either maps, books or charts, by those who continually drudge from Monday morning until Sunday noon? O, ye fairer sisters, whose hands are never soiled, whose nerves and muscles are never strained, go learn by experience! Had we had the opportunity that you have had, to improve our moral and mental faculties, what would have hindered our intellects from being as bright, and our manners from being as dignified as yours? Had it been our lot to have been nursed in the lap of affluence and ease, and to have basked beneath the smiles and sunshine of fortune, should we not have naturally supposed that we were never made to toil? And why are not our forms as delicate, and our constitutions as slender, as yours? Is not the workmanship as curious and complete? Have pity upon us— have pity upon us, O ye who have hearts to feel for others' woes; for the hand of God has touched us. Owing to the disadvantages under which we labor, there are many flowers among us that are

> born to bloom unseen,
> And waste their fragrance on the desert air.

My beloved brethren, as Christ has died in vain for those who will not accept of offered mercy, so will it be in vain for the advocates of freedom to spend their breath in our behalf, unless with united hearts and souls you make some mighty efforts to raise your sons and daughters from the horrible state of servitude and degradation in which they are placed. It is upon you that woman depends; she can do but little besides using her influence; and it is for her sake and yours that I have come forward and made myself a hissing and a reproach amongst the people; for I am also one of the wretched and miserable daughters of the descendants of fallen Africa. Do you ask—Why are you wretched and miserable? I reply, look at many of the most worthy and interesting of us doomed to spend our lives in gentlemen's kitchens. Look at our young men, smart, active and energetic, with souls filled with ambitious fire; if they look forward, alas! what are their prospects? They can be nothing but the humblest laborers, on account of their dark complexions; hence many of them lose their ambition, and become worthless. Look at our middle-aged men, clad in their rusty plaids and coats—in winter, every cent they earn goes to buy their wood and pay their rents; their poor wives also toil beyond their strength to help support their families. Look at our aged sires, who heads are whitened with the frosts of seventy winters, with their old wood saws on their backs. Alas, what keeps us so? Prejudice, ignorance and poverty. But ah! methinks our oppression is soon to come to an end; yea, before the majesty of heaven, our groans and cries have reached the ears of the Lord of Sabaoth. As the prayers and tears of Christians will avail the finally impenitent nothing; neither will the prayers and tears of the friends of humanity avail us anything, unless we possess a spirit of virtuous emulation within our breasts. Did the Pilgrims, when they first landed on these shores, quietly compose themselves, and say, "The Britons have all the money and all the power, and we must continue their servants forever?" Did they sluggishly sigh and say, "Our lot is hard—the Indians own the soil, and we cannot cultivate it?" No—they first made powerful efforts to raise themselves and then God raised up those illustrious patriots, Washington and Lafayette, to assist and defend them. And, my brethren, have you made a powerful effort? Have you prayed the legislature for mercy's sake to grant you all the rights and privileges of free citizens, that your daughters may rise to that degree of respectability which true merit deserves, and your sons above the servile situations which most of them fill?

AN ADDRESS DELIVERED AT THE AFRICAN MASONIC HALL

Boston, February 27, 1833

African rights and liberty is a subject that ought to fire the breast of every free man of color in these United States, and excite in his bosom a lively, deep, decided, and heart-felt interest. When I cast my eyes on the long list of illustrious names that are enrolled on the bright annals of fame among the whites, I turn my eyes within, and ask my thoughts, "Where are the names of *our* illustrious ones?" It must certainly have been for the want of energy on the part of the free people of color, that they have been long willing to bear the yoke of oppression. It must have been the want of ambition and force that has given the whites occasion to say that our natural abilities are not as good, and our capacities by nature inferior to theirs. They boldly assert that, did we possess a natural independence of soul, and feel a love for liberty within our breasts, some one of our sable race long before this would have testified it, notwithstanding the disadvantages under which we labor. We have made ourselves appear altogether unqualified to speak in our own defence, and are therefore looked upon as objects of pity and commiseration. We have been imposed upon, insulted and derided on every side; and now, if we complain, it is considered as the height of impertinence. We have suffered ourselves to be considered as dastards, cowards, mean, faint-hearted wretches; and on this account, (not because of our complexion) many despise us, and would gladly spurn us from their presence.

These things have fired my soul with a holy indignation, and compelled me thus to come forward, and endeavor to turn their attention to knowledge and improvement; for knowledge is power. I would ask, is it blindness of mind, or stupidity of soul, or the want of education, that has caused our men who are 60 or 70 years of age, never to let their voices be heard, nor their hands be raised in behalf of their color? Or has it been for the fear of offending the whites? If it has, O ye fearful ones, throw off your fearfulness, and come forth in the name of the Lord, and in the strength of the God of Justice, and make yourselves useful and active members in society; for they admire a noble and patriotic spirit in others; and should they not admire it in us? If you are men, convince them that you possess the spirit of men; and as your day, so shall your strength be. Have the sons of Africa no souls? Feel they no ambitious desires? Shall the chains of ignorance forever confine them? Shall the insipid appellation of "clever negroes," or "good creatures," any longer content them? Where can we find among ourselves the man of science, or a philosopher, or an able statesman, or a counsellor at law? Show me our fearless and brave, our noble and gallant ones. Where are our lecturers on natural history, and our critics in useful knowledge? There may be a few such men among us, but they are rare. It is true, our fathers bled and died in the revolutionary war, and others fought bravely under the command of Jackson, in defence

of liberty. But where is the man that has distinguished himself in these modern days by acting wholly in the defence of African rights and liberty? There was one; although he sleeps, his memory lives.

I am sensible that there are many highly intelligent gentlemen of color in these United States, in the force of whose arguments, doubtless, I should discover my inferiority; but if they are blest with wit and talent, friends and fortune, why have they not made themselves men of eminence, by striving to take all the reproach that is cast upon the people of color, and in endeavoring to alleviate the woes of their brethren in bondage? Talk, without effort, is nothing; you are abundantly capable, gentlemen, of making yourselves men of distinction; and this gross neglect, on your part, causes my blood to boil within me. Here is the grand cause which hinders the rise and progress of the people of color. It is their want of laudable ambition and requisite courage.

Individuals have been distinguished according to their genius and talents, ever since the first formation of man, and will continue to be while the world stands. The different grades rise to honor and respectability as their merits may deserve. History informs us that we sprung from one of the most learned nations of the whole earth; from the seat, if not the parent of science; yes, poor, despised Africa was once the resort of sages and legislators of other nations, was esteemed the school for learning, and the most illustrious men in Greece flocked thither for instruction. But it was our gross sins and abominations that provoked the Almighty to frown thus heavily upon us, and give our glory unto others. Sin and prodigality have caused the downfall of nations, kings and emperors; and were it not that God in wrath remembers mercy, we might indeed despair; but a promise is left us; "Ethiopia shall again stretch forth her hands unto God."

But it is of no use for us to boast that we sprung from this learned and enlightened nation, for this day a thick mist of moral gloom hangs over millions of our race. Our condition as a people has been low for hundreds of years, and it will continue to be so, unless, by true piety and virtue, we strive to regain that which we have lost. White Americans, by their prudence, economy and exertions, have sprung up and become one of the most flourishing nations in the world, distinguished for their knowledge of the arts and sciences, for their polite literature. While our minds are vacant, and starving for want of knowledge, theirs are filled to overflowing. Most of our color have been taught to stand in fear of the white man, from their earliest infancy, to work as soon as they could walk, and call "master," before they scarce could lisp the name of *mother*. Continual fear and laborious servitude have in some degree lessened in us that natural force and energy which belong to man; or else, in defiance of opposition, our men, before this, would have nobly and boldly contended for their rights. But give the man of color an equal opportunity with the white from the cradle to manhood, and from manhood to the grave, and you would discover the dignified statesman, the man of science, and the philosopher. But there is no such opportunity for the sons of Africa, and I fear that our powerful ones are fully determined that there never shall be. Forbid, ye Powers on high, that it should any longer be said that our men possess no force. O ye sons of Africa, when will your voices be heard in our legislative halls, in defiance of your enemies, contending for equal rights and liberty? How can you, when you reflect from what you have fallen, refrain from crying mightily unto God, to turn away from us the fierceness of his anger, and remember our transgressions against us no more forever. But a God of infinite purity will not regard the prayers of those who hold religion in one hand, and prejudice, sin and pollution in the other; he will not regard the prayers of self-righteousness and hypocrisy. Is it possible, I exclaim, that for the want of knowledge, we have labored for hundreds of years to support others, and been content to receive what they chose to give us in return? Cast

your eyes about, look as far as you can see; all, all is owned by the lordly white, except here and there a lowly dwelling which the man of color, midst deprivations, fraud and opposition, has been scarce able to procure. Like king Solomon, who put neither nail nor hammer to the temple, yet received the praise; so also have the white Americans gained themselves a name, like the names of the great men that are in the earth, while in reality we have been their principal foundation and support. We have pursued the shadow, they have obtained the substance; we have performed the labor, they have received the profits; we have planted the vines, they have eaten the fruits of them.

I would implore our men, and especially our rising youth, to flee from the gambling board and the dance-hall; for we are poor, and have no money to throw away. I do not consider dancing as criminal in itself, but it is astonishing to me that our young men are so blind to their own interest and the future welfare of their children, as to spend their hard earnings for this frivolous amusement; for it has been carried on among us to such an unbecoming extent, that it has became absolutely disgusting. "Faithful are the wounds of a friend, but the kisses of an enemy are deceitful." Had those men among us, who have had an opportunity, turned their attention as assiduously to mental and moral improvement as they have to gambling and dancing, I might have remained quietly at home, and they stood contending in my place. These polite accomplishments will never enrol your names on the bright annals of fame, who admire the belle void of intellectual knowledge, or applaud the dandy that talks largely on politics, without striving to assist his fellow in the revolution, when the nerves and muscles of every other man forced him into the field of action. You have a right to rejoice, and to let your hearts cheer you in the days of your youth; yet remember that for all these things, God will bring you into judgment. Then, O ye sons of Africa, turn your mind from these perishable objects, and contend for the cause of God and the rights of man. Form yourselves into temperance societies. There are temperate men among you; then why will you any longer neglect to strive, by your example, to suppress vice in all its abhorrent forms? You have been told repeatedly of the glorious results arising from temperance, and can you bear to see the whites arising in honor and respectability, without endeavoring to grasp after that honor and respectability also?

But I forbear. Let our money, instead of being thrown away as heretofore, be appropriated for schools and seminaries of learning for our children and youth. We ought to follow the example of the whites in this respect. Nothing would raise our respectability, add to our peace and happiness, and reflect so much honor upon us, as to be ourselves the promoters of temperance, and the supporters, as far as we are able, of useful and scientific knowledge. The rays of light and knowledge have been hid from our view; we have been taught to consider ourselves as scarce superior to the brute creation; and have performed the most laborious part of American drudgery. Had we as a people received one half the early advantages the whites have received, I would defy the government of these United States to deprive us any longer of our rights.

I am informed that the agent of the Colonization Society has recently formed an association of young men, for the purpose of influencing those of us to go to Liberia who may feel disposed. The colonizationists are blind to their own interest, for should the nations of the earth make war with America, they would find their forces much weakened by our absence; or should we remain here, can our "brave soldiers," and "fellow-citizens," as they were termed in time of calamity, condescend to defend the rights of the whites, and be again deprived of their own, or sent to Liberia in return? Or, if the colonizationists are real friends to Africa, let them expend the money which they collect, in erecting a college to educate her injured sons in this land of gospel light and liberty; for it would be most thankfully received on our part, and convince us of the truth of their professions, and save

time, expense and anxiety. Let them place before us noble objects, worthy of pursuit, and see if we prove ourselves to be those unambitious negroes they term us. But ah! methinks their hearts are so frozen towards us, they had rather their money should be sunk in the ocean than to administer it to our relief; and I fear, if they dared, like Pharaoh, king of Egypt, they would order every male child among us to be drowned. But the most high God is still as able to subdue the lofty pride of these white Americans, as He was the heart of that ancient rebel. They say, though we are looked upon as *things,* yet we sprang from a scientific people. Had our men the requisite force and energy, they would soon convince them by their efforts both in public and private, that they were men, or things in the shape of men. Well may the colonizationists laugh us to scorn for our negligence; well may they cry, "Shame to the sons of Africa." As the burden of the Israelites was too great for Moses to bear, so also is our burden too great for our noble advocate to bear. You must feel interested, my brethren, in what he undertakes, and hold up his hands by your good works, or in spite of himself, his soul will become discouraged, and his heart will die within him; for he has, as it were, the strong bulls of Bashan to contend with.

It is of no use for us to wait any longer for a generation of well educated men to arise. We have slumbered and slept too long already; the day is far spent; the night of death approaches; and you have sound sense and good judgment sufficient to begin with, if you feel disposed to make a right use of it. Let every man of color throughout the United States, who possesses the spirit and principles of a man, sign a petition to Congress, to abolish slavery in the District of Columbia, and grant you the rights and privileges of common free citizens; for if you had had faith as a grain of mustard seed, long before this the mountains of prejudice might have been removed. We are all sensible that the Anti-Slavery Society has taken hold of the arm of our whole population, in order to raise them out of the mire. Now all we have to do is, by a spirit of virtuous ambition to strive to raise ourselves; and I am happy to have it in my power thus publicly to say, that the colored inhabitants of this city, in some respects, are beginning to improve. Had the free people of color in these United States nobly and boldly contended for their rights, and showed a natural genius and talent, although not so brilliant as some; had they held up, encouraged and patronized each other, nothing could have hindered us from being a thriving and flourishing people. There has been a fault among us. The reason why our distinguished men have not made themselves more influential is, because they fear that the strong current of opposition through which they must pass, would cause their downfall and prove their overthrow. And what gives rise to this opposition? Envy. And what has it amounted to? Nothing. And who are the cause of it? Our whited sepulchres, who want to be great, and don't know how; who love to be called of men 'Rabbi, Rabbi, who put on false sanctity, and humble themselves to their brethren, for the sake of acquiring the highest place in the synagogue, and the upper-most seats at the feast. You, dearly beloved, who are the genuine followers of our Lord Jesus Christ, the salt of the earth and the light of the world, are not so culpable. As I told you, in the very first of my writing, I tell you again, I am but as a drop in the bucket—as one particle of the small dust of the earth. God will surely raise up those among us who will plead the cause of virtue, and the pure principles of morality, more eloquently than I am able to do.

It appears to me that America has become like the great city of Babylon, for she has boasted in her heart, "I sit a queen, and am no widow, and shall see no sorrow?" She is indeed a seller of slaves and the souls of men; she has made the Africans drunk with the wine of her fornication; she has put them completely beneath her feet, and she means to keep them there; her right hand supports the reins of government, and her left hand the wheel of power, and she is determined not to let go her grasp. But many powerful sons and daughters of Africa will shortly arise, who will put down vice and immorality among us, and declare by Him that sitteth upon the throne, that they will have their rights; and if refused, I am afraid they will spread horror and devastation around. I believe that the oppression of injured Africa has come up before the Majesty of Heaven; and when our cries shall have reached the ears of the Most High, it will be a tremendous day for the people of this land; for strong is the arm of the Lord God Almighty.

Life has almost lost its charms for me; death has lost its sting and the grave its terrors; and at times I have a strong desire to depart and dwell with Christ, which is far better. Let me entreat my white brethren to awake and save our sons from dissipation, and our daughters from ruin. Lend the hand of assistance to feeble merit, plead the cause of virtue among our sable race; so shall our curses upon you be turned into blessings; and though you should endeavor to drive us from these shores, still we will cling to you the more firmly; nor will we attempt to rise above you: we will presume to be called your equals only.

The unfriendly whites first drove the native American from his much loved home. Then they stole our fathers from their peaceful and quiet dwellings, and brought them hither, and made bond-men and bond-women of them and their little ones; they have obliged our brethren to labor, kept them in utter ignorance, nourished them in vice, and raised them in degradation; and now that we have enriched their soil, and filled their coffers, they say that we are not capable of becoming like white men, and that we never can rise to respectability in this country. They would drive us to a strange land. But before I go, the bayonet shall pierce me through. African rights and liberty is a subject that ought to fire the breast of every free man of color in these United States, and excite in his bosom a lively, deep, decided and heart-felt interest.

Appeal of Forty Thousand Citizens, Threatened with Disfranchisement, to the People of Pennsylvania

Robert Purvis

Philadelphia, March 14, 1838. A very numerous and respectable meeting of the colored citizens of Pennsylvania, was held in the Presbyterian Church, Seventh Street, below Shippen, on the evening of the 14th inst. The meeting was organized by calling John P. Burr to the Chair, and appointing Thomas Butler and Stephen H. Gloucester Vice-Presidents, and *James Cornish* and *James Forten, jr.,* Secretaries. After an appropriate prayer by the Rev. Charles W. Gardner, the Chairman, with some suitable observations, stated the object of the meeting,—which was to receive the report of a Committee consisting of the following gentlemen: Robert Purvis, James Cornish, J. C. Bowers, Robert B. Forten, J. J. G. Bias, James Needham, and John P. Burr—appointed at a public meeting held prior to the above, in St. Paul's Lutheran Church, Quince Street, to prepare an appeal in behalf of forty thousand citizens, threatened with disfranchisement, to their fellow citizens, remonstrating against the late cruel act of the Reform Convention. Robert Purvis, Chairman of said Committee, presented and read the appeal; it was accepted, and remarks were then made by James Forten, sr., Robert Purvis, J. C. Bowers, F. A. Hinton, Charles W. Gardner, and several others, after which it was adopted with a unanimity and spirit equalled only by the memorable meeting of 1817.

The following resolutions were unanimously adopted:

Source: Appeal of Forty Thousand Citizens, Threatened with Disfranchisement, to the People of Pennsylvania. (Philadelphia: Merrihew and Gunn, 1838).

1. *Resolved,* That our warm and grateful thanks are due those gentlemen who, on the floor of the Convention, stood by us in the hour of need, in the able assertion and advocacy of our rights, and to others who voted against the insertion of the word "white." Also, that like thanks are due to our Abolition friends for their active though unavailing exertions to prevent the unrighteous act.

2. *Resolved,* That a committee of five be appointed to draw up a remonstrance against the Colonization Society, to be presented to the various Churches, Presbyterys, Conferences, and Conventions. The following persons were appointed:—James Forten, sr., S. H. Gloucester, Robert Douglass, Charles W. Gardner, and Bishop Brown.

John P. Burr, President.

Thomas Butler, \
S. H. Gloucester, } Vice-Presidents.

James Cornish, \
James Forten, jr., } Secretaries.

APPEAL

Fellow Citizens: We appeal to you from the decision of the "Reform Convention," which has stripped us of a right peaceably enjoyed during forty-seven years under the Constitution of this commonwealth. We honor Pennsylvania and her noble institutions too much to part with our birthright, as her free citizens, without a struggle. To all her citizens the right of suffrage is valuable in proportion as she is free; but surely there are none who can so ill afford to spare it as ourselves.

Was it the intention of the people of this commonwealth that the Convention to which the Constitution was committed for revision and amendment, should tear up and cast away its first principles? Was it made the business of the Convention to deny "that all men are born equally free," by making political rights depend upon the skin in which a man is born? or to divide what our fathers bled to unite, to wit, TAXATION and REPRESENTATION? We will not allow ourselves for one moment to suppose, that the majority of the people of Pennsylvania are not too respectful of the rights and too liberal towards the feelings of others, as well as too much enlightened to their own interests, to deprive of the right of suffrage a single individual who may safely be trusted with it. And we cannot believe that you have found among those who bear the burdens of taxation any who have proved, by their abuse of the right, that it is not safe in their hands. This is a question, fellow citizens, in which we plead *your* cause as well as our own. It is the safeguard of the strongest that he lives under a government which is obliged to respect the voice of the weakest. When you have taken from an individual his right to vote, you have made the government, in regard to him, a mere despotism; and you have taken a step towards making it a despotism to all.—To your women and children, their inability to vote at the polls may be no evil, because they are united by consanguinity and affection with those who can do it. To foreigners and paupers the want of the right may be tolerable, because a little time or labor will make it theirs. They are candidates for the privilege, and hence substantially enjoy its benefits. But when a distinct class of the community, already sufficiently the objects of prejudice, are wholly, and for ever, disfranchised and excluded, to the remotest posterity, from the possibility of a voice in regard to the laws under which they are to live—it is the same thing as if their abode were transferred to the dominions of the Russian Autocrat, or of the Grand Turk. They have lost their check upon oppression, their wherewith to buy friends, their panoply of manhood; in short, they are thrown upon the mercy of a despotic majority. Like every other despot, this despot majority, will believe in the mildness of its own sway; but who will the more willingly submit to it for that?

To us our right under the Constitution has been more precious, and our deprivation of it will be the more grievous, because our expatriation has come to be a darling project with many of our fellow citizens. Our abhorrence of a scheme which comes to us in the guise of Christian benevolence, and asks us to suffer ourselves to be transplanted to a distant and barbarous land, *because we are a "nuisance" in this,* is not more deep and thorough than it is reasonable. We love our native country, much as it has wronged us; and in the peaceable exercise of our inalienable rights, we will cling to it. The immortal Franklin, and his fellow laborers in the cause of humanity, have bound us to our homes here with chains of gratitude. We are PENNSYLVANIANS, and we hope to see the day when Pennsylvania will have reason to be proud of us, as we believe she has now none to be ashamed. Will you starve our patriotism? Will you cast our hearts out of the treasury of the commonwealth? Do you count our enmity better than our friendship?

Fellow citizens, we entreat you, in the name of fair dealing, to look again at the just and noble charter of Pennsylvania freedom, which you are asked to narrow down to the lines of caste and color. The Constitution reads as follows:—

> "*Art.* 3, § 1. In elections by the citizens, every freeman, of the age of twenty-one years, having resided in the State two years next before the election, and within that time paid a State or county tax, which shall have been assessed at least six months before the election, shall enjoy the rights of an elector, &c.

This clause guaranties the right of suffrage to us as fully as to any of our fellow citizens whatsoever, for

1. Such was the intention of the framers. In the original draft, reported by a committee of nine, the word "WHITE" stood before "FREEMAN." On motion of Albert Gallatin it was stricken out,

for the express purpose of including colored citizens within the pale of the elective franchise. (See *Minutes of the Convention, 1790.*)

2. We are citizens. This, we believe, would never have been denied, had it not been for the scheme of expatriation to which we have already referred. But as our citizenship has been doubted by some who are not altogether unfriendly to us, we beg leave to submit some proofs, which we think you will not hastily set aside.

We were regarded as *citizens* by those who drew up the articles of confederation between the States, in 1778. The fourth of the said articles contains the following language:—"The free inhabitants of each of these States, paupers, vagabonds, and fugitives from justice excepted, shall be entitled to all privileges and immunities of free *citizens* in the several States." That we were not excluded under the phrase "paupers, vagabonds, and fugitives from justice," any more than our while countrymen, is plain from the debates that preceded the adoption of the article. For, on the 25th of June, 1778, "the delegates from South Carolina moved the following amendment *in behalf of their State.* In article fourth, between the words *free* inhabitants, insert *white*. Decided in the negative; ayes, two States; nays, eight States: one State divided." Such was the solemn decision of the revolutionary Congress, concurred in by the entire delegation from our own commonwealth. On the adoption of the present Constitution of the United States no change was made as to the rights of citizenship. This is explicitly proved by the Journal of Congress. Take, for example, the following resolution passed in the House of Representatives, Dec. 21, 1803:

On motion, *Resolved,* That the Committee appointed to enquire and report whether any further provisions are necessary for the more effectual protection of American seamen, do enquire into the expediency of granting protections to such American seamen, *citizens of the United States,* as *are free persons of color,* and that they report by bill, or otherwise.

Journ. H. Rep., 1st Sess., 8th Cong., p. 224.

Proofs might be multiplied. In almost every State we have been spoken of, either expressly or by implication, as *citizens*. In the very year before the adoption of the present Constitution, 1789, the "Pennsylvania Society for Promoting the Abolition of Slavery, &c.," put forth an address, signed by "BENJAMIN FRANKLIN, *President,*" in which they stated one of their objects to be, "to *qualify* those who have been restored to freedom, for the exercise and enjoyment of CIVIL LIBERTY." The Convention of 1790, by striking out the word "WHITE," fixed the same standard of *qualification* for all; and, in fact, granted and guarantied "civil liberty" to all who possessed that qualification. Are we now to be told, that the Convention did not intend to include colored men, and that BENJAMIN FRANKLIN did not know what he was about, forasmuch as it was impossible for a colored man to become a citizen of the commonwealth?

It may here be objected to us, that in point of fact we have lost by the recent decision of the Supreme Court, in the case of *Fogg* vs. *Hobbs,* whatever claim to the right of suffrage we may have had under the Constitution of 1790; and hence have no reason to oppose the amended Constitution. Not so. We hold our rights under the present Constitution none the cheaper for the decision. The section already cited gives us all that we ask—all that we can conceive it in the power of language to convey. Reject, fellow citizens, the partial, disfranchising Constitution offered you by the Reform Convention, and we shall confidently expect that the Supreme Court will do us the justice and itself the honor to retract its decision. Should it not, our appeal will still be open to the conscience and common sense of the people, who through their chief magistrate and a majority of two-thirds of both branches of the Legislature may make way to the bench of the Supreme Court, for expounders of the Constitution who will not do violence to its most sacred and fundamental principles.

We cannot forbear here to refer you to some points in the published opinion of the

Court as delivered by Chief Justice Gibson, which we believe will go far to strip it of the weight and authority ordinarily conceded to the decision of the highest tribunal (save the elections) of this commonwealth.

1. The Court relies much on a decision *said to have been had "about"* forty-three years ago, the claim of which to a place in the repository of the Pennsylvania law is thus set forth by the Court itself:—

> About the year 1795, as I have it from James Gibson, Esq., of the Philadelphia bar, the very point before us was ruled by the High Court of Errors and Appeals, against the right of Negro suffrage. Mr. Gibson declined an invitation to be concerned in the argument, and therefore has no memorandum of the cause to direct us to the record. I have had the office searched for it; but the papers had fallen into such disorder as to preclude a hope of its recovery. Most of them were imperfect, and many were lost or misplaced. *But Mr. Gibson's remembrance of the decision is perfect and entitled to full confidence.*

Now, suppressing doubt, and supposing such a decision actually to have emanated from the then highest tribunal of the commonwealth, does not the fact that it was so utterly forgotten as not to have regulated the polls within the memory of the present generation, nor to have brought up against us in the Reform Convention, prove that it was virtually retracted? And if retracted, is it now to be revived to the overthrow of rights enjoyed without contradiction during the average life of man?

2. The Court argues that colored men are not *freemen*, and hence not entitled by the present Constitution to vote, because under laws prior to the Constitution there *might be* individuals who were not slaves, and yet were not *freemen!* The deduction is, that as the word "freeman" was, *before* the present Constitution, used in a restricted sense, it must have been used in the same sense *in* it. The correctness of this interpretation will be tested by substituting, in Art. 3, Sec. 1, for the word "freeman" the meaning which the Court chooses to have attached to it. This

meaning appears from the passages cited by the Court to be, *an elector.** Making the substitution, the article reads, "In elections by the citizens, every *elector,* of the age of twenty-one years, &c. &c., shall enjoy the right of an *elector,* &c."—a proposition which sheds a very faint light upon the question of the extent of the elective franchise, and from which it would appear that they may be electors who are *not* to enjoy the rights of electors. But taking the less restricted term *citizen,* which the Court also seems to think of the same force with "freeman," the article will read more sensibly, that "In elections by the citizens, every *citizen* of the age of twenty-one," who has paid taxes, &c. "shall enjoy the right of an elector." To what evidence does the Court refer to show that a *colored* man may not be a *citizen*? To none whatever. We have too much respect for old Pennsylvania to believe that such puerile absurdity can become her fixed and irreversible law.

3. Since the argument above referred to, such as it is, does not rest upon color, it is not less applicable to the descendants of Irish and German ancestors than to ourselves. If there ever have been within the common-wealth, men, or sets of men, who though personally free were not technically *freemen,* it is unconstitutional, according to the doctrine of the Court, for their descendants to exercise the right of suffrage, pay what taxes they may, till in "the discretion of the judges," their blood has "become so diluted in successive descents as to lose its dis-

---

*"Thus," says the Chief Justice, "till the instant when the phrase on which the question turns was penned, the term freeman had a peculiar and specific sense, being used like the term *citizen* which supplanted it, to denote one who had a voice in public affairs. The citizens were denominated freemen even in the Constitution of 1776—and under the present Constitution, the word, through dropped in the style, was used in the legislative acts convertibly with *electors,* so late as the year 1798 when it grew into disuse."

tinctive character." Is this the doctrine of Pennsylvania freedom?

4. Lastly, the Court openly rests its decision on the authority of a *wrong*, which this commonwealth so long ago as 1780 solemnly acknowledged, and, to the extent of its power, for ever repealed. To support the same *wrong* in *other States*, the Constitution of *this*, when it uses the words "every freeman," must be understood to exclude every freeman of a certain color! The Court is of opinion that the people of this commonwealth had no power to confer the rights of citizenship upon one who, were he in another State, *might be* loaded by its laws with "countless disabilities." Now, since in some of the States men may be found in slavery who have not the slightest trace of African blood, it is difficult to see, on the doctrine of the Court, how the Constitution of Pennsylvania could confer the right of citizenship upon any person; and, indeed, how it could have allowed the emancipation of slaves of any color. To such vile dependence on its own ancient *wrongs,* and on the present *wrongs* of other States, is Pennsylvania reduced by this decision!

Are we then presumptuous in the hope that this grave sentence will be as incapable of resurrection fifty years hence, as is that which the Chief Justice assures us was pronounced *"about* the year 1795?" No. The blessings of the broad and impartial charter of Pennsylvania rights can no more be wrested from us by legal subtilty, than the beams of our common sun or the breathing of our common air.

What have we done to forfeit the inestimable benefits of this charter? Why should tax-paying colored men, any more than other tax-payers, be deprived of the right of voting for their representatives? It was said in the Convention, that this government belongs to the *Whites.* We have already shown this to be false, as to the past. Those who established our present government designed it equally for all. It is for you to decide whether it shall be confined to the European complexion in future. Why should you exclude us from a fair participation in the ben-

efits of the republic? Have we oppressed the whites? Have we used our right to the injury of any class? Have we disgraced it by receiving bribes? Where are the charges written down, and who will swear to them? We challenge investigation. We put it to the conscience of every Pennsylvanian, whether there is, or ever has been, in the commonwealth, either a political party or religious sect which has less deserved than ourselves to be thus disfranchised. As to the charge of idleness, we fling it back indignantly. Whose brows have sweat for our livelihood but our own? As to vice, if it disqualifies us for civil liberty, why not apply the same rule to the whites, so far as they are vicious? Will you punish the innocent for the crimes of the guilty? The execution of the laws is in the hands of the whites. If we are bad citizens let them apply the proper remedies. We do not ask the right of suffrage for the inmates of our jails and penitentiaries, but for those who honestly and industriously contribute to bear the burdens of the State. As to inferiority to the whites, if indeed we are guilty of it, either by nature or education, we trust our enjoyment of the rights of freemen will on that account be considered the less dangerous. If we are incompetent to fill the offices of State, it will be the fault of the whites only if we are suffered to disgrace them. We are in too feeble a minority to cherish a mischievous ambition. Fair protection is all that we aspire to.

We ask your attention, fellow citizens, to facts and testimonies which go to show that, considering the circumstances in which we have been placed, our country has no reason to be ashamed of us, and that those have the most occasion to blush to whom nature has given the power.

By the careful inquiry of a committee appointed by the "Pennsylvania Society for Promoting the Abolition of Slavery," it has been ascertained that the colored population of Philadelphia and its suburbs, numbering 18,768 souls, possess at the present time, of real and personal estate, not less that $1,350,000. They have paid for taxes during the last year $3,252.83, for house, water, and ground rent, $166,963.50. This committee estimate the income to the holders of real estate occupied by the colored people, to be 7½ per cent. on a capital of about $2,000,000. Here is an addition to the wealth of their white brethren. But the rents and taxes are not all; to pay them, the colored people must be employed in labor, and here is another profit to the whites, for no man employs another unless he can make his labor profitable to himself. For a similar reason, a profit is made by all the whites who sell to colored people the necessaries or luxuries of life. Though the aggregate amount of the wealth derived by the whites from our people can only be conjectured, its importance is worthy of consideration by those who would make it less by lessening our motive to accumulate for ourselves.

Nor is the profit derived from us counterbalanced by the sums which we in any way draw from the public treasures. From a statement published by order of the Guardians of the Poor of Philadelphia, in 1830, it appears that out of 549 out-door poor relieved during the year, only 22 were persons of color, being about four per cent. of the whole number, while the ratio of our population to that of the city and suburbs exceeds 8¼ per cent. By a note appended to the printed report above referred to, it appears that the colored *paupers* admitted into the almshouse for the same period, did not exceed four per cent. of the whole. Thus it has been ascertained that they pay more than they receive in the support of their own poor. The various "mutual relief" societies of Philadelphia expend upwards of $7,000 annually, for the relief of their members when sick or disabled.

That we are not neglectful of our religious interests, nor of the education of our children, is shown by the fact that there are among us in Philadelphia, Pittsburg, York, West Chester, and Columbia, 22 churches, 48 clergymen, 26 day schools, 20 Sabbath schools, 125 Sabbath school teachers, 4 literary societies, 2 public libraries, consisting of about 800 volumes, besides 8,333 volumes in private libraries, 2 tract societies, 2 Bible societies, and 7 temperance societies.

In other parts of the State we are confident our condition will compare very favorably with that in Philadelphia, although we are not furnished with accurate statistics.

Our fathers shared with yours the trials and perils of the wilderness. Among the facts which illustrate this, it is well known that the founder of your capital, from whom it bears the name of Harrisburg, was rescued by a *colored man,* from a party of Indians, who had captured, and bound him to the stake for execution. In gratitude for this act, he *invited colored persons* to settle in his town, and offered them land on favorable terms. When our common country has been invaded by a foreign foe, colored men have hazarded their lives in its defence. Our fathers fought by the side of yours in the struggle which made us an independent republic. We offer the following testimonies.

Hon. Mr. Burgess, of Rhode Island, said on the floor of Congress, January 28th, 1828—

At the commencement of the revolutionary war, Rhode Island had a number of this description of people, (slaves.) A regiment of them were enlisted into the continental service, and no *braver* men met the enemy in battle; but not one of them was permitted to be a soldier until he had first been made a *freeman.*

Said the Hon. Mr. Martindale, of New York, in Congress, January 22d, 1828—

Slaves, or Negroes, who had been slaves, were enlisted as soldiers in the war of the revolution; and I myself saw a battalion of them, as fine martial looking men as I ever saw, attached to the northern army, in the last war, on its march from Plattsburg to Sacketts Harbor.

Said the Hon. Charles Miner, of Pennsylvania, in Congress, February 7th, 1828—

The African race make excellent soldiers. Large numbers of them were with Perry, and aided to gain the brilliant victory on lake Erie.

A whole battalion of them was distinguished for its soldierly appearance.

The Hon. Mr. Clarke, in the Convention which revised the Constitution of New York, in 1821, said, in regard to the right of suffrage of colored men—

In the war of the revolution these people helped to fight your battles by land and by sea. Some of your States were glad to turn out corps of colored men, and to stand shoulder to shoulder with them. In your late war they contributed largely towards some of your most splendid victories. On lakes Erie and Champlain, where your fleets triumphed over a foe superior in numbers and engines of death, they were manned in a large proportion with men of color. And in this very house, in the fall of 1814, a bill passed, receiving the approbation of all the branches of your government, authorizing the governor to accept the services of 2,000 free people of color.

On the 20th of March, 1779, it was recommended by Congress to the States of Georgia and South Carolina to raise 3,000 colored troops who were to be rewarded for their services by their freedom. The delegations from those States informed Congress that such a body of troops would be not only "formidable to the enemy," but would "lessen the danger of revolts and desertions" among the slaves themselves. (See *Secret Journal of the Old Congress,* Vol. I. pages 105–107.)

During the last war the free colored people were called to the defence of the country by GENERAL JACKSON, and received the following testimony to the value of their services, in which let it be remarked that they are addressed as *fellow citizens* with the *whites:*

Soldiers! When, on the banks of the Mobile, I called you to take up arms, inviting you to partake the perils and glory of your white fellow citizens, I expected much from you—for I was not ignorant that you possessed qualities most formidable to an invading enemy. I knew with what fortitude you could endure hunger and thirst, and all the fatigues of a campaign. I knew well how you loved your native country, and that you had, as well as ourselves, to defend what man holds most dear, his parents, relations, wife, children, and property. You have done more than I expected. In addition to the qualities which I previously knew you to possess, I find, moreover, among you a noble enthusiasm, which leads you to the performance of great things. SOLDIERS—the President of the United States shall hear how praise-worthy was your conduct in the hour of danger, and the representatives of the American people will, I doubt not, give you the praise which your deeds deserve. Your General anticipates them in applauding your noble ardor, &c.

By order, (*Signed*)   Thomas Butler, *Aid-de-Camp.*

Are we to be thus looked to for help in the "hour of danger," but trampled under foot in the time of peace? In which of the battles of the revolution did not our fathers fight as bravely as yours, for American liberty? Was it that their children might be disfranchised and loaded with insult that they endured the famine of Valley Forge, and the horrors of the Jersey Prison Ship? Nay, among those from whom you are asked to wrench the birthright of CIVIL LIBERTY, are those who themselves shed their blood on the snows of Jersey, and faced British bayonets in the most desperate hour of the revolution.

In other hours of danger, too, colored men have shown themselves the friends of their white countrymen. When the yellow fever ravaged Philadelphia in 1793, and the whites fled, and there were not found enough of them in the city to bury their own dead, the colored people volunteered to do that painful and dangerous duty. They appointed two of their own number to superintend the sad work, who afterwards received the following testimonial:—

Having, during the prevalence of the late malignant disorder, had almost daily opportunities of seeing the conduct of Absalom Jones and Richard Allen, and the people employed by them to bury the dead, I with cheerfulness give this testimony of my approbation of their proceedings, as far as the same came under my notice. Their diligence, attention, and decency of deportment, afforded me at the time much satisfaction.

(*Signed*) Matthew Clarkson, *Mayor.*
Philadelphia, Jan. 23, 1794.

It is notorious that many whites who were forsaken by their own relations and left to the mercy of this fell disease, were nursed *gratuitously* by the colored people. Does this speak an enmity which would abuse the privileges of civil liberty to the injury of the whites? We have the testimony of a committee of the Senate of this commonwealth, no longer ago than 1830, who were appointed to report upon the expediency of restricting the emigration of colored people into the commonwealth. The following extract from their report, signed by the Hon. Mr. Breck, chairman, testifies to our character:

On this subject your committee beg to remark, that by the last census our colored population amounted to about 36,000, of whom 30,000 inhabit the eastern district, and only 6,000 the western. And this number, so small compared with the white population, is scattered among 1,500,000 of our own color, making 1 colored to 42 whites. So few of these, it is believed by your committee, need not at present be an object of uneasiness, and would not seem to require the enactment of any restrictive laws; MORE ESPECIALLY AS THEY ARE, FOR THE GREATER PART, INDUSTRIOUS, PEACEABLE, AND USEFUL PEOPLE.

Be it remembered, fellow citizens, that it is only for the "*industrious, peaceable, and useful*" part of the colored people that we plead. We would have the right of suffrage only as the reward of industry and worth. We care not how high the qualification be placed. All we ask is, that no man shall be excluded on account of his *color,* that the same rule shall be applied to all.

Are we to be disfranchised, lest the purity of the *white* blood should be sullied by an intermixture with ours? It seems to us that our white brethren might well enough reserve

their fear, till we seek such alliance with them. We ask no social favors. We would not willingly darken the doors of those to whom the complexion and features, which our Maker has given us, are disagreeable. The territories of the commonwealth are sufficiently ample to afford us a home without doing violence to the delicate nerves of our white brethren, for centuries to come. Besides, we are not intruders here, nor were our ancestors. Surely you ought to bear as unrepiningly the evil consequences of your fathers' guilt, as we those of our fathers' misfortune. Proscription and disfranchisement are the last things in the world to alleviate these evil consequences. Nothing, as shameful experience has already proved, can so powerfully promote the evil which you profess to deprecate, as the degradation of our race by the oppressive rule of yours. Give us that fair and honorable ground which self-respect requires to stand on, and the dreaded amalgamation, if it take place at all, shall be by your own fault, as indeed it always has been. We dare not give full vent to the indignation we feel on this point, but we will not attempt wholly to conceal it. We ask a voice in the disposition of those public resources which we ourselves have helped to earn; we claim a right to be heard, according to our numbers, in regard to all those great public measures which involve our lives and fortunes, as well as those of our fellow citizens; we assert our right to vote at the polls as a shield against that strange species of benevolence which seeks legislative aid to banish us—and we are told that our white fellow citizens cannot submit to an *intermixture of the races!* Then let the indentures, title-deeds, contracts, notes of hand, and all other evidences of bargain, in which colored men have been treated as *men,* be torn and scattered on the winds. Consistency is a jewel. Let no white man hereafter ask his colored neighbor's *consent* when he wants his property or his labor, lest he should endanger the Anglo-Saxon purity of his descendants? Why should not the same principle hold good between neighbor and neighbor, which is deemed necessary, as a fundamental principle in the Constitution itself? Why should you be ashamed to act in private business, as the Reform Convention would have you act in the capacity of a commonwealth? But, no! we do not believe our fellow citizens, while with good faith they hold ourselves bound by their contracts with us, and while they feel bound to deal with us only by fair contract, will ratify the arbitrary principle of the Convention, howmuchsoever they may prefer the complexion in which their Maker has pleased to clothe themselves.

We would not misrepresent the motives of the Convention, but we are constrained to believe that they have laid our rights a sacrifice on the altar of slavery. We do not believe our disfranchisement would have been proposed, but for the desire which is felt by political aspirants to gain the favor of the slaveholding States. This is not the first time that northern statesmen have "bowed the knee to the dark spirit of slavery," but it is the first time that they have bowed so low! Is Pennsylvania, which abolished slavery in 1780, and enfranchised her tax-paying colored citizens in 1790, now, in 1838, to get upon her knees and repent of her humanity, to gratify those who disgrace the very name of American Liberty, by holding our brethren as goods and chattels? We freely acknowledge our brotherhood to the slave, and our interest in his welfare. Is this a crime for which we should be ignominiously punished? The very fact that we are deeply interested for our kindred in bonds, shows that we are the right sort of stuff to make good citizens of. Were we not so, we should better deserve a lodging in your penitentiaries than a franchise at your polls. Doubtless it will be well pleasing to the slave-holders of the South to see us degraded. They regard our freedom from chains as a dangerous example, much more our political freedom. They see in every thing which fortifies our rights, an obstacle to the recovery of their fugitive property. Will Pennsylvania go backwards towards slavery, for the better safety of southern slave property? Be assured

the South will never be satisfied till the old "Keystone" has returned to the point from which she started in 1780. And since the number of colored men in the commonwealth is so inconsiderable, the safety of slavery *may* require still more. It may demand that a portion of the white tax-payers should be unmanned and turned into chattels—we mean those whose hands are hardened by daily toil. Fellow citizens, will you take the first step towards reimposing the chains which have now rusted for more than fifty years? Need we inform you that every colored man in Pennsylvania is exposed to be arrested as a fugitive from slavery? and that it depends not upon the verdict of a jury of his peers but upon the decision of a judge on summary process, whether or not he shall be dragged into southern bondage? The Constitution of the United States provides that "no person shall be deprived of life, liberty, or property, without due process of law"—by which is certainly meant a TRIAL BY JURY. Yet the act of Congress of 1793, for the recovery of fugitive slaves, authorizes the claimant to seize his victim without a warrant from any magistrate, and allows him to drag him before "any magistrate of a county, city, or town corporate, where such seizure has been made," and upon proving, by "oral testimony or affidavit," to the satisfaction of such magistrate that the man is his slave, gives him a right to take him into everlasting bondage. Thus may a free-born citizen of Pennsylvania be arrested, tried without counsel, jury, or power to call witnesses, condemned by a single man, and carried across Mason and Dixon's line, within the compass of a single day. An act of this commonwealth, passed 1820, and enlarged and reenacted in 1825, it is true, puts some restraint upon the power of the claimant under the act of Congress; but it still leaves the case to the decision of a single judge, without the privilege of a jury! What unspeakably aggravates our loss of the right of suffrage at this moment is, that, while the increased activity of the slave-catchers enhances our danger, the Reform Convention has refused to amend the Constitution so as to protect our liberty by a jury trial! We entreat you to make our case your own—imagine your own wives and children to be trembling at the approach of every stranger, lest their husbands and fathers should be dragged into a slavery worse than Algerine—worse than death! Fellow citizens, if there is one of us who has abused the right of suffrage, let him be tried and punished according to law. But in the name of humanity, in the name of justice, in the name of the God you profess to worship, who has no respect of persons, do not turn into gall and wormwood the friendship we bear to yourselves by ratifying a Constitution which tears from us a privilege dearly earned and inestimably prized. We lay hold of the principles which Pennsylvania asserted in the hour which tried men's souls—which BENJAMIN FRANKLIN and his eight colleagues, in the name of the commonwealth, pledged their lives, their fortunes, and their sacred honor to sustain. We take our stand upon that solemn declaration, that to protect inalienable rights "governments are instituted among men, deriving their JUST POWERS from the CONSENT of the governed," and proclaim that a government which tears away from us and our posterity the very power of CONSENT, is a tyrannical usurpation which we will never cease to oppose. We have seen with amazement and grief the apathy of white Pennsylvanians while the "Reform Convention" has been perpetrating this outrage upon the good old principles of Pennsylvania freedom. But however others may forsake these principles, we promise to maintain them on *Pennsylvania soil,* to the last man. If this disfranchisement is designed to uproot us, it shall fail. Pennsylvania's fields, vallies, mountains, and rivers; her canals, railroads, forests, and mines; her domestic altars, and her public, religious and benevolent institutions; her Penn and Franklin, her Rush, Rawle, Wistar, and Vaux; her consecrated past and her brilliant future, are as dear to us as they can be to you. Firm upon our old Pennsylvania BILL OF RIGHTS, and trusting in a God of Truth and Justice, we lay our claim before you, with the warning that no amendments of the present Constitution can compensate for the loss of its foundation principle of equal rights, nor for the conversion into enemies of 40,000 friends.

In behalf of the Committee,
Robert Purvis, *Chairman.*

An Address to the Slaves of the United States of America

Henry Highland Garnet

Brethren and Fellow-Citizens: —Your brethren of the North, East, and West have been

Source: Henry Highland Garnet, "An Address to the Slaves of the United States of America." (1843), reprinted in Garnet, *A Memorial Discourse by Rev. Henry Highland Garnet, Delivered in the Hall of Representatives* (Philadelphia: Joseph M. Wilson, 1865), pp. 44–51.

accustomed to meet together in National Conventions, to sympathize with each other, and to weep over your unhappy condition. In these meetings we have addressed all classes of the free, but we have never, until this time, sent a word of consolation and advice to you. We have been contented in sitting still and mourning over your sorrows, earnestly hoping that before this day your sacred liberties would have been restored.

But, we have hoped in vain. Years have rolled on, and tens of thousands have been borne on streams of blood and tears, to the shores of eternity. While you have been oppressed, we have also been partakers with you; nor can we be free while you are enslaved. We, therefore, write to you as being bound with you.

Many of you are bound to us, not only by the ties of a common humanity, but we are connected by the more tender relations of parents, wives, husbands, children, brothers, and sisters, and friends. As such we most affectionately address you.

Slavery had fixed a deep gulf between you and us, and while it shuts out from you the relief and consolation which your friends would willingly render, it afflicts and persecutes you with a fierceness which we might not expect to see in the fiends of hell. But still the Almighty Father of mercies has left to us a glimmering ray of hope, which shines out like a lone star in a cloudy sky. Mankind are becoming wiser, and better—the oppressor's power is fading, and you, every day, are becoming better informed, and more numerous. Your grievances, brethren, are many. We shall not attempt, in this short address, to present to the world all the dark catalogue of this nation's sins, which have been committed upon an innocent people. Nor is it indeed necessary, for you feel them from day to day, and all the civilized world look upon them with amazement.

Two hundred and twenty-seven years ago, the first of our injured race were brought to the shores of America. They came not with glad spirits to select their homes in the New World. They came not with their own consent, to find an unmolested enjoyment of the blessings of this fruitful soil. The first dealings they had with men calling themselves Christians, exhibited to them the worst features of corrupt and sordid hearts: and convinced them that no cruelty is too great, no villainy and no robbery too abhorrent for even enlightened men to perform, when influenced by avarice and lust. Neither did they come flying upon the wings of Liberty, to a land of freedom. But they came with broken hearts, from their beloved native land, and were doomed to unrequited toil and deep degradation. Nor did the evil of their bondage end at their emancipation by death. Succeeding generations inherited their chains, and millions have come from eternity into time, and have returned again to the world of spirits, cursed and ruined by American slavery.

The propagators of the system, or their immediate ancestors, very soon discovered its growing evil, and its tremendous wickedness, and secret promises were made to destroy it. The gross inconsistency of a people holding slaves, who had themselves "ferried o'er the wave" for freedom's sake, was too apparent to be entirely overlooked. The voice of Freedom cried, "Emancipate your slaves." Humanity supplicated with tears for the deliverance of the children of Africa. Wisdom urged her solemn plea. The bleeding captive plead his innocence, and pointed to Christianity who stood weeping at the cross. Jehovah frowned upon the nefarious institution, and thunderbolts, red with vengeance, struggled to leap forth to blast the guilty wretches who maintained it. But all was vain. Slavery had stretched its dark wings of death over the land, the Church stood silently by—the priests prophesied falsely, and the people loved to have it so. Its throne is established, and now it reigns triumphant.

Nearly three millions of your fellow-citizens are prohibited by law and public opinion, (which in this country is stronger than law,) from reading the Book of Life. Your intellect has been destroyed as much as possible, and every ray of light they have attempted to shut out from your minds. The oppressors themselves have become involved in the ruin. They have become weak, sensual, and rapacious—they have cursed you—they have cursed themselves—they have cursed the earth which they have trod.

The colonists threw the blame upon England. They said that the mother country entailed the evil upon them, and that they would rid themselves of it if they could. The world thought they were sincere, and the philanthropic pitied them. But time soon tested their sincerity. In a few years the colonists grew strong, and severed themselves from the British Government. Their independence was declared, and they took their station among the sovereign powers of the earth. The declaration was a glorious document. Sages admired it, and the patriotic of every nation reverenced the God-like sentiments which it contained. When the power of Government returned to their hands, did they emancipate the slaves? No; they rather added new links to our chains. Were they ignorant of the principles of Liberty? Certainly they were not. The sentiments of their revolutionary orators fell in burning eloquence upon their hearts, and with one voice they cried, LIBERTY OR DEATH. Oh what a sentence was that! It ran from soul to soul like electric fire, and nerved the arm of thousands to fight in the holy cause of Freedom. Among the diversity of opinions that are entertained in regard to physical resistance, there are but a few found to gainsay that stern declaration. We are among those who do not.

SLAVERY! How much misery is comprehended in that single word. What mind is there that does not shrink from its direful effects? Unless the image of God be obliterated from the soul, all men cherish the love of Liberty. The nice discerning political economist does not regard the sacred right more than the untutored African who roams in the wilds of Congo. Nor has the one more right to the full enjoyment of his freedom than the other. In every man's mind the good seeds of liberty are planted, and he who brings his fellow down so low, as to make him contented with a condition of slavery, commits the highest crime against God and man. Brethren, your oppressors aim to do this. They endeavor to make you as much like brutes as possible. When they have blinded the eyes of your mind—when they have embittered the sweet waters of life—when they have shut out the light which shines from the word of God—then, and not till then, has American slavery done its perfect work.

TO SUCH DEGRADATION IT IS SINFUL IN THE EXTREME FOR YOU TO MAKE VOLUNTARY SUBMISSION. The divine commandments you are in duty bound to reverence and obey. If you do not obey them, you will surely meet with the displeasure of the Almighty. He requires you to love him supremely, and your neighbor as yourself—to keep the Sabbath day holy—to search the Scriptures—and bring up your children with respect for his laws, and to worship no other God but him. But slavery sets all these at nought, and hurls defiance in the face of Jehovah. The forlorn condition in which you are placed, does not destroy your moral obligation to God. You are not certain of heaven, because you suffer yourselves to remain in a state of slavery, where you cannot obey the commandments of the Sovereign of the universe. If the ignorance of slavery is a passport to heaven, then it is a blessing, and no curse, and you should rather desire its perpetuity than its abolition. God will not receive slavery, nor ignorance, nor any other state of mind, for love and obedience to him. Your condition does not absolve you from your moral obligation. The diabolical injustice by which your liberties are cloven down, NEITHER GOD, NOR ANGELS, OR JUST MEN, COMMAND YOU TO SUFFER FOR A SINGLE MOMENT. THEREFORE IT IS YOUR SOLEMN AND IMPERATIVE DUTY TO USE EVERY MEANS, BOTH MORAL, INTELLECTUAL, AND PHYSICAL, THAT PROMISES SUCCESS. If a band of heathen men should attempt to enslave a race of Christians, and to place their children under the influence of some false religion, surely, Heaven would frown upon the men who would not resist such aggression, even to death. If, on the other hand, a band of Christians should attempt to enslave a race of heathen men, and to entail slavery upon them, and to keep them in heathenism in the midst of Christianity, the God of heaven would smile upon every effort which the injured might make to disenthral themselves.

Brethren, it is as wrong for your lordly oppressors to keep you in slavery, as it was for the man thief to steal our ancestors from the coast of Africa. You should therefore now use the same manner of resistance, as would have been just in our ancestors, when the bloody foot-prints of the first remorseless soul-thief was placed upon the shores of our fatherland. The humblest peasant is as free in the sight of God as the proudest monarch that ever swayed a sceptre. Liberty is a spirit sent out from God, and like its great Author, is no respecter of persons.

Brethren, the time has come when you must act for yourselves. It is an old and true saying that, "if hereditary bondmen would be free, they must themselves strike the blow." You can plead your own cause, and do the work of emancipation better than any others. The nations of the old world are moving in the great cause of universal freedom, and some of them at least will, ere long, do you justice. The combined powers of Europe have placed their broad seal of disapprobation upon the African slave-trade. But in the slave-holding parts of the United States, the trade is as brisk as ever. They buy and sell you as though you were brute beasts. The North has done much—her opinion of slavery in the abstract is known. But in regard to the South, we adopt the opinion of the *New York Evangelist*—"We have advanced so far, that the cause apparently waits for a more effectual door to be thrown open than has been yet." We are about to point you to that more effectual door. Look around you, and behold the bosoms of your loving wives heaving with untold agonies! Hear the cries of your poor children! Remember the stripes your fathers bore. Think of the torture and disgrace of your noble mothers. Think of your wretched sisters, loving virtue and purity, as they are driven into concubinage and are exposed to the unbridled lusts of incarnate devils. Think of the undying glory that hangs around the ancient name of Africa:—and forget not that you are native-born American citizens, and as such, you are justly entitled to all the rights that are granted to the freest. Think how many tears you have poured out upon the soil which you have cultivated with unrequited toil and enriched with your blood; and then go to your lordly enslavers and tell them plainly, that you *are determined to be free.*

Fourth of July Speech

Frederick Douglass

. . . Fellow-citizens, pardon me, allow me to ask, why am I called upon to speak here today? What have I, or those I represent, to do with your national independence? Are the great principles of political freedom and of natural justice, embodied in that Declaration of Independence, extended to us? and am I, therefore, called upon to bring our humble

Source: Frederick Douglass, Oration delivered in Corinthian Hall (Rochester: Lee, Man & Co., 1852).

offering to the national altar, and to confess the benefits and express devout gratitude for the blessings resulting from your independence to us?

Would to God, both for your sakes and ours, that an affirmative answer could be truthfully returned to these questions! Then would my task be light, and my burden easy and delightful. For *who* is there so cold, that a nation's sympathy could not warm him? Who so obdurate and dead to the claims of gratitude, that would not thankfully acknowledge such priceless benefits? Who so stolid and selfish, that would not give his voice to swell the hallelujas of a nation's jubilee, when the chains of servitude had been torn from his limbs? I am not that man. In a case like that, the dumb might eloquently speak, and the "lame man leap as an hart."

But such is not the state of the case. I say it with a sad sense of the disparity between us. I am not included within the pale of this glorious anniversary! Your high independence only reveals the immeasurable distance between us. The blessings in which you, this day, rejoice, are not enjoyed in common.—The rich inheritance of justice, liberty, prosperity and independence, bequeathed by your fathers, is shared by you, not by me. The sunlight that brought light and healing to you, has brought stripes and death to me. This Fourth July is *yours*, not *mine. You* may rejoice, *I* must mourn. To drag a man in fetters into the grand illuminated temple of liberty, and call upon him to join you in joyous anthems, were inhuman mockery and sacrilegious irony. Do you mean, citizens, to mock me, by asking me to speak to-day? If so, there is a parallel to your conduct. And let me warn you that it is dangerous to copy the example of a nation whose crimes, towering up to heaven, were thrown down by the breath of the Almighty, burying that nation in irrevocable ruin! I can to-day take up the plaintive lament of a peeled and woe-smitten people!

> By the rivers of Babylon, there we sat down. Yea! we wept when we remembered Zion. We hanged our harps upon the willows in the midst thereof. For there, they that carried us away captive, required of us a song; and they who wasted us required of us mirth, saying, Sing us one of the songs of Zion. How can we sing the Lord's song in a strange land? If I forget thee, O Jerusalem, let my right hand forget her cunning. If I do not remember thee, let my tongue cleave to the roof of my mouth.

Fellow-citizens, above your national, tumultuous joy, I hear the mournful wail of millions! whose chains, heavy and grievous yesterday, are, to-day, rendered more intolerable by the jubilee shouts that reach them. If I do forget, if I do not faithfully remember those bleeding children of sorrow this day, "may my right hand forget her cunning, and may my tongue cleave to the roof of my mouth!" To forget them, to pass lightly over their wrongs, and to chime in with the popular theme, would be treason most scandalous and shocking, and would make me a reproach before God and the world. My subject, then, fellow-citizens, is AMERICAN SLAVERY. I shall see this day and its popular characteristics from the slave's point of view. Standing there identified with the American bondman, making his wrongs mine, I do not hesitate to declare, with all my soul, that the character and conduct of this nation never looked blacker to me than on this 4th of July! Whether we turn to the declarations of the past, or to the professions of the present, the conduct of the nation seems equally hideous and revolting. America is false to the past, false to the present, and solemnly binds herself to be false to the future. Standing with God and the crushed and bleeding slave on this occasion, I will, in the name of humanity which is outraged, in the name of liberty which is fettered, in the name of the constitution and the Bible which are disregarded and trampled upon, dare to call in question and to denounce, with all the emphasis I can command, everything that serves to perpetuate slavery—the great sin and shame of America! "I will not equivocate; I will not excuse"; I will use the severest language I can command; and yet not one word shall escape me that any man, whose judgment is not blinded by prejudice, or, who is not at heart a slaveholder, shall not confess to be right and just.

But I fancy I hear some one of my audience say, "It is just in this circumstance that you and your brother abolitionists fail to make a favorable impression on the public mind. Would you argue more, and denounce less; would you persuade more, and rebuke less; your cause would be much more likely to succeed." But, I submit, where all is plain there is nothing to be argued. What point in

moves wearily along, and the inhuman wretch who drives them. Hear his savage yells and his blood-curdling oaths, as he hurries on his affrighted captives! There, see the old man with locks thinned and gray. Cast one glance, if you please, upon that young mother, whose shoulders are bare to the scorching sun, her briny tears falling on the brow of the babe in her arms. See, too, that girl of thirteen, weeping, *yes!* weeping, as she thinks of the mother from whom she has been torn! The drove moves tardily. Heat and sorrow have nearly consumed their strength; suddenly you hear a quick snap, like the discharge of a rifle; the fetters clank, and the chain rattles simultaneously; your ears are saluted with a scream, that seems to have torn its way to the centre of your soul! The crack you heard was the sound of the slave-whip; the scream you heard was from the woman you saw with the babe. Her speed had faltered under the weight of her child and her chains! that gash on her shoulder tells her to move on. Follow this drove to New Orleans. Attend the auction; see men examined like horses; see the forms of women rudely and brutally exposed to the shocking gaze of American slave-buyers. See this drove sold and separated forever; and never forget the deep, sad sobs that arose from the scattered multitude. Tell me, citizens, WHERE, under the sun, you can witness a spectacle more fiendish and shocking. Yet this is but a glance at the American slave-trade, as it exists, at this moment, in the ruling part of the United States.

I was born amid such sights and scenes. To me the American slave-trade is a terrible reality. When a child, my soul was often pierced with a sense of its horrors. I lived on Philpot Street, Fell's Point, Baltimore, and have watched from the wharves the slave ships in the Basin, anchored from the shore, with their cargoes of human flesh, waiting for favorable winds to waft them down the Chesapeake. There was, at that time, a grand slave mart kept at the head of Pratt Street, by Austin Woldfolk. His agents were sent into every town and county in Maryland, announcing their arrival, through the papers, and on flaming *"hand-bills,"* headed CASH FOR NEGROES. These men were generally well dressed men, and very captivating in their manners; ever ready to drink, to treat, and to gamble. The fate of many a slave has depended upon the turn of a single card; and many a child has been snatched from the arms of its mother by bargains arranged in a state of brutal drunkenness.

The flesh-mongers gather up their victims by dozens, and drive them, chained, to the general depot at Baltimore. When a sufficient number has been collected here, a ship is chartered for the purpose of conveying the forlorn crew to Mobile, or to New Orleans. From the slave prison to the ship, they are usually driven in the darkness of night; for since the anti-slavery agitation, a certain caution is observed.

In the deep, still darkness of midnight, I have been often aroused by the dead, heavy footsteps, and the piteous cries of the chained gangs that passed our door. The anguish of my boyish heart was intense; and I was often consoled, when speaking to my mistress in the morning, to hear her say that the custom was very wicked; that she hated to hear the rattle of the chains and the heartrending cries. I was glad to find one who sympathized with me in my horror.

Fellow-citizens, this murderous traffic is, to-day, in active operation in this boasted republic. In the solitude of my spirit I see clouds of dust raised on the highways of the South; I see the bleeding footsteps; I hear the doleful wail of fettered humanity on the way to the slave-markets, where the victims are to be sold like *horses, sheep,* and *swine,* knocked off to the highest bidder. There I see the tenderest ties ruthlessly broken, to gratify the lust, caprice and rapacity of the buyers and sellers of men. My soul sickens at the sight.

"Is this the land your Fathers loved,
  The freedom which they toiled to win?
Is this the earth whereon they moved?
  Are these the graves they slumber in?"

But a still more inhuman, disgraceful, and scandalous state of things remains to be presented. By an act of the American Congress, not yet two years old, slavery has been nationalized in its most horrible and revolting form. By that act, Mason and Dixon's line has been obliterated; New York has become as Virginia; and the power to hold, hunt, and sell men, women and children, as slaves, remains no longer a mere state institution, but is now an institution of the whole United States. The power is co-extensive with the star-spangled banner, and American Christianity. Where these go, may also go the merciless slave-hunter. Where these are, man is not sacred. He is a bird for the sportsman's gun. By that most foul and fiendish of all human decrees, the liberty and person of every man are put in peril. Your broad republican domain is hunting ground for *men. Not* for thieves and robbers, enemies of society, merely, but for men guilty of no crime. Your law-makers have commanded all good citizens to engage in this hellish sport. Your President, your Secretary of State, your *lords, nobles,* and ecclesiastics enforce, as a duty you owe to your free and glorious country, and to your God, that you do this accursed thing. Not fewer than forty Americans have, within the past two years, been hunted down and, without a moment's warning, hurried away in chains, and consigned to slavery and excruciating torture. Some of these have had wives and children, dependent on them for bread; but of this, account was made. The right of the hunter to his prey stands superior to the right of marriage, and to *all* rights in this republic, the rights of God included! For black men there is neither law nor justice, humanity nor religion. The Fugitive Slave *Law* makes MERCY TO THEM A CRIME; and bribes the judge who tries them. An American JUDGE GETS TEN DOLLARS FOR EVERY VICTIM HE CONSIGNS *to* slavery, and five, when he fails to do so. The oath of any two villians is sufficient, under this hell-black enactment, to send the most pious and exemplary black man into the remorseless jaws of slavery! His own testimony is noth-

ing. He can bring no witnesses for himself. The minister of American justice is bound by the law to hear but *one* side; and *that* side is the side of the oppressor. Let this damning fact be perpetually told. Let it be thundered around the world that in tyrant-killing, king-hating, people-loving, democratic, Christian America the seats of justice are filled with judges who hold their offices under an open and palpable *bribe,* and are bound, in deciding the case of a man's liberty, *to hear only his accusers!*

In glaring violation of justice, in shameless disregard of the forms of administering law, in cunning arrangement to entrap the defenceless, and in diabolical intent this Fugitive Slave Law stands alone in the annals of tyrannical legislation. I doubt if there be another nation on the globe having the brass and the baseness to put such a law on the statute-book. If any man in this assembly thinks differently from me in this matter, and feels able to disprove my statements, I will gladly confront him at any suitable time and place he may select.

I take this law to be one of the grossest infringements of Christian Liberty, and, if the churches and ministers of our country were not stupidly blind, or most wickedly indifferent, they, too, would so regard it.

At the very moment that they are thanking God for the enjoyment of civil and religious liberty, and for the right to worship God according to the dictates of their own consciences, they are utterly silent in respect to a law which robs religion of its chief significance and makes it utterly worthless to a world lying in wickedness. Did this law concern the *"mint, anise, and cummin"*—abridge the right to sing psalms, to partake of the sacrament, or to engage in any of the ceremonies of religion, it would be smitten by the thunder of a thousand pulpits. A general shout would go up from the church demanding *repeal, repeal, instant repeal!*—And it would go hard with that politician who presumed to solicit the votes of the people without inscribing this motto on his banner. Further, if this demand were not complied with, another Scotland would be added to the history of religious liberty, and the stern old covenanters would be thrown into the shade. A John Knox would be seen at every church door and heard from every pulpit, and Fillmore would have no more quarter than was shown by Knox to the beautiful, but treacherous, Queen Mary of Scotland. The fact that the church of our country (with fractional exceptions) does not esteem "the Fugitive Slave Law" as a declaration of war against religious liberty, implies that that church regards religion simply as a form of worship, an empty ceremony, and *not* a vital principle, requiring active benevolence, justice, love, and good will towards man. It esteems sacrifice above mercy; psalm-singing above right doing; solemn meetings above practical righteousness. A worship that can be conducted by persons who refuse to give shelter to the houseless, to give bread to the hungry, clothing to the naked, and who enjoin obedience to a law forbidding these acts of mercy is a curse, not a blessing to mankind. The Bible addresses all such persons as "scribes, pharisees, hypocrites, who pay tithe of *mint, anise,* and *cummin,* and have omitted the weightier matters of the law, judgment, mercy, and faith."

But the church of this country is not only indifferent to the wrongs of the slave, it actually takes sides with the oppressors. It has made itself the bulwark of American slavery, and the shield of American slave-hunters. Many of its most eloquent Divines, who stand as the very lights of the church, have shamelessly given the sanction of religion and the Bible to the whole slave system. They have taught that man may, properly, be a slave; that the relation of master and slave is ordained of God; that to send back an escaped bondman to his master is clearly the duty of all the followers of the Lord Jesus Christ; and this horrible blasphemy is palmed off upon the world for Christianity.

For my part, I would say, welcome infidelity! welcome atheism! welcome anything! in preference to the gospel, *as preached by those Divines!* They convert the very name of reli-

gion into engine of tyranny and barbarous cruelty, and serve to confirm more infidels, in this age, than all the infidel writings of Thomas Paine, Voltaire, and Bolingbroke put together have done! These ministers make religion a cold and flinty-hearted thing, having neither principles of right action nor bowels of compassion. They strip the love of God of its beauty and leave the throne of religion a huge, horrible, repulsive form. It is a religion for oppressors, tyrants, man-stealers, and *thugs.* It is not that *"pure and undefiled religion"* which is from above, and which is *"first pure, then peaceable, easy to be entreated,* full of mercy and good fruits, *without partiality, and without hypocrisy."* But a religion which favors the rich against the poor; which exalts the proud above the humble; which divides mankind into two classes, tyrants and slaves; which says to the man in chains, *stay there;* and to the oppressor, *oppress on;* it is a religion which may be professed and enjoyed by all the robbers and enslavers of mankind; it makes God a respecter of persons, denies his fatherhood of the race, and tramples in the dust the great truth of the brotherhood of man. All this we affirm to be true of the popular church, and the popular worship of our land and nation— a religion, a church, and a worship which, on the authority of inspired wisdom, we pronounce to be an abomination in the sight of God. In the language of Isaiah, the American church might be well addressed, "Bring no more vain oblations; incense is an abomination unto me: the new moons and Sabbaths, the calling of assemblies, I cannot away with; it is iniquity, even the solemn meeting. Your new moons, and your appointed feast my soul hateth. They are a trouble to me; I am weary to bear them; and when ye spread forth your hands I will hide mine eyes from you. Yea! when ye make many prayers, I will not hear. YOUR HANDS ARE FULL OF BLOOD; cease to do evil, learn to do well; seek judgment; relieve the oppressed; judge for the fatherless; plead for the widow."

The American church is guilty, when viewed in connection with what it is doing to uphold slavery; but it is superlatively guilty when viewed in its connection with its ability to abolish slavery.

The sin of which it is guilty is one of omission as well as of commission. Albert Barnes but uttered what the common sense of every man at all observant of the actual state of the case will receive as truth, when he declared that "There is no power out of the church that could sustain slavery an hour, if it were not sustained in it."

Let the religious press, the pulpit, the Sunday School, the conference meeting, the great ecclesiastical, missionary, Bible and tract associations of the land array their immense powers against slavery, and slaveholding; and the whole system of crime and blood would be scattered to the winds, and that they do not do this involves them in the most awful responsibility of which the mind can conceive.

In prosecuting the anti-slavery enterprise, we have been asked to spare the church, to spare the ministry; but *how*, we ask, could such a thing be done? We are met on the threshold of our efforts for the redemption of the slave, by the church and ministry of the country, in battle arrayed against us; and we are compelled to fight or flee. From *what* quarter, I beg to know, has proceeded a fire so deadly upon our ranks, during the last two years, as from the Northern pulpit? As the champions of oppressors, the chosen men of American theology have appeared—men honored for their so-called piety, and their real learning. The LORDS of Buffalo, the SPRINGS of New York, the LATHROPS of Auburn, the COXES and SPENCERS of Brooklyn, the GANNETS and SHARPS of Boston, the DEWEYS of Washington, and other great religious lights of the land have, in utter denial of the authority of *Him* by whom they professed to be called to the ministry, deliberately taught us, against the example of the Hebrews, and against the remonstrance of the Apostles, *that we ought to obey man's law before the law of God.*

My spirit wearies of such blasphemy; and how such men can be supported, as the "standing types and representatives of Jesus Christ," is a mystery which I leave others to penetrate. In speaking of the American church, however, let it be distinctly understood that I mean the *great mass* of the religious organizations of our land. There are exceptions, and I thank God that there are. Noble men may be found, scattered all over these Northern States, of whom Henry Ward Beecher, of Brooklyn; Samuel J. May, of Syracuse; and my esteemed friend (Rev. R. R. Raymond) on the platform, are shining examples; and let me say further, that, upon these men lies the duty to inspire our ranks with high religious faith and zeal, and to cheer us on in the great mission of the slave's redemption from his chains.

One is struck with the difference between the attitude of the American church towards the anti-slavery movement, and that occupied by the churches in England towards a similar movement in that country. There, the church, true to its mission of ameliorating, elevating and improving the condition of mankind, came forward promptly, bound up the wounds of the West Indian slave, and restored him to his liberty. There, the question of emancipation was a high religious question. It was demanded in the name of humanity, and according to the law of the living God. The Sharps, the Clarksons, the Wilberforces, the Buxtons, the Burchells, and the Knibbs were alike famous for their prety and for their philanthropy. The anti-slavery movement *there* was not an anti-church movement, for the reason that the church took its full share in prosecuting that movement: and the anti-slavery movement in this country will cease to be an anti-church movement, when the church of this country shall assume a favorable instead of a hostile position towards that movement.

Americans! your republican politics, not less than your republican religion, are flagrantly inconsistent. You boast of your love of liberty, your superior civilization, and your pure Christianity, while the whole political power of the nation (as embodied in the two great political parties) is solemnly pledged to support and perpetuate the enslavement of three millions of your countrymen. You hurl your anathemas at the crowned headed tyrants of Russia and Austria and pride yourselves on your Democratic institutions, while you yourselves consent to be the mere *tools* and *body-guards* of the tyrants of Virginia and Carolina. You invite to your shores fugitives of oppression from abroad, honor them with banquets, greet them with ovations, cheer them, toast them, salute them, protect them, and pour out your money to them like water; but the fugitives from your own land you advertise, hunt, arrest, shoot, and kill. You glory in your refinement and your universal education; yet you maintain a system as barbarous and dreadful as ever stained the character of a nation—a system begun in avarice, supported in pride, and perpetuated in cruelty. You shed tears over fallen Hungary, and make the sad story of her wrongs the theme of your poets, statesmen, and orators, till your gallant sons are ready to fly to arms to vindicate her cause against the oppressor; but, in regard to the ten thousand wrongs of the American slave, you would enforce the strictest silence, and would hail him as an enemy of the nation who dares to make those wrongs the subject of public discourse! You are all on fire at the mention of liberty for France or for Ireland; but are as cold as an iceberg at the thought of liberty for the enslaved of America. You discourse eloquently on the dignity of labor; yet, you sustain a system which, in its very essence, casts a stigma upon labor. You can bare your bosom to the storm of British artillery to throw off a three-penny tax on tea; and yet wring the last hard earned farthing from the grasp of the black laborers of your country. You profess to believe "that, of one blood, God made all nations of men to dwell on the face of all the earth," and hath commanded all men, everywhere, to love one another; yet you notoriously hate (and glory in your hatred) all men whose skins are not colored like your own. You declare before the world, and are understood by the world to declare that you *"hold these truths to be self-evident, that all men are created equal; and are endowed by their Creator with certain inalienable*

rights; and that among these are, life, liberty, and the pursuit of happiness; and yet, you hold securely, in a bondage which, according to your own Thomas Jefferson, *"is worse than ages of that which your fathers rose in rebellion to oppose," a seventh part* of the inhabitants of your country.

Fellow-citizens, I will not enlarge further on your national inconsistencies. The existence of slavery in this country brands your republicanism as a sham, your humanity as a base pretense, and your Christianity as a lie. It destroys your moral power abroad; it corrupts your politicans at home. It saps the foundation of religion; it makes your name a hissing and a bye-word to a mocking earth. It is the antagonistic force in your government, the only thing that seriously disturbs and endangers your *Union.* It fetters your progress; it is the enemy of improvement; the deadly foe of education; it fosters pride; it breeds insolence; it promotes vice; it shelters crime; it is a curse to the earth that supports it; and yet you cling to it as if it were the sheet anchor of all your hopes. Oh! be warned! be warned! a horrible reptile is coiled up in your nation's bosom; the venomous creature is nursing at the tender breast of your youthful republic; *for the love of God, tear away,* and fling from you the hideous monster, and *let the weight of twenty millions crush and destroy it forever!*

But it is answered in reply to all this, that precisely what I have now denounced is, in fact, guaranteed and sanctioned by the Constitution of the United States; that, the right to hold, and to hunt slaves is a part of that Constitution framed by the illustrious Fathers of this Republic.

Then, I dare to affirm, notwithstanding all I have said before, your fathers stooped, basely stooped

> "To palter with us in a double sense:
> And keep the word of promise to the ear,
> But break it to the heart."

And instead of being the honest men I have before declared them to be, they were the veriest impostors that ever practised on mankind. This is the inevitable conclusion, and from it there is no escape; but I differ from those who charge this baseness on the framers of the Constitution of the United States. It is a slander upon their memory, at least, so I believe. There is not time now to argue the constitutional question at length; nor have I the ability to discuss it as it ought to be discussed. The subject has been handled with masterly power by Lysander Spooner, Esq., by William Goodell, by Samuel E. Sewall, Esq., and last, though not least, by Gerritt Smith, Esq. These gentlemen have, as I think, fully and clearly vindicated the Constitution from any design to support slavery for an hour.

Fellow-citizens! there is no matter in respect to which the people of the North have allowed themselves to be so ruinously imposed upon as that of the pro-slavery character of the Constitution. In that instrument I hold there is neither warrant, license, nor sanction of the hateful thing; but interpreted, as it ought to be interpreted, the Constitution is a GLORIOUS LIBERTY DOCUMENT. Read its preamble, consider its purposes. Is slavery among them? Is it at the gateway? or is it in the temple? it is neither. While I do not intend to argue this question on the present occasion, let me ask, if it be not somewhat singular that, if the Constitution were intended to be, by its framers and adopters, a slaveholding instrument, why neither slavery, slaveholding, nor slave can anywhere be found in it. What would be thought of an instrument, drawn up, legally drawn up, for the purpose of entitling the city of Rochester to a tract of land, in which no mention of land was made? Now, there are certain rules of interpretation for the proper understanding of all legal instruments. There rules are well established. They are plain, common-sense rules, such as you and I, and all of us, can understand and apply, without having passed years in the study of law. I scout the idea that the question of the constitutionality, or unconstitutionality of slavery, is not a question for the people. I hold that every American citizen has a right to form an opinion of the constitution, and to propagate that opinion, and to use all honorable means to make his opinion the prevailing one. Without this right, the liberty of an American citizen would be as insecure as that of a Frenchman. Ex-Vice-President Dallas tells us that the constitution is an object to which no American mind can be too attentive, and no American heart too devoted. He further says, the Constitution, in its words, is plain and intelligible, and is meant for the home-bred, unsophisticated understandings of our fellow-citizens. Senator Berrien tells us that the Constitution is the fundamental law, that which controls all others. The charter of our liberties, which every citizen has a personal interest in understanding thoroughly. The testimony of Senator Breese, Lewis Cass, and many others that might be named, who are everywhere esteemed as sound lawyers, so regard the constitution. I take it, therefore, that it is not presumption in a private citizen to form an opinion of that instrument.

Now, take the Constitution according to its plain reading, and I defy the presentation of a single pro-slavery clause in it. On the other hand, it will be found to contain principles and purposes, entirely hostile to the existence of slavery.

I have detained my audience entirely too long already. At some future period I will gladly avail myself of an opportunity to give this subject a full and fair discussion.

Allow me to say, in conclusion, notwithstanding the dark picture I have this day presented, of the state of the nation, I do not despair of this country. There are forces in operation which must inevitably work the downfall of slavery. "The arm of the Lord is not shortened," and the doom of slavery is certain. I, therefore, leave off where I began, with hope. While drawing encouragement from "the Declaration of Independence," the great principles it contains, and the genius of American Institutions, my spirit is also cheered by the obvious tendencies of the age. Nations do not now stand in the same relation to each other that they did ages ago.

No nation can now shut itself up from the surrounding world and trot round in the same old path of its fathers without interference. The time was when such could be done. Long established customs of hurtful character could formerly fence themselves in, and do their evil work with social impunity. Knowledge was then confined and enjoyed by the privileged few, and the multitude walked on in mental darkness. But a change has now come over the affairs of mankind. Walled cities and empires have become unfashionable. The arm of commerce has borne away the gates of the strong city. Intelligence is penetrating the darkest corners of the globe. It makes its pathway over and under the sea, as well as on the earth. Wind, steam, and lightning are its chartered agents. Oceans no longer divide, but link nations together. From Boston to London is now a holiday excursion. Space is comparatively annihilated.—Thoughts expressed on one side of the Atlantic are distinctly heard on the other.

Political Destiny of the Colored Race, on the American Continent

Martin Delany

TO THE COLORED INHABITANTS OF THE UNITED STATES

Fellow-Countrymen!—The duty assigned us is an important one, comprehending all that pertains to our destiny and that of our posterity—present and prospectively. And while it must be admitted, that the subject is one of the greatest magnitude, requiring all that talents, prudence and wisdom might adduce, and while it would be folly to pretend to give you the combined result of these three agencies, we shall satisfy ourselves with doing our duty to the best of our ability, and that in the plainest, most simple and comprehensive manner.

Our object, then, shall be to place before you our true position in this country—the United States,—the improbability of realizing our desires, and the sure, practicable and infallible remedy for the evils we now endure.

We have not addressed you as *citizens*—a term desired and ever cherished by us—because such you have never been. We have not addressed you as *freemen*,—because such privileges have never been enjoyed by any colored man in the United States. Why then should we flatter your credulity, by inducing you to believe that which neither has now, nor never before had an existence. Our oppressors are ever gratified at our manifest satisfaction, especially when that satisfaction is founded upon false premises; an assumption on our part, of the enjoyment of rights and privileges which never have been conceded, and which, according to the present system of the United States policy, we never can enjoy.

The *political policy* of this country was solely borrowed from, and shaped and modelled after, that of Rome. This was strikingly the case in the establishment of immunities,

Source: "Political Destiny of the Colored Race, on the American Continent," *Proceedings of the National Emigration Convention of Colored People.* (Philadelphia, 1854), pp. 33–43, 58–63, 69–70.

and the application of terms in their Civil and Legal regulations.

The term Citizen—politically considered—is derived from the Roman definition—which was never applied in any other sense—*Cives Ingenui;* which meant, one exempt from restraint of any kind. (*Cives,* a citizen; one who might enjoy the highest honors in his own free town—the town in which he lived—and in the country or commonwealth; and *Ingenui, freeborn*—of good extraction.) All who were deprived of citizenship—that is, the right of enjoying positions of honor and trust—were termed *Hostes* and *Peregrini;* which are public and private *enemies,* and foreigners, or *aliens* to the country. (*Hostis,* a public—and sometimes—private enemy: and *Peregrinus,* an *alien, stranger,* or *foreigner.*)

The Romans, from a national pride, to distinguish their inhabitants from those of other countries, termed them all "citizens," but consequently, were under the necessity of specifying four classes of citizens: none but the *Cives Ingenui* being unrestricted in their privileges. There was one class, called the *Jus Quiritium,* or the wailing or *supplicating* citizen—that is, one who was continually *moaning, complaining, or crying for aid or succor.* This class might also include within themselves, the *jus suffragii,* who had the privilege of *voting,* but no other privilege. They could vote for one of their superiors—the *Cives Ingenui*—but not for themselves.

Such, then, is the condition, precisely, of the black and colored inhabitants of the United States: in some of the States they answering to the latter class, having the privilege of *voting,* to elevate their superiors to positions to which they need never dare aspire, or even hope to attain.

There has, of late years, been a false impression obtained, that the privilege of *voting* constitutes, or necessarily embodies, the *rights of citizenship.* A more radical error never obtained favor among an oppressed people. Suffrage is an ambiguous term, which admits of several definitions. But according to strict political construction,

means simply "a vote, voice, approbation." Here, then, you have the whole import of the term suffrage. To have the "right of suffrage," as we rather proudly term it, is simply to have the *privilege*—there is no *right* about it—of giving our *approbation* to that which our *rulers may do,* without the privilege, on our part, of doing the same thing. Where such privileges are granted—privileges which are now exercised in but few of the States by colored men—we have but the privilege granted of saying, in common with others, who shall, for the time being, exercise *rights,* which in him, are conceded to be *inherent* and *inviolate:* Like the indented apprentice, who is summoned to give his approbation to an act which would be fully binding without his concurrence. Where there is no *acknowledged sovereignty,* there can be no binding power; hence, the suffrage of the black man, independently of the white, would be in this country unavailable.

Much might be adduced on this point to prove the insignificance of the black man, politically considered in this country, but we deem it wholly unnecessary at present, and consequently proceed at once to consider another feature of this important subject.

Let it then be understood, as a great principle of political economy, that no people can be free who themselves do not constitute an essential part of the *ruling element* of the country in which they live. Whether this element be founded upon a true or false, a just or an unjust basis; this position in community is necessary to personal safety. The liberty of no man is secure, who controls not his own political destiny. What is true of an individual, is true of a family; and that which is true of a family, is also true concerning a whole people. To suppose otherwise, is that delusion which at once induces its victim, through a period of long suffering, patiently to submit to every species of wrong; trusting against probability, and hoping against all reasonable grounds of expectation, for the granting of privileges and enjoyment of rights, which never will be attained. This delusion reveals the true secret of the power which holds in peaceable subjection, all the oppressed in every part of the world.

A people, to be free, must necessarily be *their own rulers:* that is, *each individual* must, in himself, embody the *essential ingredient*—so to speak—of the *sovereign principle* which composes the *true basis* of his liberty. This principle, when not exercised by himself, may, at his pleasure, be delegated to another—his true representative.

Said a great French writer: "A free agent, in a free government, should be his own governor," that is, he must possess within himself the *acknowledged right to govern:* this constitutes him a *governor,* though he may delegate to another the power to govern himself.

No one, then, can delegate to another a power he never possessed; that is, he cannot *give an agency* in that which he never had a right. Consequently, the colored man in the United States, being deprived of the right of inherent sovereignty, cannot *confer* a suffrage, because he possesses none to confer. Therefore, where there is no suffrage, there can neither be *freedom* nor *safety* for the disfranchised. And it is a futile hope to suppose that the agent of another's concerns, will take a proper interest in the affairs of those to whom he is under no obligations. Having no favors to ask or expect, he therefore has none to lose.

In other periods and parts of the world—as in Europe and Asia—the people being of one common, direct origin of race, though established on the presumption of difference by birth, or what was termed *blood,* yet the distinction between the superior classes and common people, could only be marked by the difference in the dress and education of the two classes. To effect this, the interposition of government was necessary; consequently, the costume and education of the people became a subject of legal restriction, guarding carefully against the privileges of the common people.

In Rome, the Patrician and Plebeian were orders in the ranks of her people—all of whom were termed citizens (*cives*)—recog-nized by the laws of the country; their dress and education being determined by law, the better to fix the distinction. In different parts of Europe, at the present day, if not the same, the distinction among the people is similar, only on a modified—and in some king-doms—probably more tolerant or deceptive policy.

In the United States, our degradation being once—as it has in a hundred instances been done—legally determined, our color is sufficient, independently of costume, education, or other distinguishing marks, to keep up that distinction.

In Europe, when an inferior is elevated to the rank of equality with the superior class, the law first comes to his aid, which, in its decrees, entirely destroys his identity as an inferior, leaving no trace of his former condition visible.

In the United States, among the whites, their color is made, by law and custom, the mark of distinction and superiority; while the color of the blacks is a badge of degradation, acknowledged by statute, organic law, and the common consent of the people.

With this view of the case—which we hold to be correct—to elevate to equality the degraded subject of law and custom, it can only be done, as in Europe, by an entire destruction of the identity of the former condition of the applicant. Even were this desirable—which we by no means admit—with the deep seated prejudices engendered by oppression, with which we have to contend, ages incalculable might reasonably be expected to roll around, before this could honorably be accomplished; otherwise, we should encourage and at once commence an indiscriminate concubinage and immoral commerce, of our mothers, sisters, wives and daughters, revolting to think of, and a physical curse to humanity.

If this state of things be to succeed, then, as in Egypt, under the dread of the inscrutable approach of the destroying angel, to appease the hatred of our oppressors, as a license to the passions of every white, let the lintel of each door of every black man, be stained with the blood of virgin purity and unsullied matron fidelity. Let it be written along the cornice in capitals, "The *will* of the white man is the rule of my household." Remove the protection to our chambers and nurseries, that the places once sacred, may henceforth become the unrestrained resort of the vagrant and rabble, always provided that the licensed commissioner of lust shall wear the indisputable impress of a *white* skin.

But we have fully discovered and comprehended the great political disease with which we are affected, the cause of its origin and continuance; and what is now left for us to do, is to discover and apply a sovereign remedy—a healing balm to a sorely diseased body—a wrecked but not entirely shattered system. We propose for this disease a remedy. That remedy is Emigration. This Emigration should be well advised, and like remedies applied to remove the disease from the physical system of man, skillfully and carefully applied, within the proper time, directed to operate on that part of the system, whose greatest tendency shall be, to benefit the whole.

Several geographical localities have been named, among which rank the Canadas. These we do not object to as places of temporary relief, especially to the fleeing fugitive—which, like a paliative, soothes for the time being the misery—but cannot commend them as permanent places upon which to fix our destiny, and that of our children, who shall come after us. But in this connexion, we would most earnestly recommend to the colored people of the United States generally, to secure by purchase all of the land they possibly can, while selling at low rates, under the British people and government. As that time may come, when, like the lands in the United States territories generally, if not as in Oregon and some other territories and States, they may be prevented entirely from settling or purchasing them; the preference being given to the white applicant.

And here, we would not deceive you by disguising the facts, that according to political tendency, the Canadas—as all British America—at no very distant day, are destined to come into the United States.

And were this not the case, the odds are against us, because the ruling element there, as in the United States, is, and ever must be, white—the population now standing, in all British America, two and a half millions of whites, to but forty thousand of the black race; or sixty-one and a fraction, whites, to one black!—the difference being eleven times greater than in the United States—so that colored people might never hope for anything more than to exist politically by mere suffrance—occupying a secondary position to the whites of the Canadas. The Yankees from this side of the lakes, are fast settling in the Canadas, infusing, with industrious success, all the malignity and Negro-hate, inseparable from their very being, as Christian Democrats and American advocates of equality.

Then, to be successful, our attention must be turned in a direction towards those places where the blacks and colored man comprise, by population, and constitute by necessity of numbers, the *ruling element* of the body politic. And where, when occasion shall require it, the issue can be made and maintained on this basis. Where our political enclosure and national edifice can be reared, established, walled, and proudly defended on this great elementary principle of original identity. Upon this solid foundation rests the fabric of every substantial political structure in the world, which cannot exist without it; and so soon as a people or nation lose their original identity, just so soon must that nation or people become extinct.—Powerful though they may have been, they must fall. Because the nucleus which heretofore held them together, becoming extinct, there being no longer a centre of attraction, or basis for a union of the parts, a dissolution must as naturally ensue, as the result of the nutrality of the basis of adhesion among the particles of matter.

This is the secret of the eventful downfall of Egypt, Carthage, Rome, and the former Grecian States, once so powerful—a loss of original identity; and with it, a loss of interest in maintaining their fundamental principles of nationality.

This, also, is the great secret of the present strength of Great Britain, Russia, the United States, and Turkey; and the endurance of the French nation, whatever its strength and power, is attributable only to their identity as Frenchmen.

And doubtless the downfall of Hungary, brave and noble as may be her people, is mainly to be attributed to the want of identity of origin, and consequently, a union of interests and purpose. This fact it might not have been expected would be admitted by the great Magyar, in his thrilling pleas for the restoration of Hungary, when asking aid, both national and individual, to enable him to throw off the ponderous weight placed upon their shoulders by the House of Hapsburg.

Hungary consisted of three distinct "races"—as they call themselves—of people, all priding in and claiming rights based on their originality—the Magyars, Celts, and Sclaves. On the encroachment of Austria, each one of these races—declaring for nationality—rose up against the House of Hapsburg, claiming the right of self-government, premised on their origin. Between the three a compromise was effected—the Magyars, being the majority, claimed the precedence. They made an effort, but the want of a unity of interests—and identity of origin, the noble Hungarians failed.—All know the result.

Nor is this the only important consideration. Were we content to remain as we are, sparsely interspersed among our white fellow-countrymen, we never might be expected to equal them in any honorable or respectable competition for a livelihood. For the reason that, according to the customs and policy of the country, we for ages would be kept in a secondary position, every situation of respectability, honor, profit or trust, either as mechanics, clerks, teachers, jurors, councilmen, or legislators, being filled by white men, consequently, our energies must become paralysed or enervated for the want of proper encouragement.

This example upon our children, and the colored people generally, is pernicious and degrading in the extreme. And how could it otherwise be, when they see every place of respectability filled and occupied by the whites, they pandering to their vanity, and existing among them merely as a thing of conveniency.

Our friends in this and other countries, anxious for our elevation, have for years been erroneously urging us to lose our identity as a distinct race, declaring that we were the same as other people; while at the very same time their own representative was traversing the world and propagating the doctrine in favor of a *universal Anglo-Saxon predominance*. The "Universal Brotherhood," so ably and eloquently advocated by that Polyglot Christian Apostle* of this doctrine, had established as its basis, a universal acknowledgment of the Anglo-Saxon rule.

The truth is, we are not identical with the Anglo-Saxon or any other race of the Caucasian or pure white type of the human family, and the sooner we know and acknowledge this truth, the better for ourselves and posterity.

The English, French, Irish, German, Italian, Turk, Persion, Greek, Jew, and all other races, have their native or inherent peculiarities, and why not our race? We are not willing, therefore, at all times and under all circumstances to be moulded into various shapes of eccentricity, to suit the caprices and conveniences of every kind of people. We are more suitable to everybody than everybody is suitable to us; therefore, no more like other people than others are like us.

We have then inherent traits, attributes—so to speak—and native characteristics, pe-

*Elihu Burritt.

culiar to our race—whether pure or mixed blood—and all that is required of us is to cultivate these and develope them in their purity, to make them desirable and emulated by the rest of the world.

That the colored races have the highest traits of civilization, will not be disputed. They are civil, peaceable and religious to a fault. In mathematics, sculpture and architecture, as arts and sciences, commerce and internal improvements as enterprises, the white race may probably excel; but in languages, oratory, poetry, music and painting as arts and sciences, and in ethics, metaphysics, theology and legal jurisprudence; in plain language—in the true principles of morals, correctness of thought, religion, and law or civil government, there is no doubt but the black race will yet instruct the world.

It would be duplicity longer to disguise the fact, that the great issue, sooner or later, upon which must be disputed the world's destiny, will be a question of black and white; and every individual will be called upon for his identity with one or the other. The blacks and colored races are four-sixths of all the population of the world; and these people are fast tending to a common cause with each other. The white races are but one-third of the population of the globe—or one of them to two of us—and it cannot much longer continue, that two-thirds will passively submit to the universal domination of this one-third. And it is notorious that the only progress made in territorial domain, in the last three centuries, by the whites, has been a usurpation and encroachment on the rights and native soil of some of the colored races.

The East Indies, Java, Sumatria, the Azores, Madeira, Canary, and Capo Verde Islands; Socotra, Guardifui and the Isle of France; Algiers, Tunis, Tripoli, Barca and Egypt in the North, Sierra Leon in the West, and Cape Colony in the South of Africa; besides many other Islands and possessions not herein named. Australia, the Ladrone Islands, together with many others of Oceania; the seizure and appropriation of a great portion of the Western Continent, with all its Islands, were so many encroachments of the whites upon the rights of the colored races. Nor are they yet content, but, intoxicated with the success of their career, the Sandwich Islands are now marked out as the next booty to be seized, in the ravages of their exterminating crusade.

We regret the necessity of stating the fact—but duty compels us to the task—that for more than two thousand years, the determined aim of the whites has been to crush the colored races wherever found. With a determined will, they have sought and pursued them in every quarter of the globe. The Anglo-Saxon has taken the lead in this work of universal subjugation. But the Anglo-American stands pre-eminent for deeds of injustice and acts of oppression, unparalleled perhaps in the annals of modern history.

We admit the existence of great and good people in America, England, France, and the rest of Europe, who desire a unity of interests among the whole human family, of whatever origin or race.

But it is neither the moralist, Christian, nor philanthropist whom we now have to meet and combat, but the politician—the civil engineer and skillful economist, who direct and control the machinery which moves forward with mighty impulse, the nations and powers of the earth. We must, therefore, if possible, meet them on vantage ground, or, at least, with adequate means for the conflict.

Should we encounter an enemy with artillery, a prayer will not stay the cannon shot; neither will the kind words nor smiles of philanthropy shield his spear from piercing us through the heart. We must meet mankind, then, as they meet us—prepared for the worst, though we may hope for the best. Our submission does not gain us an increase of friends nor respectability—as the white race will only respect those who oppose their usurpation, and acknowledge as equals those who will not submit to their rule. This may be no new discovery in political economy, but it certainly is a subject worthy the consideration of the black race.

After a due consideration of these facts, as herein recounted, shall we stand still and continue inactive—the passive observers of the great events of the times and age in which we live; submitting indifferently to the usurpation, by the white race, of every right belonging to the blacks? Shall the last vestage of an opportunity, outside of the continent of Africa, for the national development of our race, be permitted, in consequence of our slothfulness, to elude our grasp and fall into the possession of the whites? This, may Heaven forbid. May the sturdy, intelligent Africo-American sons of the Western Continent forbid.

Longer to remain inactive, it should be borne in mind, may be to give an opportunity to despoil us of every right and possession sacred to our existence, with which God has endowed us as a heritage on the earth. For let it not be forgotten, that the white race—who numbers but *one* of them to *two* of us—originally located in Europe, besides possessing all of that continent, have now got hold of a large portion of Asia, Africa, all North America, a portion of South America, and all of the great Islands of both Hemispheres, except Paupau, or New Guinea, inhabited by Negroes and Malays, in Oceanica; the Japanese Islands, peopled and ruled by the Japanese; Madigascar, peopled by Negroes, near the coast of Africa; and the Island of Haiti, in the West Indies, peopled by as brave and noble descendants of Africa, as they who laid the foundation of Thebias, or constructed the everlasting pyramids and catecombs of Egypt.—A people who have freed themselves by the might of their own will, the force of their own power, the unfailing strength of their own right arms, and their unflinching determination to be free.

Let us, then, not survive the disgrace and ordeal of Almighty displeasure, of two to one, witnessing the universal possession and control by the whites, of every habitable portion of the earth. For such must inevitably be the case, and that, too, at no distant day, if black men do not take advantage of the opportunity, by grasping hold of those places where chance is in their favor, and establishing the rights and power of the colored race.

We must make an issue, create an event, and establish for ourselves a position. This is essentially necessary for our effective elevation as a people, in shaping our national development, directing our destiny, and redeeming ourselves as a race.

If we but determine it shall be so, it *will* be so; and there is nothing under the sun can prevent it. We shall then be but in pursuit of our legitimate claims to inherent rights, bequeathed to us by the will of Heaven—the endowment of God, our common parent. A distinguished economist has truly said, "God has implanted in man an infinite progression in the career of improvement. A soul capacitated for improvement ought not to be bounded by a tyrant's landmarks." This sentiment is just and true, the application of which to our case, is adapted with singular fitness.

Having glanced hastily at our present political position in the world generally, and the United States in particular—the fundamental disadvantages under which we exist, and the improbability of ever attaining citizenship and equality of rights in this country—we call your attention next, to the places of destination to which we shall direct Emigration.

The West Indies, Central and South America, are the countries of our choices, the advantages of which shall be made apparent to your entire satisfaction.

Though we have designated them as countries, they are in fact but one country—relatively considered—a part of this, the Western Continent. . . .

There is but one question presents itself for our serious consideration, upon which we *must* give a decisive reply—Will we transmit as an inheritance to our children, the blessings of unrestricted civil liberty, or shall we entail upon them, as our only political legacy, the degradation and oppression left us by our fathers?

Shall we be persuaded that we can live and prosper nowhere but under the authority and power of our North American white oppressors; that this (the United States,) is the country most—if not the only one—favorable to our improvement and progress? Are we willing to admit that we are incapable of self-government, establishing for ourselves such political privileges, and making such internal improvements as we delight to enjoy, after American white men have made them for themselves?

No! Neither is it true that the United States is the country best adapted to *our* improvement. But that country is the best in which our manhood—morally, mentally and physically—can be *best developed*—in which we have an untrammeled right to the enjoyment of civil and religious liberty; and the West Indies, Central and South America, present now such advantages, superiorly preferable to all other countries.

That the continent of America was designed by Providence as a reserved asylum for the various oppressed people of the earth, of all races, to us seems very apparent.

From the earliest period after the discovery, various nations sent a representative here, either as adventurers and speculators, or employed laborers, seamen, or soldiers, hired to work for their employers. And among the earliest and most numerous class who found their way to the new world, were those of the African race. And it has been ascertained to our minds beyond a doubt, that when the Continent was discovered, there were found in the West Indies and Central America, tribes of the black race, fine looking people, having the usual characteristics of color and hair, identifying them as being originally of the African race; no doubt, being a remnant of the Africans who, with the Carthagenian expedition, were adventitiously cast upon this continent, in their memorable adventure to the "Great Island," after sailing many miles distant to the West

of the "Pillars of Hercules"—the present Straits of Gibralter.

We would not be thought to be superstitious, when we say, that in all this we can "see the finger of God." Is it not worthy of a notice here, that while the ingress of foreign white to this continent has been voluntary and constant, and that of the blacks involuntary and but occasional, yet the whites in the southern part have *decreased* in numbers, *degenerated* in character, and become mentally and physically *enervated* and imbecile; while the blacks and colored people have studiously *increased* in numbers, *regenerated* in character, and have grown mentally and physically vigorous and active, developing every function of their manhood, and are now, in their elementary character, decidedly superior to the white race? So then the white race could never successfully occupy the southern portion of the continent; they must of necessity, every generation, be repeopled from another quarter of the globe. The fatal error committed by the Spaniards, under Pizarro, was the attempt to exterminate the Incas and Peruvians, and fill their places by European whites. The Peruvian Indians, a hale, hardy, vigorous, intellectual race of people, were succeeded by those who soon became idle, vicious, degenerated and imbecile. But Peru, like all the other South American States, is regaining her former potency, just in proportion as the European race decreases among them. All the labor of the country is performed by the aboriginal natives and the blacks; the few Europeans there, being the merest excrescences on the body politic—consuming drones in the social hive.

Had we no other claims than those set forth in a foregoing part of this Address, they are sufficient to induce every black and colored person to remain on this continent, unshaken and unmoved.

But the West Indians, Central and South Americans, are a noble race of people; generous, sociable and tractible—just the people with whom we desire to unite, who are susceptible of progress, improvement and re-form of every kind. They now desire all the improvements of North America, but being justly jealous of their rights, they have no confidence in the whites of the United States, and consequently peremptorily refuse to permit an indiscriminate settlement among them of this class of people; but placing every confidence in the black and colored people of North America.

The example of the unjust invasion and forcible seizure of a large portion of the territory of Mexico, is still fresh in their memory; and the oppressive disfranchisement of a large number of native Mexicans, by the Americans—because of the color and race of the natives—will continue to rankle in the bosom of the people of those countries, and prove a sufficient barrier henceforth against the inroads of North American whites among them.

Upon the American continent, then, we are determined to remain despite every opposition that may be urged against us.

You will doubtless be asked—and that, too, with an air of seriousness—why, if desirable to remain on this continent, not be content to remain *in* the United States. The objections to this—and potent reasons, too, in our estimation—have already been clearly shown.

But notwithstanding all this, were there still any rational, nay, even the most futile grounds for hope, we still might be stupid enough to be content to remain, and yet through another period of unexampled patience and suffering, continue meekly to drag the galling yoke and clank the chain of servility and degradation. But whether or not in this, God is to be thanked and Heaven blessed, we are not permitted, despite our willingness and stupidity, to indulge even the most distant glimmer of a hope of attaining to the level of a well protected slave.

For years, we have been studiously and jealously observing the course of political events and policy, on the part of this country, both in a national and individual State capacity, as pursued toward the colored peo-ple. And he who, in the midst of them, can live with observation, is either excusably ignorant, or reprehensibly deceptious and untrustworthy.

We deem it entirely unnecessary to tax you with anything like the history of even one chapter of the unequalled infamies perpetrated on the part of the various States, and national decrees, by legislation, against us. But we shall call your particular attention to the more recent acts of the United States; because whatever privileges we may enjoy in any individual State, will avail nothing, when not recognized as such by the United States.

When the condition of the inhabitants of any country is fixed by legal grades of distinction, this condition can never be changed except by express legislation. And it is the height of folly to expect such express legislation, except by the inevitable force of some irresistible internal political pressure. The force necessary to this imperative demand on our part, we never can obtain, because of our numerical feebleness.

Were the interests of the common people identical with ours, we, in this, might succeed, because we, as a class, would then be numerically the superior. But this is not a question of the rich against the poor, nor the common people against the higher classes but a question of white against black—every white person, by legal right, being held superior to a black or colored person.

In Russia, the common people might obtain an equality with the aristocracy; because, of the sixty-five millions of her population, forty-five millions are serfs or peasants—leaving but twenty millions of the higher classes, royalty, nobility and all included.

The rights of no oppressed people have ever yet been obtained by a voluntary act of justice on the part of the oppressors. Christians, philanthropists, and moralists, may preach, argue and philosophise as they may to the contrary; facts are against them. Voluntary acts, it is true, which are in themselves just, may sometimes take place on the part of the oppressor; but these are always actuated by the force of some outward circumstances of self-interest, equal to a compulsion.

The boasted liberties of the American people were established by a Constitution, borrowed from and modeled after the British *magna charta.* And this great charter of British liberty, so much boasted of and vaunted as a model bill of rights, was obtained only by force and extortion.

The Barons, an order of noblemen, under the reign of King John, becoming dissatisfied at the terms submitted to by their sovereign, which necessarily brought degradation upon themselves—terms prescribed by the insolent Pope Innocent III, the haughty sovereign Pontiff of Rome; summoned his majesty to meet them on the plains of the memorable meadow of Runnimede, where presenting to him their own Bill of Rights—a bill dictated by themselves, and drawn up by their own hands—at the unsheathed points of a thousand glittering swords, they commanded him, against his will, to sign the extraordinary document. There was no alternative; he must either do or die. With a puerile timidity, he leaned forward his rather commanding but imbecile person, and with a trembling hand and single dash of the pen, the name King John stood forth in bold relief, sending more terror throughout the world, than the mystic hand-writing of Heaven throughout the dominions of Nebuchadnezzar, blazing on the walls of Babylon. A consternation, not because of the *name* of the King, but because of the rights of *others,* which the name acknowledged.

The King, however, soon became dissatisfied, and determining on a revocation of the act—an act done entirely contary to his will—at the head of a formidable army, spread fire and sword throughout the kingdom.

But the Barons, though compelled to leave their castles—their houses and homes—and fly for their lives, could not be induced to undo that which they had so nobly done; the achievement of their rights and privileges. Hence, the act has stood throughout all suc-

ceeding time, because never annulled by those who *willed* it.

It will be seen that the first great modern Bill of Rights was obtained only by a force of arms: a resistence of the people against the injustice and intolerance of their rulers. We say the people—because that which the Barons demanded for themselves, was afterwards extended to the common people. Their only hope was based on their *superiority of numbers.*

But can we in this country hope for as much? Certainly not.—Our case is a hopeless one. There was but *one* John, with his few sprigs of adhering royalty; and but *one* heart at which the threatening points of their swords were directed by a thousand Barons; while in our case, there is but a handful of the oppressed, without a sword to point, and *twenty millions* of Johns or Jonathans—as you please—with as many hearts, tenfold more relentless than that of Prince John Lackland, and as deceptious and hypocritical as the Italian heart of Innocent III.

Where, then, is our hope of success in this country? Upon what is it based? Upon what principle of political policy and sagacious discernment, do our political leaders and acknowledged great men—colored men we mean—justify themselves by telling us, and insisting that we shall believe them, and submit to what they say—to be patient, remain where we are; that there is a "bright prospect and glorious future" before us in this country! May Heaven open our eyes from their Bartemian obscurity.

But we call your attention to another point of our political degradation. The acts of State and general governments.

In a few of the States, as in New York, the colored inhabitants have a partial privilege of voting a white man into office. This privilege is based on a property qualification of two hundred and fifty dollars worth of real estate. In others, as in Ohio, in the absence of organic provision, the privilege is granted by judicial decision, based on a ratio of blood, of an admixture of more than one-half white; while in many of the States, there is no privilege allowed, either partial or unrestricted.

The policy of the above named States will be seen and detected at a glance, which while seeming to extend immunities, is intended especially for the object of degradation.

In the State of New York, for instance, there is a constitutional distinction created among colored men—almost necessarily compelling one part to feel superior to the other; while among the whites no such distinctions dare be known. Also, in Ohio, there is a legal distinction set up by an upstart judiciary, creating among the colored people, a privileged class by birth! All this must necessarily sever the cords of union among us, creating almost insurmountable prejudices of the most stupid and fatal kind, paralysing the last bracing nerve which promised to give us strength.

It is upon this same principle, and for the self same object, that the General Government has long been endeavoring, and is at present knowingly designing to effect a recognition of the independence of the Dominican Republic, while disparagingly refusing to recognize the independence of the Haitien nation—a people four-fold greater in numbers, wealth and power. The Haitiens, it is pretended, are refused because they are *Negroes* while the Dominicans, as is well known to all who are familiar with the geography, history, and political relations of that people, are identical—except in language, they speaking the Spanish tongue—with those of the Haitiens; being composed of Negroes and a mixed race. The government may shield itself by the plea that it is not familiar with the origin of those people. To this we have but to reply, that if the government is thus ignorant of the relations of its near neighbors, it is the heighth of presumption, and no small degree of assurance, for it to set up itself as capable of prescribing terms to the one, or conditions to the other.

Should they accomplish their object, they then will have succeeded in forever establishing a barrier of impassable separation, by the creation of a political distinction between those people, of superiority and inferiority of origin or national existence. Here, then, is another strategem of this most determined and untiring enemy of our race—the government of the United States.

We come now to the crowning act of infamy on the part of the General Government towards the colored inhabitants of the United States—an act so vile in its nature, that rebellion against its demands should be promptly made, in every attempt to enforce its infernal provisions.

In the history of national existence, there is not to be found a parallel to the tantalising and aggravating despotism of the provisions of Millard Fillmore's Fugitive Slave Bill, passed by the thirty-third Congress of the United States, with the approbation of a majority of the American people, in the year of the Gospel of Jesus Christ, eighteen hundred and fifty.

This Bill had but one object in its provisions, which was fully accomplished in its passage; that is the reduction of every colored person in the United States—save those who carry free papers of emancipation, or bills of sale from former claimants or owners—to a state of relative *slavery*; placing each and every one of us at the *disposal of any and every white* who might choose to *claim* us, and the caprice of any and every upstart knave bearing the title of "Commissioner."

Did any of you, fellow-countrymen, reside in a country the provisions of whose laws were such that any person of a certain class, who whenever he, she or they pleased might come forward, lay a claim to, make oath before (it might be,) some stupid and heartless person, authorized to decide in such cases, and take, at their option, your horse, cow, sheep, house and lot, or any other property, bought and paid for by your own earnings—the result of your personal toil and labor—would you be willing, or could you be induced, by any reasoning, however great the source from which it came, to remain in that country? We pause, fellow-countrymen, for a reply.

If there be not one yea, of how much more importance, then, is your *own personal safety,* than that of property? Of how much more concern is the safety of a wife or husband, than that of a cow or horse; a child, than a sheep; the destiny of your family, to that of a house and lot?

And yet this is precisely our condition. Any one of us, at any moment, is liable to be *claimed, seized* and *taken* into custody by the white as his or her property—to be *enslaved for life*—and there is no remedy, because it is the *law of the land!* And we dare predict, and take this favorable opportunity to forewarn you, fellow-countrymen, that the time is not far distant, when there will be carried on by the white men of this nation, an extensive commerce in the persons of what now compose the free colored people of the North. We forewarn you, that the general enslavement of the whole of this class of people, is now being contemplated by the whites.

At present, we are liable to enslavement at any moment, provided we are taken *away* from our homes. But we dare venture further to forewarn you, that the scheme is in mature contemplation and has even been mooted in high places, of harmonizing the two discordant political divisions in the country, by again reducing the free to slave States.

The completion of this atrocious scheme, only becomes necessary for each and every one of us to find an owner and master at our own doors. Let the general government but pass such a law, and the States will comply as an act of harmony. Let the South but *demand* it, and the North will comply as a *duty* of compromise.

If Pennsylvania, New York and Massachusetts can be found arming their sons as watchdogs for southern slave hunters; if the United States may, with impunity, garrison with troops the Court House of the freest city in America; blockade the streets; station armed ruffians of dragoons, and spiked artillery in

hostile awe of the people; if free, white, high-born and bred gentlemen of Boston and New York, are smitten down to the earth,* refused an entrance on professional business, into the Court Houses, until inspected by a slave hunter and his counsel; all to put down the liberty of the black man; then, indeed, is there no hope for us in this country! . . .

That, then, which is left for us to do, is to *secure* our liberty; a position which shall fully *warrant* us *against* the *liability* of such monstrous political crusade and riotous invasions of our rights.—Nothing less than a national indemnity, indelibly fixed by virtue of our own sovereign potency, will satisfy us as a redress of grievances for the unparalleled wrongs, undisguised impositions, and unmitigated oppression, which we have suffered at the hands of this American people.

And what wise politician would otherwise conclude and determine? None we dare say. And a people who are incapable of this discernment and precaution, are incapable of self-government, and incompetent to direct their own political destiny. For our own part, we spurn to treat for liberty on any other terms or conditions.

It may not be inapplicable, in this particular place, to quote from high authority, lan-

---

*John Jay, Esq., of New York, son of the late distinguished jurist, Hon. Wm. Jay, was, in 1852, as the counsel of a Fugitive Slave brutally assaulted and struck in the face by the slave catching agent and counsel, Busteed.

Also, Mr. Dana, an honorable gentleman, counsel for the fugitive Burns, one of the first literary men of Boston, was arrested on his entrance into the Court House, and not permitted to pass the guard of slave catchers, till the slave agent and counsel, Loring, together with the overseer, Suttle, *inspected* him, and ordered that he might be *allowed* to pass in! After which, in passing along the street, Mr. Dana was ruffianly assaulted and murderously fallen to the earth, by the minions of the dastardly southern overseer.

guage which has fallen under our notice, since this report has been under consideration. The quotation is worth nothing, except to show that the position assumed by us, is a natural one, which constitutes the essential basis of self-protection.

Said Earl Aberdeen recently in the British House of Lords, when referring to the great question which is now agitating Europe:— "One thing alone is certain, that the only way to obtain a sure and honorable peace, is to *acquire a position* which may *command it;* and to gain such a position *every nerve and sinew* of the empire should be strained. The pickpocket who robs us is not to be let off because he offers to restore our purse," and his Grace might have justly added, "should never thereafter be entrusted or confided in."

The plea doubtless will be, as it already frequently has been raised, that to remove from the United States, our slave brethren would be left without a hope. They already find their way in large companies to the Canadas, and they have only to be made sensible that there is as much freedom for them South, as there is North; as much protection in Mexico as in Canada and the fugitive slave will find it a much pleasanter journey and more easy of access, to wend his way from Louisiana and Arkansas to Mexico, than thousands of miles through the slaveholders of the South and slave-catchers of the North, to Canada. Once into Mexico, and his farther exit to Central and South America and the West Indies, would be certain. There would be no obstructions whatever. No miserable, half-starved, servile Northern slave-catchers by the way, waiting cap in hand, ready and willing to do the bidding of their contemptible southern masters.

No prisons, nor Court Houses, as slave-pens and garrisons, to secure the fugitive and rendezvous the mercenary gangs, who are bought as military on such occasions. No perjured Marshals, bribed Commissioners, nor hireling counsel, who, spaniel-like, crouch at the feet of Southern slave-holders, and cringingly tremble at the crack of their whip. No,

not as may be encountered throughout his northern flight, there are none of these to be found or met with in his travels from the Bravo del Norte to the dashing Oronoco— from the borders of Texas to the boundaries of Peru.

Should anything occur to prevent a successful emigration to the South—Central, South America and the West Indies—we have no hesitancy, rather than remain in the United States, the merest subordinates and serviles of the whites, should the Canadas still continue separate in their political relations from this country, to recommend to the great body of our people, to remove to Canada West, where being politically equal to the whites, physically united with each other by a concentration of strength; when worse comes to worse, we may be found, not as a scattered, weak and impotent people, as we now are separated from each other throughout the Union, but a united and powerful body of freemen, mighty in politics, and terrible in any conflict which might ensue, in the event of an attempt at the disturbance of our political relations, domestic repose, and peaceful firesides.

Now, fellow-countrymen, we have done. Into your ears have we recounted your own sorrows; before your own eyes have we exhibited your wrongs; into your own hands have we committed your own cause. If there should prove a failure to remedy this dreadful evil, to assuage this terrible curse which has come upon us; the fault will be yours and not ours; since we have offered you a healing balm for every sorely aggravated wound.

Martin R. Delany, Pa.
William Webb, Pa.
Augustus R. Green, Ohio
Edward Butler, Mo.
H. S. Douglass, La.
A. Dudley, Wis.
Conaway Barbour, Ky.
Wm. J. Fuller, R. I.
Wm. Lambert, Mich.
J. Theodore Holly, N. Y.
T. A. White, Ind.
John A. Warren, Canada

Address to a Meeting in Boston

John S. Rock

Ladies and Gentlemen: You will not expect a lengthened speech from me to-night. My health is too poor to allow me to indulge much in speech-making. But I have not been able to resist the temptation to unite with you in this demonstration of respect for some of my noble but misguided ancestors.

White Americans have taken great pains to try to prove that we are cowards. We are often insulted with the assertion, that if we had had the courage of the Indians or the white man, we would never have submitted to be slaves. I ask if Indians and white men have never been slaves? The white man tested the Indian's courage here when he had his organized armies, his battle-grounds, his places of retreat, with everything to hope for and everything to lose. The position of the African slave has been very different. Seized a prisoner of war, unarmed, bound hand and foot, and conveyed to a distant country among what to him were worse than cannibals; brutally beaten, half-starved, closely watched by armed men, with no means of knowing their own strength or the strength of their enemies, with no weapons, and without a probability of success. But if the white man will take the trouble to fight the black man in Africa or in Hayti, and fight him as fair as the black man will fight him there—if the black man does not come off victor, I am deceived in his prowess. But, take a man, armed or unarmed, from his home, his country, or his friends, and place him among savages, and who is he that would not make good his retreat? 'Discre-

tion is the better part of valor,' but for a man to resist where he knows it will destroy him, shows more fool-hardiness than courage. There have been many Anglo-Saxons and Anglo-Americans enslaved in Africa, but I have never heard that they successfully resisted any government. They always resort to running indispensables.

The courage of the Anglo-Saxon is best illustrated in his treatment of the negro. A score or two of them can pounce upon a poor negro, tie and beat him, and then call him a coward because he submits. Many of their most brilliant victories have been achieved in the same manner. But the greatest battles which they have fought have been upon paper. We can easily account for this; their trumpeter is dead. He died when they used to be exposed for sale in the Roman market, about the time that Cicero cautioned his friend Atticus not to buy them, on account of their stupidity. A little more than half a century ago, this race, in connection with their Celtic neighbors, who have long been considered (by themselves, of course,) the bravest soldiers in the world, so far forgot themselves, as to attack a few cowardly, stupid negro slaves, who, according to their accounts, had not sense enough to go to bed. And what was the result? Why, sir, the negroes drove them out from the island like so many sheep, and they have never dared to show their faces, except with hat in hand.

Our true and tried friend, Rev. Theodore Parker, said, in his speech at the State House, a few weeks since, that 'the stroke of the axe would have settled the question long ago, but the black man would not strike.' Mr. Parker makes a very low estimate of the courage of his race, if he means that one, two, or three millions of these ignorant

Source: John S. Rock, "Address to a Meeting in Boston." In *Liberator* (March 12, 1858).

and cowardly black slaves could without means, have brought to their knees five, ten, or twenty millions of intelligent, brave white men, backed up by a rich oligarchy. But I know of no one who is more familiar with the true character of the Anglo-Saxon race than Mr. Parker. I will not dispute this point with him, but I will thank him or any one else to tell us how it could have been done. His remark calls to my mind the day which is to come, when one shall chase a thousand, and two put ten thousand to flight. But when he says that 'the black man *would not* strike,' I am prepared to say that he does us great injustice. The black man is not a coward. The history of the bloody struggles for freedom in Hayti, in which the blacks whipped the French and the English, and gained their independence, in spite of the perfidy of that villainous First Consul, will be a lasting refutation of the malicious aspersions of our enemies. The history of the struggles for the liberty of the U.S. ought to silence every American calumniator. I have learned that even so late as the Texan war, a number of black men were silly enough to offer themselves as living sacrifices for our country's shame. A gentleman who delivered a lecture before the New York Legislature, a few years since, whose name I do not now remember, but whose language I give with some precision, said, 'In the Revolution, colored soldiers fought side by side with you in your struggles for liberty, and there is not a battlefield from Maine to Georgia that has not been crimsoned with their blood, and whitened with their bones.' In 1814, a bill passed the Legislature of New York, accepting the services of 2000 colored volunteers. Many black men served under Com. McDonough when he conquered on lake Champlain. Many were in the battles of Plattsburgh and Sackett's Harbor, and General Jackson called out colored troops from Louisiana and Alabama, and in a solemn proclamation attested to their fidelity and courage.

The white man contradicts himself who says, that if he were in our situation, he would throw off the yoke. Thirty millions of white men of this proud Caucasian race are at this moment held as slaves, and bought and sold with horses and cattle. The iron heel of oppression grinds the masses of all European races to the dust. They suffer every kind of oppression, and no one dares to open his mouth to protest against it. Even in the Southern portion of this boasted land of liberty, no white man dares advocate so much of the Declaration of Independence as declares that 'all men are created free and equal, and have an inalienable right to life, liberty,' &c.

White men have no room to taunt us with tamely submitting. If they were black men, they would work wonders; but, as white men, they can do nothing. 'O, Consistency, thou art a jewel!'

Now, it would not be surprising if the brutal treatment which we have received for the past two centuries should have crushed our spirits. But this is not the case. Nothing but a superior force keeps us down. And when I see the slaves rising up by hundreds annually, in the majesty of human nature, bidding defiance to every slave code and its penalties, making the issue Canada or death, and that too while they are closely watched by paid men armed with pistols, clubs and bowic-knives, with the army and navy of this great Model Republic arrayed against them, I am disposed to ask if the charge of cowardice does not come with ill-grace.

But some men are so steeped in folly and imbecility; so lost to all feelings of their own littleness; so destitute of principle, and so regardless of humanity, that they dare attempt to destroy everything which exists in opposition to their interests or opinions which their narrow comprehensions cannot grasp.

We ought not to come here simply to honor those brave men who shed their blood for freedom, or to protest against the Dred Scott decision, but to take counsel of each other, and to enter into new vows of duty. Our fathers fought nobly for freedom, but they were not victorious. They fought for liberty, but they got slavery. The white man was benefitted, but the black man was injured. I do not envy the white American the little liberty which he enjoys. It is his right, and he ought to have it. I wish him success, though I do not think he deserves it. But I would have all men free. We have had much sad experience in this country, and it would be strange indeed if we do not profit by some of the lessons which we have so dearly paid for. Sooner or later, the clashing of arms will be heard in this country, and the black man's services will be needed: 150,000 freemen capable of bearing arms, and not all cowards and fools, and three quarters of a million slaves, wild with the enthusiasm caused by the dawn of the glorious opportunity of being able to strike a genuine blow for freedom, will be a power which white men will be "bound to respect." Will the blacks fight? Of course they will. The black man will never be neutral. He could not if he would, and he would not if he could. Will he fight for this country, right or wrong? This the common sense of every one answers; and when the time comes, and come it will, the black man will give an intelligent answer. Judge Taney may outlaw us; Caleb Cushing may show the depravity of his heart by abusing us; and this wicked government may oppress us; but the black man will live when Judge Taney, Caleb Cushing and this wicked government are no more. White man may despise, ridicule, slander and abuse us; they may seek as they always have done to divide us, and make us feel degraded; but no man shall cause me to turn my back upon my race. With it I will sink or swim.

The prejudice which some white men have, or affected to have, against my color gives me no pain. If any man does not fancy my color, that is his business, and I shall not meddle with it. I shall give myself no trouble because he lacks good taste. If he judges my intellectual capacity by my color, he certainly cannot expect much profundity, for it is only skin deep, and is really of no very great importance to any one but myself. I will not deny that I admire the talents and noble characters of many white men. But I cannot say that I am particularly pleased with their physical appearance. If old mother nature had held out as well as she commenced, we should, probably, have had fewer varieties in the races. When I contrast the fine tough muscular system, the beautiful, rich color, the full broad features, and the gracefully frizzled hair of the Negro, with the delicate physical organization wan color, sharp features and lank hair of the Caucasian, I am inclined to believe that when the white man was created, nature was pretty well exhausted—but determined to keep up appearances, she pinched up his features and did the best she could under the circumstances. (Great laughter.)

I would have you understand, that I not only love my race, but am pleased with my color; and while many colored persons may feel degraded by being called negroes, and wish to be classed among other races more favored, I shall feel it my duty, my pleasure and my pride, to concentrate my feeble efforts in elevating to a fair position a race to which I am especially identified by feelings and by blood.

My friends, we can never become elevated until we are true to ourselves. We can come here and make brilliant speches, but our field of duty is elsewhere. Let us go to work—each man in his place, determined to do what he can for himself and his race. Let us try to carry out some of the resolutions which we have made, and are so fond of making. If we do this, friends will spring up in every quarter, and where we least expect them. But we must not rely on them. They cannot elevate us. Whenever the colored man is elevated, it will be by his own exertions. Our friends can do what many of them are nobly doing, assist us to remove the obstacles which prevent our elevation, and stimulate the worthy to persevere. The colored man who, by dint of perseverance and industry, educates and elevates himself, prepares the way for others, gives character to the race, and hastens the day of general emancipation. While the negro who hangs around the corners of the streets, or lives in the grog-shops or by gambling, or who has no higher ambition than to serve, is by his vocation forging fetters for the slave, and is 'to all intents and purposes' a curse to his race. It is true, considering the circumstances under which we have been placed by our white neighbors, we have a right to ask them not only to cease to oppress us, but to give us that encouragement which our talents and industry may merit. When this is done, they will see our minds expand, and our pockets filled with rocks. How very few colored men are encouraged in their trades or business! Our young men see this, and become disheartened. In this country, where money is the great sympathetic nerve which ramifies society, and has a ganglia in every man's pocket, a man is respected in proportion to his success in business. When the avenues to wealth are opened to us, we will then become educated and wealthy, and then the roughest looking colored man that you ever saw, or ever will see, will be pleasanter than the harmonies of Orpheus, and black will be a very pretty color. It will make our jargon, wit—our words, oracles; flattery will then take the place of slander, and you will find no prejudice in the Yankee whatever. We do not expect to occupy a much better position than we now do, until we shall have our educated and wealthy men, who can wield a power that cannot be misunderstood. Then, and not till then, will the tongue of slander be silenced, and the lip of prejudice sealed. Then, and not till then, will we be able to enjoy true equality, which can exist only among peers.

SUGGESTED READINGS

Leonard P. Curry, *The Free Black in Urban America, 1800–1850: The Shadow of the Dream* (Chicago, 1981)

Eddie S. Glaude, Jr. *Exodus! Religion, Race, and Nation in Early Nineteenth-Century Black America* (Chicago, 1999)

Stanley Harrold, *Subversives: Antislavery Community in Washington, D.C., 1820–1865* (Baton Rouge, La., 2003)

Peter P. Hinks, *To Awaken My Afflicted Brethren: David Walker and the Problem of Antebellum Slave Resistance* (University Park, Pa., 1997)

Graham Russell Hodges, *Root and Branch: African Americans in New York and East Jersey, 1613–1863* (Chapel Hill, N.C., 1999)

James Oliver and Lois P. Horton, *In Hope of Liberty: Culture, Community, and Protest Among Northern Free Blacks, 1700–1860* (New York, 1997)

Leon F. Litwack, *North of Slavery: The Negro in the Free States, 1790–1860* (Chicago, 1961)

Waldo E. Martin, Jr., *The Mind of Frederick Douglass* (Chapel Hill, N.C., 1984)

Gary Nash, *Forging Freedom: The Formation of Philadelphia's Black Community, 1720–1840* (Cambridge, Mass., 1988)

Benjamin Quarles, *Black Abolitionists* (New York, 1969)

Patrick Rael, *Black Identity and Black Protest in the Antebellum North* (Chapel Hill, N.C., 2002)

Harry Reed, *Platform for Change: The Foundations of the Northern Free Black Community, 1775–1865* (East Lansing, Mich., 1994)

John Stauffer, *The Black Hearts of Men: Radical Abolitionists and the Transformation of Race* (Cambridge, Mass., 2002)

Julie Winch, *A Gentleman of Color: The Life of James Forten* (Cambridge, Mass., 2002)

Shirley J. Yee, *Black Women Abolitionists: A Study in Activism, 1828–1860* (Knoxville, Tenn., 1992)

COME AND JOIN US BROTHERS.
PUBLISHED BY THE SUPERVISORY COMMITTEE FOR RECRUITING COLORED REGIMENTS
1210 CHESTNUT ST. PHILADELPHIA.

A recruitment poster for African Americans during the Civil War depicts a regiment of black Union soldiers adjacent to their white commander. (*Source:* The Chicago Historical Socety.)

Chapter 5

The Negro's Civil War

The rise of the sectional conflict over the expansion of slavery in the trans-Mississippi West forced the issue of slavery into the center of national politics after the Mexican War. The struggle for the abolition of slavery and the actions of the slaves themselves also made most Americans, north and south, confront the problem of racial slavery. The first two documents in this chapter, the "Fugitive Slave Act" and the "Dred Scott Decision," represent two important instances of contestation between the north and south and were brought on by the actions of African Americans. Slave runaways created the fugitive slave problem, and Dred Scott in suing for his freedom made the United States Supreme Court comment on African American citizenship and the sectional dispute over the expansion of slavery.

During the Civil War, thousands of slaves ran into Union Army lines and forced the antislavery Lincoln administration to move on emancipation. The testimony of the Superintendent of contrabands, as runaway slaves were called, gives evidence of this flight of slaves from southern plantations to the Union Army encampments. The historic Emancipation Proclamation issued by Abraham Lincoln, who had always expressed his moral abhorrence of slavery, made the war for the Union into a war against slavery. The two Civil War spirituals reveal slaves' reaction to freedom, or as they called it, "the Day of Jubilee," vesting emancipation with religious and historical significance. The speech of Frederick Douglass asking black men to enlist in the Union Army and the description of black Union soldiers' bravery in the Battle of Port Hudson are indicative of the black military experience. Around 180,000 black soldiers, most of them former slaves, served in the Union Army and another ten thousand black men served in the Union Navy. The three Civil War Songs, the "Battle Hymn of the Republic," and two versions of it, "John Brown's Body" and the "Marching Song of the First Arkansas Colored Regiment," reveal the abolitionist and African American understanding of the war as a war for the liberation of the slaves. The last two selections from Susie King Taylor and Elizabeth Keckley detail the wartime experiences of two black women. Taylor lived in an army camp during the Civil War, and Keckley gained notoriety as Mary Todd Lincoln's personal dressmaker. The Civil War has often been called the second American Revolution, as emancipation, in Lincoln's memorable words, gave rise "to a new birth of freedom" in the American Republic. However, as Taylor King's memoirs reveal, black Americans saw their rights systematically denied in the south after the Civil War and Reconstruction, and the expectation for freedom and racial equality raised by emancipation were fulfilled only in the twentieth century with the success of the Civil Rights Movement.

The Fugitive Slave Act, 1850

Be it enacted by the Senate and House of Representatives of the United States of America in Congress assembled, That the persons who have been, or may hereafter be, appointed commissioners, in virtue of any act of Congress, by the Circuit Courts of the United States, and Who, in consequence of such appointment, are authorized to exercise the powers that any justice of the peace, or other magistrate of any of the United States, may exercise in respect to offenders for any crime or offense against the United States, by arresting, imprisoning, or bailing the same under and by the virtue of the thirty-third section of the act of the twenty-fourth of September seventeen hundred and eighty-nine, entitled "An Act to establish the judicial courts of the United States" shall be, and are hereby, authorized and required to exercise and discharge all the powers and duties conferred by this act.

SEC. 2. And be it further enacted, That the Superior Court of each organized Territory of the United States shall have the same power to appoint commissioners to take acknowledgments of bail and affidavits, and to take depositions of witnesses in civil causes, which is now possessed by the Circuit Court of the United States; and all commissioners who shall hereafter be appointed for such purposes by the Superior Court of any organized Territory of the United States, shall possess all the powers, and exercise all the duties, conferred by law upon the commissioners appointed by the Circuit Courts of the United States for similar purposes, and shall moreover exercise and discharge all the powers and duties conferred by this act.

SEC. 3. And be it further enacted, That the Circuit Courts of the United States shall from time to time enlarge the number of the commissioners, with a view to afford reasonable facilities to reclaim fugitives from labor, and to the prompt discharge of the duties imposed by this act.

SEC. 4. And be it further enacted, That the commissioners above named shall have concurrent jurisdiction with the judges of the Circuit and District Courts of the United States, in their respective circuits and districts within the several States, and the judges of the Superior Courts of the Territories, severally and collectively, in term-time and vacation; shall grant certificates to such claimants, upon satisfactory proof being made, with authority to take and remove such fugitives from service or labor, under the restrictions herein contained, to the State or Territory from which such persons may have escaped or fled.

SEC. 5. And be it further enacted, That it shall be the duty of all marshals and deputy marshals to obey and execute all warrants and precepts issued under the provisions of this act, when to them directed; and should any marshal or deputy marshal refuse to receive such warrant, or other process, when tendered, or to use all proper means diligently to execute the same, he shall, on conviction thereof, be fined in the sum of one thousand dollars, to the use of such claimant, on the motion of such claimant, by the Circuit or District Court for the district of such marshal; and after arrest of such fugitive, by such marshal or his deputy, or whilst at any time in his custody under the provisions of this act, should such fugitive escape, whether with or without the assent of such marshal or his deputy, such marshal shall be liable, on his official bond, to be prosecuted for the benefit of such claimant, for the full value of the service or labor of said fugitive in the State, Territory, or District whence he escaped: and the better to enable the said commissioners, when thus appointed, to execute their duties faithfully and efficiently, in conformity with the re-

Source: The Fugitive Slave Act, 1850.

quirements of the Constitution of the United States and of this act, they are hereby authorized and empowered, within their counties respectively, to appoint, in writing under their hands, any one or more suitable persons, from time to time, to execute all such warrants and other process as may be issued by them in the lawful performance of their respective duties; with authority to such commissioners, or the persons to be appointed by them, to execute process as aforesaid, to summon and call to their aid the bystanders, or posse comitatus of the proper county, when necessary to ensure a faithful observance of the clause of the Constitution referred to, in conformity with the provisions of this act; and all good citizens are hereby commanded to aid and assist in the prompt and efficient execution of this law, whenever their services may be required, as aforesaid, for that purpose; and said warrants shall run, and be executed by said officers, any where in the State within which they are issued.

SEC. 6. And be it further enacted, That when a person held to service or labor in any State or Territory of the United States, has heretofore or shall hereafter escape into another State or Territory of the United States, the person or persons to whom such service or labor may be due, or his, her, or their agent or attorney, duly authorized, by power of attorney, in writing, acknowledged and certified under the seal of some legal officer or court of the State or Territory in which the same may be executed, may pursue and reclaim such fugitive person, either by procuring a warrant from some one of the courts, judges, or commissioners aforesaid, of the proper circuit, district, or county, for the apprehension of such fugitive from service or labor, or by seizing and arresting such fugitive, where the same can be done without process, and by taking, or causing such person to be taken, forthwith before such court, judge, or commissioner, whose duty it shall be to hear and determine the case of such claimant in a summary manner; and upon satisfactory proof being made, by deposition or affidavit, in writing, to be taken and certi-

fied by such court, judge, or commissioner, or by other satisfactory testimony, duly taken and certified by some court, magistrate, justice of the peace, or other legal officer authorized to administer an oath and take depositions under the laws of the State or Territory from which such person owing service or labor may have escaped, with a certificate of such magistracy or other authority, as aforesaid, with the seal of the proper court or officer thereto attached, which seal shall be sufficient to establish the competency of the proof, and with proof, also by affidavit, of the identity of the person whose service or labor is claimed to be due as aforesaid, that the person so arrested does in fact owe service or labor to the person or persons claiming him or her, in the State or Territory from which such fugitive may have escaped as aforesaid, and that said person escaped, to make out and deliver to such claimant, his or her agent or attorney, a certificate setting forth the substantial facts as to the service or labor due from such fugitive to the claimant, and of his or her escape from the State or Territory in which he or she was arrested, with authority to such claimant, or his or her agent or attorney, to use such reasonable force and restraint as may be necessary, under the circumstances of the case, to take and remove such fugitive person back to the State or Territory whence he or she may have escaped as aforesaid. In no trial or hearing under this act shall the testimony of such alleged fugitive be admitted in evidence; and the certificates in this and the first [fourth] section mentioned, shall be conclusive of the right of the person or persons in whose favor granted, to remove such fugitive to the State or Territory from which he escaped, and shall prevent all molestation of such person or persons by any process issued by any court, judge, magistrate, or other person whomsoever.

SEC. 7. And be it further enacted, That any person who shall knowingly and willingly obstruct, hinder, or prevent such claimant, his agent or attorney, or any person or persons lawfully assisting him, her, or them, from arresting such a fugitive from service or labor, either with or without process as aforesaid, or shall rescue, or attempt to rescue, such fugitive from service or labor, from the custody of such claimant, his or her agent or attorney, or other person or persons lawfully assisting as aforesaid, when so arrested, pursuant to the authority herein given and declared; or shall aid, abet, or assist such person so owing service or labor as aforesaid, directly or indirectly, to escape from such claimant, his agent or attorney, or other person or persons legally authorized as aforesaid; or shall harbor or conceal such fugitive, so as to prevent the discovery and arrest of such person, after notice or knowledge of the fact that such person was a fugitive from service or labor as aforesaid, shall, for either of said offences, be subject to a fine not exceeding one thousand dollars, and imprisonment not exceeding six months, by indictment and conviction before the District Court of the United States for the district in which such offence may have been committed, or before the proper court of criminal jurisdiction, if committed within any one of the organized Territories of the United States; and shall moreover forfeit and pay, by way of civil damages to the party injured by such illegal conduct, the sum of one thousand dollars for each fugitive so lost as aforesaid, to be recovered by action of debt, in any of the District or Territorial Courts aforesaid, within whose jurisdiction the said offence may have been committed.

Sec. 8. And be it further enacted, That the marshals, their deputies, and the clerks of the said District and Territorial Courts, shall be paid, for their services, the like fees as may be allowed for similar services in other cases; and where such services are rendered exclusively in the arrest, custody, and delivery of the fugitive to the claimant, his or her agent or attorney, or where such supposed fugitive may be discharged out of custody for the want of sufficient proof as aforesaid, then such fees are to be paid in whole by such claimant, his or her agent or attorney;

and in all cases where the proceedings are before a commissioner, he shall be entitled to a fee of ten dollars in full for his services in each case, upon the delivery of the said certificate to the claimant, his agent or attorney; or a fee of five dollars in cases where the proof shall not, in the opinion of such commissioner, warrant such certificate and delivery, inclusive of all services incident to such arrest and examination, to be paid, in either case, by the claimant, his or her agent or attorney. The person or persons authorized to execute the process to be issued by such commissioner for the arrest and detention of fugitives from service or labor as aforesaid, shall also be entitled to a fee of five dollars each for each person he or they may arrest, and take before any commissioner as aforesaid, at the instance and request of such claimant, with such other fees as may be deemed reasonable by such commissioner for such other additional services as may be necessarily performed by him or them; such as attending at the examination, keeping the fugitive in custody, and providing him with food and lodging during his detention, and until the final determination of such commissioners; and, in general, for performing such other duties as may be required by such claimant, his or her attorney or agent, or commissioner in the premises, such fees to be made up in conformity with the fees usually charged by the officers of the courts of justice within the proper district or county, as near as may be practicable, and paid by such claimants, their agents or attorneys, whether such supposed fugitives from service or labor be ordered to be delivered to such claimant by the final determination of such commissioner or not.

SEC. 9. And be it further enacted, That, upon affidavit made by the claimant of such fugitive, his agent or attorney, after such certificate has been issued, that he has reason to apprehend that such fugitive will be rescued by force from his or their possession before he can be taken beyond the limits of the State in which the arrest is made, it shall be the duty of the officer making the arrest to retain such fugitive in his custody, and to remove him to the State whence he fled, and there to deliver him to said claimant, his agent, or attorney. And to this end, the officer aforesaid is hereby authorized and required to employ so many persons as he may deem necessary to overcome such force, and to retain them in his service so long as circumstances may require. The said officer and his assistants, while so employed, to receive the same compensation, and to be allowed the same expenses, as are now allowed by law for transportation of criminals, to be certified by the judge of the district within which the arrest is made, and paid out of the treasury of the United States.

SEC. 10. And be it further enacted, That when any person held to service or labor in any State or Territory, or in the District of Columbia, shall escape therefrom, the party to whom such service or labor shall be due, his, her, or their agent or attorney, may apply to any court of record therein, or judge thereof in vacation, and make satisfactory proof to such court, or judge in vacation, of the escape aforesaid, and that the person escaping owed service or labor to such party. Whereupon the court shall cause a record to be made of the matters so proved, and also a general description of the person so escaping, with such convenient certainty as may be; and a transcript of such record, authenticated by the attestation of the clerk and of the seal of the said court, being produced in any other State, Territory, or district in which the person so escaping may be found, and being exhibited to any judge, commissioner, or other office, authorized by the law of the United States to cause persons escaping from service or labor to be delivered up, shall be held and taken to be full and conclusive evidence of the fact of escape, and that the service or labor of the person escaping is due to the party in such record mentioned. And upon the production by the said party of other and further evidence if necessary, either oral or by affidavit, in addition to what is contained in the said record of the identity of the person escaping, he or she shall be delivered up to the claimant, And the said court, commissioner, judge, or other person authorized by this act to grant certificates to claimants or fugitives, shall, upon the production of the record and other evidences aforesaid, grant to such claimant a certificate of his right to take any such person identified and proved to be owing service or labor as aforesaid, which certificate shall authorize such claimant to seize or arrest and transport such person to the State or Territory from which he escaped: Provided, That nothing herein contained shall be construed as requiring the production of a transcript of such record as evidence as aforesaid. But in its absence the claim shall be heard and determined upon other satisfactory proofs, competent in law.

Approved, September 18, 1850.

The Dred Scott Decision, 1857

Roger Taney

DRED SCOTT, PLAINTIFF IN ERROR, V. JOHN F. A. SANDFORD.

December Term, 1856

Mr. Chief Justice Taney: . . . There are two leading questions presented by the record:

1. Had the Circuit Court of the United States jurisdiction to hear and determine the case between these parties? And
2. If it had jurisdiction, is the judgment it has given erroneous or not?

The plaintiff in error, who was also the plaintiff in the court below, was, with his wife and children, held as slaves by the defendant, in the State of Missouri; and he brought this action in the Circuit Court of the United States for that district, to assert the title of himself and his family to freedom.

The declaration is in the form usually adopted in that State to try questions of this description, and contains the averment necessary to give the court jurisdiction; that he and the defendant are citizens of different States; that is, that he is a citizen of Missouri, and the defendant a citizen of New York.

The defendant pleaded in abatement to the jurisdiction of the court, that the plaintiff was not a citizen of the State of Missouri, as alleged in his declaration, being a negro of African descent, whose ancestors were of pure African blood, and who were brought into this country and sold as slaves. . . .

The question is simply this: Can a negro, whose ancestors were imported into this country, and sold as slaves, become a member of the political community formed and brought into existence by the Constitution of the United States, and as such become entitled to all the rights, and privileges, and immunities, guarantied by that instrument to

the citizen? One of which rights is the privilege of suing in a court of the United States in the cases specified in the Constitution.

It will be observed, that the plea applies to that class of persons only whose ancestors were negroes of the African race, and imported into this country, and sold and held as slaves. The only matter in issue before the court, therefore, is, whether the descendants of such slaves, when they shall be emancipated, or who are born of parents who had become free before their birth, are citizens of a State, in the sense in which the word citizen is used in the Constitution of the United States. And this being the only matter in dispute on the pleadings, the court must be understood as speaking in this opinion of that class only, that is, of those persons who are the descendants of Africans who were imported into this country, and sold as slaves. . . .

The question then arises, whether the provisions of the Constitution, in relation to the personal rights and privileges to which the citizen of a State should be entitled, embraced the negro African race, at that time in this country, or who might afterwards be imported, who had then or should afterwards be made free in any State; and to put it in the power of a single State to make him a citizen of the United States, and endue him with the full rights of citizenship in every other State without their consent? Does the Constitution of the United States act upon him whenever he shall be made free under the laws of a State, and raised there to the rank of a citizen, and immediately clothe him with all the privileges of a citizen in every other State, and in its own courts?

The court thinks the affirmative of these propositions cannot be maintained. And if it cannot, the plaintiff in error could not be a citizen of the State of Missouri, within the meaning of the Constitution of the United

States, and, consequently, was not entitled to sue in its courts. . . .

In the opinion of the court, the legislation and histories of the times, and the language used in the Declaration of Independence, show, that neither the class of persons who had been imported as slaves, nor their descendants, whether they had become free or not, were then acknowledged as a part of the people, nor intended to be included in the general words used in that memorable instrument.

It is difficult at this day to realize the state of public opinion in relation to that unfortunate race, which prevailed in the civilized and enlightened portions of the world at the time of the Declaration of Independence, and when the Constitution of the United States was framed and adopted. But the public history of every European nation displays it in a manner too plain to be mistaken.

They had for more than a century before been regarded as beings of an inferior order, and altogether unfit to associate with the white race, either in social or political relations; and so far inferior, that they had no rights which the white man was bound to respect; and that the negro might justly and lawfully be reduced to slavery for his benefit. He was bought and sold, and treated as an ordinary article of merchandise and traffic, whenever a profit could be made by it. This opinion was at that time fixed and universal in the civilized portion of the white race. It was regarded as an axiom in morals as well as in politics, which no one thought of disputing, or supposed to be open to dispute; and men in every grade and position in society daily and habitually acted upon it in their private pursuits, as well as in matters of public concern, without doubting for a moment the correctness of this opinion.

And in no nation was this opinion more firmly fixed or more uniformly acted upon than by the English Government and English people. They not only seized them on the coast of Africa, and sold them or held them in slavery for their own use; but they took them as ordinary articles of merchan-

dise to every country where they could make a profit on them, and were far more extensively engaged in this commerce than any other nation in the world.

The opinion thus entertained and acted upon in England was naturally impressed upon the colonies they founded on this side of the Atlantic. And, accordingly, a negro of the African race was regarded by them as an article of property, and held, and bought and sold as such, in every one of the thirteen colonies which united in the Declaration of Independence, and afterwards formed the Constitution of the United States. The slaves were more or less numerous in the different colonies, as slave labor was found more or less profitable. But no one seems to have doubted the correctness of the prevailing opinion of the time. . . .

No one of that race had ever migrated to the United States voluntarily; all of them had been brought here as articles of merchandise. The number that had been emancipated at that time were but few in comparison with those held in slavery; and they were identified in the public mind with the race to which they belonged, and regarded as a part of the slave population rather than the free. It is obvious that they were not even in the minds of the framers of the Constitution when they were conferring special rights and privileges upon the citizens of a State in every other part of the Union.

Indeed, when we look to the condition of this race in the several States at the time, it is impossible to believe that these rights and privileges were intended to be extended to them.

And if we turn to the legislation of the States where slavery had worn out, or measures taken for its speedy abolition, we shall find the same opinions and principles equally fixed and equally acted upon. . . .

But so far as mere rights of person are concerned, the provision in question is confined to citizens of a State who are temporarily in another State without taking up their residence there. It gives them no political rights in the State, as to voting or holding office, or in any other respect. For a citizen of one State has no right to participate in the government of another. But if he ranks as a citizen in the State to which he belongs, within the meaning of the Constitution of the United States, then, whenever he goes into another State, the Constitution clothes him, as to the rights of person, will all the privileges and immunities which belong to citizens of the State. And if persons of the African race are citizens of a State, and of the United States, they would be entitled to all of these privileges and immunities in every State, and the State could not restrict them; for they would hold these privileges and immunities under the paramount authority of the Federal Government, and its courts would be bound to maintain and enforce them, the Constitution and laws of the State to the contrary notwithstanding. And if the States could limit or restrict them, or place the party in an inferior grade, this clause of the Constitution would be unmeaning, and could have no operation; and would give no rights to the citizen when in another State. He would have none but what the State itself chose to allow him. This is evidently not the construction or meaning of the clause in question. It guaranties rights to the citizen, and the State cannot withhold them. And these rights are of a character and would lead to consequences which make it absolutely certain that the African race were not included under the name of citizens of a State, and were not in the contemplation of the framers of the Constitution when these privileges and immunities were provided for the protection of the citizen in other States. . . .

. . . [T]he court is of opinion, that, upon the facts stated in the plea in abatement, Dred Scott was not a citizen of Missouri within the meaning of the Constitution of the United States, and not entitled as such to sue in its courts; and, consequently, that the Circuit Court had no jurisdiction of the case, and that the judgment on the plea in abatement is erroneous.

We are aware that doubts are entertained by some of the members of the court, whether the plea in abatement is legally before the court upon this writ of error; but if that plea is regarded as waived, or out of the case upon any other ground, yet the question as to the jurisdiction of the Circuit Court is presented on the face of the bill of exception itself, taken by the plaintiff at the trial; for he admits that he and his wife were born slaves, but endeavors to make out his title to freedom and citizenship by showing that they were taken by their owner to certain places, hereinafter mentioned, where slavery could not by law exist, and that they thereby became free, and upon their return to Missouri became citizens of that State.

Now, if the removal of which he speaks did not give them their freedom, then by his own admission he is still a slave; and whatever opinions may be entertained in favor of the citizenship of a free person of the African race, no one supposes that a slave is a citizen of the State or of the United States. If, therefore, the acts done by his owner did not make them free persons, he is still a slave, and certainly incapable of suing in the character of a citizen. . . .

The case before us still more strongly imposes upon this court the duty of examining whether the court below has not committed an error, in taking jurisdiction and giving a judgment for costs in favor of the defendant; . . . in this case it does appear that the plaintiff was born a slave; and if the facts upon which he relies have not made him free, then it appears affirmatively on the record that he is not a citizen, and consequently his suit against Sandford was not a suit between citizens of different States, and the court had no authority to pass any judgment between the parties. The suit ought, in this view of it, to have been dismissed by the Circuit Court, and its judgment in favor of Sandford is erroneous, and must be reversed. . . .

But in considering the question before us, it must be borne in mind that there is no law of nations standing between the people of the United States and their Government, and interfering with their relation to each other. The powers of the Government, and the rights of the citizen under it, are positive and practical regulations plainly written down. The people of the United States have delegated to it certain enumerated powers, and forbidden it to exercise others. It has no power over the person or property of a citizen but what the citizens of the United States have granted. And no laws or usages of other nations, or reasoning of statesmen or jurists upon the relations of master and slave, can enlarge the powers of the Government, or take from the citizens the rights they have reserved. And if the Constitution recognises the right of property of the master in a slave, and makes no distinction between that description of property and other property owned by a citizen, no tribunal, acting under the authority of the United States, whether it be legislative, executive, or judicial, has a right to draw such a distinction, or deny to it the benefit of the provisions and guarantees which have been provided for the protection of private property against the encroachments of the Government.

Now, as we have already said in an earlier part of this opinion, upon a different point, the right of property in a slave is distinctly and expressly affirmed in the Constitution. The right to traffic in it, like an ordinary article of merchandise and property, was guarantied to the citizens of the United States, in every State that might desire it, for twenty years. And the Government in express terms is pledged to protect it in all future time, if the slave escapes from his owner. This is done in plain words—too plain to be misunderstood. And no word can be found in the Constitution which gives Congress a greater power over slave property, or which entitles property of that kind to less protection that property of any other description. The only power conferred is the power coupled with the duty of guarding and protecting the owner in his rights.

Upon these considerations, it is the opinion of the court that the act of Congress which prohibited a citizen from holding and owning property of this kind in the territory of the United States north of the line therein mentioned, is not warranted by the Constitution, and is therefore void; and that neither Dred Scott himself, nor any of his family, were made free by being carried into this territory; even if they had been carried there by the owner, with the intention of becoming a permanent resident.

We have so far examined the case, as it stands under the Constitution of the United States, and the powers thereby delegated to the Federal Government.

But there is another point in the case which depends on State power and State law. And it is contended, on the part of the plaintiff, that he is made free by being taken to Rock Island, in the State of Illinois, independently of his residence in the territory of the United States; and being so made free, he was not again reduced to a state of slavery by being brought back to Missouri. . . .

So in this case. As Scott was a slave when taken into the State of Illinois by his owner, and was there held as such, and brought back in that character, his status, as free or slave, depended on the laws of Missouri, and not of Illinois.

It has, however, been urged in the argument, that by the laws of Missouri he was free on his return, and that this case, therefore, cannot be governed by the case of Strader et al. v. Graham, where it appeared, by the laws of Kentucky, that the plaintiffs continued to be slaves on their return from Ohio. But whatever doubts or opinions may, at one time, have been entertained upon this subject, we are satisfied, upon a careful examination of all the cases decided in the State courts of Missouri referred to, that it is now firmly settled by the decisions of the highest court in the State, that Scott and his family upon their return were not free, but were, by the laws of Missouri, the property of the defendant; and that the Circuit Court of the United States had no jurisdiction, when, by the laws of the State, the plaintiff was a slave, and not a citizen. . . .

Upon the whole, therefore, it is the judgment of this court, that it appears by the record before us that the plaintiff in error is not a citizen of Missouri, in the sense in which that word is used in the Constitution; and that the Circuit Court of the United States, for that reason, had no jurisdiction in the case, and could give no judgment in it.

Its judgment for the defendant must, consequently, be reversed, and a mandate issued, directing the suit to be dismissed for want of jurisdiction.

Testimony by the Superintendent of Contrabands at Fortress Monroe, Virginia, Before the American Freedman's Inquiry Commission

Capt. C. B. Wilder

[*Fortress Monroe, Va.,*] **May 9, 1863.** *Question* How many of the people called contrabands, have come under your observation?

Answer Some 10,000 have come under our control, to be fed in part, and clothed in part, but I cannot speak accurately in regard to the number. This is the rendezvous. They come here from all about, from Richmond and 200 miles off in North Carolina. There was one gang that started from Richmond 23 strong and only 3 got through.

Q In your opinion, is there any communication between the refugees and the black men still in slavery?

A Yes Sir, we have had men here who have gone back 200 miles.

Q In your opinion would a change in our policy which would cause them to be treated with fairness, their wages punctually paid and employment furnished them in the army, become known and would it have any effect upon others in slavery?

Source: "Testimony by the Superintendent of Contrabands at Fortress Monroe, Virginia, Before the American Freedmen's Inquiry Commission." In Ira Berlin et al., eds. *Freedom: A Documentary History of Emancipation, 1861–1867* (Cambridge University Press, 1985), pp. 88–90.

A Yes—Thousands upon Thousands. I went to Suffolk a short time ago to enquire into the state of things there—for I found I could not get any foot hold to make things work there, through the Commanding General, and I went to the Provost Marshall and all hands—and the colored people actually sent a deputation to me one morning before I was up to know if we put black men in irons and sent them off to Cuba to be sold or set them at work and put balls on their legs and whipped them, just as in slavery; because that was the story up there, and they were frightened and didn't know what to do. When I got at the feelings of these people I found they were not afraid of the slaveholders. They said there was nobody on the plantations but women and they were not afraid of them. One woman came through 200 miles in Men's clothes. The most valuable information we received in regard to the Merrimack and the operations of the rebels came from the colored people and they got no credit for it. I found hundreds who had left their wives and families behind. I asked them "Why did you come away and leave them there?" and I found they had heard these stories, and wanted to come and see how it was. "I am going back again after my wife" some of them have said "When I have earned a little money" What as far as that?" "Yes" and I have had them come to me to borrow money, or to get their pay, if they had earned a months wages, and to get passes. "I am going for my family" they say. "Are you not afraid to risk it?" "No I know the Way" Colored men will help colored men and they will work along the by paths and get through. In that way I have known quite a number who have gone up from time to time in the neighborhood of Richmond and several have brought back their families; some I have never heard from. As I was saying they do not feel afraid now. The white people have nearly all gone, the blood hounds are not there now to hunt them and they are not afraid, before they were afraid to stir. There are hundreds of negroes at Williamsburgh with their families working for nothing. They would not get pay here and they had rather stay where they are. "We are not afraid of being carried back" a great many have told us and "if we are, we can get away again" Now that they are getting their eyes open they are coming in. Fifty came this morning from Yorktown who followed Stoneman's Cavalry when they returned from their raid. The officers reported to their Quartermaster that they had so many horses and fifty or sixty negroes. "What did you bring them for" "Why they followed us and we could not stop them." I asked one of the men about it and he said they would leave their work in the field as soon as they found the Soldiers were Union

men and follow them sometimes without hat or coat. They would take best horse they could get and every where they rode they would take fresh horses, leave the old ones and follow on and so they came in. I have questioned a great many of them and they do not feel much afraid; and there are a great many courageous fellows who have come from long distances in rebeldom. Some men who came here from North Carolina, knew all about the Proclammation and they started on the belief in it; but they had heard these stories and they wanted to know how it was. Well, I gave them the evidence and I have no doubt their friends will hear of it. Within the last two or three months the rebel guards have been doubled on the line and the officers and privates of the 99th New York between Norfolk and Suffolk have caught hundreds of fugitives and got pay for them.

Q Do I understand you to say that a great many who have escaped have been sent back?

A Yes Sir, The masters will come in to Suffolk in the day time and with the help of some of the 99th carry off their fugitives and by and by smuggle them across the lines and the soldier will get his $20. or $50.

Emancipation Proclamation

Abraham Lincoln

BY THE PRESIDENT OF THE UNITED STATES OF AMERICA

A Proclamation.

Whereas on the 22d day of September, A. D. 1862, a proclamation was issued by the President of the United States, containing, among other things, the following, to wit:

Source: Emancipation Proclamation, January 1, 1863.

That on the 1st day of January, A. D. 1863, all persons held as slaves within any State or designated part of a State the people whereof shall then be in rebellion against the United States shall be then, thenceforward, and forever free; and the executive government of the United States, including the military and naval authority thereof, will recognize and maintain the freedom of such persons and will do no act or acts to repress such persons, or any of them, in any efforts they may make for their actual freedom.

That the Executive will on the 1st day of January aforesaid, by proclamation, designate the States and parts of States, if any, in which the people thereof, respectively, shall then be in rebellion against the United States; and the fact that any State or the people thereof shall on that day be in good faith represented in the Congress of the United States by members chosen thereto at elections wherein a majority of the qualified voters of such States shall have participated shall, in the absence of strong countervailing testimony, be deemed conclusive evidence that such State and the people thereof are not then in rebellion against the United States.

Now, therefore, I, Abraham Lincoln, President of the United States, by virtue of the power in me vested as Commander in Chief of the Army and Navy of the United States in time of actual armed rebellion against the authority and Government of the United States, and as a fit and necessary war measure for suppressing said rebellion, do, on this 1st day of January, A. D. 1863, and in accordance with my purpose so to do, publicly proclaimed for the full period of one hundred days from the day first above mentioned, order and designate as the States and parts of States wherein the people thereof, respectively, are this day in rebellion against the United States the following, to wit:

Arkansas, Texas, Louisiana (except the parishes of St. Bernard, Plaquemines, Jefferson, St. John, St. Charles, St. James, Ascension, Assumption, Terrebonne, Lafourche, St. Mary, St. Martin, and Orleans, including the city of New Orleans), Mississippi, Alabama, Florida, Georgia, South Carolina, North Carolina, and Virginia (except the forty-eight counties designated as West Virginia, and also the counties of Berkeley, Accomac, Northampton, Elizabeth City, York, Princess Anne, and Norfolk, including the cities of Norfolk and Portsmouth), and which excepted parts are for the present left precisely as if this proclamation were not issued.

And by virtue of the power and for the purpose aforesaid, I do order and declare that all persons held as slaves within said designated States and parts of States are and hence-forward shall be free, and that the executive government of the United States, including the military and naval authorities thereof, will recognize and maintain the freedom of said persons.

And I hereby enjoin upon the people so declared to be free to abstain from all violence, unless in necessary self-defense; and I recommend to them that in all cases when allowed they labor faithfully for reasonable wages.

And I further declare and make known that such persons of suitable condition will be received into the armed service of the United States to garrison forts, positions, stations, and other places and to man vessels of all sorts in said service.

And upon this act, sincerely believed to be an act of justice, warranted by the Constitution upon military necessity, I invoke the considerate judgment and mankind and the gracious favor of Almighty God.

In witness whereof I have hereunto set my hand and caused the seal of the United States to be affixed.

Done at the city of Washington, this 1st day of January, A. D. 1863, and of the Independence of the United States of America the eighty-seventh.

Abraham Lincoln.

African American Emancipation Songs

Many Thousand Gone

No more auction block for me,
No more, no more,
No more auction block for me,
Many thousand gone.

No more driver's lash for me,
No more, no more,
No more driver's lash for me,
Many thousand gone.

No more peck of salt for me,
No more, no more,
No more peck of salt for me,
Many thousand gone.

No more iron chain for me,
No more, no more,
No more iron chain for me,
Many thousand gone.

Kingdom Coming

Say, darkeys, hab you seen de massa,
Wid de muff-stash on his face,
Go long de road some time dis mornin',
Like he gwine to leab de place?
He seen a smoke, way up de ribber,
Whar de Linkum gumboats lay;
He took his hat, an' lef berry sudden,
An' I spec he's run away!

Source: "Many Thousands Gone" and "Kingdom Coming." In Louis A. Banks, ed., *Immortal Songs of Camp and Field* (Cleveland, 1899), pp. 140–44.

Chorus:

De massa run? ha, ha!
De darkey stay? ho, ho!
It mus' be now de kingdom comin',
An' de year ob Jubilo!

He six foot one way, two foot tudder,
An' he weigh tree hundred pound.
His coat so big, he couldn't pay de tailor,
An' it won't go half way round.
He drill so much dey call him Cap'an,
And he get so drefful tanned,
I spec he try an' fool dem Yankees
For to tink he's contraband.

De darkeys feel so lonesome libing
In de log-house on de lawn,
Dey move dar tings to massa's parlor
For to keep it while he's gone.
Dar's wine an' cider in de kitchen,
An' de darkeys dey'll hab some;
I spose dey'll all be confiscated
When de Linkum sojers come.

De oberseer he made us trubbel,
An' he dribe us round a spell;
We lock him up in de smoke-house cellar,
Wid de key trown in de well.
De whip is lost, de hand-cuff's broken,
But de massa'll hab his pay.
He's ole enough, big enough, ought to known
    better
Dan to went an' run away.

Speech of Frederick Douglass

Frederick Douglass

Mr. President and Fellow Citizens: I shall not attempt to follow Judge Kelley and Miss Dickinson in their eloquent and thrilling appeals to colored men to enlist in the service of the United States. They have left nothing to be desired on that point. I propose to look at the subject in a plain and practical common-sense light. There are obviously two views to be taken of such enlistments—a broad view and a narrow view. I am willing to take both, and consider both. The narrow view of this subject is that which respects the matter of dollars and cents. There are those among us who say they are in favor of taking a hand in this tremendous war, but add they wish to do so on terms of equality with white men. They say if they enter the service, endure all the hardships, perils and suffering—if they make bare their breasts, and with strong arms and courageous hearts confront rebel cannons, and wring victory from the jaws of death, they should have the same pay, the same rations, the same bounty, and the same favorable conditions every way afforded to other men.

I shall not oppose this view. There is something deep down in the soul of every man present which assents to the justice of the claim thus made, and honors the manhood and self respect which insists upon it. I say at once, in peace and in war, I am content with nothing for the black man short of equal and exact justice. The only question I have, and the point at which I differ from those who

refuse to enlist, is whether the colored man is more likely to obtain justice and equality while refusing to assist in putting down this tremendous rebellion than he would be if he should promptly, generously and earnestly give his hand and heart to the salvation of the country in this its day of calamity and peril. Nothing can be more plain, nothing more certain than that the speediest and best possible way open to us to manhood, equal rights and elevation, is that we enter this service. For my own part, I hold that if the Government of the United States offered nothing more, as an inducement to colored men to enlist, than bare subsistence and arms, considering the moral effect of compliance upon ourselves, it would be the wisest and best thing for us to enlist. There is something ennobling in the possession of arms, and we of all other people in the world stand in need of their ennobling influence.

The case presented in the present war, and the light in which every colored man is bound to view it, may be stated thus. There are two governments struggling now for the possession of and endeavoring to bear rule over the United States—one has its capital in Richmond, and is represented by Mr. Jefferson Davis, and the other has its capital at Washington, and is represented by "Honest Old Abe." These two governments are today face to face, confronting each other with vast armies, and grappling each other upon many a bloody field, north and south, on the banks of the Mississippi, and under the shadows of the Alleghanies. Now, the question for every colored man is, or ought to be, what attitude is assumed by these respective governments and armies towards the rights and liberties of the colored race in this country; which is for us, and which against us!

Now, I think there can be no doubt as to the attitude of the Richmond or Confederate

Source: "Speech of Mr. Frederick Douglass," in *Addresses of the Hon. W. D. Kelley, Miss Anna E. Dickinson and Frederick Douglass, at a mass meeting, held at National Hall, Philadelphia, July 6, 1863, for the Promotion of Colored Enlistments* (Philadelphia, 1863), pp. 5–7.

Government. Wherever else there has been concealment, here all is frank, open, and diabolically straightforward. Jefferson Davis and his government make no secret as to the cause of this war, and they do not conceal the purpose of the war. That purpose is nothing more nor less than to make the slavery of the African race universal and perpetual on this continent. It is not only evident from the history and logic of events, but the declared purpose of the atrocious war now being waged against the country. Some, indeed, have denied that slavery has anything to do with the war, but the very same men who do this affirm it in the same breath in which they deny it, for they tell you that the abolitionists are the cause of the war. Now, if the abolitionists are the cause of the war, they are the cause of it only because they have sought the abolition of slavery. View it in any way you please, therefore, the rebels are fighting for the existence of slavery—they are fighting for the privilege, the horrid privilege, of sundering the dearest ties of human nature—of trafficking in slaves and the souls of men—for the ghastly privilege of scourging women and selling innocent children.

I say this is not the concealed object of the war, but the openly confessed and shamelessly proclaimed object of the war. Vice-President Stephens has stated, with the utmost clearness and precision, the difference between the fundamental ideas of the Confederate Government and those of the Federal Government. One is based upon the idea that colored men are an inferior race, who may be enslaved and plundered forever and to the hearts' content of any men of a different complexion, while the Federal Government recognizes the natural and fundamental equality of all men.

I say, again, we all know that this Jefferson Davis government holds out to us nothing but fetters, chains, auction blocks, bludgeons, branding-irons, and eternal slavery and degradation. If it triumphs in this contest, woe, woe, ten thousands woes, to the black man! Such of us as are free, in all the likelihoods of the case, would be given over to the most excruciating tortures, while the last hope of the long crushed bondman would be extinguished forever.

Now, what is the attitude of the Washington Government towards the colored race? What reasons have we to desire its triumph in the present contest? Mind, I do not ask what was its attitude towards us before this bloody rebellion broke out. I do not ask what was its disposition when it was controlled by the very men who are now fighting to destroy it when they could no longer control it. I do not even ask what it was two years ago, when McClellan shamelessly gave out that in a war between loyal slaves and disloyal masters, he would take the side of the masters, against the slaves—when he openly proclaimed his purpose to put down slave insurrections with an iron hand—when glorious Ben. Butler, now stunned into a conversion to anti-slavery principles, (which I have every reason to believe sincere,) proffered his services to the Governor of Maryland, to suppress a slave insurrection, while treason ran riot in that State, and the warm, red blood of Massachusetts soldiers still stained the pavements of Baltimore.

I do not ask what was the attitude of this Government when many of the officers and men who had undertaken to defend it, openly threatened to throw down their arms and leave the service if men of color should step forward to defend it, and be invested with the dignity of soldiers. Moreover, I do not ask what was the position of this Government when our loyal camps were made slave hunting grounds, and United States officers performed the disgusting duty of slave dogs to hunt down slaves for rebel masters. These were all dark and terrible days for the republic. I do not ask you about the dead past. I bring you to the living present. Events more mighty than men, eternal Providence, all-wise and all-controlling, have placed us in new relations to the Government and the Government to us. What that Government is to us today, and what it will be tomorrow, is made evident by a very few facts. Look at them, colored men. Slavery in the District of Columbia is abolished forever; slavery in all the territories of the United States is abolished forever; the foreign slave trade, with its ten thousand revolting abominations, is rendered impossible; slavery in ten States of the Union is abolished forever; slavery in the five remaining States is as certain to follow the same fate as the night is to follow the day. The independence of Haiti is recognized; her Minister sits beside our Prime Minister, Mr. Seward, and dines at his table in Washington, while colored men are excluded from the cars in Philadelphia; showing that a black man's complexion in Washington, in the presence of the Federal Government, is less offensive than in the city of brotherly love. Citizenship is no longer denied us under this government.

Under the interpretation of our rights by Attorney General Bates, we are American citizens. We can import goods, own and sail ships, and travel in foreign countries with American passports in our pockets; and now, so far from there being any opposition, so far from excluding us from the army as soldiers, the President at Washington, the Cabinet and the Congress, the generals commanding the whole army of the nation unite in giving us one thunderous welcome to share with them in the honor and glory of suppressing treason and upholding the star-spangled banner. The revolution is tremendous, and it becomes us as wise men to recognize the change, and to shape our action accordingly.

I hold that the Federal Government was never, in its essence, anything but an anti-slavery government. Abolish slavery tomorrow, and not a sentence or syllable of the Constitution need be altered. It was purposely so framed as to give no claim, no sanction to the claim, of property in man. If in its origin slavery had any relation to the government, it was only as the scaffolding to the magnificent structure, to be removed as soon as the building was completed. There is in the Constitution no East, no West, no North, no South, no black, no white, no

slave, no slaveholder, but all are citizens who are of American birth.

Such is the government, fellow-citizens, you are now called upon to uphold with your arms. Such is the government that you are called upon to co-operate with in burying rebellion and slavery in a common grave. Never since the world began was a better chance offered to a long enslaved and oppressed people. The opportunity is given as to be men. With one courageous resolution we may blot out the hand-writing of the ages against us. Once let the black man get upon his person the brass letters U. S.; let him get an eagle on his button, and a musket on his shoulder, and bullets in his pocket, and there is no power on the earth or under the earth which can deny that he has earned the right of citizenship in the United States. I say again, this is our chance, and woe betide us if we fail to embrace it. The immortal bard hath told us:

"There is a tide in the affairs of men,
Which, taken at the flood, leads on to fortune.
Omitted, all the voyage of their life
Is bound in shallows and in miseries.
We must take the current when it serves,
Or lose our ventures."

Do not flatter yourselves, my friends, that you are more important to the government than the government is to you. You stand but as the plank to the ship. This rebellion can be put down without your help. Slavery can be abolished by white men; but liberty so won for the black man, while it may leave him an object of pity, can never make him an object of respect.

Depend upon it, this is no time for hesitation. Do you say you want the same pay that white men get? I believe that the justice and magnanimity of your country will speedily grant it. But will you be overnice about this matter? Do you get as good wages now as white men get by staying out of the service? Don't you work for less every day than white men get? You know you do. Do I hear you say you want black officers? Very well, and I have not the slightest doubt that in the progress of this war, we shall see black officers, black colonels, and generals even. But is it not ridiculous in us in all at once refusing to be commanded by white men in time of war, when we are everywhere commanded by white men in time of peace? Do I hear you say still that you are a son, and want your mother provided for in your absence?—a husband and want your wife cared for?—a brother, and want your sister secured against want? I honor you for your solicitude. Your mothers, your wives, and your sisters ought to be cared for, and an association of gentlemen, composed of responsible white and colored men, is now being organized in this city for this very purpose.

Do I hear you say you offered your services to Pennsylvania and were refused? I know it. But what of that? The State is not more than the nation. The greater includes the lesser. Be-

cause the State refuses, you should all the more readily turn to the United States. When the children fall out, they should refer the quarrel to the parent. "You came unto your own, and your own received you not." But the broad gates of the United States stand open night and day. Citizenship in the United States will, in the end, secure your citizenship in the State.

Young men of Philadelphia, you are without excuse. The hour has arrived, and your place is in the Union army. Remember that the musket—the United States musket with its bayonet of steel—is better than all mere parchment guarantees of liberty. In your hands that musket means liberty; and should your constitutional right at the close of this war be denied, which, in the nature of things, it cannot be, your brethren are safe while you have a Constitution which proclaims your right to keep and bear arms.

Battle of Port Hudson

William Wells Brown

On the 26th of May, 1863, the wing of the army under Major-Gen. Banks was brought before the rifle-pits and heavy guns of Port Hudson. Night fell—the lovely Southern night—with its silvery moonshine on the gleaming waters of the Mississippi, that passed directly by the intrenched town. The glistening stars appeared suspended in the upper air as globes of liquid light, while the fresh soft breeze was bearing such sweet

scents from the odoriferous trees and plants, that a poet might have fancied angelic spirits were abroad, making the atmosphere luminous with their pure presence, and every breeze fragrant with their luscious breath. The deep-red sun that rose on the next morning indicated that the day would be warm; and, as it advanced, the heat became intense. The earth had been long parched, and the hitherto green verdure had begun to turn yellow. Clouds of dust followed every step and movement of the troops. The air was filled with dust: clouds gathered, frowned upon the earth, and hastened away.

The weatherwise watched the red masses of the morning, and still hoped for a shower to cool the air, and lay the dust, before the

Source: "Battle of Port Hudson," in William Wells Brown, *The Negro in the American Rebellion: His Heroism and His Fidelity* (Boston: Lee and Separd, 1867), pp. 167–76.

work of death commenced; but none came, and the very atmosphere seemed as if it were from an overheated oven. The laying-aside of all unnecessary articles or accoutrements, and the preparation that showed itself on every side, told all present that the conflict was near at hand. Gen. Dwight, whose antecedents with regard to the rights of the Negro, and his ability to fight, were not of the most favorable character, was the officer in command over the colored brigade; and busy Rumor, that knows every thing, had whispered it about that the valor of the black man was to be put to the severest test that day.

The black forces consisted of the First Louisiana, under Lieut-Col. Bassett, and the Third Louisiana, under Col. Nelson. The line-officers of the Third were white; and the regiment was composed mostly of freedmen, many of whose backs still bore the marks of the lash, and whose brave, stout hearts beat high at the thought that the hour had come when they were to meet their proud and unfeeling oppressors. The First was the noted regiment called "The Native Guard," which Gen. Butler found when he entered New Orleans, and which so promptly offered its services to aid in crushing the Rebellion. The line-officers of this regiment were all colored, taken from amongst the most wealthy and influential of the free colored people of New Orleans. It was said that not one of them was worth less than twenty-five thousand dollars. The brave, the enthusiastic, and the patriotic, found full scope for the development of their powers in this regiment, of which all were well educated; some were fine scholars. One of the most efficient officers was Capt. André Callioux, a man whose identity with his race could not be mistaken; for he prided himself on being the blackest man in the Crescent City. Whether in the drawing-room or on the parade, he was ever the centre of attraction. Finely educated, polished in his manners, a splendid horseman, a good boxer, bold, athletic, and daring, he never lacked admirers. His men were ready at any time to follow him to the cannon's mouth; and he was as ready to

lead them. This regiment petitioned their commander to allow them to occupy the post of danger in the battle, and it was granted.

As the moment of attack drew near, the greatest suppressed excitement existed; but all were eager for the fight. Capt. Callioux walked proudly up and down the line, and smilingly greeted the familiar faces of his company. Officers and privates of the white regiments looked on as they saw these men at the front, and asked each other what they thought would be the result. Would these blacks stand fire? Was not the test by which they were to be tried too severe? Col. Nelson being called to act as brigadier-general, Lieut-Col. Finnegas took his place. The enemy in his stronghold felt his power, and bade defiance to the expected attack. At last the welcome word was given, and our men started. The enemy opened a blistering fire of shell, canister, grape, and musketry. The first shell thrown by the enemy killed and wounded a number of the blacks; but on they went. "Charge" was the word.

> "Charge!" Trump and drum awoke:
> Onward the bondmen broke;
> Bayonet and sabre-stroke
> Vainly opposed their rush."

At every pace, the column was thinned by the falling dead and wounded. The blacks closed up steadily as their comrades fell, and advanced within fifty paces of where the rebels were working a masked battery, situated on a bluff where the guns could sweep the whole field over which the troops must charge. This battery was on the left of the charging line. Another battery of three or four guns commanded the front, and six heavy pieces raked the right of the line as it formed, and enfiladed its flank and rear as it charged on the bluff. It was ascertained that a bayou ran under the bluff where the guns lay,—a bayou deeper than a man could ford. This charge was repulsed with severe loss. Lieut-Col. Finnegas was then ordered to charge, and in a well-dressed steady line his men went on the double-quick down over the field of death. No matter how gallantly the men behaved, no matter how bravely they were led, it was not in the course of things that this gallant brigade should take these works by charge. Yet charge after charge was ordered and carried out under all these disasters with Spartan firmness. Six charges in all were made. Col. Nelson reported to Gen. Dwight the fearful odds he had to contend with. Says Gen. Dwight, in reply, "Tell Col. Nelson I shall consider that he has accomplished nothing unless he take those guns." Humanity will never forgive Gen. Dwight for this last order; for he certainly saw that he was only throwing away the lives of his men. But what were his men? "Only niggers." Thus the last charge was made under the spur of desperation.

The ground was already strewn with the dead and wounded, and many of the brave officers had fallen early in the engagement. Among them was the gallant and highly cultivated Anselmo. He was a standard-bearer, and hugged the stars and stripes to his heart as he fell forward upon them pierced by five balls. Two corporals near by struggled between themselves as to who should have the honor of again raising those bloodstained emblems to the breeze. Each was eager for the honor; and during the struggle a missile from the enemy wounded one of them, and the other corporal shouldered the dear old flag in triumph, and bore it through the charge in the front of the advancing lines.

> "Now," the flag-sergeant cried,
> "Though death and hell betide,
> Let the whole nation see
> If we are fit to be
> Free in this land, or bound
> Down, like the whining hound,—
> Bound with red stripes and pain
> In our old chains again."
> Oh! what a shout there went
> From the black regiment!

Shells from the rebel guns cut down trees three feet in diameter, and they fell, at one time burying a whole company beneath their branches. Thus they charged bravely on certain destruction, till the ground was slippery with the gore of the slaughtered, and cumbered with the bodies of the maimed. The last charge was made about one o'clock. At this juncture, Capt. Callioux was seen with his left arm dangling by his side,—for a ball had broken it above the elbow,—while his right hand held his unsheathed sword gleaming in the rays of the sun; and his hoarse, faint voice was heard cheering on his men. A moment more, and the brave and generous Callioux was struck by a shell, and fell far in advance of his company. The fall of this officer so exasperated his men, that they appeared to be filled with new enthusiasm; and they rushed forward with a recklessness that probably has never been surpassed. Seeing it to be a hopeless effort, the taking of these batteries, order was given to change the programme; and the troops were called off. But had they accomplished any thing more than the loss of many of their brave men? Yes: they had. The self-forgetfulness, the undaunted heroism, and the great endurance of the Negro, as exhibited that day, created a new chapter in American history for the colored man.

Many Persians were slain at the battle of Thermopylae; but history records only the fall of Leonidas and his four hundred companions. So in the future, when we shall have passed away from the stage, and rising generations shall speak of the conflict at Port Hudson, and the celebrated charge of the Negro brigade, they will forget all others in their admiration for André Callioux and his colored associates. Gen. Banks, in his report of the battle of Port Hudson, says, "Whatever doubt may have existed heretofore as to the efficiency of organizations of this character, the history of this day proves conclusively to those who were in a condition to observe the conduct of these regiments, that the Government will find in this class of troops effective supporters and defenders. The severe test to which they were subjected, and the determined manner in which they encountered the enemy, leaves upon my mind no doubt of their ultimate success."

Hon. B. F. Flanders paid them the following tribute:—

> The unanimous report of all those who were in the recent battle at Port Hudson, in regard to the Negroes, is, that they fought like devils. They have completely conquered the prejudice of the army against them. Never before was there such an extraordinary revolution of sentiment as that of this army in respect to the Negroes as soldiers.

This change was indeed needed; for only a few days previous to the battle, while the regiments were at Baton Rouge, the line-officers of the New-England troops, either through jealously or hatred to the colored men on account of their complexion, demanded that the latter, as officers, should be dismissed. And, to the disgrace of these white officers, the colored men, through the mean treatment of their superiors in office, the taunts and jeers of their white assailants, were compelled to throw up their commissions. The colored soldiers were deeply pained at seeing the officers of their own color and choice taken from them; for they were much attached to their commanders, some of whom were special favorites with the whole regiment. Among these were First Lieut. Joseph Howard of Company I, and Second Lieut. Joseph G. Parker, of Company C. These gentlemen were both possessed of ample wealth, and had entered the army, not as a matter of speculation, as too many have done, but from a love of military life. Lieut. Howard was a man of more than ordinary ability in military tactics; and a braver or more daring officer could not be found in the Valley of the Mississippi. He was well educated, speaking the English, French, and Spanish languages fluently, and was considered a scholar of rare literary attainments. He, with his friend Parker, felt sorely the humiliation attending their dismissal from the

army, and seldom showed themselves on the streets of their native city, to which they had returned. When the news reached New Orleans of the heroic charge made by the First Louisiana Regiment, at Port Hudson, on the 27th of May, Howard at once called on Parker; and they were so fired with the intelligence, that they determined to proceed to Port Hudson, and to join their old regiment as *privates.* That night they took passage, and the following day found them with their former friends in arms. The regiment was still in position close to the enemy's works, and the appearance of the two lieutenants was hailed with demonstrations of joy. Instead of being placed as privates in the ranks, they were both immediately assigned the command of a company each, not from any compliment to them, but from sheer necessity, because the *white officers* of these companies, feeling that the colored soldiers were put in front of the battle owing to their complexion, were not willing to risk their lives, and had thrown up their commissions.

On the 5th of June, these two officers were put to the test, and nobly did they maintain their former reputation for bravery. Capt. Howard leading the way, they charged upon the rebel's rifle-pits, drove them out, and took possession, and held them for three hours, in the face of a raking fire of artillery. Several times the blacks were so completely hidden from view by the smoke of their own guns and the enemy's heavy cannon, that they could not be seen. It was at this time, that Capt. Howard exhibited his splendid powers as a commander. The Negroes never hesitated. Amid the roar of artillery, and the rattling of musketry, the groans of the wounded, and the ghastly appearance of the dead, the heroic and intrepid Howard was the same. He never said to his men, "Go," but always, "Follow me." At last, when many of their men were killed, and the severe fire of the enemy's artillery seemed to mow down every thing before it, these brave men were compelled to fall back from the pits which they had so triumphantly taken. At nightfall, Gen. Banks paid the Negro officers a high compliment, shaking the hand of Capt. Howard, and congratulating him on his return, and telling his aides that this man was worthy of a more elevated position.

Although the First Louisiana had done well, its great triumph was reserved for the 14th of June, when Capt. Howard and his associates in arms won for themselves immortal renown. Never, in the palmy days of Napoleon, Wellington, or any other general, was more true heroism shown. The effect of the battle of the 27th of May, is thus described in "The New-York Herald," June 6:—

The First Regiment Louisiana Native Guard, Col. Nelson, were in this charge. *They went on the advance, and, when they came out, six hundred out of nine hundred men could not be accounted for. It is said on every side that they fought with the desperation of tigers.* One Negro was observed with a rebel soldier in his grasp, tearing the flesh from his face with his teeth, other weapons having failed him. There are other incidents connected with the conduct of this regiment that have raised them very much in my opinion as soldiers. *After firing one volley, they did not deign to load again, but went in with bayo-*

nets; and, wherever they had a chance, it was all up with the rebels.

From "The New-York Tribune," June 8:—

Nobly done, First Regiment of Louisiana Native Guard! though you failed to carry the rebel works against overwhelming numbers, you did not charge and fight and fall in vain. That heap of six hundred corpses, lying there dark and grim and silent before and within the rebel works, is a better proclamation of freedom than even President Lincoln's. A race ready to die thus was never yet retained in bondage, and never can be. Even the Wood copperheads, who will not fight themselves, and try to keep others out of the Union ranks, will not dare to mob Negro regiments if this is their style of fighting.

Thus passes one regiment of blacks to death and everlasting fame.

Humanity should not forget, that, at the surrender of Port Hudson, not a single colored man could be found alive, although thirty-five were known to have been taken prisoners during the siege. All had been murdered.

Three Versions of the Battle Hymn of the Republic

The Battle Hymn of the Republic

Julia Ward Howe

Mine eyes have seen the glory of the coming of the Lord;
He is trampling out the vintage where the grapes of wrath are stored;
He hath loosed the fateful lightning of His terrible swift sword;
His truth is marching on.

Glory! Glory! Hallelujah!
Glory! Glory! Hallelujah!
Glory! Glory! Hallelujah!
His truth is marching on.

I have seen Him in the watch fires of a hundred circling camps
They have builded Him an altar in the evening dews and damps;
I can read His righteous sentence by the dim and flaring lamps;
His day is marching on.

Glory! Glory! Hallelujah!
Glory! Glory! Hallelujah!
Glory! Glory! Hallelujah!
His day is marching on.

He has sounded forth the trumpet that shall
    never call retreat;
He is sifting out the hearts of men before His
    judgement seat;
Oh, be swift, my soul, to answer Him; be jubi-
    lant, my feet;
Our God is marching on.

Glory! Glory! Hallelujah!
Glory! Glory! Hallelujah!
Glory! Glory! Hallelujah!
Our God is marching on.

In the beauty of the lilies Christ was born
    across the sea,
With a glory in His bosom that transfigures
    you and me;
As He died to make men holy, let us die to
    make men free;
While God is marching on.

Glory! Glory! Hallelujah!
Glory! Glory! Hallelujah!
Glory! Glory! Hallelujah!
While God is marching on.

John Brown's Body

John Brown's body lies a-mouldering in the
    grave,
John Brown's body lies a-mouldering in the
    grave,
But his soul goes marching on.

Chorus
Glory, glory, hallelujah,
Glory, glory, hallelujah,
His soul goes marching on.

He's gone to be a soldier in the Army of the
    Lord,
He's gone to be a soldier in the Army of the
    Lord,
His soul goes marching on.
Chorus

John Brown's knapsack is strapped upon his
    back,
John Brown's knapsack is strapped upon his
    back,
His soul goes marching on.
Chorus

John Brown died that the slaves might be free,
John Brown died that the slaves might be free,
His soul goes marching on.
Chorus

The stars above in Heaven now are looking
    kindly down,
The stars above in Heaven now are looking
    kindly down,
His soul goes marching on.
Chorus

*Marching Song of the First Arkansas Colored
Regiment of the Union Army*

Oh, we're the bully soldiers of the First of
    Arkansas
We are fighting for the Union, we are fighting
    for the law
We can hit a Rebel further than a white man
    ever saw,
As we go marching on!

Glory Glory hallelujah
Glory Glory hallelujah
Glory Glory hallelujah
As we go marching on!

See, there above the center where the flag is
    waving bright,
We are going out of slavery; we're bound for
    freedom's light,
We mean to show Jeff Davis how the Africans
    can fight
As we go marching on!

Glory Glory hallelujah
Glory Glory hallelujah
Glory Glory hallelujah
As we go marching on!

We are done with hoeing cotton! We are done
    with hoeing corn
We are colored Yankee soldiers now, as sure as
    you are born
When the masters hear us yellin', they'll think
    us Gabriel's horn
As we go marching on!

Glory Glory hallelujah
Glory Glory hallelujah
Glory Glory hallelujah
As we go marching on!

They said, Now colored brethren, you shall be
    forever free
From the first of January, eighteen hundred
    sixty-three.
We heard it in the river going rushing to the
    sea,
As it went sounding on.

Glory Glory hallelujah
Glory Glory hallelujah
Glory Glory hallelujah
As we go marching on!

Father Abraham has spoken and the message
    has been sent
The prison doors be opened, and out the
    pris'ners went
To join the sable army of the African descent
As we go marching on

Glory Glory hallelujah
Glory Glory hallelujah
Glory Glory hallelujah
As we go marching on

Behind the Scenes: Thirty Years a Slave and Four Years in the White House

Elizabeth Keckley

WHERE I WAS BORN

My life has been an eventful one. I was born a slave—was the child of slave parents—therefore I came upon the earth free in God-like thought, but fettered in action. My birthplace was Dinwiddie Court-House, in Virginia. My recollections of childhood are distinct, perhaps for the reason that many stirring incidents are associated with that period. I am now on the shady side of forty, and as I sit alone in my room the brain is busy, and a rapidly moving panorama brings scene after scene before me, some pleasant and others sad; and when I thus greet old familiar faces, I often find myself wondering if I am not living the past over again. . . .

I was nearly eighteen when we removed from Virginia to Hillsboro', North Carolina, where young Mr. Burwell took charge of a

church. The salary was small, and we still had to practise the closest economy. Mr. Bingham, a hard, cruel man, the village schoolmaster, was a member of my young master's church, and he was a frequent visitor to the parsonage. She whom I called mistress seemed to be desirous to wreak vengeance on me for something, and Bingham became her ready tool. During this time my master was unusually kind to me; he was naturally a good-hearted man, but was influenced by his wife. It was Saturday evening, and while I was bending over the bed, watching the baby that I had just hushed into slumber, Mr. Bingham came to the door and asked me to go with him to his study. Wondering what he meant by his strange request, I followed him, and when we had entered the study he closed the door, and in his blunt way remarked: "Lizzie, I am going to flog you." I was thunderstruck, and tried to think if I had been remiss in anything. I could not recollect of doing anything to deserve punishment, and with surprise exclaimed: "Whip me, Mr. Bingham! what for?"

"No matter," he replied, "I am going to whip you, so take down your dress this instant."

Recollect, I was eighteen years of age, was a woman fully developed, and yet this man coolly bade me take down my dress. I drew myself up proudly, firmly, and said: "No, Mr. Bingham, I shall not take down my dress before you. Moreover, you shall not whip me unless you prove the stronger. Nobody has a right to whip me but my own master, and nobody shall do so if I can prevent it."

My words seemed to exasperate him. He seized a rope, caught me roughly, and tried to tie me. I resisted with all my strength, but he was the stronger of the two, and after a hard struggle succeeded in binding my hands and tearing my dress from my back. Then he picked up a raw-hide, and began to ply it freely over my shoulders. With steady hand and practised eye he would raise the instrument of torture, nerve himself for a blow, and with fearful force the raw-hide descended upon the quivering flesh. It cut the skin, raised great welts, and the warm blood trickled down my back. Oh God! I can feel the torture now—the terrible, excruciating agony of those moments. I did not scream; I was too proud to let my tormentor know what I was suffering. I closed my lips firmly, that not even a groan might escape from them, and I stood like a statue while the keen lash cut deep into my flesh. As soon as I was released, stunned with pain, bruised and bleeding, I went home and rushed into the presence of the pastor and his wife, wildly exclaiming: "Master Robert, why did you let Mr. Bingham flog me? What have I done that I should be so punished?"

"Go away," he gruffly answered, "do not bother me."

I would not be put off thus. "What *have* I done? I *will* know why I have been flogged."

I saw his cheeks flush with anger, but I did not move. He rose to his feet, and on my refusing to go without an explanation, seized a chair, struck me, and felled me to the floor. I rose, bewildered, almost dead with pain, crept to my room, dressed my bruised arms and back as best I could, and then lay down, but not to sleep. No, I could not sleep, for I was suffering mental as well as bodily torture. My spirit rebelled against the unjustness that had been inflicted upon me, and though I tried to smother my anger and to forgive those who had been so cruel to me, it was impossible. The next morning I was more calm, and I believe that I could then have for given everything for the sake of one kind word. But the kind word was not proffered, and it may be possible that I grew somewhat wayward and sullen. Though I had faults, I know now, as I felt then, harshness was the poorest inducement for the correction of them. It seems that Mr. Bingham had pledged himself to Mrs. Burwell to subdue what he called my "stubborn pride." On Friday following the Saturday on which I was so savagely beaten, Mr. Bingham again directed me to come to his study. I went, but with the determination to offer resistance should he attempt to flog me again. On entering the room I found him prepared with a new rope and a new cowhide. I told him that I was ready to die, but that he could not conquer me. In struggling with him I bit his finger severely, when he seized a heavy stick and beat me with it in a shameful manner. Again I went home sore and bleeding, but with pride as strong and defiant as ever. The following Thursday Mr. Bingham again tried to conquer me, but in vain. We struggled, and he struck me many savage blows. As I stood bleeding before him, nearly exhausted with his efforts, he burst into tears, and declared that it would be a sin to beat me any more. My suffering at last subdued his hard heart; he asked my forgiveness, and afterwards was an altered man. He was never known to strike one of his servants from that day forward. Mr. Burwell, he who preached the love of Heaven, who glorified the precepts and examples of Christ, who expounded the Holy Scriptures Sabbath after Sabbath from the pulpit, when Mr. Bingham refused to whip me any more, was urged by his wife to punish me himself. One morning he went to the wood-pile, took an oak broom, cut the handle off, and with this heavy handle attempted to conquer me. I fought him, but he proved the strongest. At the sight of my bleeding form, his wife fell upon her knees and begged him to desist. My distress even touched her cold, jealous heart. I was so badly bruised that I was unable to leave my bed for five days. I will not dwell upon the bitter anguish of these hours, for even the thought of them now makes me shudder. The Rev. Mr. Burwell was not yet satisfied. He resolved to make another attempt to subdue my proud, rebellious spirit—made the attempt and again failed, when he told me, with an air of penitence, that he should never strike me another blow; and faithfully he kept his word. These revolting scenes created a great sensation at the time, were the talk of the town and neighborhood, and I flatter myself that the actions of those who had conspired against me were not viewed in a light to reflect much credit upon them.

The savage efforts to subdue my pride were not the only things that brought me suffering and deep mortification during my residence at Hillsboro'. I was regarded as fair-looking for one of my race, and for four years a white man—I spare the world his name—had base designs upon me. I do not care to dwell upon this subject, for it is one that is fraught with pain. Suffice it to say, that he persecuted me for four years, and I— I—became a mother. The child of which he was the father was the only child that I ever brought into the world. If my poor boy ever suffered any humiliating pangs on account of birth, he could not blame his mother, for God knows that she did not wish to give him life; he must blame the edicts of that society which deemed it no crime to undermine the virtue of girls in my then position.

HOW I GAINED MY FREEDOM.

. . . My troubles in North Carolina were brought to an end by my unexpected return to Virginia, where I lived with Mr. Garland, who had married Miss Ann Burwell, one of my old master's daughters. His life was not a prosperous one, and after struggling with the world for several years he left his native State, a disappointed man. He moved to St. Louis, hoping to improve his fortune in the West; but ill luck followed him there, and he seemed to be unable to escape from the influence of the evil star of his destiny. When his family, myself included, joined him in his new home on the banks of the Mississippi, we found him so poor that he was unable to pay the dues on a letter advertised as in the post-office for him. The necessities of the family were so great, that it was proposed to place my mother out at service. The idea was shocking to me. Every gray hair in her old head was dear to me, and I could not bear the thought of her going to work for strangers. She had been raised in the family, had watched the growth of each child from infancy to maturity; they had been the objects of her kindest care, and she was wound round about them as the vine winds itself about the rugged oak. They had been the central figures in her dream of life—a dream beautiful to her, since she had basked in the sunshine of no other. And now they proposed to destroy each tendril of affection, to cloud the sunshine of her existence when the day was drawing to a close, when the shadows of solemn night were rapidly approaching. My mother, my poor aged mother, go among strangers to toil for a living! No, a thousand times no! I would rather work my fingers to the bone, bend over my sewing till the film of blindness gathered in my eyes; nay, even beg from street to street. I told Mr. Garland so, and he gave me permission to see what I could do. I was fortunate in obtaining work, and in a short time I had acquired something of a reputation as a seamstress and dress-maker. The best ladies in St. Louis were my patrons, and when my reputation was once established I never lacked for orders. With my needle I kept bread in the mouths of seventeen persons for two years and five months. While I was working so hard that others might live in comparative comfort, and move in those circles of society to which their birth gave them entrance, the thought often occurred to me whether I was really worth my salt or not; and then perhaps the lips curled with a bitter sneer. It may seem strange that I should place so much emphasis upon words thoughtlessly, idly spoken; but then we do many strange things in life, and cannot always explain the motives that actuate us. The heavy task was too much for me, and my health began to give way. About this time Mr. Keckley, whom I had met in Virginia, and learned to regard with more than friendship, came to St. Louis. He sought my hand in marriage, and for a long time I refused to consider his proposal; for I could not bear the thought of bringing children into slavery—of adding one single recruit to the millions bound to hopeless servitude, fettered and shackled with chains stronger and heavier than manacles of iron. I made a proposition to buy myself and son; the proposition was bluntly declined, and I was commanded never to broach the subject again. I would not be put off thus, for hope pointed to a freer, brighter life in the future. Why should my son be held in slavery? I often asked myself. He came into the world through no will of mine, and yet, God only knows how I loved him. The Anglo-Saxon blood as well as the African flowed in his veins; the two currents commingled—one singing of freedom, the other silent and sullen with generations of despair. Why should not the Anglo-Saxon triumph—why should it be weighed down with the rich blood typical of the tropics? Must the life-current of one race bind the other race in chains as strong and enduring as if there had been no Anglo-Saxon taint? By the laws of God and nature, as interpreted by man, one-half of my boy was free, and why should not this fair birthright of freedom remove the curse from the other half—raise it into the bright, joyous sunshine of liberty? I could not answer these questions of my heart that almost maddened me, and I learned to regard human philosophy with distrust. Much as I respected the authority of my master, I could not remain silent on a subject that so nearly concerned me. One day, when I insisted on knowing whether he would permit me to purchase myself, and what price I must pay for myself, he turned to me in a petulant manner, thrust his hand into his pocket, drew forth a bright silver quarter of a dollar, and proffering it to me, said:

"Lizzie, I have told you often not to trouble me with such a question. If you really wish to leave me, take this: it will pay the passage of yourself and boy on the ferry-boat, and when you are on the other side of the river you will be free. It is the cheapest way that I know of to accomplish what you desire."

I looked at him in astonishment, and earnestly replied: "No, master, I do not wish to be free in such a manner. If such had been my wish, I should never have troubled you about obtaining your consent to my purchasing myself. I can cross the river any day, as you well know, and have frequently done so, but will never leave you in such a manner. By the laws of the land I am your slave—you are my master, and I will only be free by such means as the laws of the country provide." He expected this answer, and I knew that he was pleased. Some time afterwards he told me that he had reconsidered the question; that I had served his family faithfully; that I deserved my freedom, and that he would take $1200 for myself and boy.

This was joyful intelligence for me, and the reflection of hope gave a silver lining to the dark cloud of my life—faint, it is true, but still a silver lining.

Taking a prospective glance at liberty, I consented to marry. The wedding was a great event in the family. The ceremony took place in the parlor, in the presence of the family and a number of guests. Mr. Garland gave me away, and the pastor, Bishop Hawks, performed the ceremony, who had solemnized the bridals of Mr. G.'s own children. The day was a happy one, but it faded all too soon. Mr. Keckley—let me speak kindly of his faults—proved dissipated, and a burden instead of a helpmate. More than all, I learned that he was a slave instead of a free man, as he represented himself to be. With the simple explanation that I lived with him eight years, let charity draw around him the mantle of silence.

I went to work in earnest to purchase my freedom, but the years passed, and I was still a slave. Mr. Garland's family claimed so much of my attention—in fact, I supported them—that I was not able to accumulate anything. In the mean time Mr. Garland died, and Mr. Burwell, a Mississippi planter, came to St. Louis to settle up the estate. He was a kind-hearted man, and said I should be free, and would afford me every facility to raise the necessary amount to pay the price of my liberty. Several schemes were urged upon me by my friends. At last I formed a resolution to go to New York, state my case, and appeal to the benevolence of the people. The plan seemed feasible, and I made preparations to carry it out. When I was almost ready to turn my face north-ward, Mrs. Garland told me that she would require the names of six gentlemen who would vouch for my return, and become responsible for the amount at which I was valued. I had many friends in St. Louis, and as I believed that they had confidence in me, I felt that I could readily obtain the names desired. I started out, stated my case, and obtained five signatures to the paper, and my heart throbbed with pleasure, for I did not believe that the sixth would refuse me. I called, he listened patiently, then remarked:

"Yes, yes, Lizzie; the scheme is a fair one, and you shall have my name. But I shall bid you good-by when you start."

"Good-by for a short time," I ventured to add.

"No, good-by for all time," and he looked at me as if he would read my very soul with his eyes.

I was startled. "What do you mean, Mr. Farrow? Surely you do not think that I do not mean to come back?"

"No."

"No, what then?"

"Simply this: you *mean* to come back, that is, you *mean* so *now,* but you never will. When you reach New York the abolitionists will tell you what savages we are, and they will prevail on you to stay there; and we shall never see you again."

"But I assure you, Mr. Farrow, you are mistaken. I not only *mean* to come back, but *will* come back, and pay every cent of the twelve hundred dollars for myself and child."

I was beginning to feel sick at heart, for I could not accept the signature of this man when he had no faith in my pledges. No; slavery, eternal slavery rather than be regarded with distrust by those whose respect I esteemed.

"But—I am not mistaken," he persisted. "Time will show. When you start for the North I shall bid you good-by."

The heart grew heavy. Every ray of sun-shine was eclipsed. With humbled pride, weary step, tearful face, and a dull, aching pain, I left the house. I walked along the street mechanically. The cloud had no silver lining now. The rose-buds of hope had withered and died without lifting up their heads to receive the dew kiss of morning. There was no morning for me—all was night, dark night.

I reached my own home, and weeping threw myself upon the bed. My trunk was packed, my luncheon was prepared by mother, the cars were ready to bear me where I would not hear the clank of chains, where I would breathe the free, invigorating breezes of the glorious North. I had dreamed such a happy dream, in imagination had drunk of the water, the pure, sweet crystal water of life, but now—now—the flowers had withered before my eyes; darkness had settled down upon me like a pall, and I was left alone with cruel mocking shadows.

The first paroxysm of grief was scarcely over, when a carriage stopped in front of the house; Mrs. Le Bourgois, one of my kind patrons, got out of it and entered the door. She seemed to bring sunshine with her handsome cheery face. She came to where I was, and in her sweet way said:—

"Lizzie, I hear that you are going to New York to beg for money to buy your freedom. I have been thinking over the matter, and told Ma it would be a shame to allow you to go North to *beg* for what we should *give* you. You have many friends in St. Louis, and I am going to raise the twelve hundred dollars required among them. I have two hundred dollars put away for a present; am indebted to you one hundred dollars; mother owes you fifty dollars, and will add another fifty to it, and as I do not want the present, I will make the money a present to you. Don't start for New York now until I see what I can do among your friends."

Like a ray of sunshine she came, and like a ray of sunshine she went away. The flowers no longer were withered, drooping. Again they seemed to bud and grow in fragrance and beauty. Mrs. Le Bourgois, God bless her dear good heart, was more than successful. The twelve hundred dollars were raised, and at last my son and myself were free. Free, free! what a glorious ring to the word. Free! the bitter heart-struggle was over. Free! the soul could go out to heaven and to God with no chains to clog its flight or pull it down. Free! the earth wore a brighter look, and the very stars seemed to sing with joy. Yes, free! free by the laws of man and the smile of God—and Heaven bless them who made me so! . . .

I left St. Louis in the spring of 1860, taking the cars direct for Baltimore, where I stopped six weeks, attempting to realize a sum of money by forming classes of young colored women, and teaching them my system of cutting and fitting dresses. The scheme was not successful, for after six weeks of labor and vexation, I left Baltimore with scarcely money enough to pay my fare to Washington. Arriving in the capital, I sought and obtained work at two dollars and a half per day. However, as I was notified that I could only remain in the city ten days without obtaining a license to do so, such being the law, and as I did not know whom to apply to for assistance, I was sorely troubled. I also had to have some one vouch to the authorities that I was a free woman. My means were too scanty, and my profession too precarious to warrant my purchasing license. In my perplexity I called on a lady for whom I was sewing, Miss Ringold, a member of Gen. Mason's family, from Virginia. I stated my case, and she kindly volunteered to render me all the assistance in her power. She called on Mayor Burritt with me, and Miss Ringold suc-

ceeded in making an arrangement for me to remain in Washington without paying the sum required for a license; moreover, I was not to be molested. I rented apartments in a good locality, and soon had a good run of custom. The summer passed, winter came, and I was still in Washington. Mrs. Davis, wife of Senator Jefferson Davis, came from the South in November of 1860, with her husband. Learning that Mrs. Davis wanted a modiste, I presented myself, and was employed by her on the recommendation of one of my patrons and her intimate friend, Mrs. Captain Hetsill. I went to the house to work, but finding that they were such late risers, and as I had to fit many dresses on Mrs. Davis, I told her that I should prefer giving half the day to her, working the other in my own room for some of my other lady patrons. Mrs. D. consented to the proposition, and it was arranged that I should come to her own house every day after 12 M. It was the winter before the breaking out of that fierce and bloody war between the two sections of the country; and as Mr. Davis occupied a leading position, his house was the resort of politicians and statesmen from the South. Almost every night, as I learned from the servants and other members of the family, secret meetings were held at the house; and some of these meetings were protracted to a very late hour. The prospects of war were freely discussed in my presence by Mr. and Mrs. Davis and their friends. The holidays were approaching, and Mrs. Davis kept me busy in manufacturing articles of dress for herself and children. She desired to present Mr. Davis on Christmas with a handsome dressing-gown. The material was purchased, and for weeks the work had been under way. Christmas eve came, and the gown had been laid aside so often that it was still unfinished. I saw that Mrs. D. was anxious to have it completed, so I volunteered to remain and work on it. Wearily the hours dragged on, but there was no rest for my busy fingers. I persevered in my task, notwithstanding my head was aching. Mrs. Davis was busy in the adjoining room, arranging the Christmas tree for the children. I looked at the clock, and the hands pointed to a quarter of twelve. I was arranging the cords on the gown when the Senator came in; he looked somewhat careworn, and his step seemed to be a little nervous. He leaned against the door, and expressed his admiration of the Christmas tree, but there was no smile on his face. Turning round, he saw me sitting in the adjoining room, and quickly exclaimed:

"That you, Lizzie! why are you here so late? Still at work; I hope that Mrs. Davis is not too exacting!"

"No, sir," I answered. "Mrs. Davis was very anxious to have this gown finished tonight, and I volunteered to remain and complete it."

"Well, well, the case must be urgent," and he came slowly towards me, took the gown in his hand, and asked the color of the silk, as he said the gas-light was so deceptive to his old eyes.

"It is a drab changeable silk, Mr. Davis," I answered; and might have added that it was rich and handsome, but did not, well knowing that he would make the discovery in the morning.

He smiled curiously, but turned and walked from the room without another question. He inferred that the gown was for him, that it was to be the Christmas present from his wife, and he did not wish to destroy the pleasure that she would experience in believing that the gift would prove a surprise. In this respect, as in many others, he always appeared to me as a thoughtful, considerate man in the domestic circle. As the clock struck twelve I finished the gown, little dreaming of the future that was before it. It was worn, I have not the shadow of a doubt, by Mr. Davis during the stormy years that he was the President of the Confederate States.

The holidays passed, and before the close of January the war was discussed in Mr. Davis's family as an event certain to happen in the future. Mrs. Davis was warmly attached to Washington, and I often heard her say that she disliked the idea of breaking up old associations, and going South to suffer from trouble and deprivation. One day, while discussing the question in my presence with one of her intimate friends, she exclaimed: "I would rather remain in Washington and be kicked about, than go South and be Mrs. President." Her friend expressed surprise at the remark, and Mrs. Davis insisted that the opinion was an honest one.

While dressing her one day, she said to me: "Lizzie, you are so very handy that I should like to take you South with me."

"When do you go South, Mrs. Davis?" I inquired.

"Oh, I cannot tell just now, but it will be soon. You know there is going to be war, Lizzie?"

"No!"

"But I tell you yes."

"Who will go to war?" I asked.

"The North and South," was her ready reply. "The Southern people will not submit to the humiliating demands of the Abolition party; they will fight first."

"And which do you think will whip?"

"The South, of course. The South is impulsive, is in earnest, and the Southern soldiers will fight to conquer. The North will yield, when it sees the South is in earnest, rather than engage in a long and bloody war."

"But, Mrs. Davis, are you certain that there will be war?"

"Certain!—I know it. You had better go South with me; I will take good care of you. Besides, when the war breaks out, the colored people will suffer in the North. The Northern people will look upon them as the cause of the war, and I fear, in their exasperation, will be inclined to treat you harshly. Then, I may come back to Washington in a few months, and live in the White House. The Southern people talk of choosing Mr. Davis for their President. In fact, it may be considered settled that he will be their President. As soon as we go South and secede from the other States, we will raise an army and march on Washington, and then I shall live in the White House."

I was bewildered with what I heard. I had served Mrs. Davis faithfully, and she had learned to place the greatest confidence in me. At first I was almost tempted to go South with her, for her reasoning seemed plausible. At the time the conversation was closed, with my promise to consider the question.

I thought over the question much, and the more I thought the less inclined I felt to accept the proposition so kindly made by Mrs. Davis. I knew the North to be strong, and believed that the people would fight for the flag that they pretended to venerate so highly. The Republican party had just emerged from a heated campaign, flushed with victory, and I could not think that the hosts composing the party would quietly yield all they had gained in the Presidential canvass. A show of war from the South, I felt, would lead to actual war in the North; and with the two sections bitterly arrayed against each other, I preferred to cast my lot among the people of the North.

I parted with Mrs. Davis kindly, half promising to join her in the South if further deliberation should induce me to change my views.

MY INTRODUCTION TO MRS. LINCOLN

Ever since arriving in Washington I had a great desire to work for the ladies of the White House, and to accomplish this end I was ready to make almost any sacrifice consistent with propriety.

The streets of the capital were thronged with people, for this was Inauguration day. A new President, a man of the people from the broad prairies of the West, was to accept the solemn oath of office, was to assume the responsibilities attached to the high position of Chief Magistrate of the United States. Never was such deep interest felt in the inauguration proceedings as was felt to-day; for threats of assassination had been made, and every breeze from the South came heavily laden with the rumors of war. . . .

With a nervous step I passed on, and knocked at Mrs. Lincoln's door. A cheery voice bade me come in, and a lady, inclined to stoutness, about forty years of age, stood before me.

"You are Lizzie Keckley, I believe."

I bowed assent.

"The dress-maker that Mrs. McClean recommended?"

"Yes, madam."

"Very well; I have not time to talk to you now, but would like to have you call at the White House, at eight o'clock to-morrow morning, where I shall then be."

I bowed myself out of the room, and returned to my apartments. The day passed slowly, for I could not help but speculate in relation to the appointed interview for the morrow. My long-cherished hope was about to be realized, and I could not rest.

Tuesday morning, at eight o'clock, I crossed the threshold of the White House for the first time. I was shown into a waiting-room, and informed that Mrs. Lincoln was at breakfast. In the waiting-room I found no less than three mantua-makers waiting for an interview with the wife of the new President. It seems that Mrs. Lincoln had told several of her lady friends that she had urgent need for a dress-maker, and that each of these friends had sent her mantua-maker to the White House. Hope fell at once. With so many rivals for the position sought after, I regarded my chances for success as extremely doubtful. I was the last one summoned to Mrs. Lincoln's presence. All the others had a hearing, and were dismissed. I went up-stairs timidly, and entering the room with nervous step, discovered the wife of the President standing by a window, looking out, and engaged in lively conversation with a lady, Mrs. Grimsly, as I afterwards learned. Mrs. L. came forward, and greeted me warmly.

"You have come at last. Mrs. Keckley, who have you worked for in the city?"

"Among others, Mrs. Senator Davis has been one of my best patrons," was my reply.

"Mrs. Davis! So you have worked for her, have you? Of course you gave satisfaction; so far, good. Can you do my work?"

"Yes, Mrs. Lincoln. Will you have much work for me to do?"

"That, Mrs. Keckley, will depend altogether upon your prices. I trust that your terms are reasonable. I cannot afford to be extravagant. We are just from the West, and are poor. If you do not charge too much, I shall be able to give you all my work."

"I do not think there will be any difficulty about charges, Mrs. Lincoln; my terms are reasonable."

"Well, if you will work cheap, you shall have plenty to do. I can't afford to pay big prices, so I frankly tell you so in the beginning." . . .

I became the regular modiste of Mrs. Lincoln. I made fifteen or sixteen dresses for her during the spring and early part of the summer, when she left Washington; spending the hot weather at Saratoga, Long Branch, and other places. In the mean time I was employed by Mrs. Senator Douglas, one of the loveliest ladies that I ever met, Mrs. Secretary Wells, Mrs. Secretary Stanton, and others. Mrs. Douglas always dressed in deep mourning, with excellent taste, and several of the leading ladies of Washington society were extremely jealous of her superior attractions. . . .

One fair summer evening I was walking the streets of Washington, accompanied by a friend, when a band of music was heard in the distance. We wondered what it could mean, and curiosity prompted us to find out its meaning. We quickened our steps, and discovered that it came from the house of Mrs. Farnham. The yard was brilliantly lighted, ladies and gentlemen were moving about, and the band was playing some of its sweetest airs. We approached the sentinel on duty at the gate, and asked what was going on. He told us that it was a festival given for the benefit of the sick and wounded soldiers in the city. This suggested an idea to me. If the white people can give festivals to raise funds for the relief of suffering soldiers, why should not the well-to-do colored people go to work to do something for the benefit of the suffering blacks? I could not rest. The thought was ever present with me, and the next Sunday I made

a suggestion in the colored church, that a society of colored people be formed to labor for the benefit of the unfortunate freedmen. The idea proved popular, and in two weeks "the Contraband Relief Association" was organized, with forty working members.

In September of 1862, Mrs. Lincoln left Washington for New York, and requested me to follow her in a few days, and join her at the Metropolitan Hotel. I was glad of the opportunity to do so, for I thought that in New York I would be able to do something in the interests of our society. Armed with credentials, I took the train for New York, and went to the Metropolitan, where Mrs. Lincoln had secured accommodations for me. The next morning I told Mrs. Lincoln of my project; and she immediately headed my list with a subscription of $200. I circulated among the colored people, and got them thoroughly interested in the subject, when I was called to Boston by Mrs. Lincoln, who wished to visit her son Robert, attending college in that city. I met Mr. Wendell Phillips, and other Boston philanthropists, who gave me all the assistance in their power. We held a mass meeting at the Colored Baptist Church, Rev. Mr. Grimes, in Boston, raised a sum of money, and organized there a branch society. The society was organized by Mrs. Grimes, wife of the pastor, assisted by Mrs. Martin, wife of Rev. Stella Martin. This branch of the main society, during the war, was able to send us over eighty large boxes of goods, contributed exclusively by the colored people of Boston. Returning to New York, we held a successful meeting at the Shiloh Church, Rev. Henry Highland Garnet, pastor. The Metropolitan Hotel, at that time as now, employed colored help. I suggested the object of my mission to Robert Thompson, Steward of the Hotel, who immediately raised quite a sum of money among the dining-room waiters. Mr. Frederick Douglass contributed $200, besides lecturing for us. Other prominent colored men sent in liberal contributions. From England a large quantity of stores was received. Mrs. Lincoln made frequent contributions, as also did the President. In 1863 I was re-elected President of the Association, which office I continue to hold. . . .

THE SECOND INAUGURATION

Mrs. Lincoln came to my apartments one day towards the close of the summer of 1864, to consult me in relation to a dress. And here let me remark, I never approved of ladies, attached to the Presidential household, coming to my rooms. I always thought that it would be more consistent with their dignity to send for me, and let me come to them, instead of their coming to me. I may have peculiar notions about some things, and this may be regarded as one of them. No matter, I have recorded my opinion. I cannot forget the associations of my early life. Well, Mrs. Lincoln came to my rooms, and, as usual, she had much to say about the Presidential election.

After some conversation, she asked: "Lizzie, where do you think I will be this time next summer?"

"Why, in the White House, of course."

"I cannot believe so. I have no hope of the re-election of Mr. Lincoln. The canvass is a heated one, the people begin to murmur at the war, and every vile charge is brought against my husband."

"No matter," I replied, "Mr. Lincoln will be re-elected. I am so confident of it, that I am tempted to ask a favor of you."

"A favor! Well, if we remain in the White House I shall be able to do you many favors. What is the special favor?"

"Simply this, Mrs. Lincoln—I should like for you to make me a present of the right-hand glove that the President wears at the first public reception after his second inaugural."

"You shall have it in welcome. It will be so filthy when he pulls it off, I shall be tempted to take the tongs and put it in the fire. I cannot imagine, Lizabeth, what you want with such a glove."

"I shall cherish it as a precious memento of the second inauguration of the man who has done so much for my race. He has been a Je-

hovah to my people—has lifted them out of bondage, and directed their footsteps from darkness into light. I shall keep the glove, and hand it down to posterity."

"You have some strange ideas, Lizabeth. Never mind, you shall have the glove; that is, if Mr. Lincoln continues President after the 4th of March next."

I held Mrs. Lincoln to her promise. That glove is now in my possession, bearing the marks of the thousands of hands that grasped the honest hand of Mr. Lincoln on that eventful night. Alas! it has become a prouder, sadder memento than I ever dreamed—prior to making the request—it would be.

In due time the election came off, and all of my predictions were verified. The loyal States decided that Mr. Lincoln should continue at the nation's helm. Autumn faded, winter dragged slowly by, and still the country resounded with the clash of arms. The South was suffering, yet suffering was borne with heroic determination, and the army continued to present a bold, defiant front. With the first early breath of spring, thousands of people gathered in Washington to witness the second inauguration of Abraham Lincoln as President of the United States. It was a stirring day in the National Capital, and one that will never fade from the memory of those who witnessed the imposing ceremonies. The morning was dark and gloomy; clouds hung like a pall in the sky, as if portending some great disaster. But when the President stepped forward to receive the oath of office, the clouds parted, and a ray of sunshine streamed from the heavens to fall upon and gild his face. It is also said that a brilliant star was seen at noon-day. It was the noon-day of life with Mr. Lincoln, and the star, as viewed in the light of subsequent events, was emblematic of a summons from on high. This was Saturday, and on Monday evening I went to the White House to dress Mrs. Lincoln for the first grand levee. While arranging Mrs. L.'s hair, the President came in. It was the first time I had seen him since the inauguration, and I went up to him, proffering my hand with words of congratulation.

He grasped my outstretched hand warmly, and held it while he spoke: "Thank you. Well, Madam Elizabeth"—he always called me Madam Elizabeth—"I don't know whether I should feel thankful or not. The position brings with it many trials. We do not know what we are destined to pass through. But God will be with us all. I put my trust in God." He dropped my hand, and with solemn face walked across the room and took his seat on the sofa. Prior to this I had congratulated Mrs. Lincoln, and she had answered with a sigh, "Thank you, Elizabeth; but now that we have won the position, I almost wish it were otherwise. Poor Mr. Lincoln is looking so broken-hearted, so completely worn out, I fear he will not get through the next four years." Was it a presentiment that made her take a sad view of the future? News from the front was never more cheering. On every side the Confederates were losing ground, and the lines of blue were advancing in triumph. As I would look out my window almost every day, I could see the artillery going past on its way to the open space of ground, to fire a salute in honor of some new victory. From every point came glorious news of the success of the soldiers that fought for the Union. And yet, in their private chamber, away from the curious eyes of the world, the President and his wife wore sad, anxious faces.

I finished dressing Mrs. Lincoln, and she took the President's arm and went below. It was one of the largest receptions ever held in Washington. Thousands crowded the halls and rooms of the White House, eager to shake Mr. Lincoln by his hand, and receive a gracious smile from his wife. The jam was terrible, and the enthusiasm great. The President's hand was well shaken, and the next day, on visiting Mrs. Lincoln, I received the soiled glove that Mr. Lincoln had worn on his right hand that night.

Many colored people were in Washington, and large numbers had desired to attend the levee, but orders were issued not to admit them. A gentleman, a member of Congress, on his way to the White House, recognized Mr. Frederick Douglass, the eloquent colored orator, on the outskirts of the crowd.

"How do you do, Mr. Douglass? A fearful jam to-night. You are going in, of course?"

"No—that is, no to your last question."

"Not going in to shake the President by the hand! Why, pray?"

"The best reason in the world. Strict orders have been issued not to admit people of color."

"It is a shame, Mr. Douglass, that you should thus be placed under ban. Never mind; wait here, and I will see what can be done."

The gentleman entered the White House, and working his way to the President, asked permission to introduce Mr. Douglass to him.

"Certainly," said Mr. Lincoln. "Bring Mr. Douglass in, by all means. I shall be glad to meet him."

The gentleman returned, and soon Mr. Douglass stood face to face with the President. Mr. Lincoln pressed his hand warmly, saying: "Mr. Douglass, I am glad to meet you. I have long admired your course, and I value your opinions highly."

Mr. Douglass was very proud of the manner in which Mr. Lincoln received him. On leaving the White House he came to a friend's house where a reception was being held, and he related the incident with great pleasure to myself and others.

On the Monday following the reception at the White House, everybody was busy preparing for the grand inaugural ball to come off that night. I was in Mrs. Lincoln's room the greater portion of the day. While dressing her that night, the President came in, and I remarked to him how much Mr. Douglass had been pleased on the night he was presented to Mr. Lincoln. Mrs. L. at once turned to her husband with the inquiry, "Father, why was not Mr. Douglass introduced to me?"

"I do not know. I thought he was presented."

"But he was not."

"It must have been an oversight then, mother; I am sorry you did not meet him.". . .

During my residence in the Capital I made my home with Mr. and Mrs. Walker Lewis, people of my own race, and friends in the truest sense of the word.

The days passed without any incident of particular note disturbing the current of life. On Friday morning, April 14th—alas! what American does not remember the day—I saw Mrs. Lincoln but for a moment. She told me that she was to attend the theatre that night with the President, but I was not summoned to assist her in making her toilette. Sherman had swept from the northern border of Georgia through the heart of the Confederacy down to the sea, striking the death-blow to the rebellion. Grant had pursued General Lee beyond Richmond, and the army of Virginia, that had made such stubborn resistance, was crumbling to pieces. Fort Sumter had fallen;—the stronghold first wrenched from the Union, and which had braved the fury of Federal guns for so many years, was restored to the Union; the end of the war was near at hand, and the great pulse of the loyal North thrilled with joy. The dark war-cloud was fading, and a white-robed angel seemed to hover in the sky, whispering "Peace—peace on earth, good-will toward men!" Sons, brothers, fathers, friends, sweethearts were coming home. Soon the white tents would be folded, the volunteer army be disbanded, and tranquillity again reign. Happy, happy day!—happy at least to those who fought under the banner of the Union. There was great rejoicing throughout the North. From the Atlantic to the Pacific, flags were gayly thrown to the breeze, and at night every city blazed with its tens of thousand lights. But scarcely had the fireworks ceased to play, and the lights been taken down from the windows, when the lightning flashed the most appalling news over the magnetic wires. "The President has been murdered!" spoke the swift-winged messenger, and the loud huzza died upon the lips. A nation suddenly paused in the midst of festivity, and stood paralyzed with horror—transfixed with awe.

Oh, memorable day! Oh, memorable night! Never before was joy so violently contrasted with sorrow.

At 11 o'clock at night I was awakened by an old friend and neighbor, Miss M. Brown, with the startling intelligence that the entire Cabinet had been assassinated, and Mr. Lincoln shot, but not mortally wounded. When I heard the words I felt as if the blood had been frozen in my veins, and that my lungs must collapse for the want of air. Mr. Lincoln shot! the Cabinet assassinated! What could it mean? The streets were alive with wondering, awe-stricken people. Rumors flew thick and fast, and the wildest reports came with every new arrival. The words were repeated with blanched cheeks and quivering lips. I waked Mr. and Mrs. Lewis, and told them that the President was shot, and that I must go to the White House. I could not remain in a state of uncertainty. I felt that the house would not hold me. They tried to quiet me, but gentle words could not calm the wild tempest. They quickly dressed themselves, and we sallied out into the street to drift with the excited throng. We walked rapidly towards the White House, and on our way passed the residence of Secretary Seward, which was surrounded by armed soldiers, keeping back all intruders with the point of the bayonet. We hurried on, and as we approached the White House, saw that it too was surrounded with soldiers. Every entrance was strongly guarded, and no one was permitted to pass. The guard at the gate told us that Mr. Lincoln had not been brought home, but refused to give any other information. More excited than ever, we wandered down the street. Grief and anxiety were making me weak, and as we joined the outskirts of a large crowd, I began to feel as meek and humble as a penitent child. A gray-haired old man was passing. I caught a glimpse of his face, and it seemed so full of kindness and sorrow that I gently touched his arm, and imploringly asked:

"Will you please, sir, to tell me whether Mr. Lincoln is dead or not?"

"Not dead," he replied, "but dying. God help us!" and with a heavy step he passed on.

"Not dead, but dying! then indeed God help us!"

We learned that the President was mortally wounded—that he had been shot down in his box at the theatre, and that he was not expected to live till morning; when we returned home with heavy hearts, I could not sleep. I wanted to go to Mrs. Lincoln, as I pictured her wild with grief; but then I did not know where to find her, and I must wait till morning. Never did the hours drag so slowly. Every moment seemed an age, and I could do nothing but walk about and hold my arms in mental agony.

Morning came at last, and a sad morning was it. The flags that floated so gayly yesterday now were draped in black, and hung in silent folds at half-mast. The President was dead, and a nation was mourning for him. Every house was draped in black, and every face wore a solemn look. People spoke in subdued tones, and glided whisperingly, wonderingly, silently about the streets.

About eleven o'clock on Saturday morning a carriage drove up to the door, and a messenger asked for "Elizabeth Keckley."

"Who wants her?" I asked.

"I come from Mrs. Lincoln. If you are Mrs. Keckley, come with me immediately to the White House."

I hastily put on my shawl and bonnet, and was driven at a rapid rate to the White House. Everything about the building was sad and solemn. I was quickly shown to Mrs. Lincoln's room, and on entering, saw Mrs. L. tossing uneasily about upon a bed. The room was darkened, and the only person in it besides the widow of the President was Mrs. Secretary Welles, who had spent the night with her. Bowing to Mrs. Welles, I went to the bedside.

"Why did you not come to me last night, Elizabeth—I sent for you?" Mrs. Lincoln asked in a low whisper.

"I did try to come to you, but I could not find you," I answered, as I laid my hand upon her hot brow.

I afterwards learned, that when she had partially recovered from the first shock of the terrible tragedy in the theatre, Mrs. Welles asked:

"Is there no one, Mrs. Lincoln, that you desire to have with you in this terrible affliction?"

"Yes, send for Elizabeth Keckley. I want her just as soon as she can be brought here."

Three messengers, it appears, were successively despatched for me, but all of them mistook the number and failed to find me.

Shortly after entering the room on Saturday morning, Mrs. Welles excused herself, as she said she must go to her own family, and I was left alone with Mrs. Lincoln.

She was nearly exhausted with grief, and when she became a little quiet, I asked and received permission to go into the Guests' Room, where the body of the President lay in state. When I crossed the threshold of the room, I could not help recalling the day on which I had seen little Willie lying in his coffin where the body of his father now lay. I remembered how the President had wept over the pale beautiful face of his gifted boy, and now the President himself was dead. The last time I saw him he spoke kindly to me, but alas! the lips would never move again. The light had faded from his eyes, and when the light went out the soul went with it. What a noble soul was his—noble in all the noble attributes of God! Never did I enter the solemn chamber of death with such palpitating heart and trembling footsteps as I entered it that day. No common mortal had died. The Moses of my people had fallen in the hour of his triumph. Fame had woven her choicest chaplet for his brow. Though the brow was cold and pale in death, the chaplet should not fade, for God had studded it with the glory of the eternal stars.

When I entered the room, the members of the Cabinet and many distinguished officers of the army were grouped around the body of their fallen chief. They made room for me, and, approaching the body, I lifted the white cloth from the white face of the man that I had worshipped as an idol—looked upon as a demi-god. Not-withstanding the violence of the death of the President, there was something beautiful as well as grandly solemn in the expression of the placid face. There lurked the sweetness and gentleness of childhood, and the stately grandeur of god-like intellect. I gazed long at the face, and turned away with tears in my eyes and a choking sensation in my throat. Ah! never was man so widely mourned before. The whole world bowed their heads in grief when Abraham Lincoln died.

Reminiscences of My Life in Camp

Susie Taylor King

II

My Childhood

I was born under the slave law in Georgia, in 1848, and was brought up by my grandmother in Savannah. There were three of us with her, my younger sister and brother. My brother and I being the two eldest, we were sent to a friend of my grandmother, Mrs. Woodhouse, a widow, to learn to read and write. She was a free woman and lived on Bay Lane, between Habersham and Price streets, about half a mile from my house. We went every day about nine o'clock, with our books wrapped in paper to prevent the police or white persons from seeing them. We went in, one at a time, through the gate, into the yard to the L kitchen, which was the schoolroom. She had twenty-five or thirty children whom she taught, assisted by her daughter, Mary Jane. The neighbors would see us going in sometimes, but they supposed we were there learning trades, as it was the custom to give children a trade of some kind. After school we left the same way we entered, one by one, when we would go to a square, about a block from the school, and wait for each other. We would gather laurel leaves and pop them on our hands, on

our way home. I remained at her school for two years or more, when I was sent to a Mrs. Mary Beasley, where I continued until May, 1860, when she told my grandmother she had taught me all she knew, and grandmother had better get some one else who could teach me more, so I stopped my studies for a while.

I had a white playmate about this time, named Katie O'Connor, who lived on the next corner of the street from my house, and who attended a convent. One day she told me, if I would promise not to tell her father, she would give me some lessons. On my promise not to do so, and getting her mother's consent, she gave me lessons about four months, every evening. At the end of this time she was put into the convent permanently, and I have never seen her since.

A month after this, James Blouis, our landlord's son, was attending the High School, and was very fond of grandmother, so she asked him to give me a few lessons, which he did until the middle of 1861, when the Savannah Volunteer Guards, to which he and his brother belonged, were ordered to the front under General Barton. In the first battle of Manassas, his brother Eugene was killed, and James deserted over to the Union side, and at the close of the war went to Washington, D.C., where he has since resided.

I often wrote passes for my grandmother, for all colored persons, free or slaves, were compelled to have a pass; free colored people having a guardian in place of a master. These passes were good until 10 or 10.30

Source: Susie Taylor King, *Reminiscences of My Life in Camp.* (Boston, 1902), pp. 5–10, 11–17, 19, 21, 22–30, 31–35, 42–44, 45–52, 61–62, 65–66, 67–68, 75–76.

P. M. for one night or every night for one month. The pass read as follows:—

Savannah, Ga., March 1st, 1860.
Pass the bearer——from 9 to 10.30. P. M.
VALENTINE GREST.

Every person had to have this pass, for at nine o'clock each night a bell was rung, and any colored persons found on the street after this hour were arrested by the watchman, and put in the guard-house until next morning, when their owners would pay their fines and release them. I knew a number of persons who went out at any time at night and were never arrested, as the watchman knew them so well he never stopped them, and seldom asked to see their passes, only stopping them long enough, sometimes, to say "Howdy," and then telling them to go along.

About this time I had been reading so much about the "Yankees" I was very anxious to see them. The whites would tell their colored people not to go to the Yankees, for they would harness them to carts and make them pull the carts around, in place of horses. I asked grandmother, one day, if this was true. She replied, "Certainly not!" that the white people did not want slaves to go over to the Yankees, and told them these things to frighten them. "Don't you see those signs pasted about the streets? one reading, 'I am a rattlesnake; if you touch me I will strike!' Another reads, 'I am a wild-cat! Beware,' etc. These are warnings to the North; so don't mind what the white people say." I wanted to see these wonderful "Yankees" so much, as I heard my parents say the Yankee was going to set all the slaves free. Oh, how those people prayed for freedom! I remember, one night, my grandmother went out into the suburbs of the city to a church meeting, and they were fervently singing this old hymn,—

"Yes, we all shall be free,
Yes, we all shall be free,
Yes, we all shall be free,
When the Lord shall appear,"—

when the police came in and arrested all who were there, saying they were planning freedom, and sang "the Lord," in place of "Yankee," to blind any one who might be listening. Grandmother never forgot that night, although she did not stay in the guard-house, as she sent to her guardian, who came at once for her; but this was the last meeting she ever attended out of the city proper.

On April 1, 1862, about the time the Union soldiers were firing on Fort Pulaski, I was sent out into the country to my mother. I remember what a roar and din the guns made. They jarred the earth for miles. The fort was at last taken by them. Two days after the taking of Fort Pulaski, my uncle took his family of seven and myself to St. Catherine Island. We landed under the protection of the Union fleet, and remained there two weeks, when about thirty of us were taken aboard the gunboat P——, to be transferred to St. Simon's Island; and at last, to my unbounded joy, I saw the "Yankee."

After we were all settled aboard and started on our journey, Captain Whitmore, commanding the boat, asked me where I was from. I told him Savannah, Ga. He asked if I could read; I said, "Yes!" "Can you write?" he next asked. "Yes, I can do that also," I replied, and as if he had some doubts of my answers he handed me a book and a pencil and told me to write my name and where I was from. I did this; when he wanted to know if I could sew. On hearing I could, he asked me to hem some napkins for him. He was surprised at my accomplishments (for they were such in those days), for he said he did not know there were any negroes in the South able to read or write. He said, "You seem to be so different from the other colored people who came from the same place you did." "No!" I replied, "the only difference is, they were reared in the country and I in the city, as was a man from Darien, Ga., named Edward King." That seemed to satisfy him, and we had no further conversation that day on the subject. . . .

III

On St. Simon's Island

1862 Next morning we arrived at St. Simon's, and the captain told Commodore Goldsborough about this affair, and his reply was, "Captain Whitmore, you should not have allowed them to return; you should have kept them." After I had been on St. Simon's about three days, Commodore Goldsborough heard of me, and came to Gaston Bluff to see me. I found him very cordial. He said Captain Whitmore had spoken to him of me, and that he was pleased to hear of my being so capable, etc., and wished me to take charge of a school for the children on the island. I told him I would gladly do so, if I could have some books. He said I should have them, and in a week or two I received two large boxes of books and testaments from the North. I had about forty children to teach, beside a number of adults who came to me nights, all of them so eager to learn to read, to read above anything else. Chaplain French, of Boston, would come to the school, sometimes, and lecture to the pupils on Boston and the North.

About the first of June we were told that there was going to be a settlement of the war. Those who were on the Union side would remain free, and those in bondage were to work three days for their masters and three for themselves. It was a gloomy time for us all, and we were to be sent to Liberia. Chaplain French asked me would I rather go back to Savannah or go to Liberia. I told him the latter place by all means. We did not know when this would be, but we were prepared in case this settlement should be reached. However, the Confederates would not agree to the arrangement, or else it was one of the many rumors flying about at the time, as we heard nothing further of the matter. There were a number of settlements on this island of St. Simon's, just like little villages, and we would go from one to the other on business, to call, or only for a walk.

One Sunday, two men, Adam Miller and Daniel Spaulding, were chased by some rebels as they were coming from Hope Place (which was between the Beach and Gaston Bluff), but the latter were unable to catch them. When they reached the Beach and told this, all the men on the place, about ninety, armed themselves, and next day (Monday), with Charles O'Neal as their leader, skirmished the island for the "rebs." In a short while they discovered them in the woods, hidden behind a large log, among the thick underbrush. Charles O'Neal was the first to see them, and he was killed; also John Brown, and their bodies were never found. Charles O'Neal was an uncle of Edward King, who later was my husband and a sergeant in Co. E., U. S. I. Another man was shot, but not found for three days. On Tuesday, the second day, Captain Trowbridge and some soldiers landed, and assisted the skirmishers. Word having been sent by the mail-boat Uncas to Hilton Head, later in the day Commodore Goldsborough, who was in command of the naval station, landed about three hundred marines, and joined the others to oust the rebels. On Wednesday, John Baker, the man shot on Monday, was found in a terrible condition by Henry Batchlott, who carried him to the Beach, where he was attended by the surgeon. He told us how, after being shot, he lay quiet for a day. On the second day he managed to reach some wild grapes growing near him. These he ate, to satisfy his hunger and intense thirst, then he crawled slowly, every movement causing agony, until he got to the side of the road. He lived only three months after they found him.

On the second day of the skirmish the troops captured a boat which they knew the Confederates had used to land in, and having this in their possession, the "rebs" could not return; so pickets were stationed all around the island. There was an old man, Henry Capers, who had been left on one of the places by his old master, Mr. Hazzard, as he was too old to carry away. These rebels went to his house in the night, and he hid them up in the loft. On Tuesday all hands went to this man's house with a determination to burn it down, but Henry Batchlott pleaded with the men to spare it. The rebels were in hiding, still, waiting a chance to get off the island. They searched his house, but neglected to go up into the loft, and in so doing missed the rebels concealed there. Late in the night Henry Capers gave them his boat to escape in, and they got off all right. This old man was allowed by the men in charge of the island to cut grass for his horse, and to have a boat to carry this grass to his home, and so they were not detected, our men thinking it was Capers using the boat. After Commodore Goldsborough left the island, Commodore Judon sent the old man over to the mainland and would not allow him to remain on the island.

There were about six hundred men, women, and children on St. Simon's, the women and children being in the majority, and we were afraid to go very far from our own quarters in the daytime, and at night even to go out of the house for a long time, although the men were on the watch all the time; for there were not any soldiers on the island, only the marines who were on the gunboats along the coast. The rebels, knowing this, could steal by them under cover of the night, and getting on the island would capture any persons venturing out alone and carry them to the mainland. Several of the men disappeared, and as they were never heard from we came to the conclusion they had been carried off in this way.

The latter part of August, 1862, Captain C. T. Trowbridge, with his brother John and Lieutenant Walker, came to St. Simon's Island from Hilton Head, by order of General Hunter, to get all the men possible to finish filling his regiment which he had organized in March, 1862. He had heard of the skirmish on this island, and was very much pleased at the bravery shown by these men. He found me at Gaston Bluff teaching my little school, and was much interested in it. When I knew him better I found him to be a thorough gentleman and a staunch friend to my race.

Captain Trowbridge remained with us until October, when the order was received to evacuate, and so we boarded the Ben-De-Ford, a transport, for Beaufort, S. C. When we arrived in Beaufort, Captain Trowbridge and the men he had enlisted went to camp at Old Fort, which they named "Camp Saxton." I was enrolled as laundress.

The first suits worn by the boys were red coats and pants, which they disliked very much, for, they said, "The rebels see us, miles away."

The first colored troops did not receive any pay for eighteen months, and the men had to depend wholly on what they received from the commissary, established by General Saxton. A great many of these men had large families, and as they had no money to give them, their wives were obliged to support themselves and children by washing for the officers of the gunboats and the soldiers, and making cakes and pies which they sold to the boys in camp. Finally, in 1863, the government decided to give them half pay, but the men would not accept this. They wanted "full pay" or nothing. They preferred rather to give their services to the state, which they did until 1864, when the government granted them full pay, with all the back pay due.

I remember hearing Captain Heasley telling his company, one day, "Boys, stand up for your full pay! I am with you, and so are all the officers." This captain was from Pennsylvania, and was a very good man; all the men liked him. N. G. Parker, our first lieutenant, was from Massachusetts. H. A. Beach was from New York. He was very delicate, and had to resign in 1864 on account of ill health.

I had a number of relatives in this regiment,—several uncles, some cousins, and a husband in Company E, and a number of cousins in other companies. Major Strong, of this regiment, started home on a furlough, but the vessel he was aboard was lost, and he never reached his home. He was one of the best officers we had. After his death, Captain C. T. Trowbridge was promoted major, August, 1863, and filled Major Strong's place until December, 1864, when he was promoted lieutenant-colonel, which he remained until he was mustered out, February 6, 1866.

In February, 1863, several cases of varioloid broke out among the boys, which caused some anxiety in camp. Edward Davis, of Company E (the company I was with), had it very badly. He was put into a tent apart from the rest of the men, and only the doctor and camp steward, James Cummings, were allowed to see or attend him; but I went to see this man every day and nursed him. The last thing at night, I always went in to see that he was comfortable, but in spite of the good care and attention he received, he succumbed to the disease.

I was not in the least afraid of the smallpox. I had been vaccinated, and I drank sassafras tea constantly, which kept my blood purged and prevented me from contracting this dread scourge, and no one need fear getting it if they will only keep their blood in good condition with this sassafras tea, and take it before going where the patient is.

IV

Camp Saxton—Proclamation and Barbecue

1863 On the first of January, 1863, we held services for the purpose of listening to the reading of President Lincoln's proclamation by Dr. W. H. Brisbane, and the presentation of two beautiful stands of colors, one from a lady in Connecticut, and the other from Rev. Mr. Cheever. The presentation speech was made by Chaplain French. It was a glorious day for us all, and we enjoyed every minute of it, and as a fitting close and the crowning event of this occasion we had a grand barbecue. A number of oxen were roasted whole, and we had a fine feast. Although not served as tastily or correctly as it would have been at home, yet it was enjoyed with keen appetites and relish. The soldiers had a good time. They sang or shouted "Hurrah!" all through the camp, and seemed overflowing with fun and frolic until taps were sounded, when many, no doubt, dreamt of this memorable day. . . .

I did not go any more until the regiment was ordered to our new camp, which was named after our hero, Colonel Shaw, who at that time was at Beaufort with his regiment, the 54th Massachusetts.

I taught a great many of the comrades in Company E to read and write, when they were off duty. Nearly all were anxious to learn. My husband taught some also when it was convenient for him. I was very happy to know my efforts were successful in camp, and also felt grateful for the appreciation of my services. I gave my services willingly for four years and three months without receiving a dollar. I was glad, however, to be allowed to go with the regiment, to care for the sick and afflicted comrades.

V

Military Expeditions, and Life in Camp

. . . March 10, 1863, we were ordered to Jacksonville, Florida. Leaving Camp Saxton between four and five o'clock, we arrived at Jacksonville about eight o'clock next morning, accompanied by three or four gunboats. When the rebels saw these boats, they ran out of the city, leaving the women behind, and we found out afterwards that they thought we had a much larger fleet than we really had. Our regiment was kept out of sight until we made fast at the wharf where it landed, and while the gunboats were shelling up the river and as far inland as possible, the regiment landed and marched up the street, where they spied the rebels who had fled from the city. They were hiding behind a house about a mile or so away, their faces blackened to disguise themselves as negroes, and our boys, as they advanced toward them, halted a second, saying, "They are black men! Let them come to us, or we will make them know who we are." With this, the firing was opened and several of our men were wounded and killed. The rebels had a number wounded and killed. It was through this way the discovery was made that they were white men. Our men drove them some distance in retreat and then threw out their pickets.

While the fighting was on, a friend, Lizzie Lancaster, and I stopped at several of the rebel homes, and after talking with some of the women and children we asked them if they had any food. They claimed to have only some hard-tack, and evidently did not care to give us anything to eat, but this was not surprising. They were bitterly against our people and had no mercy or sympathy for us.

The second day, our boys were reinforced by a regiment of white soldiers, a Maine regiment, and by cavalry, and had quite a fight. On the third day, Edward Herron, who was a fine gunner on the steamer John Adams, came on shore, bringing a small cannon, which the men pulled along for more than five miles. This cannon was the only piece for shelling. On coming upon the enemy, all secured their places, and they had a lively fight, which lasted several hours, and our boys were nearly captured by the Confederates; but the Union boys carried out all their plans that day, and succeeded in driving the enemy back. After this skirmish, every afternoon between four and five o'clock the Confederate General Finegan would send a flag of truce to Colonel Higginson, warning him to send all women and children out of the city, and threatening to bombard it if this was not done. Our colonel allowed all to go who wished, at first, but as General Finegan grew more hostile and kept sending these communications for nearly a week, Colonel Higginson thought it not best or necessary to send any more out of the city, and so informed General Finegan. This angered the general, for that night the rebels shelled directly toward Colonel Higginson's headquarters. The shelling was so heavy that the colonel told my captain to have me taken up into the town to a hotel, which was used as a hospital. As my quarters were just in the rear of the colonel's, he was compelled to leave his also before the night was over. I expected every moment to be killed by a shell, but on arriving at the hospital I knew I was safe, for

the shells could not reach us there. It was plainly to be seen now, the ruse of the flag of truce coming so often to us. The bearer was evidently a spy getting the location of the headquarters, etc., for the shells were sent too accurately to be at random.

Next morning Colonel Higginson took the cavalry and a regiment on another tramp after the rebels. They were gone several days and had the hardest fight they had had, for they wanted to go as far as a station which was some distance from the city. The gunboats were of little assistance to them, yet notwithstanding this drawback our boys returned with only a few killed and wounded, and after this we were not troubled with General Finegan.

We remained here a few weeks longer, when, about April first, the regiment was ordered back to Camp Saxton, where it stayed a week, when the order came to go to Port Royal Ferry on picket duty. It was a gay day for the boys. By seven o'clock all tents were down, and each company, with a commissary wagon, marched up the shell road, which is a beautiful avenue ten or twelve miles out of Beaufort. We arrived at Seabrooke at about four o'clock, where our tents were pitched and the men put on duty. We were here a few weeks, when Company E was ordered to Barnwell plantation for picket duty.

Some mornings I would go along the picket line, and I could see the rebels on the opposite side of the river. Sometimes as they were changing pickets they would call over to our men and ask for something to eat, or for tobacco, and our men would tell them to come over. Sometimes one or two would desert to us, saying, they "had no negroes to fight for." Others would shoot across at our picket, but as the river was so wide there was never any damage done, and the Confederates never attempted to shell us while we were there.

I learned to handle a musket very well while in the regiment, and could shoot straight and often hit the target. I assisted in cleaning the guns and used to fire them off, to see if the cartridges were dry, before cleaning and reloading, each day. I thought this great fun. I was also able to take a gun all apart, and put it together again.

Between Barnwell and the mainland was Hall Island. I went over there several times with Sergeant King and other comrades. One night there was a stir in camp when it was found that the rebels were trying to cross, and next morning Lieutenant Parker told me he thought they were on Hall Island; so after that I did not go over again.

While planning for the expedition up the Edisto River, Colonel Higginson was a whole night in the water, trying to locate the rebels and where their picket lines were situated. About July the boys went up the Edisto to destroy a bridge on the Charleston and Savannah road. This expedition was twenty or more miles into the mainland. Colonel Higginson was wounded in this fight and the regiment nearly captured. The steamboat John Adams always assisted us, carrying soldiers, provisions, etc. She carried several guns and a good gunner, Edward Herron. Henry Batchlott, a relative of mine, was a steward on this boat. There were two smaller boats, Governor Milton and the Enoch Dean, in the fleet, as these could go up the river better than the larger ones could. I often went aboard the John Adams. It went with us into Jacksonville, to Cole and Folly Island, and Gunner Herron was always ready to send a shell at the enemy.

One night, Companies K and E, on their way to Pocotaligo to destroy a battery that was situated down the river, captured several prisoners. The rebels nearly captured Sergeant King, who, as he sprang and caught a "reb," fell over an embankment. In falling he did not release his hold on his prisoner. Although his hip was severely injured, he held fast until some of his comrades came to his aid and pulled them up. These expeditions were very dangerous. Sometimes the men had to go five or ten miles during the night over on the rebel side and capture or destroy whatever they could find.

While at Camp Shaw, there was a deserter who came into Beaufort. He was allowed his freedom about the city and was not molested.

He remained about the place a little while and returned to the rebels again. On his return to Beaufort a second time, he was held as a spy, tried, and sentenced to death, for he was a traitor. The day he was shot, he was placed on a hearse with his coffin inside, a guard was placed either side of the hearse, and he was driven through the town. All the soldiers and people in town were out, as this was to be a warning to the soldiers. Our regiment was in line on dress parade. They drove with him to the rear of our camp, where he was shot. I shall never forget this scene.

While at Camp Shaw, Chaplain Fowler, Robert Defoe, and several of our boys were captured while tapping some telegraph wires. Robert Defoe was confined in the jail at Walterborough, S. C., for about twenty months. When Sherman's army reached Pocotaligo he made his escape and joined his company (Company G). He had not been paid, as he had refused the reduced pay offered by the government. Before we got to camp, where the pay-rolls could be made out, he sickened and died of small-pox, and was buried at Savannah, never having been paid one cent for nearly three years of service. He left no heirs and his account was never settled.

In winter, when it was very cold, I would take a mess-pan, put a little earth in the bottom, and go to the cook-shed and fill it nearly full of coals, carry it back to my tent and put another pan over it; so when the provost guard went through camp after taps, they would not see the light, as it was against the rules to have a light after taps. In this way I was heated and kept very warm.

A mess-pan is made of sheet iron, something like our roasting pans, only they are nearly as large round as a peck measure, but not so deep. We had fresh beef once in a while, and we would have soup, and the vegetables they put in this soup were dried and pressed. They looked like hops. Salt beef was our stand-by. Sometimes the men would have what we called slap-jacks. This was flour, made into bread and spread thin on the bottom of the mess-pan to cook. Each man had one of them, with a pint of tea, for his supper, or a pint of tea and five or six hard-tack. I often got my own meals, and would fix some dishes for the non-commissioned officers also.

Mrs. Chamberlain, our quartermaster's wife, was with us here. She was a beautiful woman; I can see her pleasant face before me now, as she, with Captain Trowbridge, would sit and converse with me in my tent two or three hours at a time. She was also with me on Cole Island, and I think we were the only women with the regiment while there. I remember well how, when she first came into camp, Captain Trowbridge brought her to my tent and introduced her to me. I found her then, as she remained ever after, a lovely person, and I always admired her cordial and friendly ways.

Our boys would say to me sometimes, "Mrs. King, why is it you are so kind to us? you treat us just as you do the boys in your own company." I replied, "Well, you know, all the boys in other companies are the same to me as those in my Company E; you are all doing the same duty, and I will do just the same for you." "Yes," they would say, "we know that, because you were the first woman we saw when we came into camp, and you took an interest in us boys ever since we have been here, and we are very grateful for all you do for us."

When at Camp Shaw, I visited the hospital in Beaufort, where I met Clara Barton. There were a number of sick and wounded soldiers there, and I went often to see the comrades. Miss Barton was always very cordial toward me, and I honored her for her devotion and care of those men. . . .

VI

On Morris and Other Islands

Fort Wagner being only a mile from our camp, I went there two or three times a week, and would go up on the ramparts to watch the gunners send their shells into Charleston (which they did every fifteen minutes), and had a full view of the city from that point. Outside of the fort were many skulls lying about; I have often moved them one side out of the path. The comrades and I would have quite a debate as to which side the men fought on. Some thought they were the skulls of our boys; others thought they were the enemy's; but as there was no definite way to know, it was never decided which could lay claim to them. They were a gruesome sight, those fleshless heads and grinning jaws, but by this time I had become accustomed to worse things and did not feel as I might have earlier in my camp life.

It seems strange how our aversion to seeing suffering is overcome in war,—how we are able to see the most sickening sights, such as men with their limbs blown off and mangled by the deadly shells, without a shudder; and instead of turning away, how we hurry to assist in alleviating their pain, bind up their wounds, and press the cool water to their parched lips, with feelings only of sympathy and pity.

About the first of June, 1864, the regiment was ordered to Folly Island, staying there until the latter part of the month, when it was ordered to Morris Island. We landed on Morris Island between June and July, 1864. This island was a narrow strip of sandy soil, nothing growing on it but a few bushes and shrubs. The camp was one mile from the boat landing, called Pawnell Landing, and the landing one mile from Fort Wagner.

Colonel Higginson had left us in May of this year, on account of wounds received at Edisto. All the men were sorry to lose him. They did not want him to go, they loved him so. He was kind and devoted to his men, thoughtful for their comfort, and we missed his genial presence from the camp.

The regiment under Colonel Trowbridge did garrison duty, but they had troublesome times from Fort Gregg, on James Island, for the rebels would throw a shell over on our island every now and then. Finally orders were received for the boys to prepare to take Fort

Gregg, each man to take 150 rounds of cartridges, canteens of water, hard-tack, and salt beef. This order was sent three days prior to starting, to allow them to be in readiness. I helped as many as I could to pack haversacks and cartridge boxes.

The fourth day, about five o'clock in the afternoon, the call was sounded, and I heard the first sergeant say, "Fall in, boys, fall in," and they were not long obeying the command. Each company marched out of its street, in front of their colonel's headquarters, where they rested for half an hour, as it was not dark enough, and they did not want the enemy to have a chance to spy their movements. At the end of this time the line was formed with the 103d New York (white) in the rear, and off they started, eager to get to work. It was quite dark by the time they reached Pawnell Landing. I have never forgotten the good-bys of that day, as they left camp. Colonel Trowbridge said to me as he left, "Good-by, Mrs. King, take care of yourself if you don't see us again." I went with them as far as the landing, and watched them until they got out of sight, and then I returned to the camp. There was no one at camp but those left on picket and a few disabled soldiers, and one woman, a friend of mine, Mary Shaw, and it was lonesome and sad, now that the boys were gone, some never to return.

Mary Shaw shared my tent that night, and we went to bed, but not to sleep, for the fleas nearly ate us alive. We caught a few, but it did seem, now that the men were gone, that every flea in camp had located my tent, and caused us to vacate. Sleep being out of the question, we sat up the remainder of the night.

About four o'clock, July 2, the charge was made. The firing could be plainly heard in camp. I hastened down to the landing and remained there until eight o'clock that morning. When the wounded arrived, or rather began to arrive, the first one brought in was Samuel Anderson of our company. He was badly wounded. Then others of our boys, some with their legs off, arm gone, foot off, and wounds of all kinds imaginable. They had to wade through creeks and marshes, as

they were discovered by the enemy and shelled very badly. A number of the men were lost, some got fastened in the mud and had to cut off the legs of their pants, to free themselves. The 103d New York suffered the most, as their men were very badly wounded.

My work now began. I gave my assistance to try to alleviate their sufferings. I asked the doctor at the hospital what I could get for them to eat. They wanted soup, but that I could not get; but I had a few cans of condensed milk and some turtle eggs, so I thought I would try to make some custard. I had doubts as to my success, for cooking with turtle eggs was something new to me, but the adage has it, "Nothing ventured, nothing done," so I made a venture and the result was a very delicious custard. This I carried to the men, who enjoyed it very much. My services were given at all times for the comfort of these men. I was on hand to assist whenever needed. I was enrolled as company laundress, but I did very little of it, because I was always busy doing other things through camp, and was employed all the time doing something for the officers and comrades....

IX

Capture of Charleston

On February 28, 1865, the remainder of the regiment were ordered to Charleston, as there were signs of the rebels evacuating that city. Leaving Cole Island, we arrived in Charleston between nine and ten o'clock in the morning, and found the "rebs" had set fire to the city and fled, leaving women and children behind to suffer and perish in the flames. The fire had been burning fiercely for a day and night. When we landed, under a flag of truce, our regiment went to work assisting the citizens in subduing the flames. It was a terrible scene. For three or four days the men fought the fire, saving the property and effects of the people, yet these white men and women could not tolerate our black Union soldiers, for many of them had formerly been their slaves; and although these brave men risked life and limb to assist them in their distress, men and even women would sneer and molest them whenever they met them.

I had quarters assigned me at a residence on South Battery Street, one of the most aristocratic parts of the city, where I assisted in caring for the sick and injured comrades. After getting the fire under control, the regiment marched out to the race track, where they camped until March 12, when we were ordered to Savannah, Ga. We arrived there on the 13th, about eight o'clock in the evening, and marched out to Fairlong, near the A. & G. R. R., where we remained about ten days, when we were ordered to Augusta, Ga., where Captain Alexander Heasley, of Co. E, was shot and killed by a Confederate. After his death Lieutenant Parker was made captain of the company, and was with us until the regiment was mustered out. He often told me about Massachusetts, but I had no thought at that time that I should ever see that State, and stand in the "Cradle of Liberty."

The regiment remained in Augusta for thirty days, when it was ordered to Hamburg, S. C., and then on to Charleston. It was while on their march through the country, to the latter city, that they came in contact with the bushwhackers (as the rebels were called), who hid in the bushes and would shoot the Union boys every chance they got. Other times they would conceal themselves in the cars used to transfer our soldiers, and when our boys, worn out and tired, would fall asleep, these men would come out from their hiding places and cut their throats. Several of our men were killed in this way, but it could not be found out who was committing these murders until one night one of the rebels was caught in the act, trying to cut the throat of a sleeping soldier. He was put under guard, court-martialed, and shot at Wall Hollow.

First Lieutenant Jerome T. Furman and a number of soldiers were killed by these South Carolina bushwhackers at Wall Hollow. After this man was shot, however, the regiment marched through unmolested to Charleston.

X

Mustered Out

The regiment, under Colonel Trowbridge, reached Charleston in November, 1865, and camped on the race track until January, when they returned to Morris Island, and on February 9, 1866, the following "General Orders" were received and the regiment mustered out.

They were delighted to go home, but oh! how they hated to part from their commanding chief, Colonel C. T. Trowbridge. He was the very first officer to take charge of black soldiers. We thought there was no one like him, for he was a "man" among his soldiers. All in the regiment knew him personally, and many were the jokes he used to tell them. I shall never forget his friendship and kindness toward me, from the first time I met him to the end of the war. There was never any one from the North who came into our camp but he would bring them to see me.

While on a visit South in 1888, I met a comrade of the regiment, who often said to me, "You up North, Mrs. King, do you ever see Colonel Trowbridge? How I should like to see him! I don't see why he does not come South sometime. Why, I would take a day off and look up all the 'boys' I could find, if I knew he was coming." I knew this man meant what he said, for the men of the regiment knew Colonel Trowbridge first of all the other officers. He was with them on St. Simon and at Camp Saxton. I remember when the company was being formed, we wished Captain C. T. was our captain, because most of the men in Co. E were the men he brought with him from St. Simon, and they were attached to him. He was always jolly and pleasing with all. I remember, when going into Savannah in 1865, he said that he had been there before the war, and told me many things I did not know about the river. Although this was my home, I had never been on it before. No officer in the army was more beloved than our late lieutenant-colonel, C. T. Trowbridge.

[*Copy of General Orders.*]
"GENERAL ORDERS.
"HEADQUARTERS 33D U. S. C. T.,
"LATE 1ST SO. CAROLINA VOLUNTEERS,
"MORRIS ISLAND, S. C., Feb. 9, 1866.

"*General Order,*
"*No.* 1.

"COMRADES: The hour is at hand when we must separate forever, and nothing can take from us the pride we feel, when we look upon the history of the 'First South Carolina Volunteers,' the first black regiment that ever bore arms in defense of freedom on the continent of America.

"On the 9th day of May, 1862, at which time there were nearly four millions of your race in bondage, sanctioned by the laws of the land and protected by our flag,—on that day, in the face of the floods of prejudice that well-nigh deluged every avenue to manhood and true liberty, you came forth to do battle for your country and kindred.

"For long and weary months, without pay or even the privilege of being recognized as soldiers, you labored on, only to be disbanded and sent to your homes without even a hope of reward, and when our country, necessitated by the deadly struggle with armed traitors, finally granted you the opportunity again to come forth in defense of the nation's life, the alacrity with which you responded to the call gave abundant evidence of your readiness to strike a manly blow for the liberty of your race. And from that little band of hopeful, trusting, and brave men who gathered at Camp Saxton, on Port Royal Island, in the fall of '62, amidst the terrible prejudices that surrounded us, has grown an army of a hundred and forty thousand black soldiers, whose valor and heroism has won for your race a name which will live as long as the undying pages of history shall endure; and by whose efforts, united with those of the white man, armed rebellion has been conquered, the millions of bondsmen have been emancipated, and the fundamental law of the land has been so altered as to remove forever the possibility of human slavery being established within the borders of redeemed America. The flag of our fathers, restored to its rightful significance, now floats over every foot of our territory, from Maine to California, and beholds only free men! The prejudices which formerly existed against you are well-nigh rooted out.

"Soldiers, you have done your duty and acquitted yourselves like men who, actuated by such ennobling motives, could not fail; and as the result of your fidelity and obedience you have won your freedom, and oh, how great the reward! It seems fitting to me that the last hours of our existence as a regiment should be passed amidst the unmarked graves of your comrades, at Fort Wagner. Near you rest the bones of Colonel Shaw, buried by an enemy's hand in the same grave with his black soldiers who fell at his side; where in the future your children's children will come on pilgrimages to do homage to the ashes of those who fell in this glorious struggle.

"The flag which was presented to us by the Rev. George B. Cheever and his congregation, of New York city, on the 1st of January, 1863,—the day when Lincoln's immortal proclamation of freedom was given to the world,—and which you have borne so nobly through the war, is now to be rolled up forever and deposited in our nation's capital. And while there it shall rest, with the battles in which you have participated inscribed upon its folds, it will be a source of pride to us all to remember that it has never been disgraced by a cowardly faltering in the hour of danger, or polluted by a traitor's touch.

"Now that you are to lay aside your arms, I adjure you, by the associations and history of the past, and the love you bear for your liberties, to harbor no feelings of hatred toward your former masters, but to seek in the paths of honesty, virtue, sobriety, and industry, and by a willing obedience to the laws of the land, to grow up to the full stature of American citizens. The church, the school-house, and the right forever to be free are now secured to you, and every prospect before you is full of hope and encouragement. The nation guarantees to you full protection and justice, and will require from you in return that respect for the laws and orderly department which will prove to every one your right to all the privileges of freemen. To the officers of the regiment I would say, your toils are ended, your mission is fulfilled, and we separate forever. The fidelity, patience, and patriotism with which you have discharged your duties to your men and to your country entitle you to a far higher tribute than any words of thankfulness which I can give you from the bottom of my heart. You will find your reward in the proud conviction that the cause for which you have battled so nobly has been crowned with abundant success.

"Officers and soldiers of the 33d U. S. Colored Troops, once the First So. Carolina Volunteers, I bid you all farewell!

"By order of
"Lt. Colonel C. T. Trowbridge,
"*Commanding regiment.*
"E. W. Hyde,
"1st Lieut. 33d U. S. C. T. and acting adjutant."

I have one of the original copies of these orders still in my possession.

My dear friends! do we understand the meaning of war? Do we know or think of that war of '61? No, we do not, only those brave soldiers, and those who had occasion to be in it, can realize what it was. I can and shall never forget that terrible war until my eyes close in death. The scenes are just as fresh in my mind to-day as in '61. I see now each scene,—the roll-call, the drum tap, "lights out," the call at night when there was danger from the enemy, the double force of pickets, the cold and rain. How anxious I would be, not knowing what would happen before morning! Many times I would dress, not sure but all would be captured. Other times I would stand at my tent door and try to see what was going on, because night was the time the rebels would try to get into our lines and capture some of the boys. It was mostly at night that our men went out for their scouts, and often had a hand to hand fight with the rebels, and although our men came out sometimes with a few killed or wounded, none of them ever were captured.

We do not, as the black race, properly appreciate the old veterans, white or black, as we ought to. I know what they went through, especially those black men, for the Confederates had no mercy on them; neither did they show any toward the white Union soldiers. I have seen the terrors of that war. I was the wife of one of those men who did not get a penny for eighteen months for their services, only their rations and clothing.

I cannot praise General David Hunter too highly, for he was the first man to arm the black man, in the beginning of 1862. He had a hard struggle to hold all the southern division, with so few men, so he applied to Congress; but the answer to him was, "Do not bother us," which was very discouraging. As the general needed more men to protect the islands and do garrison duty, he organized two companies.

I look around now and see the comforts that our younger generation enjoy, and think of the blood that was shed to make these comforts possible for them, and see how little some of them appreciate the old soldiers. My heart burns within me, at this want of appreciation. There are only a few of them left now, so let us all, as the ranks close, take a deeper interest in them. Let the younger generation take an interest also, and remember that it was through the efforts of these veterans that they and we older ones enjoy our liberty to-day.

XIII

Thoughts on Present Conditions

Living here in Boston where the black man is given equal justice, I must say a word on the general treatment of my race, both in the North and South, in this twentieth century. I wonder if our white fellow men realize the true sense or meaning of brotherhood? For two hundred years we had toiled for them; the war of 1861 came and was ended, and we thought our race was forever freed from bondage, and that the two races could live in unity with each other, but when we read almost every day of what is being done to my race by some whites in the South, I sometimes ask, "Was the war in vain? Has it brought freedom, in the full sense of the word, or has it not made our condition more hopeless?"

In this "land of the free" we are burned, tortured, and denied a fair trial, murdered for any imaginary wrong conceived in the brain of the negro-hating white man. There is no redress for us from a government which promised to protect all under its flag. It seems a mystery to me. They say, "One flag, one nation, one country indivisible." Is this true? Can we say this truthfully, when one race is allowed to burn, hang, and inflict the most horrible torture weekly, monthly, on another?

No, we cannot sing, "My country, 't is of thee, Sweet land of Liberty"! It is hollow mockery. The Southland laws are all on the side of the white, and they do just as they like to the negro, whether in the right or not.

I do not uphold my race when they do wrong. They ought to be punished, but the innocent are made to suffer as well as the guilty, and I hope the time will hasten when it will be stopped forever. Let us remember God says, "He that sheds blood, his blood shall be required again." I may not live to see it, but the time is approaching when the South will again have cause to repent for the blood it has shed of innocent black men, for their blood cries out for vengeance. For the South still cherishes a hatred toward the blacks, although there are some true Southern gentlemen left who abhor the stigma brought upon them, and feel it very keenly, and I hope the day is not far distant when the two races will reside in peace in the Southland, and we will sing with sincere and truthful hearts, "My country, 't is of thee, Sweet land of Liberty, of thee I sing.". . .

I read an article, which said the ex-Confederate Daughters had sent a petition to the managers of the local theatres in Tennessee to prohibit the performance of "Uncle Tom's Cabin," claiming it was exaggerated (that is, the treatment of the slaves), and would have a very bad effect on the children who might see the drama. I paused and thought back a few years of the heart-rending scenes I have witnessed; I have seen many times, when I was a mere girl, thirty or forty men, handcuffed, and as many women and children, come every first Tuesday of each month from Mr. Wiley's trade office to the auction blocks, one of them being situated on Drayton Street and Court Lane, the other on Bryant Street, near the Pulaski House. The route was down our principal street, Bull Street, to the court-house, which was only a block from where I resided.

All people in those days got all their water from the city pumps, which stood about a block apart throughout the city. The one we used to get water from was opposite the court-house, on Bull Street. I remember, as if it were yesterday, seeing droves of negroes going to be sold, and I often went to look at them, and I could hear the auctioneer very plainly from my house, auctioning these poor people off.

Do these Confederate Daughters ever send petitions to prohibit the atrocious lynchings and wholesale murdering and torture of the negro? Do you ever hear of them fearing this would have a bad effect on the children? Which of these two, the drama or the present state of affairs, makes a degrading impression upon the minds of our young generation? In my opinion it is not "Uncle Tom's Cabin," but it should be the one that has caused the world to cry "Shame!" It does not seem as if our land is yet civilized. It is like times long past, when rulers and high officers had to flee for their lives, and the negro has been dealt with in the same way since the war by those he lived with and toiled for two hundred years or more. I do not condemn all the Caucasian race because the negro is badly treated by a few of the race. No! for had it not been for the true whites, assisted by God and the prayers of our forefathers, I should not be here to-day. . . .

There are many people who do not know what some of the colored women did during the war. There were hundreds of them who assisted the Union soldiers by hiding them and helping them to escape. Many were punished for taking food to the prison stockades for the prisoners. When I went into Savannah, in 1865, I was told of one of these stockades which was in the suburbs of the city, and they said it was an awful place. The Union soldiers were in it, worse than pigs, without any shelter from sun or storm, and the colored women would take food there at night and pass it to them, through the holes in the fence. The soldiers were starving, and these women did all they could towards relieving those men, although they knew the penalty, should they be caught giving them aid. Others assisted in various ways the Union army. These things should be kept in history before the people. There has never been a greater war in the United States than the one of 1861, where so many lives were lost,—not men alone but noble women as well.

Let us not forget that terrible war, or our brave soldiers who were thrown into Andersonville and Libby prisons, the awful agony they went through, and the most brutal treatment they received in those loathsome dens, the worst ever given human beings; and if the white soldiers were subjected to such treatment, what must have been the horrors inflicted on the negro soldiers in their prison pens? Can we forget those cruelties? No, though we try to forgive and say, "No North, no South," and hope to see it in reality before the last comrade passes away.

We are similar to the children of Israel, who, after many weary years in bondage, were led into that land of promise, there to thrive and be forever free from persecution; and I don't despair, for the Book which is our guide through life declares, "Ethiopia shall stretch forth her hand."

What a wonderful revolution! In 1861 the Southern papers were full of advertisements for "slaves," but now, despite all the hindrances and "race problems," my people are striving to attain the full standard of all other races born free in the sight of God, and in a number of instances have succeeded. Justice we ask,—to be citizens of these United States, where so many of our people have shed their blood with their white comrades, that the stars and stripes should never be polluted.

SUGGESTED READINGS

Ira Berlin, Barbara J. Fields, Steven F. Miller, Joseph P. Reidy, and Leslie S. Rowland, *Slave No More: Three Essays on Emancipation and the Civil War* (Cambridge, England, 1992)

David W. Blight, *Frederick Douglass' Civil War: Keeping Faith in Jubilee* (Baton Rouge, La., 1989)

LaWanda Cox, *Lincoln and Black Freedom: A Study in Presidential Leadership* (Columbia, S.C., 1981)

Don E. Fehrenbacher, *The Dred Scott Case: Its Significance in American Law and Politics* (New York, 1978)

Paul Finkelman, *An Imperfect Union: Slavery, Federalism and Comity* (Chapel Hill, N.C., 1981)

Eric Foner, *Free Soil, Free Labor, Free Men: The Ideology of the Republican Party Before the Civil War* (New York, 1970)

John Hope Franklin, *The Emancipation Proclamation* (New York, 1963)

Jospeh T. Glathaar, *Forged in Battle: The Civil War Alliance of Black Soldiers and White Officers* (New York, 1990)

Leon F. Litwack, *Been in the Storm So Long: The Aftermath of Slavery* (New York, 1979)

James M. McPherson, *Battle Cry of Freedom: The Civil War Era* (New York, 1988)

James M. McPherson, *The Negro's Civil War: How American Negroes Felt and Acted During the War for the Union* (New York, 1965)

David M. Potter, *The Impending Crisis, 1848–1861* (New York, 1976)

Benjamin Quarles, *Lincoln and the Negro* (New York, 1962)

Benjamin Quarles, *The Negro in the Civil War* (New York, 1953)

Manisha Sinha, *The Counterrevolution of Slavery: Politics and Ideology in Antebellum South Carolina* (Chapel Hill, N.C., 2000)

Michael Vorenberg, *Final Freedom: The Civil War, The Abolition of Slavery, and the Thirteenth Amendment* (Cambridge, England, 2001)

Carol Wilson, *Freedom at Risk: The Kidnapping of Free Blacks in America, 1780–1865* (Lexington, Ky., 1994)

Entered according to act of Congress in the year 1872 by Currier & Ives, in the Office of the Librarian of Congress at Washington.

ROBERT C. DE LARGE, M.C. of S.Carolina.   JEFFERSON H. LONG, M.C. of Georgia.

U.S. Senator H.R.REVELS, of Mississippi   BENJ. S. TURNER, M.C. of Alabama.   JOSIAH T. WALLS, M.C. of Florida.   JOSEPH H. RAINY, M.C. of S.Carolina.   R. BROWN ELLIOT, M.C. of S.Carolina.

THE FIRST COLORED SENATOR AND REPRESENTATIVES,

In the 41ˢᵗ and 42ⁿᵈ Congress of the United States.

NEW YORK, PUBLISHED BY CURRIER & IVES, 125 NASSAU STREET

The first seven African Americans to serve in the U.S. Senate and the U.S. House of Representatives. (Courtesy of the Library of Congress.)

Chapter 6

Black Reconstruction

The end of the Civil War and the destruction of slavery raised black hopes to unprecedented levels. African Americans actively sought to define the contours and content of their freedom during Reconstruction. Lincoln's assassination led to a brief period of Presidential Reconstruction under Andrew Johnson. During this time, white southerners, taking advantage of Johnson's pardons, attempted to push freed people back into conditions as close to slavery as possible by instituting "Black Codes" that denied them basic civil and political rights. However, by 1866, black southerners and their radical Republican allies inaugurated Congressional Reconstruction, which nullified the Black Codes and established the legal foundations for African American citizenship. African Americans sought to give meaning to their freedom by reconstituting families that had been torn apart by slavery; acquiring education; developing their own institutions, such as the church and benevolent and fraternal associations; and demanding all the rights of American citizenship and property ownership.

The Freedmen's Bureau, established by the federal government to ease the transition from slavery to freedom, was the first large-scale government agency created to address social problems. One of the most remarkable achievements of Reconstruction was black enfranchisement

(excluding women) and the rapid ascension of African Americans to positions of power in local, state, and federal government. Despite black demands and the support of some radical politicians, land in the south was not redistributed to the freed people, and African Americans, though legally free, were forced to labor as agricultural workers, tenants, and sharecroppers. Moreover, most white southerners resisted black rights by every means possible, including the employment of wholesale vigilante violence and racial intimidation through newly founded organizations such as the Ku Klux Klan. The fall of Reconstruction and the disfranchisement of African Americans put an end to the promise of an interracial democracy in the south.

The first document on the Colloquy with black ministers shows how former slaves tried to define their freedom by demanding political rights and economic autonomy. This conversation led to Sherman's famous Field Order Number 15, which settled African Americans in lowcountry South Carolina and Georgia on forty acres of land and gave them a mule. Johnson revoked this order. The role of the Freedman's Bureau and northern "Gideonites," who traveled to the south to teach in freedmen's schools, is amply illustrated by the selection from J.W. Alvord's book. The three Reconstruction amendments and the

Civil Rights Act of 1875 dramatically expanded citizenship and civil rights for black people. The selection from the proceedings of the South Carolina Constitutional Convention of 1868 that inaugurated Reconstruction there reveals the debate over land reform. Racial violence during Reconstruction is epitomized by the description of the famous Hamburg Riot of 1876. The speeches by Henry Turner and George White protesting their expulsion from the Georgia legislature and Congress are examples of the feeling of betrayal among African Americans once Reconstruction came to an end, accompanied by the demise of black political power. In 1883, the Supreme Court overturned the Civil Rights Act of 1875, prompting Frederick Douglass to protest this betrayal of the legacy of the Civil War and Reconstruction. This retreat paved the way for the instituting of racial segregation in the south. Two documents, the memorial from former slaves in Indian territory and noted black Senator Blanche K. Bruce's speech, illustrate the complex interaction between African Americans and Native Americans. Frances Ellen Watkins Harper's speech to the Women's Congress affirms the role of African American women in the struggle for black equality during Reconstruction.

Colloquy with Colored Ministers[1]

On the evening of Thursday, the 12th day of January, 1865, the following persons of African descent met, by appointment, to hold an interview with Edwin M. Stanton, Secretary of War, and Major-General Sherman, to have a conference upon matters relating to the freedmen of the State of Georgia, to wit:

1. *William J. Campbell,* aged fifty-one years, born in Savannah; slave until 1849, and then liberated by will of his mistress, Mrs. Mary Maxwell; for ten years pastor of the First Baptist Church of Savannah, numbering about eighteen hundred members; average congregation nineteen hundred; the church property belonging to the congregation (trustees white) worth eighteen thousand dollars.

2. *John Cox,* aged fifty-eight years, born in Savannah; slave until 1849, when he bought his freedom for eleven hundred dollars; pastor of the Second African Baptist Church; in the ministry fifteen years; congregation twelve hundred and twenty-two persons; church property worth ten thousand dollars, belonging to the congregation.

3. *Ulysses L. Houston,* aged forty-one years, born in Grahamsville, South Carolina; slave 'until the Union army entered Savannah'; owned by Moses Henderson, Savannah; and pastor of Third African Baptist Church, congregation numbering four hundred; church property worth five thousand dollars, belongs to congregation; in the ministry about eight years.

Source: "Colloquy with Colored Ministers," *Journal of Negro History,* vol. XVI, No. 1, January, 1931, pp. 88–94. Copyright 1931 Journal of Negro History.

[1]This colloquy is valuable not only for the information concerning the war but for understanding the status of Negroes in Georgia: the effect of the war on them, and their prospects in 1865.

4. *William Bentley,* aged seventy-two years, born in Savannah; slave until twenty-five years of age, when his master, John Waters, emancipated him by will; pastor of Andrew's Chapel, Methodist Episcopal Church (only one of that denomination in Savannah), congregation numbering three hundred and sixty members; church property worth about twenty thousand dollars, and is owned by the congregation; been in the ministry about twenty years; a member of Georgia Conference.

5. *Charles Bradwell,* aged forty years, born in Liberty County, Georgia; slave until 1851; emancipated by will of his master, J. L. Bradwell; local preacher, in charge of the Methodist Episcopal congregation (Andrew's Chapel) in the absence of the minister; in the ministry ten years.

6. *William Gaines,* aged forty-one years, born in Wills County, Georgia; slave 'until the Union forces freed me'; owned by Robert Toombs, formerly United States Senator, and his brother, Gabriel Toombs; local preacher of the Methodist Episcopal Church (Andrew's Chapel); in the ministry sixteen years.

7. *James Hill,* aged fifty-two years, born in Bryan County, Georgia; slave 'up to the time the Union army come in'; owned by H. F. Willings, of Savannah; in the ministry sixteen years.

8. *Glasgow Taylor,* aged seventy-two years, born in Wilkes County, Georgia; slave 'until the Union army come'; owned by A. P. Wetter; is a local preacher of the Methodist Episcopal Church (Andrew's Chapel); in the ministry thirty-five years.

9. *Garrison Frazier,* aged sixty-seven years, born in Granville County, North Carolina; slave until eight years ago, when he bought himself and wife, paying one thousand dollars in gold and silver; is an ordained minister in the Baptist Church, but, his health failing, has now charge of no congregation; has been in the ministry thirty-five years.

10. *James Mills,* aged fifty-six years, born in Savannah; freeborn, and is a licensed preacher of the First Baptist Church; has been eight years in the ministry.

11. *Abraham Burke,* aged forty-eight years, born in Bryan County, Georgia; slave until twenty years ago, when he bought himself for eight hundred dollars; has been in the ministry about ten years.

12. *Arthur Wardell,* aged forty-four years, born in Liberty County, Georgia; slave until 'freed by the Union army'; owned by A. A. Solomons, Savannah, and is a licensed minister in the Baptist Church; has been in the ministry six years.

13. *Alexander Harris,* aged forty-seven years, born in Savannah; free-born; licensed minister of Third African Baptist Church; licensed about one month ago.

14. *Andrew Neal,* aged sixty-one years, born in Savannah; slave 'until the Union army liberated me'; owned by Mr. William Gibbons, and has been deacon in the Third Baptist Church for ten years.

15. *James Porter,* aged thirty-nine years, born in Charleston, South Carolina; free-born, his mother having purchased her freedom; is lay-reader and president of the board of wardens and vestry of St. Stephen's Protestant Episcopal Colored Church in Savannah; has been in communion nine years; the congregation numbers about two hundred persons; the church property is worth about ten thousand dollars, and is owned by the congregation.

16. *Adolphus Delmotte,* aged twenty-eight years, born in Savannah; free-born; is a licensed minister of the Missionary Baptist Church of Milledgeville, congregation numbering about three or four hundred persons; has been in the ministry about two years.

17. *Jacob Godfrey,* aged fifty-seven years, born in Marion, South Carolina; slave 'until the Union army freed me'; owned by James E. Godfrey, Methodist preacher, now in the rebel army; is a classleader, and steward of Andrew's Chapel since 1836.

18. *John Johnson,* aged fifty-one years, born in Bryan County, Georgia; slave 'up to the time the Union army came here'; owned by

W. W. Lincoln, of Savannah; is class-leader, and treasurer of Andrew's Chapel for sixteen years.

19. *Robert N. Taylor,* aged fifty-one years, born in Wilkes County, Georgia; slave 'to the time the Union army come'; was owned by Augustus P. Wetter, Savannah, and is class-leader in Andrew's Chapel—for nine years.

20. *James Lynch,* aged twenty-six years, born in Baltimore, Maryland; free-born; is presiding elder of the Methodist Episcopal Church, and missionary to the Department of the South; has been seven years in the ministry, and two years in the South.

Garrison Frazier being chosen by the persons present to express their common sentiments upon the matters of inquiry, makes answers to inquiries as follows:

1. State what your understanding is in regard to the acts of Congress, and President Lincoln's proclamation, touching the condition of the colored people in the rebel States.

Answer. So far as I understand President Lincoln's proclamation to the rebellious States, it is, that if they would lay down their arms and submit to the laws of the United States before the 1st of January, 1863, all should be well; but if they did not, then all the slaves in the rebel States should be free, henceforth and forever: that is what I understood.

2. State what you understand by slavery, and the freedom that was to be given by the President's Proclamation.

Answer. Slavery is receiving by irresistible power the work of another man, and not by his consent. The freedom, as I understand it, promised by the proclamation, is taking us from under the yoke of bondage and placing us where we could reap the fruit of our own labor, and take care of ourselves, and assist the Government in maintaining our freedom.

3. State in what manner you think you can take care of yourselves, and how can you best assist the Government in maintaining your freedom.

Answer. The way we can best take care of ourselves is to have land, and turn in and till it by our labor—that is, by the labor of the women, and children, and old men—and we can soon maintain ourselves and have something to spare; and to assist the Government, the young men should enlist in the service of the Government, and serve in such manner as they may be wanted (the rebels told us that they piled them up and made batteries of them, and sold them to Cuba, but we don't believe that). We want to be placed on land until we are able to buy it and make it our own.

4. State in what manner you would rather live, whether scattered among the whites, or in colonies by yourselves.

Answer. I would prefer to live by ourselves, for there is a prejudice against us in the South that will take years to get over; but I do not know that I can answer for my brethren.

[*Mr. Lynch* says he thinks they should not be separated, but live together. All the other persons present being questioned, one by one, answer that they agree with 'brother *Frazier.'*]

5. Do you think that there is intelligence enough among the slaves of the South to maintain themselves under the Government of the United States, and the equal protection of its laws, and maintain good and peaceable relations among yourselves and with your neighbors?

Answer. I think there is sufficient intelligence among us to do so.

6. State what is the feeling of the black population of the South toward the Government of the United States; what is the understanding in respect to the present war, its causes and object, and their disposition to aid either side; state fully your views.

Answer. I think you will find there is thousands that are willing to make any sacrifice to assist the Government of the United States, while there is also many that are not willing to take up arms. I do not suppose there is a dozen men that is opposed to the Government. I understand as to the war that the South is the aggressor. President Lincoln was elected President by a majority of the

United States, which guaranteed him the right of holding the office and exercising that right over the whole United States. The South, without knowing what he would do, rebelled. The war was commenced by the rebels before he came into the office. The object of the war was not, at first, to give the slaves their freedom, but the sole object of the war was, at first to bring the rebellious States back into the Union, and their loyalty to the laws of the United States. Afterwards, knowing the value that was set on the slaves by the rebels, the President thought that his proclamation would stimulate them to lay down their arms, reduce them to obedience, and help to bring back the rebel States; and their not doing so has now made the freedom of the slaves a part of the war. It is my opinion that there is not a man in this city that could be started to help the rebels one inch, for that would be suicide. There was two black men left with the rebels, because they had taken an active part for the rebels, and thought something might befall them if they staid behind, but there is not another man. If the prayers that have gone up for the Union army could be read out, you would not get through them these two weeks.

7. State whether the sentiments you now express are those only of the colored people in the city, or do they extend to the colored population through the country, and what are your means of knowing the sentiments of those living in the country?

Answer. I think the sentiments are the same among the colored people of the State. My opinion is formed by personal communication in the course of my ministry, and also from the thousands that followed the Union army, leaving their homes and undergoing suffering. I did not think there would be so many; the number surpassed my expectation.

8. If the rebel leaders were to arm the slaves, what would be its effect?

Answer. I think they would fight as long as they were before the bayonet, and just as soon as they could get away they would desert, in my opinion.

9. What, in your opinion, is the feeling of the colored people about enlisting and serving as soldiers of the United States, and what kind of military service do they prefer?

Answer. A large number have gone as soldiers to Port Royal to be drilled and put in the service, and I think there is thousands of the young men that will enlist; there is something about them that, perhaps, is wrong; they have suffered so long from the rebels, that they want to meet and have a chance with them in the field. Some of them want to shoulder the musket, others want to go into the quartermaster or the commissary's service.

10. Do you understand the mode of enlistment of colored persons in the rebel States, by State agents, under the act of Congress; if yea, state what your understanding is?

Answer. My understanding is that colored persons enlisted by State agents are enlisted as substitutes, and give credit to the States, and do not swell the army, because every black man enlisted by a State agent leaves a white man at home; and, also, that larger bounties are given or promised by the State agents than are given by the States. The great object should be to push through this rebellion the shortest way, and there seems to be something wanting in the enlistment by State agents, for it don't strengthen the army, but takes one away for every colored man enlisted.

11. State what in your opinion is the best way to enlist colored men for soldiers.

Answer. I think, sir, that all compulsory operations should be put a stop to. The ministers would talk to them, and the young men would enlist. It is my opinion that it would be far better for the State agents to stay at home, and the enlistments to be made for the United States under the direction of General Sherman.

In the absence of General Sherman, the following question was asked:

12. State what is the feeling of the colored people in regard to General Sherman, and how far do they regard his sentiments and

actions as friendly to their rights and interests, or otherwise?

Answer. We looked upon General Sherman, prior to his arrival, as a man, in the providence of God, specially set apart to accomplish this work, and we unanimously felt inexpressible gratitude to him, looking upon him as a man that should be honored for the faithful performance of his duty. Some of us called upon him immediately upon his arrival, and it is probable he did not meet the Secretary with more courtesy than he met us. His conduct and deportment towards us characterized him as a friend

and a gentleman. We have confidence in General Sherman, and think that what concerns us could not be under better hands. This is our opinion now from the short acquaintance and intercourse we have had.

[*Mr. Lynch* states that, with his limited acquaintance with General Sherman, he is unwilling to express an opinion. All others present declare their agreement with Mr. *Frazier* about General Sherman.]

Some conversation upon general subjects relating to General Sherman's march then ensued, of which no note was taken."

From the Journals of Charlotte Forten Grimke

Charlotte Forten Grimke

Tuesday, October 28, 1862. It was nearly dark when we reached St. Helena's, where we found Miss T. [owne]'s carriage awaiting us, and then we three and our driver, had a long drive along the lonely roads in the dark night. How easy it sh'ld have been for a band of guerilas—had any chanced that way—to seize and hang us. But we found nothing of the kind. We were in a jubilant state of mind and sang "John Brown" with a will as we drove through the pines and palmettos. Arrived at the Superintendent's house[;] we were kindly greeted by him and the ladies and shown into a lofty *ceilinged* parlor where a cheerful wood fire glowed in the grate, and we soon began to feel quite at home in the very heart of Rebeldom; only that I do not at all realize yet that we are in S.[outh] C.[arolina]. It is all a strange wild

dream, from which I am constantly expecting to awake.

Wednesday, October 29. We left Oaklands and drove to the school. It is kept by Miss [Ellen] Murray and Miss Towne in the little Baptist Church, which is beautifully situated in a grove of live oaks. Never saw anything more beautiful than these trees. It is strange that we do not hear of them at the North. They are the first objects that attract one's attention here. They are large, noble trees with small glossy green leaves. Their beauty consists in the long bearded moss with which every branch is heavily draped. This moss is singularly beautiful, and gives a solemn almost funeral aspect to the trees.

We went into the school, and heard the children read and spell. The teachers tell us that they have made great improvement in a very short time, and I noticed with pleasure how bright, how eager to learn many of them seem. The singing delighted me most. They sang beautifully in their rich, sweet

Source: From *The Journals of Charlotte Forten Grimke, 1854–1892.* Ms. Moorland-Spingarn Library, Howard University.

clear tones, and with that peculiar swaying motion which I had noticed before in the older people, and which seems to make their singing all the more effective. Besides several other tunes they sang "Marching Along" with much spirit, and then one of their own hymns "Down in the Lonesome Valley," which is sweetly solemn and most beautiful. Dear children! born in slavery, but free at last? May God preserve to you all the blessings of freedom, and may you be in every possible way fitted to enjoy them. My heart goes out to you. I shall be glad to do all that I can to help you.—

Sunday, November 2. Drove to church to-day—to the same little Baptist Church that the school is held in. The people came in slowly. They have no way of telling the time. About eleven they had all assembled; the church was full. Old and young were there assembled in their Sunday dresses. Clean gowns on, clean head handkerchiefs, bright colored, of course, I noticed that some had even reached the dignity of straw hats, with bright feathers. The services were very interesting. The minister, Mr. P.[hillips?] is an earnest N.[ew] E.[ngland] man. The singing was very beautiful, sat there in a kind of trance and listened to it, and while I listened looked through the open windows into the beautiful grove of oaks with their moss drapery. "Ah w'ld that my tongue c'ld utter the thoughts that arise in me." But it cannot. The sermon was quite good. But I enjoyed nothing so much as the singing—the wonderful, beautiful singing. There can be no doubt that these people have a great deal of musical talent. It was a beautiful sight,— their enthusiasm. After the service two couples were married. Then the meeting was out. The various groups under the trees forming a very pretty picture. We drove to the Episcopal Church afterward where the aristocracy of Rebeldom was to worship.

Saturday, November 8. Spent part of the morn. in the store which was more crowded than ever. So much gold and silver I've not seen for many months. These people must have been hoarding it up for a long time. They are rather unreasonable, and expect one to wait on a dozen at once. But it is not strange. Miss T.[owne] came this afternoon, and gave medicine to Tilla's baby, which seems, I think, a little better; and all the other children. Everyone of them has the whooping cough.'

Monday, November 10. We taught—or rather commenced teaching the children "John Brown" which they entered into eagerly. I felt to the full the significance of *that* song being sung here in S.[outh] C.[arolina] by little negro children, by those whom he— the glorious old man—died to save. Miss [Laura] T.[owne] told them about him. A poor mulatto man is in one of our people's houses, a man from the North, who assisted Mr. [Samuel D.] Phillips (a nephew of Wendell P.[hillips]) when he was here, in teaching school; he seems to be quite an intelligent man. He is suffering from fever. I shall be glad to take as good care of him as I can. It is so sad to be ill, helpless and poor, and so far away from home.

Thursday, November 13. Talked to the children a little while to-day about the noble Toussaint. They listened very attentively. It is well that they sh'ld know what one of their own color c'ld do for his race. I long to inspire them with courage and ambition (of a noble sort), and high purposes. It is noticeable how very few mulattoes there are here. Indeed in our school, with one or two exceptions, the children are all black.

A little mulatto child strayed into the school house yesterday—a pretty little thing with large beautiful black eyes and lovely long lashes. But so dirty! I longed to seize and thoroughly cleanse her. The mother is a good-looking woman, but quite black. "Thereby," I doubt not, "hangs a tale."

This eve. Harry, one of the men on the place, came in for a lesson. He is most eager to learn, and is really a scholar to be proud of. He learns rapidly. I gave him his first lesson in writing to-night, and his progress was wonderful. He held his pen almost perfectly right the first time. He will very soon learn to write, I think. I must inquire who w'ld like to take lessons at night. Whenever I am well enough it will be a real pleasure to teach them.

Monday, November 17. Had a dreadfully wearying day in school, of which the less said the better. Afterward drove the ladies to "The Corner," a collection of negro houses, whither Miss T.[owne] went on a doctoring expedition. The people there are very pleasant. Saw a little baby, just borne [*sic*] today—and another—old Venus' great grandchild for whom I made the little pink frock. These people are very grateful. The least kindness that you do them they insist on repaying in some way. We have had a quantity of eggs and potatoes brought us despite our remonstrances. Today one of the women gave me some Tanias. Tania is a queer looking root. After it is boiled it looks a little like potato, but is much larger. I don't like the taste.

Tuesday, November 18. After school went to the Corner again. Stopped at old Susy's house to see some sick children. Old Susy is a character. Miss T.[owne] asked her if she wanted her old master to come back again. Most emphatically she answered. "No *indeed*, missus, no indeed dey treat we too bad. Dey tuk ebery one of my chilen away from me. When we sick and c'ldnt work dey tuk away all our food from us; gib us nutten to eat. Dey's orful hard Missis." When Miss T.[owne] told her that some of the people wanted their old masters to come back, a look of supreme contempt came to old Susy's withered face. "That's cause dey's got no sense den, missus," she said indignantly. Susy has any quantity of children and grandchildren, and she thanks God that she can now have some of them with her in her old age. To-night gave Cupid a lesson in the alphabet. He is not a brilliant scholar, but he tries hard to learn, and so I am sure will succeed in time. A man from another plantation

came in for a lesson. L.[izzie Hunn] attended to him while I had Cupid. He knows his letters, and seems very bright.

Sunday, November 23. Attended church to-day. T'was even a pleasanter experience than before. Saw several new arrivals there—old ones returned, rather—among them Mr. S.[amuel] Phillips, a nephew of *the* Phillips. He has not the glorious beauty of his illustrious relative, but still has some-what the Phillips style of face. He is not at all handsome; has bright red hair, but a pleasant face, and an air *distingue*. After the sermon an old negro made a touching and most effective prayer. Then the minister read Gen. Saxton's Proclamation for Thanksgiving—which is grand—the very best and noblest that c'ld have been penned. I like and admire the Gen.[eral] more than ever now. Six couples were married to-day. Some of the dresses were unique. Am sure one must have worn a cast-off dress of her mistress's. It looked like white silk covered with lace. The lace sleeves, and other trimmings were in rather a decayed state and the white cotton gloves were well ventilated. But the bride looked none the less happy for that. Only one had the slightest claim to good looks, and she was a demure little thing with a neat, plain silk dress on. T'was amusing to see some of the headresses. One, of tattered flowers and ribbons, was very ridiculous. But no matter for that. I am *truly* glad that the poor creatures are trying to live right and virtuous lives. As usual we had some fine singing. It was very pleasant to be at church again. For two Sundays past I had not been, not feeling well.

This eve. our boys and girls with others from across the creek came in and sang a long time for us. Of course we had the old favorites "Down in the Lonesome Valley," and "Roll, Jordan, Roll," and "No man can hender me," and beside those several shouting tunes that we had not heard before; they are very wild and strange. It was impossible for me to understand many of the words although I asked them to repeat them for me. I only know that one had something about "De Nell Am Ringing." I think that was the refrain; and of another, some of the words were "Christ build the church widout no hammer nor nail." "Jehovah Halleluhiah," which is a grand thing, and "Hold the light," an especial favorite of mine—they sang also with great spirit. The leader of the singing was Prince, a large black boy, from Mr. R. [uggle]'s place. He was full of the shouting spirit, and c'ld not possibly keep still. It was amusing to see his gymnastic performances. They were quite in the Ethiopian Methodists' style. He has really a very fine bass voice. I enjoyed their singing so much, and sh'ld have enjoyed it so much more if some dear ones who are far away c'ld have listened it to [sic] with me.

How delighted they would have been. The effect of the singing has been to make me feel a little sad and lonely to-night. A yearning for congenial companionship *will* sometimes come over me in the few leisure moments I have in the house. 'Tis well they are so few. Kindness, most invariable,—for which I am most grateful—I meet with constantly, but congeniality I find not at all in this house. But silence, foolish murmurer. He who knows all things knows that it was for no selfish motive that I came here, far from the few who are so dear to me. Therefore let me not be selfish now. Let the work to which I have solemnly pledged myself fill up my whole existence to the exclusion of all vain longings.

Thursday, November 27. Thanksgiving Day. This, according to Gen. [Rufus] Saxton's noble Proclamation, was observed as a day of "Thanksgiving and praise." It has been a lovely day—cool, delicious air, golden, gladdening sunlight, deep blue sky, with soft white clouds floating over it. Had we no other causes the glory and beauty of the day alone make it a day for which to give thanks. But we have other causes, great and glorious, which unite to make this peculiarly a day of thanksgiving and praise. It has been a general holiday. According to Gen. Saxton's

orders an animal was killed on each plantation that the people might to-day eat fresh meat, which is a great luxury to them, and indeed to all of us here. This morning a large number—Superintendents, teachers, and freed people, assembled in the little Baptist church. It was a sight that I shall not soon forget—that crowd of eager, happy black faces from which the shadow of slavery had forever passed. "Forever free!" "Forever free!" Those magical words were all the time singing themselves in my soul, and never before have I felt so truly grateful to God. The singing was, as usual, very beautiful. I thought I had never heard my favorite "Down in the Lonesome Valley" so well sung. After an appropriate prayer and sermon by Rev. Mr. Phillips, Gen. Saxton made a short but spirited speech to the people— urging the young men to enlist in the regiment now forming under Col. T. [homas] W. [entworth] Higginson. That was the first intimation I had had of Mr. H. [igginson]'s being down here. I am greatly rejoiced thereat. He seems to me of all fighting men the one best fitted to command a regiment of colored soldiers. The mention of his [name] recalled the happy days passed last summer in Mass. [achusetts], when day after day, in the streets of W. [orcester] we used to see the indefatigable *Capt.* H. [igginson] drilling his white company. I never saw him so full of life and energy—entering with his whole soul into his work—without thinking what a splendid general he w'ld make. And that too may come about. Gen. Saxton said today that he hoped to see him commander of an army of black men. The Gen. told the people how nobly Mr. H. [igginson] had stood by Anthony Burns, in the old dark days, even suffering imprisonment for his sake; and assured [them] that they might feel sure of meeting with no injustice under the leadership of such a man; that he w'ld see to it that they were not wronged in any way. Then he told them the story of Robert Small[s], and added "Today Robt. came to see me. I asked him how he was getting on in the store which he is keeping for the freed people. He said he was doing very well—making fifty dollars a week, sometimes. 'But,' said he[,] 'Gen. I'm going to stop keeping store. I'm going to enlist!' When you can make fifty doll[ar]s. a week keeping store? 'Yes Sir,' he replied, 'I'm going to enlist as a private in the black regiment. How can I expect to keep my freedom if I'm not willing to fight for it? Suppose the Secesh sh'ld get back here again? what good w'ld my fifty doll[ar]s. do me then? Yes, Sir, I sh'ld enlist if I were making a thousand dollars a week.' " Mrs. [Francis] Gage then made a few beautiful and earnest remarks. She told the people about the slaves in Santa Cruz, how they rose and conquered their masters, and declared themselves free, and no one dared to oppose them. And how, soon after, the governor rode into the market-place and proclaimed emancipation to all the people of the Danish W.[est] I.[ndies]. She then made a beautiful appeal to the mothers, urging them not to keep back their sons from the war fearing they might be killed but to send them forth willingly and gladly as she had done hers, to fight for liberty. It must have been something very novel and strange to them to hear a woman speak in public, but they listened with great attention and seemed much moved by what she said. Then Gen. Saxton made a few more remarks. I think what he said will have much effect on the young men here. There has been a good deal of distrust about joining the regiment[,] the soldiers were formerly so unjustly treated by the Government. But they trust Gen. Saxton. He told them what a victory the black troops had lately won on the Georgian coast, and what a great good they had done for their race in winning: they had proved to their enemies that the black man can and will fight for his freedom. After the Gen. had done speaking the people [sang] "Marching Along," with great spirit. After church there was a wedding. This is a very common occurrence here. Of course the bridal costumes are generally very unique and comical, but the principal actors are fortunately quite unconscious of it, and look so proud and

happy while enjoying this—one of the many privileges that freedom has bestowed upon them—that it is quite pleasant to see them. Beside the Gen. and Miss. G.[age] there were several other strangers present;—ladies from the North who come down here to teach. In Miss T.[owne]'s box came my parcel—so long looked for—containing letters from my dear Mary S.[hepard], Aunt M.[argaretta], Nellie A.[lexander?] and Mrs. J. and a "Liberator," the first that I have seen since leaving home. How great a pleasure it is to see it. It is familiar and delightful to look upon as the face of an old friend. It is of an old date—October 31st—but it is not the less welcome for that. And what a significant fact it is that one may now sit here in safety— here in the rebellious little Palmetto State and read the "Liberator," and display it to one's friends, rejoicing over it in the fulness of one's heart as a very great treasure. It is fitting that we sh'ld give to this—the pioneer paper in the cause of human rights—a hearty welcome to the land where, until so recently, those rights have been most barbarously trampled upon. We do not forget that it is in fact directly traceable to the exertions of the editor of this paper and those who have labored so faithfully with him, that the Northern people now occupy in safety the S.[outh] C.[arolina] shore; that freedom now blesses it, that it is, for the first time, a place worth living in. This eve. commenced a long letter to Mr. [William Lloyd] Garrison. Composed partly of to-day's journalism, and partly of other things that I thought w'ld interest him. He can publish it in the "Liberator," if he thinks it worth printing, which I do not. Truly this has been a delightful day to me. I recal [sic] with pleasure the pleasant Thanks-giving days passed in N.[ew] E.[ngland] in Mass.[achusetts], which I believe I am in the habit of considering as *all* N.[ew] E.[ngland]. But this has been the happiest, the most jubilant Thanksgiving day of my life. We hear of cold weather and heavy snow-storms up in the North land. But here roses and oleanders are blooming in the open air. Figs and oranges are ripening, the sunlight is warm and bright, and over all shines gloriously the blessed light of Freedom—Freedom forevermore!

Sunday November 30. Am in a writing mood to-night, and think I will give to you, my dearest A.[,] a more minute description of the people around than I've yet given to anyone. I shall write down their names too, that I may remember them always. Don't know them thoroughly enough yet to say much about their characters. To begin with the older ones.

First there is old Harriet. She is a very kind, pleasant old soul. Comes from Darien G.[eorgia]. Her parents were Africans. She speaks a *very* foreign tongue. Three of her children have been sold from her. Her master's son killed somebody in a duel, and was obliged to "pay money" H.[arriet] says. I suppose she means to give bail. And she and her children were sold to this place, to raise the money. Then there is her daughter Tillah. Poor creature, she has a dear little baby, Annie, who for weeks has been dangerously ill with whooping cough and fever. Our good Miss T.[owne] attends it, and does all that can be done, but the baby is still very ill. For Tillah's sake I hope it will get well. She is devoted to it night and day. T.[illah]'s husband is a gallant looking young soldier—a member of the black regiment. H.[arriet]'s mother, Bella, is rather a querulous body. But who can blame her? She has had enough to try her sorely. One by one her children at a tender age have been dragged from her to work in the cotton fields. She herself has been made to work when most unfit for it. She has had to see her own children cruelly beaten. Is it strange that these things sh'ld have embittered her? But she has much of the milk of human kindness left her yet. She nurses her poor baby faithfully, and often, old as she is, sits up the entire night with it. Harry is another of her sons. I have told you, dear A., how bright, how eager to learn, he is. His wife, Tamar, is a good-natured easy soul. She has several nice little children, and

the baby—Mary Lincoln—as Mr. [T. Edwin] R.[uggles] the Superintendent has named her—is a very cunning little creature, an especial pet of ours. Celia is one of the best women on the place. She is a cripple. Her feet and limbs were so badly frozen by exposure that her legs were obliged to be amputated just above the knees. But she manages to get about almost as actively as any of the others. Her husband, Thomas, has been a soldier, and is now quite ill with pneumonia. She has several children—Rose, who is our little maid, Olivia the eldest, Dolly, a bright little thing who goes to school with me every morn. and who likes to go. Lastly Aikin, whose proper name is Thomas. He is an odd little fellow, very much spoiled. Amaretta, Celia's sister is our laundress and cook. I like her very much. Then there is Wilhelmina, a mulatto (the others are all black). She comes from Virginia, and speaks therefore quite intelligibly. She is a good sensible woman, and both she and her husband Robt.,—who is one of my night pupils—are most anxious for their three little ones to learn. Cupid our major-domo. is as obliging as possible. A shrewd fellow, who knows well what he is about. His wife Patience, is Tamar's sister, and lives across the creek at Pollywana. Their children—two of them—come to our school. They are good scholars. I do enjoy hearing Cupid and Harry tell about the time that the Secesh had to flee. The time of the "gun shoot," as they call the taking of Bay Point, which is opposite Hilton Head. It delights them greatly to recall that time. Their master had the audacity to venture back even while the Union troops were occupying Beaufort. H.[arry] says he tried to persuade him to go back with him, assuring him that the Yankees w'ld shoot them all when they came. "Bery well sur," he replied[,] "if I go wid you I be good as dead, so if I got the dead, I might's well dead here as anywhere. So I'll stay and wait for the Yankees." He told me that he knew all the time that his master was not telling the truth. Cupid says the master told the people to get all the furniture together and take it over to Pollywana, and to stay on that side themselves, "so" says Cupid, "dey c'ld jus' swap us all and put us in de boat. And he telled me to row Patience and de chilens down to a certain pint, and den I c'ld come back if I choose." "Jus' as if I was gwine to be sich a goat" adds Cupid, with a look and gesture of ineffable contempt. The *finale* of the story is that the people left the premises and hid themselves so that when the master returned not one of all his "faithful servants" was to be found to go into slavery with him, and he was obliged to return, a disappointed, but it is to be hoped, a wiser man.

As I sat on the stand and looked around on the various groups, I thought I had never seen a sight so beautiful. There were the black soldiers, in their blue coats and scarlet pants, the officers of this and other regiments in their handsome uniforms, and crowds of lookers-on, men, women and children, grouped in various attitudes, under the trees. The faces of all wore a happy, eager, expectant look. The exercises commenced by a prayer from Rev. Mr. [James H.] Fowler, Chaplain of the Reg. An ode written for the occasion by Prof. [John] Zachos, originally a Greek, now Sup.[erintendent] of Paris Island, was read by himself, and then sung by the whites. Col. H.[igginson] introduced Dr. [William] Brisbane in a few elegant and graceful words. He (Dr. B.[risbane]) read the President's Proclamation, which was warmly cheered. Then the beautiful flags presented by Dr. [George] Cheever's Church were presented to Col. H.[igginson] for the Reg. in an excellent and enthusiastic speech, by Rev. Mr. [Mansfield] French. Immediately at the conclusion, some of the colored people—of their own accord sang "My Country Tis of Thee." It was a touching and beautiful incident, and Col. Higginson, in accepting the flags made it the occasion of some happy remarks. He said that *that* tribute was far more effecting than any speech he c'ld make. He spoke for some time, and all that he said was grand, glorious. He seemed inspired. Nothing c'ld have been better, more perfect. And Dr. R.[ogers] told

me afterward that the Col. was much affected. That tears were in his eyes. He is as Whittier says, truly a "sure man." The men all admire and love him. There is a great deal of personal magnetism about him, and his kindness is proverbial. After he had done speaking he delivered the flags to the color-bearers with a few very impressive remarks to them. They each then, Prince Rivers, and Robert Sutton, made very good speeches indeed, and were loudly cheered. Gen. Saxton and Mrs. Gage spoke very well. The good Gen. was received with great enthusiasm, and throughout the morning—every little while it seemed to me three cheers were given for him. A Hymn written I believe, by Mr. Judd, was sung, and then all the people united with the Reg. in singing "John Brown." It was grand. During the exercises, it was announced that [John C.] Fremont was appointed Commander-in-Chief of the Army, and this was received with enthusiastic and prolonged cheering.

Saturday January 31. In B.[eaufort] we spent nearly all our time at Harriet Tubman's otherwise [*sic*] "Moses." She is a wonderful woman—a real heroine. Has helped off a large number of slaves, after taking her own freedom. She told us that she used to hide them in the woods during the day and go around to get provisions for them. Once she had with her a man named Joe, for whom a reward of $1500 was offered. Frequently, in different places she found hand-bills exactly describing him, but at last they reached in safety the Suspension Bridge over the Falls and found themselves in Canada. Until then, she said, Joe had been very silent. In vain had she called his attention to the glory of the Falls. He sat perfectly still—moody, it seemed, and w'ld not even glance at them. But when she said, "Now we are in Can.[ada]" he sprang to his feet—with a great shout and sang and clapped his hands in a perfect delirium of joy. So when they got out, and he first touched *free* soil, he shouted and hurrahed "as if he were crazy"—she said. How exciting it was to hear her tell the story. And to hear her sing the very scraps of jubilant hymns that he sang. She said the ladies crowded around them, and some laughed and some cried. My own eyes were full as I listened to her—the heroic woman! A reward of $10,000 was offered for her by the Southerners, and her friends deemed it best that she sh'ld, for a time find refuge in Can.[ada]. And she did so, but only for a short time. She came back and was soon at the good brave work again. She is living in B.[eaufort] now; keeping an eating house. But she wants to go North, and will probably do so ere long. I am glad I saw her—*very* glad.

United States Constitution: Reconstruction Amendments

AMENDMENT XIII [1865]

Section 1. Neither slavery nor involuntary servitude, except as a punishment for crime whereof the party shall have been duly convicted, shall exist within the United States, or any place subject to their jurisdiction.

Section 2. Congress shall have power to enforce this article by appropriate legislation.

AMENDMENT XIV [1868]

Section 1. All persons born or naturalized in the United States, and subject to the jurisdiction thereof, are citizens of the United States and of the State wherein they reside. No State shall make or enforce any law which shall abridge the privileges or immunities of citizens of the United States; nor shall any State deprive any person of life, liberty, or property, without due process of law; nor deny to any person within its jurisdiction the equal protection of the laws.

Section 2. Representatives shall be apportioned among the several States according to their respective numbers, counting the whole number of persons in each State, excluding Indians not taxed. But when the right to vote at any election for the choice of electors for President and Vice President of the United States, Representatives in Congress, the Executive and Judicial officers of a State, or the members of the Legislature thereof, is denied to any of the male inhabitants of such State, being twenty-one years of age, and citizens of the United States, or in any way abridged, except for participation in rebellion, or other crime, the basis of representation therein shall be reduced in the proportion which the number of such male citizens shall bear to the whole number of male citizens twenty-one years of age in such State.

Section 3. No person shall be a Senator or Representative in Congress, or elector of President and Vice President, or hold any office, civil or military, under the United States, or under any State, who, having previously taken an oath, as a member of Congress, or as an officer of the United States, or as a member of any State legislature, or as an executive or judicial officer of any State, to support the Constitution of the United States, shall have engaged in insurrection or rebellion against the same, or given aid or comfort to the enemies thereof. But Congress may by a vote of two-thirds of each House, remove such disability.

Section 4. The validity of the public debt of the United States, authorized by law, including debts incurred for payment of pensions and bounties for services in suppressing insurrection or rebellion, shall not be questioned. But neither the United States nor any State shall assume or pay any debt or obligation incurred in aid of insurrection or rebellion against the United States, or any claim for the loss or emancipation of any slave; but all such debts, obligations and claims shall be held illegal and void.

Section 5. The Congress shall have power to enforce, by appropriate legislation, the provisions of this article.

AMENDMENT XV [1870]

Section 1. The right of citizens of the United States to vote shall not be denied or abridged by the United States or by any State on account of race, color, or previous condition of servitude.

Section 2. The Congress shall have power to enforce this article by appropriate legislation.

Excerpts from the Proceedings of the Constitutional Convention of South Carolina

The Committee on Petitions, to whom was referred the preamble and resolution relative to petitioning Congress for a grant of one million dollars to be appropriated for the purchase of lands in this State, ask leave to report that they have duly considered the same, and are of the opinion that the prayer of your petitioner should be granted, and that the President of this Convention be requested to transmit a copy of the preamble and resolution to the Congress of the United States at as early a date as practicable.

W. E. Rose, *Chairman.*

... **Mr. Cain.** I offer this resolution with good intentions. I believe there is need of

Source: From *Proceedings of the Constitutional Convention of South Carolina.* (Charleston: Denny and Perry, 1868), Vol. I, pp. 376, 378–82, 400–406, 419–24, 438.

immediate relief to the poor people of the State. I know from my experience among the people, there is pressing need of some measures to meet the wants of the utterly destitute. The gentleman says it will only take money out of the Treasury. Well that is the intention. I do not expect to get it anywhere else. I expect to get the money, if at all, through the Treasury of the United States, or some other department. It certainly must come out of the Government. I believe such an appropriation would remove a great many of the difficulties now in the State and do a vast amount of good to poor people. It may be that we will not get it, but that will not debar us from asking. It is our privilege and right. Other Conventions have asked from Congress appropriations. Georgia and other States have sent in their petitions. One has asked for $30,000,000 to be appropriated to the Southern States. I do not see any inconsistency in the proposition presented by myself.... This is a measure of relief to those thousands of freed people who now have no lands of their own. I believe the possession of lands and homesteads is one of the best means by which a people is made industrious, honest and advantageous to the State. I believe it is a fact well known, that over three hundred thousand men, women and children are homeless, landless. The abolition of slavery has thrown these people upon their own resources. How are they to live. I know the philosopher of the New York Tribune says, "root hog or die;" but in the meantime we ought to have some place to root. My proposition is simply to give the hog some place to root. I believe if the proposition is sent to Congress, it will certainly receive the attention of our friends. I believe the whole country is desirous to see that this State shall return to the Union in peace and quiet, and that every inhabitant of the State shall be made industrious and profitable to the State. I am opposed to this Bureau system. I want a system adopted that will do away with the Bureau, but I cannot see how it can be done unless the people have homes. As long as people are working on shares and contracts, and at the end of every year are in debt, so long will they and the country suffer. But give them a chance to buy lands, and they become steady, industrious men. That is the reason I desire to bring this money here and to assist them to buy lands. It will be the means of encouraging them to industry if the petition be granted by Congress. It will be the means of meeting one of the great wants of the present among the poor. It will lay the foundation for the future prosperity of the country as no other measure will at this time, because it will bring about a reconciliation in the minds of thousands of these helpless people, which nothing else can. This measure, if carried out, will bring capital to the State and stimulate the poor to renewed efforts in life, such as they never had before. Such a measure will give to the landholders relief from their embarrassments financially, and enable them to get fair compensation for their

lands. It will relieve the Government of the responsibility of taking care of the thousands who now are fed at the Commissaries and fostered in laziness, I have gone through the country and on every side I was besieged with questions: How are we to get homesteads, to get lands? I desire to devise some plan, or adopt some measure by which we can dissipate one of the arguments used against us, that the African race will not work. I do not believe the black man hates work any more than the white man does. Give these men a place to work, and I will guarantee before one year passes, there will be no necessity for the Freedman's Bureau, or any measure aside from those measures which a people may make in protecting themselves.

But a people without homes become wanderers. If they possess lands they have an interest in the soil, in the State, in its commerce, its agriculture, and in everything pertaining to the wealth and welfare of the State. If these people had homes along the lines of railroads, and the lands were divided and sold in small farms, I will guarantee our railroads will make fifty times as much money, banking systems will be advanced by virtue of the settlement of the people throughout the whole State. We want these large tracts of land cut up. The land is productive, and there is nothing to prevent the greatest and highest prosperity. What we need is a system of small farms. Every farmer owning his own land will feel he is in possession of something. It will have a tendency to settle the minds of the people in the State and settle many difficulties. In the rural districts now there is constant discontent, constant misapprehension between the parties, a constant disregard for each other. One man won't make an engagement to work, because he fears if he makes a contract this year, he will be cheated again as he thinks he was last year. We have had petitions from planters asking the Convention to disabuse the minds of the freedmen of the thought that this Convention has any lands at its disposal, but I do desire this Convention to do something at least to relieve the wants of these poor suffering people. I believe this measure, if adopted and sent to Congress, will indicate to the people that this Convention does desire they shall possess homes and have relief.

Some of my friends say that the sum is too small, and ask why I do not make it more. I made it a million, because I thought there would be more probability of getting one million than five. It might be put into the hands of the Bureau, and I am willing to trust the Bureau. . . . I do not desire to have a foot of land in this State confiscated. I want every man to stand upon his own character. I want these lands purchased by the government, and the people afforded an opportunity to buy from the government. I believe every man ought to carve out for himself a character and position in this life. I believe every man ought to be made to work by some means or other, and if he does not, he must go down. I believe if the same amount of money that has been employed by the Bureau in feeding lazy, worthless men and women, had been expended in purchasing lands, we would to-day have no need of the Bureau. Millions upon millions have been expended, and it is still going on *ad infinitum.* I propose to let the poor people buy these lands, the government to be paid back in five years time. It is one of the great cries of the enemies of reconstruction, that Congress has constantly fostered laziness. I want to have the satisfaction of showing that the freedmen are as capable and willing to work as any men on the face of the earth. This measure will save the State untold expenses. I believe there are hundreds of persons in the jail and penitentiary cracking rock to-day who have all the instincts of honesty, and who, had they an opportunity of making a living, would never have been found in such a place. I think if Congress will accede to our request, we shall be benefited beyond measure, and save the State from taking charge of paupers, made such by not having the means to earn a living for themselves.

I can look to a part of my constituency, men in this hall, mechanics, plasterers, carpenters, engineers, men capable of doing all kind of work, now idle because they cannot find any work in the city. Poverty stares them in the face, and their children are in want. They go to the cotton houses, but can find no labor. They are men whose honesty and integrity has never been called in question. They are suffering in consequence of the poverty-stricken condition of the city and State. I believe the best measure is to open a field where they can labor, where they can take the hoe and the axe, cut down the forest, and make the whole land blossom as the Garden of Eden, and prosperity pervade the whole land.

Now, the report of Major General Howard gives a surplus of over seven millions in the Freedman's Bureau last year. Out of that seven millions I propose we ask Congress to make an appropriation of one million, which will be properly distributed and then leave several millions in that Department, my friend from Barnwell notwithstanding.

I think there could be no better measure for this Convention to urge upon Congress. If that body should listen to our appeal, I have no doubt we shall be benefited. This measure of relief, it seems to me, would come swiftly. It is a swift messenger that comes in a week's time after it is passed; so that in the month of February or March the people may be enabled to go to planting and raising crops for the ensuring year. One gentleman says it will take six months or a year, but I hope, with the assistance of the Government, we could accomplish it in less time. . . . If this measure is carried out, the results will be that we will see all along our lines of railroad and State roads little farms, log cabins filled with happy families, and thousands of families coming on the railroads with their products. There will also spring up depots for the reception of cotton, corn and all other cereals. Prosperity will return to the State, by virtue of the people being happy, bound to the Government by a tie that cannot be broken. The taxes, that are so heavy now that men are compelled to sell their horses, will be lightened. I want to see the State alive, to hear the hum of the spindle and the mills! I want to see cattle and horses, and fowls, and everything that makes up a happy home and family. I want to see the people shout with joy and gladness. There shall then be no antagonism between white men and black men, but we shall all realize the end of our being, and realize that we are all made to dwell upon the earth in peace and happiness. The white man and the black man then work in harmony, and secure prosperity to all coming generations. . . .

Mr. W. J. Whipper. In attempting to speak upon this question, it is with no view of defeating the resolution or adoption of the report of the Committee. I intend to vote against the measure, and take this opportunity of saying so. I am the more zealous to do so when I find members of this body oscillating as they are, and openly declaring that they are going to vote for it, though believing it wrong. I am the more zealous of doing so when I find members afraid to follow their honest convictions; and then meet their constituency. Whatever may be my conviction as to the policy of this measure, I, in my heart of hearts, believe it will be detrimental to the people and detrimental to the State, and for that reason shall record my vote against it. I am not afraid to meet my constituents, nor afraid to meet the people of South Carolina, and answer for all that I shall do here, believing it to be for their best interest. I am willing that time should decide as to the propriety of the course I pursue in this body. I say it is my earnest desire that that petition should be voted down, as it should have been without discussion.

With regard to the gentleman from Barnwell, upon whom it has been the province of the delegates to pounce so wickedly, I would say he has told much that is true, and much that they will find hereafter incontrovertible.

As to the office seeking of the Charleston delegates, I have nothing to do.

In the first place, I regard the petition a failure. I am opposed to one million of dollars being brought to the State of South Carolina to be disposed of as that petition proposes. I am in favor of any measure of relief that will affect the people permanently; but if we can devise no other measure than this, then I am opposed to it. Admitting it can be done, that Congress may appropriate one million of dollars, what will be the result? The gentleman from Charleston tells you it will give homes to one-fourth of the people of the State. What kind of homes would they be? It would place them in possession of five and one-seventh acres; just about enough to starve to death decently that one-fourth of the people. If you want to make a man an everlasting pauper, do as the United States did in my district, make him the owner of some ten acres. He cannot raise more than enough to feed his babies upon it. Men in this State must have more land. . . . I claim that this measure will not benefit the people of South Carolina, and upon that ground I oppose it. The very moment this resolution passes and the papers publish that a petition has been sent to Congress to buy lands for the poor of this State, a clamor for land will at once arise, the freedmen will forsake their contracts and at once leave their places of employment. You raise the hopes of the entire poor people of the country, you draw around the land offices, which they will inevitably create, a multitude, three fourths of whom will be compelled to go away with shattered hopes. Let me give you an illustration. In my district quite a scarcity of provisions existed. The Bureau, in its wisdom and charity, sent to that district twelve hundred bushels of corn, and I know that I am speaking the sentiments of my constituents when I say that that distribution of corn had an injurious effect upon labor.

This miserable meagre measure of relief but looses the laborer from the land and raises his hopes, leading him to believe he is to realize all he has longed for for years, and with that object in view goes to the land office perhaps, only to return to his house disappointed, and see his prospects for another year frustrated. You will have three-fourth without an inch of land, and another fourth with but five and one-seventh acres. If you wish to see such a state of affairs, vote for that petition. If Congress does not, in its wisdom, see fit to withhold this loan, you will see that condition of affairs to your satisfaction.

It is said we must do something here, or the people will never ratify the Constitution. There is no one would be prouder to do something that would give permanent relief than I would. If we can give any thing, give the poor man property in his labor, and we will have effected that relief. There cannot be a delegate from the coast but knows of the dire effect of holding out inducements to hold land, produced upon the laborers on the adjacent islands. Only about two years ago the Commissioner was compelled, with the bayonet, to force the people to go to work for the very reason that these inducements, with regard to owning land, had been held out to them. They had been made to believe they should hold them. The sooner the public mind is disabused of that impression, the sooner every man knows that to acquire land he must earn it; the sooner he feels the Government has no lands to dispose of or to give him, the better. Do what is necessary to protect the laborer in his labor and you will effect the greatest possible good. All these temporary and meagre measures of relief that are gotten up, I fear are too much for political purposes. I believe a majority of the members of this body do not believe this measure is permanent in its character. They look upon it as a measure of relief that in its details must fail. But they ask, must we face our constituency—go home and say we voted against that which certain members said was calculated to relieve the poor? Must we say we voted against a donation? No, it will frustrate our future prospects. But to whatever political

death it may consign me, I shall vote against it.

I know members upon this floor have said in the last twenty-four hours that they intend to swim with the tide. I regret to see this disposition, for in my judgment if a measure does not meet the conscientious convictions of the members, they should vote against it and take the consequences. I believe the adoption of this measure would bring interminable difficulties upon the Assistant Commissioner of your district. But I warn you, gentlemen, against the final results. Are you not going to disappointment the people beyond all expectation? I warn you against the indignation of the people whom you may deceive by that measure, and whose hopes you raise only to be blasted a few months hence. You may establish a measure giving to the poor man property in his labor. Do that, and you further the permanent interests of the State, build up the waste places, erect school houses, give encouragement to the mechanic and the laborer, and furnish the means for the cultivation of those lands.

If you create property in labor, the landholder will be compelled to divide and sell his lands, and the laborer will be able to purchase a home for himself. I desire to see established a system of taxation which will make it unprofitable for a man to keep lands uncultivated. We are not here to enter into any begging scheme, even if expedient to do so. I do not believe that it is for the interest of the people of this State. But protect labor and secure the laborer in all his right, and with their own strong arms and willing hands the people will accumulate property for themselves, and purchase homesteads with the results of honest industry. . . .

. . . **Mr. F. L. Cardozo.** This question has been mingled by some of the opposition with a great deal of personality. They freely imputed the most malicious motives to their opponents, and while I sat listening to those imputations I was forcibly reminded of the proverb, "It takes a rogue to catch a rogue." I will make one remark, and then will be done with personalities. The gentleman from Barnwell has referred constantly to the gentleman from Charleston; but it is believed that the gentleman from Barnwell is an old cast off Charleston politician. I remember his obtaining a hall of me and asking me to go help him at Barnwell. I positively refused to do it, because I thought, as the gentleman from Edgefield has said, that he (Leslie) was *non compos mentis.*

I am surprised at the gentleman from Beaufort, who just about two weeks ago rose in this Convention and advocated two measures of relief for the planters of this State, to save their property from going under the hammer of the auctioneer for debts contracted for the purchase of slaves. He was very eloquent in favor of those two measures of relief that would save to the rebel planters their old estates. But now, when a measure comes up to request help for the poor colored people, the very same eloquence is employed on the opposite side.

I would only say to him who imputed improper motives to the gentleman who originated this measure, it is currently reported that he is the tool of rebels, and his course has certainly justified that report. I opposed those two measures of relief that he favored, for two reasons; first, I said they were unjust in themselves. Men had contracted debts with their eyes wide open, knew the risks they run, took those risks, and if they were honest men, would pay their debts; but if they were dishonest, I claim they ought to be made to pay their debts. They contracted those debts in the rebel cause, to keep poor colored people down, to perpetuate slavery, and, having done that, they should suffer the consequences. Let their large estates be divided, and the poor colored people would have a better opportunity of buying lands. Those measures of relief were passed. This Convention refused to give the colored people that legal opportunity, and I would say to the gentlemen who voted for those measures of relief, if they are consistent, if they are the friends of the colored man, they may,

with equal consistency, vote for this measure. The argument is used that we are not likely to get the money asked for. But how can they tell? I think we are just as likely to get it, and more likely to obtain it, than the thirty millions asked by the Georgia Convention for the planters of the South, who have tried to reduce the colored man again to slavery or its equivalent condition—serfdom.

The gentleman from Beaufort argued that this was an impolitic measure, because it would not give all the colored people lands, and I would say better that than none at all. It will do a great deal of good. It is precisely what the Assistant Commissioner of this State has been doing in this District. No later than last night he told me that he had a large quantity of provisions, amounting to a large sum, to aid the people of this State, and had been told to give it out freely. He wrote to General Howard, stating that it would be better to assist the planters, taking a lien on the crops, and he sent him word to do so: took a lien upon the crops, and said when he got the money he would build school houses with it. But the crops have failed, and it is probable he will have no return. That was a help to the white planter. The Assistant Commissioner, however, made no invidious distinction, for a truer and nobler friend, both to the colored and white man does not exist in our State. He helps all alike, and assists all alike. The poor freedmen were induced, by many Congressmen even, to expect confiscation. They held out the hope of confiscation. General Sherman did confiscate, gave the lands to the freedmen; and if it were not for President Johnson, they would have them now. The hopes of the freedmen have not been realized, and I do not think that asking for a loan of one million, to be paid by a mortgage upon the land, will be half as bad as has been supposed. I have been told by the Assistant Commissioner that he has been doing on a private scale what this petition proposes to do. I say every opportunity for helping the colored man should be seized upon. I think the adoption of this measure will do honor to the Convention. We should certainly vote for some measure of relief for the colored men, as we have to the white men, who mortgaged their property to perpetuate slavery, and whom they have liberated from their bonds.

. . . [Mr. R. H. Cain.] The appropriations could be made in three directions; first, to the purchase of lands; second, to the purchase of sites; third, to the purchase of necessary agricultural implements. It was said that this appropriation, if carried out, would give homes to but few. I think it was said that it would give one hundred and twenty-five thousand persons homes. According to my friend from Beaufort (Mr. Whipper), it would allow but five and one-seventh acres to each head of a family, and he claims that that would not be sufficient to do any good. Well, if we can give homes to one hundred and twenty-five thousand persons, we shall thereby take out from the jurisdiction of the Freedman's Bureau that number who still linger at the door of the Commissary, waiting for something to eat. It will, therefore, be a measure of relief to three parties; first, a measure of relief to the poor; second, to the Freedman's Bureau; third, to the landholders who will receive just compensation for the lands they own, and thus spread a million of dollars in circulation, giving to every class of men something to eat and something to do. That much good will be accomplished. But to answer the gentleman, that it will give discontent to the poor colored people, is it not better to give one hundred and twenty-five thousand people homes by a measure so judicious, so complete and so swift as this will be, than to let four hundred thousand go without any homes at all. It is objected by the gentleman also, that it will create discontent in the minds of others. I prefer to cut off one hundred and twenty-five thousand grumblers than none at all. I believe it a measure of relief, such as the people do need, such as they want, and such as they shall have.

I can see no reason why any gentleman should object to the proposition; I believe the Government will be benefited by it, and I reiterate what I said last week. I am opposed to the people constantly going up to the Commissary Department and receiving rations; I believe that if the money expended by the Commissary Department of the Freedman's Bureau was given for the purchase of land it would have a more permanent and beneficial effect. Four hundred and fifty thousand dollars has been expended in that Bureau in five months for the simple item of rations, yet that Bureau has not reached one-tenth of the people in this State. Again, I would not call into question the honesty of the officers of the Bureau, I believe there are some honest men there at any rate. . . . I believe that the gentlemen at the head of that Bureau, from their antecedents and long experience in these matters, will do justice in this case.

The gentleman from Beaufort opposed the measure on the ground that it would create discontent, but was in favor of bringing up a resolution either in the Convention or by the Legislature, fixing such a tax upon the lands as to compel the sale of those lands, whether the owners wanted to or not.

Mr. W. J. Whipper. I deny it.

Mr. R. H. Cain. I may be mistaken, but I watched very closely the arguments made by the gentleman last Saturday, and I distinctly understood him to say he was in favor of taxing the lands so as to compel the sale of them, and throw them into the market. The poor would then have a chance to buy. I am unqualifiedly opposed to any measure of taxation for the simple purpose of compelling the owners to sell their lands. I believe the best measure to be adopted is to bring capital to the State, and instead of causing revenge and unpleasantness, I am for even-handed justice. I am for allowing the parties who own lands to bring them into the market and sell them upon such terms as will be satisfactory to both sides. I believe a measure of this kind has a double effect: first, it brings capital, what the people want; second, it puts the people to work; its gives homesteads, what we need; it relieves the Government and takes away its responsibility of feeding the people; it inspires every man with a noble manfulness, and by the thought that he is the possessor of something in the State; it adds also to the revenue of the country. By these means men become interested in the country as they never were before. It was said that five and one-seventh acres were not enough to live on. If South Carolina, in its sovereign power, can devise any plan for the purchase of the large plantations in this State now lying idle, divide and sell them out at a reasonable price, it will give so many people work. I will guarantee to find persons to work every five acres. I will also guarantee that after one year's time, the Freedman's Bureau will not have to give any man having one acre of land anything to eat. This country has a genial clime, rich soil, and can be worked to advantage. The man who can not earn a living on five acres, will not do so on twenty-five. I regret that another position taken by gentlemen in the opposition, is that they do not believe that we will get what we ask for. I believe that the party, now in power in the Congress of the United States, will do whatever they can for the welfare of the people of this State and of the South. I believe that the noble men who have maintained the rights of the freedmen before and since their liberation, will continue to do everything possible to forward these great interests. I am exceedingly anxious, if possible, to allay all unpleasant feeling—I would not have any unpleasant feeling among ourselves.

I would not have any unpleasant feelings between the races. If we give each family in the State an opportunity of purchasing a home, I think they will all be better satisfied.

But it is also said that it will disturb all the agricultural operations in the State. I do not believe if the Congress of the United States shall advance one million of dollars to make purchase of lands, the laborers will abandon their engagement and run off. I have more confidence in the people I represent. I believe all who have made contracts will fulfill those contracts, and when their contracts have expired, they will go on their own lands, as all freemen ought to go. I claim it would do no harm. It would be a wonderful concatenation of circumstances indeed, to find that because the Government had appropriated one million of dollars for the purchase of lands, to see all of four hundred thousand people, rushing pell mell down to Charleston to get a homestead. I know the ignorance of the people with whom I am identified is great. I know that four hundred years of bondage has degraded them, but I have more confidence in humanity then to believe the people will leave their homes and their families to come to Charleston just to get five acres of land.

If I understood the speaker in the opposition this morning, he offered it because he said it was simply a scheme for colored men. I wish to state this question right. If there was one thing on which I thought I had been specific, it was on that point. The clock had struck two and I had dashed down my pen when the thought struck me it might be misunderstood. I retraced my steps and so shaped the petition as simply to state the poor of any class. I bore in mind the poor whites of the upper districts. I saw, not long ago, a poor white woman walk eighteen miles barefooted to receive a bag of corn and four pounds of meat, resting all night on the roadside, eating one-half and then go away, living on roots afterwards and half starved. I desire that class of people to have homes as well as the black man. I have lost long since that hateful idea that the complexion of a man makes any difference as far as rights are concerned. The true principle of progress and civilization is to recognize the great brotherhood of man, and a man's wants, whatever he may be, or whatever clime he comes from, are as sacred to me as any other class of men. I believe this measure will advance the interests of all classes.

A few more words and I am done. Gentlemen of the Convention, I wish to appeal to you and ask have we not had suffering enough in this country? Has not the rude hands of war, with its fiery sword, trampled out the commercial interests of the States? Hath not the rude hand of war laid up the ships in our harbors, torn down fences and barns, and left our country almost a wilderness? Hath not war set the whole country in commotion? Look at the former rich white man, now walking poor and penniless; look at those formerly in opulence, now poor and brought down low. Can the gentleman from Barnwell, formerly from New York, last from Charleston, understand the fact that the people of the State want relief? I came to identify myself with the interests of the country. If she falls, I fall with her. If she rises, I rise with her. I have a kind of South Carolina pride, because my broad heart reaches out to all men's interests wherever I am. I have identified myself with the country, and I claim it is no time in the reconstruction of the State to seek revenge upon the head of any person, or to disregard the cries of millions for relief. The freed people, in connection with the poor whites of this State, are in great want. Let us see the number of destitute in this State. General Howard reports in South Carolina five thousand colored and five thousand whites, March 7th, 1867. There are other reports here which show a larger number of persons, and as I before remarked, the Bureau hath not met one-tenth of the wants of the people. This measure, if carried out, therefore, will meet a want which the Bureau never can meet. A man may have rations to-day and not tomorrow, but when he gets land and a homestead, and is once fixed on that land, he never will want to go to the Commissary again. It is said that I depicted little farms by the roadside, chickens roosting on the fence, and all those poetical beauties. But however poetical the gentlemen may be in his remarks, I prefer to see chickens roosting on the fence, and the lambs frisking round the place, and all other things which may be desired, than to see four hundred thousand people without homes, without owning even the sand they carry in their shoes. I prefer to see each one of them the owner of a log cabin, than to be compelled to work for five or ten dollars per month. I prefer to see that than to see the bayonets of the United States brought into requisition to drive poor, helpless men, women and children, because of the relentless hearts of those planters who will not pay. I prefer this to seeing strong men working for the paltry sum of five or ten dollars a month, and some for even three dollars a month. How can a man live at that rate. I hate the contract system as I hate the being of whom my friend from Orangeburg (Mr. Randolph) spoke last week (the devil). It has ruined the people. After fifty men have gone on a plantation, worked the whole year at raising twenty thousand bushels of rice, and then go to get their one-third, by the time they get through the division, after being charged by the landlord twenty-five or thirty cents a pound for bacon, two or three dollars for a pair of brogans that costs sixty cents, for living that costs a mere song, two dollars a bushel for corn that can be bought for one dollar; after I say, these people have worked the whole season, and at the end make up their accounts, they find themselves in debt. The planters sell their cotton, for it is said that a Negro has not brain enough to sell his own cotton. He can raise anything; he can dig ditches, pick cotton, but has not the sense to sell it. I deprecate that idea. I would rather see these people have little cottages and farms for themselves.

It is but a few days ago I went to a plantation on Cooper river. The first place I visited, I said to the men there, go to work, work honestly, stay on the plantation, do the best you can, make yourselves as comfortable as possible. After awhile your old masters may do you justice. Those people have remained on those plantations. What was the result.

Week before last they came and said to me, we took your advice, have worked hard, but as God is our judge, we have not as much as when these men got back their place again. I looked and saw four mule teams rolling off bales of cotton. I saw corn cribs piled with corn, and fodder houses filled with fodder. I went into the cabin of the Negroes and found but a scanty morsel of corn dodger and a scanty ration of bacon.

I say, therefore, it is time to relieve these people, and if this is not a measure of relief I know not what is. I desire to relieve all classes. I desire to relieve the planters of the large plantations they cannot attend to, and which must be so great a burden on their minds. They are pressed down; do now know what to do with their great plantations. I propose to bring money and say to them, "here gentlemen, you want to sell, we want to buy; we will give you a reasonable price; you will have the greenbacks, we will have the land; you can apply that money to banking purposes or buy bank stock, we will deposit the money with you." I want to see a change in this country. Instead of the colored people being always penniless, I want to see them coming in with their mule teams and ox teams. I want to see them come with their corn and potatoes and exchange for silks and satins. I want to see school houses and churches in every parish and township. I want to see children coming forth to enjoy life as it ought to be enjoyed. This people know nothing of what is good and best for mankind until they get homesteads and enjoy them.

With these remarks, I close. I hope the Convention will vote for the proposition. Let us send up our petition. The right to petition is a jealous right. It was a right guaranteed to the Barons of England. The American people have always been jealous of that right, and regarded it as sacred and inviolate. That right we propose to maintain. It is said here that some high officers are opposed to it. I do not care who is opposed to it. It is none of their business. I do not care whether General Scott, General Grant, or General anybody else is opposed to it, we will petition in spite of them. I appeal to the delegates to pass this resolution. It will do no harm if it does no good, and I am equally confident that some gentleman will catch what paddy gave the drum when they go back to their constituents. . . .

[After further debate, the resolution was finally passed in an amended and watered-down form.]

Resolved, That the President of the Convention be authorized to telegraph to the President of the United States Senate and Speaker of the national House of Representatives, and request them to present before their respective branches of Congress the great need of our people, and their homeless and landless condition, with the view of securing an early expression from the Government as to whether a petition of every member of this Convention would be productive of a loan from the national Treasury to enable our people to buy farms on a reasonable credit, and if so, how large an amount should be petitioned for.

Speech on the Eligibility of Colored Members to Seats in the Georgia Legislature

Henry M. Turner

Mr. Speaker: Before proceeding to argue this question upon its intrinsic merits, I wish the Members of this House to understand the position that I take. I hold that I am a member of this body. Therefore, sir, I shall neither fawn nor cringe before any party, nor stoop to *beg* them for my rights. Some of my colored fellow-members, in the course of their remarks, took occasion to appeal to the *sympathies* of Members on the opposite side, and to eulogize their character for magnanimity. It reminds me very much, sir, of slaves begging under the lash. I am here to demand my rights, and to hurl thunderbolts at the men who would dare to cross the threshold of my manhood. There is an old aphorism which says, "Fight the Devil with fire," and if I should observe the rule in this instance, I wish gentlemen to understand that it is but fighting them with their own weapon.

The scene presented in this House, to-day, is one unparalleled in the history of the world. From this day, back to the day when God breathed the breath of life into Adam, no analogy for it can be found. Never, in the history of the world, has a man been arraigned before a body clothed with legislative, judicial or executive functions, charged with the offence of being of a darker hue than his fellow-men. I know that questions have been before the Courts of this country, and of other countries, involving topics not altogether dissimilar to that which is being discussed here to-day. But, sir, never, in all the history of the great nations of this

world—never before—has a man been arraigned, charged with an offence committed by the God of Heaven himself. Cases may be found where men have been deprived of their rights for crimes and misdemeanors; but it has remained for the State of Georgia, in the very heart of the nineteenth century, to call a man before the bar, and there charge him with an act for which he is no more responsible than for the head which he carries upon his shoulders. The Anglo-Saxon race, sir, is a most surprising one. No man has ever been more deceived in that race than I have been for the last three weeks. I was not aware that there was in the character of that race so much cowardice, or so much pusillanimity. The treachery which has been exhibited by gentleman belonging to that race has shaken my confidence in it more than anything that has come under my observation from the day of my birth.

What is the question at issue? Why, sir, this Assembly, to-day, is discussing and deliberating on a matter upon which Angels would tremble to sit in judgment; there is not a Cherubim that sits around God's Eternal Throne, to-day, that would not tremble—even were an order issued by the Supreme God himself—to come down here and sit in judgment on my manhood. Gentlemen may look at this question in whatever light they choose, and with just as much indifference as they may think proper to assume, but I tell you, sir, that this is a question which will not die to-day. This event shall be remembered by posterity for ages yet to come, and while the sun shall continue to climb the hills of heaven.

Whose Legislature is this? Is it a white man's Legislature, or is it a black man's legislature? Who voted for a Constitutional

Source: Henry M. Turner, *Speech on the Eligibility of Colored Members to Seats in the Georgia Legislature, . . . September 3, 1868.* (Augusta: E. H. Pughe, 1868).

Convention, in obedience to the mandate of the Congress of the United States? Who first rallied around the standard of Reconstruction? Who set the ball of loyalty rolling in the State of Georgia? And whose voice was heard on the hills and in the valleys of this State? It was the voice of the brawny-armed Negro, with the few humanitarian-hearted white men who came to our assistance. I claim the honor, sir, of having been the instrument of convincing hundreds—yea, thousands—of white men, that to reconstruct under the measures of the United States Congress was the safest and the best course for the interest of the State.

Let us look at some facts in connection with this matter. Did half the white men of Georgia vote for this Legislature? Did not the great bulk of them fight, with all their strength, the Constitution under which we are acting? And did they not fight against the organization of this Legislature? And further, sir, did they not *vote* against it? Yes, sir! And there are persons in this Legislature, to day, who are ready to spit their poison in my face, while they themselves opposed, with all their power; the ratification of this Constitution. They question my right to a seat in this body, to represent the people whose legal votes elected me. This objection, sir, is an unheard of monopoly of power. No analogy can be found for it, except it be the case of a man who should go into my house, take possession of my wife and children, and then tell me to walk out. I stand very much in the position of a criminal before your bar, because I dare to be the exponent of the views of those who sent me here. Or, in other words, we are told that if black men want to speak, they must speak through white trumpets; if black men want their sentiments expressed, they must be adulterated and sent through white messengers, who will quibble, and equivocate, and evade, as rapidly as the pendulum of a clock. If this be not done, then the black men have committed an outrage, and their Representatives must be denied the right to represent their constituents.

The great question, sir, is this: Am I a man? If I am such, I claim the rights of a man. Am I not a man, because I happen to be of a darker hue than honorable gentlemen around me? Let me see whether I am or not. I want to convince the House, to-day, that I am entitled to my seat here. A certain gentleman has argued that the Negro was a mere development similar to the ourang-outang or chimpanzee, but it so happens that, when a Negro is examined, physiologically, phrenologically and anatomically, and, I may say, physiognomically, he is found to be the same as persons of different color. I would like to ask any gentleman on this floor, where is the analogy? Do you find me quadruped, or do you find me a man? Do you find three bones less in my back than in that of the white man? Do you find less organs in the brain? If you know nothing of this, I do, for I have helped to dissect fifty men, black and white, and I assert that by the time you take off the mucous pigment—the color of the skin—you cannot, to save your life, distinguish between the black man and the white. Am I a man? Have I a soul to save, as you have? Am I susceptible of eternal development, as you are? Can I learn all the arts and sciences that you can—has it ever been demonstrated in the history of the world? Have black men ever exhibited bravery, as white men have done? Have they ever been in the professions? Have they not as good articulative organs as you? Some people argue that there is a very close similarity between the larynx of the Negro and that of the ourang-outang. Why, sir, there is not so much similarity between them as there is between the larynx of the man and that of the dog, and this fact I dare any Member of this House to dispute. God saw fit to vary everything in Nature. There are no two men alike—no two voices alike—no two trees alike. God has weaved and tissued variety and versatility throughout the boundless space of His creation.— Because God saw fit to make some red, and some white, and some black, and some brown, are we to sit here in judgment upon what God has seen fit to do? As well might one play with the thunderbolts of heaven as with that creature that bears God's image—God's photograph.

The question is asked: "What is it that the Negro race has done?" Well, Mr. Speaker, all I have to say upon the subject is this: that if we are the class of people that we are generally represented to be, I hold that we are a very great people. It is generally considered that we are the Children of Canaan, and that the curse of a father rests upon our heads, and has rested, all through history. Sir, I deny that the curse of Noah has anything to do with the Negro. We are not the Children of Canaan; and if we were, sir, where should we stand? Let us look a little into history. Melchisedeck was a Canaanite; all the Phœnicians—all those inventors of the arts and sciences—were the posterity of Canaan; but, sir, the Negro is not. We are the children of Cush, and Canaan's curse has nothing whatever to do with the Negro. If we belong to that race, Ham belonged to it, under whose instructions Napoleon Bonaparte studied military tactics. If we belong to that race, St. Augustine belonged to it. Who was it that laid the foundation of the great Reformation? Martin Luther, who lit the light of Gospel Truth—a light that will never go out until the sun shall rise to set no more; and, long ere then, Democratic principles will have found their level in the regions of Pluto and of Proserpine.

The Negro is here charged with holding office. Why, sir, the Negro never wanted office. I recollect that when we wanted candidates for the Constitutional Convention, we went from door to door in the "Negro belt," and begged white men to run. Some promised to do so; and yet, on the very day of election, many of them first made known their determination not to comply with their promises. They told black men, everywhere, that they would rather see *them* run; and it was this encouragement of the white men that induced the colored man to place his name upon the ticket as a candidate for the Convention. In many instances, these white men voted for us. We did not want them, nor ask them, to do it. All we wanted them to do was, to stand still and allow us to walk up to the polls and deposit our ballots. They would not come here themselves, but would insist upon sending us. Ben. Hill told them it was a nigger affair, and advised them to stay away from the polls—a piece of advice which they took very liberal advantage of. If the "niggers" had "office on the brain," it was the white man that put it there—not carpet-baggers, either, nor Yankees, nor scalawags, but the high-bred and dignified Democracy of the South. And if any one is to blame for having Negroes in these Legislative Halls—if blame attaches to it at all—it is the Democratic party. Now, however, a change has come over the spirit of their dream. They want to turn the "nigger" out; and, to support their argument, they say that the black man is debarred from holding office by the Reconstruction measures of Congress. Let me tell them one thing for their information. Black men have held office, and are now holding office, under the United States Government. Andrew Johnson, President of the United States, in 1865, commissioned me as United States Chaplain, and I would have been Chaplain today, had I not resigned—not desiring to hold office any longer. Let the Democratic party, then, go to Mr. Johnson, and ask him why he commissioned a Negro to that position? And if they inquire further, they will ascertain that black men have been commissioned as Lieutenants, Captains, Majors, Brevet Colonels, Surgeons, and other offices of trust and responsibility, under the United States Government. Black men, today, in Washington City, hold positions as Clerks, and the only reason why Mr. Langston is not at this time a Consul Diplomat or Minister Plenipotentiary in some foreign country, is, because he would not be corrupted by President Johnson and made to subscribe to his wicked designs. Is not that an office, and is it not a great deal better office than any seat held in this body?

The honorable gentleman from Whitfield (Mr. Shumate), when arguing this question, a day or two ago, put forth the proposition that to be a Representative was not to be an officer—"it was a privilege that citizens. had a right to enjoy." These are his words. It was not an office it was a "privilege." Every gentleman here knows that he denied that to be a Representative was to be an officer. Now, he is recognized as a leader of the Democratic party in this House, and generally cooks victuals for them to eat; makes that remarkable declaration, and how are you, gentlemen on the other side of the House, to ignore that declaration? Are you going to expel me from this House, because I am an officer, when one of your great lights says that I am *not* an officer? If you deny my right—the right of my constituents to have representation here—because it is a "privilege," then, sir, I will show you that I have as many privileges as the whitest man on this floor. If I am not permitted to occupy a seat here, for the purpose of representing my constituents, I want to know how white men can be permitted to do so? How can a white man represent a colored constituency, if a colored man cannot do it? The great argument is: "Oh, we have inherited" this, that and the other. Now, I want gentlemen to come down to cool, common sense. Is the created greater than the Creator? Is man greater than God? It is very strange, if a white man can occupy on this floor *a seat created by colored votes,* and a black man cannot do it. Why, gentlemen, it is the most shortsighted reasoning in the world. A man can see better than that with half an eye; and even if he had no eye at all, he could forge one, as the Cyclops did, or punch one with his finger, which would enable him to see through that.

It is said that Congress never gave us the right to hold office. I want to know, sir, if the Reconstruction measures did not base their action on the ground that no distinction should be made on account of race, color, or previous condition! Was not that the grand fulcrum on which they rested? And did not every reconstructed State have to reconstruct on the idea that no discrimination, in any sense of the term, should be made?

There is not a man here who will dare say, "No." If Congress has simply given me merely sufficient civil and political rights to make me a mere political slave for Democrats, or anybody else—giving them the opportunity of jumping on my back, in order to leap into political power—I do not thank Congress for it. Never, so help me, God, shall I be a political slave. I am not now speaking for those colored men who sit with me in this House, nor do I say that they endorse my sentiments [cries from the colored Members, "We do!"], but I am speaking simply and solely for myself. Congress, after assisting Mr. Lincoln to take me out of servile slavery, did not intend to put me and my race into *political* slavery. If they did, let them take away my ballot—I do not want it, and shall not have it. [Several colored Members: "Nor we!"] I don't want to be a mere tool of that sort. I have been a slave long enough already.

I tell you what I would be willing to do: I am willing that the question should be submitted to Congress for an explanation as to what was meant in the passage of these Reconstruction measures, and of the Constitutional Amendment. Let the Democratic party in this House pass a Resolution giving this subject that direction, and I shall be content. I dare you, gentlemen, to do it. Come up to the question openly, whether it meant that the Negro might hold office, or whether it meant that he should merely have the right to vote. If you are honest men, you will do it. If, however, you will not do that, I would make another proposition: Call together, again, the Convention that framed the Constitution under which we are acting; let them take a vote upon the subject, and I am willing to abide their decision.

In the course of this discussion, a good deal of reference has been made to the Constitution of the United States. I hold, sir, that, under that Constitution, I am as much a man as anybody else. I hold that that document is neither proscripted, or has it ever, in the first instance, sanctioned slavery.

The Constitution says that any person escaping from service in one State, and going to another, shall, on demand, be given up. That has been the clause under which the Democratic fire-eaters have maintained that that document sanctioned slavery in man. I shall show you that it meant no such thing. It was placed there, according to Mr. Madison, altogether for a different purpose. In the Convention that drafted the Constitution,

> Mr. Madison declared, he "thought it wrong to admit in the Constitution the idea that there could be property in man." On motion of Mr. Randolph, the word "servitude" was struck out, and "service" unanimously inserted—the former being thought to express the condition of SLAVES, and the latter the obligation of free persons.—3D MAD. PAP., 1429 and 1569.

Now, if you can, make anything out of that that you find in it. It comes from one of the fathers of the Constitution. Sir, I want the gentleman to know that the Constitution, as Mr. Alexander H. Stephens said, I think, in 1854, so far as slavery is concerned, is neutral. He said, that if slavery existed in Georgia, it existed under the Constitution and by the authority of the Constitution; that if slavery did not exist in Pennsylvania, or in New York, *it was equally under the Constitution.*

That is a distinct avowal that the Constitution was neutral, and it is the opinion of a man who is acknowledged to be a man of great mind and large acquaintance with political affairs. Again: the Constitution of the United States has the following clause:

> This Constitution, and *and all laws made in pursuance thereof,* shall be the supreme law of the land.

Every law, therefore, which is passed under the Constitution of the United States, is a portion of the supreme law of the land, and you are bound to obey it.

But gentlemen say that the Democrats did not pass the Reconstruction measures. I know they did not. Such Democrats as we

are having in this State come pretty well under the description given of the Bourbons by Napoleon Bonaparte, who said that they never originated a new idea, nor ever forgot an old one. They certainly never would pass such measures. Did the Revolutionary Fathers intend to perpetuate slavery? Many say they did; I say they did not. What was meant by the clause which states that no bill of attainder or *ex-post facto* law shall be passed? I will tell you what I believe the Revolutionary Fathers meant: I believe it was intended to put a clause there which should eventually work out the emancipation of the slaves. It was not intended that because the father has served in slavery the curse should descend.

One of the strongest objections to the Negro holding office is based upon the fact that he has been a slave, and had no rights; but the Fathers of this country framed a Constitution and Laws, whose spirit and letter condemn this everlasting proscription of the Negro.

Let us take, for example, an extract from a memorial sent to Congress in 1794. It was written by a Committee of which Dr. Rush was Chairman, and is signed by such men as Samuel Adams, John Adams, Isaac Law, Stephen Hopkins, and a host of other prominent gentlemen. This memorial says:

> Many reasons concur in persuading us to abolish slavery in our country. It is inconsistent with the safety of the liberties of the United States. Freedom and slavery cannot long exist together.

Let it be remembered that some of the gentlemen who signed this memorial had been Presidents of the United States. It is also well known that General Washington, in his will, earnestly expresses a desire that all his slaves should receive their freedom upon the death of his wife. He says:

> Upon the decease of my wife, it is my will and desire that all the slaves held by me in my own right should receive their freedom. And I do

most pointedly and solemnly enjoin on my Executors to see that the clause regarding my slaves, and every part thereof, be religiously fulfilled.

Did *he* intend to perpetutate slavery or Negro proscription? What says he, when writing to General Lafayette?—

There is not a man living who wishes more sincerely than I do, to see a plan adopted for the abolition of slavery, but there is only one plan by which it can be accomplished. That is by legislative authority, and this, so far, as my suffrage will go, shall not be wanting.

General Lafayette once said:

I never thought, when I was fighting for America, that I was fighting to perpetuate slavery. I never should have drawn my sword in her defence, if I suspected such a thing.

Jefferson says:

And can the liberties of the nation be thought secure, when we have removed the only firm basis—the conviction of the minds of the people that liberty is the gift of God? Indeed, I tremble for my country, when I reflect that God is just, and that injustice cannot last forever.

I could quote from such men for days and weeks together, to show the spirit that was in them upon this subject, if I thought it necessary to my cause.

We are told that we have no right to hold office, because it was never conferred upon us by "specific enactment." *Were we ever made slaves by specific enactment?* I hold, sir, that there never was a law passed in this country, from its foundation to the Emancipation, which enacted us slaves. Even the great Mr. Calhoun said: "I doubt whether there is a single State in the South that *ever enacted them slaves.*" If, then, you have no laws enacting me a slave, how can you question my right to my freedom? Judge Lump-

kin, one of the ablest jurists that Georgia ever had, said that there never was any positive law in the State of Georgia that forbade Negroes from testifying in Courts; "and they are," said he, "only debarred by their ignorance and ignoble status." Neither did Queen Elizabeth, when she gave to Sir John Hawkins a charter to bring Negroes to this country, give him that right with any other understanding than that no violence or force should be used therefor; and she never intended that they should be anything more than apprentices. Mr. Madison, in speaking upon the subject of jury-trials for Negroes, says: "Proof would have to be brought forward that slavery was established by preexisting laws;" "and," said he, "it will be impossible to comply with such a request, *for no such law could be produced.*" Why, then, do gentlemen clamor for proof of our being free "by virtue of specific enactment?" Show me any specific law of Georgia, or of the United States, that enacted black men to be slaves, and I will then tell you that, before we can enjoy our rights as free men, such law must be repealed.

I stand here to-day, sir, pleading for ninety thousand black men—voters—of Georgia; and I shall stand and plead the cause of my race until God, in His providence, shall see proper to take me hence. I trust that He-will give me strength to stand, and power to accomplish the simple justice that I seek for them.

Why did your forefathers come to this country? Did they not flee from oppression? They came to free themselves from the chains of tyranny, and to escape from under the heel of the Autocrat. Why, sir, in England, for centuries together, men—and *white* men at that—wore metal collars around their necks, bearing, in graven characters, the names by which they were known. Your great and noble race were sold in the slave-marts of Rome. The Irish, also, held many white slaves, until 1172; and even Queen Elizabeth, in her day, had to send a deputation to inquire into the condition of such white slaves as had been born in England.

King Alfred the Great, in his time, provided that for seven years' work the slave should be set free. And, going back to more ancient and more valuable authority, did not God himself, when he had brought the Children of Israel out of Egypt, say unto them: "Remember that you were slaves in Egypt?" I say to you, white men, to-day, that the great deliverance of the recent past is not altogether dissimilar to the great deliverance of ancient times. Your Democratic party may be aptly said to represent Pharaoh; the North to represent one of the walls, and the South the other. Between these two great walls the black man passes out to freedom, while your Democratic party—the Pharaoh of to-day—follows us with hasty strides and lowering visage.

The gentleman from Floyd (Mr. Scott) went down amid the chambers of the dead, and waked up the musty decision of Judge Taney in the Dred Scott case. Why, the very right on which he denied citizenship to Dred Scott, was, that if he were a citizen, he would be a free man, and invested with all rights of citizenship. The Constitution says that

> All persons born or naturalized in the United States, and residents in this State, are hereby declared citizens of this State; and no law shall be made or enforced that shall abridge the privileges or immunities of citizens of the United States, or of this State, or deny to any person within its jurisdiction the equal protection of its laws.

For what purpose was this clause inserted in that Constitution? It was placed there, sir, to protect the rights of every man—the Heaven-granted, inalienable, unrestricted rights of mine, and of my race. Great God, if I had the voice of seven thunders, to-day, I would make the ends of the earth to hear me. The Code of Laws known as Irwin's Code of Georgia, clearly states the rights of citizens. Section 1648 is as follows:

> Among the rights of citizens are the enjoyment of personal security, of personal liberty, private

property and the disposition thereof, the elective franchise, the right to hold office, to appeal to the Courts, to testify as a witness to perform any civil function, and to keep and bear arms.

Section 1649 of the same Code says:

> All citizens are entitled to exercise of their right as such, unless specially prohibited by law.

I would like to ascertain, Mr. Speaker, what prohibition has been put upon me, or upon my race, and what can be put upon it, under the provision of the Constitution, which would deprive us of holding office. The Constitution of Georgia, Article 2, Section 2, says that

> Every male person who has been born or naturalized, or who has legally declared his intention to become a citizen of the United States, twenty years old or upward, who shall have resided in this State six months next preceding the election, and shall have resided thirty days in the county in which he offers to vote, and shall have paid all taxes which may have been required of him, and which he may have had an opportunity of paying, agreeably to law, for the year next preceding the election (except as hereinafter provided), shall be declared an elector; and every male citizen of the United States, of the age aforesaid (except as hereinafter provided), who may be a resident of the State at the time of the adoption of this Constitution, shall be deemed an elector, and shall have all the rights of an elector as aforesaid.

Now let me read to you the meaning of the word "citizen," as given by Mr. Bouvier in his Law Dictionary:

> In American law, one who, under the Constitution and Laws of the United States, has a right to vote for Representatives in Congress and other public officers, and who is qualified to fill offices in the gift of the people. Any white person born in the United States, or nat-

uralized persons born out of the same, who has not lost his right as such.

Now, sir, I claim to be a citizen, I claim to be an elector, and I claim to be entitled to hold office.

We have heard a good deal said about Greece and Rome, and the great nations of antiquity, and of such great men as Socrates, Seneca, Aristotle, Plato, Herodotus, Horace, and Homer. Well, I make a reference or two to these times and nations. A freedman among the Romans was nothing more than, in the time of slavery in this country, a free Negro would be. He could not come in contact with the citizen upon an equal footing, but when the Empire came under the sway of Constantine, he provided that all slaves who were made free upon account of meritorious conduct should be enfranchised. Go back, then, Georgians, to the days of Constantine, and learn from him a lesson of wisdom. In the days of Justinian, too, provision was made that every slave who was made free should be enfranchised and made a full citizen of Rome. The celebrated Roman writer, Horace, boasted that he was the son of a freedman; and I would remind you, also, that one of the Emperors and rulers of Rome had a slave mother. Another provision of those times was, that a slave could become free and a citizen by the consent of six thousand other citizens. Now, sir, even following the example of Rome, am I not a citizen? Have not more than six thousand white citizens voted me my rights as such? And have not forty thousand white citizens voted for the Constitution which grants me my rights as such?

We learn some peculiar points in regard to slavery from many of the writers of ancient times. Tacitus, for instance, tells us that, amongst the ancient Germans, if, in gaming, the slave should win, the master became his property and and slave, while he became master. Mohammed gave political rights to all slaves who defended his religion; and so, indeed, in general, did the Crusaders; and the Popes of Rome used to teach their flocks that all men were the Lord's freemen. St. Jerome once remarked that a man's right to enfranchisement existed in his knowledge of the truth. I might quote for hours from such authorities as these upon the rights which rested in, and were acquired by, the slaves of old, but I deem it unnecessary to do so at this time.

These colored men, who are unable to express themselves with all the clearness, and dignity, and force of rhetorical eloquence, are laughed at in derision by the Democracy of the country. It reminds me very much of the man who looked at himself in a mirror, and, imagining that he was addressing another person, exclaimed: "My God, how ugly you are!" [Laughter.] These gentlemen do not consider for a moment the dreadful hardships which these people have endured, and especially those who in any way endeavored to acquire an education. For myself, sir, I was raised in the cotton field of South Carolina, and, in order to prepare myself for usefulness, as well to myself as to my race, I determined to devote my spare hours to study. When the overseer retired at night to his comfortable couch, I sat and read, and thought, and studied, until I heard him blow his horn in the morning. He frequently told me, with an oath, that if he discovered me attempting to learn, he would whip me to death, and I have no doubt he would have done so, if he had found an opportunity. I prayed to Almighty God to assist men, and He did, and I thank Him with my whole heart and soul.

Personally, I have the highest regard for the gentleman from Floyd (Mr. Scott), but I need scarcely say that I heartily despise the political sentiments which he holds. I would pledge myself to do this, however: To take the Holy Bible and read it in as many different languages as he will. If *he* reads it in English, *I* will do it; if *he* reads it in Latin, *I* will do the same; if in Greek, *I* will read it in that language, too; and if in Hebrew, *I* will meet *him,* also, there. It can scarcely, then, be upon the plea of ignorance that he would debar me from the exercise of political rights.

I must now direct your attention to a point which shows the intention of the framers of the Constitution of Georgia, which you have sworn to support. In the "Proceedings of the Constitutional Convention," which framed this Constitution, I find, under date of March 3d, 1868, that, on motion of Mr. Akerman, the report of the Judiciary Committee on the subject of the qualifications of persons for membership to the first General Assembly, after the ratification and adoption of the Constitution, was taken up, and, without amendment, adopted. That report is as follows:

> *Be it ordained by the people of Georgia, in Convention assembled*, That the persons eligible as members of the General Assembly, at the first election held under the Constitution framed by this Convention, shall be citizens of the United States who shall have been inhabitants of this State for six months, and of the district or county for which they shall be elected for three months next preceding such election, and who, in the case of Senators, shall have attained the age of twenty-five years, and, in the case of Representatives, the age of twenty-one years, at the time of such election.

Gentlemen will observe the word "inhabitant" in that Ordinance; and it was put there especially, in order that no question could arise as to who were eligible to fill the positions of Senator and Representative.

So far as I am personally concerned, no man in Georgia has been more conservative than I. "Anything to please the white folks" has been my motto; and so closely have I adhered to that course, that many among my own party have classed me as a Democrat. One of the leaders of the Republican party in Georgia has not been at all favorable to me for some time back, because he believed that I was too "conservative" for a Republican. I can assure you, however, Mr. Speaker, that I have had quite enough, and to spare, of such "conservatism."

The "conservative" element has pursued a somewhat erratic course in the reconstruction of Georgia. In several instances—as, for instance, in Houston county—they placed Negroes on their tickets for county offices, and *elected* them, too, and *they are holding office to-day*. And this policy is perfectly consistent with the doctrine taught, in public and in private, by the great lights of Democracy, all through the last canvass. They objected to the Constitution, "because," said they, "it confers upon the niggers the right to hold office." Even Mr. Alexander H. Stephens—one of the greatest men, if not *the greatest* man, in the South, to-day, and one for whom I have the utmost respect—in a conversation that I had with him before the Legislature convened (Governor Brown's Marietta speech being one of the topics under consideration very generally throughout the State at the time), said: "Governor Brown says that the black man cannot hold office under that Constitution, but he *knows* that he can."

But, Mr. Speaker, I do not regard this movement as a thrust at me. It is a thrust at the Bible—a thrust at the God of the Universe, for making man and not finishing him; it is simply calling the Great Jehovah a fool. Why, sir, though we are not white, we have accomplished much. We have pioneered civilization here; we have built up your country; we have worked in your fields, and garnered your harvests, for two hundred and fifty years! And what do we ask of you in return? Do we ask you for compensation for the sweat our fathers bore for you—for the tears you have caused, and the hearts you have broken, and the lives you have curtailed, and the blood you have spilled? Do we ask retaliation? We ask it not. We are willing to let the dead past bury its dead; but we ask you, now, for our RIGHTS. You have all the elements of superiority upon your side; you have our money and your own: you have our education and your own; and you have our land and your own, too. We, who number hundreds of thousands in Georgia, including our wives and families, with not a foot of land to call our own—strangers in the land of our birth; without money, without education, without aid, without a roof to cover us while we live, nor sufficient clay to cover us when we die! It is extraordinary that a race such as yours, professing gallantry, and chivalry, and education, and superiority, living in a land where ringing chimes call child and sire to the Church of God—a land where Bibles are read and Gospel truths are spoken, and where courts of justice are presumed to exist; it is extraordinary, I say, that, with all these advantages on your side, you can make war upon the poor defenceless black man. You know we have no money, no railroads, no telegraphs, no advantages of any sort, and yet all manner of injustice is placed upon us. You know that the black people of this country acknowledge you as their superiors, by virtue of your education and advantages.

There was a Resolution passed here at the early part of this session stating that all persons who were in their seats were eligible thereto, What are gentlemen going to do, with that Resolution staring them in the face? Your children and my children will read that Resolution, and they will be this House that is contemplated to-day, I will call a colored Convention, and I will say to my friends: Let us send North for carpet-baggers and Yankees, and let us send to Europe and all over the world for immigrants, and when they come here, we will give them every vote we have, and send them to the Legislature, in preference to sending a Georgian there.

Go on with your oppressions. Babylon fell. Where is Greece? Where is Nineveh? and where is Rome, the mistress Empire of the world? Why is it that she stands, to-day, in broken fragments throughout Europe? Because oppression killed her. Every act that we commit is like a bounding ball. If you curse a man, that curse rebounds upon you; and when you bless a man, the blessing returns to you; and when you oppress a man, the oppression, also, will rebound. Where have you ever heard of four millions of freemen being governed by laws, and yet have no hand in their making? Search the records of the world, and you will find no example. "Governments derive their just powers from the consent of the governed." How dare you to make laws by which to try me and my wife and children, and deny me a voice in the making of these laws? I know you can establish a monarchy, an autocracy, an oligarchy, or any other kind of an "ocracy" that you please: and that you can declare whom you please to be sovereign; but tell me, sir, how you can clothe me with more power than another, where all are sovereigns alike? How can you say you have a Republican form of Government, when you make such distinction and enact such proscriptive laws?

Gentlemen talk a good deal about the Negroes "building no monuments." I can tell the gentlemen one thing that is, that we could have built monuments of fire while the war was in progress. We could have fired your woods, your barns and fences, and called you home. Did we do it? No, sir! And God grant that the Negro may never do it, or do anything else that would destroy the good opinion of his friends. No epithet is sufficiently opprobrious for us now. I say, sir, that we have built a monument of docility, of obedience, of respect, and of self-control, that will endure longer than the Pyramids of Egypt.

We are a persecuted people. Luther was persecuted; Galileo was persecuted; good men in all nations have been persecuted; but the persecutors have been handed down to posterity with shame and ignominy. If you pass this Bill, you will never get Congress to pardon or enfranchise another rebel in your lives. You are going to fix an everlasting disfranchisement upon Mr. Toombs and the other leading men of Georgia. You may think you are doing yourselves honor by expelling us from this House; but when we go, we will do as Wickliffe and as Latimer did. We will light a torch of truth that will never be extinguished—the impression that will run through the country, as people picture in their mind's eye these poor black men, in all parts of this Southern country, pleading for their rights. When you expel us, you make us forever your political foes, and you will never find a black man to vote a Democratic ticket again; for, so help me, God, astonished that persons, claiming to be men, with souls and consciences, should, contrary to the express provision of that Resolution, turn the colored man out of his seat in this Hall. Another Resolution came before this House, a short time ago, praying Congress to remove all political disabilities from the white people of Georgia. I stood up in my place here, sir, and advocated that Resolution, and advised all colored Members to do the same; and almost every one of them voted for it. We were willing to give the white man every right which he ever rightfully possessed, and, were there forty Negroes in this country to one white man, I would have precisely the same feeling, and act precisely the same way. The action of the House reminds me very much of a couple of lines of verse which we occasionally read:

> "When the Devil was sick, the Devil a saint would be;
> When the Devil was well, the Devil a saint was he."

When this House was "sick" with fear for the safety of the seats of ineligible Democrats, they were all very gracious and polite. But, when the Resolution was passed, declaring, in the face of facts, that all who were in their seats were eligible, then the foot was raised which was to trample on the poor Negro, and that, too, by those who claim bravery and chivalry.

You may expel us, gentlemen, but I firmly believe that you will some day repent it. The black man cannot protect a country, if the country doesn't protect him; and if, to-morrow, a war should arise, I would not raise a musket to defend a country where my manhood is denied. The fashionable way in Georgia, when hard work is to be done, is, for the white man to sit at his ease, while the black man does the work; but, sir, I will say this much to the colored men of Georgia, as, if I should be killed in this campaign, I may have no opportunity of telling them at any

other time: Never lift a finger nor raise a hand in defence of Georgia, unless Georgia acknowledges that you are men, and invests you with the rights pertaining to manhood. Pay your taxes, however, obey all orders from your employers, take good counsel from friends, work faithfully, earn an honest living, and show, by your conduct, that you can be good citizens.

I want to take your memories back to 1862. In that year, the Emperor of Russia, with one stroke of his pen, freed twenty-two millions of serfs. What did Russia do, then? Did she draw lines of distinction between those who had been serfs and her other citizens? No! That noble Prince, upon whose realm the sun never sets, after having freed these serfs, invested them with all the political rights enjoyed by his other subjects. America boasts of being the most enlightened, intelligent and enterprising nation in the world, and many people look upon Russia as not altogether perfectly civilized. But, look at what Russia has done for her slaves; there were twenty-two millions of them, while there are but four millions of us in the whole South, and only half a million in Georgia. If the action is taken in I will go through all the length and breadth of the land, where a man of my race is to be found, and advise him to beware of the Democratic party. Justice is the great doctrine taught in the Bible. God's Eternal Justice is founded upon Truth, and the man who steps from Justice steps from Truth, and cannot make his principles to prevail.

I have now, Mr. Speaker, said all that my physical condition will allow me to say. Weak and ill, though I am, I could not sit passively here and see the sacred rights of my race destroyed at one blow. We are in a position somewhat similar to that of the famous "Light Brigade," of which Tennyson says, they had

> "Cannon to right of them,
> Cannon to left of them,
> Cannon in front of them,
> Volleyed and thundered."

I hope our poor, down-trodden race may act well and wisely through this period of trial, and that they will exercise patience and discretion under all circumstances.

You may expel us, gentlemen, by your votes, to-day; but, while you do it, remember that there is a just God in Heaven, whose All-Seeing Eye beholds alike the acts of the oppressor and the oppressed, and who, despite the machinations of the wicked, never fails to vindicate the cause of Justice, and the sanctity of His own handiwork.

Letters from the South, Relating to the Condition of the Freedman

J. W. Alvord

Major General O. O. Howard.
                    Columbia, S. C., *January* 7, 1870.
Dear General: I will not report in detail the Schools in Columbia, as you were an eye witness to their condition.

The absence of advanced and older pupils, is said to be from the fact that young colored men here, who were boys during the war, grew up especially vicious, and are now, therefore, comparatively indifferent to an education. From the younger class we are undoubtedly to expect the largest results in all parts of the South, as well as in this city.

These colored schools are the only public schools of the Capital of South Carolina, and in their well arranged and spacious building, under the fine direction of so efficient a corps of teachers, will certainly accomplish great good.

The older colored people of the city and surrounding country, as I learned, are unusually intelligent and prosperous—one man, a skillful mechanic, being worth $50,000. More than forty heads of families have within the last six months purchased city property for homes, at from $500 to $1,200 each. It is the testimony of well-informed gentlemen that the whole colored population of upper South Carolina is, in general, in a thriving condition—with better houses, clothing, and family comforts from year to year.

South Carolina appropriated last year $200,000 to buy land in the upper part of the State which has been sold to Freedmen for homesteads. Upwards of 40,000 acres of this land have been actually sold during the year to poor men of all colors. The Governor says he intends this year to recommend for the same purpose an appropriation of $400,000. Colored members of the Legislature, whom I met in the interior counties, asked me earnestly for more schools for their children, which were promised as strongly as I dared.

I have been much interested in witnessing the social elevation of the Freedmen at this place. The Governor, General R. K. Scott, in his receptions makes no distinction among the members of the Legislature, (125 of whom are colored); all are taken equally by the hand with the graceful urbanity for which his honor is distinguished. All alike, on such occasions, crowd around his luxurious refreshment tables, where, as his accomplished lady told me, no invidious distinctions are made.

Source: From J. W. Alvord, *Letters from the South, Relating to the Condition of the Freedman* (Washington: Howard University Press, 1870), pp. 5–28.

You will remember at the dinner party given on your account by the Governor, and at which I had the honor of being a guest, his Secretary of State, the Hon. F. L. Cardozo and lady, (both colored,) received equal attention with other officials, and ladies and gentlemen of the highest standing. I could but feel as I looked around upon that agreeable circle that *equality of character and culture were the true conditions of equality in social life.* I learned of other occasions when the Governor had followed the same rule, and in conversation he assured me he could allow himself to adopt none other.

His opinion is that in our higher institutions of learning *cultured* youth of both colors will come, at length, to associate on equal terms, and that scholarship and general refinement on each side will gradually settle the whole question of mixed schools.

At Orangeburg I found the Claflin University in the large and beautiful building (late the Orangeburg Female Academy, bought recently by the Methodist Episcopal Society, and repaired by Major Deane, of the Bureau, at an expense of $2,500,) with about one hundred students, under the efficient training of Dr. Webster. This is a very promising Institution, and in a commanding and well chosen locality. It will probably ask for further assistance from the Bureau.

Will write you next from Charleston.

I have the honor to be yours, &c., very respectfully,

J. W. Alvord,
Gen. Supt. Ed., Bu. R., F., & A. L.

Major General O. O. Howard.
Charleston, S. C., *January* 11, 1870.

Dear General: In Charleston I have visited the schools, eight in number, with, in all, about 2,500 pupils, and, with one or two exceptions find them in good condition. The "Avery Institute" and the "Shaw Memorial" rank first. Each of these have an enrollment of about 300 pupils. The Morris Street School, with 800 pupils, in charge of the City Board, is conducted on the Southern plan; strict in discipline, but with less that culti-

vates the mind and heart. It is, however, an honor to the city. The Orphan School, (100 inmates,) now in charge of the State, is much neglected. The lady manager, Miss Boorn, is energetic, but needs assistants and more means. I have directed Mr. Cook to send her books, and will see the trustee to-day. South Carolina is at present too much immersed in politics to care thoroughly for orphans.

The "Freedmen's *Pay* School," (150 pupils,) with colored teachers, is a landmark, showing the progress of these people. All its expenses are met by *the Freedmen.* The school of the Episcopal Society, in the old Marine Hospital, is respectable in conduct and attainment, with 160 pupils, but the building needs repairs. I went thoroughly through Rev. A. T. Porter's "Parochial Orphan School" with much interest; eighty boys, well kept and taught, and the whole Institution on a larger scale than I expected. Mr. Porter deserves much credit for his earnest labors, and in my judgment what you have done for him has been within the law and well deserved.

Since I was in Charleston, three years ago, there has been great progress in our educational work, seen not only in the schools themselves, but in the *general* elevation of the whole colored population.

We are not to contrast these people with the white race, long favored with opportunities. Their history of utter demoralization is to be constantly kept in mind, and progress only (in comparison) from that stand-point noted.

In this advancing civilization, nothing is more apparent than the altered *apparel* of the Freedmen. From linsey wolsey, ragged garments, clumsy brogans, or bare feet of former times, we notice the change to clothes of modern material; shoes or gaiters on the feet of boys and girls; whole schools as tidily dressed as most of the common schools at the North. While the same make of clothing, bought with their own money from the shops, or skillfully made with their own hands, is everywhere to be seen. It gives the adult population in the streets and churches an air strikingly in contrast with the menial raiment with which slavery had clothed them. It is the costume of freedom, each choosing his or her dress, according to taste, and all mainly in the respectable raiment of society around them.

The point to be gained in our schools is to retain more permanently the advanced pupils; they pass away two [sic] soon, called by the stern necessities of life.

Some *liberal fund* is needed to keep choice, select scholars for two or three years until they can be thoroughly prepared as teachers and leaders of the people.

The *Normal* Schools and classes, of all the Northern Associations, should be more thorough, with special effort and expenditure to carry pupils entirely through the course.

On the whole, I am satisfied that educational matters in this State are running in the *right direction,* and if the new State school bill passes, we shall be able to accomplish much more than at present.

With respect, yours, &c.,

J. W. Alvord,
General Superintendent of Education.

Major General O. O. Howard.

Savannah, Ga., *January* 13, 1870.

Dear General: In Charleston and on Sea Island plantations I had excellent opportunity of seeing the Freedmen's condition. The statements of Mr. Pillsbury are exaggerations; extreme cases, as there are, would not justify his account of things.

I have visited the same class of plantations and Negroes, and from all parties, have usually, a flat contradiction and denial of such allegations as he made, especially from the old planters and the more intelligent Freedmen. As a very respectable old colored preacher said to me, "Whoever say such tings don't speak de trut." Possibly, mothers and babes do not have the care which slavery gave them when the birth and life of the latter was of such pecuniary advantage; but in spite of neglect and poverty, I have invariably seen around cabin doors respectable

squads of juveniles—"children enough," everybody says.

Infanticide, as such, is never known. An eminent Southern physician, whom I consulted, remarked that "the Negroes, with their strong domestic affection, were incapable of such a crime."

Similar testimony comes from planters, freedmen, preachers, cottonfactors on the wharves, and officials of both parties. Among the latter are the mayors and both chiefs of police in Charleston and this city. The people are poor, and their children die, as do the suffering poor everywhere, but not as the result of deliberate barbarity.

As to intemperance there is certainly quite too much of it among the Freedmen. Three reasons have been given me for its prevalence: 1st. In the interior the "whiskey wagons" perambulating the country; 2d. The unrestrained sale of liquors in towns and cities; 3d. The Negroes now have money. The general admission, however, is that there is not as much drunkenness among the blacks as whites. Your friend, Gen. Robt. Anderson, chief of police of this city, (as did his first lieutenant,) assured me that this was so. The arrests for this crime may be greater among the Negroes, for as these officers said, "they are usually boisterous when intoxicated." "We do not," said they, "arrest a drunken man who is quietly trying to get home.

I will send you soon a synopsis of the police reports of crime from Charleston and Savannah for the last three months as in comparison between the whites and blacks. It will show you the precise facts, which are vouched for respectively as correct by both the mayors. Also, I will send the mortuary reports from the officers of the city clerks showing how Freedmen do not "die off" as reported.

It is remarkable what a general reputation the Freedmen have for good behavior and industry. "They work well when paid," is a universal remark. "We don't want Chinamen," said a planter to me, and he pointed around to the cabins of his laborers, saying, "these people are used to our work, and we are used to them." Mr. Wm. Whaley, acknowledges that "the people on Edisto are industrious and well behaved," and, said he, "we are satisfied with their labor." He will plant next season six hundred acres.

The Freedmen are very eager for land. The savings they have placed in our Banks, and the profits of cotton this year, are enabling them to make large purchases. In Orangeburg County, South Carolina, hundreds of colored men have bought lands and are building and settling upon them. In a single day, in our Charleston Savings Bank, I took the record of seventeen Freedmen who were drawing their money to pay for farms they had been buying, generally forty or fifty acres each, paying about $10 per acre. I met at a cotton merchant's in that city ten Freedmen who had clubbed together with the proceeds of their crop and bought a whole Sea Island plantation of seven hundred acres. The merchant was that day procuring their deed. He told me that the entire purchase price was paid in cash from the balance due them on the crop of the season. Here, then, besides supporting their families with provisions raised, these men had each, by the profits of a single year, bought a farm of seventy acres. What northern laborer could do better?

I found on the Islands other clubs forming to do the same thing, and this in a season when the caterpillar has destroyed one-half their cotton. A leading cotton broker in Charleston told me that he thought nearly half the cotton on the Islands belonged to colored men. He had himself already 126 consignments from them, and the amount of his sales on their account had reached over $30,000. As I learned, the average of the Freedmen's crop, or share of crop, of Sea Island cotton is from three to six hundred pounds each.

Much excitement prevails here in political matters, and we are seeing the worse side of things. Much, indeed, to be deplored among all classes, but leading men are preparing, as I can see, to accept what Congress will give

them; these men will gradually allow the Freedmen all their immunities. Wages for labor are too low, but prices must improve as the large cotton crop of the next season goes in.

The planters beg off strongly on payment for the "supplies," yet acknowledge that this is a debt of honor, and must be met, unless Congress grant them relief. Mr. Bennett, your agent, is hopeful of immediate collections.

General Anderson sends his compliments to you—a fellow student, I believe, at West Point—and assures me that he is interested in our work. He has aided me most cheerfully in obtaining facts, and testifies strongly to what he says is "the magnificent conduct of the Negroes." I presented him with your last report.

I have the honor to be yours, &c., very respectfully,

J. W. Alvord,
Gen. Supt. Ed. Bu. R., F., & A. L.

Major General O. O. Howard,
Commissioner, &c.

Savannah, Ga., *January,* 14, 1870.
Dear General: I find in this city the "Beach Institute," with three hundred pupils and seven teachers in the different departments, all in excellent condition and making good progress. The building is large, (erected by the Bureau,) of the most improved modern construction, and well kept. Although the children and colored population generally here, are not as far advanced as in Charleston, yet this Institute is a credit to our work, and seems to command the respect of all classes.

This is a continuation of the schools we started when your army from Atlanta met us on the coast. Changes have taken place but the organization, as you recollect, with a colored educational committee and ten colored teachers, was placed under the general patronage of the American Missionary Association, occupying, by leave of General Geary, who was left in command of the city, the old "Bryan Slave Mart." *Now* we have a *permanent Institution,* under the best possible direction and well endowed, having had a total expenditure by the Association and Bureau of over $40,000. One thousand dollars were given by the Freedmen at the time of starting.

I called together the old colored educational committee (these are the men whom Secretary Stanton met and conferred with when at Savannah in 1865,) for examination of these schools. These fathers were highly gratified with the wonderful exhibition and progress made, and promised to visit the Institution, in an advisory way, on the first Tuesday of each month. This will continue their own interest and help the association in the estimation of all the colored people.

I visited the private schools taught by colored men. They are quite respectable, with, in all, about one hundred and twenty pupils.

The Catholics have a school of sixty pupils, managed by the Bishop and taught by the St. Joseph Sisters, an order in France trained expressly for African missions. By especial dispensation of the Pope a band of them have been sent here, and others to St. Augustine and Jacksonville, Florida; they have a small school, as I should have informed you, at Charleston. After looking in upon one of these schools, with very polite reception by the teacher, I called upon the acting bishop. The call was in every way agreeable. He complained, however, that your officers had refused to their church the aid given, under the law, to other parties.

I promised, on his invitation, to examine the school more thoroughly, and if found to be teaching the *elements of an English education w*ould report in favor of its receiving such assistance. But knocking for admission next morning, the teacher held the door partly open and positively forbade my entrance—said *"the father* (after my call) had ordered her so to do." I was of course surprised, but parleyed pleasantly; told her that *"the father" had invited me to "visit the school whenever I wished,"* but in vain. She "presumed the permission had been reconsidered," and said that "the teachers were a

priesthood," "took no pay," "were mainly teaching religion," &c., and reiterated her positive refusal to admit me. I could only express my regrets, and on leaving sent my official card to "Father Hamilton," with the message that I was very sorry not to be able to see the school; that our government made no distinction in religious denominations, and that if the school could *be reported on our blanks,* the usual Bureau aid would be most cheerfully granted. On the back of the card I noted that I should be happy to see him at the Beach Institute at any time during the day, but he did not call. This bishop should not complain of you hereafter.

The general testimony of the citizens of Savannah (I saw all classes) is that our schools are a great benefit to the Freedmen. Old families exclude our teachers from their social circles, yet no longer denounce their Christian work.

The industry of the Freedmen is also admitted, and the good influence of the Savings Bank. The mayor and other officials were quite surprised when I told them the branch in their city had on deposit over $80,000. A prominent physician assured me that in constitutional health Negroes had suffered from the influences of slavery; that in their extreme poverty, no doubt, many infants died from want of care. "In the old time," he said, *"they were cared for as animals to be bred."*

I went through the public market, along the wharves, out into the suburbs, noting carefully the conduct of the colored population, and can only say there are signs of constant improvement. I was in business in this city when a young man, nearly forty years ago; often visiting the place since, and cannot be mistaken.

The *general* condition of the Freedmen along all this coast, (city, county, and islands,) is comparatively low, but so far as my observation goes, they compare favorably with other laboring classes in moral conduct, temperance, chastity, especially in a desire for quiet home-life, wherever they can buy and settle upon lands. The taxes upon their accumulating property and homesteads are already swelling the revenue of both the city and surrounding parishes. And these Freedmen have just reached a condition to make, if elevating influences are continued, still more rapid progress.

I have the honor to be yours, &c., very respectfully,

J. W. Alvord,
General Superintendent of Education.

Major General O. O. Howard.
Commissioner, &c.

Augusta, Ga., *January* 17, 1870.

Dear General: Arrived at this place, by night train, yesterday morning.

The schools in Augusta are among the best I have seen, not so much in advancement as in high tone and enthusiasm. The older classes are well sustained.

They are under the care, as you know, of the "Baptist Home Mission Society," with the exception of one (sixty pupils) supported by county commissioners, and two smaller schools, the expenses of which are paid by the Freemen themselves. I am happy to report the above society as doing so well. The superintendent, Rev. W. D. Seigfreid, appears, in all ways to be the right man. Their seven teachers (three of whom are colored) are accomplished and thorough. Mr. S. has also a class of seventeen men who are studying the Scriptures, in order to become preachers. The county school is well conducted by one of the excellent teachers of the American Missionary Association, but she fails of prompt pay from the county commissioners. Excellent singing was noted in this school.

In the evening we had an enthusiastic meeting in one of the churches, when the subjects of education, savings bank, and general prosperity of the Freedmen were the themes; a number of the speakers were colored; audience deeply interested.

One half the population of Augusta, numbering in all 12,000, is colored. With much to struggle against, and some division among themselves in religious matters, the Freedmen here are fully meeting our expectations. As a body they are more intelligent and enterprising than those on the coast.

Just out of the city is a settlement of about one hundred families—something like the Barry Farm at Washington—where small homesteads have been purchased and are being paid for; average value of each from $100 to $500. These families are joyously cultivating their own gardens and provision grounds, also finding work in the city. The Bureau has erected for them a convenient house, now used for a school and chapel.

Further in the interior the Freedmen are buying or renting land and raising their own crops. A community of such families, about thirty miles out, (in South Carolina,) came in, a few days since, to market their crops for the season. They had chartered a railroad car for $140 the round trip, and loading it with cotton, corn, &c. exchanged the same for clothing, furniture, implements of husbandry, and supplies for putting in their next crop. They came to us on returning, and begged very hard that a teacher might be sent to their settlement, promising to pay all expenses. These are indications of the *drift* of these people towards independent home life and profitable labor. Although the savings bank here is one of the most recently established, it has had deposited over $60,000, of which 31,000 is still to their credit.

One of the worse habits of Freedmen in Augusta is spending money for lottery tickets. Lottery offices are on every business street, tempting the unwary, and by an occasional prize, these ignorant people (not all of them) are lured to this species of gambling Mr. Ritter, the cashier of the bank, told me that probably more was thus wasted than is brought to the bank.

A trifling incident at the above meeting may interest you. Without my expecting it, one of the prominent colored men rose at the close of the addresses, and said he had heard that "the Bureau was to be abolished," and wished all who were opposed would raise their hands. Instantly their came up a whole forest of *arms* from all parts of the house. Of course I gave assurances that their request should be reported to Congress.

I regret to find that the educational association in Georgia, spoken of in my former reports, composed of both white and colored men, is embarrassed by the political conflicts of the State. The colored men are greatly incensed that some of their leaders are tampering with the rebel element. Almost to a man the entire freed people of the State are intensely loyal; and colored members-elect of the approaching Legislature will vote to sustain the action of Congress, and the enactment of a code of laws providing for universal education.

I have the honor to be yours, &c.,

J. W. Alvord,
General Superintendent of Education.

Major General O. O. Howard.

Macon, Ga., *January* 18, 1870.

Dear General: I enclose to you a synopsis of criminal arrests from records of the Mayor's court in Savannah. You perceive cases marked "colored" predominate. This differs from the record at Charleston, a copy of which, made with great care, I sent you, which showed nearly an equality as to color. The disparity is more apparent than real: 1. At this season of the year laborers come, in great numbers, from the plantations outside of Savannah to help in shipping cotton. They become what are called "long-shoremen," have small jobs on the wharves at twenty-five-cents per hour, and are exposed to every species of temptation. I counted twenty-five square-rigged cotton ships in port, with crews of idle sailors on shore demoralizing both sexes. This greatly swells the criminal calender of the city at the present time.

2. The authorities and police in Savannah are of the old rebel class, (Charleston has Northern men,) and the colored race in court suffers in comparison with the white. You notice the record is one of "*arrests.*" A Negro with firearms about him, and many now feel obliged to carry them, or any considerable sum of money in his hand, is liable to arrest on suspicion. Not so with white men. The latter also, when intoxicated, are often conveyed home, while the former are sure to be held for trial, when comparatively far less testimony convicts the black. The old slavery feeling remains, and, from past Negro habit and character, presupposes that the accused is surely guilty; respectable parties declare that in Southern cities, if still governed by a native magistracy, at least twenty-five per cent. should on this account be abated from the colored criminal list. It has been to me a noticeable fact that where recorded crime is against color, the verbal admission of magistrates has been that "there is less drunkenness with Freedmen than among the white population."

Allow me to add my own observation. I have now travelled 1,200 miles, through city and country, conversing with fellow passengers, mingling with numerous colored assemblies, making excursions on the coast and islands by row-boat, carriage, and on foot, always going in the lowest purlieus and carefully observing all classes, and I declare to you, General, I have not seen one colored man or woman who appeared intoxicated. I did see white men in this condition. Before reaching my hotel, as I entered Charleston, two gentlemen of high (political) standing, whose names I could give, were pointed out to me reeling in locked arms along the street, helping each other home!

I beg you will note that those who make statements in regard to the morality of Freedmen seem to have forgotten the deplorable influences of slavery; the embruted condition from which these people have been so lately taken. A few months, or years, even, are only sufficient to make the first stand against such moral ruin. Give us time to rally them, so as to start fair in the race with the hitherto privileged class. A generation at least should be granted for an even chance, and all judgment (as to comparison at present) should be stayed, or else made with this reasonable allowance.

Those of us who have often seen the Negro, both before and since emancipation, feel assured that such progress as has already been made is evidence of a *vitality* prophetic of a rapidly rising people. Notwithstanding delinquencies and admissions, we must not ignore the evidences of improvement in all private, social, industrial, educational, moral, and religious life.

The following is the abstract above referred to:

To J. W. Alvord:

Arrests by police force of the City of Savannah, from October 1 to December 31, 1868, inclusive:

Month	No. White.	No. Colored.	Total
October	61	90	151
November	101	156	257
December	144	173	317
	306	419	725

R. H. Anderson, *Chief of Police*

If space permitted I would state in specific detail the various crimes in the abstract here given.

Yours, &c., very respectfully,

J. W. Alvord,
General Superintendent of Education.

Major General O. O. Howard.

Atlanta, *January* 18, 1870.

Dear General: My Sabbath was in Macon visiting colored schools and congregations, observing the religious habits of this people, and addressing them. On Monday examined schools, banks, business marts, police stations, &c.

More general prosperity is apparent than in the lower part of the State; cotton crop abundant, and of the 80,000 bales already sent to the Macon market, 10,000 bales are the property of Freedmen. Not less than $1,000,000 (as the brokers say) have been paid them in that city for this crop the present season. It is supposed by good judges that one-third of the cotton in all upper Georgia belongs to colored men. This has been raised generally on shares or rented land. There are three methods of working on shares: 1. The laborer has one-third of the corn and one-fourth of the cotton, with all supplies found. 2. He has one-third of all crops and found. 3. One-half of all, and shares equally in expenses.

Rents of land are from $1 to $2 per acre. These rentals are much more common than heretofore. With the proceeds of the present crop a large amount of land will be purchased.

I find the following history of the Freedmen's labor: The first year they worked for bare subsistence; second year they bought stock—mules, implements, &c.; third year many rented lands; and now, the fourth year, large numbers are prepared to buy. This is the record of the most industrious, others are following at a slower pace. In this process difficulties have been encountered—low wages, fraud, ill-treatment, &c., some becoming discouraged, but the majority are determined to rise. As illustrations: Several Freedmen in Houston county have bought from 100 to 600 acres of land each. One man is now planting for fifty bales of cotton. A colored company (called Peter Walker's) own 1,500 acres. Two brothers (Warren) saved in the bank $600, and with it obtained a title to 1,500 acres, having credit for the balance, and both are now building houses and preparing to make a crop which they expect will clear off their whole debt. In Americus fully one hundred houses and lots belong to colored people.

Wages in this part of the State are better than below, usually $12 per month, and for the coming season promise to be still higher. I saw a group of laborers at the mart contracting with planters for from $150 to $175 per year. Emigration for laboring purposes is rapidly going from Georgia to the west and southwest especially to the lower Mississippi. The train on which I came to this city had a large company—poor whites as well as blacks. This will soon relieve the depressed population of the coast, and help to increase wages throughout the State.

The testimony of all parties in Macon is that the freed people are industrious, more sober than the whites; though there are worthless characters, and all spend too much money in childish shows, circuses and lotteries, yet as a people they are becoming saving and thrifty. Mr. William P. Goodall, cashier of the city bank—a southern man—with whom I conferred on banking affairs, spoke of the Freedmen, as a whole, in terms of high commendation.

The Speaker of the State Senate, Mr. Conly, of Augusta, said to me: "I have been in this State forty years, and I never knew a Christmas and New Years pass off with so little intemperance among the colored population as the recent one." I was travelling," he said, "and saw hundreds about the depots, but none were drunk."

Our schools in Georgia have silenced open opposition, even in this time of fearful political excitement. I, as yet, hear of no increased violence to teachers. In Macon the schools of the American Missionary Association, (five hundred pupils,) under the care of Mr. Sawtell, are in excellent order, and the large and substantial building which the Bureau has erected, is admirably arranged and kept in good repair. I could not find a pin scratch on a single desk. Some others, especially the private schools, are not in as good condition.

The thing to be deplored is that the *older* classes cannot be retained and carried forward to the completion of their studies. The "fund," to which I alluded in a former letter, for the support of worthy youth is greatly needed. These are almost sure now to be forced away by the incessant calls of actual life. Who can be drawn upon? Will the Northern people do this or the General Government? I asked Mr. C. R. Robert, of New York, whom I met at Macon, if he could not start such an educational fund. He admitted its urgent necessity, but pointed to his "Lookout Mountain" enterprise. These Southern States may do well in *legislation*, but if left to themselves will not take earnest hold of this school work for years to come.

The bank is starting well—a colored cashier of good ability. On deposit, $15,000. Chapel and church enterprise by the American Missionary Association promising. We had delightful services on the Sabbath, with more special religious interest than I have before seen.

Of the political status in this city (Atlanta) you are, of course, informed by the daily press. General Terry is very firm and the commission on membership is earnestly at work. One old friend of ours (I need not give his name) seems to be foolishly selling himself and his party, if he can, to the opposition. Not a colored member goes with him in either House. Even though he were honest in saying that he "can now hold the balance of power and afterwards turn it into the hands of the Republicans," he greatly overestimates his strength. His best friends in all the State will drop him.

Passing through the halls of the House, I overheard a group of Democratic leaders cursing him in the most blasphemous terms, and then, in an undertone, saying, "but we've got to use him; can then throw him out," &c. Don't credit his telegrams and letterwriters. I have had a number of interviews with him, and he told me distinctly "he'd rather the whole Republican party in Georgia should be a failure than that Bullock should triumph." His more intimate advisers, I have seen, and know their character, and can assure you that no true Republican here stands by him.

Yours, &c., very respectfully,

J. W. Alvord,
General Superintendent of Education.

Major General O. O. Howard,
Commissioner, &c.

Atlanta University, *January* 22, 1870.

Dear General: I look out upon these entrenchments, which flank the grounds of this university, in wonder at the change which four short years have made. These earthworks, where rebels defied the approach of freedom, have now risen in walls of brick and stone to shelter the children of the free, and endow them with the power of knowledge. The roar of batteries is now exchanged for the music of school songs and recitations.

We are asked for progress! Such altered position is enough. Is not this progress? The institution of such a school in such a place and these fine classes of students, is but the beginning of the end. I have listened to them from the model department to the highest in languages and mathematics, and can testify to the accuracy and enthusiasm of both pupils and teachers. Blackboard demonstrations especially showed ready brains and skillful fingers.

At the opening of the evening session in the large public hall the pupils requested in childlike simplicity permission to sing for me *"We are rising,"* evidently supposing the song at least, if not the incident, to which the genius of Whittier has given world-wide fame, would be new to me. They rendered it in exact time and with much spirit. At the close, I suggested that this must not merely be true in *song* but in *fact;* that it *is true,* perhaps, far beyond what they were aware of. I then made a brief statement of our three thousand or four thousand colored schools of different kinds, varying grades, advancement, &c., from the lowest primary to those of full college classes. I described commencement graduations of such classes which I had witnessed, and positions which the graduates are now occupying; mentioned your honored name as commissioner, and the interest you feel in regard to all especially Atlanta University.

The whole school bent forward as I spoke, every face beaming with intense interest. I could not avoid the remark, in closing, that if any had message to send you I should be most happy to bear them. A silent pause of about half a minute, and a tall boy, in a distant corner, slowly arose, stood a moment in thought, and then said, "Tell General Howard we are all thankful for what he is doing for us. We will endeavor to improve these privileges, and prepare ourselves for usefulness;" a short pause, and he added, *"socially, religiously,* and *politically."* I give his exact words as pencilled at the moment, uttered with deliberation and most appropriate emphasis.

Before leaving next morning the enclosed written messages, each in the handwriting of its author, accumulated in my hands. I send them without correction, expressed as you see in great simplicity, but they are the voice of those young hearts to yours.

The lad who in this school two years ago gave you the message immortalized by Whittier, is now a half-grown young man and a promising scholar. I am sorry to say he was not present. His mother aids him all in her power, but a step-father (an intemperate man) has taken him from school, insisting that he help support himself and the family. I did not hesitate to sanction measures to have him returned. Will not some one become patron of this interesting boy? His name is Richard B. Wright. He was pointed out to me to-day in front of our Savings bank, (just being opened,) gazing up at the new sign. "Have you any money here?" I inquired. "No, sir," said he, "but I mean to have."

To Chattanooga in the morning.

Yours, &c., very respectfully,

J. W. Alvord,
General Superintendent of Education.

The following are specimens of the messages to General Howard referred to in the above letter:

FROM THE MODEL SCHOOL

Atlanta, Ga., 21*st. January.*

Gen. Howard—*Sir:* It is true that we were in bondage, and if it had not been for the kind people of the North we should have been slaves this day. Instead we are free. Oh, how thankful I feel because we have learned to pray.

Wright Kemp.

[Wright Kemp, the above boy, has lost his right arm, and is about fourteen years old.]

Atlanta, Ga., *Jan.* 21, 1870.

Sir: You will please tell Gen. Howard we are trying to rise as fast as possible, and I hope we shall soon be able to do much good among our people. And I hope his name will ever be remembered among our people as one that has done much good.

Yours respectfully,

Melinda A. Griffin.
Of Augusta, Ga.

Atlanta University, *Jan.* 21, 1870.

Sir: Will you please to tell the General that we have been expecting him for some time in our city with great joy. I hope we *are* rising as a people. We are striving with all our strength and minds to progress, both in our books and also in our duty to God. We will ever remember him in our prayers, and do return him sincere thanks for his kindness in aiding us so much.

Respectfully,

Lucy Sauey, *Of Macon, Ga.*

Atlanta, Ga., *Jan.* 21.

Dear Sir: We are glad to hear you have done so much for us, and we will never forget you so long as the world stands.

Your friend.

J. W. Marlow.

Major General O. O. Howard.

Marietta, Ga., *January* 22, 1870.

Dear General: Left Atlanta a few hours since, and here under the shadow of Kenesaw and Lost mountains, still bearing on their flanks the greatest scars of your victories, I stop to look about and make a few notes. The town (county seat of Cobb county) was much torn by troops in the rebellion, but is now rebuilding, in a region, as you remember, beautifully picturesque, and by the war made classic ground. This mountains region (so New England like) gives to the traveler refreshing relief from the piney levels or slightly rolling country on the coast, and slopes of this Alleghany range. From Atlanta the way is thick with localities of interest. Tourists will hereafter often trace its scenes of thrilling history. Marietta has two colored day schools and two on the Sabbath. They are not large, but will increase as the town recovers its former population.

We have seen along the road more emigration to the West and Southwest. Yesterday a train with 150 freedmen passed through the capital, and to-day we met another train, well loaded. Labor agents go through the country, contract with and conduct these laboring people to their destination. These agents have much opportunity for fraud. Some, with whom I conversed, appeared heartily interested in their welfare—told me that firstclass hands would get $15 per month. One had them in families, and his whole company were stopping a day for the funeral of one of their children.

A recent tour of Colonel Lewis, superintendent, to the States on the Mississippi river, reveals some contrasts to what is found in Georgia. More general immorality prevails. Frauds on colored soldiers having claims against the Government are attempted, and so complicated that their fellow-freedmen are often involved in them. As accomplices of dishonest men, they are taught to deceive and cheat each other. Would it not be wise to have pensions and bounties for colored soldiers, which sharpers are so apt to get from them, (even after the money is in their own hands,) placed, in some way, in the savings bank as a deposit-ary or receiver, thus affording these soldiers its friendship and some legal hinderance against their enemies?

Your officers in Georgia are excellent and efficient men, diligently at work in all the interests of the freedmen.

On that most interesting of questions, the industry and economy of these people, permit me to add another fact: Mr. Harris, our inspector, who resides at Beaufort, S.C., and whom I find earnestly examining the freedmen's banks in this region, has given me the record of nearly two thousand families now settled on Sea Island lands owned by themselves. For these purchases most of them had saved their money in the savings bank, at Beaufort.

I distributed bank papers to-day from the cars which were eagerly taken by the younger freedmen who could read.

Our train is off in a few minutes.
Yours, &c., very respectfully,

J. W. Alvord,
General Superintendent of Education.

Civil Rights Act of 1875

AN ACT TO PROTECT ALL CITIZENS IN THEIR CIVIL AND LEGAL RIGHTS*

Whereas, it is essential to just government we recognize the equality of all men before the law, and hold that it is the duty of government in its dealings with the people to mete out equal and exact justice to all, of whatever nativity, race, color, or persuasion, religious or political; and it being the appropriate object of legislation to enact great fundamental principles into law: Therefore,

Be it enacted by the Senate and House of Representatives of the United States of America in Congress assembled, That all persons within the jurisdiction of the United States shall be entitled to the full and equal enjoyment of the accommodations, advantages, facilities, and privileges of inns, public conveyances on land or water, theaters, and other places of public amusement; subject only to the conditions and limitations established by law, and applicable alike to citizens of every race and color, regardless of any previous condition of servitude.

Sec. 2. That any person who shall violate the foregoing section by denying to any citizen, except for reasons by law applicable to citizens of every race and color, and regardless of any previous condition of servitude,

the full enjoyment of any of the accommodations, advantages, facilities, or privileges in said section enumerated, or by aiding or inciting such denial, shall, for every such offense, forfeit and pay the sum of five hundred dollars to the person aggrieved thereby, to be recovered in an action of debt, with full costs; and shall also, for every such offense, be deemed guilty of a misdemeanor, and, upon conviction thereof, shall be fined not less than five hundred nor more than one thousand dollars, or shall be imprisoned not less than thirty days nor more than one year: *Provided,* That all persons may elect to sue for the penalty aforesaid or to proceed under their rights at common law and by State statutes; and having so elected to proceed in the one mode or the other, their right to proceed in the other jurisdiction shall be barred. But this proviso shall not apply to criminal proceedings, either under this act or the criminal law of any State: *And provided further,* That a judgment for the penalty in favor of the party aggrieved, or a judgment upon an indictment, shall be a bar to either prosecution respectively.

Sec. 3. That the district and circuit courts of the United States shall have, exclusively of the courts of the several States, cognizance of all crimes and offenses against, and violations of, the provisions of this act; and actions for the penalty given by the preceding section may be prosecuted in the territorial,

---

*18 Stat. 335 (1875).

district, or circuit courts of the United States wherever the defendant may be found, without regard to the other party; and the district attorneys, marshals, and deputy marshals of the United States, and commissioners appointed by the circuit and territorial courts of the United States, with powers of arresting and imprisoning or bailing offenders against the laws of the United States, are hereby specially authorized and required to institute proceedings against every person who shall violate the provisions of this act, and cause him to be arrested and imprisoned or bailed, as the case may be, for trial before such court of the United States, or territorial court, as by law has cognizance of the offense, except in respect of the right of action accruing to the person aggrieved; and such district attorneys shall cause such proceedings to be prosecuted to their termination as in other cases: *Provided,* That nothing contained in this section shall be construed to deny or defeat any right of civil action accruing to any person, whether by reason of this act or otherwise; and any district attorney who shall willfully fail to institute and prosecute the proceedings herein required, shall, for every such offense, forfeit and pay the sum of five hundred dollars to the person aggrieved thereby, to be recovered by an action of debt, with full costs, and shall, on conviction thereof, be deemed guilty of a misdemeanor, and be fined not less than one thousand nor more than five thousand dollars: *And provided further,* That a judgment for the penalty in favor of the party aggrieved against any such district attorney, or a judgment upon an indictment against any such district attorney, shall be a bar to either prosecution respectively.

Sec. 4. That no citizen possessing all other qualifications which are or may be prescribed by law shall be disqualified for service as grand or petit juror in any court of the United States, or of any State, on account of race, color, or previous condition of servitude; and any officer or other person charged with any duty in the selection or summoning of jurors who shall exclude or fail to summon any citizen for the cause aforesaid shall, on conviction thereof, be deemed guilty of a misdemeanor, and be fined not more than five thousand dollars.

Sec. 5. That all cases arising under the provisions of this act in the courts of the United States shall be reviewable by the Supreme Court of the United States, without regard to the sum in controversy, under the same provisions and regulations as are now provided by law for the review of other causes in said court.

Approved, March 1, 1875.

Hamburg Riot of 1876

D. L. ADAMS—AIKEN COUNTY

Columbia, S. C., *December* 16, 1876.

D. L. Adams (colored) sworn and examined. By Mr. Cameron:

Question. Where do you live?—*Answer.* I live in Hamburgh.

Q. How long have you lived there?—*A.* I have been living in Hamburgh about two years and six months, I guess.

Q. What is your age?—*A.* I was thirty-eight years old on the 4th day of July.

Q. Where did you live before you went to Hamburgh?—*A.* In Augusta, Ga.

Q. How long did you live there?—*A.* I have lived there about twenty-five or twenty-six years—about twenty-six years, I guess.

Q. Of what State are you a native?—*A.* I was born in the upper part of Georgia, Talbot County.

Q. Where had you worked or lived?—*A.* I generally have worked in Augusta, Ga., up to the 8th of July. I haven't been in Augusta since that time.

Q. On what day did the Hamburgh massacre take place?—*A.* On the 8th of July.

Q. Where were you on the 4th of July?—*A.* I was also in Hamburgh.

Q. I will ask you if you were captain of the colored militia company in Hamburgh at that time?—*A.* Yes, sir.

Q. Of how many men did that company of militia consist?—*A.* It consisted of eighty-four members. It was called Company A, Eighteenth Regiment National Guards.

Q. State whether or not it was organized under the State laws?—*A.* It was organized under the State laws.

Source: Hamburg Riot of 1876. From *South Carolina in 1876*, 44th Congress, 2nd Session, Senate Miscellaneous Document # 48 (Washington: 1887), Volume I, pp. 34–45, 47.

Q. How long had it been an organized company?—*A.* It had been an organized company some five or six years, I think, or probably more.

Q. How long had you been captain of the company?—*A.* I had been captain of the company, I guess, about seven or eight months—somewhere about that, as near as I could come at it.

Q. Who were the other commissioned officers of the company?—*A.* Louis Cartiledge was first lieutenant; A. T. Attaway was second lieutenant.

Q. How frequently did the company meet for military drill or exercise?—*A.* According to the rule and according to the law we drilled once every month; but after I got to be captain of the company I drilled them about once or twice a week.

Q. State whether or not the company had a hall or armory?—*A.* It had a hall; we called it an armory.

Q. How was the company armed?—*A.* With thumb-loading rifles.

Q. State what occurred in the fourth day of July; begin with the beginning and go through with the narrative.—*A.* On the fourth day of July, about six o'clock in the evening, or probably half past five, to be sure of it, I took the company out on parade. As we were going up a street in Hamburgh called Market street, about six or half past six o'clock, I guess it was, there was a man by the name of Henry Getsen, and Tom Butler, son of R. J. Butler, and also a son-in-law of R. J. Butler, all white men. They had been on one side of the street, sitting in a buggy, looking at us drill up and down the street, I reckon, for about half an hour. After a while they went back down the street from where we were drilling, and went around on the street called Main street. Afterward they came back on the street. I was at the upper part of the street, and we were going down, marching by fours, in what is called an interval march, open order, having an interval between ranks, I suppose, of twenty or thirty feet.

Q. How wide was the street?—*A.* It was one hundred and fifty-eight feet wide, and we were about the center of the street going down. They turned the corner and came up the street in a slow trot. I saw that they intended to drive through the company, and I halted the company, and then they stopped. I was at the head of the company, and I went around in front of their buggy and said to him, "Mr. Getsen, I do not know for what reason you treat me in this manner." He asked me "What?" I said, "Aiming to drive through my company, when you have room enough on the outside to drive in the road." He said, "Well, this is the rut I always travel." Said I, "That may be true; but if ever you had a company out here I should not have treated you in this kind of a manner." Said I, "I would have gone around and showed some respect to you." 'Well,' said he, "this is the rut that I always travel, and I don't intend to get out of it for no d—d niggers." Said I, "All right; I won't hold any contention with you; I will let you through." So I gave command to the company to "open order," and let him go through; so he went on through, and I then went on down to the hall. Some of the men seemed to have got a little flustrated because they drove through the company, and commenced talking, but I ordered them to hush, and carried them in the hall and dismissed the company. On Monday his father-in-law came down and took out a warrant.

Q. Mr. Getson's father-in-law?—A. Yes, sir.

Q. What was his name?—A. Robert J. Butler. He took out a warrant, and on Tuesday morning I received a summons. The constable brought it to me, and, after looking at it, I told him that it was all right; I would be there at the time designated. Sure enough I went.

Q. Before what justice?—A. Before Trial-Justice Prince Rivers. So I went down to the court at the time designated, and when I got there Rivers read—I don't know what you call it—but anyhow he did not say that it was a warrant. I asked him if it was a warrant, and he said it was not. He was general of the militia organization, major-general of the State.

Q. Butler was?—A. Rivers was. And he said he wanted to find out from the evidence in the case—he wanted to hear the officers' testimony and afterward he wanted to find out whether it would be a case that would be suitable or a case calling for his court-martialing officers, or whether it would be a case to prosecute them before a court. He went on to hear Getsen's testimony, and after he got through, if I mistake not, he heard Tommy Miller's evidence—no, he had just heard Getsen's evidence. After he got through, he told me, "As you have no counsel you can ask any question of the witness you desire." So I asked him a few questions, and at the same time, said I, "Mr. Gesten, did I treat you with any disrespect when I spoke to you or didn't I treat you politely?" He said, "I can't say that you treated me with any disrespect, but I can say this much, that there was one or two members of the company that showed some impudence to me, and also I saw them load their guns." I said, "Mr. Getsen, didn't you see me examining the cartridge-boxes and also the pockets of the members of the company to see if they had any ammunition, before they went on drill?" He said, "Yes," he did. Said I, "Did you see any?" He said "No, I didn't." I made him recollect this; said I, "Didn't you know that I found one man with a cartridge in his pocket and I took it away from him and scolded him about it?" He said "Yes," he did. Said I, "Well, then, are you certain that these men loaded their guns?" He said, "I saw them move their guns and I thought they loaded." Whilst I was asking that question, Rivers, the trial justice, said to me, says he, "I don't want you to treat my court with contempt." Said I to him, "Judge, I don't mean to do that, if I know myself. I never expect to treat any lawful officer with any contempt," and said I, "I was only asking the question, and if the question is not legal then I don't want to ask him." Before he could say anything to me I was taking my seat, and said I, "I will ask the witness no more questions, but will leave it to your discretion." He then said that sitting down was contempt of court. I told him if it was he must excuse me, as I was not accustomed to law, and if it was any contempt I was then asking his pardon for it, for I did not mean contempt of the court. He said it was contempt and he would put me under arrest, and he dismissed the court until Thursday; I think it was Thursday; it was on the 8th of July, anyhow. I was also, then, under arrest with the constable. He went out to his dinner and came back again, and when he came back he asked me if I would retract. I told him I did not know what he meant. He said if I was willing to beg pardon of the court he would excuse me from the fine. I told him, well, if I had contempted the court I was willing to ask pardon of the court. He said, well he would relieve me of the fine, and I was to appear again on the 8th of July, at half past four o'clock. I told him all right, I would appear. So it passed off, then, until the 8th of July. During that time I heard a great many threats that were made. These persons would send me notice at different times of what they had heard; what they were going to do with me on that day. I did not pay any attention to them; did not give no notice to them at all. The day before the trial, (on the 7th of July,) I went home to dinner at one o'clock, and when I got home to dinner it was not ready, and it was very warm, and the company's drill-room was joining my house where I lived; it was a part of the house, and I could pass right out of my bed-room into the drill-room; so I went out of my bed-room into the drill-room, and I was sitting by the window when a man by the name of Mr. Melen, [Meling,] (a white man and a preacher,) him and some other white man were together, and were right by the drill-room, and I got up and looked out of my window and I heard them say, "That's where that d——d militia company drills;" and, said he, "To-morrow thay are going to have a trial, and we intend to kill the captain of that company before he gets away from that court." Well, I heard a great deal of big talk and of threats, but I did not pay any attention to them. Sure enough, on the 8th of July I came home from work as usual, and I did not go back with the expectation of attending to court. About two o'clock R. J. Butler and Tommy Butler, his son, and Henry Getsen, his son-in-law, and Harrison Butler, another son of his, were there, and I was standing out before my door when they came on down. Henry Getsen had a gun; I supposed it to be a sixteen-shooter; it might not have been; there was another fashion of gun at that time, but it appeared to be a sixteen-shooter which he had across his saddle. R. J. Butler and his son Tommy were in the buggy together, and had a sixteen-shooter in the buggy. I supposed from the looks of it they had about seven or eight pistols in the buggy; large Navy pistols. They went on down in the town, and yet I did not pay much attention to that. In a little while there was about thirty men came, armed with sixteen-shooters and double-barreled shot-guns; they were coming in from Edgefield.

Q. How far does R. J. Butler live from Hamburgh?—A. One part of his place is in Hamburgh and the other just out; I guess from the main part of town he lives three-quarters of a mile, or it may be a mile. I saw about thirty of these men come in, but I did not get scared yet; so about half past two o'clock I reckon there was about one hundred men in the town of Hamburgh, all armed, some with pistols and some with guns also.

Q. White men?—A. White men; they were getting drunk very fast, or drinking liquor and appearing like they were drunk, and saying they were going to kill every God damned nigger in Hamburgh that day, and especially Dock Adams; that was myself. So, hearing all this, I went down to Judge Rivers's house and told him, said I, "Judge Rivers, I can't appear before your court to-day for I feel that you are unable, and your court is unable, to protect my life, and I believe my life to be unsafe; I am willing that you should go to work and draw up a bond that you think proper and I am willing to give bond to a higher court, where I think my life will be safe. The reason I come to you to tell you, is because I don't want you to suppose that I treated your court with any disrespect by not coming, but it is because I don't think my life is safe." He stopped and said to me, "Well, you must use your own judgment of course, if your life is unsafe, and if these men intended to take your life of course I can't protect you. I haven't protection enough to protect you; my constable can't do much." Said I, "That is my belief, and for that reason I don't want to go before your court without you force me to, and then if I am killed you will be responsible." He said, "You can use your own judgment; I shall go to court at the usual time; your name, of course, will be called, and if you don't answer to your name—well," he says, "you won't be there; that is all; you won't be there to answer." So, sure enough, before I got through talking with him a white man by the name of Sparnick—I forget his other name—before I got out of the house this man Sparnick came up to his house and knocked at the door and came in. He said that Mr. M. C. Butler had met him at the store that they call George Damm's, and he said that he would like to see me; that he appeared as counsel for R. J. Butler, and he would like to settle the matter without any difficulty and without going before the court, if it could be settled. I told him, "Well, there is no one more readier to settle it than I am." He said that Mr. Butler wanted the officers of the company, in fact, to meet him. Whilst he was talking another man came in, by the name of Sam. P. Spencer, and said that M. C. Butler also had said that he would like to have a conference with the officers of the company. I told him, "Well, I will go;" but afterward I went to the door and I saw a great crowd down at his place, all armed men, and they were drunk, or playing off drunk; they appeared to be drunk, any way. I went back and told Mr. Spencer to go and tell General Butler that I would meet him, but I would like for him to come away from where those men were, and that I was willing to meet him at Spencer's house. So Spencer went back and told him, and he agreed to meet me there. In this time I was in my shirt-sleeves; I had just come from work and had pulled off my coat; so I went back and put on my coat to go down there, and sent word that I would come and meet him. One of the officers refused to go. I told him, well, I would go, and I supposed if I went it would be sufficient; and the first lieutenant agreed to go, but the second lieutenant wouldn't go, because he believed he would be killed; he expressed the reason in that way. I went on down to meet Mr. Butler. Before getting there Mr. Butler left; in fact he didn't go to Spencer's house; he left Mr. Damm's store, after promising to meet me, but he did not go. He got in the buggy and went on across the river to Augusta. I desire to alter that; he didn't go to Augusta at that time; he went on to the court, where we were to meet the court at. He came on up where Rivers lived and said that the time to meet the court had come and he was ready to go to court and he was going on there. Rivers got his book and went on down to the court. I didn't go, but they went. I couldn't tell you—I couldn't tell you, but if I was to tell you it would be what I heard, and that wouldn't be relative, I suppose. General Butler came back from the court and sent word for me to meet him at the council-chamber; that was at the town hall. I sent word back expressing more reasons, that the men were still gathering in the town and that they had expressed themselves as going to kill me on sight, but that I was willing to meet him to settle the matter any way that it could be settled, that was right, but that I couldn't go down to

the council-chamber; that his men were all around him, and he had already expressed himself that he couldn't control them; that they were drunk, and that I wouldn't be able to go to him, but that if he was willing and wanted to see me of course he could go where I could make it convenient to see him. He said he wasn't going nowhere else, and right there I had to come. So I said I wasn't going to that place. Then he left the council chamber and went on around to Augusta.

Q. About what time did he go to Augusta?—*A.* He went to Augusta about 5 o'clock in the afternoon, as near as I can guess at it. He came back from Augusta with a man by the name of S. B. Picksley, who, I think, was on the committee; and he met him and had a talk with him. I don't know what that talk was.

Q. How long did he remain at Augusta?—*A.* He remained, I suppose about twenty-five or thirty minutes. He came on back. The intendant of the town went to him and told him that there was a great many women and children, and he believed there was going to be a fuss, and he would like to have some time to get the women and children out. He told me, I think, that he would give him fifteen minutes to get them out. He asked him, then, wasn't there any way in the world that that matter could be settled without a difficulty. He said the only thing that would settle the matter was for the company to surrender the arms and the officers to him, and he wanted an answer from me. I sent word back to him that the arms that were borne by that company belonged to the State; that I had received those arms in my charge, and was responsible for them, and I couldn't give them up to no private citizen; but if any officer who had a right to take them would come to me for them, I would give them to him. The intendant of the town asked him, in case the arms were surrendered to him, would he guarantee the safety of the town. He said it depended entirely upon how they behaved. He afterward turned around and said he wouldn't vouch for anything; he had nothing to do with that part. So I sent word, in reply to his answer, that I couldn't give them to him; that I had no right, but he could send any officer that had a right to receive them that would relieve me from responsibility, and I would give them to him. So the major-general came, (that is, Rivers,) and told me what Mr. Butler had said, and all about it, and what he said he would do, and that if we didn't give them up he was going to melt the ball down before 10 o'clock that night. I said to him, "General, I see you are major-general of this State, are you not?" He said, "Yes, I am." I said, "Do you demand these arms? If you do, I will give them to you." He says, "I have no right to do it under the law." I says, "Well, I know, come down to the law about a matter of law, of course I don't believe you have a right to do it; but if you do demand them, to relieve the responsibility of any blood being shed in the town from me, I will give them to you." He said, "No, I don't demand them; I have no right to do it; you must use your own discretion about it." I said, "Well, if that is the way you leave me, I am not going to give them to General Butler." I then wrote a note to General Butler, saying in the note: "General Butler, these guns are placed in my hands, and I am responsible for them, and I have no right to give them up to no private citizen; I can't surrender them to you." He sent me word back that he was going to have them in fifteen minutes. I told him, well, then he would have to take them by force, and then I would not be responsible for them. So then, after that, he commenced placing his men; in the first place, about twenty-five or thirty horsemen—men mounted on horses—in front of the drill-room, near the river bank.

Q. How far from the drill-room were they?—A. I suppose they were about seventy-five or eighty yards. Then he placed behind the first abutment of the N. and C. C. R. R., he placed about fifteen or twenty, as near as I can guess at it without counting. Down below, on the river, under a large tree, he had some thirty or forty. And there was a well about two hundred yards from the drill-room, and just beyond the well, about fifty or sixty feet, there stood, I suppose, 800 men, all in arms. He placed them all around the square, back of the drill-room, on the street. I forget the name of the street; but it was back of the drill-room. He had men placed all around there, and up on a hill, about five hundred or six hundred yards—may be a little more. I could see him placing men all around town.

Q. He was stationing them there himself?—A. Yes, sir. He was with the men that was doing it. Pick Butler was also in the crowd. Colonel Butler was also carrying out the orders. I could go up on top of the drill-room and see them,

and I did so. Then I came down off the top of the drill-room into the drill-room, and I placed my men then where they wouldn't get hurt.

By Mr. Christiancy

Q. How many had you in the drill-room?—A. Thirty-eight; I suppose about twenty-five were members of the company, and some others were taking refuge there. Those I didn't call in myself, I only had twenty-five members of the company in the drill-room. After he got all the men placed he sent word back to me to know if I was going to give the guns up; that the time was out. I sent word back to him that I could not give them up; that I didn't desire any fuss, and we had gone out of the streets into our hall for the safety of our lives, and there I was going to remain; that I was not going to give the guns to anybody. He did not send no more answer then. About the time he must have got the word his men commenced firing. There was a signal-gun fired; I suppose it was a signal-gun; it was down the river, sorter. It looked like it fired right up into the air. These horsemen that I was telling you about, that had been placed in front of the drill-room, they were removed before the firing commenced, and went down the street back of the square. I didn't see them after they got out of sight, and don't know where they went; and these men, when that signal-gun was fired behind the abutment of the bridge, fired upon the drill-room. They fired rapidly, I suppose, for about half an hour. They shot out nearly all the window-panes in the building. There were four windows in front, and they shot mighty near all the panes out; I don't think there were two panes left standing in each one of the windows, but there may be three; anyhow, the most of them was shot out; the glass rattled all over the floor. There was side glass and transom lights over the door, and all those were shot out; the men were standing between the windows and behind the wall. After awhile, just about half past six o'clock, I guess, they kept closing up like they were coming up to the drill-room, and after awhile I gave orders to fire, for it was the only chance of our lives to fire, and they commenced firing then. The firing was kept up, I suppose, for about a half an hour from the drill-room, but only every now and then; not regularly. During that time this man that was said to have been shot (Mackey Merrivale) was killed. He was one of the men that was firing from behind this abutment. Then I went upon the top of the drill-room to see where the largest body of men was. I had heard somebody holler down the street, and I recognized it to be A. P. Butler's voice; I was very familiar with it; he hollered to a man by the name of Walker McFeeny to go over the river and bring two kegs of powder; that they were going to blow that building up. There was one part of the building that we couldn't see nobody from it. It had then got sort of dark anyway; it was moonshiny, but it was so dark from the trees and houses that were handy to it that we couldn't see them. Of course, then I was afraid that they might do something of that kind, believing that they could do it. I then went to work, and tore up some lumber, and made a ladder, and got out of the back way of the building; there was no way to get down without a ladder; and we escaped from the building the back way.

Q. All of you went out?—*A.* Yes, sir; we all went out. But before I went out of the building I sent the men out. I seen that in the back part of the yard there was no firing; everything was perfectly still. I had been outside of the building, and went down the street, I suppose, between 200 and 300 yards, to see where the men were, and went all around. I went back in front of the building, and went through front door, the entrance leading up in the hall, and told this Ataway, the first lieutenant; he had got outside somehow or other; he had got scared, and left the building before I knew it. I told him to go down first and receive all the men that were in the building, and keep them together till I came out; that I would stay up there with two or three men, and every once in a while fire and make them think we were in the building, while they were escaping. So he went out, and he got scared, and, I suppose, got excited—I couldn't allege it to be anything else—and controlled off the best part of the company; so when I got to them there wasn't but fifteen men with myself. So I asked for Lieutenant Ataway and the balance of the men, and they told me that he had gone off and tried to carry them off. They said they couldn't tell me where he had gone. Said I, "Men, we are surrounded." I think there was over three thousand men there; they were coming from Augusta at all times, three and four hundred

together, all around; the lower part of Market street had been completely blocked up with them for about 200 yards; it looked like just as thick as they could stand; and in the rear street it was the same way, and also on the street called Main street, which runs across. So I told these few men that were there, said I "Men, I don't know how we will get out of here, and there is but one way;" and said I, "You will have to fight pretty rapidly to get out that way."

Q. Had you your guns with you?—*A.* Yes, sir; we all had our guns. We went out that way, and got out on the street, and had to fight pretty rapidly; in fact, the fight lasted until about half past one o'clock that night before we did get out. None of the men that was with me got killed. One of them got wounded in the thigh, but he managed to get away; he didn't fall or anything of the sort. I carried them away in the upper part of the street and put them down next to the river in R. J. Butler's field. Of course they didn't expect us to go there, he being such an enemy to us. I carried them in there, and put them over by the side of a little branch, where it was very thick with bushes. I was very troubled about these men that had hid themselves, and wanted to get them out. I believed if they were caught they would be killed; the men with the second lieutenant. So after I got these men safe—they were out of ammunition then; they hadn't had very much any way—said I, "You stay here now, and I will go back and find the men, if I can. I will try to work my way back, and will try to bring them out." So I did go back. I was shot at, I reckon, over two hundred times before I got in the square; however, I didn't turn my course; I went on. I went back in the square, and I went under most every house there was in the square; that is, I went far enough to call under-it. Some one or two, probably three, men answered; the balance wouldn't answer. They were scared, I suppose, and wouldn't answer. I got three of them. By that time I was surrounded and couldn't get out on more, but I carried those three men where I thought they would be safe. I knocked out some bricks under a brick house with the butt of my gun, and told them to crawl under there. That was under a house that was very near to the ground, and was bricked up all the way from the ground. After they got in there I placed the bricks all back all back just like they were before, very smooth so you couldn't discover any hole, especially in the night. Then I went back in pursuit of these other men, but I didn't find them. While standing in a little corner field, near a garden, looking out, one of the men, which was the town marshal, run across the garden, and I called him, but I suppose he didn't recognize my voice, as he didn't stop. He ran on and jumped over the fence, and I managed to get up on some part of the trestle of the railroad and could see through it. The moon was shining very bright, The corn made a shade where I was, and of course they didn't see me. They stopped the town marshal; his name was Jeems Cook. Henry Getsen, a man by the name of Bill Morgan, and I recognized one of the men I thought to be Kenlo Chaffee, but I was not certain whether it was him or not, but I knew Henry Gibson and Bill Morgan. I recognized their voices. They stopped him and told him "God damn you! we have got you. You have been town marshal here going about here arresting democrats, but you won't arrest any more after tonight." Said he, "Mr. Getsen, I know you and will ask you to save my life. I haven't done anything to you. I have only done my duty as town marshal." "Yes," says he, "God damn you, your knowing me ain't nothing; I don't care anything about your marshalship; we are going to kill you;" and they fired. There was four or five men in the crowd, and all of them shot him. He fell. I staid there and saw them taking his boots off, and they took his watch out of his pocket.

By Mr. Cameron:

Q. Who did that?—A. They were all down in a huddle and I couldn't see who it was took the watch. So some of them said. "By God, I reckon some of us had better go over in the corn-field." Then I moved out of the corn field. Louis Shiller—his house was in the same square—I went then in his office.

Q. Was Shiller a white man?—A. Shiller was a white man, and a trial-justice also. I went in his office, right under his house. I remained there, I suppose, about an hour. They were breaking in the houses everywhere and shooting people. This time they came to the front door, and broke in the front door of the office. So I went out of the back door into the back yard. They came in there, and they looked around and found what I didn't find the whole hour that I was in there. I suppose they had lights, and found these men that were in there who wouldn't answer me when I called them. They found one of two colored men in there and took them out. I heard them cursing and say, "God damn you, we have got you." They were beating them with sticks and guns, or something.

Q. Did you know any of the men that went into Shiller's house?—A. No; I didn't know any of them. Whilst I was standing in the back yard I could look right into my bed-room window, and also into my sitting-room window, and I saw them taking down my pictures and breaking up the furniture. They broke up everything I had in the world; took all my clothes, my mattresses and feather-bed, and cut it in pieces and scattered it everywhere, destroying everything that I had. I didn't have a suit of clothes only what I had on my back. They took all my wife's clothes, and broke up all my furniture and everything. By that time they commenced getting very thick in the square, and as they commenced getting thick, I jumped over a little cross fence in Shiller's yard; and as I got up on the fence I heard somebody say "Halt!" and I looked over the fence and I saw old man R. J. Butler run out the back part of Lafayette Davis's store, and he shot and I heard him say, "God damn him! I have got him." This was a man by the name of Moses Parks. So he shot him. He turned around and said, "God damn him! I have got him," and shot Parks and killed him. I went then up in the post-master's house, where he lived. His name is Rawles. I forget his other name. It was a two-story house, and I went up stairs in the veranda, and it had slats all along on the top of the banisters along there in front. It was like the house fronted one street, this way. (Illustrating by diagram on paper.) I was on the back part of it, and here came another street. Right on this street, I suppose, there was over a thousand men. They had their head-quarters there, and Gen. M. C. Butler was among that crowd, and every time a party would come in and bring a colored man that they had captured they would bring him right up there to what they called the "dead-ring." They had a "dead-ring" down below me there—I suppose about seventy-five or eighty yards, and that is where they would bring the colored men that they would capture. Every time they would come in General Butler would yell, "Good boys! God damn it! turn your hounds loose, and bring the last one in." That was General M. C. Butler, and also Pick. Butler. They were together most of the time, and they would ask, "God damn it! can't you find that Dock Adams? We want to get him," (that was myself;) and some asked what kind of a man I was, and some would try and agree what sort of a man I was—"a man with side-wiskers and moustache"—and some would roll up their sleeves and write it on their cuffs. One man wrote down my description on the bosom of his shirt, and said, "We'll have him before day;" and I was standing right there, looking at him. I was looking through the blinds, where, I reckon, there was about a half-dozen slabs broke out right at the end, and I could stand there and look at them. I could move back where they could not see me, and it was dark anyhow. So I staid right there till day. I guess that was about between two and three o'clock. So finally time commenced running out, and they said, "Well, we had better go to work and kill all the niggers we have got. We won't be able to find that son of a bitch."

Q. Could you distinguish who said that?—A. Well, I don't think I could tell who it was that made use of the expression. It was made in the crowd. Some said, "We had better kill all," and some would say, "We had better find out." From what I heard men say, General Butler had moved men around to the corner house, on Main street, in the rear of the building, and had made that his headquarters. Some would say, "We will go around to 'Davis's store and there we will find General Butler," and then he says, "We will do just whatever he says." Some of the men would say, "We had better kill all, because, if we don't, they will give testimony against us some day to come." So they had quite a wrangle among themselves at one time, because some of them did not want to kill all. They wanted to pick out certain men, and some wanted to kill all, and they got up quite a fuss, and talked about shooting among themselves about it. Finally, there was a man from Augusta—I know the man well, but I can't think of his name now, to save my life; he has a kind of a curious name, and I have been trying to think of his name ever since I have been here; but anyhow he told them that they had better have a court-martial of twenty men, and whatever that court-martial decided on, then do it. So they agreed to that; they went

off, and when they came back they had the men's names that they intended to kill down on paper, and called them out one by one and would carry them off across the South Carolina Railroad, by that corn-field, and stand them up there and shoot them. I saw M. C. Butler. He came around there once, about the time the court-martial was decided, and was telling them what men to kill and what men he wanted to be killed; and I heard him call Attaway's name distinctly, and another by the name of Dave Phillips. The other names I could not hear. They wanted to kill some who got away.

Q. You heard Butler call those names as the names of the persons who were to be killed?—A. Yes, sir; I did. The men seemed to be very much dissatisfied, and they said that General Butler ought to kill the last one of them. They wanted to kill all of them, and they were sort of dissatisfied about it. Some said they would go off home, because they would not kill all.

By Mr. Christiancy:

Q. What did this Georgia man do?—A. He said there ought to be a court-martial; he was not in favor of killing all. There was one or two men taken out of the ring that they wanted to kill, and carried-over in Georgia by some one or two of the Georgians. They got a man by the name of Spencer Harris, who was in the dead-ring, and they slipped him off; also Gilbert Miller; and they carried another young man by the name of Frank Robinson across the river to save his life. A man by the name of Pompey Curry, he was to be killed. They called him, and when they called him he answered to his name, and then jumped and run at the same time. They shot him down, but he got up and got away at last, he lingered a good while, but he is up there now. He has never been able to be out much since.

By Mr. Cameron:

Q. What time of the day were these last men that you have mentioned shot?—A. They were shot, I guess, about 3 or 4 o'clock in the morning.

Q. Was it daylight?—A. No, sir; it wasn't quite daylight; the moon was shining very bright—about as bright as ever you seem it shine. It appeared to me that the moon shone brighter than it ever did before.

By Mr. Christiancy:

Q. You did not want it to shine half so brightly?—*A.* No, sir.

By Mr. Cameron:

Q. How many were shot at that time?—*A.* There was four men killed out of that dead-ring.

Q. Give the names of those who were killed.—*A.* The first was A. T. Ataway, the first lieutenant; the next was David Phillips.

Q. Was he a member of your company?—*A.* He was; he was the armorer. The third one was Alfred Minyon.

Q. Was he member of your company?—*A.* Yes, sir; he was. There was another one—I can't think of his first name, but his last name was Stephens; but he was not a member of the company. . . .

Q. How long did you remain in the house?—*A.* I remained in the house until the main crowd had dispersed, except some few stragglers. I remained there until you could just discover day. I came down then out of the building from where I was and went out of the back lot and looked at Jimmy Cook, the town marshal, that was killed by Getsen and Morgan; and afterward I went right on out through the back way down and got on the South Carolina Railroad, and I then came to Aiken.

Q. How far is that from Hamburgh?—*A.* Seventeen miles from Hamburgh. We had a good many in this dead ring. I suppose some twenty-five or thirty. They just went into their houses and took them out of their houses—men who had taken refuge in their own houses to save themselves, and had nothing to do with the affair.

Q. They did not kill them?—*A.* No, sir, only Stephens; they took him out of his house and killed him. I heard—I am not able to say who the men were, there was such a crowd—but right near where I was standing they expressed their reasons why Minyon and Stephens were killed. A man by the name of Lamar, (I forget his other name—I am sorry I can't recollect it,) but it was from some previous falling out that they had had at some sale prior to that, and he wanted him killed on that account; that was expressed in my hearing by some of the men. Also Stephens was another man that some man had a grudge against him; but these others were killed down there simply because they were leading republicans, and also belonged to that company. . . .

Q. During the night while that crowd of armed men were around there, and when they were killing these colored men, was anything said about politics?—*A.* Yes, sir; that was the whole talk all the time. You could just hear it all the time: "By God! we will carry South Carolina now; about the time we kill four or five hundred more we will scare the rest." You could hear them say, "This is only the beginning of it. We have got to have South Carolina; we have got to go through; the State has got to be democratic; the white man has got to rule; this is a white man's government!" Politics was used all night long, all the time; even in the evening, before it begun, you could hear, "We are going to redeem South Carolina to-day!" You could hear them singing it on the streets, "This is the beginning of the redemption of South Carolina." And they allowed there was no court in South Carolina that would try them; that every hundred years the law run out, and there was no law now. They tell it constantly up about Hamburgh that they ain't begun to kill out what they are going to kill. They, most all of them around there, say they intend to kill me, if I am the last man on earth; and I have received from time to time, I reckon, a dozen notes. I have got some now, and I wish I had known I would be called in and I should have presented them.

Q. Do you think it safe for you to return to Hamburgh?—*A.* No, sir; it is not safe for me to be there, but I am compelled to be there; when I am elsewhere I am on expenses; I haven't been able to make five cents since that time; I am afraid to work.

By Mr. Cameron:

Q. What is your business?—*A.* I am a boss-carpenter by trade.

Q. Have you heard threats made to colored people since the Hamburgh riot, or at any time during the summer?—*A.* Every day.

Q. State generally what the nature of these threats was?—*A.* Well, even up to the election and since the election, it has been usually expressed that they were going to kill out all the radicals, and all those that didn't vote the democratic ticket they would kill. They said there would be clubs after the election until the next election, and every colored man that didn't join the clubs they were going to kill, if they lived in South Carolina. . . .

Frederick Douglass Protests the Supreme Court Decision in the Civil Rights Cases

Frederick Douglass

Friends and Fellow-Citizens:

I have only a very few words to say to you this evening, and in order that those few words shall be well-chosen, and not liable to be misunderstood, distorted, or misrepresented, I have been at the pains of writing them out in full. It may be, after all, that the hour calls more loudly for silence than for speech. Later on in this discussion, when we shall have the full text of the recent decision of the Supreme Court before us, and the dissenting opinion of Judge Harlan, who must have weighty reasons for separating from all his associates, and incurring thereby, as he must, an amount of criticism from which even the bravest man might shrink, we may be in better frame of mind, better supplied with facts, and better prepared to speak calmly, correctly, and wisely, than now. The temptation at this time, is of course, to speak more from feeling than reason, more from impulse than reflection.

We have been, as a class, grievously wounded, wounded in the house of our friends, and this wound is too deep and too painful for ordinary measured speech.

"When a deed is done for Freedom,
Through the broad earth's aching breast
Runs a thrill of joy prophetic,
Trembling on from east to west."

But when a deed is done from slavery, caste and oppression, and a blow is struck at

Source: Frederick Douglass Protests the Supreme Court Decision in the Civil Rights Cases. From *Proceedings of the Civil Rights Mass-meeting, Held at Lincoln Hall [Washington], October 22, 1883* (Washington, 1883).

human progress, whether so intended or not, the heart of humanity sickens in sorrow and writhes in pain. It makes us feel as if some one were stamping upon the graves of our mothers, or desecrating our sacred temples of worship. Only base men and oppressors can rejoice in a triumph of injustice over the weak and defenceless, for weakness ought itself to protect from assaults of pride, prejudice and power.

The cause which has brought us here to-night is neither common nor trivial. Few events in our national history have surpassed it in magnitude, importance and significance. It has swept over the land like a moral cyclone, leaving moral desolation in its track.

We feel it, as we felt the furious attempt, years ago, to force the accursed system of slavery upon the soil of Kansas, the enactment of the Fugitive Slave Bill, the repeal of the Missouri Compromise, the Dred Scott decision. I look upon it as one more shocking development of that moral weakness in high places which has attended the conflict between the spirit of liberty and the spirit of slavery from the beginning, and I venture to predict that it will be so regarded by after-coming generations.

Far down the ages, when men shall wish to inform themselves as the real state of liberty, law, religion and civilization in the United States at this juncture of our history, they will overhaul the proceedings of the Supreme Court, and read the decision declaring the Civil Rights Bill unconstitutional and void.

From this they will learn more than from many volumes, how far we have advanced, in this year of grace, from barbarism toward civilization.

Fellow-citizens: Among the great evils which now stalk abroad in our land, the one, I think, which most threatens to undermine and destroy the foundations of our free institutions, is the great and apparently increasing want of respect entertained for those to whom are committed the responsibility and the duty of administering our government. On this point, I think all good men must agree, and against this evil I trust you feel, and we feel, the deepest repugnance, and that we will, neither here nor elsewhere, give it the least breath of sympathy or encouragement. We should never forget, that, whatever may be the incidental mistakes or misconduct of rulers, government is better than anarchy, and patient reform is better than violent revolution.

But while I would increase this feeling, and give it the emphasis of a voice from heaven, it must not be allowed to interfere with free speech, honest expression, and fair criticism. To give up this would be to give up liberty, to give up progress, and to consign the nation to moral stagnation, putrefaction, and death.

In the matter of respect for dignitaries, it should never be forgotten, however, that duties are reciprocal, and while the people should frown down every manifestation of levity and contempt for those in power, it is the duty of the possessors of power so to use it as to deserve and to insure respect and reverence.

To come a little nearer to the case now before us. The Supreme Court of the United States, in the exercise of its high and vast constitutional power, has suddenly and unexpectedly decided that the law intended to secure to colored people the civil rights guaranteed to them by the following provision of the Constitution of the United States, is unconstitutional and void. Here it is:

"No State," says the 14th Amendment, "shall make or enforce any law which shall abridge the privileges or immunities of citizens of the United States; nor shall any State deprive any person of life, liberty, or property without due process of law; nor deny any person within its jurisdiction the equal protection of the laws."

Now, when a bill has been discussed for weeks and months, and even years, in the press and on the platform, in Congress and out of Congress; when it has been calmly debated by the clearest heads, and the most skillful and learned lawyers in the land; when every argument against it has been over and over again carefully considered and fairly answered; when its constitutionality has been especially discussed, pro and con; when it has passed the United States House of Representatives, and has been solemnly enacted by the United States Senate, perhaps the most imposing legislative body in the world; when such a bill has been submitted to the Cabinet of the Nation, composed of the ablest men in the land; when it has passed under the scrutinizing eye of the Attorney-General of the United States; when the Executive of the Nation has given to it his name and formal approval; when it has taken its place upon the statute-book, and has remained there for nearly a decade, and the country has largely assented to it, you will agree with me that the reasons for declaring such a law unconstitutional and void, should be strong, irresistible and absolutely conclusive.

Inasmuch as the law in question is a law in favor of liberty and justice, it ought to have had the benefit of any doubt which could arise as to its strict constitutionality. This, I believe, will be the view taken of it, not only by laymen like myself, but by eminent lawyers as well.

All men who have given any thought to the machinery, the structure, and practical operation of our Government, must have recognized the importance of absolute harmony between its various departments of powers and duties. They must have seen clearly the mischievous tendency and danger to the body politic of any antagonisms between its various branches. To feel the force of this thought, we have only to remember the administration of President

Johnson, and the conflict which then took place between the National Executive and the National Congress, when the will of the people was again and again met by the Executive veto, and when the country seemed upon the verge of another revolution. No patriot, however bold, can wish for his country a repetition of those gloomy days.

Now let me say here, before I go on a step further in this discussion, if any man has come here to-night with his breast heaving with passion, his heart flooded with acrimony, wishing and expecting to hear violent denunciation of the Supreme Court, on account of this decision, he has mistaken the object of this meeting, and the character of the men by whom it is called.

We neither come to bury Caesar, nor to praise him. The Supreme Court is the autocratic point in our National Government. No monarch in Europe has a power more absolute over the laws, lives and liberties of his people, than that Court has over our laws, lives, and liberties. Its Judges live, and ought to live, an eagle's flight beyond the reach of fear or favor, praise or blame, profit or loss. No vulgar prejudice should touch the members of that Court, anywhere. Their decisions should come down to us like the calm, clear light of Infinite justice. We should be able to think of them and to speak of them with profoundest respect for their wisdom, and deepest reverence for their virtue; for what His Holiness, the Pope, is to the Roman Catholic church, the Supreme Court is to the American State. Its members are men, to be sure, and may not claim infallibility, like the Pope, but they are the Supreme power of the Nation, and their decisions are law.

What will be said here to-night, will be spoken, I trust, more in sorrow than in anger, more in a tone of regret than of bitterness.

We cannot, however, overlook the fact that though not so intended, this decision has inflicted a heavy calamity upon seven millions of the people of this country, and left them naked and defenceless against the action of a malignant, vulgar, and pitiless prejudice.

It presents the United States before the world as a Nation utterly destitute of power to protect the rights of its own citizens upon its own soil.

It can claim service and allegiance, loyalty and life, of them, but it cannot protect them against the most palpable violation of the rights of human nature, rights to secure which, governments are established. It can tax their bread and tax their blood, but has no protecting power for their persons. Its National power extends only to the District of Columbia, and the Territories—where the people have no votes—and where the land has no people. All else is subject to the States. In the name of common sense, I ask, what right have we to call ourselves a Nation, in view of this decision, and this utter destitution of power?

In humiliating the colored people of this country, this decision has humbled the Nation. It gives to a South Carolina, or a Mississippi, Railroad Conductor, more power than it gives to the National Government. He may order the wife of the Chief Justice of the United States into a smoking-car, full of hirsute men and compel her to go and listen to the coarse jests of a vulgar crowd. It gives to a hotel-keeper who may, from a prejudice born of the rebellion, wish to turn her out at midnight into the darkness of the storm, power to compel her to go. In such a case, according to this decision of the Supreme Court, the National Government has no right to interfere. She must take her claim for protection and redress, not to the Nation, but to the State, and when the State, as I understand it, declares there is upon its Statute book, no law for her protection, the function and power of the National Government is exhausted, and she is utterly without redress.

Bad, therefore, as our case is under this decision, the evil principle affirmed by the court is not wholly confined to or spent upon persons of color. The wife of Chief Justice Waite—I speak of respectfully—is protected to-day, not by law, but solely by the accident of her color. So far as the law of the land is concerned, she is in the same condition as that of the humblest colored woman in the Republic. The difference between colored and white, here, is, that the one, by reason of color, needs legal protection, and the other, by reason of color, does not need protection. It is nevertheless true, that manhood is insulted, in both cases. No man can put a chain about the ankle of his fellow man, without at last finding the other end of it fastened about his own neck.

The lesson of all the ages on this point is, that a wrong done to one man, is a wrong done to all men. It may not be felt at the moment, and the evil day may be long delayed, but so sure as there is a moral government of the universe, so sure will the harvest of evil come.

Color prejudice is not the only prejudice against which a Republic like ours should guard. The spirit of caste is dangerous everywhere. There is the prejudice of the rich against the poor, the pride and prejudice of the idle dandy against the hard handed working man. There is, worst of all, religious prejudice; a prejudice which has stained a whole continent with blood. It is, in fact, a spirit infernal, against which every enlightened man should wage perpetual war. Perhaps no class of our fellow citizens has carried this prejudice against color to a point more extreme and dangerous than have our Catholic Irish fellow citizens, and yet no people on the face of the earth have been more relentlessly persecuted and oppressed on account of race and religion, than the Irish people.

But in Ireland, persecution has at last reached a point where it reacts terribly upon her persecutors. England to-day is reaping the bitter consequences of her injustice and oppression. Ask any man of intelligence to-day, "What is the chief source of England's weakness?" "What has reduced her to the rank of a second-class power?" and the answer will be *"Ireland!"* Poor, ragged, hungry, starving and oppressed as she is, she is strong enough to be a standing menace to the power and glory of England.

Fellow-citizens! We want no black Ireland in America. We want no aggrieved class in America. Strong as we are without the Negro, we are stronger with him than without him. The power and friendship of seven millions of people scattered all over the country, however humble, are not to be despised.

To-day, our Republic sits as a Queen among the nations of the earth. Peace is within her walls of plenteousness within her palaces, but he is a bolder and a far more hopeful man than I am, who will affirm that this peace and prosperity will always last. History repeats itself. What has happened once may happen again.

The Negro, in the Revolution, fought for us and with us. In the war of 1812 Gen. Jackson, at New Orleans, found it necessary to call upon the colored people to assist in its defence against England. Abraham Lincoln found it necessary to call upon the Negro to defend the Union against rebellion, and the Negro responded gallantly in all cases.

Our legislators, our Presidents, and our judges should have a care, lest, by forcing these people outside of law, they destroy that love of country which is needful to the Nation's defense in the day of trouble.

I am not here, in this presence, to discuss the constitutionality or unconstitutionality of this decision of the Supreme Court. The decision may or may not be constitutional. That is a question for lawyers, and not for laymen, and there are lawyers on this platform as learned, able, and eloquent as any who have appeared in this case before the Supreme Court, or is any in the land. To these I leave the exposition of the Constitution; but I claim the right to remark upon a strange and glaring inconsistency with former decisions, in the action of the court on this Civil Rights Bill. It is a new departure, entirely out of the line of the precedents and decisions of the Supreme Court at other times and in other directions where the rights of colored men were concerned. It has utterly ignored and rejected the force and application of object and intention as a rule of interpretation. It has construed the Constitution in defiant disregard of what was the object and intention of the adoption of the Fourteenth Amendment. It has made no account whatever of the intention and purpose of Congress and the President in putting the Civil Rights Bill upon the Statute Book of the Nation. It has seen fit in this case, affecting a weak and much persecuted people, to be guided by the narrowest and most restricted rules of legal interpretation. It has viewed both the Constitution and the law with a strict regard to their letter, but without any generous recognition of their broad and liberal spirit. Upon those narrow principles the decision is logical and legal, of course. But what I complain of, and what every lover of liberty in the United States has a right to complain of, is this sudden and causeless reversal of all the great rules of legal interpretation by which this Court was governed in other days, in the construction of the Constitution and of laws respecting colored people.

In the dark days of slavery, this Court, on all occasions, gave the greatest importance to *intention* as a guide to interpretation. The object and *intention* of the law, it was said, must prevail. Everything in favor of slavery and against the Negro was settled by this object and *intention*. The Constitution was construed according to its *intention*. We were over and over again referred to what the framers *meant,* and plain language was sacrificed that the so affirmed *intention* of these framers might be positively asserted. When we said in behalf of the Negro that the Constitution of the United States was intended to establish justice and to secure the blessings of liberty to ourselves and our posterity, we were told that the words said so but that that was obviously not its *intention;* that it was intended to apply only to white people, and that the *intention* must govern.

When we came to that clause of the Constitution which declares that the immigration or importation of such persons as any of the States may see fit to admit shall not be prohibited, and the friends of liberty declared that that provision of the Constitution did not describe the slave-trade, they were told that while its language applied not to slaves, but to persons, still the object and *intention* of that clause of the Constitution was plainly to protect the slave-trade, and that that *intention* was the law. When we came to that clause of the Constitution which declares that "No person held to service or labor in one State, under the laws thereof, escaping into another, shall in consequence of any law or regulation therein be discharged from such service or labor, but shall be delivered up on claim of the party to whom such service or labor may be due," we insisted that it neither described nor applied to slaves; that it applied only to persons owing service and labor; that slaves did not and could not owe service and labor; that this clause of the Constitution said nothing of slaves or the masters of slaves; that it was silent as to slave States or free States; that it was simply a provision to enforce a contract; to discharge an obligation between two persons capable of making a contract, and not to force any man into slavery, for the slave could not owe service or make a contract.

We affirmed that it gave no warrant for what was called the "Fugitive Slave Bill," and we contended that that bill was therefore unconstitutional; but our arguments were laughed to scorn by that Court. We were told that the *intention* of the Constitution was to enable masters to recapture their slaves, and that the law of Ninety-three and the Fugitive Slave law of 1850 were constitutional.

Fellow-citizens! While slavery was the base line of American society, while it ruled the church and the state, while it was the interpreter of our law and the exponent of our religion, it admitted no quibbling, no narrow rules of legal or scriptural interpretations of

Bible or Constitution. It sternly demanded its pound of flesh, no matter how much blood was shed in the taking of it. It was enough for it to be able to show the *intention* to get all it asked in the Courts or out of the Courts. But now slavery is abolished. Its reign was long, dark and bloody. Liberty *now,* is the base line of the Republic. Liberty has supplanted slavery, but I fear it has not supplanted the spirit or power of slavery. Where slavery was strong, liberty is now weak.

O for a Supreme Court of the United States which shall be as true to the claims of humanity as the Supreme Court formerly was to the demands of slavery! When that day comes, as come it will, a Civil Rights Bill will not be declared unconstitutional and void, in utter and flagrant disregard of the objects and *intentions* of the National legislature by which it was enacted, and of the rights plainly secured by the Constitution.

This decision of the Supreme Court admits that the Fourteenth Amendment is a prohibition on the States. It admits that a State shall not abridge the privileges or immunities of citizens of the United States, but commits the seeming absurdity of allowing the people of a State to do what it prohibits the State itself from doing.

It used to be thought that the whole was more than a part; that the greater included the less, and that what was unconstitutional for a State to do was equally unconstitutional for an individual member of a State to do. What is a State, in the absence of the people who compose it? Land, air and water. That is all. As individuals, the people of the State of South Carolina may stamp out the rights of the Negro wherever they please, so long as they do not do so as a State. All the parts can violate the Constitution, but the whole cannot. It is not the act itself, according to this decision, that is unconstitutional. The unconstitutionality of the case depends wholly upon the party committing the act. If the State commits it, it is wrong, if the citizen of the State commits it, it is right.

O consistency, thou art indeed a jewel! What does it matter to a colored citizen that a State may not insult and outrage him, if a citizen of a State may? The effect upon him is the same, and it was just this effect that the framers of the Fourteenth Amendment plainly intended by that article to prevent.

It was the act, not the instrument, which was prohibited. It meant to protect the newly enfranchised citizen from injustice and wrong, not merely from a State, but from the individual members of a State. It meant to give him the protection to which his citizenship, his loyalty, his allegiance, and his services entitled him, and this meaning, and this purpose, and this intention, is now declared unconstitutional and void, by the Supreme Court of the United States.

I say again, fellow-citizens, O for a Supreme Court which shall be as true, as vigilant, as active, and exacting in maintaining laws enacted for the protection of human rights as in other days was that Court for the destruction of human rights!

It is said that this decision will make no difference in the treatment of colored people; that the Civil Rights Bill was a dead letter, and could not be enforced. There is some truth in all this, but it is not the whole truth. That bill, like all advance legislation, was a banner on the outer wall of American liberty, a noble moral standard, uplifted for the education of the American people. There are tongues in trees, books, in the running brooks,—sermons in stones. This law, though dead, did speak. It expressed the sentiment of justice and fair play, common to every honest heart. Its voice was against popular prejudice and meanness. It appealed to all the noble and patriotic instincts of the American people. It told the American people that they were all equal before the law; that they belonged to a common country and were equal citizens. The Supreme Court has hauled down this flag of liberty in open day, and before all the people, and has thereby given joy to the heart of every man in the land who wishes to deny to others what he claims for himself. It is a concession to race pride, selfishness and meanness, and will be received with joy by every upholder of caste in the land, and for this I deplore and denounce that decision.

It is a frequent and favorite device of an indefensible cause to misstate and pervert the views of those who advocate a good cause, and I have never seen this device more generally resorted to than in the case of the late decision on the Civil Rights Bill. When we dissent from the opinion of the Supreme Court, and give the reasons why we think that opinion unsound, we are straightway charged in the papers with denouncing the Court itself, and thus put in the attitude of bad citizens. Now, I utterly deny that there has ever been any denunciation of the Supreme Court on this platform, and I defy any man to point out one sentence or one syllable of any speech of mine in denunciation of that Court.

Another illustration of this tendency to put opponents in a false position, is seen in the persistent effort to stigmatize the "Civil Rights Bill" as a "Social Rights Bill." Now, nowhere under the whole heavens, outside of the United States, could any such perversion of truth have any chance of success. No man in Europe would ever dream that because he has a right to ride on a railway, or stop at a hotel, he therefore has the right to enter into social relations with anybody. No one has a right to speak to another without that other's permission. Social equality and civil equality rest upon an entirely different basis, and well enough the American people know it; yet to inflame a popular prejudice, respectable papers like the New York *Times* and the Chicago *Tribune*, persist in describing the Civil Rights Bill as a Social Rights Bill.

When a colored man is in the same room or in the same carriage with white people, as a servant, there is no talk of social equality, but if he is there as a man and a gentleman, he is an offence. What makes the difference? It is not color, for his color is unchanged. The whole essence of the thing is a studied pur-pose to degrade and stamp out the liberties of a race. It is the old spirit of slavery, and nothing else. To say that because a man rides in the same car with another, he is therefore socially equal, is one of the wildest absurdities.

When I was in England, some years ago, I rode upon highways, byways, steamboats, stage coaches, omnibuses; I was in the House of Commons, in the House of Lords, in the British Museum, in the Coliseum, in the National Gallery, everywhere; sleeping sometimes in rooms where lords and dukes had slept; sitting at tables where lords and dukes were sitting; but I never thought that those circumstances made me socially the equal of lords and dukes. I hardly think that some of our Democratic friends would be regarded among those lords as their equals. If riding in the same car makes one equal, I think that the little poodle I saw sitting in the lap of a lady was made equal by riding in the same car. Equality, social equality, is a matter between individuals. It is a reciprocal understanding. I don't think when I ride with an educated polished rascal, that he is thereby made my equal, or when I ride with a numbskull that it makes me his equal, or makes him my equal. Social equality does not necessarily follow from civil equality, and yet for the purpose of a hell black and damning prejudice, our papers still insist that the Civil Rights Bill is a Bill to establish social equality.

If it is a Bill for social equality, so is the Declaration of Independence, which declares that all men have equal rights; so is the Sermon on the Mount, so is the Golden Rule, that commands us to do to others as we would that others should do to us; so is the Apostolic teaching, that of one blood God has made all nations to dwell on all the face of the earth; so is the Constitution of the United States, and so are the laws and customs of every civilized country in the world; for no where, outside of the United States is any man denied civil rights on account of his color.

Colored Women of America

Francis Ellen Watkins Harper

The women as a class are quite equal to the men in energy and executive ability. In fact I find by close observation, that the mothers are the levers which move in education. The men talk about it, especially about election time, if they want an office for self or their candidate, but the women work most for it. They labour in many ways to support the family, while the children attend school. They make great sacrifices to spare their own children during school hours. I know of girls from sixteen to twenty-two who iron till midnight that they may come to school in the day. Some of our scholars, aged about nineteen, living about thirty miles off, rented land, ploughed, planted, and then sold their cotton, in order to come to us. A woman near me, urged her husband to go in debt 500 dollars for a home, as the titles to the land they built on were insecure, and she said to me, "We have five years to pay it in, and I shall begin to-day to do it, if life is spared. I will make a hundred dollars at washing, for I have done it." Yet they have seven little children to feed, clothe, and educate. In the field the women receive the same wages as the men, and are often preferred, clearing land, hoeing, or picking cotton, with equal ability.

In different departments of business, coloured women have not only been enabled to keep the wolf from the door, but also to acquire property, and in some cases the coloured woman is the mainstay of the family, and when work fails the men in large cities, the money which the wife can obtain by washing, ironing, and other services, often keeps pauperism at bay. I do not suppose, considering the state of her industrial lore and her limited advantages, that there is among the poorer classes a more helpful woman than the coloured woman as a labourer. When I was in Mississippi, I stopped with Mr. Montgomery, a former slave of Jefferson Davis's brother. His wife was a woman capable of taking on her hands 130 acres of land, and raising one hundred and seven bales of cotton by the force which she could organise. Since then I have received a very interesting letter from her daughter, who for years has held the position of Assistant Post-mistress. In her letter she says: "There are many women around me who would serve as models of executiveness anywhere. They do double duty, a man's share in the field, and a woman's part at home. They do any kind of field work, even ploughing, and at home the cooking, washing, milking, and gardening. But these have husbands; let me tell you of some widows and unaided women:—

"1st. Mrs. Hill, a widow, has rented, cultivated, and solely managed a farm of five acres for five years. She makes her garden, raises poultry, and cultivates enough corn and cotton to live comfortably, and keep a surplus in the bank. She saves something every year, and this is much, considering the low price of cotton and unfavourable seasons.

"2nd. Another woman, whose husband died in the service during the war, cultivated one acre, making vegetables for sale, besides a little cotton. She raises poultry, spins thread, and knits hose for a living. She supports herself comfortably, never having to ask credit or to borrow.

"[3rd.] Mrs. Jane Brown and Mrs. Halsey formed a partnership about ten years ago,

Source: Francis Ellen Watkins Harper, "Colored Women of America," *Englishwoman's Review* (January 15, 1878).

leased nine acres and a horse, and have cultivated the land all that time, just the same as men would have done. They have saved considerable money from year to year, and are living independently. They have never had any expenses for labour, making and gathering the crops themselves.

"4th. Mrs. Henry, by farming and peddling cakes, has the last seven years laid up seven hundred dollars. She is an invalid, and unable to work at all times. Since then she has been engaged in planting sweet potatoes and raising poultry and hogs. Last year she succeeded in raising 250 hogs, but lost two-thirds by disease. She furnished eggs and chickens enough for family use, and sold a surplus of chickens, say fifty dozen chickens. On nine acres she made 600 bushels of sweet potatoes. The present year she has planted ten acres of potatoes. She has 100 hogs, thirty dozen chickens, a small lot of ducks and turkeys, and also a few sheep and goats. She has also a large garden under her supervision, which is planted in cabbages. She has two women and a boy to assist. Miss Montgomery, a coloured lady, says: 'I have constantly been engaged in bookkeeping for eight years, and for ten years as assistant post-mistress, doing all the work of the office. Now, instead of bookkeeping, I manage a school of 133 pupils, and I have an assistant, and I am still attending to the post-office." Of her sister she says, she is a better and swifter worker than herself; that she generally sews, but that last year she made 100 dozen jars of preserved fruit for sale. An acquaintance of mine, who lives in South Carolina, and has been engaged in mission work, reports that, in supporting the family, women are the mainstay; that two-thirds of the truck gardening is done by them in South Carolina; that in the city they are more industrious than the men; that when the men lose their work through their political affiliations, the women stand by them, and say, 'stand by your principles.' And I have been informed by the same person that a number of women have homes of their own,

bought by their hard earnings since freedom. Mr. Stewart, who was employed in the Freedmen's bank, says he has seen scores of coloured women in the South working and managing plantations of from twenty to 100 acres. They and their boys and girls doing all the labour, and marketing in the fall from ten to fifty bales of cotton. He speaks of a mulatto woman who rented land, which she and her children worked until they had made enough to purchase a farm of 130 acres. She then lived alone upon it, hiring help and working it herself, making a comfortable living, and assisting her sons in the purchase of land. The best sugar maker, he observes, he ever saw was a stupid looking coloured woman, apparently twenty-five years old. With a score or more of labourers, she was the 'boss,' and it was her eye which detected the exact consistency to which the syrup had boiled, and while tossing it in the air, she told with certainty the point of granulation."

In higher walks of life too, the coloured women have made progress. The principal of the Coloured High School in Philadelphia was born a slave in the District of Columbia; but in early life she was taken North, and she resolved to get knowledge. When about fifteen years old, she obtained a situation as a house servant, with the privilege of going every other day to receive instruction. Poverty was in her way, but instead of making it a stumbling block, she converted it into a stepping stone. She lived in one place about six years, and received seven dollars a month. A coloured lady presented her a scholarship, and she entered Oberlin as a pupil. When she was sufficiently advanced, Oberlin was brave enough to accord her a place as a teacher in the preparatory department of the college, a position she has held for several years, graduating almost every year a number of pupils, a part of whom are scattered abroad as teachers in different parts of the country. Nearly all the coloured teachers in Washington are girls and women, a large percentage of whom were educated in the district of Columbia. Nor is it only in the ranks of teachers that coloured women are content to remain. Some years since, two coloured women were studying in the Law School of Howard University. One of them, Miss Charlotte Ray, a member of this body, has since graduated, being, I believe, the first coloured woman in the country who has ever gained the distinction of being a graduated lawyer. Others have gone into medicine and have been practising in different States of the Union. In the Woman's Medical College of Pennsylvania, two coloured women were last year pursuing their studies as Matriculants, while a young woman, the daughter of a former fugitive slave, has held the position of an assistant resident physician in one of the hospitals. Miss Cole, of Philadelphia, held for some time the position of physician in the State Orphan Asylum in South Carolina.

In literature and art we have not accomplished much, although we have a few among us who have tried literature. Miss Foster has written for the *Atlantic Monthly,* and Mrs. Mary Shadd Cary for years edited a paper called the *Provincial Freeman,* and another coloured woman has written several stories, poems, and sketches, which have appeared in different periodicals. In art, we have Miss Edmonia Lewis, who is, I believe, allied on one side to the negro race. She exhibited several pieces of statuary, among which is Cleopatra, at the Centennial.

The coloured women have not been backward in promoting charities for their own sex and race. One of the most efficient helpers is Mrs. Madison, who although living in a humble and unpretending home, had succeeded in getting up a home for aged coloured women. By organized effort, coloured women have been enabled to help each other in sickness, and provide respectable funerals for the dead. They have institutions under different names; one of the oldest, perhaps the oldest in the country, has been in existence, as I have been informed, about fifty years, and has been officered and managed almost solely by women for about half a century. There are also, in several States, homes for aged coloured women: the largest I know of being in Philadelphia. This home was in a measure built by Stephen and Harriet Smith, coloured citizens of the State of Pennsylvania. Into this home men are also admitted. The city of Philadelphia has also another home for the homeless, which, besides giving them a temporary shelter, provides a permanent home for a number of aged coloured women. In looking over the statistics of miscellaneous charities, out of a list of fifty-seven charitable institutions, I see only nine in which there is any record of coloured inmates. Out of twenty-six Industrial Schools, I counted four. Out of a list of one hundred and fifty-seven orphan asylums, miscellaneous charities, and industrial schools, I find fifteen asylums in which there is some mention of coloured inmates. More than half the reform schools in 1874, had admitted coloured girls. The coloured women of Philadelphia have formed a Christian Relief Association, which has opened sewing schools for coloured girls, and which has been enabled, year after year, to lend a hand to some of the more needy of their race, and it also has, I understand, sustained an employment office for some time.

Memorial from Negroes of Indian Territory

James Ladd, Richard Brashears, and N. C. Coleman

To the Senate and House of Representatives in Congress assembled: The undersigned, a committee on behalf of the colored people of the Choctaw and Cherokee tribes of Indians, appointed at a convention held by said colored people near Scullyville, Indian Territory, on the 15th of January, 1870, would respectfully represent to your honorable bodies—

That, although freed from slavery by the result of the late war, we enjoy few, if any, of the benefits of freedom.

Being deprived as yet of every political right, we are still wholly in the power of our late masters, who were almost a unit on the side of the rebellion against the government, and who, from having been compelled to relinquish their ownership in us, regard our presence among them with no favorable eye.

That we, under these circumstances and in our helpless condition, have suffered, and still do suffer, many ills and outrages, even to the loss of many a life, may be readily surmised, and is a notorious fact.

By the treaty held at Fort Smith, Ark., in September, 1865, the following stipulations were enacted in our behalf, viz:

Art. 3. The Choctaws and Chickasaws, in consideration of the sum of $300,000, hereby cede to the United States the territory west of the 98° west longitude, known as the leased district, provided that the said sum shall be invested and held by the United States, at an interest not less than 5%, in trust for said nations, until the legislatures of the Choctaw and Chickasaw nations respectively shall have made such laws, rules, and regulations as may be necessary to give all persons of African descent, resident in

Source: Memorial from Negroes of Indian Territory. *Senate Miscellaneous Documents No. 106,* 41st Cong., 2nd Sess., (1870).

the said nations at the date of the treaty of Fort Smith, and their descendants, heretofore held in slavery among said nations, all the rights, privileges, and immunities, including the right of suffrage, of citizens of said nations, except in the annuities, moneys, and public domain claimed by, or belonging to, said nations respectfully; and also to give to such persons who were residents as aforesaid, and their descendants, 40 acres each of the land of said nations on the same terms as the Choctaws and Chickasaws, to be selected on the survey of said land, after the Choctaws and Chickasaws and Kansas Indians have made their selections as herein provided; and immediately on the enactment of such laws, rules, and regulations, the said sum of $300,000 shall be paid to the said Choctaw and Chickasaw nations in the proportion of 3/4 to the former and 1/4 to the latter, less such sum, at the rate of $100 *per capita,* as shall be sufficient to pay such persons of African descent before referred to as within 90 days after the passage of such laws, rules, and regulations shall elect to remove from the said nations respectively. And should the said laws, rules, and regulations not be made by the legislatures of the said nations respectively within two years from the ratification of this treaty, then the said sum of $300,000 shall cease to be held in trust for the said Choctaw and Chickasaw nations, and be held for the use and benefit of such of said persons of African descent as the United States shall remove from the said territory in such manner as the United States shall deem proper, the United States agreeing, within 90 days from the expiration of the said two years, to remove from said nations all such persons of African descent as may be willing to remove; those remaining or returning after having been removed from said nations to have no benefit of said sum of $300,000, or any part thereof, but shall be upon the same footing as other citizens of the United States in the said nations.

Art. 4. The said nations further agree that all Negroes, not otherwise disqualified or disabled, shall be competent witnesses in all civil and criminal suits and proceedings in the Choctaw and Chickasaw courts, any law to the contrary notwithstanding; and they fully recognize the right of the freedmen to a fair remuneration on reasonable and equitable contracts for their labor, which the law should aid them to enforce. And they agree, on the part of their respective nations, that all laws shall be equal in their operation upon Choctaws, Chickasaws, and Negroes, and that no distinction affecting the latter shall at any time be made, and that they shall be treated with kindness and be protected against injury; and they further agree, that while the said freedmen now in the Choctaw and Chickasaw nations remain in said nations, respectively, they shall be entitled to as much land as they may cultivate for the support of themselves and families, in cases where they do not support themselves and families by hiring, not interfering with existing improvements without the consent of the occupant, it being understood that in the event of the making of the laws, rules, and regulations aforesaid, the 40 acres aforesaid shall stand in place of the land cultivated as last aforesaid.

But thus far none of the conditions contained in the above articles has been fulfilled, and the time set for their fulfillment has long since expired.

We sought to bring our grievances to the notice of your honorable bodies at the last session of Congress, and for this purpose held a mass meeting on the 16th of February, 1869, but before we could perfect arrangements to send our petition by a trusty messenger, Congress had adjourned.

On the 25th of September, 1869, the colored people residing in the eastern portion of the Choctaw and Chickasaw country held a convention at Scullyville, near the western boundary of Arkansas, to take in consideration of their condition, and there passed the following resolutions:

Whereas, the Choctaws and Chickasaws utterly failed and wilfully neglected to fulfill the stipulations of the treaty made with the government of the United States, and approved July, 1866, in regard to the colored people of said nations: therefore be it

Resolved, That we do no longer consider those stipulations in relation to us as of any force whatever.

Resolved, That we consider ourselves full citizens of those nations, and fully entitled to all the rights, privileges, and benefits as such, the same as any citizen of Indian extraction.

Resolved, That as we can claim no other country as ours except this Territory, we desire to continue to live in it in peace and harmony with all others living therein.

Resolved, That we are in favor of having this Indian country sectionized and a certain amount of land allotted to each inhabitant as his own.

Resolved, That we are in favor of opening this territory to white immigration, and of selling to them, for the benefit of the whole people of these nations, our surplus lands.

Resolved, That this convention elect three trusty men to act for us as delegates, whenever our interest demands it.

A convention to be held by the colored people of the western portion of the Territory, to take similar action in relation to their condition, was frustrated by the Indians, who threatened the life of any colored man attempting to meet at the appointed place and time, tore down and destroyed the printed posters giving notice of the proposed convention, and had a leading colored man, on his way to the place of meeting, arrested through the United States agent.

Upon this, another meeting of the colored people was held on the 15th of January last, at Scullyville, Indian Territory, at which they reaffirmed the resolutions of September 26, 1869, and passed the following additional resolutions, viz:

Whereas, the colored people of the Choctaw and Chickasaw nations were, by force, intimidation and threats against their lives, prevented from holding a peaceable convention in which to deliberate upon an amelioration of their deplorable condition, and bring it to the notice of the government;

Resolved, That we regard the action of those engaged in preventing us from exercising the right of assemblying peaceably as unwarranted, unjust and tyrannical.

Resolved, That we regard the arrest of Richard Brashears, while on his way to the proposed Armstrong Academy convention, at the instigation of the United States agent and by the United States marshal, as a most outrageous and flagrant violation of our rights as freemen, and a disgrace to the government.

Resolved, That we are less than ever inclined to leave our native country, and more than ever claim protection from the government, equal rights with the Indians, and a speedy throwing open of the Territory to white settlement.

And whereas not a single stipulation of the treaty of Fort Smith concerning us has been kept by our late masters; and whereas, by a most insidious clause in said treaty, a large number of our brethren, who at the time were either still in the Union army or had not ventured to return to their country, are debarred from again becoming residents of their native country;

Resolved, That we earnestly entreat the national government not to permit so cruel an outrage to be inflicted on its own defenders, and not to allow rebels to punish loyal men for their loyalty;

Resolved, That James Ladd, Richard Brashears, and N. C. Coleman be, and are hereby, authorized to act as delegates for us, the colored people of the Choctaw and Chickasaws nations, to lay this our petition for relief before Congress, and in case they are unable to proceed thither, to authorize Hon. V. Dell, of Fort Smith, Ark., to be our representative at Washington.

Believing, as we do, that your honorable bodies have the power and the will to redress our grievances as well as the *right,* notwithstanding all "treaties," so called, of which so much only is kept by our late masters as suits their convenience, we trustfully turn to you to afford us the desired relief, and to secure to us those rights to which we claim to be entitled as men, as citizens of these United States, and as natives of the Indian Territory. And as in duty bound we will ever pray,

James Ladd
Richard Brashears
N. C. Coleman
Committee on the part of the Colored People of the Choctaw and Chickasaw Nations

Speech on Indian Policy

Blanche K. Bruce

Mr. President, I shall support the pending bill, and without attempting a discussion of the specific features of the measure, I desire to submit a few remarks upon the general subject suggested by it.

Our Indian policy and administration seem to me to have been inspired and controlled by a stern selfishness, with a few

Source: Blanche K. Bruce, Speech on Indian policy, April 7, 1880 in Congressional Record, 46th Congress, 2nd Session, Part 3, pp. 2195–96.

honorable exceptions. Indian treaties have generally been made as the condition and instrument of acquiring the valuable territory occupied by the several Indian nations and have been changed and revised from time to time as it became desirable that the steadily growing, irrepressible white races should secure more room for their growth and more lands for their occupancy; and wars, bounties and beads have been used as auxiliaries for the purpose of temporary peace and security for the whites, and as the preliminary to further aggressions upon the red man's lands, with the ultimate view of his expulsion and extinction from the continent.

No set purpose has been evinced in adequate, sufficient measure to build him up, to civilize him, and to make him part of the great community of states. Whatever of occasional and spasmodic effort has been made for his redemption from savagery and his perpetuity as a race, has been only sufficient to supply that class of exceptions to the rule necessary to prove the selfishness of the policy that we allege to have been practiced toward him.

The political or governmental idea underlying the Indian policy is to maintain the paramount authority of the United States over the Indian Territory and over the Indian tribes, yet recognizing tribal independence and autonomy and a local government, un-American in structure and having no reference to the Constitution or laws of the United States, so far as the tribal governments affect the persons, lives and rights of the members of the tribe alone. Currently with the maintenance of a policy thus based, under treaty obligations, the government of the United States contributes to the support, equipments and comforts of these Indians, not only by making appropriations for food and raiment but by sustaining blacksmiths, mechanics, farmers, millers and schools in the midst of the Indian reservations. This government also, in its treaties and its enforcement thereof, encourages and facilitates the missionary enterprises of the different churches which look to the Christianization and education of the Indians distributed throughout the public domain. The effort, under these circumstances, to preserve peace among the Indian tribes in their relations to each other and in their relations to the citizens of the United States becomes a very onerous and difficult endeavor, and has not heretofore produced results that have either satisfied the expectations and public sentiment of the country, vindicated the wisdom of the policy practiced toward this people, or honored the Christian institutions and civilizations of our great country.

We have in the effort to realize a somewhat intangible ideal—to wit, the preservation of Indian liberty and the administration and exercise of national authority—complicated an essentially difficult problem by surrounding it with needless and equivocal adjuncts; we have rendered a questionable policy more difficult of successful execution by basing it upon a political theory which is un-American in character, and which, in its very structure, breeds and perpetuates the difficulties sought to be avoided and overcome.

Our system of government is complex in that it recognizes a general and local jurisdiction, and seeks to subserve and protect the rights of the individual and of the different political communities and the great aggregates of society making up the nation, by a division of authority distributed among general and local agencies, which are required like "the wheels within wheels" of Ezekiel's vision, to so move in their several appropriate spheres as shall not only prevent attrition and collision, but as shall secure unity in the system, in its fullest integrity, currently with the enjoyment of the largest liberty by the citizen.

Our system, I repeat, is complex, but it is nevertheless homogeneous. It is not incongruous; the general and local organisms belong to the same great class; they are both American, and they are moved by and respond to the same great impulse—the popular will of the American people.

Now, the political system that underlies our Indian policy is not only complex but it is incongruous, and one of the governments embraced in the system, ostensibly to secure the largest license and independence to the red race affected by the subject of this nondescript policy, is foreign in its character; the individuals and the system of laws are neither American. All the contradictions, the absurdities, and impossibilities developed and cropping out on the surface of our administration of Indian affairs are referable to this singular philosophy upon which, as a political theory, the Indian policy of the United States rests.

Now, sir, there must be a change in the Indian policy if beneficent practical results are expected, and any change that gives promise of solving this red-race problem must be a change based upon an idea in harmony, and not at war, with our free institutions. If the Indian is expected and required to respond to federal authority; if this people are expected to grow up into organized and well-ordered society; if they are to be civilized, in that the best elements of their natures are to be developed in the exercise of their best functions, so as to produce individual character and social groups characteristic of enlightened people; if this is to be done under our system, its ultimate realization requires an adoption of a political philosophy that shall make the Indians, as an individual and as a tribe, subjects of American law and beneficiaries of American institutions, by making them first American citizens, and clothing them, as rapidly as their advancement and location will permit, with the protective and ennobling prerogatives of such citizenship.

I favor the measure pending, because it is a step in the direction that I have indicated. You propose to give the Indian not temporary but permanent residence as a tribe, and not tribal location, but by a division of lands in severalty you secure to him the individual property rights which, utilized, will sustain life for himself and family better than his nomadic career. By this location you lay the foundation for that love of country essential to the patriotism and growth of a people, and by the distribution of lands to the individual, in severalty, you appeal to and develop that essential constitutional quality of humanity, the disposition to accumulate, upon which, when healthily and justly developed, depends the wealth, the growth, the power, the comfort, the refinement and the glory of the nations of the earth.

The measure also, with less directness, but as a necessary sequence to the provisions that I have just characterized, proposes, as preliminary to bringing the red race under the operation of our laws, to present the best phases of civilized life. Having given the red man a habitat, having identified the individual as well as the tribe with his new home, by securing his individual interests and rights therein, having placed these people where law can reach them, govern them and protect them, you purpose a system of administration that shall bring them in contact not with the adventurer of the border, not a speculative Indian agent, not an armed blue-coated soldier, but with the American people, in the guise and fashion in which trade, commerce, arts—useful and attractive—in the panoply that loving peace supplies, and with the plenty and comforts that follow in the footsteps of peace, and for the first time in the Indian's history, he will see the industrial, commercial, comfortable side of the character of the American people, will find his contact and form his associations with the citizens of the great Republic, and not simply and exclusively its armed men—its instruments of justice and destruction. So much this measure, if it should be a type of the new policy, will do for the Indian; and the Indian problem—heretofore rendered difficult of solution because of the false philosophy underlying it and the unjust administration too frequently based upon it, a policy that has kept the Indian a fugitive and a vagabond, that has bred discontent, suspicion and hatred in the mind of the red man—will be settled, not immediately, in a day or a year, but it will be put in course of settlement, and the question will be placed where a successful issue will be secured beyond a peradventure.

Mr. President, the red race are not a numerous people in our land, not equaling probably a half million souls, but they are the remnants of a great and multitudinous nation, and their hapless fortunes heretofore not only appeal to sympathy and to justice in any measures that we may take affecting them, but the vigor, energy, bravery and integrity of this remnant entitle them to consideration on the merits of the question.

Our age has been signalized by the grand scientific and mechanical discoveries and inventions which have multiplied the productive forces of the world. The power of nature has been harnessed to do the work of man, and every hour some new discovery contributes to swell the volume of the physical energies and its utilization, human ingenuity and thought have already been directed to the conservation, to the economy against the waste, of the physical forces. The man is considered a public benefactor who can utilize waste fuel, who can convert to some practical end some physical energy still lost, to a percent at least, through the imperfection of the machinery employed.

Now, sir, the Indian is a physical force; a half million vigorous, physical, intellectual agents ready for the plastic hand of Christian civilization, living in a country possessing empires of untilled and uninhabited lands. The Indian tribes, viewed from this utilitarian standpoint, are worth preservation, conservation, utilization and civilization, and I believe that we have reached a period when the public sentiment of the country demands such a modification in the Indian policy, in its purposes and in its methods, as shall save and not destroy these people.

There is nothing in the matter of obstructions, as suggested by the opponents of this measure, to convince me that the new policy is either impracticable or visionary. As a people, our history is full of surmounted obstacles; we have been solving difficult problems for more than a hundred years; we have been settling material, moral and great political questions that, before our era, had been unsolved, and the possible solution of which, even among the timid in our midst, was questioned.

The Indian is human, and no matter what his traditions or his habits, if you will locate him and put him in contact, and hold him in contact, with the forces of our civilization, his fresh, rugged nature will respond, and the fruit of his endeavor, in his civilization and development, will be the more permanent and enduring because his nature is so strong and obdurate. When you have no longer made it necessary for him to be a vagabond and fugitive; when you have allowed him to see the lovable and attractive side of our civilization as well as the stern military phase; when you have made the law apply to him as it does to others, so that the ministers of the law shall not only be the executors of its penalties but the administrators of its saving, shielding, protecting provisions, he will become trustful and reliable; and when he is placed in position in which not only to become an industrial force—to multiply his comforts and those of his people—but the honest, full sharer of the things he produces, savage life will lose its attractions, and the hunter will become the herdsman, the herdsman in his turn the farmer, and the farmer the mechanic, and out of the industries and growth of the Indian homes will spring up commercial interests and men competent to foster and handle them.

The American people are beginning to reach the conscientious conviction that redemption and civilization are due to the Indian tribes of the United States, and the present popular purpose is not to exterminate them but to perpetuate them on this continent.

The Indian policy has never attracted so much attention as at the present time, and the public sentiment demands that the new departure on this question shall ultimate in measures, toward the wild tribes of America, that shall be Christian and righteous in their character. The destruction of this vigorous race, rather than their preservation and development, is coming to be considered not only an outrage against Christian civilization, but an economic wrong to the people of the United States; and the people of America demand that the measures and administration of government relative to these people shall proceed upon the wise and equitable principles that regulate the conduct of public affairs relative to every other race in the Republic, and when rightful conceptions obtain in the treatment of the red race, the Indian question, with its cost, anxieties and wars, will disappear.

Address to the United States House of Representatives

George E. White

Mr. Chairman: I want to enter a plea for the colored man, the colored woman, the colored boy, and the colored girl of this country. I would not thus digress from the question at issue and detain the House in a discussion of the interests of this particular people at this time but for the constant and the persistent efforts of certain gentlemen upon this floor to mold and rivet public sentiment against us as a people, and to lose no opportunity to hold up the unfortunate few, who commit crimes and depredations and lead lives of infamy and shame, as other races do, as fair specimens of representatives of the entire colored race. And at no time, perhaps, during the 56th Congress were these charges and countercharges, containing, as they do, slanderous statements, more persistently magnified and pressed upon the attention of the nation than during the consideration of the recent reapportionment bill, which is now a law. As stated some days ago on this floor by me, I then sought diligently to obtain an opportunity to answer some of the statements made by gentlemen from different states, but the privilege was denied me; and I therefore must embrace this opportunity to say, out of season perhaps, that which I was not permitted to say in season.

I would like to advance the statement that the musty records of 1868, filed away in the archives of Southern capitols, as to what the Negro was thirty years ago, is not a proper standard by which the Negro living on the threshold of the twentieth century should be measured. Since that time we have reduced the illiteracy of the race at least 45 percent. We have written and published nearly five hundred books. We have nearly eight hundred newspapers, three of which are dailies. We have now in practice over two thousand lawyers, and a corresponding number of doctors. We have accumulated over $12,000,000 worth of school property and about $40,000,000 worth of church property. We have about 140,000 farms and homes, valued in the neighborhood of $750,000,000, and personal property valued about $170,000,000. We have raised about $11,000,000 for educational purposes, and the property per capita for every colored man, woman and child in the United States is estimated at $75.

We are operating successfully several banks, commercial enterprises among our people in the Southland, including one silk mill and one cotton factory. We have 32,000 teachers in the schools of the country; we have built, with the aid of our friends about 20,000 churches, and support seven colleges, seventeen academies, fifty high schools, five law schools, five medical schools and twenty-five theological seminaries. We have over 600,000 acres of land in the South alone. The cotton produced, mainly by black labor, has increased from 4,669,770 bales in 1860 to 11,235,000 in 1899. All this was done under the most adverse circumstances. We have done it in the face of lynching, burning at the stake, with the humiliation of Jim Crow cars, the disfranchisement of our male citizens, slander and degradation of our women, with the factories closed against us, no Negro permitted to be conductor on the railway cars, whether run through the streets of our cities or across the prairies of our great country, no Negro permitted to run as engineer on a locomotive, most of the mines closed against us.

Source: George E. White, "Address to the United States House of Representatives," on January 29, 1901. In Congressional Record, 56th Congress, 2nd Session, 1634–1638.

Labor unions—carpenters, painters, brick masons, machinists, hackmen and those supplying nearly every conceivable avocation for livelihood—have banded themselves together to better their condition, but, with few exceptions, the black man has been left out. The Negroes are seldom employed in our mercantile stores. At this we do not wonder. Some day we hope to have them employed in our own stores. With all these odds against us we are forging our way ahead, slowly perhaps, but surely. You may tie us and then taunt us for a lack of bravery, but some day we will break the bonds. You may use our labor for two and a half centuries and then taunt us for poverty, but let me remind you we will not always remain poor. You may withhold even the knowledge of how to read God's word and learn the way from earth to glory and then taunt us for our ignorance, but we will remind you that there is plenty of room at the top, and we are climbing.

After enforced debauchery with many kindred horrors incident to slavery, it comes with ill grace from the perpetrators of these deeds to hold up the shortcomings of some of our race to ridicule and scorn.

The new man, the slave who has grown out of the ashes of thirty-five years ago, is inducted into the political and social system, cast into the arena of manhood, where he constitutes a new element and becomes a competitor for all its emoluments. He is put upon trial to test his ability to be counted worthy of freedom, worthy of the elective franchise; and after thirty-five years of struggling against almost insurmountable odds, under conditions but little removed from slavery itself, he makes a fair and just judgment, not of those whose prejudice has endeavored to forestall, to frustrate, his every forward movement, rather those who have lent a helping hand, that he might demonstrate the truth of the "fatherhood of God and the brotherhood of man."

Now, Mr. Chairman, before concluding my remarks I want to submit a brief recipe for the solution of the so-called American Negro problem. He asks no special favors, but simply demands that he be given the same chance for existence, for earning a livelihood, for raising himself in the scales of manhood and womanhood, that are accorded to kindred nationalities. Treat him as a man; go into his home and learn of his social conditions; learn of his cares, his troubles and his hope for the future; gain his confidence; open the doors of industry to him; let the word "Negro," "colored," and "black" be stricken from all the organizations enumerated in the Federation of Labor.

Help him to overcome his weaknesses, punish the crime-committing class by the courts of the land, measure the standard of the race by its best material, cease to mold prejudicial and unjust public sentiment against him, and—my word for it—he will learn to support, hold up the hands of, and join in with that political party, that institution, whether secular or religious, in every community where he lives, which is destined to do the greatest good for the greatest number. Obliterate race hatred, party prejudice, and help us to achieve nobler ends, greater results and become satisfactory citizens to our brother in white.

This, Mr. Chairman, is perhaps the Negro's temporary fare-well to the American Congress; but let me say, phoenixlike he will rise up some day and come again. These parting words are in behalf of an outraged, heartbroken, bruised and bleeding, but God-fearing, people, faithful, industrious, loyal people, rising people, full of potential force.

Mr. Chairman, in the trial of Lord Bacon, when the court disturbed the counsel for the defendants, Sir Walter Raleigh raised himself up to his full height and addressing the court, said, "Sir, I am pleading for the life of a human being."

The only apology that I have to make for the earnestness with which I have spoken is that I am pleading for the life, the liberty, the future happiness, and manhood suffrage for one eighth of the entire population of the United States.

SUGGESTED READINGS

James Anderson, *The Education of Blacks in the South, 1860–1935* (Chapel Hill, N. C., 1988)

Stephen Ward Angell, *Bishop Henry McNeal Turner and African American Religion in the South* (Knoxville, Tenn., 1992)

Melba Joyce Boyd, *Discarded Legacy: Politics and Poetics in the Life of Francis E. W. Harper, 1825–1911* (Detroit, 1994)

W. E. B. Du Bois, *Black Reconstruction in America: An Essay toward a History of the Part which Black Folk Played in an Attempt to Reconstruct Democracy in America, 1860–1880* (New York, 1935)

Laura Edwards, *Gendered Strife and Confusion: The Political Culture of Reconstruction* (Urbana, Ill., 1997)

Eric Foner, *Reconstruction: America's Unfinished Revolution, 1863–1877* (New York, 1988)

Thomas C. Holt, *Black Over White: Negro Political Leadership in South Carolina During Reconstruction* (Urbana, Ill., 1977)

Gerald David Jaynes, *Branches Without Roots: Genesis of the Black Working Class in the American South, 1862–1882* (New York, 1986)

Jacqueline Jones, *Labor of Love, Labor of Sorrow: Black Women, Work, and the Family from Slavery to the Present* (New York, 1985)

Edward Magdol, *A Right to the Land: Essays on the Freedmen's Community* (Westport, Conn., 1977)

Robert C. Morris, *Reading, 'Riting, and Reconstruction: The Education of Freedmen in the South, 1861–1870* (Chicago, 1981)

Claude F. Oubre, *Forty Acres and a Mule: The Freedmen's Bureau and Black Landownership* (Baton Rouge, La., 1978)

Nell Irvin Painter, *Exodusters: Black Migration to Kansas After Reconstruction* (New York, 1976)

Howard N. Rabinowitz, ed., *Southern Black Leaders of the Reconstruction Era* (Urbana 1982)

Peter J. Rachleff, *Black Labor in the South: Richmond, Virginia, 1865–1890* (Philadelphia, 1984)

Roger L. Ransom and Richard Sutch, *One Kind of Freedom: The Economic Consequences of Emancipation* (Cambridge, England, 1977)

Wille Lee Rose, *Rehearsal for Reconstruction: The Port Royal Experiment* (Indianapolis, 1964)

Julie Saville, *The Work of Reconstruction: From Slave to Wage Laborer in South Carolina, 1860–1870* (Cambridge, England, 1994)

Leslie A. Schwalm, *A Hard Fight for We: Women's Transition from Slavery to Freedom in South Carolina* (Urbana, Ill., 1997)

Amy Dru Stanley, *From Bondage to Contract: Wage Labor, Marriage and the Market in the Age of Slave Emancipation* (Cambridge, England, 1998)

Allen W. Trelease, *White Terror: The Ku Klux Klan Conspiracy and Southern Reconstruction* (New York, 1971)

Clarence Earl Walker, *A Rock in a Weary Land: The African Methodist Episcopal Church during Civil War and Reconstruction* (Baton Rouge, La., 1982)